NewAmerican Standard
NEW TESTAMENT

Soul Winner's Edition

Holman Bible Publishers
Nashville

W9-ABU-293

© Copyright The Lockman Foundation
1960, 1962, 1963, 1971, 1972

The text of the New American Standard Bible Copyright 1960, 1962, 1963, 1971, 1972 by The Lockman Foundation, a corporation not for profit, La Habra, California 90631. All rights reserved. No part may be reproduced in any manner without permission in writing from The Lockman Foundation, except brief quotations used in connection with a review in a magazine or newspaper.

© Copyright The Clift Brannon Evangelistic Association, Inc., 1972, 1975

The references, notes, helps and outlines appearing outside the text of the New American Standard New Testament and appearing in this Soul Winner's Edition, are copyrighted by The Clift Brannon Evangelistic Association, Inc., a corporation not for profit, P.O. Box 1441, Longview, Texas 75601. All rights reserved. No part of said references, notes, helps and outlines may be reproduced in any manner without permission in writing from The Clift Brannon Evangelistic Association, Inc., except brief quotations used in connection with a review in a magazine or newspaper.

6 7 8 9 89 88 87
Printed in the United States of America

TABLE OF CONTENTS

FOREWORD

The New American Standard Bible has been produced with the conviction that the words of Scripture as originally penned in the Hebrew and Greek were inspired by God. Being the eternal Word of God, the Holy Scriptures speak with fresh power to each generation, to give us wisdom that leads to salvation, that we may serve to the glory of Christ.

The Editorial Board had a two-fold purpose in making this translation: to adhere as closely as possible to the original languages of the Holy Scriptures, and to make the translation in a fluent and readable style according to current English usage. (This translation follows the principles used in the American Standard Version 1901 known as the Rock of Biblical Honesty.)

SCRIPTURAL PROMISE

"The grass withers, the flower fades, but the Word of our God stands forever."   Isaiah 40:8

FOUR-FOLD AIM

OF

The Lockman Foundation Publications

1. These publications shall be true to the original Greek.

2. They shall be grammatically correct.

3. They shall be understandable to the masses.

4. They shall give the Lord Jesus Christ His proper place, the place which the Word gives Him, and no work will ever be personalized.

EXPLANATION OF GENERAL FORMAT

MARGINAL NOTES AND CROSS REFERENCES have been deleted from this edition. Footnotes are used only where the text requires them for clarification.

PARAGRAPHS are designated by bold face numbers or letters.

QUOTATION MARKS are used in the text in accordance with modern English usage.

PUNCTUATION CHANGES have been made in order to conform with modern practice.

"THOU, THY AND THEE" are changed to "you" except in the language of prayer when addressing Deity.

PERSONAL PRONOUNS are capitalized when pertaining to Deity.

ITALICS are used in the text to indicate words which are not found in the original Greek but implied by it.

SMALL CAPS are used in the text to indicate Old Testament quotes.

ASTERISK—Verbs marked with an asterisk (*) represent historical presents in the Greek which have been translated with an English past tense in order to conform to modern usage. (e.g., John 1:38— "Jesus ... beheld ... and says" has been changed to "Jesus ... beheld ... and *said.")

INTRODUCTION

The Soul Winner's New American Standard New Testament is designed to reach lost men with the Word of God and to mature the saved. The gospel of Jesus Christ is clearly pointed out for easy access and the responsibility of the Christian is clearly shown.

It is the desire of the publisher that any lost person who can read the English language CAN NOW find Christ as Savior by reading the references in this book beginning on page 186; and, that any saved person can become a good minister of the manifold grace of God by using this Soul Winner's New Testament to witness with God's Word.

There are four chains of scriptures and references. The one you read first begins on page 186. Here you see "What you must do to be saved." The first scripture passage is Acts 16:30-34 and the explanation or reference is found at the bottom of page 186 and you follow the instruction on the last line to turn to page 209. There you begin the familiar Roman Road to Salvation with Romans 3:23 showing <u>WHY</u> all people Need to be saved. You continue reading all six scriptures and references until you finish page 219.

The next section consists of four scripture passages and references beginning on page 45. These deal with response of the one making a decision for Christ. It shows him how to press on to maturity and become established as a child of God. This section is entitled "How You Can Show Others You Are Saved." The subjects treated are: First, "Baptism of Believers"; second, "Church Membership of Believers"; third, "Growth in Graces of Believers"; and fourth, "Witnessing for Christ."

In our busy, confused, and complex world the unsaved too often does not respond upon the first presentation. This is due to his preoccupation. Therefore provision is made for a second visit or conversation with the prospect for salvation. The third section of scriptures and references are for this purpose beginning on page 270. They deal with the question "Is your name written in Heaven?" and show how God's word gives assurance that "you can know your name is written in Heaven." With ease the Soul Winner can return to

Section 1 to get a response from the one to whom he witnesses.

It is hoped that the timid Soul Winner will, by using this edition, gain courage to commence a conversation to introduce the unsaved to Christ; be inspired with confidence to instruct the unsaved in the scriptures leading to salvation; and, that the Holy Spirit will stir the Soul Winner's heart with compassion to give an invitation to the lost to receive Christ as Lord and Savior.

The simplicity of this edition makes it possible for a lost or unsaved man to read for himself with all ease the New Testament plan of salvation. The imperishable seed is planted in his mind and heart.

The supplemental material in the appendix is designed to teach the Soul Winner to articulate the plan of salvation with confidence and to root and ground the newborn child of God in what the Bible teaches about subjects vital to his newfound faith so he may "grow in the grace and knowledge of our Lord and Savior Jesus Christ."

HOW TO USE THIS
SOUL WINNER'S NEW TESTAMENT

Section No. 1

Many Christians desire to know the answer to the question:
What do you say to a person who—
　　Attends church,
　　　Has heard the gospel,
　　　　Lives in a Christian community,
　　　　　Has not confessed Christ as Savior, or made
　　　　　a public profession of faith?

The answer is found in six scriptures and references of explanation found below the scriptures beginning on page 186. You will observe that Scripture No. 1, Section 1 is Acts 16:30-34 and is underlined and that Reference No. 1 is entitled "What you must do to be saved." Show that person this scripture and ask him to read it aloud with you. Then read Reference No. 1, and continue through all six numbered scriptures and references in the chain as directed in the last line of each reference. Be sure to read all six links in the chain. The Holy Spirit uses this Chain of Scriptures to inform, indict and convict the unbeliever "concerning sin, and righteousness, and judgment," and inspire him to pray for forgiveness. (For further instructions, see page 353.)

Section No. 2

What do you say to a person who—
　　Says that he trusts Christ,
　　　Has given a vocal testimony of salvation, but,
　　　　Has neither been baptized, nor become a part
　　　　of the local Church to make visible his faith?

God uses the four scriptures and references of Section No. 2 beginning on page 45 to answer these questions. Ask that person to assure you he has read the six scriptures and references of Section No. 1. Then read aloud with him Scripture No. 1, Section 2, Matthew 28:18-20. When you finish paragraph 3 of the reference and before you turn to page 264, ask him to read Acts 10:46-48 and Acts 11:12 on page 177, and the explanation at the bottom of that page.

Show him that the members of the Church must hear his testimony of confession of Christ and consent or bear witness of the Holy Spirit's presence in the believer before baptism. Then turn back and finish Reference No. 1 and continue through the four links in the chain. (See page 353.)

Section No. 3

What do you say to a person who—
  Has read the plan of salvation in the Bible,
    Says privately he believes in Christ,
      But has not made a public profession?
        or to one who—
      Has been dealt with through use of the scriptures,
        But has not made public his faith?
          or to one who—
        Says he is a Christian,
          But is not sure he is going to heaven?

The Lord uses the seven scriptures and references of Section No. 3, beginning with Phil. 2:9-11, page 270, to answer the above questions. Any person who will take God at His Word will see the necessity for public acknowledgement of Christ as Savior and Lord and God's promise and assurance of his entry into heaven. (This section is recommended for a second visit to your prospect, see page 354.)

Section No. 4

What do you say to a person who—
  Does not believe in God,
    Doubts the Bible to be His Word, and
    Has not received Christ as Savior?

The scriptures you use and all you need to say to him are found in the chain of four scriptures and references beginning on page 150 with Scripture No. 1, Section 4, John 17:3, and Reference No. 1, Section 4, at the bottom of that page. You do not prove the existence of the living God for He is self-evident. You do not defend the Bible as the Word of God, you declare it and the effect is eternal. The one to whom the Word is presented will be justified or judged thereby, for there is no escape. (This section may be used on your first visit if the person is a sceptic or agnostic—see page 354.)

Jeremiah 33:3: "Call to Me, and I will answer you, and I will tell you great and mighty things, which you do not know."

You make a SIMPLE request.

God promises a SURE reply,

revealing SUPERNATURAL revelations

with SURPRISING results.

MINISTERING FOR MATURITY

Growth in Grace to maturity is the goal for your new convert, Hebrews 5:13, 14, page 298.

INVITE him to be your guest in a church that believes the <u>Bible</u>, preaches the <u>Blood</u> of Jesus as atonement for sin, and expectantly looks for the <u>Blessed</u> hope of the return of Jesus Christ. The new born babe in Christ needs a church home, page 264.

INSTRUCT him to read this book daily, beginning with John on page 122, and completing John the first week of his Christian life. Then read Acts, then Matthew, then through the New Testament. Ask him to read the word of God daily, followed by prayer, claiming the promise of Jeremiah 33:3 (see above). Ask him to study the parable on prayer, page 109 and the assurance God answers prayer, page 249. Show him that Satan will tempt him. Teach him when he sins to rebound into fellowship with God by claiming the promise of 1 John 1:9, page 322. Lead him to look for the second coming by learning the truth on page 350. Study with him page 156, the chronology of the gift of the person of the Holy Spirit. Teach him to tell why he believes what he believes about immersion by studying pages 394-401.

INSPIRE him to study and use with a lost person the message of the miracle, page 53, or the conversion of Cornelius as the result of Peter's sermon, page 176-7. Urge him to study and review the truth that God disciplines His disciples, page 238. Remind him of his highest duty and greatest obligation, page 145. He can preform this by telling The Sweetest Story Ever Told, page 125. Urge him to join you in saying: "Let us press on to maturity," Hebrews 6:1, page 298.

BOOKS OF THE NEW TESTAMENT

THE GOSPEL

ACCORDING TO

MATTHEW

THE book of the genealogy of Jesus Christ, the son of David, the son of Abraham.

2 To Abraham was born Isaac; and to Isaac, Jacob; and to Jacob, Judah and his brothers;

3 and to Judah were born Perez and Zerah by Tamar; and to Perez was born Hezron; and to Hezron, Ram;

4 and to Ram was born Amminadab; and to Amminadab, Nahshon; and to Nahshon, Salmon;

5 and to Salmon was born Boaz by Rahab; and to Boaz was born Obed by Ruth; and to Obed, Jesse;

6 and to Jesse was born David the king.

And to David was born Solomon by her *who had been the wife* of Uriah;

7 and to Solomon was born Rehoboam; and to Rehoboam, Abijah; and to Abijah, Asa;

8 and to Asa was born Jehoshaphat; and to Jehoshaphat, Joram; and to Joram, Uzziah;

9 and to Uzziah was born Jotham; and to Jotham, Ahaz; and to Ahaz, Hezekiah;

10 and to Hezekiah was born Manasseh; and to Manasseh, Amon; and to Amon, Josiah;

11 and to Josiah were born Jeconiah and his brothers, at the time of the deportation to Babylon.

12 And after the deportation to Babylon, to Jeconiah was born Shealtiel; and to Shealtiel, Zerubbabel;

13 and to Zerubbabel was born Abiud; and to Abiud, Eliakim; and to Eliakim, Azor;

14 and to Azor was born Zadok; and to Zadok, Achim; and to Achim, Eliud;

15 and to Eliud was born Eleazar; and to Eleazar, Matthan; and to Matthan, Jacob;

16 and to Jacob was born Joseph the husband of Mary, by whom was born Jesus, who is called Christ.

17 Therefore all the generations from Abraham to David are fourteen generations; and from David to the deportation to Babylon fourteen generations; and from the deportation to Babylon to *the time of* Christ fourteen generations.

18 Now the birth of Jesus Christ was as follows. When His mother Mary had been betrothed to Joseph, before they came together she was found to be with child by the Holy Spirit. (a)

19 And Joseph her husband, being a righteous man, and not wanting to disgrace her, desired to put her away secretly.

20 But when he had considered this, behold, an angel of the Lord appeared to him in a dream, saying, "Joseph, son of David, do not be afraid to take Mary as your wife; for that which has been conceived in her is of the Holy Spirit.

21 "And she will bear a Son; and you shall call His name Jesus, for it is He who will save His people from their sins."

22 Now all this took place that

(a) Virgin Birth—a cardinal truth of Christianity is the Virgin birth of Jesus Christ our Savior. He was conceived by the Holy Spirit apart from any human agency, and born of the Virgin Mary. This "Jesus" is "the Son of God," Luke 1:31, 35, p. 76.

what was spoken by the Lord through the prophet might be fulfilled, saying,

23 "BEHOLD, THE VIRGIN SHALL BE WITH CHILD, AND SHALL BEAR A SON, AND THEY SHALL CALL HIS NAME IM-MANUEL," which translated means, "GOD WITH US."

24 And Joseph arose from his sleep, and did as the angel of the Lord commanded him, and took *her* as his wife,

25 and kept her a virgin until she gave birth to a Son; and he called His name Jesus.

CHAPTER 2

NOW after Jesus was born in Bethlehem of Judea in the days of Herod the king, behold, magi from the east arrived in Jerusalem, saying,

2 "Where is He who has been born King of the Jews? For we saw His star in the east, and have come to worship Him."

3 And when Herod the king heard it, he was troubled, and all Jerusalem with him.

4 And gathering together all the chief priests and scribes of the people, he *began* to inquire of them where the Christ was to be born.

5 And they said to him, "In Bethlehem of Judea, for so it has been written by the prophet,

6 'AND YOU, BETHLEHEM, LAND OF JUDAH,

ARE BY NO MEANS LEAST AMONG THE LEADERS OF JUDAH;

FOR OUT OF YOU SHALL COME FORTH A RULER,

WHO WILL SHEPHERD MY PEO-PLE ISRAEL.'"

7 Then Herod secretly called the magi, and ascertained from them the time the star appeared.

8 And he sent them to Bethlehem, and said, "Go and make careful search for the Child; and when you have found *Him*, report to me, that I too may come and worship Him."

9 And having heard the king, they went their way; and lo, the star, which they had seen in the east, went on before them, until it came and stood over where the Child was.

10 And when they saw the star, they rejoiced exceedingly with great joy.

11 And they came into the house and saw the Child with Mary His mother; and they fell down and worshiped Him; and opening their treasures they presented to Him gifts of gold and frankincense and myrrh.

12 And having been warned *by God* in a dream not to return to Herod, they departed for their own country by another way.

13 Now when they had departed, behold, an angel of the Lord *ap-peared to Joseph in a dream, saying, "Arise and take the Child and His mother, and flee to Egypt, and remain there until I tell you; for Herod is going to search for the Child to destroy Him."

14 And he arose and took the Child and His mother by night, and departed for Egypt;

15 and was there until the death of Herod, that what was spoken by the Lord through the prophet might be fulfilled, saying, "OUT OF EGYPT DID I CALL MY SON."

16 Then when Herod saw that he had been tricked by the magi, he became very enraged, and sent and slew all the male children who were in Bethlehem and in all its environs, from two years old and under, according to the time which he had ascertained from the magi.

17 Then that which was spoken through Jeremiah the prophet was fulfilled, saying,

18 "A VOICE WAS HEARD IN RAMAH, WEEPING AND GREAT MOURN-ING,

RACHEL WEEPING FOR HER
CHILDREN;
AND SHE REFUSED TO BE COMFORTED,
BECAUSE THEY WERE NO
MORE."

19 But when Herod was dead, behold, an angel of the Lord *appeared in a dream to Joseph in Egypt, saying,

20 "Arise and take the Child and His mother, and go into the land of Israel; for those who sought the Child's life are dead."

21 And he arose and took the Child and His mother, and came into the land of Israel.

22 But when he heard that Archelaus was reigning over Judea in place of his father Herod, he was afraid to go there. And being warned by God in a dream, he departed for the regions of Galilee,

23 and came and resided in a city called Nazareth, that what was spoken through the prophets might be fulfilled, "He shall be called a Nazarene."

CHAPTER 3

N OW in those days John the Baptist *came, preaching in the wilderness of Judea, saying,

2 "Repent, for the kingdom of heaven is at hand."

3 For this is the one referred to by Isaiah the prophet, saying,

"THE VOICE OF ONE CRYING IN
THE WILDERNESS,
'MAKE READY THE WAY OF THE
LORD,
MAKE HIS PATHS STRAIGHT!' "

4 Now John himself had a garment of camel's hair, and a leather belt about his waist; and his food was locusts and wild honey.

5 Then Jerusalem was going out to him, and all Judea, and all the district around the Jordan;

6 and they were being baptized by him in the Jordan River, as they confessed their sins.

7 But when he saw many of the Pharisees and Sadducees coming for baptism, he said to them, "You brood of vipers, who warned you to flee from the wrath to come?

8 "Therefore bring forth fruit in keeping with *your* repentance;

9 and do not suppose that you can say to yourselves, 'We have Abraham for our father'; for I say to you, that God is able from these stones to raise up children to Abraham.

10 "And the axe is already laid at the root of the trees; every tree therefore that does not bear good fruit is cut down and thrown into the fire.

11 "As for me, I baptize you in water for repentance, but He who is coming after me is mightier than I, and I am not *even* fit to remove His sandals; He Himself will baptize you with the Holy Spirit and fire.

12 "And His winnowing fork is in His hand, and He will thoroughly clean His threshing floor; and He will gather His wheat into the barn, but He will burn up the chaff with unquenchable fire."

13 Then Jesus *arrived from Galilee at the Jordan *coming* to John, to be baptized by him.

14 But John tried to prevent Him, saying, "I have need to be baptized by You, and do You come to me?"

15 But Jesus answering said to him, "Permit *it* at this time; for in this way it is fitting for us to fulfill all righteousness." Then he *permitted Him.

16 And after being baptized, Jesus went up immediately from the water; and behold, the heavens were opened, and he saw the Spirit of God descending as a dove, *and* coming upon Him,

17 and behold, a voice out of the heavens, saying, "This is My beloved Son, in whom I am well-pleased."

Chapter 4

THEN Jesus was led up by the Spirit into the wilderness to be tempted by the devil.

2 And after He had fasted forty days and forty nights, He then became hungry.

3 And the tempter came and said to Him, "If You are the Son of God, command that these stones become bread."

4 But He answered and said, "It is written, 'MAN SHALL NOT LIVE ON BREAD ALONE, BUT ON EVERY WORD THAT PROCEEDS OUT OF THE MOUTH OF GOD.'"

5 Then the devil *took Him into the holy city; and he stood Him on the pinnacle of the temple,

6 and *said to Him, "If You are the Son of God throw Yourself down; for it is written,

'HE WILL GIVE HIS ANGELS
CHARGE CONCERNING YOU;
And ON THEIR HANDS THEY
WILL BEAR YOU UP,
LEST YOU STRIKE YOUR FOOT
AGAINST A STONE.'"

7 Jesus said to him, "On the other hand, it is written, 'YOU SHALL NOT TEMPT THE LORD YOUR GOD.'"

8 Again, the devil *took Him to a very high mountain, and *showed Him all the kingdoms of the world, and their glory;

9 and he said to Him, "All these things will I give You, if You fall down and worship me."

10 Then Jesus *said to him, "Begone, Satan! For it is written, 'YOU SHALL WORSHIP THE LORD YOUR GOD, AND SERVE HIM ONLY.'"

11 Then the devil *left Him; and behold, angels came and *began* to minister to Him.

12 Now when He heard that John had been taken into custody, He withdrew into Galilee;

13 and leaving Nazareth, He came and settled in Capernaum, which is by the sea, in the region of Zebulun and Naphtali.

14 *This was* to fulfill what was spoken through Isaiah the prophet, saying,

15 "THE LAND OF ZEBULUN AND
THE LAND OF NAPHTALI,
BY THE WAY OF THE SEA, BEYOND THE JORDAN, GALILEE
OF THE GENTILES—

16 "THE PEOPLE WHO WERE SITTING IN DARKNESS SAW A
GREAT LIGHT,
AND TO THOSE WHO WERE SITTING IN THE LAND AND
SHADOW OF DEATH,
UPON THEM A LIGHT DAWNED."

17 From that time Jesus began to preach and say, "Repent, for the kingdom of heaven is at hand."

18 And walking by the sea of Galilee, He saw two brothers, Simon who was called Peter, and Andrew his brother, casting a net into the sea; for they were fishermen.

19 And He *said to them, "Follow Me, and I will make you fishers of men."

20 And they immediately left the nets, and followed Him.

21 And going on from there He saw two other brothers, James the *son* of Zebedee, and John his brother, in the boat with Zebedee their father, mending their nets; and He called them.

22 And they immediately left the boat and their father, and followed Him.

23 And *Jesus* was going about in all Galilee, teaching in their synagogues, and proclaiming the gospel of the kingdom, and healing every kind of disease and every kind of sickness among the people.

24 And the news about Him went out into all Syria; and they brought to Him all who were ill, taken with various diseases and pains, demoniacs,

epileptics, paralytics; and He healed them.

25 And great multitudes followed Him from Galilee and Decapolis and Jerusalem and Judea and *from* beyond the Jordan.

CHAPTER 5

AND when He saw the multitudes, He went up on the mountain; and after He sat down, His disciples came to Him.

2 And opening His mouth He *began* to teach them, saying,

3 "Blessed are the poor in spirit, for theirs is the kingdom of heaven.

4 "Blessed are those who mourn, for they shall be comforted.

5 "Blessed are the gentle, for they shall inherit the earth.

6 "Blessed are those who hunger and thirst for righteousness, for they shall be satisfied.

7 "Blessed are the merciful, for they shall receive mercy.

8 "Blessed are the pure in heart, for they shall see God.

9 "Blessed are the peacemakers, for they shall be called sons of God.

10 "Blessed are those who have been persecuted for the sake of righteousness, for theirs is the kingdom of heaven.

11 "Blessed are you when *men* revile you, and persecute you, and say all kinds of evil against you falsely, on account of Me.

12 "Rejoice, and be glad, for your reward in heaven is great, for so they persecuted the prophets who were before you.

13 "You are the salt of the earth; but if the salt has become tasteless, how will it be made salty *again*? It is good for nothing any more, except to be thrown out and trampled under foot by men.

14 "You are the light of the world. A city set on a hill cannot be hidden.

15 "Nor do *men* light a lamp, and put it under the peck-measure, but on the lampstand; and it gives light to all who are in the house.

16 "Let your light shine before men in such a way that they may see your good works, and glorify your Father who is in heaven.

17 "Do not think that I came to abolish the Law or the Prophets; I did not come to abolish, but to fulfill.

18 "For truly I say to you, until heaven and earth pass away, not the smallest letter or stroke shall pass away from the Law, until all is accomplished.

19 "Whoever then annuls one of the least of these commandments, and so teaches others, shall be called least in the kingdom of heaven; but whoever keeps and teaches *them*, he shall be called great in the kingdom of heaven.

20 "For I say to you, that unless your righteousness surpasses *that* of the scribes and Pharisees, you shall not enter the kingdom of heaven.

21 "You have heard that the ancients were told, 'You shall not commit murder' and 'Whoever commits murder shall be liable to the court.'

22 "But I say to you that every one who is angry with his brother shall be guilty before the court; and whoever shall say to his brother, 'Raca,' shall be guilty before the supreme court; and whoever shall say, 'You fool,' shall be guilty *enough to go* into the hell of fire.

23 "If therefore you are presenting your offering at the altar, and there remember that your brother has something against you,

24 leave your offering there before the altar, and go your way; first be reconciled to your brother, and then come and present your offering.

25 "Make friends quickly with your opponent at law while you are with him on the way, in order that your

opponent may not deliver you to the judge, and the judge to the officer, and you be thrown into prison.

26 "Truly I say to you, you shall not come out of there, until you have paid up the last cent.

27 "You have heard that it was said, 'YOU SHALL NOT COMMIT ADULTERY';

28 but I say to you, that every one who looks on a woman to lust for her has committed adultery with her already in his heart.

29 "And if your right eye makes you stumble, tear it out, and throw it from you; for it is better for you that one of the parts of your body perish, than for your whole body to be thrown into hell.

30 "And if your right hand makes you stumble, cut it off, and throw it from you; for it is better for you that one of the parts of your body perish, than for your whole body to go into hell.

31 "And it was said, 'WHOEVER DIVORCES HIS WIFE, LET HIM GIVE HER A CERTIFICATE OF DISMISSAL';

32 but I say to you that every one who divorces his wife, except for *the* cause of unchastity, makes her commit adultery; and whoever marries a divorced woman commits adultery.

33 "Again, you have heard that the ancients were told, 'YOU SHALL NOT MAKE FALSE VOWS, BUT SHALL FULFILL YOUR VOWS TO THE LORD.'

34 "But I say to you, make no oath at all, either by heaven, for it is the throne of God,

35 or by the earth, for it is the footstool of His feet, or by Jerusalem, for it is THE CITY OF THE GREAT KING.

36 "Nor shall you make an oath by your head, for you cannot make one hair white or black.

37 "But let your statement be, 'Yes, yes' *or* 'No, no'; and anything beyond these is of evil.

38 "You have heard that it was said,

'AN EYE FOR AN EYE, AND A TOOTH FOR A TOOTH.'

39 "But I say to you, do not resist him who is evil; but whoever slaps you on your right cheek, turn to him the other also.

40 "And if any one wants to sue you, and take your shirt, let him have your coat also.

41 "And whoever shall force you to go one mile, go with him two.

42 "Give to him who asks of you, and do not turn away from him who wants to borrow from you.

43 "You have heard that it was said, 'YOU SHALL LOVE YOUR NEIGHBOR, and hate your enemy.'

44 "But I say to you, love your enemies, and pray for those who persecute you

45 in order that you may be sons of your Father who is in heaven; for He causes His sun to rise on *the* evil and *the* good, and sends rain on *the* righteous and *the* unrighteous.

46 "For if you love those who love you, what reward have you? Do not even the tax-gatherers do the same?

47 "And if you greet your brothers only, what do you do more *than others*? Do not even the Gentiles do the same?

48 "Therefore you are to be perfect, as your heavenly Father is perfect.

CHAPTER 6

"BEWARE of practicing your righteousness before men to be noticed by them; otherwise you have no reward with your Father who is in heaven.

2 "When therefore you give alms, do not sound a trumpet before you, as the hypocrites do in the synagogues and in the streets, that they may be honored by men. Truly I say to you, they have their reward in full.

3 "But when you give alms, do not

let your left hand know what your right hand is doing

4 that your alms may be in secret; and your Father who sees in secret will repay you.

5 "And when you pray, you are not to be as the hypocrites; for they love to stand and pray in the synagogues and on the street corners, in order to be seen by men. Truly I say to you, they have their reward in full.

6 "But you, when you pray, GO INTO YOUR INNER ROOM, AND WHEN YOU HAVE SHUT YOUR DOOR, pray to your Father who is in secret, and your Father who sees in secret will repay you.

7 "And when you are praying, do not use meaningless repetition, as the Gentiles do, for they suppose that they will be heard for their many words.

8 "Therefore do not be like them; for your Father knows what you need, before you ask Him.

9 "Pray, then, in this way:
'Our Father who art in heaven,
Hallowed be Thy name.

10 'Thy kingdom come.
Thy will be done,
On earth as it is in heaven.

11 'Give us this day our daily bread.

12 'And forgive us our debts, as we also have forgiven our debtors.

13 'And do not lead us into temptation, but deliver us from evil. [For Thine is the kingdom, and the power, and the glory, forever. Amen].'

14 "For if you forgive men for their transgressions, your heavenly Father will also forgive you.

15 "But if you do not forgive men, then your Father will not forgive your transgressions.

16 "And whenever you fast, do not put on a gloomy face as the hypocrites *do*, for they neglect their appearance in order to be seen fasting by men. Truly I say to you, they have their reward in full.

17 "But you, when you fast, anoint your head, and wash your face

18 so that you may not be seen fasting by men, but by your Father who is in secret; and your Father who sees in secret will repay you.

19 "Do not lay up for yourselves treasures upon earth, where moth and rust destroy, and where thieves break in and steal.

20 "But lay up for yourselves treasures in heaven, where neither moth nor rust destroys, and where thieves do not break in or steal;

21 for where your treasure is, there will your heart be also.

22 "The lamp of the body is the eye; if therefore your eye is clear, your whole body will be full of light.

23 "But if your eye is bad, your whole body will be full of darkness. If therefore the light that is in you is darkness, how great is the darkness!

24 "No one can serve two masters; for either he will hate the one and love the other, or he will hold to one and despise the other. You cannot serve God and Mammon.

25 "For this reason I say to you, do not be anxious for your life, *as to* what you shall eat, or what you shall drink; nor for your body, *as to* what you shall put on. Is not life more than food, and the body than clothing?

26 "Look at the birds of the air, that they do not sow, neither do they reap, nor gather into barns, and *yet* your heavenly Father feeds them. Are you not worth much more than they?

27 "And which of you by being anxious can add a *single* cubit to his life's span?

28 "And why are you anxious about clothing? Observe how the lilies of the field grow; they do not toil nor do they spin,

29 yet I say to you that even Solomon in all his glory did not clothe himself like one of these.

30 "But if God so arrays the grass of the field, which is *alive* today and tomorrow is thrown into the furnace, *will He* not much more *do so for* you, O men of little faith?

31 "Do not be anxious then, saying, 'What shall we eat?' or 'What shall we drink?' or 'With what shall we clothe ourselves?'

32 "For all these things the Gentiles eagerly seek; for your heavenly Father knows that you need all these things.

33 "But seek first His kingdom and His righteousness; and all these things shall be added to you.

34 "Therefore do not be anxious for tomorrow; for tomorrow will care for itself. *Each* day has enough trouble of its own.

Chapter 7

"Do not judge lest you be judged *yourselves.*

2 "For in the way you judge, you will be judged; and by your standard of measure, it shall be measured to you.

3 "And why do you look at the speck in your brother's eye, but do not notice the log that is in your own eye?

4 "Or how can you say to your brother, 'Let me take the speck out of your eye,' and behold, the log is in your own eye?

5 "You hypocrite, first take the log out of your own eye, and then you will see clearly *enough* to take the speck out of your brother's eye.

6 "Do not give what is holy to dogs, and do not throw your pearls before swine, lest they trample them under their feet, and turn and tear you to pieces.

7 "Ask, and it shall be given to you;

seek, and you shall find; knock, and it shall be opened to you.

8 "For every one who asks receives, and he who seeks finds, and to him who knocks it shall be opened.

9 "Or what man is there among you, when his son shall ask him for a loaf, will give him a stone?

10 "Or if he shall ask for a fish, he will not give him a snake, will he?

11 "If you then, being evil, know how to give good gifts to your children, how much more shall your Father who is in heaven give what is good to those who ask Him!

12 "Therefore whatever you want others to do for you, do so for them, for this is the Law and the Prophets.

13 "Enter by the narrow gate; for the gate is wide, and the way is broad that leads to destruction, and many are those who enter by it.

14 "For the gate is small, and the way is narrow that leads to life, and few are those who find it.

15 "Beware of the false prophets, who come to you in sheep's clothing, but inwardly are ravenous wolves.

16 "You will know them by their fruits. Grapes are not gathered from thornbushes, nor figs from thistles, are they?

17 "Even so, every good tree bears good fruit; but the rotten tree bears bad fruit.

18 "A good tree cannot produce bad fruit, nor can a rotten tree produce good fruit.

19 "Every tree that does not bear good fruit is cut down and thrown into the fire.

20 "So then, you will know them by their fruits.

21 "Not every one who says to Me, 'Lord, Lord,' will enter the kingdom of heaven; but he who does the will of My Father who is in heaven.

22 "Many will say to Me on that day, 'Lord, Lord, did we not prophesy in Your name, and in Your name cast

out demons, and in Your name perform many miracles?'

23 "And then I will declare to them, 'I never knew you; DEPART FROM ME, YOU WHO PRACTICE LAWLESSNESS.'

24 "Therefore every one who hears these words of Mine, and acts upon them, may be compared to a wise man, who built his house upon the rock.

25 "And the rain descended, and the floods came, and the winds blew, and burst against that house; and *yet* it did not fall, for it had been founded upon the rock.

26 "And every one who hears these words of Mine, and does not act upon them, will be like a foolish man, who built his house upon the sand.

27 "And the rain descended, and the floods came, and the winds blew, and burst against that house; and it fell, and great was its fall."

28 The result was that when Jesus had finished these words, the multitudes were amazed at His teaching;

29 for He was teaching them as *one* having authority, and not as their scribes.

CHAPTER 8

AND when He had come down from the mountain, great multitudes followed Him.

2 And behold, a leper came to Him, and bowed down to Him, saying, "Lord, if You are willing, You can make me clean."

3 And stretching out His hand, He touched him, saying, "I am willing; be cleansed." And immediately his leprosy was cleansed.

4 And Jesus *said to him, "See that you tell no one; but go, SHOW YOURSELF TO THE PRIEST, and present the offering that Moses prescribed, for a testimony to them."

5 And when He had entered Capernaum, a centurion came to Him, entreating Him,

6 and saying, "Sir, my servant is lying paralyzed at home, suffering great pain."

7 And He *said to him, "I will come and heal him."

8 But the centurion answered and said, "Lord, I am not qualified for You to come under my roof, but just say the word, and my servant will be healed.

9 "For I, too, am a man under authority, with soldiers under me; and I say to this one, 'Go!' and he goes, and to another, 'Come!' and he comes, and to my slave, 'Do this!' and he does *it*."

10 Now when Jesus heard *this*, He marveled, and said to those who were following, "Truly I say to you, I have not found such great faith with anyone in Israel.

11 "And I say to you, that many shall come from east and west, and recline *at table* with Abraham, and Isaac, and Jacob, in the kingdom of heaven;

12 but the sons of the kingdom shall be cast out into the outer darkness; in that place there shall be weeping and gnashing of teeth."

13 And Jesus said to the centurion, "Go your way; let it be done to you as you have believed." And the servant was healed that *very* hour.

14 And when Jesus had come to Peter's home, He saw his mother-in-law lying sick in bed with a fever.

15 And He touched her hand, and the fever left her; and she arose, and began to wait on Him.

16 And when evening had come, they brought to Him many who were demon-possessed; and He cast out the spirits with a word, and healed all who were ill

17 in order that what was spoken through Isaiah the prophet might be fulfilled, saying, "HE HIMSELF TOOK

OUR INFIRMITIES, AND CARRIED AWAY OUR DISEASES."

18 Now when Jesus saw a crowd around Him, He gave orders to depart to the other side.

19 And a certain scribe came and said to Him, "Teacher, I will follow You wherever You go."

20 And Jesus *said to him, "The foxes have holes, and the birds of the air *have* nests; but the Son of Man has nowhere to lay His head."

21 And another of the disciples said to Him, "Lord, permit me first to go and bury my father."

22 But Jesus *said to him, "Follow Me; and allow the dead to bury their own dead."

23 And when He got into the boat, His disciples followed Him.

24 And behold, there arose a great storm in the sea, so that the boat was covered with the waves; but He Himself was asleep.

25 And they came to *Him*, and awoke Him, saying, "Save *us*, Lord; we are perishing!"

26 And He *said to them, "Why are you timid, you men of little faith?" Then He arose, and rebuked the winds and the sea; and it became perfectly calm.

27 And the men marveled, saying, "What kind of a man is this, that even the winds and the sea obey Him?"

28 And when He had come to the other side into the country of the Gadarenes, two men who were demon-possessed met Him as they were coming out of the tombs; *they were* so exceedingly violent that no one could pass by that road.

29 And behold, they cried out, saying, "What do we have to do with You, Son of God? Have you come here to torment us before the time?"

30 Now there was at a distance from them a herd of many swine feeding.

31 And the demons *began* to entreat Him, saying, "If You are *going to* cast us out, send us into the herd of swine."

32 And He said to them, "Begone!" And they came out, and went into the swine, and behold, the whole herd rushed down the steep bank into the sea and perished in the waters.

33 And the herdsmen fled, and went away to the city, and reported everything, including the *incident* of the demoniacs.

34 And behold, the whole city came out to meet Jesus; and when they saw Him, they entreated *Him* to depart from their region.

CHAPTER 9

AND getting into a boat, He crossed over, and came to His own city.

2 And behold, they were bringing to Him a paralytic, lying on a bed; and Jesus seeing their faith said to the paralytic, "Take courage, *My* son, your sins are forgiven."

3 And behold, some of the scribes said to themselves, "This *fellow* blasphemes."

4 And Jesus knowing their thoughts said, "Why are you thinking evil in your hearts?

5 "For which is easier, to say, 'Your sins are forgiven,' or to say, 'Rise, and walk'?

6 "But in order that you may know that the Son of Man has authority on earth to forgive sins"—then He *said to the paralytic, "Rise, take up your bed, and go home."

7 And he rose, and went to his home.

8 But when the multitudes saw *this*, they were filled with awe, and glorified God, who had given such authority to men.

9 And as Jesus passed on from there, He saw a man, called Matthew, sitting in the tax office; and He *said to him, "Follow Me!" And he rose, and followed Him.

10 And it happened that as He was reclining *at table* in the house, behold many tax-gatherers and sinners came and joined Jesus and His disciples *at the table.*

11 And when the Pharisees saw *this*, they said to His disciples, "Why does your Teacher eat with the tax-gatherers and sinners?"

12 But when He heard this, He said, "*It is* not those who are healthy who need a physician, but those who are ill.

13 "But go and learn what *this* means, 'I DESIRE COMPASSION, AND NOT SACRIFICE,' for I did not come to call *the* righteous, but sinners."

14 Then the disciples of John *came to Him, saying, "Why do we and the Pharisees fast, but Your disciples do not fast?"

15 And Jesus said to them, "The attendants of the bridegroom cannot mourn, as long as the bridegroom is with them, can they? But the days will come when the bridegroom is taken away from them, and then they will fast.

16 "But no one puts a patch of unshrunk cloth on an old garment; for the patch pulls away from the garment, and a worse tear results.

17 "Nor do *men* put new wine into old wineskins; otherwise the wineskins burst, and the wine pours out, and the wineskins are ruined; but they put new wine into fresh wineskins, and both are preserved."

18 While He was saying these things to them, behold, there came a synagogue official, and bowed down before Him, saying, "My daughter has just died; but come and lay Your hand on her, and she will live."

19 And Jesus rose and *began* to follow him, and *so did* His disciples.

20 And behold, a woman who had been suffering from a hemorrhage for twelve years, came up behind Him and touched the fringe of His cloak;

21 for she was saying to herself, "If I only touch His garment, I shall get well."

22 But Jesus turning and seeing her said, "Daughter, take courage; your faith has made you well." And at once the woman was made well.

23 And when Jesus came into the official's house, and saw the flute-players, and the crowd in noisy disorder,

24 He *began* to say, "Depart; for the girl is not dead, but is asleep." And they were laughing at Him.

25 But when the crowd had been put out, He entered and took her by the hand; and the girl arose.

26 And this news went out into all that land.

27 And as Jesus passed on from there, two blind men followed Him, crying out, and saying, "Have mercy on us, Son of David!"

28 And after He had come into the house, the blind men came up to Him, and Jesus *said to them, "Do you believe that I am able to do this?" They *said to Him, "Yes, Lord."

29 Then He touched their eyes, saying, "Be it done to you according to your faith."

30 And their eyes were opened. And Jesus sternly warned them, saying, "See *here*, let no one know *about this!*"

31 But they went out, and spread the news about Him in all that land.

32 And as they were going out, behold, a dumb man, demon-possessed, was brought to Him.

33 And after the demon was cast out, the dumb man spoke; and the multitudes marveled, saying, "Nothing like this was ever seen in Israel."

34 But the Pharisees were saying, "He casts out the demons by the ruler of the demons."

35 And Jesus was going about all the cities and the villages, teaching in their synagogues, and proclaiming the gospel of the kingdom, and healing every kind of disease and every kind of sickness.

36 And seeing the multitudes, He felt compassion for them, because they were distressed and downcast like sheep without a shepherd.

37 Then He *said to His disciples, "The harvest is plentiful, but the workers are few.

38 "Therefore beseech the Lord of the harvest to send out workers into His harvest."

CHAPTER 10

AND having summoned His twelve disciples, He gave them authority over unclean spirits, to cast them out, and to heal every kind of disease and every kind of sickness.

2 Now the names of the twelve apostles are these: The first, Simon, who is called Peter, and Andrew his brother; and James the *son* of Zebedee, and John his brother;

3 Philip and Bartholomew; Thomas and Matthew the tax-gatherer; James the *son* of Alphaeus, and Thaddaeus;

4 Simon the Cananaean, and Judas Iscariot, the one who betrayed Him.

5 These twelve Jesus sent out after instructing them, saying, "Do not go in *the* way of *the* Gentiles, and do not enter *any* city of the Samaritans;

6 but rather go to the lost sheep of the house of Israel.

7 "And as you go, preach, saying, 'The kingdom of heaven is at hand.'

8 "Heal *the* sick, raise *the* dead, cleanse *the* lepers, cast out demons; freely you received, freely give.

9 "Do not acquire gold, or silver, or copper for your money belts;

10 or a bag for *your* journey, or even two tunics, or sandals, or a staff;

for the worker is worthy of his support.

11 "And into whatever city or village you enter, inquire who is worthy in it; and abide there until you go away.

12 "And as you enter the house, give it your greeting.

13 "And if the house is worthy, let your *greeting of* peace come upon it; but if it is not worthy, let your *greeting of* peace return to you.

14 "And whoever does not receive you, nor heed your words, as you go out of that house or that city, shake off the dust of your feet.

15 "Truly I say to you, it will be more tolerable for *the* land of Sodom and Gomorrah in the day of judgment, than for that city.

16 "Behold, I send you out as sheep in the midst of wolves; therefore be shrewd as serpents, and innocent as doves.

17 "But beware of men; for they will deliver you up to *the* courts, and scourge you in their synagogues;

18 and you shall even be brought before governors and kings for My sake, as a testimony to them and to the Gentiles.

19 "But when they deliver you up, do not become anxious about how or what you will speak; for it shall be given you in that hour what you are to speak.

20 "For it is not you who speak, but *it is* the Spirit of your Father who speaks in you.

21 "And brother will deliver up brother to death, and a father *his* child; and CHILDREN WILL RISE UP AGAINST PARENTS, and cause them to be put to death.

22 "And you will be hated by all on account of My name, but it is the one who has endured to the end who will be saved.

23 "But whenever they persecute you in this city, flee to the next; for truly I say to you, you shall not finish

going through the cities of Israel, until the Son of Man comes.

24 "A disciple is not above his teacher, nor a slave above his master.

25 "It is enough for the disciple that he become as his teacher, and the slave as his master. If they have called the head of the house Beelzebul, how much more the members of his household!

26 "Therefore do not fear them, for there is nothing covered that will not be revealed, and hidden that will not be known.

27 "What I tell you in the darkness, speak in the light; and what you hear *whispered* in *your* ear, proclaim upon the housetops.

28 "And do not fear those who kill the body, but are unable to kill the soul; but rather fear Him who is able to destroy both soul and body in hell.

29 "Are not two sparrows sold for a cent? And *yet* not one of them will fall to the ground apart from your Father.

30 "But the very hairs of your head are all numbered.

31 "Therefore do not fear; you are of more value than many sparrows.

SCRIPTURE No. 2, SEC. 3

32 "Every one therefore who shall confess Me before men, I will also confess him before My Father who is in heaven.

33 "But whoever shall deny Me before men, I will also deny him before My Father who is in heaven. (r2)

34 "Do not think that I came to bring peace on the earth; I did not come to bring peace, but a sword.

(r2) REFERENCE NO. 2, SEC. 3—

HAS JESUS CONFESSED YOUR NAME IN HEAVEN?

"Everyone who shall confess Me before men, I will also confess him before My Father who is in heaven."

This verse teaches three things:

First, Jesus said, "Confess Me." That is, you confess or acknowledge a person. In prayer you confess your sins to God believing that Christ died for our sins, "He was buried, and that He was raised on the third day." Since you turned to Him, put your trust in Him, you received the Holy Spirit into your heart. You tell that you trust Jesus as Lord by the Holy Spirit.

Second, Jesus said your confession is "before men." It must be public. A private acknowledgement of Christ is not enough. In the house of Cornelius there were "six brethren," Peter said, who "went with Me." They heard those converted "speaking ... and exalting God." That is, they confessed Christ before the members of the Jerusalem Church. And the brethren agreed their testimony proved they were saved. When you are saved, "the Spirit Himself bears Witness" in the children of God who hear your testimony.

Third, Jesus promises to confess everyone in heaven who confesses Him "before men." Jesus keeps His promise. You are saved by "His precious and magnificent promises." Now when you tell before men you have received Him, He tells heaven. You can rely on Jesus.

"But whoever shall deny Me before men, I will also deny him before my Father who is in Heaven." What peril to be denied by Christ before the Father! God says, "that every tongue should confess that Jesus Christ is Lord, to the glory of God the Father." If you fail or refuse to confess Christ before men then Jesus will say before the Father, "I never knew you; depart from Me."

Do you see that it is necessary to confess Christ before men? If so, say:

"I understand that I must confess Jesus Christ as Lord before men."

Now turn to page 104, Scripture No. 3, Sec. 3, Luke 15:10.

35 "For I came to SET A MAN AGAINST HIS FATHER, AND A DAUGHTER AGAINST HER MOTHER, AND A DAUGHTER-IN-LAW AGAINST HER MOTHER-IN-LAW;

36 and A MAN'S ENEMIES WILL BE THE MEMBERS OF HIS HOUSEHOLD.

37 "He who loves father or mother more than Me is not worthy of Me; and he who loves son or daughter more than Me is not worthy of Me.

38 "And he who does not take his cross and follow after Me is not worthy of Me.

39 "He who has found his life shall lose it, and he who has lost his life for My sake shall find it.

40 "He who receives you receives Me, and he who receives Me receives Him who sent Me.

41 "He who receives a prophet in *the* name of a prophet shall receive a prophet's reward; and he who receives a righteous man in the name of a righteous man shall receive a righteous man's reward.

42 "And whoever in the name of a disciple gives to one of these little ones even a cup of cold water to drink, truly I say to you he shall not lose his reward."

CHAPTER 11

AND it came about that when Jesus had finished giving instructions to His twelve disciples, He departed from there to teach and preach in their cities.

2 Now when John in prison heard of the works of Christ, he sent *word* by his disciples,

3 and said to Him, "Are You the Coming One, or shall we look for someone else?"

4 And Jesus answered and said to them, "Go and report to John the things which you hear and see:

5 *the* BLIND RECEIVE SIGHT and *the* lame walk, *the* lepers are cleansed and *the* deaf hear, and *the* dead are raised up, and *the* POOR HAVE THE GOSPEL PREACHED to them.

6 "And blessed is he who keeps from stumbling over Me."

7 And as these were going *away*, Jesus began to say to the multitudes concerning John, "What did you go out into the wilderness to look at? A reed shaken by the wind?

8 "But what did you go out to see? A man dressed in soft *clothing*? Behold, those who wear soft *clothing* are in kings' palaces.

9 "But why did you go out? To see a prophet? Yes, I tell you, and one who is more than a prophet.

10 "This is the one about whom it was written,

'BEHOLD, I SEND MY MESSENGER BEFORE YOUR FACE,
WHO WILL PREPARE YOUR WAY BEFORE YOU.'

11 "Truly, I say to you, among those born of women there has not arisen *anyone* greater than John the Baptist; yet he who is least in the kingdom of heaven is greater than he.

12 "And from the days of John the Baptist until now the kingdom of heaven suffers violence, and violent men take it by force.

13 "For all the prophets and the Law prophesied until John.

14 "And if you care to accept *it*, he himself is Elijah, who was to come.

15 "He who has ears to hear, let him hear.

16 "But to what shall I compare this generation? It is like children sitting in the market places, who call out to the other *children*,

17 and say, 'We played the flute for you, and you did not dance; we sang a dirge, and you did not mourn.'

18 "For John came neither eating nor drinking, and they say, 'He has a demon!'

19 "The Son of Man came eating and drinking, and they say, 'Behold, a gluttonous man and a drunkard, a

friend of tax-gatherers and sinners!' Yet wisdom is vindicated by her deeds."

20 Then He began to reproach the cities in which most of His miracles were done, because they did not repent.

21 "Woe to you, Chorazin! Woe to you, Bethsaida! For if the miracles had occurred in Tyre and Sidon which occurred in you, they would have repented long ago in sackcloth and ashes.

22 "Nevertheless I say to you, it shall be more tolerable for Tyre and Sidon in *the* day of judgment, than for you.

23 "And you, Capernaum, will not be exalted to heaven, will you? You shall DESCEND TO HADES; for if the miracles had occurred in Sodom which occurred in you, it would have remained to this day.

24 "Nevertheless I say to you that it shall be more tolerable for the land of Sodom in *the* day of judgment, than for you."

25 At that time Jesus answered and said, "I praise Thee, O Father, Lord of heaven and earth, that Thou didst hide these things from *the* wise and intelligent and didst reveal them to babes.

26 "Yes, Father, for thus it was well-pleasing in Thy sight.

27 "All things have been handed over to Me by My Father; and no one knows the Son, except the Father; nor does anyone know the Father, except the Son, and anyone to whom the Son wills to reveal *Him.*

28 "Come to Me, all who are weary and heavy laden, and I will give you rest.

29 "Take My yoke upon you, and learn from Me, for I am gentle and humble in heart; and YOU SHALL FIND REST FOR YOUR SOULS.

30 "For My yoke is easy, and My load is light."

CHAPTER 12

A T that time Jesus went on the Sabbath through the grainfields, and His disciples became hungry and began to pick the heads *of grain* and eat.

2 But when the Pharisees saw it, they said to Him, "Behold, Your disciples do what is not lawful to do on a Sabbath."

3 But He said to them, "Have you not read what David did, when he became hungry, he and his companions;

4 how he entered the house of God, and they ate the consecrated bread, which was not lawful for him to eat, nor for those with him, but for the priests alone?

5 "Or have you not read in the Law, that on the Sabbath the priests in the temple break the Sabbath, and are innocent?

6 "But I say to you, that something greater than the temple is here.

7 "But if you had known what this means, 'I DESIRE COMPASSION, AND NOT A SACRIFICE,' you would not have condemned the innocent.

8 "For the Son of Man is Lord of the Sabbath."

9 And departing from there, He went into their synagogue.

10 And behold, *there was* a man with a withered hand. And they questioned Him, saying, "Is it lawful to heal on the Sabbath?"—in order that they might accuse Him.

11 And He said to them, "What man shall there be among you, who shall have one sheep, and if it falls into a pit on the Sabbath, will he not take hold of it, and lift it out?

12 "Of how much more value then is a man than a sheep! So then, it is lawful to do good on the Sabbath."

13 Then He *said to the man, "Stretch out your hand!" And he stretched it out, and it was restored to normal, like the other.

14 But the Pharisees went out, and counseled together against Him, *as to* how they might destroy Him.

15 But Jesus, aware of *this*, withdrew from there. And many followed Him, and He healed them all,

16 and warned them not to make Him known,

17 in order that what was spoken through Isaiah the prophet, might be fulfilled, saying,

18   "BEHOLD, MY SERVANT WHOM
              I HAVE CHOSEN;
           MY BELOVED IN WHOM MY
              SOUL IS WELL-PLEASED;
           I WILL PUT MY SPIRIT UPON
              HIM,
           AND HE SHALL PROCLAIM JUS-
              TICE TO THE GENTILES.

19   "HE WILL NOT QUARREL, NOR
              CRY OUT;
           NOR WILL ANY ONE HEAR HIS
              VOICE IN THE STREETS.

20   "A BATTERED REED HE WILL
              NOT BREAK OFF,
           AND A SMOLDERING WICK HE
              WILL NOT PUT OUT,
           UNTIL HE LEADS JUSTICE TO
              VICTORY.

21   "AND IN HIS NAME THE GEN-
              TILES WILL HOPE."

22 Then there was brought to Him a demon-possessed man *who was* blind and dumb, and He healed him, so that the dumb man spoke and saw.

23 And all the multitudes were amazed, and *began* to say, "This *man* cannot be the Son of David, can he?"

24 But when the Pharisees heard it, they said, "This man casts out demons only by Beelzebul the ruler of the demons."

25 And knowing their thoughts He said to them, "Any kingdom divided against itself is laid waste; and any city or house divided against itself shall not stand.

26 "And if Satan casts out Satan, he is divided against himself; how then shall his kingdom stand?

27 "And if I by Beelzebul cast out demons, by whom do your sons cast them out? Consequently they shall be your judges.

28 "But if I cast out demons by the Spirit of God, then the kingdom of God has come upon you.

29 "Or how can anyone enter the strong man's house and carry off his property, unless he first binds the strong *man*? And then he will plunder his house.

30 "He who is not with Me is against Me; and he who does not gather with Me scatters.

31 "Therefore I say to you, any sin and blasphemy shall be forgiven men, but blasphemy against the Spirit shall not be forgiven.

32 "And whoever shall speak a word against the Son of Man, it shall be forgiven him; but whoever shall speak against the Holy Spirit, it shall not be forgiven him, either in this age, or in the *age* to come.

33 "Either make the tree good, and its fruit good; or make the tree rotten, and its fruit rotten; for the tree is known by its fruit.

34 "You brood of vipers, how can you, being evil, speak what is good? For the mouth speaks out of that which fills the heart.

35 "The good man out of *his* good treasure brings forth what is good; and the evil man out of *his* evil treasure brings forth what is evil.

36 "And I say to you, that every careless word that men shall speak, they shall render account for it in the day of judgment.

37 "For by your words you shall be justified, and by your words you shall be condemned."

38 Then some of the scribes and Pharisees answered Him, saying, "Teacher, we want to see a sign from You."

39 But He answered and said to

them, "An evil and adulterous generation craves for a sign; and *yet* no sign shall be given to it but the sign of Jonah the prophet;

40 for just as JONAH WAS THREE DAYS AND THREE NIGHTS IN THE BELLY OF THE SEA MONSTER, so shall the Son of Man be three days and three nights in the heart of the earth.

41 "The men of Nineveh shall stand up with this generation at the judgment, and shall condemn it because they repented at the preaching of Jonah; and behold, something greater than Jonah is here.

42 "*The* Queen of *the* South shall rise up with this generation at the judgment and shall condemn it, because she came from the ends of the earth to hear the wisdom of Solomon; and behold, something greater than Solomon is here.

43 "Now when the unclean spirit goes out of a man, it passes through waterless places, seeking rest, and does not find *it*.

44 "Then it says, 'I will return to my house from which I came'; and when it comes, it finds it unoccupied, swept, and put in order.

45 "Then it goes, and takes along with it seven other spirits more wicked than itself, and they go in and live there; and the last state of that man becomes worse than the first. That is the way it will also be with this evil generation."

46 While He was still speaking to the multitudes, behold, His mother and His brothers were standing outside, seeking to speak to Him.

47 And someone said to Him, "Behold, Your mother and Your brothers are standing outside seeking to speak to You."

48 But He answered the one who was telling Him and said, "Who is My mother and who are My brothers?"

49 And stretching out His hand toward His disciples, He said, "Behold, My mother and My brothers!

50 "For whoever shall do the will of My Father who is in heaven, he is My brother and sister and mother."

CHAPTER 13

ON that day Jesus went out of the house, and was sitting by the sea.

2 And great multitudes gathered about Him, so that He got into a boat and sat down, and the whole multitude was standing on the beach.

3 And He spoke many things to them in parables, saying, "Behold, the sower went out to sow;

4 and as he sowed, some *seeds* fell beside the road, and the birds came and devoured them.

5 "And others fell upon the rocky places, where they did not have much soil; and immediately they sprang up, because they had no depth of soil.

6 "But when the sun had risen, they were scorched; and because they had no root, they withered away.

7 "And others fell among the thorns, and the thorns came up and choked them out.

8 "And others fell on the good soil, and *yielded a crop, some a hundredfold, some sixty, and some thirty.

9 "He who has ears, let him hear."

10 And the disciples came and said to Him, "Why do You speak to them in parables?"

11 And He answered and said to them, "To you it has been granted to know the mysteries of the kingdom of heaven, but to them it has not been granted.

12 "For whoever has, to him shall *more* be given, and he shall have an abundance; but whoever does not have, even what he has shall be taken away from him.

13 "Therefore I speak to them in

parables; because while seeing they do not see, and while hearing they do not hear, nor do they understand.

14 "And in their case the prophecy of Isaiah is being fulfilled, which says,

> 'You will keep on hearing,
>   but will not understand;
> And you will keep on seeing,
>   but will not perceive;
15 For the heart of this people
>   has become dull,
> And with their ears they
>   scarcely hear,
> And they have closed their
>   eyes
> Lest they should see with
>   their eyes,
> And hear with their ears,
> And understand with their
>   heart and turn again,
> And I should heal them.'

16 "But blessed are your eyes, because they see; and your ears, because they hear.

17 "For truly I say to you, that many prophets and righteous men desired to see what you see, and did not see *it*; and to hear what you hear, and did not hear *it*.

18 "Hear then the parable of the sower.

19 "When any one hears the word of the kingdom, and does not understand it, the evil *one* comes and snatches away what has been sown in his heart. This is the one on whom seed was sown beside the road.

20 "And the one on whom seed was sown on the rocky places, this is the man who hears the word, and immediately receives it with joy;

21 yet he has no *firm* root in himself, but is *only* temporary, and when affliction or persecution arises because of the word, immediately he falls away.

22 "And the one on whom seed was sown among the thorns, this is the man who hears the word, and the worry of the world, and the deceitfulness of riches choke the word, and it becomes unfruitful.

23 "And the one on whom seed was sown on the good ground, this is the man who hears the word and understands it; who indeed bears fruit, and brings forth, some a hundredfold, some sixty, and some thirty."

24 He presented another parable to them, saying, "The kingdom of heaven may be compared to a man who sowed good seed in his field.

25 "But while men were sleeping, his enemy came and sowed tares also among the wheat, and went away.

26 "But when the wheat sprang up and bore grain, then the tares became evident also.

27 "And the slaves of the landowner came and said to him, 'Sir, did you not sow good seed in your field? How then does it have tares?'

28 "And he said to them, 'An enemy has done this!' And the slaves *said to him, 'Do you want us, then, to go and gather them up?'

29 "But he *said, 'No; lest while you are gathering up the tares, you may root up the wheat with them.

30 'Allow both to grow together until the harvest; and in the time of the harvest I will say to the reapers, "First gather up the tares and bind them in bundles to burn them up; but gather the wheat into my barn."'"

31 He presented another parable to them, saying, "The kingdom of heaven is like a mustard seed, which a man took and sowed in his field;

32 and this is smaller than all *other* seeds; but when it is full grown, it is larger than the garden plants, and becomes a tree, so that the birds of the air come and nest in its branches."

33 He spoke another parable to them, "The kingdom of heaven is like leaven, which a woman took, and hid

in three pecks of meal, until it was all leavened."

34 All these things Jesus spoke to the multitudes in parables, and He was not talking to them without a parable,

35 so that what was spoken through the prophet might be fulfilled, saying,

"I WILL OPEN MY MOUTH IN PARABLES;

I WILL UTTER THINGS HIDDEN SINCE THE FOUNDATION OF THE WORLD."

36 Then He left the multitudes, and went into the house. And His disciples came to Him, saying, "Explain to us the parable of the tares of the field."

37 And He answered and said, "The one who sows the good seed is the Son of Man,

38 and the field is the world; and *as for* the good seed, these are the sons of the kingdom; and the tares are the sons of the evil *one;*

39 and the enemy who sowed them is the devil, and the harvest is the end of the age; and the reapers are angels.

40 "Therefore just as the tares are gathered up and burned with fire, so shall it be at the end of the age.

41 "The Son of Man will send forth His angels, and they will gather out of His kingdom all STUMBLING BLOCKS, AND THOSE WHO COMMIT LAWLESSNESS,

42 and will cast them into the furnace of fire; in that place there shall be weeping and gnashing of teeth.

43 "Then THE RIGHTEOUS WILL SHINE FORTH AS THE SUN in the kingdom of their Father. He who has ears, let him hear.

44 "The kingdom of heaven is like a treasure hidden in the field, which a man found and hid; and from joy over it he goes and sells all that he has, and buys that field.

45 "Again, the kingdom of heaven is like a merchant seeking fine pearls,

46 and upon finding one pearl of great value, he went and sold all that he had, and bought it.

47 "Again, the kingdom of heaven is like a dragnet cast into the sea, and gathering *fish* of every kind;

48 and when it was filled, they drew it up on the beach; and they sat down, and gathered the good *fish* into containers, but the bad they threw away.

49 "So it will be at the end of the age; the angels shall come forth, and take out the wicked from among the righteous,

50 and will cast them into the furnace of fire; there shall be weeping and gnashing of teeth.

51 "Have you understood all these things?" They *said to Him, "Yes."

52 And He said to them, "Therefore every scribe who has become a disciple of the kingdom of heaven is like a head of a household, who brings forth out of his treasure things new and old."

53 And it came about that when Jesus had finished these parables, He departed from there.

54 And coming to His home town He *began* teaching them in their synagogue, so that they became astonished, and said, "Where *did* this man *get* this wisdom, and *these* miraculous powers?

55 "Is not this the carpenter's son? Is not His mother called Mary, and His brothers, James and Joseph and Simon and Judas?

56 "And His sisters, are they not all with us? Where then *did* this man *get* all these things?"

57 And they took offense at Him. But Jesus said to them, "A prophet is not without honor except in his home town, and in his *own* household."

58 And He did not do many miracles there because of their unbelief.

CHAPTER 14

AT that time Herod the tetrarch heard the news about Jesus,

2 and said to his servants, "This is John the Baptist; he has risen from the dead; and that is why miraculous powers are at work in him."

3 For Herod had seized John, and bound him, and put him in prison on account of Herodias, the wife of his brother Philip.

4 For John had been saying to him, "It is not lawful for you to have her."

5 And although he wanted to put him to death, he feared the multitude, because they regarded him as a prophet.

6 But when Herod's birthday came, the daughter of Herodias danced before *them* and pleased Herod.

7 Thereupon he promised with an oath to give her whatever she asked.

8 And having been prompted by her mother, she *said, "Give me here on a platter the head of John the Baptist."

9 And although he was grieved, the king commanded *it* to be given because of his oaths, and because of his dinner guests.

10 And he sent and had John beheaded in the prison.

11 And his head was brought on a platter and given to the girl; and she brought *it* to her mother.

12 And his disciples came and took away the body and buried it; and they went and reported to Jesus.

13 Now when Jesus heard *it*, He withdrew from there in a boat, to a lonely place by Himself; and when the multitudes heard *of this*, they followed Him on foot from the cities.

14 And when He came out, He saw a great multitude, and felt compassion for them, and healed their sick.

15 And when it was evening, the disciples came to Him, saying, "The place is desolate, and the time is already past; so send the multitudes away, that they may go into the villages and buy food for themselves."

16 But Jesus said to them, "They do not need to go away; you give them *something* to eat!"

17 And they *said to Him, "We have here only five loaves and two fish."

18 And He said, "Bring them here to Me."

19 And ordering the multitudes to recline on the grass, He took the five loaves and the two fish, and looking up toward heaven, He blessed *the food*, and breaking the loaves He gave them to the disciples, and the disciples *gave* to the multitudes,

20 and they all ate, and were satisfied. And they picked up what was left over of the broken pieces, twelve full baskets.

21 And there were about five thousand men who ate, aside from women and children.

22 And immediately He made the disciples get into the boat, and go ahead of Him to the other side, while He sent the multitudes away.

23 And after He had sent the multitudes away, He went up to the mountain by Himself to pray; and when it was evening, He was there alone.

24 But the boat was already many stadia away from the land, battered by the waves; for the wind was contrary.

25 And in the fourth watch of the night He came to them, walking upon the sea.

26 And when the disciples saw Him walking on the sea, they were frightened, saying, "It is a ghost!" And they cried out for fear.

27 But immediately Jesus spoke to them, saying, "Take courage, it is I; do not be afraid."

28 And Peter answered Him and said, "Lord, if it is You, command me to come to You on the water."

29 And He said, "Come!" And Peter got out of the boat, and walked on the water and came toward Jesus.

30 But seeing the wind, he became afraid, and beginning to sink, he cried out, saying, "Lord, save me!"

31 And immediately Jesus stretched out His hand and took hold of him, and *said to him, "O you of little faith, why did you doubt?"

32 And when they got into the boat, the wind stopped.

33 And those who were in the boat worshiped Him, saying, "You are certainly God's Son!"

34 And when they had crossed over, they came to land at Gennesaret.

35 And when the men of that place recognized Him, they sent into all that surrounding district and brought to Him all who were ill;

36 and they *began* to entreat Him that they might just touch the fringe of His cloak; and as many as touched *it* were cured.

CHAPTER 15

T HEN some Pharisees and scribes *came to Jesus from Jerusalem, saying,

2 "Why do Your disciples transgress the tradition of the elders? For they do not wash their hands when they eat bread."

3 And He answered and said to them, "And why do you yourselves transgress the commandment of God for the sake of your tradition?

4 "For God said, 'HONOR YOUR FATHER AND MOTHER,' and, 'HE WHO SPEAKS EVIL OF FATHER OR MOTHER, LET HIM BE PUT TO DEATH.'

5 "But you say, 'Whoever shall say to *his* father or mother, "Anything of mine you might have been helped by has been given *to God*,"

6 he is not to honor his father or his mother.' And *thus* you invalidated the word of God for the sake of your tradition.

7 "You hypocrites, rightly did Isaiah prophesy of you, saying,

8 'THIS PEOPLE HONORS ME WITH THEIR LIPS,

BUT THEIR HEART IS FAR AWAY FROM ME.

9 BUT IN VAIN DO THEY WORSHIP ME,

TEACHING AS THEIR DOCTRINES THE PRECEPTS OF MEN.' ''

10 And He called to Himself the multitude, and said to them, "Hear, and understand.

11 "Not what enters into the mouth defiles the man, but what proceeds out of the mouth, this defiles the man."

12 Then the disciples *came and *said to Him, "Do You know that the Pharisees were offended when they heard this statement?"

13 But He answered and said, "Every plant which My heavenly Father did not plant shall be rooted up.

14 "Let them alone; they are blind guides of the blind. And if a blind man guides a blind man, both will fall into a pit."

15 And Peter answered and said to Him, "Explain the parable to us."

16 And He said, "Are you also still without understanding?

17 "Do you not understand that everything that goes into the mouth passes into the stomach, and is eliminated?

18 "But the things that proceed out of the mouth come from the heart, and those defile the man.

19 "For out of the heart come evil thoughts, murders, adulteries, fornications, thefts, false witness, slanders.

20 "These are the things which defile the man; but to eat with unwashed hands does not defile the man."

21 And Jesus went away from there, and withdrew into the district of Tyre and Sidon.

22 And behold, a Canaanite woman came out from that region, and *began* to cry out, saying, "Have mercy on me, O Lord, Son of David; my daughter is cruelly demon-possessed."

23 But He did not answer her a word. And His disciples came to *Him* and kept asking Him, saying, "Send her away, for she is shouting out after us."

24 But He answered and said, "I was sent only to the lost sheep of the house of Israel."

25 But she came and *began* to bow down before Him, saying, "Lord, help me!"

26 And He answered and said, "It is not good to take the children's bread and throw *it* to the dogs."

27 But she said, "Yes, Lord; but even the dogs feed on the crumbs which fall from their master's table."

28 Then Jesus answered and said to her, "O woman, your faith is great; be it done for you as you wish." And her daughter was healed at once.

29 And departing from there, Jesus went along by the sea of Galilee, and having gone up to the mountain, He was sitting there.

30 And great multitudes came to Him, bringing with them *those who were* lame, crippled, blind, dumb, and many others, and they laid them down at His feet; and He healed them,

31 so that the multitude marveled as they saw the dumb speaking, the crippled restored, and the lame walking, and the blind seeing; and they glorified the God of Israel.

32 And Jesus summoned to Himself His disciples, and said, "I feel compassion for the multitude, because they have remained with Me now for three days and have nothing to eat; and I do not wish to send them away hungry, lest they faint on the way."

33 And the disciples *said to Him, "Where would we get so many loaves in a desert place to satisfy such a great multitude?"

34 And Jesus *said to them, "How many loaves do you have?" And they said, "Seven, and a few small fish."

35 And He directed the multitude to sit down on the ground;

36 and He took the seven loaves and the fish; and giving thanks, He broke *them* and started giving *them* to the disciples, and the disciples *in turn*, to the multitudes.

37 And they all ate, and were satisfied, and they picked up what was left over of the broken pieces, seven full baskets.

38 And those who ate were four thousand men, besides women and children.

39 And dismissing the multitudes, He got into the boat, and came to the region of Magadan.

CHAPTER 16

AND the Pharisees and Sadducees came up, and testing Him asked Him to show them a sign from heaven.

2 But He answered and said to them, "When it is evening, you say, '*It will be* fair weather, for the sky is red.'

3 "And in the morning, '*There will be* a storm today, for the sky is red and threatening.' Do you know how to discern the appearance of the sky, but cannot *discern* the signs of the times?

4 "An evil and adulterous generation seeks after a sign; and a sign will not be given it, except the sign of Jonah." And He left them, and went away.

5 And the disciples came to the other side and had forgotten to take bread.

6 And Jesus said to them, "Watch out and beware of the leaven of the Pharisees and Sadducees."

7 And they began to discuss among themselves, saying, "*It is* because we took no bread."

8 But Jesus, aware of this, said, "You men of little faith, why do you discuss among yourselves because you have no bread?

9 "Do you not yet understand or remember the five loaves of the five thousand, and how many large baskets you took up?

10 "Or the seven loaves of the four thousand, and how many baskets you took up?

11 "How is it that you do not understand that I did not speak to you concerning bread? But beware of the leaven of the Pharisees and Sadducees."

12 Then they understood that He did not say to beware of the leaven of bread, but of the teaching of the Pharisees and Sadducees.

13 Now when Jesus came into the district of Caesarea Philippi, He *began* asking His disciples, saying, "Who do people say that the Son of Man is?"

14 And they said, "Some *say* John the Baptist; some, Elijah; and others, Jeremiah, or one of the prophets."

15 He *said to them, "But who do you say that I am?"

SCRIPTURE No. 2, SEC. 4

16 And Simon Peter answered and said, "Thou art the Christ, the Son of the living God." (r2)

(r2) REFERENCE NO. 2, SEC. 4—
"WHAT YOU SHOULD KNOW ABOUT JESUS CHRIST"
"Thou art the Christ, the Son of the living God."

Jesus Christ is the Son of the living God. "Before the world was," "He existed in the form of God." He said, "I and the Father are one," so there was "equality with God." But He was willing to give up "the glory" which He had with the Father and was "made in the likeness of men." He was born of a virgin because Mary, His mother, "was found to be with child by the Holy Spirit, and in appearance as a man appeared as a "baby as He lay in the manger in Bethlehem."

The Lord Jesus Christ "knew no sin." He was "holy, innocent, undefiled" because He "committed no sin, nor was deceit found in His mouth." His Father, the Living God said, "This is My beloved Son, in Whom I am well pleased." "In Him was life, and the life was the light of men."

"He humbled Himself by becoming obedient to the point of death, even death on a Cross." Just before His crucifixion Jesus said, "This is My blood of the Covenant, which is to be shed on behalf of many for forgiveness of sins." "He offered up Himself," so "that by the grace of God He might taste death for everyone." "Greater love has no one than this, that one lay down his life for his friends."

"He was declared with power to be the Son of God by the resurrection from the dead." To His disciples after His resurrection, Jesus "presented Himself alive by many convincing proofs, appearing to them over a period of forty days."

Now "if you confess with your mouth Jesus as Lord, and believe in your heart that God raised Him from the dead, you shall be saved."

"Through His name everyone who believes in Him has received forgiveness of sins."

Forty days after His resurrection He ascended into heaven. "He was lifted up while they were looking on, and a cloud received Him out of their sight." Then, "Two men

(Turn to next page.)

17 And Jesus answered and said to him, "Blessed are you, Simon Bar-jona, because flesh and blood did not reveal *this* to you, but My Father who is in heaven.

18 "And I also say to you that you are Peter, and upon this rock I will build My church; and the gates of Hades shall not overpower it.

19 "I will give you the keys of the kingdom of heaven; and whatever you shall bind on earth shall have been bound in heaven, and whatever you shall loose on earth shall have been loosed in heaven."

20 Then He warned the disciples that they should tell no one that He was the Christ.

21 From that time Jesus Christ began to show His disciples that He must go to Jerusalem, and suffer many things from the elders and chief priests and scribes, and be killed, and be raised up on the third day.

22 And Peter took Him aside and began to rebuke Him, saying, "God forbid *it*, Lord! This shall never happen to You."

23 But He turned and said to Peter, "Get behind Me, Satan! You are a stumbling block to Me; for you are not setting your mind on God's interests, but man's."

24 Then Jesus said to His disciples, "If any one wishes to come after Me, let him deny himself, and take up his cross, and follow Me.

25 "For whoever wishes to save his life shall lose it; but whoever loses his life for My sake shall find it.

26 "For what will a man be profited, if he gains the whole world, and forfeits his soul? Or what will a man give in exchange for his soul?

27 "For the Son of Man is going to come in the glory of His Father with His angels; and WILL THEN RECOMPENSE EVERY MAN ACCORDING TO HIS DEEDS.

28 "Truly I say to you, there are some of those who are standing here who shall not taste death until they see the Son of Man coming in His kingdom."

CHAPTER 17

AND six days later Jesus *took with Him Peter and James and John his brother, and *brought them up to a high mountain by themselves.

2 And He was transfigured before them; and His face shone like the sun, and His garments became as white as light.

3 And behold, Moses and Elijah appeared to them, talking with Him.

4 And Peter answered and said to Jesus, "Lord, it is good for us to be here; if You wish, I will make three tabernacles here, one for You, and one for Moses, and one for Elijah."

5 While he was still speaking, behold, a bright cloud overshadowed them; and behold, a voice out of the cloud, saying, "This is My beloved

---

(Continued from page 23.)

in white clothing stood beside them; and they also said, 'This Jesus, who has been taken up from you into heaven, will come in just the same way as you have watched Him go into heaven'."

Therefore believe "Jesus is the Christ, the Son of God." He "knew no sin," and "died for sins once for all, the Just for the unjust." But "God raised Him up again" and He "was received up into heaven." He "sat down at the right hand of the throne of God." And He promised, "I will come again, and receive you to Myself."

Will you accept these facts concerning Jesus Christ, the Son of the living God? If so, say:

"I believe the Lord Jesus Christ is the Son of God."

Now turn to page 148, Scripture No. 3, Sec. 4, John 15:26.

Son, with whom I am well-pleased; hear Him!"

6 And when the disciples heard *this*, they fell on their faces and were much afraid.

7 And Jesus came to *them* and touched them and said, "Arise, and do not be afraid."

8 And lifting up their eyes, they saw no one, except Jesus Himself alone.

9 And as they were coming down from the mountain, Jesus commanded them, saying, "Tell the vision to no one until the Son of Man has risen from the dead."

10 And His disciples asked Him, saying, "Why then do the scribes say that Elijah must come first?"

11 And He answered and said, "Elijah is coming and will restore all things;

12 but I say to you, that Elijah already came, and they did not recognize him, but did to him whatever they wished. So also the Son of Man is going to suffer at their hands."

13 Then the disciples understood that He had spoken to them about John the Baptist.

14 And when they came to the multitude, a man came up to Him, falling on his knees before Him, and saying,

15 "Lord, have mercy on my son, for he is an epileptic, and is very ill; for he often falls into the fire, and often into the water.

16 "And I brought him to Your disciples, and they could not cure him."

17 And Jesus answered and said, "O unbelieving and perverted generation, how long shall I be with you? How long shall I put up with you? Bring him here to Me."

18 And Jesus rebuked him, and the demon came out of him, and the boy was cured at once.

19 Then the disciples came to Je-sus privately and said, "Why could we not cast it out?"

20 And He *said to them, "Because of the littleness of your faith; for truly I say to you, if you have faith as a mustard seed, you shall say to this mountain, 'Move from here to there,' and it shall move; and nothing shall be impossible to you.

21 ["But this kind does not go out except by prayer and fasting."]

22 And while they were gathering together in Galilee, Jesus said to them, "The Son of Man is going to be delivered into the hands of men;

23 and they will kill Him, and He will be raised again on the third day." And they were deeply grieved.

24 And when they had come to Capernaum, those who collected the two-drachma *tax* came to Peter, and said, "Does your teacher not pay the two-drachma *tax*?"

25 He *said, "Yes." And when he came into the house, Jesus spoke to him first, saying, "What do you think, Simon? From whom do the kings of the earth collect customs or poll-tax, from their sons or from strangers?"

26 And upon his saying, "From strangers," Jesus said to him, "Consequently the sons are exempt.

27 "But, lest we give them offense, go to the sea, and throw in a hook, and take the first fish that comes up; and when you open its mouth, you will find a stater. Take that and give it to them for you and Me."

CHAPTER 18

AT that time the disciples came to Jesus, saying, "Who then is greatest in the kingdom of heaven?"

2 And He called a child to Himself and stood him in their midst,

3 and said, "Truly I say to you, unless you are converted and become like children, you shall not enter the kingdom of heaven.

4 "Whoever then humbles himself as this child, he is the greatest in the kingdom of heaven.

5 "And whoever receives one such child in My name receives Me;

6 but whoever causes one of these little ones who believe in Me to stumble, it is better for him that a heavy millstone be hung around his neck, and that he be drowned in the depth of the sea.

7 "Woe to the world because of *its* stumbling blocks! For it is inevitable that stumbling blocks come; but woe to that man through whom the stumbling block comes!

8 "And if your hand or your foot causes you to stumble, cut it off and throw it from you; it is better for you to enter life crippled or lame, than having two hands or two feet, to be cast into the eternal fire.

9 "And if your eye causes you to stumble, pluck it out, and throw it from you. It is better for you to enter life with one eye, than having two eyes, to be cast into the hell of fire.

10 "See that you do not despise one of these little ones, for I say to you, that their angels in heaven continually behold the face of My Father who is in heaven.

11 ["For the Son of Man has come to save that which was lost.]

12 "What do you think? If any man has a hundred sheep, and one of them has gone astray, does he not leave the ninety-nine on the mountains and go and search for the one that is straying?

13 "And if it turns out that he finds it, truly I say to you, he rejoices over it more than over the ninety-nine which have not gone astray.

14 "Thus it is not *the* will of your Father who is in heaven that one of these little ones perish.

15 "And if your brother sins, go and reprove him in private; if he listens to you, you have won your brother.

16 "But if he does not listen *to you,*

take one or two more with you, so that BY THE MOUTH OF TWO OR THREE WITNESSES EVERY FACT MAY BE CONFIRMED.

17 "And if he refuses to listen to them, tell it to the church; and if he refuses to listen even to the church, let him be to you as a Gentile and a tax-gatherer.

18 "Truly I say to you, whatever you shall bind on earth shall have been bound in heaven; and whatever you loose on earth shall have been loosed in heaven.

19 "Again I say to you, that if two of you agree on earth about anything that they may ask, it shall be done for them by My Father who is in heaven.

20 "For where two or three have gathered together in My name, there I am in their midst."

21 Then Peter came and said to Him, "Lord, how often shall my brother sin against me and I forgive him? Up to seven times?"

22 Jesus *said to him, "I do not say to you, up to seven times, but up to seventy times seven.

23 "For this reason the kingdom of heaven may be compared to a certain king who wished to settle accounts with his slaves.

24 "And when he had begun to settle *them*, there was brought to him one who owed him ten thousand talents.

25 "But since he did not have *the means* to repay, his lord commanded him to be sold, along with his wife and children and all that he had, and repayment to be made.

26 "The slave therefore falling down, prostrated himself before him, saying, 'Have patience with me, and I will repay you everything.'

27 "And the lord of that slave felt compassion and released him and forgave him the debt.

28 "But that slave went out and found one of his fellow-slaves who

owed him a hundred denarii; and he seized him and *began* to choke *him*, saying, 'Pay back what you owe.'

29 "So his fellow-slave fell down and *began* to entreat him, saying, 'Have patience with me and I will repay you.'

30 "He was unwilling however, but went and threw him in prison until he should pay back what was owed.

31 "So when his fellow-slaves saw what had happened, they were deeply grieved and came and reported to their lord all that had happened.

32 "Then summoning him, his lord *said to him, 'You wicked slave, I forgave you all that debt because you entreated me.

33 'Should you not also have had mercy on your fellow-slave, even as I had mercy on you?'

34 "And his lord, moved with anger, handed him over to the torturers until he should repay all that was owed him.

35 "So shall My heavenly Father also do to you, if each of you does not forgive his brother from your heart."

CHAPTER 19

AND it came about that when Jesus had finished these words, He departed from Galilee, and came into the region of Judea beyond the Jordan;

2 and great multitudes followed Him, and He healed them there.

3 And *some* Pharisees came to Him, testing Him, and saying, "Is it lawful *for a man* to divorce his wife for any cause at all?"

4 And He answered and said, "Have you not read, that He who created *them* from the beginning MADE THEM MALE AND FEMALE,

5 and said, 'FOR THIS CAUSE A MAN SHALL LEAVE HIS FATHER AND MOTHER, AND SHALL CLEAVE TO HIS WIFE; AND THE TWO SHALL BECOME ONE FLESH'?

6 "Consequently they are no more two, but one flesh. What therefore God has joined together, let no man separate."

7 They *said to Him, "Why then did Moses command to GIVE HER A CERTIFICATE AND DIVORCE HER?"

8 He *said to them, "Because of your hardness of heart, Moses permitted you to divorce your wives; but from the beginning it has not been this way.

9 "And I say to you, whoever divorces his wife, except for immorality, and marries another commits adultery."

10 The disciples *said to Him, "If the relationship of the man with his wife is like this, it is better not to marry."

11 But He said to them, "Not all men *can* accept this statement, but *only* those to whom it has been given.

12 "For there are eunuchs who were born that way from their mother's womb; and there are eunuchs who were made eunuchs by men; and there are *also* eunuchs who made themselves eunuchs for the sake of the kingdom of heaven. He who is able to accept *this*, let him accept *it*."

13 Then *some* children were brought to Him so that He might lay His hands on them and pray; and the disciples rebuked them.

14 But Jesus said, "Let the children alone, and do not hinder them from coming to Me; for the kingdom of heaven belongs to such as these."

15 And after laying His hands on them, He departed from there.

16 And behold, one came to Him and said, "Teacher, what good thing shall I do that I may obtain eternal life?"

17 And He said to him, "Why are you asking Me about what is good? There is *only* One who is good; but if

you wish to enter into life, keep the commandments."

18 He *said to Him, "Which ones?" And Jesus said, "You shall not commit murder; You shall not commit adultery; You shall not steal; You shall not bear false witness;

19 Honor your father and mother; and You shall love your neighbor as yourself."

20 The young man *said to Him, "All these things I have kept; what am I still lacking?"

21 Jesus said to him, "If you wish to be complete, go and sell your possessions and give to the poor, and you shall have treasure in heaven; and come, follow Me."

22 But when the young man heard this statement, he went away grieved; for he was one who owned much property.

23 And Jesus said to His disciples, "Truly I say to you, it is hard for a rich man to enter the kingdom of heaven.

24 "And again I say to you, it is easier for a camel to go through the eye of a needle, than for a rich man to enter the kingdom of God."

25 And when the disciples heard this, they were very astonished and said, "Then who can be saved?"

26 And looking upon them Jesus said to them, "With men this is impossible, but with God all things are possible."

27 Then Peter answered and said to Him, "Behold, we have left everything and followed You; what then will there be for us?"

28 And Jesus said to them, "Truly I say to you, that you who have followed Me, in the regeneration when the Son of Man will sit on His glorious throne, you also shall sit upon twelve thrones, judging the twelve tribes of Israel.

29 "And everyone who has left houses or brothers or sisters or father or mother or children or farms for My name's sake, shall receive many times as much, and shall inherit eternal life.

30 "But many who are first will be last; and the last, first.

Chapter 20

" **F**OR the kingdom of heaven is like a landowner who went out early in the morning to hire laborers for his vineyard.

2 "And when he had agreed with the laborers for a denarius for the day, he sent them into his vineyard.

3 "And he went out about the third hour and saw others standing idle in the market place;

4 and to those he said, 'You too go into the vineyard, and whatever is right I will give you.' And so they went.

5 "Again he went out about the sixth and the ninth hour, and did the same thing.

6 "And about the eleventh hour he went out, and found others standing; and he *said to them, 'Why have you been standing here idle all day long?'

7 "They *said to him, 'Because no one hired us.' He *said to them, 'You too go into the vineyard.'

8 "And when evening had come, the owner of the vineyard *said to his foreman, 'Call the laborers and pay them their wages, beginning with the last group to the first.'

9 "And when those hired about the eleventh hour came, each one received a denarius.

10 "And when those hired first came, they thought that they would receive more; and they also received each one a denarius.

11 "And when they received it, they grumbled at the landowner,

12 saying, 'These last men have worked only one hour, and you have made them equal to us who have

borne the burden and the scorching heat of the day.'

13 "But he answered and said to one of them, 'Friend, I am doing you no wrong; did you not agree with me for a denarius?

14 'Take what is yours and go your way, but I wish to give to this last man the same as to you.

15 'Is it not lawful for me to do what I wish with what is my own? Or is your eye envious because I am generous?'

16 "Thus the last shall be first, and the first last."

17 And as Jesus was about to go up to Jerusalem, He took the twelve *disciples* aside by themselves, and on the way He said to them,

18 "Behold, we are going up to Jerusalem; and the Son of Man will be delivered up to the chief priests and scribes, and they will condemn Him to death,

19 and will deliver Him up to the Gentiles to mock and scourge and crucify *Him*, and on the third day He will be raised up."

20 Then the mother of the sons of Zebedee came to Him with her sons, bowing down, and making a request of Him.

21 And He said to her, "What do you wish?" She *said to Him, "Command that in Your kingdom these two sons of mine may sit, one on Your right and one on Your left."

22 But Jesus answered and said, "You do not know what you are asking for. Are you able to drink the cup that I am about to drink?" They *said to Him, "We are able."

23 He *said to them, "My cup you shall drink; but to sit on My right and on *My* left, this is not Mine to give, but *it is* for those for whom it has been prepared by My Father."

24 And hearing *this*, the ten became indignant at the two brothers.

25 But Jesus called them to Himself, and said, "You know that the

rulers of the Gentiles lord it over them, and *their* great men exercise authority over them.

26 "It is not so among you, but whoever wishes to become great among you shall be your servant,

27 and whoever wishes to be first among you shall be your slave;

28 just as the Son of Man did not come to be served, but to serve, and to give His life a ransom for many."

29 And as they were going out from Jericho, a great multitude followed Him.

30 And behold, two blind men sitting by the road, hearing that Jesus was passing by, cried out, saying, "Lord, have mercy on us, Son of David!"

31 And the multitude sternly told them to be quiet; but they cried out all the more, saying, "Lord, have mercy on us, Son of David!"

32 And Jesus stopped and called them, and said, "What do you wish Me to do for you?"

33 They *said to Him, "Lord, we want our eyes to be opened."

34 And moved with compassion, Jesus touched their eyes; and immediately they received their sight, and followed Him.

Chapter 21

AND when they had approached Jerusalem and had come to Bethphage, to the Mount of Olives, then Jesus sent two disciples,

2 saying to them, "Go into the village opposite you, and immediately you will find a donkey tied *there* and a colt with her; untie *them*, and bring *them* to Me.

3 "And if anyone says something to you, you shall say, 'The Lord has need of them;' and immediately he will send them."

4 Now this took place that what was spoken through the prophet might be fulfilled, saying,

5   "SAY TO THE DAUGHTER OF
ZION,
'BEHOLD YOUR KING IS COMING
TO YOU,
GENTLE, AND MOUNTED UPON A
DONKEY,
EVEN UPON A COLT, THE FOAL
OF A BEAST OF BURDEN.' "

6   And the disciples went and did
just as Jesus had directed them,

7   and brought the donkey and
the colt, and laid on them their garments, on which He sat.

8   And most of the multitude
spread their garments in the road, and
others were cutting branches from the
trees, and spreading them in the road.

9   And the multitudes going before Him, and those who followed
after were crying out, saying,
"HOSANNA to the Son of David;
BLESSED IS HE WHO COMES IN
THE NAME OF THE LORD;
HOSANNA in the highest!"

10   And when He had entered Jerusalem, all the city was stirred, saying,
"Who is this?"

11   And the multitudes were saying, "This is the prophet Jesus, from
Nazareth in Galilee."

12   And Jesus entered the temple
and cast out all those who were buying and selling in the temple, and
overturned the tables of the moneychangers and the seats of those who
were selling doves.

13   And He *said to them, "It is
written, 'MY HOUSE SHALL BE CALLED A
HOUSE OF PRAYER'; but you are making
it a robbers' den."

14   And *the* blind and *the* lame
came to Him in the temple, and He
healed them.

15   But when the chief priests and
the scribes saw the wonderful things
that He had done, and the children
who were crying out in the temple and
saying, "Hosanna to the Son of David," they became indignant,

16   and said to Him, "Do You hear
what these are saying?" And Jesus
*said to them, "Yes; have you never
read, 'OUT OF THE MOUTH OF INFANTS
AND NURSING BABES THOU HAST PREPARED PRAISE FOR THYSELF'?"

17   And He left them and went out
of the city to Bethany, and lodged
there.

18   Now in the morning, when He
returned to the city, He became hungry.

19   And seeing a lone fig tree by the
road, He came to it, and found nothing on it except leaves only; and He
*said to it, "No longer shall there ever
be *any* fruit from you." And at once
the fig tree withered.

20   And seeing *this*, the disciples
marveled, saying, "How did the fig
tree wither at once?"

21   And Jesus answered and said to
them, "Truly I say to you, if you have
faith, and do not doubt, you shall not
only do what was done to the fig tree,
but even if you say to this mountain,
'Be taken up and cast into the sea,' it
shall happen.

22   "And everything you ask in
prayer, believing, you shall receive."

23   And when He had come into
the temple, the chief priests and the
elders of the people came to Him as
He was teaching, and said, "By what
authority are You doing these things,
and who gave You this authority?"

24   But Jesus answered and said to
them, "I will ask you one thing too,
which if you tell Me, I will also tell
you by what authority I do these
things.

25   "The baptism of John was from
what *source*, from heaven or from
men?" And they *began* reasoning
among themselves, saying, "If we say,
'From heaven,' He will say to us,
'Then why did you not believe him?'

26   "But if we say, 'From men,' we
fear the multitude; for they all hold
John to be a prophet."

27   And they answered Jesus and

said, "We do not know." He also said to them, "Neither will I tell you by what authority I do these things.

28 "But what do you think? A man had two sons, and he came to the first and said, 'Son, go work today in the vineyard.'

29 "And he answered and said, 'I will, sir'; and he did not go.

30 "And he came to the second and said the same thing. But he answered and said, 'I will not'; *yet* he afterward regretted *it* and went.

31 "Which of the two did the will of his father?" They *said, "The latter." Jesus *said to them, "Truly I say to you that the tax-gatherers and harlots will get into the kingdom of God before you.

32 "For John came to you in the way of righteousness and you did not believe him; but the tax-gatherers and harlots did believe him; and you, seeing this, did not even feel remorse afterward so as to believe him.

33 "Listen to another parable. There was a landowner who PLANTED A VINEYARD AND PUT A WALL AROUND IT AND DUG A WINE PRESS IN IT, AND BUILT A TOWER, and rented it out to vine-growers, and went on a journey.

34 "And when the harvest time approached, he sent his slaves to the vine-growers to receive his produce.

35 "And the vine-growers took his slaves and beat one, and killed another, and stoned a third.

36 "Again he sent another group of slaves larger than the first; and they did the same thing to them.

37 "But afterward he sent his son to them, saying, 'They will respect my son.'

38 "But when the vine-growers saw the son, they said among themselves, 'This is the heir; come, let us kill him, and seize his inheritance.'

39 "And they took him, and cast him out of the vineyard, and killed *him.*

40 "Therefore when the owner of the vineyard comes, what will he do to those vine-growers?"

41 They *said to Him, "He will bring those wretches to a wretched end, and will rent out the vineyard to other vine-growers, who will pay him the proceeds at the *proper* seasons."

42 Jesus *said to them, "Did you never read in the Scriptures,

'THE STONE WHICH THE BUILD-
ERS REJECTED,
THIS BECAME THE CHIEF COR-
NER *stone;*
THIS CAME ABOUT FROM THE
LORD,
AND IT IS MARVELOUS IN OUR
EYES'?

43 "Therefore I say to you, the kingdom of God will be taken away from you, and be given to a nation producing the fruit of it.

44 "And he who falls on this stone will be broken to pieces; but on whomever it falls, it will scatter him like dust."

45 And when the chief priests and the Pharisees heard His parables, they understood that He was speaking about them.

46 And when they sought to seize Him, they became afraid of the multitudes, because they held Him to be a prophet.

CHAPTER 22

AND Jesus answered and spoke to them again in parables, saying,

2 "The kingdom of heaven may be compared to a king, who gave a wedding feast for his son.

3 "And he sent out his slaves to call those who had been invited to the wedding feast, and they were unwilling to come.

4 "Again he sent out other slaves saying, 'Tell those who have been invited, "Behold, I have prepared my dinner; my oxen and my fattened live-

stock are *all* butchered and everything is ready; come to the wedding feast." '

5 "But they paid no attention and went their way, one to his own farm, another to his business,

6 and the rest seized his slaves and mistreated them and killed them.

7 "But the king was enraged and sent his armies, and destroyed those murderers, and set their city on fire.

8 "Then he *said to his slaves, 'The wedding is ready, but those who were invited were not worthy.

9 'Go therefore to the main highways, and as many as you find *there*, invite to the wedding feast.'

10 "And those slaves went out into the streets, and gathered together all they found, both evil and good; and the wedding hall was filled with dinner guests.

11 "But when the king came in to look over the dinner guests, he saw there a man not dressed in wedding clothes,

12 and he *said to him, 'Friend, how did you come in here without wedding clothes?' And he was speechless.

13 "Then the king said to the servants, 'Bind him hand and foot, and cast him into the outer darkness; in that place there shall be weeping and gnashing of teeth.'

14 "For many are called, but few *are* chosen."

15 Then the Pharisees went and counseled together how they might trap Him in what He said.

16 And they *sent their disciples to Him, along with the Herodians, saying, "Teacher, we know that You are truthful and teach the way of God in truth, and defer to no one; for You are not partial to any.

17 "Tell us therefore, what do You think? Is it lawful to give a poll-tax to Caesar, or not?"

18 But Jesus perceived their malice, and said, "Why are you testing Me, you hypocrites?

19 "Show Me the coin *used* for the poll-tax." And they brought Him a denarius.

20 And He *said to them, "Whose likeness and inscription is this?"

21 They *said to Him, "Caesar's." Then He *said to them, "Then render to Caesar the things that are Caesar's; and to God the things that are God's."

22 And hearing *this*, they marveled, and leaving Him, they went away.

23 On that day *some* Sadducees (who say there is no resurrection) came to Him and questioned Him,

24 saying, "Teacher, Moses said, 'IF A MAN DIES, HAVING NO CHILDREN, HIS BROTHER AS NEXT OF KIN SHALL MARRY HIS WIFE, AND RAISE UP AN OFFSPRING TO HIS BROTHER.'

25 "Now there were seven brothers with us; and the first married and died, and having no offspring left his wife to his brother;

26 so also the second, and the third, down to the seventh.

27 "And last of all, the woman died.

28 "In the resurrection therefore whose wife of the seven shall she be? For they all had her."

29 But Jesus answered and said to them, "You are mistaken, not understanding the Scriptures, or the power of God.

30 "For in the resurrection they neither marry, nor are given in marriage, but are like angels in heaven.

31 "But regarding the resurrection of the dead, have you not read that which was spoken to you by God, saying,

32 'I AM THE GOD OF ABRAHAM, AND THE GOD OF ISAAC, AND THE GOD OF JACOB'? God is not *the God* of *the* dead but of *the* living."

33 And when the multitudes heard *this*, they were astonished at His teaching.

34 But when the Pharisees heard that He had put the Sadducees to silence, they gathered themselves together.

35 And one of them, a lawyer, asked Him a question, testing Him,

36 "Teacher, which is the great commandment in the Law?"

37 And He said to him, " 'YOU SHALL LOVE THE LORD YOUR GOD WITH ALL YOUR HEART, AND WITH ALL YOUR SOUL, AND WITH ALL YOUR MIND.'

38 "This is the great and foremost commandment.

39 "And a second is like it, 'YOU SHALL LOVE YOUR NEIGHBOR AS YOURSELF.'

40 "On these two commandments depend the whole Law and the Prophets."

41 Now while the Pharisees were gathered together, Jesus asked them a question,

42 saying, "What do you think about the Christ, whose son is He?" They *said to Him, "*The son* of David."

43 He *said to them, "Then how does David in the Spirit call Him 'Lord,' saying,

44 'THE LORD SAID TO MY LORD, "SIT AT MY RIGHT HAND, UNTIL I PUT THINE ENEMIES BENEATH THY FEET." '

45 "If David then calls Him 'Lord', how is He his son?"

46 And no one was able to answer Him a word, nor did anyone dare from that day on to ask Him another question.

CHAPTER 23

THEN Jesus spoke to the multitudes and to His disciples,

2 saying, "The scribes and the Pharisees have seated themselves in the chair of Moses;

3 therefore all that they tell you, do and observe, but do not do according to their deeds; for they say *things*, and do not do *them*.

4 "And they tie up heavy loads, and lay them on men's shoulders; but they themselves are unwilling to move them with *so much as* a finger.

5 "But they do all their deeds to be noticed by men; for they broaden their phylacteries, and lengthen the tassels *of their garments*.

6 "And they love the place of honor at banquets, and the chief seats in the synagogues,

7 and respectful greetings in the market places, and being called by men, Rabbi.

8 "But do not be called Rabbi; for One is your Teacher, and you are all brothers.

9 "And do not call *anyone* on earth your father; for One is your Father, He who is in heaven.

10 "And do not be called leaders; for One is your Leader, *that is*, Christ.

11 "But the greatest among you shall be your servant.

12 "And whoever exalts himself shall be humbled; and whoever humbles himself shall be exalted.

13 "But woe to you, scribes and Pharisees, hypocrites, because you shut off the kingdom of heaven from men; for you do not enter in yourselves, nor do you allow those who are entering to go in.

14 ["Woe to you, scribes and Pharisees, hypocrites, because you devour widows' houses, even while for a pretense you make long prayers; therefore you shall receive greater condemnation.]

15 "Woe to you, scribes and Pharisees, hypocrites, because you travel about on sea and land to make one proselyte; and when he becomes one, you make him twice as much a son of hell as yourselves.

16 "Woe to you, blind guides, who say, 'Whoever swears by the temple, that is nothing; but whoever swears by the gold of the temple, he is obligated.'

17 "You fools and blind men; which is more important, the gold, or the temple that sanctified the gold?

18 "And, 'Whoever swears by the altar, *that* is nothing, but whoever swears by the offering upon it, he is obligated.'

19 "You blind men, which is more important, the offering or the altar that sanctifies the offering?

20 "Therefore he who swears, swears *both* by the altar and by everything on it.

21 "And he who swears by the temple, swears *both* by the temple and by Him who dwells within it.

22 "And he who swears by heaven, swears *both* by the throne of God and by Him who sits upon it.

23 "Woe to you, scribes and Pharisees, hypocrites! For you tithe mint and dill and cummin, and have neglected the weightier provisions of the law: justice and mercy and faithfulness; but these are the things you should have done without neglecting the others.

24 "You blind guides, who strain out a gnat and swallow a camel!

25 "Woe to you, scribes and Pharisees, hypocrites! For you clean the outside of the cup and of the dish, but inside they are full of robbery and self-indulgence.

26 "You blind Pharisee, first clean the inside of the cup and of the dish, so that the outside of it may become clean also.

27 "Woe to you, scribes and Pharisees, hypocrites! For you are like whitewashed tombs which on the outside appear beautiful, but inside they are full of dead men's bones and all uncleanness.

28 "Even so you too outwardly appear righteous to men, but inwardly you are full of hypocrisy and lawlessness.

29 "Woe to you, scribes and Pharisees, hypocrites! For you build the tombs of the prophets and adorn the monuments of the righteous,

30 and say, 'If we had been *living* in the days of our fathers, we would not have been partners with them in *shedding* the blood of the prophets.'

31 "Consequently you bear witness against yourselves, that you are sons of those who murdered the prophets.

32 "Fill up then the measure *of the guilt* of your fathers.

33 "You serpents, you brood of vipers, how shall you escape the sentence of hell?

34 "Therefore, behold, I am sending you prophets and wise men and scribes; some of them you will kill and crucify, and some of them you will scourge in your synagogues, and persecute from city to city,

35 that upon you may fall *the guilt of* all the righteous blood shed on earth, from the blood of righteous Abel to the blood of Zechariah, the son of Berechiah, whom you murdered between the temple and the altar.

36 "Truly I say to you, all these things shall come upon this generation.

37 "O Jerusalem, Jerusalem, who kills the prophets and stones those who are sent to her! How often I wanted to gather your children together, the way a hen gathers her chicks under her wings, and you were unwilling.

38 "Behold, your house is being left to you desolate!

39 "For I say to you, from now on you shall not see Me until you say, 'Blessed is He who comes in the name of the Lord!' "

CHAPTER 24

AND Jesus came out from the temple and was going away when His disciples came up to point out the temple buildings to Him.

2 And He answered and said to them, "Do you not see all these things? Truly I say to you, not one stone here shall be left upon another, which will not be torn down."

3 And as He was sitting on the Mount of Olives, the disciples came to Him privately, saying, "Tell us, when will these things be, and what *will be* the sign of Your coming, and of the end of the age?"

4 And Jesus answered and said to them, "See to it that no one misleads you.

5 "For many will come in My name, saying, 'I am the Christ,' and will mislead many.

6 "And you will be hearing of wars and rumors of wars; see that you are not frightened, for *those things* must take place, but *that* is not yet the end.

7 "For nation will rise against nation, and kingdom against kingdom, and in various places there will be famines and earthquakes.

8 "But all these things are *merely* the beginning of birth pangs.

9 "Then they will deliver you up to tribulation, and will kill you, and you will be hated by all nations on account of My name.

10 "And at that time many will fall away and will betray one another and hate one another.

11 "And many false prophets will arise, and will mislead many.

12 "And because lawlessness is increased, most people's love will grow cold.

13 "But the one who endures to the end, it is he who shall be saved.

14 "And this gospel of the kingdom shall be preached in the whole world for a witness to all the nations, and then the end shall come.

15 "Therefore when you see the ABOMINATION OF DESOLATION which was spoken of through Daniel the prophet, standing in the holy place (let the reader understand),

16 then let those who are in Judea flee to the mountains;

17 let him who is on the housetop not go down to get the things out that are in his house;

18 and let him who is in the field not turn back to get his cloak.

19 "But woe to those who are with child and to those who nurse babes in those days!

20 "But pray that your flight may not be in the winter, or on a Sabbath;

21 for then there will be a great tribulation, such as has not occurred since the beginning of the world until now, nor ever shall.

22 "And unless those days had been cut short, no life would have been saved; but for the sake of the elect those days shall be cut short.

23 "Then if any one says to you, 'Behold, here is the Christ,' or 'There *He is*,' do not believe *him*.

24 "For false Christs and false prophets will arise and will show great signs and wonders, so as to mislead, if possible, even the elect.

25 "Behold, I have told you in advance.

26 "If therefore they say to you, 'Behold, He is in the wilderness,' do not go forth, *or*, 'Behold, He is in the inner rooms,' do not believe *them*.

27 "For just as the lightning comes from the east, and flashes even to the west, so shall the coming of the Son of Man be.

28 "Wherever the corpse is, there the vultures will gather.

29 "But immediately after the tribulation of those days THE SUN WILL BE DARKENED, AND THE MOON WILL NOT GIVE ITS LIGHT, AND THE

STARS WILL FALL from the sky, and the POWERS OF THE HEAVENS WILL BE shaken,

30 and then the sign of the Son of Man will appear in the sky, and then all the tribes of the earth will mourn, and they will see the SON OF MAN COMING ON THE CLOUDS OF THE SKY with power and great glory.

31 "And He will send forth His angels WITH A GREAT TRUMPET and THEY WILL GATHER TOGETHER His elect FROM THE FOUR WINDS, FROM ONE END OF THE SKY TO THE OTHER.

32 "Now learn the parable from the fig tree: when its branch has already become tender, and puts forth its leaves, you know that summer is near;

33 even so you too, when you see all these things, recognize that He is near, *right* at the door.

34 "Truly I say to you, this generation will not pass away until all these things take place.

35 "Heaven and earth will pass away, but My words shall not pass away.

36 "But of that day and hour no one knows, not even the angels of heaven, nor the Son, but the Father alone.

37 "For the coming of the Son of Man will be just like the days of Noah.

38 "For as in those days which were before the flood they were eating and drinking, they were marrying and giving in marriage, until the day that NOAH ENTERED THE ARK,

39 and they did not understand until the flood came and took them all away, so shall the coming of the Son of Man be.

40 "Then there shall be two men in the field; one will be taken, and one will be left.

41 "Two women *will be* grinding at the mill; one will be taken, and one will be left.

42 "Therefore be on the alert, for you do not know which day your Lord is coming.

43 "But be sure of this, that if the head of the house had known at what time of the night the thief was coming, he would have been on the alert and would not have allowed his house to be broken into.

44 "For this reason you be ready too; for the Son of Man is coming at an hour when you do not think *He will.*

45 "Who then is the faithful and sensible slave whom his master put in charge of his household to give them their food at the proper time?

46 "Blessed is that slave whom his master finds so doing when he comes.

47 "Truly I say to you, that he will put him in charge of all his possessions.

48 "But if that evil slave says in his heart, 'My master is not coming for a long time,'

49 and shall begin to beat his fellow-slaves and eat and drink with drunkards;

50 the master of that slave will come on a day when he does not expect *him* and at an hour which he does not know,

51 and shall cut him in pieces and assign him a place with the hypocrites; weeping shall be there and the gnashing of teeth.

CHAPTER 25

"THEN the kingdom of heaven will be comparable to ten virgins, who took their lamps, and went out to meet the bridegroom.

2 "And five of them were foolish, and five were prudent.

3 "For when the foolish took their lamps, they took no oil with them,

4 but the prudent took oil in flasks along with their lamps.

5 "Now while the bridegroom was delaying, they all got drowsy and *began* to sleep.

6 "But at midnight there was a shout, 'Behold, the bridegroom! Come out to meet *him*.'

7 "Then all those virgins arose, and trimmed their lamps.

8 "And the foolish said to the prudent, 'Give us some of your oil, for our lamps are going out.'

9 "But the prudent answered, saying, 'No, there will not be enough for us and you *too*; go instead to the dealers and buy *some* for yourselves.'

10 "And while they were going away to make the purchase, the bridegroom came, and those who were ready went in with him to the wedding feast; and the door was shut.

11 "And later the other virgins also came, saying, 'Lord, Lord, open up for us.'

12 "But he answered and said, 'Truly I say to you, I do not know you.'

13 "Be on the alert then, for you do not know the day nor the hour.

14 "For *it is* just like a man *about* to go on a journey, who called his own slaves, and entrusted his possessions to them.

15 "And to one he gave five talents, to another, two, and to another, one, each according to his own ability; and he went on his journey.

16 "Immediately the one who had received the five talents went and traded with them, and gained five more talents.

17 "In the same manner the one who had *received* the two *talents* gained two more.

18 "But he who received the one *talent* went away and dug in the ground, and hid his master's money.

19 "Now after a long time the master of those slaves *came and *settled accounts with them.

20 "And the one who had received the five talents came up and brought five more talents, saying, 'Master, you entrusted five talents to me; see, I have gained five more talents.'

21 "His master said to him, 'Well done, good and faithful slave; you were faithful with a few things, I will put you in charge of many things, enter into the joy of your master.'

22 "The one also who had *received* the two talents came up and said, 'Master, you entrusted to me two talents; see, I have gained two more talents.'

23 "His master said to him, 'Well done, good and faithful slave; you were faithful with a few things, I will put you in charge of many things; enter into the joy of your master.'

24 "And the one also who had received the one talent came up and said, 'Master, I knew you to be a hard man, reaping where you did not sow, and gathering where you scattered no *seed*.

25 'And I was afraid, and went away and hid your talent in the ground; see, you have what is yours.'

26 "But his master answered and said to him, 'You wicked, lazy slave, you knew that I reap where I did not sow, and gather where I scattered no *seed*.

27 'Then you ought to have put my money in the bank, and on my arrival I would have received my *money* back with interest.

28 'Therefore take away the talent from him, and give it to the one who has the ten talents.'

29 "For to everyone who has shall *more* be given, and he shall have an abundance; but from the one who does not have, even what he does have shall be taken away.

30 "And cast out the worthless slave into the outer darkness; in that place there shall be weeping and gnashing of teeth.

31 "But when the Son of Man

comes in His glory, and all the angels with Him, then He will sit on His glorious throne.

32 "And all the nations will be gathered before Him; and He will separate them from one another, as the shepherd separates the sheep from the goats;

33 and He will put the sheep on His right, and the goats on the left.

34 "Then the King will say to those on His right, 'Come, you who are blessed of My Father, inherit the kingdom prepared for you from the foundation of the world.

35 'For I was hungry, and you gave Me *something* to eat; I was thirsty, and you gave Me drink; I was a stranger, and you invited Me in;

36 naked, and you clothed Me; I was sick, and you visited Me; I was in prison, and you came to Me.'

37 "Then the righteous will answer Him, saying, 'Lord, when did we see You hungry, and feed You, or thirsty, and give You drink?

38 'And when did we see You a stranger, and invite You in, or naked, and clothe You?

39 'And when did we see You sick, or in prison, and come to You?'

40 "And the King will answer and say to them, 'Truly I say to you, to the extent that you did it to one of these brothers of Mine, *even* the least *of them,* you did it to Me.'

41 "Then He will also say to those on His left, 'Depart from Me, accursed ones, into the eternal fire which has been prepared for the devil and his angels;

42 for I was hungry, and you gave Me *nothing* to eat; I was thirsty, and you gave Me nothing to drink;

43 I was a stranger, and you did not invite Me in; naked, and you did not clothe Me; sick, and in prison, and you did not visit Me.'

44 "Then they themselves also will answer, saying, 'Lord, when did we see You hungry, or thirsty, or a stranger, or naked, or sick, or in prison, and did not take care of You?'

45 "Then He will answer them, saying, 'Truly I say to you, to the extent that you did not do it to one of the least of these, you did not do it to Me.'

46 "And these will go away into eternal punishment, but the righteous into eternal life."

CHAPTER 26

AND it came about that when Jesus had finished all these words, He said to His disciples,

2 "You know that after two days the Passover is coming, and the Son of Man is *to be* delivered up for crucifixion."

3 Then the chief priests and the elders of the people were gathered together in the court of the high priest, named Caiaphas;

4 and they plotted together to seize Jesus by stealth, and kill *Him.*

5 But they were saying, "Not during the festival, lest a riot occur among the people."

6 Now when Jesus was in Bethany, at the home of Simon the leper,

7 a woman came to Him with an alabaster vial of very costly perfume, and she poured it upon His head as He reclined *at table.*

8 But the disciples were indignant when they saw *this,* and said, "What is the point of this waste?

9 "For this *perfume* might have been sold for a high price and *the money* given to the poor."

10 But Jesus, aware of this, said to them, "Why do you bother the woman? For she has done a good deed to Me.

11 "For the poor you have with you

always; but you do not always have Me.

12 "For when she poured this perfume upon My body, she did it to prepare Me for burial.

13 "Truly I say to you, wherever this gospel is preached in the whole world, what this woman has done shall also be spoken of in memory of her."

14 Then one of the twelve, named Judas Iscariot, went to the chief priests,

15 and said, "What are you willing to give me to deliver Him up to you?" And they weighed out to him thirty pieces of silver.

16 And from then on he *began* looking for a good opportunity to betray Him.

17 Now on the first *day* of the *Feast* of Unleavened Bread the disciples came to Jesus, saying, "Where do You want us to prepare for You to eat the Passover?"

18 And He said, "Go into the city to a certain man, and say to him, 'The Teacher says, "My time is at hand; I *am* to keep the Passover at your house with My disciples." ' "

19 And the disciples did as Jesus had directed them; and they prepared the Passover.

20 Now when evening had come, He was reclining *at table* with the twelve disciples.

21 And as they were eating, He said, "Truly I say to you that one of you will betray Me."

22 And being deeply grieved, they each one began to say to Him, "Surely not I, Lord?"

23 And He answered and said, "He who dipped his hand with Me in the bowl is the one who will betray Me.

24 "The Son of Man *is to* go, just as it is written of Him; but woe to that man through whom the Son of Man

is betrayed! It would have been good for that man if he had not been born."

25 And Judas, who was betraying Him, answered and said, "Surely it is not I, Rabbi?" He *said to him, "You have said *it* yourself."

26 And while they were eating, Jesus took *some* bread, and after a blessing, He broke it and gave *it* to the disciples, and said, "Take, eat; this is My body."

27 And He took a cup and gave thanks, and gave *it* to them, saying, "Drink from it, all of you;

28 for this is My blood of the covenant, which is *to be* shed on behalf of many for forgiveness of sins.

29 "But I say to you, I will not drink of this fruit of the vine from now on until that day when I drink it new with you in My Father's kingdom."

30 And after singing a hymn, they went out to the Mount of Olives.

31 Then Jesus *said to them, "You will all fall away because of Me this night, for it is written, 'I WILL STRIKE DOWN THE SHEPHERD, AND THE SHEEP OF THE FLOCK SHALL BE SCATTERED.'

32 "But after I have been raised, I will go before you to Galilee."

33 But Peter answered and said to Him, "*Even* though all may fall away because of You, I will never fall away."

34 Jesus said to him, "Truly I say to you that this *very* night, before a cock crows, you shall deny Me three times."

35 Peter *said to Him, "Even if I must die with You, I will not deny You." All the disciples said the same thing too.

36 Then Jesus *came with them to a place called Gethsemane, and *said to His disciples, "Sit here while I go over there and pray."

37 And He took with Him Peter

and the two sons of Zebedee, and began to be grieved and distressed.

38 Then He *said to them, "My soul is deeply grieved, to the point of death; remain here and keep watch with Me."

39 And He went a little beyond *them*, and fell on His face and prayed, saying, "My Father, if it is possible, let this cup pass from Me; yet not as I will, but as Thou wilt."

40 And He *came to the disciples and *found them sleeping, and *said to Peter, "So, you *men* could not keep watch with Me for one hour?

41 "Keep watching and praying, that you may not enter into temptation; the spirit is willing, but the flesh is weak."

42 He went away again a second time and prayed, saying, "My Father, if this cannot pass away unless I drink it, Thy will be done."

43 And He came back and found them sleeping, for their eyes were heavy.

44 And He left them again, and went away and prayed a third time, saying the same thing once more.

45 Then He *came to the disciples, and *said to them, "Are you still sleeping and taking your rest? Behold, the hour is at hand and the Son of Man is being betrayed into the hands of sinners.

46 "Arise, let us be going; behold, the one who betrays Me is at hand!"

47 And while He was still speaking, behold, Judas, one of the twelve, came up, accompanied by a great multitude with swords and clubs, from the chief priests and elders of the people.

48 Now he who was betraying Him gave them a sign, saying, "Whomever I shall kiss, He is the one; seize Him."

49 And immediately he came to Jesus and said, "Hail, Rabbi!" and kissed Him.

50 And Jesus said to him, "Friend, *do* what you have come for." Then they came and laid hands on Jesus and seized Him.

51 And behold, one of those who were with Jesus reached and drew out his sword, and struck the slave of the high priest, and cut off his ear.

52 Then Jesus *said to him, "Put your sword back into its place; for all those who take up the sword shall perish by the sword.

53 "Or do you think that I cannot appeal to My Father, and He will at once put at My disposal more than twelve legions of angels?

54 "How then shall the Scriptures be fulfilled, that it must happen this way?"

55 At that time Jesus said to the multitudes, "Have you come out with swords and clubs to arrest Me as though I *were* a robber? Every day I used to sit in the temple teaching and you did not seize Me.

56 "But all this has taken place that the Scriptures of the prophets may be fulfilled." Then all the disciples left Him and fled.

57 And those who had seized Jesus led Him away to Caiaphas, the high priest, where the scribes and the elders were gathered together.

58 But Peter also followed Him at a distance as far as the courtyard of the high priest, and entered in, and sat down with the officers to see the outcome.

59 Now the chief priests and the whole Council kept trying to obtain false testimony against Jesus, in order that they might put Him to death;

60 and they did not find it, even though many false witnesses came forward. But later on two came forward,

61 and said, "This man stated, 'I am able to destroy the temple of God and to rebuild it in three days.'"

62 And the high priest stood up

and said to Him, "Do You make no answer? What is it that these men are testifying against You?"

63　But Jesus kept silent. And the high priest said to Him, "I adjure You by the living God, that You tell us whether You are the Christ, the Son of God."

64　Jesus *said to him, "You have said it *yourself*; nevertheless I tell you, hereafter you shall see THE SON OF MAN SITTING AT THE RIGHT HAND OF POWER, *and* COMING ON THE CLOUDS OF HEAVEN."

65　Then the high priest tore his robes, saying, "He has blasphemed! What further need do we have of witnesses? Behold, you have now heard the blasphemy;

66　what do you think?" They answered and said, "He is deserving of death!"

67　Then they spat in His face and beat Him with their fists; and others slapped Him,

68　and said, "Prophesy to us, You Christ; who is the one who hit You?"

69　Now Peter was sitting outside in the courtyard, and a certain servant-girl came to him and said, "You too were with Jesus the Galilean."

70　But he denied *it* before them all, saying, "I do not know what you are talking about."

71　And when he had gone out to the gateway, another *servant-girl* saw him and *said to those who were there, "This man was with Jesus of Nazareth."

72　And again he denied *it* with an oath, "I do not know the man."

73　And a little later the bystanders came up and said to Peter, "Surely you too are *one* of them; for the way you talk gives you away."

74　Then he began to curse and swear, "I do not know the man!" And immediately a cock crowed.

75　And Peter remembered the word which Jesus had said, "Before a cock crows, you will deny Me three times." And he went out and wept bitterly.

CHAPTER 27

NOW when morning had come, all the chief priests and the elders of the people took counsel against Jesus to put Him to death;

2　and they bound Him, and led Him away, and delivered Him up to Pilate the governor.

3　Then when Judas, who had betrayed Him, saw that He had been condemned, he felt remorse and returned the thirty pieces of silver to the chief priests and elders,

4　saying, "I have sinned by betraying innocent blood." But they said, "What is that to us? See *to that* yourself!"

5　And he threw the pieces of silver into the sanctuary and departed; and he went away and hanged himself.

6　And the chief priests took the pieces of silver and said, "It is not lawful to put them into the temple treasury, since it is the price of blood."

7　And they counseled together and with the money bought the Potter's Field as a burial place for strangers.

8　For this reason that field has been called the Field of Blood to this day.

9　Then that which was spoken through Jeremiah the prophet was fulfilled, saying, "AND THEY TOOK THE THIRTY PIECES OF SILVER, THE PRICE OF THE ONE WHOSE PRICE HAD BEEN SET BY THE SONS OF ISRAEL;

10　AND THEY GAVE THEM FOR THE POTTER'S FIELD, AS THE LORD DIRECTED ME."

11　Now Jesus stood before the governor, and the governor questioned Him, saying, "Are You the King of the Jews?" And Jesus said to him, "*It is as* you say."

12 And while He was being accused by the chief priests and elders, He made no answer.

13 Then Pilate *said to Him, "Do You not hear how many things they testify against You?"

14 And He did not answer him with regard to even a single charge, so that the governor was quite amazed.

15 Now at *the* feast the governor was accustomed to release for the multitude *any* one prisoner whom they wanted.

16 And they were holding at that time a notorious prisoner, called Barabbas.

17 When therefore they were gathered together, Pilate said to them, "Whom do you want me to release for you? Barabbas, or Jesus who is called Christ?"

18 For he knew that because of envy they had delivered Him up.

19 And while he was sitting on the judgment seat, his wife sent to him, saying, "Have nothing to do with that righteous Man; for last night I suffered greatly in a dream because of Him."

20 But the chief priests and the elders persuaded the multitudes to ask for Barabbas, and to put Jesus to death.

21 But the governor answered and said to them, "Which of the two do you want me to release for you?" And they said, "Barabbas."

22 Pilate *said to them, "What then shall I do with Jesus who is called Christ?" They all *said, "Let Him be crucified!"

23 And he said, "Why, what evil has He done?" But they kept shouting all the more, saying, "Let Him be crucified!"

24 And when Pilate saw that he was accomplishing nothing, but rather that a riot was starting, he took water and washed his hands in front of the multitude, saying, "I am innocent of this Man's blood; see *to that* yourselves."

25 And all the people answered and said, "His blood *be* on us and on our children!"

26 Then he released Barabbas for them; but Jesus he scourged and delivered over to be crucified.

27 Then the soldiers of the governor took Jesus into the Praetorium and gathered the whole *Roman* cohort around Him.

28 And they stripped Him, and put a scarlet robe on Him.

29 And after weaving a crown of thorns, they put it on His head, and a reed in His right hand; and they kneeled down before Him and mocked Him, saying, "Hail, King of the Jews!"

30 And they spat on Him, and took the reed and *began* to beat Him on the head.

31 And after they had mocked Him, they took His robe off and put His garments on Him, and led Him away to crucify *Him*.

32 And as they were coming out, they found a certain Cyrenian named Simon; this man they pressed into service to bear His cross.

33 And when they had come to a place called Golgotha, which means Place of a Skull,

34 THEY GAVE HIM WINE TO DRINK MINGLED WITH GALL; and after tasting *it*, He was unwilling to drink.

35 And when they had crucified Him, THEY DIVIDED UP HIS GARMENTS AMONG THEMSELVES, CASTING LOTS;

36 and sitting down, they *began* to keep watch over Him there.

37 And they put up above His head the charge against Him which read, "THIS IS JESUS THE KING OF THE JEWS."

38 At that time two robbers *were

crucified with Him, one on the right and one on the left.

39 And those who were passing by were hurling abuse at Him, WAGGING THEIR HEADS,

40 and saying, "You who destroy the temple and rebuild it in three days, save Yourself! If You are the Son of God, come down from the cross."

41 In the same way the chief priests, along with the scribes and elders, were mocking *Him*, and saying,

42 "He saved others; He cannot save Himself. He is the King of Israel; let Him now come down from the cross, and we shall believe in Him.

43 "HE TRUSTS IN GOD; LET HIM DELIVER *Him* now, IF HE TAKES PLEASURE IN HIM; for He said, 'I am the Son of God.'"

44 And the robbers also who had been crucified with Him were casting the same insult at Him.

45 Now from the sixth hour darkness fell upon all the land until the ninth hour.

46 And about the ninth hour Jesus cried out with a loud voice, saying, "ELI, ELI, LAMA SABACHTHANI?" that is, "MY GOD, MY GOD, WHY HAST THOU FORSAKEN ME?"

47 And some of those who were standing there, when they heard it, *began* saying, "This man is calling for Elijah."

48 And immediately one of them ran, and taking a sponge, he filled it with sour wine, and put it on a reed, and gave Him a drink.

49 But the rest *of them* said, "Let us see whether Elijah will come to save Him."

50 And Jesus cried out again with a loud voice, and yielded up *His* spirit.

51 And behold, the veil of the temple was torn in two from top to bottom, and the earth shook; and the rocks were split,

52 and the tombs were opened; and many bodies of the saints who had fallen asleep were raised;

53 and coming out of the tombs after His resurrection they entered the holy city and appeared to many.

54 Now the centurion, and those who were with him keeping guard over Jesus, when they saw the earthquake and the things that were happening, became very frightened and said, "Truly this was the Son of God!"

55 And many women were there looking on from a distance, who had followed Jesus from Galilee, ministering to Him,

56 among whom was Mary Magdalene, *along with* Mary the mother of James and Joseph, and the mother of the sons of Zebedee.

57 And when it was evening, there came a rich man from Arimathea, named Joseph, who himself had also become a disciple of Jesus.

58 This man came to Pilate and asked for the body of Jesus. Then Pilate ordered *it* to be given over *to him*.

59 And Joseph took the body and wrapped it in a clean linen cloth,

60 and laid it in his own new tomb, which he had hewn out in the rock; and he rolled a large stone against the entrance of the tomb and went away.

61 And Mary Magdalene was there, and the other Mary, sitting opposite the grave.

62 Now on the next day, which is *the one* after the preparation, the chief priests and the Pharisees gathered together with Pilate,

63 and said, "Sir, we remember that when He was still alive that deceiver said, 'After three days I *am to* rise again.'

64 "Therefore, give orders for the grave to be made secure until the third day, lest the disciples come and steal Him away and say to the people,

'He has risen from the dead,' and the last deception will be worse than the first."

65 Pilate said to them, "You have a guard; go, make it *as* secure as you know how."

66 And they went and made the grave secure, and along with the guard they set a seal on the stone.

Chapter 28

NOW late on the Sabbath, as it began to dawn toward the first *day* of the week, Mary Magdalene and the other Mary came to look at the grave.

2 And behold, a severe earthquake had occurred, for an angel of the Lord descended from heaven and came and rolled away the stone and sat upon it.

3 And his appearance was like lightning, and his garment as white as snow;

4 and the guards shook for fear of him, and became like dead men.

5 And the angel answered and said to the women, "Do not be afraid; for I know that you are looking for Jesus who has been crucified.

6 "He is not here, for He has risen, just as He said. Come, see the place where He was lying. (a)

7 "And go quickly and tell His disciples that He has risen from the dead; and behold, He is going before you into Galilee, there you will see Him; behold, I have told you." (b)

8 And they departed quickly from the tomb with fear and great joy and ran to report it to His disciples.

9 And behold, Jesus met them and greeted them. And they came up and took hold of His feet and worshiped Him.

10 Then Jesus *said to them, "Do not be afraid; go and take word to My brethren to leave for Galilee, and there they shall see Me."

11 Now while they were on their way, behold, some of the guard came into the city and reported to the chief priests all that had happened.

12 And when they had assembled with the elders and counseled together, they gave a large sum of money to the soldiers,

13 and said, "You are to say, 'His disciples came by night and stole Him away while we were asleep.'

14 "And if this should come to the governor's ears, we will win him over and keep you out of trouble."

15 And they took the money and did as they had been instructed; and this story was widely spread among the Jews, *and is* to this day.

The RESURRECTION OF CHRIST WAS

(a) FORETOLD by Jesus. "The Son of Man must suffer many things and be rejected by the leaders and chief priests and scribes, and be killed, and be raised up the third day," Luke 9:22 page 92, and "Just as He said" is a

(b) FACT OF HISTORY. "He is risen from the dead." "He Himself stood in their midst" and said, "See My hands and My Feet, that it is I Myself; touch Me and see, for a spirit does not have flesh and bones as you see that I have," Luke 24:36, 39 page 121. Now you must have

(c) FAITH IN HIS RESURRECTION TO BE SAVED. "If you confess with your mouth Jesus as Lord, and believe in your heart that God raised Him from the dead, you shall be saved," Rom. 10:9 page 219.

16 But the eleven disciples proceeded to Galilee, to the mountain which Jesus had designated.

17 And when they saw Him, they worshiped *Him*; but some were doubtful.

SCRIPTURE NO. 1, SEC. 2

18 And Jesus came up and spoke to them, saying, "All authority has been given to Me in heaven and on earth.

19 "Go therefore and make disciples of all the nations, baptizing them in the name of the Father and the Son and the Holy Spirit,

20 teaching them to observe all that I commanded you; and lo, I am with you always, even to the end of the age." (r1)

Have you read the preceding references? It is best that you first read the six references in section one on "What you must do to be saved" beginning on page 186 with Acts 16:30–34.

The following is the first of four references concerning scriptures on the subject.

"How You Can Show Others You Are Saved."

(r1) REFERENCE NO. 1, SEC. 2—

BAPTISM OF BELIEVERS SHOWS SALVATION.

Jesus said, "Go . . . make disciples . . . baptizing them in the name of the Father and the Son and the Holy Spirit, teaching them to observe all that I command you."

When you believe in your heart and call upon the name of the Lord in true repentance and confess your faith in Him you become His disciple. Now, as a believer, you should be baptized as Jesus commanded.

Baptism is a picture of the gospel showing the death, burial and resurrection of Jesus. For you are "buried with Him through baptism into death." And Just "as Christ was raised from the dead through the glory of the Father," by this living Lord you "too might walk in newness of life." In baptism, you show how you consider yourself "to be dead to sin, but alive to God in Christ Jesus." This pictures how you are buried with Him "and raised to walk in newness of life."

Baptism is an act of obedience that follows salvation. Cornelius, "his relatives and close friends" heard Peter speak "words . . . by which you will be saved, you and all your household." "While Peter was still speaking these words, the Holy Spirit fell upon all those who were listening to the message." The "believers who had come with Peter . . . heard them speaking . . . and exalting God. Then Peter answered, surely no one can refuse the water for these to be baptized who have received the Holy Spirit just as we did, can he? And he ordered them to be baptized." In keeping with Jesus' command to His disciples they were "buried with Him in baptism" and "raised up with Him through faith in the working of God."

See page 177, Acts 10:46–48, Acts 11:12, and the explanation on that page, which shows the church members heard the testimony of the new believers.

If you have called upon the name of the Lord and received Jesus Christ as Savior, and confessed Him as your Lord, show your love and obey His command to be baptized.

Will you obey God's command to be baptized? If so, say:

"I will obey Him and be baptized."

Now turn to page 264, Scripture 2, Sec. 2, Eph. 3:20,21.

THE GOSPEL

ACCORDING TO

MARK

THE beginning of the gospel of Jesus Christ, the Son of God.

2 As it is written in Isaiah the prophet,

"BEHOLD, I SEND MY MESSEN-
GER BEFORE YOUR FACE,
WHO WILL PREPARE YOUR
WAY;

3 "THE VOICE OF ONE CRYING IN
THE WILDERNESS,
'MAKE READY THE WAY OF THE
LORD,
MAKE HIS PATHS STRAIGHT.'"

4 John the Baptist appeared in the wilderness preaching a baptism of repentance for the forgiveness of sins.

5 And all the country of Judea was going out to him, and all the people of Jerusalem; and they were being baptized by him in the Jordan River, confessing their sins.

6 And John was clothed with camel's hair and *wore* a leather belt around his waist, and his diet was locusts and wild honey.

7 And he was preaching, and saying, "After me comes One who is mightier than I, and I am not *even* fit to stoop down and untie the thong of His sandals.

8 "I baptized you with water; but He will baptize you with the Holy Spirit."

9 And it came about in those days that Jesus came from Nazareth in Galilee, and was baptized by John in the Jordan.

10 And immediately coming up out of the water, He saw the heavens opening, and the Spirit like a dove descending upon Him;

11 and a voice came out of the heavens: "Thou art My beloved Son, in Thee I am well-pleased."

12 And immediately the Spirit *impelled Him *to go* out into the wilderness.

13 And He was in the wilderness forty days being tempted by Satan; and He was with the wild beasts, and the angels were ministering to Him.

14 And after John had been taken into custody, Jesus came into Galilee, preaching the gospel of God,

15 and saying, "The time is fulfilled, and the kingdom of God is at hand; repent and believe in the gospel."

16 And as He was going along by the sea of Galilee, He saw Simon and Andrew, the brother of Simon, casting a net in the sea; for they were fishermen.

17 And Jesus said to them, "Follow Me, and I will make you become fishers of men."

18 And they immediately left the nets and followed Him.

19 And going on a little farther, He saw James the *son* of Zebedee, and John his brother, who were also in the boat mending the nets.

20 And immediately He called them; and they left their father Zebe-

dee in the boat with the hired servants, and went away to follow Him.

21 And they *went into Capernaum; and immediately on the
Sabbath He entered the synagogue
and *began* to teach.

22 And they were amazed at His
teaching; for He was teaching them as
one having authority, and not as the
scribes.

23 And just then there was in their
synagogue a man with an unclean
spirit; and he cried out,

24 saying, "What do we have to do
with You, Jesus of Nazareth? Have
You come to destroy us? I know who
You are—the Holy One of God!"

25 And Jesus rebuked him, saying,
"Be quiet, and come out of him!"

26 And throwing him into convulsions, the unclean spirit cried out with
a loud voice, and came out of him.

27 And they were all amazed, so
that they debated among themselves,
saying, "What is this? A new teaching
with authority! He commands even
the unclean spirits, and they obey
Him."

28 And immediately the news
about Him went out everywhere into
all the surrounding district of Galilee.

29 And immediately after they
had come out of the synagogue, they
came into the house of Simon and
Andrew, with James and John.

30 Now Simon's mother-in-law
was lying sick with a fever; and immediately they *spoke to Him about her.

31 And He came to her and raised
her up, taking her by the hand, and
the fever left her, and she began to
wait on them.

32 And when evening had come,
after the sun had set, they *began*
bringing to Him all who were ill and
those who were demon-possessed.

33 And the whole city had gathered at the door.

34 And He healed many who were
ill with various diseases, and cast out
many demons; and He was not per-
mitting the demons to speak, because
they knew who He was.

35 And in the early morning, while
it was still dark, He arose and went
out and departed to a lonely place,
and was praying there.

36 And Simon and his companions
hunted for Him;

37 and they found Him, and *said
to Him, "Everyone is looking for
You."

38 And He *said to them, "Let us
go somewhere else to the towns
nearby, in order that I may preach
there also; for that is what I came out
for."

39 And He went into their synagogues throughout all Galilee,
preaching and casting out the demons.

40 And a leper *came to Him, be-
seeching Him and falling on his knees
before Him, and saying to Him, "If
You are willing, You can make me
clean."

41 And moved with compassion,
He stretched out His hand and
touched him, and *said to him, "I am
willing; be cleansed."

42 And immediately the leprosy
left him and he was cleansed.

43 And He sternly warned him and
immediately sent him away,

44 and He *said to him, "See that
you say nothing to anyone; but go,
show yourself to the priest and offer
for your cleansing what Moses commanded, for a testimony to them."

45 But he went out and began to
proclaim it freely and to spread the
news about, to such an extent that
Jesus could no longer publicly enter a
city, but stayed out in unpopulated
areas; and they were coming to Him
from everywhere.

CHAPTER 2

AND when He had come back to

Capernaum several days afterward, it was heard that He was at home.

2 And many were gathered together, so that there was no longer room, even near the door; and He was speaking the word to them.

3 And they *came, bringing to Him a paralytic, carried by four men.

4 And being unable to get to Him on account of the crowd, they removed the roof above Him; and when they had dug an opening, they let down the pallet on which the paralytic was lying.

5 And Jesus seeing their faith *said to the paralytic, "My son, your sins are forgiven."

6 But there were some of the scribes sitting there and reasoning in their hearts,

7 "Why does this man speak that way? He is blaspheming; who can forgive sins but God alone?"

8 And immediately Jesus, perceiving in His spirit that they were reasoning that way within themselves, *said to them, "Why are you reasoning about these things in your hearts?

9 "Which is easier, to say to the paralytic, 'Your sins are forgiven'; or to say, 'Arise, and take up your pallet and walk'?

10 "But in order that you may know that the Son of Man has authority on earth to forgive sins," He *said to the paralytic,

11 "I say to you, rise, take up your pallet and go home."

12 And he rose and immediately took up the pallet and went out in the sight of all; so that they were all amazed and were glorifying God, saying, "We have never seen anything like this."

13 And He went out again by the seashore; and all the multitude were coming to Him, and He was teaching them.

14 And as He passed by, He saw Levi the *son* of Alpheus sitting in the tax office, and He *said to him, "Follow Me!" And he rose and followed Him.

15 And it came about that He was reclining *at table* in his house, and many tax-gatherers and sinners were dining with Jesus and His disciples; for there were many of them, and they were following Him.

16 And when the scribes of the Pharisees saw that He was eating with the sinners and tax-gatherers, they *began* saying to His disciples, "Why is He eating and drinking with tax-gatherers and sinners?"

17 And hearing this, Jesus *said to them, "*It is not* those who are healthy who need a physician, but those who are sick; I did not come to call *the* righteous, but sinners."

18 And John's disciples and the Pharisees were fasting; and they *came and *said to Him, "Why do John's disciples and the disciples of the Pharisees fast, but Your disciples do not fast?"

19 And Jesus said to them, "While the bridegroom is with them, the attendants of the bridegroom do not fast, do they? So long as they have the bridegroom with them, they cannot fast.

20 "But the days will come when the bridegroom is taken away from them, and then they will fast in that day.

21 "No one sews a patch of unshrunk cloth on an old garment; otherwise the patch pulls away from it, the new from the old, and a worse tear results.

22 "And no one puts new wine into old wineskins; otherwise the wine will burst the skins, and the wine is lost, and the skins *as well*; but *one puts* new wine into fresh wineskins."

23 And it came about that He was passing through the grainfields on the Sabbath, and His disciples began to

make their way along while picking the heads *of grain.*

24 And the Pharisees were saying to Him, "See here, why are they doing what is not lawful on the Sabbath?"

25 And He *said to them, "Have you never read what David did when he was in need and became hungry, he and his companions:

26 how he entered into the house of God in the time of Abiathar *the* high priest, and ate the consecrated bread, which is not lawful for *anyone* to eat except the priests, and he gave *it* also to those who were with him?"

27 And He was saying to them, "The Sabbath was made for man, and not man for the Sabbath.

28 "Consequently, the Son of Man is Lord even of the Sabbath."

CHAPTER 3

AND He entered again into a synagogue; and a man was there with a withered hand.

2 And they were watching Him *to see* if He would heal him on the Sabbath, in order that they might accuse Him.

3 And He *said to the man with the withered hand, "Rise and *come* forward!"

4 And He *said to them, "Is it lawful on the Sabbath to do good or to do harm, to save a life or to kill?" But they kept silent.

5 And after looking around at them with anger, grieved at their hardness of heart, He *said to the man, "Stretch out your hand." And he stretched it out, and his hand was restored.

6 And the Pharisees went out and immediately *began* taking counsel with the Herodians against Him, *as to* how they might destroy Him.

7 And Jesus withdrew to the sea with His disciples; and a great multitude from Galilee followed; and *also* from Judea,

8 and from Jerusalem, and from Idumea, and beyond the Jordan, and the vicinity of Tyre and Sidon, a great multitude heard of all that He was doing and came to Him.

9 And He told His disciples that a boat should stand ready for Him because of the multitude, in order that they might not crowd Him;

10 for He had healed many, with the result that all those who had afflictions pressed about Him in order to touch Him.

11 And whenever the unclean spirits beheld Him, they would fall down before Him and cry out, saying, "You are the Son of God!"

12 And He earnestly warned them not to reveal His identity.

13 And He *went up to the mountain and *summoned those whom He Himself wanted, and they came to Him.

14 And He appointed twelve, that they might be with Him, and that He might send them out to preach,

15 and to have authority to cast out the demons.

16 And He appointed the twelve: Simon (to whom He gave the name Peter),

17 and James, the *son* of Zebedee, and John the brother of James (to them He gave the name Boanerges, which means, "Sons of Thunder");

18 and Andrew, and Philip, and Bartholomew, and Matthew, and Thomas, and James the *son* of Alphaeus, and Thaddaeus, and Simon the Cananaean;

19 and Judas Iscariot, who also betrayed Him.

20 And He *came home, and the multitude *gathered again, to such an extent that they could not even eat a meal.

21 And when His own people heard *of this*, they went out to take custody of Him; for they were saying, "He has lost His senses."

22 And the scribes who came down from Jerusalem were saying, "He is possessed by Beelzebul," and "He casts out the demons by the ruler of the demons."

23 And He called them to Himself and began speaking to them in parables, "How can Satan cast out Satan?

24 "And if a kingdom is divided against itself, that kingdom cannot stand.

25 "And if a house is divided against itself, that house will not be able to stand.

26 "And if Satan has risen up against himself and is divided, he cannot stand, but he is finished!

27 "But no one can enter the strong man's house and plunder his property unless he first binds the strong man, and then he will plunder his house.

28 "Truly I say to you, all sins shall be forgiven the sons of men, and whatever blasphemies they utter;

29 but whoever blasphemes against the Holy Spirit never has forgiveness, but is guilty of an eternal sin" —

30 because they were saying, "He has an unclean spirit."

31 And His mother and His brothers *arrived, and standing outside they sent *word* to Him, and called Him.

32 And a multitude was sitting around Him, and they *said to Him, "Behold, Your mother and Your brothers are outside looking for You."

33 And answering them, He *said, "Who are My mother and My brothers?"

34 And looking about on those who were sitting around Him, He *said, "Behold, My mother and My brothers!

35 "For whoever does the will of God, he is My brother and sister and mother."

Chapter 4

And He began to teach again by the seashore. And such a very great multitude gathered before Him that He got into a boat in the sea and sat down; and all the multitude were by the seashore on the land.

2 And He was teaching them many things in parables, and was saying to them in His teaching,

3 "Listen *to this*! Behold, the sower went out to sow;

4 and it came about that as he was sowing, some *seed* fell beside the road, and the birds came and ate it up.

5 "And other *seed* fell on the rocky *ground* where it did not have much soil; and immediately it sprang up because it had no depth of soil.

6 "And after the sun had risen, it was scorched; and because it had no root, it withered away.

7 "And other *seed* fell among the thorns, and the thorns grew up and choked it, and it yielded no crop.

8 "And other *seeds* fell into the good soil and as they grew up and increased, they were yielding a crop and were producing thirty, sixty, and a hundredfold."

9 And He was saying, "He who has ears to hear, let him hear."

10 And as soon as He was alone, His followers, along with the twelve, *began* asking Him *about* the parables.

11 And He was saying to them, "To you has been given the mystery of the kingdom of God; but those who are outside get everything in parables,

12 in order that WHILE SEEING, THEY MAY SEE AND NOT PERCEIVE; AND WHILE HEARING, THEY MAY HEAR AND NOT UNDERSTAND LEST THEY RETURN AGAIN AND BE FORGIVEN."

13 And He *said to them, "Do you not understand this parable? And how will you understand all the parables?

14 "The sower sows the word.

15 "And these are the ones who are beside the road where the word is sown; and when they hear, immediately Satan comes and takes away the word which has been sown in them.

16 "And in a similar way these are the ones on whom seed was sown on the rocky *places*, who, when they hear the word, immediately receive it with joy;

17 and they have no *firm* root in themselves, but are *only* temporary; then, when affliction or persecution arises because of the word, immediately they fall away.

18 "And others are the ones on whom seed was sown among the thorns; these are the ones who have heard the word,

19 and the worries of the world, and the deceitfulness of riches, and the desires for other things enter in and choke the word, and it becomes unfruitful.

20 "And those are the ones on whom seed was sown on the good ground; and they hear the word and accept it, and bear fruit, thirty, sixty, and a hundredfold."

21 And He was saying to them, "A lamp is not brought to be put under a peck-measure, is it, or under a bed? Is it not *brought* to be put on the lampstand?

22 "For nothing is hidden, except to be revealed; nor has *anything* been secret, but that it should come to light.

23 "If any man has ears to hear, let him hear."

24 And He was saying to them, "Take care what you listen to. By your standard of measure it shall be measured to you; and more shall be given you besides.

25 "For whoever has, to him shall *more* be given; and whoever does not have, even what he has shall be taken away from him."

26 And He was saying, "The kingdom of God is like a man who casts seed upon the ground;

27 and goes to bed at night and gets up by day, and the seed sprouts up and grows — how, he himself does not know.

28 "The earth produces crops by itself; first the blade, then the head, then the mature grain in the head.

29 "But when the crop permits, he immediately puts in the sickle, because the harvest has come."

30 And He said, "How shall we picture the kingdom of God, or by what parable shall we present it?

31 "*It is* like a mustard seed, which, when sown upon the ground, though it is smaller than all the seeds that are upon the ground,

32 yet when it is sown, grows up and becomes larger than all the garden plants and forms large branches; so that the birds of the air can nest under its shade."

33 And with many such parables He was speaking the word to them as they were able to hear it;

34 and He was not speaking to them without parables; but He was explaining everything privately to His own disciples.

35 And on that day, when evening had come, He *said to them, "Let us go over to the other side."

36 And leaving the multitude they *took Him along with them, just as He was, in the boat; and other boats were with Him.

37 And there *arose a fierce gale of wind, and the waves were breaking

over the boat so much that the boat was already filling up.

38 And He Himself was in the stern, asleep on the cushion; and they *awoke Him and *said to Him, "Teacher, do You not care that we are perishing?"

39 And being aroused, He rebuked the wind and said to the sea, "Hush, be still." And the wind died down and it became perfectly calm.

40 And He said to them, "Why are you so timid? How is it that you have no faith?"

41 And they became very much afraid and said to one another, "Who then is this, that even the wind and the sea obey Him?"

CHAPTER 5

AND they came to the other side of the sea, into the country of the Gerasenes.

2 And when He had come out of the boat, immediately a man from the tombs with an unclean spirit met Him,

3 and he had his dwelling among the tombs. And no one was able to bind him any more, even with a chain;

4 because he had often been bound with shackles and chains, and the chains had been torn apart by him, and the shackles broken in pieces, and no one was strong enough to subdue him.

5 And constantly night and day, among the tombs and in the mountains, he was crying out and gashing himself with stones.

6 And seeing Jesus from a distance, he ran up and bowed down before Him;

7 and crying out with a loud voice, he *said, "What do I have to do with You, Jesus, Son of the Most High God? I implore You by God, do not torment me!"

8 For He had been saying to him,

"Come out of the man, you unclean spirit!"

9 And He was asking him, "What is your name?" And he *said to Him, "My name is Legion; for we are many."

10 And he *began* to entreat Him earnestly not to send them out of the country.

11 Now there was a big herd of swine feeding there on the mountain side.

12 And they entreated Him, saying, "Send us into the swine so that we may enter them."

13 And He gave them permission. And coming out, the unclean spirits entered the swine; and the herd rushed down the steep bank into the sea, about two thousand *of them*; and they were drowned in the sea.

14 And those who tended them ran away and reported it in the city and *out* in the country. And *the people* came to see what it was that had happened.

15 And they *came to Jesus and *observed the man who had been demon-possessed sitting down, clothed and in his right mind, the very man who had had the "legion"; and they became frightened.

16 And those who had seen it described to them how it had happened to the demon-possessed man, and *all* about the swine.

17 And they began to entreat Him to depart from their region.

18 And as He was getting into the boat, the man who had been demon-possessed was entreating Him that he might accompany Him.

19 And He did not let him, but He *said to him, "Go home to your people and report to them what great things the Lord has done for you, and *how* He had mercy on you."

20 And he went off and began to proclaim in Decapolis what great things Jesus had done for him; and everyone marveled.

21 And when Jesus had crossed over again in the boat to the other side, a great multitude gathered about Him; and He stayed by the seashore.

22 And one of the synagogue officials named Jairus *came up, and upon seeing Him, *fell at His feet,

23 and *entreated Him earnestly, saying, "My little daughter is at the point of death; *please* come and lay Your hands on her, that she may get well and live."

24 And He went off with him; and a great multitude was following Him and pressing in on Him. (r1)

25 And a woman who had had a hemorrhage for twelve years, (a)

26 and had endured much at the hands of many physicians, and had spent all that she had and was not helped at all, but rather had grown worse, (b)

27 after hearing about Jesus, came up in the crowd behind *Him,* and touched His cloak.

28 For she thought, "If I just touch His garments, I shall get well." (c)

29 And immediately the flow of her blood was dried up; (d) and she

---

(r1) THE MESSAGE OF THE MIRACLE. Miracles were performed by Jesus for the purpose of revealing His Messiahship, see John 20:30, 31, p. 157.

(a) CONDITION—The physical condition of the woman's diseased body suffering "a hemorrhage for twelve years" portrays the fate of the sinner. She faced the fate or peril of physical death. The sinner faces the fate of the death of his soul, "Sin . . . brings forth death," James 1:15, p. 309; Rom. 6:23, p. 214.

(b) CONDEMNATION—The words "had grown worse" shows the woman was condemned to die because of the disease. Her failure to find a remedy sealed her fate. The sinner has no human remedy for the disease of sin, Eph. 2:8, 9, p 263. She had no hope. The sinner has no human hope, Eph. 2:12, p. 263. The sinner is "condemned already" "without Christ" John 3:18, p. 126. She had "spent all" and came as a pauper empty handed to Jesus. The sinner must come "empty handed" to Christ, acknowledging his failure.

(c) CONFIDENCE—"After hearing about Jesus" she came to Him. Her faith grew out of the message she heard about the power of Jesus to heal. She was told by someone who knew of her peril. For the sinner "faith comes from hearing, and hearing by the Word of Christ," Rom. 10:17, p. 220. Her faith was expressed in an act. She came to Him. The sinner must come to Jesus as an act of faith, Matt. 11:28, p. 15, John 5:40, p. 130.

(d) COMPLETE CURE—"The words, "immediately . . . dried up," indicate two things. First, the woman was cured instantly. That is a picture of salvation. It is instant as an event. "He who believes has eternal life," John 5:24, p. 130. Second, the woman was healed completely as shown in the words "dried up." In her peril she experienced His power and found perfect healing. Likewise the sinner passes "out of death into life . . . and does not come into judgment." It is instant and complete salvation.

(Turn to next page.)

felt in her body that she was healed of her affliction. (e)

30 And immediately Jesus, perceiving in Himself that the power *proceeding* from Him had gone forth, turned around in the crowd and said, "Who touched My garments?"

31 And His disciples said to Him, "You see the multitude pressing in on You, and You say, 'Who touched Me?' "

32 And He looked around to see the woman who had done this.

33 But the woman fearing and trembling, aware of what had happened to her, came and fell down before Him, and told Him the whole truth. (f)

34 And He said to her, "Daughter, your faith has made you well; go in peace, and be healed of your affliction." (g)

35 While He was still speaking, they *came from the *house of* the synagogue official, saying, "Your daughter has died; why trouble the Teacher any more?"

36 But Jesus, overhearing what was being spoken, *said to the synagogue official, "Do not be afraid *any longer,* only believe."

37 And He allowed no one to follow with Him, except Peter and James and John the brother of James.

38 And they *came to the house of the synagogue official; and He *beheld a commotion, and *people* loudly weeping and wailing.

39 And entering in, He *said to them, "Why make a commotion and

---

(Continued from page 53.)

(e) CONSCIOUSNESS—"She felt in her body that she was healed." How perfect was her healing. She knew she was healed. Likewise the sinner who is saved is made conscious. He "has the witness in himself." It is written "in order that you may know that you have eternal life." I John 5:10-13, pages 325 and 326. But notice the woman did not feel her healing until she believed Jesus first. The sinner believes Jesus, then feels salvation, for feeling follows faith.

(f) CONFESSION—Her faith overcame her fears. She "told Him the whole truth." She confesses that the miracle of Christ had healed her body to be a fact. She told publicly of her peril, her faith in His power, and the perfect healing she experienced. The sinner, when saved, tells the world Jesus Christ is Lord and Savior, Rom. 10:9, p. 219 and Matt. 10:32, p. 13.

(g) CHILD OF GOD—"a woman" becomes "daughter" she gained a future in the family of God. What a relationship. The sinner becomes a son "of God through faith in Christ Jesus," Gal. 3:26, p. 259. "Go in peace, and be healed of your affliction assured a future free from fear. She came in a state of peril. She experienced His power in healing. She went home in peace. The sinner in peril of Hell can experience God's great salvation in the power of Christ and go in peace Rom. 5:1, p. 211. What is your relationship to God? Are you just a man or a woman? You can be a daughter or a son of God. Put your faith in Christ's death, burial and resurrection.

See Rom. 10:9-14, page 219, and Reference No. 6, Sec. 1. Pray the prayer suggested there.

weep? The child has not died, but is asleep."

40 And they were laughing at Him. But putting them all out, He *took along the child's father and mother and His own companions, and *entered the *room* where the child was.

41 And taking the child by the hand, He *said to her, "Talitha kum!" (which translated means, "Little girl, I say to you, arise!")

42 And immediately the girl got up and *began* to walk; for she was twelve years old. And immediately they were completely astounded.

43 And He gave them strict orders that no one should know about this; and He said that *something* should be given her to eat.

CHAPTER 6

AND He went out from there, and He *came into His home town; and His disciples *followed Him.

2 And when the Sabbath had come, He began to teach in the synagogue; and the many listeners were astonished, saying, "Where did this man *get* these things, and what is *this* wisdom given to Him, and such miracles as these performed by His hands?

3 "Is not this the carpenter, the son of Mary, and brother of James, and Joses, and Judas, and Simon? Are not His sisters here with us?" And they took offense at Him.

4 And Jesus said to them, "A prophet is not without honor except in his home town and among his *own* relatives and in his *own* household."

5 And He could do no miracle there except that He laid His hands upon a few sick people and healed them.

6 And He wondered at their unbelief.

And He was going around the villages teaching.

7 And He *summoned the twelve and began to send them out in pairs; and He was giving them authority over the unclean spirits;

8 and He instructed them that they should take nothing for *their* journey, except a mere staff; no bread, no bag, no money in their belt;

9 but *to* wear sandals; and *He* added, "Do not put on two tunics."

10 And He said to them, "Wherever you enter a house, stay there until you leave town.

11 "And any place that does not receive you or listen to you, as you go out from there, shake off the dust from the soles of your feet for a testimony against them."

12 And they went out and preached that *men* should repent.

13 And they were casting out many demons and were anointing with oil many sick people and healing them.

14 And King Herod heard *of it,* for His name had become well known; and *people* were saying, "John the Baptist has risen from the dead, and therefore these miraculous powers are at work in him."

15 But others were saying, "*He is* Elijah." And others were saying, "*He is* a prophet, like one of the prophets of old."

16 But when Herod heard *of it,* he kept saying, "John, whom I beheaded, he has risen!"

17 For Herod himself had sent and had John arrested and bound in prison on account of Herodias, the wife of his brother Philip, because he had married her.

18 For John had been saying to Herod, "It is not lawful for you to have your brother's wife."

19 And Herodias had a grudge against him and wanted to kill him; and could not *do so;*

20 for Herod was afraid of John, knowing that he was a righteous and

holy man, and kept him safe. And when he heard him, he was very perplexed; but he used to enjoy listening to him.

21 And a strategic day came when Herod on his birthday gave a banquet for his lords and military commanders and the leading men of Galilee;

22 and when the daughter of Herodias herself came in and danced, she pleased Herod and his dinner guests; and the king said to the girl, "Ask me for whatever you want and I will give it to you."

23 And he swore to her, "Whatever you ask of me, I will give it to you; up to half of my kingdom."

24 And she went out and said to her mother, "What shall I ask for?" And she said, "The head of John the Baptist."

25 And immediately she came in haste before the king and asked, saying, "I want you to give me right away the head of John the Baptist on a platter."

26 And although the king was very sorry, *yet* because of his oaths and because of his dinner guests, he was unwilling to refuse her.

27 And immediately the king sent an executioner and commanded *him* to bring *back* his head. And he went and beheaded him in the prison,

28 and brought his head on a platter, and gave it to the girl; and the girl gave it to her mother.

29 And when his disciples heard *about this*, they came and took away his body and laid it in a tomb.

30 And the apostles *gathered together with Jesus; and they reported to Him all that they had done and taught.

31 And He *said to them, "Come away by yourselves to a lonely place and rest a while." (For there were many *people* coming and going, and they did not even have time to eat.)

32 And they went away in the boat to a lonely place by themselves.

33 And *the people* saw them going, and many recognized *them*, and they ran there together on foot from all the cities, and got there ahead of them.

34 And disembarking, He saw a great multitude, and He felt compassion for them because they were like sheep without a shepherd; and He began to teach them many things.

35 And when it was already quite late, His disciples came up to Him and *began saying, "The place is desolate and it is already quite late;

36 send them away so that they may go into the surrounding countryside and villages and buy themselves something to eat."

37 But He answered and said to them, "You give them something to eat!" And they *said to Him, "Shall we go and spend two hundred denarii on bread and give them something to eat?"

38 And He *said to them, "How many loaves do you have? Go look!" And when they found out, they *said, "Five and two fish."

39 And He commanded them all to recline by groups on the green grass.

40 And they reclined in companies of hundreds and of fifties.

41 And He took the five loaves and the two fish, and looking up toward heaven, He blessed *the food* and broke the loaves and He kept giving *them* to the disciples to set before them; and He divided up the two fish among them all.

42 And they all ate and were satisfied.

43 And they picked up twelve full baskets of the broken pieces, and also of the fish.

44 And there were five thousand men who ate the loaves.

45 And immediately He made His disciples get into the boat and go ahead of *Him* to the other side to Bethsaida, while He Himself was sending the multitude away.

46 And after bidding them farewell, He departed to the mountain to pray.

47 And when it was evening, the boat was in the midst of the sea, and He *was* alone on the land.

48 And seeing them straining at the oars, for the wind was against them, at about the fourth watch of the night, He *came to them, walking on the sea; and He intended to pass by them.

49 But when they saw Him walking on the sea, they supposed that it was a ghost, and cried out;

50 for they all saw Him and were frightened. But immediately He spoke with them and *said to them, "Take courage; it is I, do not be afraid."

51 And He got into the boat with them, and the wind stopped; and they were greatly astonished,

52 for they had not gained any insight from the *incident of* the loaves, but their heart was hardened.

53 And when they had crossed over they came to land at Gennesaret, and moored to the shore.

54 And when they had come out of the boat, immediately *the people* recognized Him,

55 and ran about that whole country and began to carry about on their pallets those who were sick, to the place they heard He was.

56 And wherever He entered villages, or cities, or countryside, they were laying the sick in the market places, and entreating Him that they might just touch the fringe of His cloak; and as many as touched it were being cured.

CHAPTER 7

AND the Pharisees and some of the scribes gathered together around Him when they had come from Jerusalem,

2 and had seen that some of His disciples were eating their bread with impure hands, that is, unwashed.

3 (For the Pharisees and all the Jews do not eat unless they carefully wash their hands, *thus* observing the traditions of the elders;

4 and *when they come* from the market place, they do not eat unless they cleanse themselves; and there are many other things which they have received in order to observe, such as the washing of cups and pitchers and copper pots.)

5 And the Pharisees and the scribes *asked Him, "Why do Your disciples not walk according to the tradition of the elders, but eat their bread with impure hands?"

6 And He said to them, "Rightly did Isaiah prophesy of you hypocrites, as it is written,

> 'THIS PEOPLE HONORS ME WITH THEIR LIPS,
> BUT THEIR HEART IS FAR AWAY FROM ME.

7 'BUT IN VAIN DO THEY WORSHIP ME,
> TEACHING AS DOCTRINES THE PRECEPTS OF MEN.'

8 "Neglecting the commandment of God, you hold to the tradition of men."

9 He was also saying to them, "You nicely set aside the commandment of God in order to keep your tradition.

10 "For Moses said, 'HONOR YOUR FATHER AND YOUR MOTHER'; and, 'HE WHO SPEAKS EVIL OF FATHER OR MOTHER, LET HIM BE PUT TO DEATH';

11 but you say, 'If a man says to *his* father or *his* mother, anything of mine you might have been helped by is Corban (that is to say, given *to* God),'

12 you no longer permit him to do anything for *his* father or *his* mother;

13 *thus* invalidating the word of

God by your tradition which you have handed down; and you do many such things like that."

14 And summoning the multitude again, He *began* saying to them, "Listen to Me, all of you, and understand:

15 there is nothing outside the man which going into him can defile him; but the things which proceed out of the man are what defile the man."

16 (See footnote.)

17 And when leaving the multitude, He had entered the house, His disciples questioned Him about the parable.

18 And He *said to them, "Are you too so uncomprehending? Do you not see that whatever goes into the man from outside cannot defile him;

19 because it does not go into his heart, but into his stomach, and is eliminated?" (*Thus He* declared all foods clean.)

20 And He was saying, "That which proceeds out of the man, that is what defiles the man.

21 "For from within, out of the heart of men, proceed the evil thoughts of men, proceed the evil thoughts of fornications, thefts, murders, adulteries,

22 deeds of coveting *and* wickedness, *as well as* deceit, sensuality, envy, slander, pride *and* foolishness.

23 "All these evil things proceed from within and defile the man."

24 And from there He arose and went away to the region of Tyre. And when He had entered a house, He wanted no one to know *of it*; yet He could not escape notice.

25 But after hearing of Him, a woman whose little daughter had an unclean spirit, immediately came and fell at His feet.

26 Now the woman was a Gentile, of the Syrophoenician race. And she kept asking Him to cast the demon out of her daughter.

27 And He was saying to her, "Let the children be satisfied first, for it is not good to take the children's bread and throw it to the dogs."

28 But she answered and *said to Him, "Yes, Lord, *but* even the dogs under the table feed on the children's crumbs."

29 And He said to her, "Because of this answer go your way; the demon has gone out of your daughter."

30 And going back to her home, she found the child lying on the bed, the demon having departed.

31 And again He went out from the region of Tyre, and came through Sidon to the sea of Galilee, within the region of Decapolis.

32 And they *brought to Him one who was deaf and spoke with difficulty, and they *entreated Him to lay His hand upon him.

33 And He took him aside from the multitude by himself, and put His fingers into his ears, and after spitting, He touched his tongue *with the saliva;*

34 and looking up to heaven with a deep sigh, He *said to him, "Ephphatha!" that is, "Be opened!"

35 And his ears were opened, and the impediment of his tongue was removed, and he *began* speaking plainly.

36 And He gave them orders not to tell anyone; but the more He ordered them, the more widely they continued to proclaim it.

37 And they were utterly astonished, saying, "He has done all things well; He makes even the deaf to hear, and the dumb to speak."

CHAPTER 8

IN those days again, when there was a great multitude and they had noth-

---

Later mss. add verse 16: *"If any man has ears to hear, let him hear."*

ing to eat, He summoned His disciples and *said to them,

2 "I feel compassion for the multitude because they have remained with Me now three days, and have nothing to eat;

3 and if I send them away fasting to their home, they will faint on the way; and some of them have come from a distance."

4 And His disciples answered Him, "Where will anyone be able to *find enough* to satisfy these men with bread here in the wilderness?"

5 And He was asking them, "How many loaves do you have?" And they said, "Seven."

6 And He *directed the multitude to sit down on the ground; and taking the seven loaves, He gave thanks and broke them, and *began* giving them to His disciples to serve to them, and they served them to the multitude.

7 They also had a few small fish; and after He had blessed them, He ordered these to be served as well.

8 And they ate and were satisfied; and they picked up seven full baskets of what was left over of the broken pieces.

9 And about four thousand were *there*; and He sent them away.

10 And immediately He entered the boat with His disciples, and came to the district of Dalmanutha.

11 And the Pharisees came out and began to argue with Him, seeking from Him a sign from heaven, to test Him.

12 And sighing deeply in His spirit, He *said, "Why does this generation seek for a sign? Truly I say to you, no sign shall be given to this generation."

13 And leaving them, He again embarked and went away to the other side.

14 And they had forgotten to take bread; and did not have more than one loaf in the boat with them.

15 And He was giving orders to them, saying, "Watch out! Beware of the leaven of the Pharisees and the leaven of Herod."

16 And they *began* to discuss with one another *the fact* that they had no bread.

17 And Jesus, aware of this, *said to them, "Why do you discuss *the fact* that you have no bread? Do you not yet see or understand? Do you have a hardened heart?

18 "HAVING EYES, DO YOU NOT SEE? AND HAVING EARS, DO YOU NOT HEAR? And do you not remember,

19 when I broke the five loaves for the five thousand, how many large baskets full of broken pieces you picked up?" They *said to Him, "Twelve."

20 "And when I *broke* the seven for the four thousand, how many baskets full of broken pieces did you pick up?" And they *said to Him, "Seven."

21 And He was saying to them, "Do you not yet understand?"

22 And they *came to Bethsaida. And they *brought a blind man to Him, and *entreated Him to touch him.

23 And taking the blind man by the hand, He brought him out of the village; and after spitting on his eyes, and laying His hands upon him, He asked him, "Do you see anything?"

24 And he looked up and said, "I see men, for I am seeing *them* like trees, walking about."

25 Then again He laid His hands upon his eyes; and he looked intently and was restored, and *began* to see everything clearly.

26 And He sent him to his home, saying, "Do not even enter the village."

27 And Jesus went out, along with His disciples, to the villages of Caesarea Philippi; and on the way He questioned His disciples, saying to them, "Who do people say that I am?"

28 And they told Him, saying, "John the Baptist; and others *say* Elijah; but still others, one of the prophets."

29 And He *continued* by questioning them, "But who do you say that I am?" Peter *answered and *said to Him, "Thou art the Christ."

30 And He warned them to tell no one about Him.

31 And He began to teach them that the Son of Man must suffer many things and be rejected by the elders and the chief priests and the scribes, and be killed, and after three days rise again.

32 And He was stating the matter plainly. And Peter took Him aside and began to rebuke Him.

33 But turning around and seeing His disciples, He rebuked Peter, and *said, "Get behind Me, Satan; for you are not setting your mind on God's interests, but man's."

34 And He summoned the multitude with His disciples, and said to them, "If anyone wishes to come after Me, let him deny himself, and take up his cross, and follow Me.

35 "For whoever wishes to save his life shall lose it; and whoever loses his life for My sake and the gospel's shall save it.

.36 "For what does it profit a man to gain the whole world, and forfeit his soul?

37 "For what shall a man give in exchange for his soul?

38 "For whoever is ashamed of Me and My words in this adulterous and sinful generation, the Son of Man will also be ashamed of him when He comes in the glory of His Father with the holy angels."

CHAPTER 9

AND He was saying to them, "Truly I say to you, there are some of those who are standing here who shall not taste of death until they see the kingdom of God after it has come with power."

2 And six days later, Jesus *took with Him Peter and James and John, and *brought them up to a high mountain by themselves. And He was transfigured before them;

3 and His garments became radiant and exceedingly white, as no launderer on earth can whiten them.

4 And Elijah appeared to them along with Moses; and they were conversing with Jesus.

5 And Peter *answered and *said to Jesus, "Rabbi, it is good for us to be here; and let us make three tabernacles, one for You, and one for Moses, and one for Elijah."

6 For he did not know what to answer; for they became terrified.

7 Then a cloud formed, overshadowing them, and a voice came out of the cloud, "This is My beloved Son, listen to Him!"

8 And all at once they looked around and saw no one with them any more, except Jesus only.

9 And as they were coming down from the mountain, He gave them orders not to relate to anyone what they had seen, until the Son of Man should rise from the dead.

10 And they seized upon that statement, discussing with one another what rising from the dead might mean.

11 And they *began* questioning Him, saying, "Why *is it* that the scribes say that first Elijah must come?"

12 And He said to them, "Elijah does first come and restore everything. And *yet* how is it written of the Son of Man that He should suffer many things and be treated with contempt?

13 "But I say to you, that Elijah has indeed come, and they did to him whatever they wished, just as it is written of him."

14 And when they came *back* to

the disciples, they saw a large crowd around them, and *some* scribes arguing with them.

15 And immediately, when the entire crowd saw Him, they were amazed, and *began* running up to greet Him.

16 And He asked them, "What are you discussing with them?"

17 And one of the crowd answered Him, "Teacher, I brought You my son, possessed with a spirit which makes him mute;

18 and whenever it seizes him, it dashes him *to the ground* and he foams *at the mouth*, and grinds his teeth, and stiffens out. And I told Your disciples to cast it out, and they could not *do it*."

19 And He *answered them and *said, "O unbelieving generation, how long shall I be with you? How long shall I put up with you? Bring him to Me!"

20 And they brought the boy to Him. And when he saw Him, immediately the spirit threw him into a convulsion, and falling to the ground, he *began* rolling about and foaming *at the mouth*.

21 And He asked his father, "How long has this been happening to him?" And he said, "From childhood.

22 "And it has often thrown him both into the fire and into the water to destroy him. But if You can do anything, take pity on us and help us!"

23 And Jesus said to him, " 'If You can!' All things are possible to him who believes."

24 Immediately the boy's father cried out and *began* saying, "I do believe; help *me in* my unbelief."

25 And when Jesus saw that a crowd was rapidly gathering, He rebuked the unclean spirit, saying to it, "You deaf and dumb spirit, I command you, come out of him and do not enter him again."

26 And after crying out and throwing him into terrible convulsions, it came out; and *the boy* became so much like a corpse that most *of them* said, "He is dead!"

27 But Jesus took him by the hand and raised him; and he got up.

28 And when He had come into *the* house, His disciples *began* questioning Him privately, "Why is it that we could not cast it out?"

29 And He said to them, "This kind cannot come out by anything but prayer."

30 And from there they went out and *began* to go through Galilee, and He was unwilling for anyone to know *about it*.

31 For He was teaching His disciples and telling them, "The Son of Man is to be delivered up into the hands of men, and they will kill Him; and when He has been killed, He will rise again three days later."

32 But they did not understand *this* statement, and they were afraid to ask Him.

33 And they came to Capernaum; and when He was in the house, He *began* to question them, "What were you discussing on the way?"

34 But they kept silent, for on the way they had discussed with one another which *of them was* the greatest.

35 And sitting down, He called the twelve and *said to them, "If any one wants to be first, he shall be last of all, and servant of all."

36 And taking a child, He stood him in the midst of them; and taking him in His arms, He said to them,

37 "Whoever receives one child like this in My name is receiving Me; and whoever receives Me is not receiving Me, but Him who sent Me."

38 John said to Him, "Teacher, we saw someone casting out demons in Your name, and we tried to hinder him because he was not following us."

39 But Jesus said, "Do not hinder him, for there is no one who shall perform a miracle in My name, and be able soon afterward to speak evil of Me.

40 "For he who is not against us is for us.

41 "For whoever gives you a cup of water to drink because of your name as *followers* of Christ, truly I say to you, he shall not lose his reward.

42 And whoever causes one of these little ones who believe to stumble, it would be better for him if, with a heavy millstone hung around his neck, he had been cast into the sea.

43 "And if your hand causes you to stumble, cut it off; it is better for you to enter life crippled, than having your two hands, to go into hell, into the unquenchable fire.

44 (See footnote.)

45 "And if your foot causes you to stumble, cut it off; it is better for you to enter life lame, than having your two feet, to be cast into hell.

46 (See footnote.)

47 "And if your eye causes you to stumble, cast it out; it is better for you to enter the kingdom of God with one eye, than having two eyes, to be cast into hell,

48 where THEIR WORM DOES NOT DIE, AND THE FIRE IS NOT QUENCHED.

49 "For everyone will be salted with fire.

50 "Salt is good; but if the salt becomes unsalty, with what will you make it salty *again?* Have salt in yourselves, and be at peace with one another."

CHAPTER 10

AND rising up, He *went from there to the region of Judea, and be-yond the Jordan; and crowds *gathered around Him again, and, according to His custom, He once more *began* to teach them.

2 And *some* Pharisees came up to Him, testing Him, and *began* to question Him whether it was lawful for a man to divorce a wife.

3 And He answered and said to them, "What did Moses command you?"

4 And they said, "Moses permitted *a man* to write a certificate of divorce and send *her* away."

5 But Jesus said to them, "Because of your hardness of heart he wrote you this commandment.

6 "But from the beginning of creation, God MADE THEM MALE AND FEMALE.

7 "FOR THIS CAUSE A MAN SHALL LEAVE HIS FATHER AND MOTHER,

8 AND THE TWO SHALL BECOME ONE FLESH; consequently they are no longer two, but one flesh.

9 "What therefore God has joined together, let no man separate."

10 And in the house the disciples *began* questioning Him about this again.

11 And He *said to them, "Whoever divorces his wife and marries another woman commits adultery against her;

12 and if she herself divorces her husband and marries another man, she is committing adultery."

13 And they *began* bringing children to Him, so that He might touch them; and the disciples rebuked them.

14 But when Jesus saw this, He was indignant and said to them, "Permit the children to come to Me; do not hinder them; for the kingdom of God belongs to such as these.

Verses 44 and 46, which are identical with verse 48, are not found in the best ancient mss.

15 "Truly I say to you, whoever does not receive the kingdom of God like a child shall not enter it *at all*."

16 And He took them in His arms and *began* blessing them, laying His hands upon them.

17 And as He was setting out on a journey, a man ran up to Him and knelt before Him, and *began* asking Him, "Good Teacher, what shall I do to inherit eternal life?"

18 And Jesus said to him, "Why do you call Me good? No one is good except God alone.

19 "You know the commandments, 'DO NOT MURDER, DO NOT COMMIT ADULTERY, DO NOT STEAL, DO NOT BEAR FALSE WITNESS, Do not defraud, HONOR YOUR FATHER AND MOTHER.' "

20 And he said to Him, "Teacher, I have kept all these things from my youth up."

21 And looking at him, Jesus felt a love for him, and said to him, "One thing you lack: go and sell all you possess, and give *it* to the poor, and you shall have treasure in heaven; and come, follow Me."

22 But at these words his face fell, and he went away grieved, for he was one who owned much property.

23 And Jesus, looking around, *said to His disciples, "How hard it will be for those who are wealthy to enter the kingdom of God!"

24 And the disciples were amazed at His words. But Jesus *answered again and *said to them, "Children, how hard it is to enter the kingdom of God!

25 "It is easier for a camel to go through the eye of a needle than for a rich man to enter the kingdom of God."

26 And they were even more astonished and said to Him, "Then who can be saved?"

27 Looking upon them, Jesus *said, "With men it is impossible, but

not with God; for all things are possible with God."

28 Peter began to say to Him, "Behold, we have left everything and followed You."

29 Jesus said, "Truly I say to you, there is no one who has left house or brothers or sisters or mother or father or children or farms, for My sake and for the gospel's sake,

30 but that he shall receive a hundred times as much now in the present age, houses and brothers and sisters and mothers and children and farms, along with persecutions; and in the world to come, eternal life.

31 "But many *who are* first, will be last; and the last, first."

32 And they were on the road, going up to Jerusalem, and Jesus was walking on ahead of them; and they were amazed, and those who followed were fearful. And again He took the twelve aside and began to tell them what was going to happen to Him,

33 *saying*, "Behold, we are going up to Jerusalem, and the Son of Man will be delivered up to the chief priests and the scribes; and they will condemn Him to death, and will deliver Him up to the Gentiles.

34 "And they will mock Him and spit upon Him, and scourge Him, and kill *Him*, and three days later He will rise again."

35 And James and John, the two sons of Zebedee, *came up to Him, saying to Him, "Teacher, we want You to do for us whatever we ask of You."

36 And He said to them, "What do you want Me to do for you?"

37 And they said to Him, "Grant that we may sit in Your glory, one on Your right, and one on *Your* left."

38 But Jesus said to them, "You do not know what you are asking for. Are you able to drink the cup that I drink, or to be baptized with the baptism with which I am baptized?"

39 And they said to Him, "We are able." And Jesus said to them, "The cup that I drink you shall drink; and you shall be baptized with the baptism with which I am baptized.

40 "But to sit on My right or on *My* left, this is not Mine to give; but *it is for those* for whom it has been prepared."

41 And hearing this, the ten began to feel indignant toward James and John.

42 And calling them to Himself, Jesus *said to them, "You know that those who are recognized as rulers of the Gentiles lord it over them; and their great men exercise authority over them.

43 "But it is not so among you, but whoever wishes to become great among you shall be your servant;

44 and whoever wishes to be first among you shall be slave of all.

45 "For even the Son of Man did not come to be served, but to serve, and to give His life a ransom for many."

46 And they *came to Jericho. And as He was going out from Jericho with His disciples and a great multitude, a blind beggar *named* Bartimaeus, the son of Timaeus, was sitting by the road.

47 And when he heard that it was Jesus the Nazarene, he began to cry out and say, "Jesus, Son of David, have mercy on me!"

48 And many were sternly telling him to be quiet, but he *began* crying out all the more, "Son of David, have mercy on me!"

49 And Jesus stopped and said, "Call him *here.*" And they *called the blind man, saying to him, "Take courage, arise! He is calling for you."

50 And casting aside his cloak, he jumped up, and came to Jesus.

51 And answering him, Jesus said, "What do you want Me to do for you?" And the blind man said to Him, "Rabboni, *I want* to regain my sight!"

52 And Jesus said to him, "Go your way; your faith has made you well." And immediately he received his sight and *began* following Him on the road.

CHAPTER 11

AND as they *approached Jerusalem, at Bethphage and Bethany, near the Mount of Olives, He *sent two of His disciples.

2 and *said to them, "Go into the village opposite you, and immediately as you enter it, you will find a colt tied *there*, on which no one yet has ever sat; untie it and bring it *here.*

3 "And if anyone says to you, 'Why are you doing this?' you say, 'The Lord has need of it;' and immediately he will send it back here."

4 And they went away and found a colt tied at the door outside in the street; and they *untied it.

5 And some of the bystanders were saying to them, "What are you doing, untying the colt?"

6 And they spoke to them just as Jesus had told *them*, and they gave them permission.

7 And they *brought the colt to Jesus and put their garments on it; and He sat upon it.

8 And many spread their garments in the road, and others *spread* leafy branches which they had cut from the fields.

9 And those who went before, and those who followed after, were crying out,

> "HOSANNA!
> BLESSED IS HE WHO COMES IN
> THE NAME OF THE LORD;

10 Blessed *is* the coming kingdom of our father David; HOSANNA in the highest!"

11 And He entered Jerusalem *and came* into the temple; and after looking all around, He departed for Beth-

any with the twelve, since it was already late.

12 And on the next day, when they had departed from Bethany, He became hungry.

13 And seeing at a distance a fig tree in leaf, He went *to see* if perhaps He would find anything on it; and when He came to it, He found nothing but leaves, for it was not the season for figs.

14 And He answered and said to it, "May no one ever eat fruit from you again!" And His disciples were listening.

15 And they *came to Jerusalem. And He entered the temple and began to cast out those who were buying and selling in the temple, and overturned the tables of the moneychangers and the seats of those who were selling doves;

16 and He would not permit anyone to carry goods through the temple.

17 And He *began* to teach and say to them, "Is it not written, 'MY HOUSE SHALL BE CALLED A HOUSE OF PRAYER FOR ALL THE NATIONS'? But you have made it a robbers' den."

18 And the chief priests and the scribes heard *this*, and *began* seeking how to destroy Him; for they were afraid of Him, for all the multitude was astonished at His teaching.

19 And whenever evening came, they would go out of the city.

20 And as they were passing by in the morning, they saw the fig tree withered from the roots *up*.

21 And being reminded, Peter *said to Him, "Rabbi, behold, the fig tree which You cursed has withered."

22 And Jesus *answered saying to them, "Have faith in God.

23 "Truly I say to you, whoever says to this mountain, 'Be taken up and cast into the sea,' and does not doubt

in his heart, but believes that what he says is going to happen, it shall be *granted* him.

24 "Therefore I say to you, all things for which you pray and ask, believe that you have received them, and they shall be *granted* you.

25 "And whenever you stand praying, forgive, if you have anything against anyone; so that your Father also who is in heaven may forgive you your transgressions."

26 (See footnote.)

27 And they *came again to Jerusalem. And as He was walking in the temple, the chief priests, and scribes, and elders *came to Him,

28 and *began* saying to Him, "By what authority are You doing these things, or who gave You this authority to do these things?"

29 And Jesus said to them, "I will ask you one question, and you answer Me, and *then* I will tell you by what authority I do these things.

30 "Was the baptism of John from heaven, or from men? Answer Me."

31 And they *began* reasoning with one another, saying, "If we say, 'From heaven,' He will say, 'Then why did you not believe him?'

32 "But shall we say, 'From men'?" —they were afraid of the multitude, for all considered John to have been a prophet indeed.

33 And answering Jesus, they *said, "We do not know." And Jesus *said to them, "Neither will I tell you by what authority I do these things."

CHAPTER 12

AND He began to speak to them in parables: "A man PLANTED A VINEYARD, AND PUT A WALL AROUND IT, AND DUG A VAT UNDER THE WINE PRESS, AND

Later mss. add vs. 26: *"But if you do not forgive, neither will your Father who is in heaven forgive your transgressions."*

BUILT A TOWER, and rented it out to vine-growers and went on a journey.

2 "And at the *harvest* time he sent a slave to the vine-growers, in order to receive *some* of the produce of the vineyard from the vine-growers.

3 "And they took him, and beat him, and sent him away empty-handed.

4 "And again he sent them another slave, and they wounded him in the head, and treated him shamefully.

5 "And he sent another, and that one they killed; and *so with* many others, beating some, and killing others.

6 "He had one more *to send,* a beloved son; he sent him last *of all* to them, saying, 'They will respect my son.'

7 "But those vine-growers said to one another, 'This is the heir; come, let us kill him, and the inheritance will be ours!'

8 "And they took him, and killed him, and threw him out of the vineyard.

9 "What will the owner of the vineyard do? He will come and destroy the vine-growers, and will give the vineyard to others.

10 "Have you not even read this scripture:

> 'THE STONE WHICH THE BUILD-
> ERS REJECTED,
>
> THIS BECAME THE CHIEF COR-
> NER *stone;*
>
11 > THIS CAME ABOUT FROM THE
> LORD,
>
> AND IT IS MARVELOUS IN OUR
> EYES'?"

12 And they were seeking to seize Him; and *yet* they feared the multitude; for they understood that He had spoken the parable against them. And *so* they left Him, and went away.

13 And they *sent some of the Pharisees and Herodians to Him, in order to trap Him in a statement.

14 And they *came and *said to Him, "Teacher, we know that You are truthful, and defer to no one; for You are not partial to any, but teach the way of God in truth. Is it lawful to pay a poll-tax to Caesar, or not?

15 "Shall we pay, or shall we not pay?" But He, knowing their hypocrisy, said to them, "Why are you testing Me? Bring Me a denarius to look at."

16 And they brought *one.* And He *said to them, "Whose likeness and inscription is this?" And they said to Him, "Caesar's."

17 And Jesus said to them, "Render to Caesar the things that are Caesar's, and to God the things that are God's." And they were amazed at Him.

18 And *some* Sadducees (who say that there is no resurrection) *came to Him, and *began questioning Him, saying,

19 "Teacher, Moses wrote for us *a law* that IF A MAN'S BROTHER DIES, and leaves behind a wife, AND LEAVES NO CHILD, HIS BROTHER SHOULD TAKE THE WIFE, AND RAISE UP OFFSPRING TO HIS BROTHER.

20 "There were seven brothers; and the first one took a wife, and died, leaving no offspring.

21 "And the second one took her, and died, leaving behind no offspring; and the third likewise;

22 and *so* all seven left no offspring. Last of all the woman died too.

23 "In the resurrection, when they rise again, which one's wife will she be? For all seven had her as wife."

24 Jesus said to them, "Is this not the reason you are mistaken, that you do not understand the Scriptures, or the power of God?

25 "For when they rise from the dead, they neither marry, nor are given in marriage, but are like angels in heaven.

26 "But regarding the fact that the dead rise again, have you not read in

the book of Moses, in the *passage about the burning* bush, how God spoke to him, saying, 'I AM THE GOD OF ABRAHAM, AND THE GOD OF ISAAC, AND THE GOD OF JACOB'?

27 "He is not *the* God of *the* dead, but of *the* living; you are greatly mistaken."

28 And one of the scribes came and heard them arguing, and recognizing that He had answered them well, asked Him, "What commandment is the foremost of all?"

29 Jesus answered, "The foremost is, 'HEAR, O ISRAEL; THE LORD OUR GOD IS ONE LORD;

30 AND YOU SHALL LOVE THE LORD YOUR GOD WITH ALL YOUR HEART, AND WITH ALL YOUR SOUL, AND WITH ALL YOUR MIND, AND WITH ALL YOUR STRENGTH.'

31 "The second is this, 'YOU SHALL LOVE YOUR NEIGHBOR AS YOURSELF.' There is no other commandment greater than these."

32 And the scribe said to Him, "Right, Teacher, You have truly stated that HE IS ONE; AND THERE IS NO ONE ELSE BESIDES HIM;

33 AND TO LOVE HIM WITH ALL THE HEART AND WITH ALL THE UNDERSTANDING AND WITH ALL THE STRENGTH, AND TO LOVE ONE'S NEIGHBOR AS HIMSELF, is much more than all burnt offerings and sacrifices."

34 And when Jesus saw that he had answered intelligently, He said to him, "You are not far from the kingdom of God." And after that, no one would venture to ask Him any more questions.

35 And Jesus answering *began* to say, as He taught in the temple, "How *is it that* the scribes say that the Christ is the son of David?

36 "David himself said in the Holy Spirit,

'THE LORD SAID TO MY LORD,
"SIT AT MY RIGHT HAND,
UNTIL I PUT THINE ENEMIES
BENEATH THY FEET." '

37 "David himself calls Him 'Lord'; and *so* in what sense is He his son?" And the great crowd enjoyed listening to Him.

38 And in His teaching He was saying: "Beware of the scribes who like to walk around in long robes, and *like* respectful greetings in the market places,

39 and chief seats in the synagogues, and places of honor at banquets.

40 "They *are* the ones who devour widows' houses, and for appearance's sake offer long prayers; these will receive greater condemnation."

41 And He sat down opposite the treasury, and *began* observing how the multitude were putting money into the treasury; and many rich people were putting in large sums.

42 And a poor widow came and put in two small copper coins, which amount to a cent.

43 And calling His disciples to Him, He said to them, "Truly I say to you, this poor widow put in more than all the contributors to the treasury;

44 for they all put in out of their surplus, but she, out of her poverty, put in all she owned, all she had to live on."

CHAPTER 13

AND as He was going out of the temple, one of His disciples *said to Him, "Teacher, behold what wonderful stones and what wonderful buildings!"

2 And Jesus said to him, "Do you see these great buildings? Not one stone shall be left upon another which will not be torn down."

3 And as He was sitting on the Mount of Olives opposite the temple, Peter and James and John and Andrew were questioning Him privately,

4 "Tell us, when will these things be, and what *will be* the sign when all these things are going to be fulfilled?"

5 And Jesus began to say to them, "See to it that no one misleads you.

6 "Many will come in My name, saying, 'I am *He!*' and will mislead many.

7 "And when you hear of wars and rumors of wars, do not be frightened; *those things* must take place; but *that is* not yet the end.

8 "For nation will arise against nation, and kingdom against kingdom; there will be earthquakes in various places; there will *also* be famines. These things are *merely* the beginning of birth pangs.

9 "But be on your guard; for they will deliver you up to *the* courts, and you will be flogged in *the* synagogues, and you will stand before governors and kings for My sake, as a testimony to them.

10 "And the gospel must first be preached to all the nations.

11 "And when they arrest you and deliver you up, do not be anxious beforehand about what you are to say, but say whatever is given you in that hour; for it is not you who speak, but *it is* the Holy Spirit.

12 "And brother will deliver up brother to death, and a father *his* child; and children will rise up against parents and cause them to be put to death.

13 "And you will be hated by all on account of My name, but it is the one who has endured to the end who will be saved.

14 "But when you see the ABOMINATION OF DESOLATION standing where it should not be (let the reader understand), then let those who are in Judea flee to the mountains.

15 "And let him who is on the housetop not go down, or enter in, to get anything out of his house;

16 and let him who is in the field not turn back to get his cloak.

17 "But woe to those who are with child and to those who nurse babes in those days!

18 "But pray that it may not happen in the winter.

19 "For those days will be a *time of* tribulation such as has not occurred since the beginning of the creation which God created, until now, and never shall.

20 "And unless the Lord had shortened *those* days, no life would have been saved; but for the sake of the elect whom He chose, He shortened the days.

21 "And then if anyone says to you, 'Behold, here is the Christ'; or, 'Behold, *He is* there'; do not believe *him;*

22 for false Christs and false prophets will arise, and will show signs and wonders, in order, if possible, to lead the elect astray.

23 "But take heed; behold, I have told you everything in advance.

24 "But in those days, after that tribulation, THE SUN WILL BE DARKENED, AND THE MOON WILL NOT GIVE ITS LIGHT,

25 AND THE STARS WILL BE FALLING from heaven, and the POWERS THAT ARE IN THE HEAVENS WILL BE SHAKEN.

26 "AND THEN THEY SHALL SEE THE SON OF MAN COMING IN CLOUDS with great power and glory.

27 "And then He will send forth the angels, and WILL GATHER TOGETHER His elect FROM THE FOUR WINDS, FROM THE FARTHEST END of the earth, TO THE FARTHEST END OF HEAVEN.

28 "Now learn the parable from the fig tree: when its branch has already become tender, and puts forth its leaves, you know that the summer is near.

29 "Even so you too, when you see these things happening, recognize that He is near, *right* at the door.

30 "Truly I say to you, this genera-

tion will not pass away until all these things take place.

31 "Heaven and earth will pass away, but My words will not pass away.

32 "But of that day or hour no one knows, not even the angels in heaven, nor the Son, but the Father *alone*.

33 "Take heed, keep on the alert; for you do not know when the *appointed* time is.

34 "*It is* like a man, away on a journey, *who* upon leaving his house and putting his slaves in charge, *assigning* to each one his task, also commanded the doorkeeper to stay on the alert.

35 "Therefore, be on the alert — for you do not know when the master of the house is coming, whether in the evening, at midnight, at cockcrowing, or in the morning—

36 lest he come suddenly and find you asleep.

37 "And what I say to you I say to all, 'Be on the alert!' "

CHAPTER 14

N OW *the feast of* the Passover and Unleavened Bread was two days off; and the chief priests and the scribes were seeking how to seize Him by stealth, and kill *Him*;

2 for they were saying, "Not during the festival, lest there be a riot of the people."

3 And while He was in Bethany at the home of Simon the leper, and reclining *at table*, there came a woman with an alabaster vial of costly perfume of pure nard; *and* she broke the vial and poured it over His head.

4 But some were indignantly *remarking* to one another, "For what purpose has this perfume been wasted?

5 "For this perfume might have been sold for over three hundred denarii, and *the money* given to the poor." And they were scolding her.

6 But Jesus said, "Let her alone; why do you bother her? She has done a good deed to Me.

7 "For the poor you always have with you, and whenever you wish, you can do them good; but you do not always have Me.

8 "She has done what she could; she has anointed My body beforehand for the burial.

9 "And truly I say to you, wherever the gospel is preached in the whole world, that also which this woman has done shall be spoken of in memory of her."

10 And Judas Iscariot, who was one of the twelve, went off to the chief priests, in order to betray Him to them.

11 And they were glad when they heard *this*, and promised to give him money. And he *began* seeking how to betray Him at an opportune time.

12 And on the first day of *the feast of* Unleavened Bread, when the Passover *lamb* was being sacrificed, His disciples *said to Him, "Where do You want us to go and prepare for You to eat the Passover?"

13 And He *sent two of His disciples, and *said to them, "Go into the city, and a man will meet you carrying a pitcher of water; follow him;

14 and wherever he enters, say to the owner of the house, 'The Teacher says, "Where is My guest room in which I may eat the Passover with My disciples?" '

15 "And he himself will show you a large upper room furnished *and* ready; and prepare for us there."

16 And the disciples went out, and came to the city, and found *it* just as He had told them; and they prepared the Passover.

17 And when it was evening He *came with the twelve.

18 And as they were reclining *at table* and eating, Jesus said, "Truly I

say to you that one of you will betray
Me —one who is eating with Me."

19 They began to be grieved and
to say to Him one by one, "Surely not
I?"

20 And He said to them, "*It is* one
of the twelve, one who dips with Me
in the bowl.

21 "For the Son of Man *is to* go,
just as it is written of Him; but woe to
that man by whom the Son of Man is
betrayed! *It would have been* good
for that man if he had not been born."

22 And while they were eating, He
took *some* bread, and after a blessing
He broke *it;* and gave *it* to them, and
said, "Take *it;* this is My body."

23 And He took a cup, and when
He had given thanks, He gave *it* to
them; and they all drank from it.

24 And He said to them, "This is
My blood of the covenant, which is *to
be* shed on behalf of many.

25 "Truly I say to you, I shall never
again drink of the fruit of the vine
until that day when I drink it new in
the kingdom of God."

26 And after singing a hymn, they
went out to the Mount of Olives.

27 And Jesus *said to them, "You
will all fall away, because it is written,
'I WILL STRIKE DOWN THE SHEPHERD,
AND THE SHEEP SHALL BE SCATTERED.'

28 "But after I have been raised, I
will go before you to Galilee."

29 But Peter said to Him, "*Even*
though all may fall away, yet I will
not."

30 And Jesus *said to him, "Truly
I say to you, that you yourself this
very night, before a cock crows twice,
shall three times deny Me."

31 But *Peter* kept saying insis-
tently, "*Even* if I have to die with
You, I will not deny You!" And they
all were saying the same thing, too.

32 And they *came to a place
named Gethsemane; and He *said to
His disciples, "Sit here until I have
prayed."

33 And He *took with him Peter
and James and John, and began to be
very distressed and troubled.

34 And He *said to them, "My
soul is deeply grieved to the point of
death; remain here and keep watch."

35 And He went a little beyond
them, and fell to the ground, and
began praying that if it were possible,
the hour might pass Him by.

36 And He was saying, "Abba! Father! All things are possible for Thee;
remove this cup from Me; yet not
what I will, but what Thou wilt."

37 And He *came and *found
them sleeping, and *said to Peter,
"Simon, are you asleep? Could you
not keep watch for one hour?

38 "Keep watching and praying,
that you may not come into temptation; the spirit is willing, but the flesh
is weak."

39 And again He went away and
prayed, saying the same words.

40 And again He came and found
them sleeping, for their eyes were very
heavy; and they did not know what to
answer Him.

41 And He *came the third time,
and *said to them, "Are you still
sleeping and taking your rest? It is
enough; the hour has come; behold,
the Son of Man is being betrayed into
the hands of sinners.

42 "Arise, let us be going; behold,
the one who betrays Me is at hand!"

43 And immediately while He was
still speaking, Judas, one of the
twelve, *came up, accompanied by a
multitude with swords and clubs,
from the chief priests and the scribes
and the elders.

44 Now he who was betraying
Him had given them a signal, saying,
"Whomever I shall kiss, He is the
one; seize Him, and lead Him away
under guard."

45 And after coming, he immediately went up to Him, saying,
"Rabbi!" and kissed Him.

46 And they laid hands on Him, and seized Him.

47 But a certain one of those who stood by drew his sword, and struck the slave of the high priest, and cut off his ear.

48 And Jesus answered and said to them, "Have you come out with swords and clubs to arrest Me, as though I were a robber?

49 "Every day I was with you in the temple teaching, and you did not seize Me; but this has happened that the Scriptures might be fulfilled."

50 And they all left Him and fled.

51 And a certain young man was following Him, wearing nothing but a linen sheet over his naked body; and they *seized him.

52 But he left the linen sheet behind, and escaped naked.

53 And they led Jesus away to the high priest; and all the chief priests and the elders and the scribes *gathered together.

54 And Peter had followed Him at a distance, right into the courtyard of the high priest; and he was sitting with the officers, and warming himself at the fire.

55 Now the chief priests and the whole Council kept trying to obtain testimony against Jesus to put Him to death; and they were finding none.

56 For many were giving false testimony against Him, and yet their testimony was not consistent.

57 And some stood up and began to give false testimony against Him, saying,

58 "We heard Him say, 'I will destroy this temple made with hands, and in three days I will build another made without hands.' "

59 And not even in this respect was their testimony consistent.

60 And the high priest arose and came forward and questioned Jesus, saying, "Do You make no answer to what these men are testifying against You?"

61 But He kept silent, and made no answer. Again the high priest was questioning Him, and saying to Him, "Are You the Christ, the Son of the Blessed One?"

62 And Jesus said, "I am; and you shall see the SON OF MAN SITTING AT THE RIGHT HAND OF POWER, and COMING WITH THE CLOUDS OF HEAVEN."

63 And tearing his clothes, the high priest *said, "What further need do we have of witnesses?

64 "You have heard the blasphemy; how does it seem to you?" And they all condemned Him to be deserving of death.

65 And some began to spit at Him, and to blindfold Him, and to beat Him with their fists, and to say to Him, "Prophesy!" And the officers received Him with slaps in the face.

66 And as Peter was below in the courtyard, one of the servant-girls of the high priest *came,

67 and seeing Peter warming himself, she looked at him, and *said, "You, too, were with Jesus the Nazarene."

68 But he denied it, saying, "I neither know nor understand what you are talking about." And he went out onto the porch.

69 And the maid saw him, and began once more to say to the bystanders, "This is one of them!"

70 But again he was denying it. And after a little while the bystanders were again saying to Peter, "Surely you are one of them, for you are a Galilean too."

71 But he began to curse and swear, "I do not know this fellow you are talking about!"

72 And immediately a cock crowed a second time. And Peter remembered how Jesus had made the remark to him, "Before a cock crows twice, you will deny Me three times." And he began to weep.

Chapter 15

AND early in the morning the chief priests with the elders and scribes, and the whole Council, immediately held a consultation; and binding Jesus, they led Him away, and delivered Him up to Pilate.

2 And Pilate questioned Him, "Are You the King of the Jews?" And answering He *said to him, "*It is as you say.*"

3 And the chief priests *began* to accuse Him harshly.

4 And Pilate was questioning Him again, saying, "Do You make no answer? See how many charges they bring against You!"

5 But Jesus made no further answer; so that Pilate was astonished.

6 Now at *the* feast he used to release for them *any* one prisoner whom they requested.

7 And the man named Barabbas had been imprisoned with the insurrectionists who had committed murder in the insurrection.

8 And the multitude went up and began asking him *to do* as he had been accustomed to do for them.

9 And Pilate answered them, saying, "Do you want me to release for you the King of the Jews?"

10 For he was aware that the chief priests had delivered Him up because of envy.

11 But the chief priests stirred up the multitude *to ask* him to release Barabbas for them instead.

12 And answering again, Pilate was saying to them, "Then what shall I do to Him whom you call the King of the Jews?"

13 And they shouted back, "Crucify Him!"

14 But Pilate was saying to them, "Why, what evil has He done?" But they shouted all the more, "Crucify Him!"

15 And wishing to satisfy the multitude, Pilate released Barabbas for them, and after having Jesus scourged, he delivered Him over to be crucified.

16 And the soldiers took Him away into the palace (that is, the Praetorium), and they *called together the whole Roman cohort.

17 And they *dressed Him up in purple, and after weaving a crown of thorns, they put it on Him;

18 and they began to acclaim Him, "Hail, King of the Jews!"

19 And they kept beating His head with a reed, and spitting at Him, and kneeling and bowing before Him.

20 And after they had mocked Him, they took the purple off Him, and put His garments on Him. And they *led Him out to crucify Him.

21 And they *pressed into service a passerby coming from the country, Simon of Cyrene (the father of Alexander and Rufus), that he might bear His cross.

22 And they *brought Him to the place Golgotha, which is translated, Place of a Skull.

23 And they tried to give Him wine mixed with myrrh; but He did not take it.

24 And they *crucified Him, and *DIVIDED UP HIS GARMENTS AMONG THEMSELVES, CASTING LOTS FOR THEM, *to decide* what each should take.

25 And it was the third hour when they crucified Him.

26 And the inscription of the charge against Him read, "THE KING OF THE JEWS."

27 And they *crucified two robbers with Him, one on the right and one on the left.

28 (See footnote.)

Later mss. add verse 28: *And the Scripture was fulfilled which says, "And He was reckoned with transgressors."*

29 And those passing by were hurling abuse at Him, WAGGING THEIR HEADS, and saying, "Ha! You who *were going to* destroy the temple and rebuild it in three days,

30 save Yourself, and come down from the cross!"

31 In the same way the chief priests along with the scribes were also mocking *Him* among themselves and saying, "He saved others; He cannot save Himself.

32 "Let *this* Christ, the King of Israel, now come down from the cross, so that we may see and believe!" And those who were crucified with Him were casting the same insult at Him.

33 And when the sixth hour had come, darkness fell over the whole land until the ninth hour.

34 And at the ninth hour Jesus cried out with a loud voice, "ELOI, ELOI, LAMA SABACHTHANI?" which is translated, "MY GOD, MY GOD, WHY HAST THOU FORSAKEN ME?"

35 And when some of the bystanders heard it, they *began* saying, "Behold, He is calling for Elijah."

36 And someone ran and filled a sponge with sour wine, put it on a reed, and gave Him a drink, saying, "Let us see whether Elijah will come to take Him down."

37 And Jesus uttered a loud cry, and breathed His last.

38 And the veil of the temple was torn in two from top to bottom.

39 And when the centurion, who was standing right in front of Him, saw the way He breathed His last, he said, "Truly this man was the Son of God!"

40 And there were also *some* women looking on from afar, among whom *were* Mary Magdalene, and Mary the mother of James the Less and Joses, and Salome.

41 And when He was in Galilee, they used to follow Him and minister to Him; and *there were* many other women who had come up with Him to Jerusalem.

42 And when evening had already come, because it was the Preparation Day, that is, the day before the Sabbath,

43 Joseph of Arimathea came, a prominent member of the Council, a man who was himself waiting for the kingdom of God; and he gathered up courage and went in before Pilate, and asked for the body of Jesus.

44 And Pilate wondered if He was dead by this time, and summoning the centurion, he questioned him as to whether He was already dead.

45 And ascertaining this from the centurion, he granted the body to Joseph.

46 And *Joseph* bought a linen sheet, took Him down, wrapped Him in the linen sheet, and laid Him in a tomb which had been hewn out in the rock; and he rolled a stone against the entrance of the tomb.

47 And Mary Magdalene and Mary the *mother* of Joses were looking on *to see* where He was laid.

CHAPTER 16

AND when the Sabbath was over, Mary Magdalene, and Mary the *mother* of James, and Salome, bought spices, that they might come and anoint Him.

2 And very early on the first day of the week, they *came to the tomb when the sun had risen.

3 And they were saying to one another, "Who will roll away the stone for us from the entrance of the tomb?"

4 And looking up, they *saw that the stone had been rolled away, although it was extremely large.

5 And entering the tomb, they saw a young man sitting at the right, wearing a white robe; and they were amazed.

6 And he *said to them, "Do not

be amazed; you are looking for Jesus the Nazarene, who has been crucified. He has risen; He is not here; behold, *here is* the place where they laid Him.

7 "But go, tell His disciples and Peter, 'He is going before you into Galilee; there you will see Him, just as He said to you.' "

8 And they went out and fled from the tomb, for trembling and astonishment had gripped them; and they said nothing to anyone, for they were afraid.

9 [Now after He had risen early on the first day of the week, He first appeared to Mary Magdalene, from whom He had cast out seven demons.

10 She went and reported to those who had been with Him, while they were mourning and weeping.

11 And when they heard that He was alive, and had been seen by her, they refused to believe it.

12 And after that, He appeared in a different form to two of them, while they were walking along on their way to the country.

13 And they went away and reported it to the others, but they did not believe them either.

14 And afterward He appeared to the eleven themselves as they were reclining *at table*; and He reproached them for their unbelief and hardness of heart, because they had not believed those who had seen Him after He had risen.

15 And He said to them, "Go into all the world and preach the gospel to all creation.

16 "He who has believed and has been baptized shall be saved; but he who has disbelieved shall be condemned.

17 "And these signs will accompany those who have believed: in My name they will cast out demons, they will speak with new tongues;

18 they will pick up serpents, and if they drink any deadly *poison*, it shall not hurt them; they will lay hands on the sick, and they will recover."

19 So then, when the Lord Jesus had spoken to them, He was received up into heaven, and SAT DOWN AT THE RIGHT HAND OF GOD.

20 And they went out and preached everywhere, while the Lord worked with them, and confirmed the word by the signs that followed.]

THE GOSPEL

ACCORDING TO

LUKE

INASMUCH as many have undertaken to compile an account of the things accomplished among us,

2 just as those who from the beginning were eyewitnesses and servants of the Word have handed them down to us,

3 it seemed fitting for me as well, having investigated everything carefully from the beginning, to write *it* out for you in consecutive order, most excellent Theophilus;

4 so that you might know the exact truth about the things you have been taught.

5 In the days of Herod, king of Judea, there was a certain priest named Zacharias, of the division of Abijah; and he had a wife from the daughters of Aaron, and her name was Elizabeth.

6 And they were both righteous in the sight of God, walking blamelessly in all the commandments and requirements of the Lord.

7 And they had no child, because Elizabeth was barren, and they were both advanced in years.

8 Now it came about, while he was performing his priestly service before God in the *appointed* order of his division,

9 according to the custom of the priestly office, he was chosen by lot to enter the temple of the Lord and burn incense.

10 And the whole multitude of the people were in prayer outside at the hour of the incense offering.

11 And an angel of the Lord appeared to him, standing to the right of the altar of incense.

12 And Zacharias was troubled when he saw *him*, and fear gripped him.

13 But the angel said to him, "Do not be afraid, Zacharias, for your petition has been heard, and your wife Elizabeth will bear you a son, and you will give him the name John.

14 "And you will have joy and gladness, and many will rejoice at his birth.

15 "For he will be great in the sight of the Lord, and he will drink no wine or liquor; and he will be filled with the Holy Spirit, while yet in his mother's womb.

16 "And he will turn back many of the sons of Israel to the Lord their God.

17 "And it is he who will go *as a forerunner* before Him in the spirit and power of Elijah, TO TURN THE HEARTS OF THE FATHERS BACK TO THE CHILDREN, and the disobedient to the attitude of the righteous; so as to make ready a people prepared for the Lord."

18 And Zacharias said to the angel, "How shall I know this *for certain?* For I am an old man, and my wife is advanced in years."

19 And the angel answered and said to him, "I am Gabriel, who stands in the presence of God; and I have been sent to speak to you, and to bring you this good news.

20 "And behold, you shall be silent and unable to speak until the day when these things take place, because you did not believe my words, which shall be fulfilled in their proper time."

21 And the people were waiting for Zacharias, and were wondering at his delay in the temple.

22 But when he came out, he was unable to speak to them; and they realized that he had seen a vision in

the temple; and he kept making signs to them, and remained mute.

23 And it came about, when the days of his priestly service were ended, that he went back home.

24 And after these days Elizabeth his wife became pregnant; and she kept herself in seclusion for five months, saying,

25 "This is the way the Lord has dealt with me in the days when He looked *with favor* upon *me*, to take away my disgrace among men."

26 Now in the sixth month the angel Gabriel was sent from God to a city in Galilee, called Nazareth,

27 to a virgin engaged to a man whose name was Joseph, of the descendants of David; and the virgin's name was Mary.

28 And coming in, he said to her, "Hail, favored one! The Lord *is* with you."

29 But she was greatly troubled at *this* statement, and kept pondering what kind of salutation this might be.

30 And the angel said to her, "Do not be afraid, Mary; for you have found favor with God.

31 "And behold, you will conceive in your womb, and bear a son, and you shall name Him Jesus.

32 "He will be great, and will be called the Son of the Most High; and the Lord God will give Him the throne of His father David;

33 and He will reign over the house of Jacob forever; and His kingdom will have no end."

34 And Mary said to the angel, "How can this be, since I am a virgin?"

35 And the angel answered and said to her, "The Holy Spirit will come upon you, and the power of the Most High will overshadow you; and for that reason the holy offspring shall be called the Son of God.

36 "And behold, even your relative Elizabeth has also conceived a son in her old age; and she who was called barren is now in her sixth month.

37 "For nothing will be impossible with God."

38 And Mary said, "Behold, the bondslave of the Lord; be it done to me according to your word." And the angel departed from her.

39 Now at this time Mary arose and went with haste to the hill country, to a city of Judah,

40 and entered the house of Zacharias and greeted Elizabeth.

41 And it came about that when Elizabeth heard Mary's greeting, the baby leaped in her womb; and Elizabeth was filled with the Holy Spirit.

42 And she cried out with a loud voice, and said, "Blessed among women *are* you, and blessed *is* the fruit of your womb!

43 "And how has it *happened* to me, that the mother of my Lord should come to me?

44 "For behold, when the sound of your greeting reached my ears, the baby leaped in my womb for joy.

45 "And blessed *is* she who believed that there would be a fulfillment of what had been spoken to her by the Lord."

46 And Mary said:
    "My soul exalts the Lord,

47   "And my spirit has rejoiced in God my Savior.

48   "For He has had regard for the humble state of His bond-slave;
    For behold, from this time on all generations will count me blessed.

49   "For the Mighty One has done great things for me;
    And holy is His name.

50   "And His mercy is upon generation after generation Towards those who fear Him.

51   "He has done mighty deeds with His arm;

He has scattered *those who were* proud in the thoughts of their heart.

52 "He has brought down rulers from *their* thrones,

And has exalted those who were humble.

53 "HE HAS FILLED THE HUNGRY WITH GOOD THINGS;

And sent away the rich empty-handed.

54 He has given help to Israel His servant,

In remembrance of His mercy,

55 As He spoke to our fathers, To Abraham and his offspring forever."

56 And Mary stayed with her about three months, and *then* returned to her home.

57 Now the time had come for Elizabeth to give birth, and she brought forth a son.

58 And her neighbors and her relatives heard that the Lord had displayed His great mercy toward her; and they were rejoicing with her.

59 And it came about that on the eighth day they came to circumcise the child, and they were going to call him Zacharias, after his father.

60 And his mother answered and said, "No indeed; but he shall be called John."

61 And they said to her, "There is no one among your relatives who is called by that name."

62 And they made signs to his father, as to what he wanted him called.

63 And he asked for a tablet, and wrote as follows, "His name is John." And they were all astonished.

64 And at once his mouth was opened and his tongue *loosed*, and he *began* to speak in praise of God.

65 And fear came on all those living around them; and all these matters were being talked about in all the hill country of Judea.

66 And all who heard them kept them in mind, saying, "What then will this child *turn out to* be?" For the hand of the Lord was certainly with him.

67 And his father Zacharias was filled with the Holy Spirit, and prophesied, saying;

68 "Blessed *be* the Lord God of Israel,

For He has visited us and accomplished redemption for His people,

69 And has raised up a horn of salvation for us

In the house of David His servant—

70 As He spoke by the mouth of His holy prophets from of old—

71 Salvation FROM OUR ENEMIES, And FROM THE HAND OF ALL WHO HATE US;

72 To show mercy toward our fathers,

And to remember His holy covenant,

73 The oath which He swore to Abraham our father,

74 To grant us that we, being delivered from the hand of our enemies,

Might serve Him without fear,

75 In holiness and righteousness before Him all our days.

76 "And you, child, will be called the prophet of the Most High;

For you will go on BEFORE THE LORD TO PREPARE HIS WAYS;

77 To give to His people *the* knowledge of salvation

By the forgiveness of their sins,

78 Because of the tender mercy of our God,

With which the Sunrise from on high shall visit us,

79　To shine upon those who sit
　　in darkness and the
　　shadow of death,
　　To guide our feet into the way
　　of peace."

80 And the child continued to grow, and to become strong in spirit, and he lived in the deserts until the day of his public appearance to Israel.

Chapter 2

Now it came about in those days that a decree went out from Caesar Augustus, that a census be taken of all the inhabited earth.

2 This was the first census taken while Quirinius was governor of Syria.

3 And all were proceeding to register for the census, everyone to his own city.

4 And Joseph also went up from Galilee, from the city of Nazareth, to Judea, to the city of David, which is called Bethlehem, because he was of the house and family of David,

5 in order to register, along with Mary, who was engaged to him, and was with child.

6 And it came about that while they were there, the days were completed for her to give birth.

7 And she gave birth to her first-born son; and she wrapped Him in cloths, and laid Him in a manger, because there was no room for them in the inn.

8 And in the same region there were *some* shepherds staying out in the fields, and keeping watch over their flock by night.

9 And an angel of the Lord suddenly stood before them, and the glory of the Lord shone around them; and they were terribly frightened.

10 And the angel said to them, "Do not be afraid; for behold, I bring you good news of a great joy which shall be for all the people;

11 for today in the city of David there has been born for you a Savior, who is Christ the Lord.

12 "And this *will be* a sign for you: you will find a baby wrapped in cloths, and lying in a manger."

13 And suddenly there appeared with the angel a multitude of the heavenly host praising God, and saying,

14 "Glory to God in the highest,
　　And on earth peace among
　　men with whom He is
　　pleased."

15 And it came about when the angels had gone away from them into heaven, that the shepherds *began* saying to one another, "Let us go straight to Bethlehem then, and see this thing that has happened which the Lord has made known to us."

16 And they came in haste and found their way to Mary and Joseph, and the baby as He lay in the manger.

17 And when they had seen this, they made known the statement which had been told them about this Child.

18 And all who heard it wondered at the things which were told them by the shepherds.

19 But Mary treasured up all these things, pondering them in her heart.

20 And the shepherds went back, glorifying and praising God for all that they had heard and seen, just as had been told them.

21 And when eight days were completed before His circumcision, His name was *then* called Jesus, the name given by the angel before He was conceived in the womb.

22 And when the days for their purification according to the law of Moses were completed, they brought Him up to Jerusalem to present Him to the Lord

23 (as it is written in the Law of the

Lord, "EVERY *first-born* MALE THAT OPENS THE WOMB SHALL BE CALLED HOLY TO THE LORD"),

24 and to offer a sacrifice according to what was said in the Law of the Lord, "A PAIR OF TURTLEDOVES, OR TWO YOUNG PIGEONS."

25 And behold, there was a man in Jerusalem whose name was Simeon; and this man was righteous and devout, looking for the consolation of Israel; and the Holy Spirit was upon him.

26 And it had been revealed to him by the Holy Spirit that he would not see death before he had seen the Lord's Christ.

27 And he came in the Spirit into the temple; and when the parents brought in the child Jesus, to carry out for Him the custom of the Law,

28 then he took Him into his arms, and blessed God, and said,

29 "Now Lord, Thou dost let Thy
       bond-servant depart
     In peace, according to Thy
       word;

30 For mine eyes have seen Thy
       salvation,

31 Which Thou hast prepared in
       the presence of all peoples,

32 A LIGHT OF REVELATION TO
       THE GENTILES,
     And the glory of Thy people
       Israel."

33 And His father and mother were amazed at the things which were being said about Him.

34 And Simeon blessed them, and said to Mary His mother, "Behold, this *Child* is appointed for the fall and rise of many in Israel, and for a sign to be opposed —

35 and a sword will pierce even your own soul — to the end that thoughts from many hearts may be revealed."

36 And there was a prophetess, Anna the daughter of Phanuel, of the tribe of Asher. She was advanced in years, having lived with a husband seven years after her marriage,

37 and then as a widow to the age of eighty-four. And she *never* left the temple, serving night and day with fastings and prayers.

38 And at that very moment she came up and *began* giving thanks to God, and continued to speak of Him to all those who were looking for the redemption of Jerusalem.

39 And when they had performed everything according to the Law of the Lord, they returned to Galilee, to their own city of Nazareth.

40 And the Child continued to grow and become strong, increasing in wisdom; and the grace of God was upon Him.

41 And His parents used to go to Jerusalem every year at the Feast of the Passover.

42 And when He became twelve, they went up *there* according to the custom of the Feast;

43 and as they were returning, after spending the full number of days, the boy Jesus stayed behind in Jerusalem. And His parents were unaware of it,

44 but supposed Him to be in the caravan, and went a day's journey; and they *began* looking for Him among their relatives and acquaintances.

45 And when they did not find Him, they returned to Jerusalem, looking for Him.

46 And it came about that after three days they found Him in the temple, sitting in the midst of the teachers, both listening to them, and asking them questions.

47 And all who heard Him were amazed at His understanding and His answers.

48 And when they saw Him, they were astonished; and His mother said to Him, "Son, why have You treated us this way? Behold, Your father and

I have been anxiously looking for You."

49 And He said to them, "Why is it that you were looking for Me? Did you not know that I had to be in My Father's *house?*"

50 And they did not understand the statement which He had made to them.

51 And He went down with them, and came to Nazareth; and He continued in subjection to them; and His mother treasured all *these* things in her heart.

52 And Jesus kept increasing in wisdom and stature, and in favor with God and men.

CHAPTER 3

NOW in the fifteenth year of the reign of Tiberius Caesar, when Pontius Pilate was governor of Judea, and Herod was tetrarch of Galilee, and his brother Philip was tetrarch of the region of Ituraea and Trachonitis, and Lysanias was tetrarch of Abilene,

2 in the high priesthood of Annas and Caiaphas, the word of God came to John, the son of Zacharias, in the wilderness.

3 And he came into all the district around the Jordan, preaching a baptism of repentance for forgiveness of sins;

4 as it is written in the book of the words of Isaiah the prophet, "The voice of one crying in the wilderness,

'MAKE READY THE WAY OF THE LORD,

MAKE HIS PATHS STRAIGHT.

5 'EVERY RAVINE SHALL BE FILLED UP,

AND EVERY MOUNTAIN AND HILL SHALL BE BROUGHT LOW;

AND THE CROOKED SHALL BECOME STRAIGHT,

AND THE ROUGH ROADS SMOOTH;

6 AND ALL FLESH SHALL SEE THE SALVATION OF GOD.'"

7 He therefore *began* saying to the multitudes who were going out to be baptized by him, "You brood of vipers, who warned you to flee from the wrath to come?

8 "Therefore bring forth fruits in keeping with your repentance, and do not begin to say to yourselves, 'We have Abraham for our father,' for I say to you that God is able from these stones to raise up children to Abraham.

9 "And also the axe is already laid at the root of the trees; every tree therefore that does not bear good fruit is cut down and thrown into the fire."

10 And the multitudes were questioning him, saying, "Then what shall we do?"

11 And he would answer and say to them, "Let the man who has two tunics share with him who has none; and let him who has food do likewise."

12 And *some* tax-gatherers also came to be baptized, and they said to him, "Teacher, what shall we do?"

13 And he said to them, "Collect no more than what you have been ordered to."

14 And *some* soldiers were questioning him, saying, "And *what about* us, what shall we do?" And he said to them, "Do not take money from anyone by force, or accuse *anyone* falsely, and be content with your wages."

15 Now while the people were in a state of expectation and all were wondering in their hearts about John, as to whether he might be the Christ,

16 John answered and said to them all, "As for me, I baptize you with water; but He who is mightier than I is coming, and I am not fit to untie the thong of His sandals; He

Himself will baptize you in the Holy Spirit and fire.

17 "And His winnowing fork is in His hand to clean out His threshing floor, and to gather the wheat into His barn; but He will burn up the chaff with unquenchable fire."

18 So with many other exhortations also he preached the gospel to the people.

19 But when Herod the tetrarch was reproved by him on account of Herodias, his brother's wife, and on account of all the wicked things which Herod had done,

20 he added this also to them all, that he locked John up in prison.

21 Now it came about when all the people were baptized, that Jesus also was baptized, and while He was praying, heaven was opened,

22 and the Holy Spirit descended upon Him in bodily form like a dove, and a voice came out of heaven, "Thou art My beloved Son, in Thee I am well-pleased."

23 And when He began His ministry, Jesus Himself was about thirty years of age, being supposedly *the* son of Joseph, the *son* of Eli,

24 the *son* of Matthat, the *son* of Levi, the *son* of Melchi, the *son* of Jannai, the *son* of Joseph,

25 the *son* of Mattathias, the *son* of Amos, the *son* of Nahum, the *son* of Hesli, the *son* of Naggai,

26 the *son* of Maath, the *son* of Mattathias, the *son* of Semein, the *son* of Josech, the *son* of Joda,

27 the *son* of Joanan, the *son* of Rhesa, the *son* of Zerubbabel, the *son* of Shealtiel, the *son* of Neri,

28 the *son* of Melchi, the *son* of Addi, the *son* of Cosam, the *son* of Elmadam, the *son* of Er,

29 the *son* of Joshua, the *son* of Eliezer, the *son* of Jorim, the *son* of Matthat, the *son* of *Levi*,

30 the *son* of Simeon, the *son* of Judah, the *son* of Joseph, the *son* of Jonam, the *son* of Eliakim,

31 the *son* of Melea, the *son* of Menna, the *son* of Mattatha, the *son* of Nathan, the *son* of David,

32 the *son* of Jesse, the *son* of Obed, the *son* of Boaz, the *son* of Salmon, the *son* of Nahshon,

33 the *son* of Amminadab, the *son* of Admin, the *son* of Ram, the *son* of Hezron, the *son* of Perez, the *son* of Judah,

34 the *son* of Jacob, the *son* of Isaac, the *son* of Abraham, the *son* of Terah, the *son* of Nahor,

35 the *son* of Serug, the *son* of Reu, the *son* of Peleg, the *son* of Heber, the *son* of Shelah,

36 the *son* of Cainan, the *son* of Arphaxad, the *son* of Shem, the *son* of Noah, the *son* of Lamech,

37 the *son* of Methuselah, the *son* of Enoch, the *son* of Jared, the *son* of Mahalaleel, the *son* of Cainan,

38 the *son* of Enosh, the *son* of Seth, the *son* of Adam, the *son* of God.

CHAPTER 4

AND Jesus, full of the Holy Spirit, returned from the Jordan and was led about by the Spirit in the wilderness

2 for forty days, while tempted by the devil. And He ate nothing during those days; and when they had ended, He became hungry.

3 And the devil said to Him, "If You are the Son of God, tell this stone to become bread."

4 And Jesus answered him, "It is written, 'MAN SHALL NOT LIVE ON BREAD ALONE.'"

5 And he led Him up and showed Him all the kingdoms of the world in a moment of time.

6 And the devil said to Him, "I will give You all this domain and its glory; for it has been handed over to me, and I give it to whomever I wish.

7 "Therefore if You worship before me, it shall all be Yours."

8 And Jesus answered and said to

him, "It is written, 'YOU SHALL WOR-
SHIP THE LORD YOUR GOD AND SERVE
HIM ONLY.' "

9 And he led Him to Jerusalem
and set Him on the pinnacle of the
temple, and said to Him, "If You are
the Son of God, cast Yourself down
from here;

10 for it is written,

'HE WILL GIVE HIS ANGELS
CHARGE CONCERNING YOU TO
GUARD YOU,'

11 and,

'ON THEIR HANDS THEY WILL
BEAR YOU UP,
LEST YOU STRIKE YOUR FOOT
AGAINST A STONE.' "

12 And Jesus answered and said to
him, "It is said, 'YOU SHALL NOT FORCE
A TEST ON THE LORD YOUR GOD.' "

13 And when the devil had finished every temptation, he departed
from Him until an opportune time.

14 And Jesus returned to Galilee
in the power of the Spirit; and news
about Him spread through all the
surrounding district.

15 And He *began* teaching in their
synagogues and was praised by all.

16 And He came to Nazareth,
where He had been brought up; and
as was His custom, He entered the
synagogue on the Sabbath, and stood
up to read.

17 And the book of the prophet
Isaiah was handed to Him. And He
opened the book, and found the place
where it was written,

18 "THE SPIRIT OF THE LORD IS
UPON ME,
BECAUSE HE ANOINTED ME TO
PREACH THE GOSPEL TO THE
POOR.
HE HAS SENT ME TO PROCLAIM
RELEASE TO THE CAPTIVES,
AND RECOVERY OF SIGHT TO
THE BLIND,
TO SET FREE THOSE WHO ARE
DOWNTRODDEN,

19 TO PROCLAIM THE FAVORABLE
YEAR OF THE LORD."

20 And He closed the book, and
gave it back to the attendant, and sat
down; and the eyes of all in the synagogue were fixed upon Him.

21 And He began to say to them,
"Today this Scripture has been fulfilled in your hearing."

22 And all were speaking well of
Him, and wondering at the gracious
words which were falling from His
lips; and they were saying, "Is this not
Joseph's son?"

23 And He said to them, "No
doubt you will quote this proverb to
Me, 'Physician, heal yourself; whatever we heard was done at Capernaum, do here in your home town as
well.' "

24 And He said, "Truly I say to
you, no prophet is welcome in his
home town.

25 "But I say to you in truth, there
were many widows in Israel in the
days of Elijah, when the sky was shut
up for three years and six months,
when a great famine came over all the
land;

26 and yet Elijah was sent to none
of them, but only to Zarephath, in the
land of Sidon, to a woman who was a
widow.

27 "And there were many lepers in
Israel in the time of Elisha the
prophet; and none of them was
cleansed, but only Naaman the Syr-
ian."

28 And all in the synagogue were
filled with rage as they heard these
things;

29 and they rose up and cast Him
out of the city, and led Him to the
brow of the hill on which their city
had been built, in order to throw Him
down the cliff.

30 But passing through their
midst, He went His way.

31 And He came down to Capernaum, a city of Galilee. And He was
teaching them on Sabbath days;

32 and they were *continually* amazed at His teaching, for His message was with authority.

33 And there was a man in the synagogue possessed by the spirit of an unclean demon, and he cried out with a loud voice,

34 "Ha! What do we have to do with You, Jesus of Nazareth? Have You come to destroy us? I know who You are — the Holy One of God!"

35 And Jesus rebuked him, saying, "Be quiet and come out of him!" And when the demon had thrown him down in *their* midst, he went out of him without doing him any harm.

36 And amazement came upon them all, and they *began* discussing with one another, and saying, "What is this message? For with authority and power He commands the unclean spirits, and they come out."

37 And the report about Him was getting out into every locality in the surrounding district.

38 And He arose and *left* the synagogue, and entered Simon's home. Now Simon's mother-in-law was suffering from a high fever; and they made request of Him on her behalf.

39 And standing over her, He rebuked the fever, and it left her; and she immediately arose and *began* to wait on them.

40 And while the sun was setting, all who had any sick with various diseases brought them to Him; and laying His hands on every one of them, He was healing them.

41 And demons also were coming out of many, crying out and saying, "You are the Son of God!" And rebuking them, He would not allow them to speak, because they knew Him to be the Christ.

42 And when day came, He departed and went to a lonely place; and the multitudes were searching for Him, and came to Him, and tried to keep Him from going away from them.

43 But He said to them, "I must preach the kingdom of God to the other cities also, for I was sent for this purpose."

44 And He kept on preaching in the synagogues of Judea.

CHAPTER 5

NOW it came about that while the multitude were pressing around Him and listening to the word of God, He was standing by the lake of Gennesaret;

2 and He saw two boats lying at the edge of the lake; but the fishermen had gotten out of them, and were washing their nets.

3 And He got into one of the boats, which was Simon's, and asked him to put out a little way from the land. And He sat down and *began* teaching the multitudes from the boat.

4 And when He had finished speaking, He said to Simon, "Put out into the deep water and let down your nets for a catch."

5 And Simon answered and said, "Master, we worked hard all night and caught nothing, but at Your bidding I will let down the nets."

6 And when they had done this, they enclosed a great quantity of fish; and their nets *began* to break;

7 and they signaled to their partners in the other boat, for them to come and help them. And they came, and filled both of the boats, so that they began to sink.

8 But when Simon Peter saw *that*, he fell down at Jesus' feet, saying, "Depart from me, for I am a sinful man, O Lord!"

9 For amazement had seized him and all his companions because of the catch of fish which they had taken;

10 and so also James and John, sons of Zebedee, who were partners with Simon. And Jesus said to Simon,

"Do not fear, from now on you will be catching men."

11 And when they had brought their boats to land, they left everything and followed Him.

12 And it came about that while He was in one of the cities, behold, *there was* a man full of leprosy; and when he saw Jesus, he fell on his face and implored Him, saying, "Lord, if You are willing, You can make me clean."

13 And He stretched out His hand, and touched him, saying, "I am willing; be cleansed." And immediately the leprosy left him.

14 And He ordered him to tell no one, "But go and show yourself to the priest, and make an offering for your cleansing, just as Moses commanded, for a testimony to them."

15 But the news about Him was spreading even farther, and great multitudes were gathering to hear *Him* and to be healed of their sicknesses.

16 But He Himself would *often* slip away to the wilderness and pray.

17 And it came about one day that He was teaching; and there were *some* Pharisees and teachers of the law sitting *there*, who had come from every village of Galilee and Judea and *from* Jerusalem; and the power of the Lord was *present* for Him to perform healing.

18 And behold, *some* men *were* carrying on a bed a man who was paralyzed; and they were trying to bring him in, and to set him down in front of Him.

19 And not finding any *way* to bring him in because of the crowd, they went up on the roof and let him down through the tiles with his stretcher, right in the center, in front of Jesus.

20 And seeing their faith, He said, "Friend, your sins are forgiven you."

21 And the scribes and the Pharisees began to reason, saying, "Who is this *man* who speaks blasphemies? Who can forgive sins, but God alone?"

22 But Jesus, aware of their reasonings, answered and said to them, "Why are you reasoning in your hearts?

23 "Which is easier, to say, 'Your sins have been forgiven you,' or to say, 'Rise and walk'?

24 "But in order that you may know that the Son of Man has authority on earth to forgive sins," He said to the paralytic, "I say to you, rise, and take up your stretcher and go home."

25 And at once he rose up before them, and took up what he had been lying on, and went home, glorifying God.

26 And they were all seized with astonishment and *began* glorifying God; and they were filled with fear, saying, "We have seen remarkable things today."

27 And after that He went out, and noticed a tax-gatherer named Levi, sitting in the tax office, and He said to him, "Follow Me."

28 And he left everything behind, and rose up and *began* to follow Him.

29 And Levi gave a big reception for Him in his house; and there was a great crowd of tax-gatherers and other *people* who were reclining *at table* with them.

30 And the Pharisees and their scribes *began* grumbling at His disciples, saying, "Why do you eat and drink with the tax-gatherers and sinners?"

31 And Jesus answered and said to them, "*It is* not those who are well who need a physician, but those who are sick.

32 "I have not come to call righteous men but sinners to repentance."

33 And they said to Him, "The

disciples of John often fast and offer prayers; the *disciples* of the Pharisees also do the same; but Yours eat and drink."

34 And Jesus said to them, "You cannot make the attendants of the bridegroom fast while the bridegroom is with them, can you?

35 "But *the* days will come; and when the bridegroom is taken away from them, then they will fast in those days."

36 And He was also telling them a parable: "No one tears a piece from a new garment and puts it on an old garment; otherwise he will both tear the new, and the piece from the new will not match the old.

37 "And no one puts new wine into old wineskins; otherwise the new wine will burst the skins, and it will be spilled out, and the skins will be ruined.

38 "But new wine must be put into fresh wineskins.

39 "And no one, after drinking old *wine* wishes for new; for he says, 'The old is good *enough.*'"

CHAPTER 6

Now it came about on a *certain* Sabbath He was passing through *some* grainfields; and His disciples were picking and eating the heads *of wheat,* rubbing them in their hands.

2 But some of the Pharisees said, "Why do you do what is not lawful on the Sabbath?"

3 And Jesus answering them said, "Have you not even read what David did when he was hungry, he and those who were with him,

4 how he entered the house of God, and took and ate the consecrated bread which is not lawful for any to eat except the priests alone, and gave it to his companions?"

5 And He was saying to them, "The Son of Man is Lord of the Sabbath."

6 And it came about on another Sabbath, that He entered the synagogue and was teaching; and there was a man there whose right hand was withered.

7 And the scribes and the Pharisees were watching Him closely, *to see* if He healed on the Sabbath, in order that they might find *reason* to accuse Him.

8 But He knew what they were thinking, and He said to the man with the withered hand, "Arise and come forward!" And he arose and came forward.

9 And Jesus said to them, "I ask you, is it lawful on the Sabbath to do good, or to do evil, to save a life, or to destroy it?"

10 And after looking around at them all, He said to him, "Stretch out your hand!" And he did *so;* and his hand was *completely* restored.

11 But they themselves were filled with rage, and discussed together what they might do to Jesus.

12 And it was at this time that He went off to the mountain to pray, and He spent the whole night in prayer to God.

13 And when day came, He called His disciples to Him; and chose twelve of them, whom He also named as apostles:

14 Simon, whom He also named Peter, and Andrew his brother; James and John; Philip and Bartholomew;

15 Matthew and Thomas; James *the son* of Alphaeus, and Simon who was called the Zealot;

16 Judas *the son* of James, and Judas Iscariot, who became a traitor.

17 And He descended with them, and stood on a level place; and *there was* a great multitude of His disciples, and a great throng of people from all Judea and Jerusalem and the coastal region of Tyre and Sidon,

18 who had come to hear Him, and to be healed of their diseases; and

those who were troubled with unclean spirits were being cured.

19 And all the multitude were trying to touch Him, for power was coming from Him and healing *them* all.

20 And turning His gaze on His disciples, He *began* to say, "Blessed *are* you *who are* poor, for yours is the kingdom of God.

21 "Blessed *are* you who hunger now, for you shall be satisfied. Blessed *are* you who weep now, for you shall laugh.

22 "Blessed are you when men hate you, and ostracize you, and heap insults upon you, and spurn your name as evil, for the sake of the Son of Man.

23 "Be glad in that day, and leap *for joy*, for behold, your reward is great in heaven; for in the same way their fathers used to treat the prophets.

24 "But woe to you who are rich, for you are receiving your comfort in full.

25 "Woe to you who are well-fed now, for you shall be hungry. Woe *to you* who laugh now, for you shall mourn and weep.

26 "Woe *to you* when all men speak well of you, for in the same way their fathers used to treat the false prophets.

27 "But I say to you who hear, love your enemies, do good to those who hate you,

28 bless those who curse you, pray for those who mistreat you.

29 "Whoever hits you on the cheek, offer him the other also; and whoever takes away your coat, do not withhold your shirt from him either.

30 "Give to everyone who asks of you, and whoever takes away what is yours, do not demand it back.

31 "And just as you want men to treat you, treat them in the same way.

32 "And if you love those who love you, what credit is *that* to you? For

even sinners love those who love them.

33 "And if you do good to those who do good to you, what credit is *that* to you? For even sinners do the same thing.

34 "And if you lend to those from whom you expect to receive, what credit is *that* to you? Even sinners lend to sinners, in order to receive back the same *amount*.

35 "But love your enemies, and do good, and lend, expecting nothing in return; and your reward will be great, and you will be sons of the Most High; for He Himself is kind to ungrateful and evil *men*.

36 "Be merciful, just as your Father is merciful.

37 "And do not pass judgment and you will not be judged; and do not condemn, and you shall not be condemned; pardon, and you will be pardoned.

38 "Give, and it will be given to you; good measure, pressed down, shaken together, running over, they will pour into your lap. For whatever measure you deal out *to others*, it will be dealt to you in return."

39 And He also spoke a parable to them: "A blind man cannot guide a blind man, can he? Will they not both fall into a pit?

40 "A pupil is not above his teacher; but everyone, after he has been fully trained, will be like his teacher.

41 "And why do you look at the speck that is in your brother's eye, but do not notice the log that is in your own eye?

42 "Or how can you say to your brother, 'Brother, let me take out the speck that is in your eye,' when you yourself do not see the log that is in your own eye? You hypocrite, first take the log out of your own eye, and then you will see clearly to take out the speck that is in your brother's eye.

43 "For there is no good tree which produces bad fruit; nor, on the other hand, a bad tree which produces good fruit.

44 "For each tree is known by its own fruit. For men do not gather figs from thorns, nor do they pick grapes from a briar bush.

45 "The good man out of the good treasure of his heart brings forth what is good; and the evil *man* out of the evil *treasure* brings forth what is evil; for his mouth speaks from that which fills his heart.

46 "And why do you call Me, 'Lord, Lord,' and do not do what I say?

47 "Everyone who comes to Me, and hears My words, and acts upon them, I will show you whom he is like:

48 he is like a man building a house, who dug deep and laid a foundation upon the rock; and when a flood arose, the river burst against that house and could not shake it, because it had been well built.

49 "But the one who has heard, and has not acted *accordingly*, is like a man who built a house upon the ground without any foundation; and the river burst against it and immediately it collapsed, and the ruin of that house was great."

Chapter 7

WHEN He had completed all His discourse in the hearing of the people, He went to Capernaum.

2 And a certain centurion's slave, who was highly regarded by him, was sick and about to die.

3 And when he heard about Jesus, he sent some Jewish elders asking Him to come and save the life of his slave.

4 And when they had come to Jesus, they earnestly entreated Him, saying, "He is worthy for You to grant this to him;

5 for he loves our nation, and it was he who built us our synagogue."

6 Now Jesus *started* on His way with them; and when He was already not far from the house, the centurion sent friends, saying to Him, "Lord, do not trouble Yourself further, for I am not fit for You to come under my roof;

7 for this reason I did not even consider myself worthy to come to You, but just say the word, and my servant will be healed.

8 "For indeed, I am a man under authority, with soldiers under me; and I say to this one, 'Go!' and he goes; and to another, 'Come!' and he comes; and to my slave, 'Do this!' and he does it."

9 And when Jesus heard this, He marveled at him, and turned and said to the multitude that was following Him, "I say to you, not even in Israel have I found such great faith."

10 And when those who had been sent returned to the house, they found the slave in good health.

11 And it came about soon afterwards, that He went to a city called Nain; and His disciples were going along with Him, accompanied by a large multitude.

12 Now as He approached the gate of the city, behold, a dead man was being carried out, the only son of his mother, and she was a widow; and a sizeable crowd from the city was with her.

13 And when the Lord saw her, He felt compassion for her, and said to her, "Do not weep."

14 And He came up and touched the coffin; and the bearers came to a halt. And He said, "Young man, I say to you, arise!"

15 And the dead man sat up, and began to speak. And *Jesus* gave him back to his mother.

16 And fear gripped them all, and they *began* glorifying God, saying, "A

great prophet has arisen among us!" and, "God has visited His people!"

17 And this report concerning Him went out all over Judea, and in all the surrounding district.

18 And the disciples of John reported to him about all these things.

19 And summoning two of his disciples, John sent them to the Lord, saying, "Are You the One who is coming, or do we look for someone else?"

20 And when the men had come to Him, they said, "John the Baptist has sent us to You, saying, 'Are You the One who is coming, or do we look for someone else?' "

21 At that very time He cured many *people* of diseases and afflictions and evil spirits; and He granted sight to many *who were* blind.

22 And He answered and said to them, "Go and report to John what you have seen and heard: *the* BLIND RECEIVE SIGHT, *the* lame walk, *the* lepers are cleansed, and *the* deaf hear, *the* dead are raised up, *the* POOR HAVE THE GOSPEL PREACHED TO THEM.

23 "And blessed is he who keeps from stumbling over Me."

24 And when the messengers of John had left, He began to speak to the multitudes about John, "What did you go out into the wilderness to look at? A reed shaken by the wind?

25 "But what did you go out to see? A man dressed in soft clothing? Behold, those who are splendidly clothed and live in luxury are *found* in royal palaces.

26 "But what did you go out to see? A prophet? Yes, I say to you, and one who is more than a prophet.

27 "This is the one about whom it is written,

'BEHOLD, I SEND MY MESSEN-
GER BEFORE YOUR FACE,
WHO WILL PREPARE YOUR
WAY BEFORE YOU.'

28 "I say to you, among those born of women, there is no one greater than John; yet he who is least in the kingdom of God is greater than he."

29 And when all the people and the tax-gatherers heard *this*, they acknowledged God's justice, having been baptized with the baptism of John.

30 But the Pharisees and the lawyers rejected God's purpose for themselves, not having been baptized by John.

31 "To what then shall I compare the men of this generation, and what are they like?

32 "They are like children who sit in the market place and call to one another; and they say, 'We played the flute for you, and you did not dance; we sang a dirge, and you did not weep.'

33 "For John the Baptist has come eating no bread and drinking no wine; and you say, 'He has a demon!'

34 "The Son of Man has come eating and drinking; and you say, 'Behold, a gluttonous man, and a drunkard, a friend of tax-gatherers and sinners!'

35 "Yet wisdom is vindicated by all her children."

36 Now one of the Pharisees was requesting Him to dine with him. And He entered the Pharisee's house, and reclined *at table.*

37 And behold, there was a woman in the city who was a sinner; and when she learned that He was reclining *at table* in the Pharisee's house, she brought an alabaster vial of perfume,

38 and standing behind *Him* at His feet, weeping, she began to wet His feet with her tears, and kept wiping them with the hair of her head, and kissing His feet, and anointing them with the perfume.

39 Now when the Pharisee who had invited Him saw this, he said to himself, "If this man were a prophet He would know who and what sort of

person this woman is who is touching Him, that she is a sinner."

40 And Jesus answered and said to him, "Simon, I have something to say to you." And he replied, "Say it, Teacher."

41 "A certain moneylender had two debtors: one owed five hundred denarii, and the other fifty.

42 "When they were unable to repay, he graciously forgave them both. Which of them therefore will love him more?"

43 Simon answered and said, "I suppose the one whom he forgave more." And He said to him, "You have judged correctly."

44 And turning toward the woman, He said to Simon, "Do you see this woman? I entered your house; you gave Me no water for My feet, but she has wet My feet with her tears, and wiped them with her hair.

45 "You gave Me no kiss; but she, since the time I came in, has not ceased to kiss My feet.

46 "You did not anoint My head with oil, but she anointed My feet with perfume.

47 "For this reason I say to you, her sins, which are many, have been forgiven, for she loved much; but he who is forgiven little, loves little."

48 And He said to her, "Your sins have been forgiven."

49 And those who were reclining *at table* with Him began to say to themselves, "Who is this *man* who even forgives sins?"

50 And He said to the woman, "Your faith has saved you; go in peace."

CHAPTER 8

AND it came about soon afterwards, that He *began* going about from one city and village to another, proclaiming and preaching the kingdom of God; and the twelve were with Him,

2 and *also* some women who had been healed of evil spirits and sicknesses: Mary who was called Magdalene, from whom seven demons had gone out,

3 and Joanna the wife of Chuza, Herod's steward, and Susanna, and many others who were contributing to their support out of their private means.

4 And when a great multitude were coming together, and those from the various cities were journeying to Him, He spoke by way of a parable:

5 "The sower went out to sow his seed; and as he sowed, some fell beside the road; and it was trampled under foot, and the birds of the air devoured it.

6 "And other *seed* fell on rocky *soil*, and as soon as it grew up, it withered away, because it had no moisture.

7 "And other *seed* fell among the thorns; and the thorns grew up with it, and choked it out.

8 "And other *seed* fell into the good ground, and grew up, and produced a crop a hundred times as great." As He said these things, He would call out, "He who has ears to hear, let him hear."

9 And His disciples *began* questioning Him as to what this parable might be.

10 And He said, "To you it is granted to know the mysteries of the kingdom of God, but to the rest *it is* in parables; in order that SEEING THEY MAY NOT SEE, AND HEARING THEY MAY NOT UNDERSTAND.

11 "Now the parable is this: the seed is the word of God.

12 "And those beside the road are those who have heard; then the devil comes and takes away the word from their heart, so that they may not believe and be saved.

13 "And those on the rocky *soil are* those who, when they hear, receive

the word with joy; and these have no firm root; they believe for a while, and in time of temptation fall away.

14 "And the seed which fell among the thorns, these are the ones who have heard, and as they go on their way they are choked with worries and riches and pleasures of this life, and bring no fruit to maturity.

15 "And the seed in the good ground, these are the ones who have heard the word in an honest and good heart, and hold it fast, and bear fruit with perseverance.

16 "Now no one after lighting a lamp covers it over with a container, or puts it under a bed; but he puts it on a lampstand, in order that those who come in may see the light.

17 "For nothing is hidden that shall not become evident, nor anything secret that shall not be known and come to light.

18 "Therefore take care how you listen; for whoever has, to him shall more be given; and whoever does not have, even what he thinks he has shall be taken away from him."

19 And His mother came to Him and His brothers also, and they were unable to get to Him because of the crowd.

20 And it was reported to Him, "Your mother and Your brothers are standing outside, wishing to see You."

21 But He answered and said to them, "My mother and My brothers are these who hear the word of God and do it."

22 Now it came about on one of those days, that He and His disciples got into a boat, and He said to them, "Let us go over to the other side of the lake." And they launched out.

23 But as they were sailing along He fell asleep; and a fierce gale of wind descended upon the lake, and they began to be swamped and to be in danger.

24 And they came to Him and woke Him up, saying, "Master, Master, we are perishing!" And being aroused, He rebuked the wind and the surging waves, and they stopped, and it became calm.

25 And He said to them, "Where is your faith?" And they were fearful and amazed, saying to one another, "Who then is this, that He commands even the winds and the water, and they obey Him?"

26 And they sailed to the country of the Gerasenes, which is opposite Galilee.

27 And when He had come out onto the land, a certain man from the city met Him who was possessed with demons; and who had not put on any clothing for a long time, and was not living in a house, but in the tombs.

28 And seeing Jesus, he cried out and fell before Him, and said in a loud voice, "What do I have to do with You, Jesus, Son of the Most High God? I beg You, do not torment me."

29 For He had been commanding the unclean spirit to come out of the man. For it had seized him many times; and he was bound with chains and shackles and kept under guard; and yet he would burst his fetters and be driven by the demon into the deserts.

30 And Jesus asked him, "What is your name?" And he said, "Legion"; for many demons had entered him.

31 And they were entreating Him not to command them to depart into the abyss.

32 Now there was a herd of many swine feeding there on the mountain; and the demons entreated Him to permit them to enter the swine. And He gave them permission.

33 And the demons came out from the man and entered the swine; and the herd rushed down the steep bank into the lake, and were drowned.

34 And when those who tended them saw what had happened, they ran away and reported it in the city and *out* in the country.

35 And *the people* went out to see what had happened; and they came to Jesus, and found the man from whom the demons had gone out, sitting down at the feet of Jesus, clothed and in his right mind; and they became frightened.

36 And those who had seen it reported to them how the man who was demon-possessed had been made well.

37 And all the people of the country of the Gerasenes and the surrounding district asked Him to depart from them; for they were gripped with great fear; and He got into a boat, and returned.

38 But the man from whom the demons had gone out was begging Him that he might accompany Him; but He sent him away, saying,

39 "Return to your house and describe what great things God has done for you." And he departed, proclaiming throughout the whole city what great things Jesus had done for him.

40 And as Jesus returned, the multitude welcomed Him, for they had all been waiting for Him.

41 And behold, there came a man named Jairus, and he was an official of the synagogue; and he fell at Jesus' feet, and *began* to entreat Him to come to his house;

42 for he had an only daughter, about twelve years old, and she was dying. But as He went, the multitudes were pressing against Him.

43 And a woman who had a hemorrhage for twelve years, and could not be healed by anyone,

44 came up behind Him, and touched the fringe of His cloak; and immediately her hemorrhage stopped.

45 And Jesus said, "Who is the one who touched Me?" And while they were all denying it, Peter said, "Master, the multitudes are crowding and pressing upon You."

46 But Jesus said, "Someone did touch Me, for I was aware that power had gone out of Me."

47 And when the woman saw that she had not escaped notice, she came trembling and fell down before Him, and declared in the presence of all the people the reason why she had touched Him, and how she had been immediately healed.

48 And He said to her, "Daughter, your faith has made you well; go in peace."

49 While He was still speaking, someone *came from *the house of* the synagogue official, saying, "Your daughter has died; do not trouble the Teacher any more."

50 But when Jesus heard *this*, He answered him, "Do not be afraid *any longer*; only believe, and she shall be made well."

51 And when He had come to the house, He did not allow anyone to enter with Him, except Peter, John and James, and the girl's father and mother.

52 Now they were all weeping and lamenting for her; but He said, "Stop weeping, for she has not died, but is asleep."

53 And they *began* laughing at Him, knowing that she had died.

54 He, however, took her by the hand and called, saying, "Child, arise!"

55 And her spirit returned, and she rose up immediately; and He gave orders for *something* to be given her to eat.

56 And her parents were amazed; but He instructed them to tell no one what had happened.

CHAPTER 9

AND He called the twelve together, and gave them power and authority over all the demons, and to heal diseases.

2 And He sent them out to proclaim the kingdom of God, and to perform healing.

3 And He said to them, "Take nothing for *your* journey, neither a staff, nor a bag, nor bread, nor money; and do not *even* have two tunics apiece.

4 "And whatever house you enter, stay there, and take your leave from there.

5 "And as for those who do not receive you, when you depart from that city, shake off the dust from your feet as a testimony against them."

6 And departing, they *began* going about among the villages, preaching the gospel, and healing everywhere.

7 Now Herod the tetrarch heard of all that was happening; and he was greatly perplexed, because it was said by some that John had risen from the dead,

8 and by some that Elijah had appeared, and by others, that one of the prophets of old had risen again.

9 And Herod said, "I myself had John beheaded; but who is this man about whom I hear such things?" And he kept trying to see Him.

10 And when the apostles returned, they gave an account to Him of all that they had done. And taking them with Him, He withdrew privately to a city called Bethsaida.

11 But the multitudes were aware of this and followed Him; and welcoming them, He *began* speaking to them about the kingdom of God and curing those who had need of healing.

12 And the day began to decline, and the twelve came and said to Him, "Send the multitude away, that they may go into the surrounding villages and countryside and find lodging and get something to eat; for here we are in a desolate place."

13 But He said to them, "You give them something to eat!" And they said, "We have no more than five loaves and two fish, unless perhaps we go and buy food for all these people."

14 (For there were about five thousand men). And He said to His disciples, "Have them recline *to eat* in groups of about fifty each."

15 And they did so, and had them all recline.

16 And He took the five loaves and the two fish, and looking up to heaven, He blessed them, and broke *them*, and kept giving *them* to the disciples to set before the multitude.

17 And they all ate and were satisfied; and that which was left over to them of the broken pieces was picked up, twelve baskets *full.*

18 And it came about that while He was praying alone, the disciples were with Him, and He questioned them, saying, "Who do the multitudes say that I am?"

19 And they answered and said, "John the Baptist; but others *say*, Elijah; and others, that one of the prophets of old has risen again."

20 And He said to them, "But who do you say that I am?" And Peter answered and said, "The Christ of God."

21 But He warned them, and instructed *them* not to tell this to anyone,

22 saying, "The Son of Man must suffer many things, and be rejected by the elders and chief priests and scribes, and be killed, and be raised up on the third day."

23 And He was saying *to them* all, "If anyone wishes to come after Me, let him deny himself, and take up his cross daily, and follow Me.

24 "For whoever wishes to save his life shall lose it, but whoever loses his

life for My sake, he is the one who will save it.

25 "For what is a man profited if he gains the whole world, and loses or forfeits himself?

26 "For whoever is ashamed of Me and My words, of him will the Son of Man be ashamed when He comes in His glory, and *the glory* of the Father and of the holy angels.

27 "But I tell you truly, there are some of those standing here who shall not taste death until they see the kingdom of God."

28 And some eight days after these sayings, it came about that He took along Peter and John and James, and went up to the mountain to pray.

29 And while He was praying, the appearance of His face became different, and His clothing *became* white *and* gleaming.

30 And behold, two men were talking with Him; and they were Moses and Elijah,

31 who, appearing in glory, were speaking of His departure which He was about to accomplish at Jerusalem.

32 Now Peter and his companions had been overcome with sleep; but when they were fully awake, they saw His glory and the two men standing with Him.

33 And it came about, as these were parting from Him, Peter said to Jesus, "Master, it is good for us to be here; and let us make three tabernacles: one for You, and one for Moses, and one for Elijah"—not realizing what he was saying.

34 And while he was saying this, a cloud formed and *began* to overshadow them; and they were afraid as they entered the cloud.

35 And a voice came out of the cloud, saying, "This is My Son, *My* Chosen One; listen to Him!"

36 And when the voice had spoken, Jesus was found alone. And they kept silent, and reported to no one in those days any of the things which they had seen.

37 And it came about on the next day, that when they had come down from the mountain, a great multitude met Him.

38 And behold, a man from the multitude shouted out, saying, "Teacher, I beg You to look at my son, for he is my only *boy*,

39 and behold, a spirit seizes him, and he suddenly screams, and it throws him into a convulsion with foaming *at the mouth*, and as it mauls him, it scarcely leaves him.

40 "And I begged Your disciples to cast it out, and they could not."

41 And Jesus answered and said, "O unbelieving and perverted generation, how long shall I be with you, and put up with you? Bring your son here."

42 And while he was still approaching, the demon dashed him *to the ground*, and threw him into a violent convulsion. But Jesus rebuked the unclean spirit, and healed the boy, and gave him back to his father.

43 And they were all amazed at the greatness of God.

But while everyone was marveling at all that He was doing, He said to His disciples,

44 "Let these words sink into your ears; for the Son of Man is going to be delivered into the hands of men."

45 But they did not understand this statement, and it was concealed from them so that they might not perceive it; and they were afraid to ask Him about this statement.

46 And an argument arose among them as to which of them might be the greatest.

47 But Jesus, knowing what they were thinking in their heart, took a child and stood him by His side,

48 and said to them, "Whoever

receives this child in My name receives Me; and whoever receives Me receives Him who sent Me; for he who is least among you, this is the one who is great."

49 And John answered and said, "Master, we saw someone casting out demons in Your name; and we tried to hinder him because he does not follow along with us."

50 But Jesus said to him, "Do not hinder *him*; for he who is not against you is for you."

51 And it came about, when the days were approaching for His ascension, that He resolutely set His face to go to Jerusalem;

52 and He sent messengers on ahead of Him. And they went, and entered a village of the Samaritans, to make arrangements for Him.

53 And they did not receive Him, because He was journeying with His face toward Jerusalem.

54 And when His disciples James and John saw *this*, they said, "Lord, do You want us to command fire to come down from heaven and consume them?"

55 But He turned and rebuked them.

56 And they went on to another village.

57 And as they were going along the road, someone said to Him, "I will follow You wherever You go."

58 And Jesus said to him, "The foxes have holes, and the birds of the air *have* nests, but the Son of Man has nowhere to lay His head."

59 And He said to another, "Follow Me." But he said, "Permit me first to go and bury my father."

60 But He said to him, "Allow the dead to bury their own dead; but as for you, go and proclaim everywhere the kingdom of God."

61 And another also said, "I will follow You, Lord; but first permit me to say good-bye to those at home."

62 But Jesus said to him, "No one,

after putting his hand to the plow and looking back, is fit for the kingdom of God."

CHAPTER 10

Now after this the Lord appointed seventy others, and sent them two and two ahead of Him to every city and place where He Himself was going to come.

2 And He was saying to them, "The harvest is plentiful, but the laborers are few; therefore beseech the Lord of the harvest to send out laborers into His harvest.

3 "Go your ways; behold, I send you out as lambs in the midst of wolves.

4 "Carry no purse, no bag, no shoes; and greet no one on the way.

5 "And whatever house you enter, first say, 'Peace *be* to this house.'

6 "And if a man of peace is there, your peace will rest upon him; but if not, it will return to you.

7 "And stay in that house, eating and drinking what they give you; for the laborer is worthy of his wages. Do not keep moving from house to house.

8 "And whatever city you enter, and they receive you, eat what is set before you;

9 and heal those in it who are sick, and say to them, 'The kingdom of God has come near to you.'

10 "But whatever city you enter and they do not receive you, go out into its streets and say,

11 'Even the dust of your city which clings to our feet, we wipe off *in protest* against you; yet be sure of this, that the kingdom of God has come near.'

12 "I say to you, it will be more tolerable in that day for Sodom, than for that city.

13 "Woe to you, Chorazin! Woe to you, Bethsaida! For if the miracles had been performed in Tyre and Si-

don which occurred in you, they would have repented long ago, sitting in sackcloth and ashes.

14 "But it will be more tolerable for Tyre and Sidon in the judgment, than for you.

15 "And you, Capernaum, will not be exalted to heaven, will you? You will be brought down to Hades!

16 "The one who listens to you listens to Me, and the one who rejects you rejects Me; and he who rejects Me rejects the One who sent Me."

17 And the seventy returned with joy, saying, "Lord, even the demons are subject to us in Your name."

18 And He said to them, "I was watching Satan fall from heaven like lightning.

19 "Behold, I have given you authority to tread upon serpents and scorpions, and over all the power of the enemy, and nothing shall injure you.

SCRIPTURE No. 4, SEC. 3

20 "Nevertheless do not rejoice in this, that the spirits are subject to you, but rejoice that your names are recorded in heaven." (r4)

21 At that very time He rejoiced greatly in the Holy Spirit, and said, "I praise Thee, O Father, Lord of heaven and earth, that Thou didst hide these things from *the* wise and intelligent and didst reveal them to babes. Yes, Father, for thus it was well-pleasing in Thy sight.

22 "All things have been handed over to Me by My Father, and no one knows who the Son is except the Father, and who the Father is except the Son, and anyone to whom the Son wills to reveal *Him*."

23 And turning to the disciples, He said privately, "Blessed *are* the eyes which see the things you see,

24 for I say to you, that many prophets and kings wished to see the things which you see, and did not see *them*, and to hear the things which you hear, and did not hear *them*."

25 And behold, a certain lawyer stood up and put Him to the test, saying, "Teacher, what shall I do to inherit eternal life?"

26 And He said to him, "What is written in the Law? How does it read to you?"

27 And he answered and said, "YOU SHALL LOVE THE LORD YOUR GOD WITH ALL YOUR HEART, AND WITH

(r4) REFERENCE NO. 4, SEC. 3—
IS YOUR NAME RECORDED IN HEAVEN?

Jesus said to his disciples, *"Do not rejoice in this that the spirits are subject to you."* Here is a lesson in humility. The power they possessed over spirits or demons was God's gift.

Jesus told them, "Apart from Me you can do nothing." So be careful in that for which you rejoice.

He said, "But rejoice that your names are recorded in heaven." The Lord Jesus promises that your name is written when called in heaven. The recorder hears the Lord Jesus call out your name when you repent and confess Him before men. He writes your name in "the book of life."

The reason is that "the book of life" is to be opened at the "great white throne" Judgment. If you have confessed Christ before men and He has confessed you in heaven, then you will rejoice because your judgment is passed. And, "the second death has no power" over you.

Will your name be found recorded in "the book of life" in heaven? If so, say: "I want my name to be written in heaven in the book of life."

Now turn to page 307, Scripture No. 5, Sec. 3, Heb. 12:23.

ALL YOUR SOUL, AND WITH ALL YOUR
STRENGTH, AND WITH ALL YOUR
MIND; AND YOUR NEIGHBOR AS YOURSELF."

28 And He said to him, "You have answered correctly; DO THIS, AND YOU WILL LIVE."

29 But wishing to justify himself, he said to Jesus, "And who is my neighbor?"

30 Jesus replied and said, "A certain man was going down from Jerusalem to Jericho; and he fell among robbers, and they stripped him and beat him, and went off leaving him half dead.

31 "And by chance a certain priest was going down on that road, and when he saw him, he passed by on the other side.

32 "And likewise a Levite also, when he came to the place and saw him, passed by on the other side.

33 "But a certain Samaritan, who was on a journey, came upon him; and when he saw him, he felt compassion,

34 and came to him, and bandaged up his wounds, pouring oil and wine on *them;* and he put him on his own beast, and brought him to an inn, and took care of him.

35 "And on the next day he took out two denarii and gave them to the innkeeper and said, 'Take care of him; and whatever more you spend, when I return, I will repay you.'

36 "Which of these three do you think proved to be a neighbor to the man who fell into the robbers' *hands?*"

37 And he said, "The one who showed mercy toward him." And Jesus said to him, "Go and do the same."

38 Now as they were traveling along, He entered a certain village; and a woman named Martha welcomed Him into her home.

39 And she had a sister called Mary, who moreover was listening to the Lord's word, seated at His feet.

40 But Martha was distracted with all her preparations; and she came up *to Him,* and said, "Lord, do You not care that my sister has left me to do all the serving alone? Then tell her to help me."

41 But the Lord answered and said to her, "Martha, Martha, you are worried and bothered about so many things;

42 but *only* a few things are necessary, really *only* one, for Mary has chosen the good part, which shall not be taken away from her."

CHAPTER 11

AND it came about that while He was praying in a certain place, after He had finished, one of His disciples said to Him, "Lord, teach us to pray just as John also taught his disciples."

2 And He said to them, "When you pray, say:

> 'Father, hallowed be Thy name.
> Thy kingdom come.

3   'Give us each day our daily bread.

4   'And forgive us our sins,
> For we ourselves also forgive everyone who is indebted to us.
> And lead us not into temptation.' "

5 And He said to them, "Suppose one of you shall have a friend, and shall go to him at midnight, and say to him, 'Friend, lend me three loaves;

6 for a friend of mine has come to me from a journey, and I have nothing to set before him';

7 and from inside he shall answer and say, 'Do not bother me; the door has already been shut and my children and I are in bed; I cannot get up and give you *anything.*'

8 "I tell you, even though he will not get up and give him *anything* because he is his friend, yet because of his persistence he will get up and give him as much as he needs.

9 "And I say to you, ask, and it shall be given to you; seek, and you shall find; knock, and it shall be opened to you.

10 "For everyone who asks, receives; and he who seeks, finds; and to him who knocks, it shall be opened.

11 "Now suppose one of you fathers is asked by his son for a fish; he will not give him a snake instead of a fish, will he?

12 "Or *if* he is asked for an egg, he will not give him a scorpion, will he?

13 "If you then, being evil, know how to give good gifts to your children, how much more shall *your* Heavenly Father give the Holy Spirit to those who ask Him?"

14 And He was casting out a demon, *and it was* dumb; and it came about that when the demon had gone out, the dumb man spoke; and the multitudes marveled.

15 But some of them said, "He casts out demons by Beelzebul, the ruler of the demons."

16 And others, to test *Him,* were demanding of Him a sign from heaven.

17 But He knew their thoughts, and said to them, "Any kingdom divided against itself is laid waste; and a house divided against itself falls.

18 "And if Satan also is divided against himself, how shall his kingdom stand? For you say that I cast out demons by Beelzebul.

19 "And if I by Beelzebul cast out demons, by whom do your sons cast them out? Consequently they shall be your judges.

20 "But if I cast out demons by the finger of God, then the kingdom of God has come upon you.

21 "When a strong *man* fully armed guards his own homestead, his possessions are undisturbed;

22 but when someone stronger than he attacks him and overpowers him, he takes away from him all his armor on which he had relied, and distributes his plunder.

23 "He who is not with Me is against Me; and he who does not gather with Me, scatters.

24 "When the unclean spirit goes out of a man, it passes through waterless places seeking rest, and not finding any, it says, 'I will return to my house from which I came.'

25 "And when it comes, it finds it swept and put in order.

26 "Then it goes and takes *along* seven other spirits more evil than itself, and they go in and live there; and the last state of that man becomes worse than the first."

27 And it came about while He said these things, one of the women in the crowd raised her voice, and said to Him, "Blessed is the womb that bore You, and the breasts at which You nursed."

28 But He said, "On the contrary, blessed are those who hear the word of God, and observe it."

29 And as the crowds were increasing, He began to say, "This generation is a wicked generation; it seeks for a sign, and *yet* no sign shall be given to it but the sign of Jonah.

30 "For just as Jonah became a sign to the Ninevites, so shall the Son of Man be to this generation.

31 "The Queen of the South shall rise up with the men of this generation at the judgment and condemn them, because she came from the ends of the earth to hear the wisdom of Solomon; and behold, something greater than Solomon is here.

32 "The men of Nineveh shall stand up with this generation at the judgment and condemn it, because they repented at the preaching of Jo-

nah; and behold, something greater than Jonah is here.

33 "No one, after lighting a lamp, puts it away in a cellar, nor under a peck-measure, but on the lampstand, in order that those who enter may see the light.

34 "The lamp of your body is your eye; when your eye is clear, your whole body also is full of light; but when it is bad, your body also is full of darkness.

35 "Then watch out that the light in you may not be darkness.

36 "If therefore your whole body is full of light, with no dark part in it, it shall be wholly illumined, as when the lamp illumines you with its rays."

37 Now when He had spoken, a Pharisee *asked Him to have lunch with him; and He went in, and reclined *at table.*

38 And when the Pharisee saw it, he was surprised that He had not first ceremonially washed before the meal.

39 But the Lord said to him, "Now you Pharisees clean the outside of the cup and of the platter; but inside of you, you are full of robbery and wickedness.

40 "You foolish ones, did not He who made the outside make the inside also?

41 "But give that which is within as charity, and then all things are clean for you.

42 "But woe to you Pharisees! For you pay tithe of mint and rue and every *kind of* garden herb, and *yet* disregard justice and the love of God; but these are the things you should have done without neglecting the others.

43 "Woe to you Pharisees! For you love the front seats in the synagogues, and the respectful greetings in the market places.

44 "Woe to you! For you are like concealed tombs, and the people who walk over *them* are unaware *of it.*"

45 And one of the lawyers *said to Him in reply, "Teacher, when You say this, You insult us too."

46 But He said, "Woe to you lawyers as well! For you weigh men down with burdens hard to bear, while you yourselves will not even touch the burdens with one of your fingers.

47 "Woe to you! For you build the tombs of the prophets, and *it was* your fathers *who* killed them.

48 "Consequently, you are witnesses and approve the deeds of your fathers; because it was they who killed them, and you build *their tombs.*

49 "For this reason also the wisdom of God said, 'I will send to them prophets and apostles, and *some* of them they will kill and *some* they will persecute,

50 in order that the blood of all the prophets, shed since the foundation of the world, may be charged against this generation,

51 from the blood of Abel to the blood of Zechariah, who perished between the altar and the House *of God;* yes, I tell you, it shall be charged against this generation.'

52 "Woe to you lawyers! For you have taken away the key of knowledge; you did not enter in yourselves, and those who were entering in you hindered."

53 And when He left there, the scribes and the Pharisees began to be very hostile and to question Him closely on many subjects,

54 plotting against Him, to catch *Him* in something He might say.

CHAPTER 12

UNDER these circumstances, after so many thousands of the multitude had gathered together that they were stepping on one another, He began saying to His disciples first *of all*, "Beware of the leaven of the Pharisees, which is hypocrisy.

2 "But there is nothing covered up that will not be revealed, and hidden that will not be known.

3 "Accordingly whatever you have said in the dark shall be heard in the light, and what you have whispered in the inner rooms shall be proclaimed upon the housetops.

4 "And I say to you, my friends, do not be afraid of those who kill the body, and after that have no more that they can do.

5 "But I will warn you whom to fear: Fear the One who after He has killed has authority to cast into hell; yes, I tell you, fear Him!

6 "Are not five sparrows sold for two cents? And *yet* not one of them is forgotten before God.

7 "Indeed the very hairs of your head are all numbered. Do not fear; you are of more value than many sparrows.

8 "And I say to you, everyone who confesses Me before men, the Son of Man shall confess him also before the angels of God;

9 but he who denies Me before men shall be denied before the angels of God.

10 "And everyone who will speak a word against the Son of Man, it shall be forgiven him; but he who blasphemes against the Holy Spirit, it shall not be forgiven him.

11 "And when they bring you before the synagogues and the rulers and the authorities, do not become anxious about how or what you should speak in your defense, or what you should say;

12 for the Holy Spirit will teach you in that very hour what you ought to say."

13 And someone in the crowd said to Him, "Teacher, tell my brother to divide the *family* inheritance with me."

14 But He said to him, "Man, who appointed Me a judge or arbiter over you?"

15 And He said to them, "Beware, and be on your guard against every form of greed; for not *even* when one has an abundance does his life consist of his possessions."

16 And He told them a parable, saying, "The land of a certain rich man was very productive.

17 "And he began reasoning to himself, saying, 'What shall I do, since I have no place to store my crops?'

18 "And he said, 'This is what I will do: I will tear down my barns and build larger ones, and there I will store all my grain and my goods.

19 'And I will say to my soul, "Soul, you have many goods laid up for many years *to come*; take your ease, eat, drink *and* be merry." '

20 "But God said to him, 'You fool! This *very* night your soul is required of you; and *now* who will own what you have prepared?'

21 "So is the man who lays up treasure for himself, and is not rich toward God."

22 And He said to His disciples, "For this reason I say to you, do not be anxious for *your* life, *as to* what you shall eat; nor for your body, *as to* what you shall put on.

23 "For life is more than food, and the body than clothing.

24 "Consider the ravens, for they neither sow nor reap; and they have no storeroom nor barn; and *yet* God feeds them; how much more valuable you are than the birds!

25 "And which of you by being anxious can add a *single* cubit to his life's span?

26 "If then you cannot do even a very little thing, why are you anxious about other matters?

27 "Consider the lilies, how they grow; they neither toil nor spin; but I tell you, even Solomon in all his glory

did not clothe himself like one of these.

28 "But if God so *arrays* the grass in the field, which is *alive* today and tomorrow is thrown into the furnace, how much more *will He clothe* you, O men of little faith!

29 "And do not seek what you shall eat, and what you shall drink, and do not keep worrying.

30 "For all these things the nations of the world eagerly seek; but your Father knows that you need these things.

31 "But seek for His kingdom, and these things shall be added to you.

32 "Do not be afraid, little flock, for your Father has chosen gladly to give you the kingdom.

33 "Sell your possessions and give to charity; make yourselves purses which do not wear out, an unfailing treasure in heaven, where no thief comes near, nor moth destroys.

34 "For where your treasure is, there will your heart be also.

35 "Be dressed in readiness, and *keep* your lamps alight.

36 "And be like men who are waiting for their master when he returns from the wedding feast, so that they may immediately open *the door* to him when he comes and knocks.

37 "Blessed are those slaves whom the master shall find on the alert when he comes; truly I say to you, that he will gird himself *to serve*, and have them recline *at table*, and will come up and wait on them.

38 "Whether he comes in the second watch, or even in the third, and finds *them* so, blessed are those *slaves*.

39 "And be sure of this, that if the head of the house had known at what hour the thief was coming, he would not have allowed his house to be broken into.

40 "You too, be ready; for the Son of Man is coming at an hour that you do not expect."

41 And Peter said, "Lord, are You addressing this parable to us, or to everyone *else* as well?"

42 And the Lord said, "Who then is the faithful and sensible steward, whom his master will put in charge of his servants, to give them their rations at the proper time?

43 "Blessed is that slave whom his master finds so doing when he comes.

44 "Truly I say to you, that he will put him in charge of all his possessions.

45 "But if that slave says in his heart, 'My master will be a long time in coming,' and begins to beat the slaves, *both* men and women, and to eat and drink and get drunk;

46 the master of that slave will come on a day when he does not expect *him*, and at an hour he does not know, and will cut him in pieces, and assign him a place with the unbelievers.

47 "And that slave who knew his master's will and did not get ready or act in accord with his will, shall receive many *lashes*,

48 but the one who did not know *it*, and committed deeds worthy of a flogging, will receive but few. And from everyone who has been given much shall much be required; and to whom they entrusted much, of him they will ask all the more.

49 "I have come to cast fire upon the earth; and how I wish it were already kindled!

50 "But I have a baptism to undergo, and how distressed I am until it is accomplished!

51 "Do you suppose that I came to grant peace on earth? I tell you, no, but rather division;

52 for from now on five *members* in one household will be divided, three against two, and two against three.

53 "They will be divided, father against son, and son against father;

mother against daughter, and daughter against mother; mother-in-law against daughter-in-law, and daughter-in-law against mother-in-law."

54 And He was also saying to the multitudes, "When you see a cloud rising in the west, immediately you say, 'A shower is coming,' and so it turns out.

55 "And when *you see* a south wind blowing, you say, 'It will be a hot day,' and it turns out *that way.*

56 "You hypocrites! You know how to analyze the appearance of the earth and the sky, but why do you not analyze this present time?

57 "And why do you not even on your own initiative judge what is right?

58 "For while you are going with your opponent to appear before the magistrate, on *your* way *there* make an effort to settle with him, in order that he may not drag you before the judge, and the judge turn you over to the constable, and the constable throw you into prison.

59 "I say to you, you shall not get out of there until you have paid the very last cent."

CHAPTER 13

Now on the same occasion there were some present who reported to Him about the Galileans, whose blood Pilate had mingled with their sacrifices.

2 And He answered and said to them, "Do you suppose that these Galileans were *greater* sinners than all *other* Galileans, because they suffered this *fate?*

3 "I tell you, no, but, unless you repent, you will all likewise perish.

4 "Or do you suppose that those eighteen on whom the tower in Siloam fell and killed them, were *worse* culprits than all the men who live in Jerusalem?

5 "I tell you, no, but, unless you repent, you will all likewise perish."

6 And He *began* telling this parable: "A certain man had a fig tree which had been planted in his vineyard; and he came looking for fruit on it, and did not find any.

7 "And he said to the vineyard-keeper, 'Behold, for three years I have come looking for fruit on this fig tree without finding any. Cut it down! Why does it even use up the ground?'

8 "And he answered and said to him, 'Let it alone, sir, for this year too, until I dig around it and put in fertilizer;

9 and if it bears fruit next year, *fine;* but if not, cut it down.' "

10 And He was teaching in one of the synagogues on the Sabbath.

11 And behold, there was a woman who for eighteen years had had a sickness caused by a spirit; and she was bent double, and could not straighten up at all.

12 And when Jesus saw her, He called her over and said to her, "Woman, you are freed from your sickness."

13 And He laid His hands upon her; and immediately she was made erect again, and *began* glorifying God.

14 And the synagogue official, indignant because Jesus had healed on the Sabbath, *began* saying to the multitude in response, "There are six days in which work should be done; therefore come during them and get healed, and not on the Sabbath day."

15 But the Lord answered him and said, "You hypocrites, does not each of you on the Sabbath untie his ox or his donkey from the stall, and lead him away to water *him?*

16 "And this woman, a daughter of Abraham as she is, whom Satan has bound for eighteen long years, should she not have been released from this bond on the Sabbath day?"

17 And as He said this, all his opponents were being humiliated; and the entire multitude was rejoicing over all the glorious things being done by Him.

18 Therefore He was saying, "What is the kingdom of God like, and to what shall I compare it?

19 "It is like a mustard seed, which a man took and threw into his own garden; and it grew and became a tree; and the birds of the air nested in its branches."

20 And again He said, "To what shall I compare the kingdom of God?

21 "It is like leaven, which a woman took and hid in three pecks of meal, until it was all leavened."

22 And He was passing through from one city and village to another, teaching, and proceeding on His way to Jerusalem.

23 And someone said to Him, "Lord, are there *just* a few who are being saved?" And He said to them,

24 "Strive to enter by the narrow door; for many, I tell you, will seek to enter and will not be able.

25 "Once the head of the house gets up and shuts the door, and you begin to stand outside and knock on the door, saying, 'Lord, open up to us!' then He will answer and say to you, 'I do not know where you are from.'

26 "Then you will begin to say, 'We ate and drank in Your presence, and You taught in our streets';

27 and He will say, 'I tell you, I do not know where you are from; DEPART FROM ME, ALL YOU EVILDOERS.'

28 "There will be weeping and gnashing of teeth there when you see Abraham and Isaac and Jacob and all the prophets in the kingdom of God, and yourselves being cast out.

29 "And they will come from east and west, and from north and south, and will recline *at table* in the kingdom of God.

30 "And behold, *some* are last who will be first and *some* are first who will be last."

31 Just at that time some Pharisees came up, saying to Him, "Go away and depart from here, for Herod wants to kill You."

32 And He said to them, "Go and tell that fox, 'Behold, I cast out demons and perform cures today and tomorrow, and the third *day* I reach My goal.'

33 "Nevertheless I must journey on today and tomorrow and the next *day;* for it cannot be that a prophet should perish outside of Jerusalem.

34 "O Jerusalem, Jerusalem, *the city* that kills the prophets and stones those sent to her! How often I wanted to gather your children together, just as a hen *gathers* her brood under her wings, and you would not *have it!*

35 "Behold, your house is left to you *desolate;* and I say to you, you shall not see Me until *the time* comes when you say, 'Blessed *is* He who comes in the name of the Lord!'"

CHAPTER 14

AND it came about when He went into the house of one of the leaders of the Pharisees on *the* Sabbath to eat bread, that they were watching Him closely.

2 And there, in front of Him was a certain man suffering from dropsy.

3 And Jesus answered and spoke to the lawyers and Pharisees, saying, "Is it lawful to heal on the Sabbath, or not?"

4 But they kept silent. And He took hold of him, and healed him, and sent him away.

5 And He said to them, "Which one of you shall have a son or an ox fall into a well, and will not immediately pull him out on a Sabbath day?"

6 And they could make no reply to this.

7 And He *began* speaking a parable to the invited guests when He noticed how they had been picking out the places of honor *at the table*; saying to them,

8 "When you are invited by someone to a wedding feast, do not take the place of honor, lest someone more distinguished than you may have been invited by him,

9 and he who invited you both shall come and say to you, 'Give place to this man', and then in disgrace you proceed to occupy the last place.

10 "But when you are invited, go and recline at the last place, so that when the one who has invited you comes, he may say to you, 'Friend, move up higher'; then you will have honor in the sight of all who are at the table with you.

11 "For everyone who exalts himself shall be humbled, and he who humbles himself shall be exalted."

12 And He also went on to say to the one who had invited Him, "When you give a luncheon or a dinner, do not invite your friends or your brothers or your relatives or rich neighbors, lest they also invite you in return, and repayment come to you.

13 "But when you give a reception, invite *the* poor, *the* crippled, *the* lame, *the* blind,

14 and you will be blessed, since they do not have *the means* to repay you; for you will be repaid at the resurrection of the righteous."

15 And when one of those who were reclining *at table* with Him heard this, he said to Him, "Blessed is everyone who shall eat bread in the kingdom of God!"

16 But He said to him, "A certain man was giving a big dinner, and he invited many;

17 and at the dinner hour he sent his slave to say to those who had been invited, 'Come; for everything is ready now.'

18 "But they all alike began to make excuses. The first one said to him, 'I have bought a piece of land and I need to go out and look at it; please consider me excused.'

19 "And another one said, 'I have bought five yoke of oxen, and I am going to try them out; please consider me excused.'

20 "And another one said, 'I have married a wife, and for that reason I cannot come.'

21 "And the slave came *back* and reported this to his master. Then the head of the household became angry and said to his slave, 'Go out at once into the streets and lanes of the city and bring in here the poor and crippled and blind and lame.'

22 "And the slave said, 'Master, what you commanded has been done, and still there is room.'

23 "And the master said to the slave, 'Go out into the highways and along the hedges, and compel *them* to come in, that my house may be filled.

24 'For I tell you, none of those men who were invited shall taste of my dinner.' "

25 Now great multitudes were going along with Him; and He turned and said to them,

26 "If anyone comes to Me, and does not hate his own father and mother and wife and children and brothers and sisters, yes, and even his own life, he cannot be My disciple.

27 "Whoever does not carry his own cross and come after Me cannot be My disciple.

28 "For which one of you, when he wants to build a tower, does not first sit down and calculate the cost, to see if he has enough to complete it?

29 "Otherwise, when he has laid a foundation, and is not able to finish, all who observe it begin to ridicule him,

30 saying, 'This man began to build and was not able to finish.'

31 "Or what king, when he sets out to meet another king in battle, will not first sit down and take counsel whether he is strong enough with ten thousand *men* to encounter the one coming against him with twenty thousand?

32 "Or else, while the other is still far away, he sends a delegation and asks terms of peace.

33 "So therefore, no one of you can be My disciple who does not give up all his own possessions.

34 "Therefore, salt is good; but if even salt has become tasteless, with what will it be seasoned?

35 "It is useless either for the soil or for the manure pile; it is thrown out. He who has ears to hear, let him hear."

CHAPTER 15

N OW all the tax-gatherers and the sinners were coming near Him to listen to Him.

2 And both the Pharisees and the scribes *began* to grumble, saying, "This man receives sinners and eats with them."

3 And He told them this parable, saying,

4 "What man among you, if he has a hundred sheep and has lost one of them, does not leave the ninety-nine in the open pasture, and go after the one which is lost, until he finds it?

5 "And when he has found it, he lays it on his shoulders, rejoicing.

6 "And when he comes home, he calls together his friends and his neighbors, saying to them, 'Rejoice with me, for I have found my sheep which was lost!'

7 "I tell you that in the same way, there will be *more* joy in heaven over one sinner who repents, than over ninety-nine righteous persons who need no repentance.

8 "Or what woman, if she has ten silver coins and loses one coin, does not light a lamp and sweep the house and search carefully until she finds it?

9 "And when she has found it, she calls together her friends and neighbors, saying, 'Rejoice with me, for I have found the coin which I had lost!'

SCRIPTURE NO. 3, SEC. 3

10 "In the same way, I tell you, there is joy in the presence of the angels of God over one sinner who repents." (r3)

(r3) REFERENCE NO. 3, SEC. 3—
HAVE THOSE IN HEAVEN HEARD YOUR NAME CALLED THERE?

"There is joy in the presence of the angels of God over one sinner who repents."
What happens in heaven when you are truly saved? Your repentance brings rejoicing. Because "you turned to God from idols to serve a living and true God."

When you show your true repentance by telling you trust Jesus as Lord "before men," then instantly Jesus Christ calls your name before the Father in heaven as one who has put your faith in Him. "In the presence of the angels of God" are also those believers in Christ Jesus who are "absent from the body" and are "at home with the Lord." When your name is called they "know fully" what has happened and "there is joy."

When you repent and believe in Christ you are justified. This means, just as if you had never sinned. You pass "out of death into life" and will "not come into judgment." So that is another reason for joy.

Do you see there will be joy in heaven when Christ confesses your name there? If so, say:

"I know there will be joy in heaven when Jesus Christ confesses my name there."
Now turn to page 95, Scripture No. 4, Sec. 3, Luke 10:20.

11 And He said, "A certain man had two sons;

12 and the younger of them said to his father, 'Father, give me the share of the estate that falls to me.' And he divided his wealth between them.

13 "And not many days later, the younger son gathered everything together and went on a journey into a distant country, and there he squandered his estate with loose living.

14 "Now when he had spent everything, a severe famine occurred in that country, and he began to be in need.

15 "And he went and attached himself to one of the citizens of that country, and he sent him into his fields to feed swine.

16 "And he was longing to fill his stomach with the pods that the swine were eating, and no one was giving *anything* to him.

17 "But when he came to his senses, he said, 'How many of my father's hired men have more than enough bread, but I am dying here with hunger!

18 'I will get up and go to my father, and will say to him, "Father, I have sinned against heaven, and in your sight;

19 "I am no longer worthy to be called your son; make me as one of your hired men." '

20 "And he got up and came to his father. But while he was still a long way off, his father saw him, and felt compassion *for him*, and ran and embraced him, and kissed him.

21 "And the son said to him, 'Father, I have sinned against heaven and in your sight; I am no longer worthy to be called your son.'

22 "But the father said to his slaves, 'Quickly bring out the best robe and put it on him, and put a ring on his hand and sandals on his feet;

23 and bring the fattened calf, kill it, and let us eat and be merry;

24 for this son of mine was dead,

and has come to life again; he was lost, and has been found.' And they began to be merry.

25 "Now his older son was in the field, and when he came and approached the house, he heard music and dancing.

26 "And he summoned one of the servants and *began* inquiring what these things might be.

27 "And he said to him, 'Your brother has come, and your father has killed the fattened calf, because he has received him back safe and sound.'

28 "But he became angry, and was not willing to go in; and his father came out and *began* entreating him.

29 "But he answered and said to his father, 'Look! For so many years I have been serving you, and I have never neglected a command of yours; and *yet* you have never given me a kid, that I might be merry with my friends;

30 but when this son of yours came, who has devoured your wealth with harlots, you killed the fattened calf for him.'

31 "And he said to him, '*My* child, you have always been with me, and all that is mine is yours.

32 'But we had to be merry and rejoice, for this brother of yours was dead and *has begun* to live, and *was* lost and has been found.' "

CHAPTER 16

NOW He was also saying to the disciples, "There was a certain rich man who had a steward, and this *steward* was reported to him as squandering his possessions.

2 "And he called him and said to him, 'What is this I hear about you? Give an account of your stewardship, for you can no longer be steward.'

3 "And the steward said to himself, 'What shall I do, since my master is taking the stewardship away from me? I am not strong enough to dig; I am ashamed to beg.

4 'I know what I shall do, so that when I am removed from the stewardship, they will receive me into their homes.'

5 "And he summoned each one of his master's debtors, and he *began* saying to the first, 'How much do you owe my master?'

6 "And he said, 'A hundred measures of oil.' And he said to him, 'Take your bill, and sit down quickly and write fifty.'

7 "Then he said to another, 'And how much do you owe?' And he said, 'A hundred measures of wheat.' He *said to him, 'Take your bill, and write eighty.'

8 "And his master praised the unrighteous steward because he had acted shrewdly; for the sons of this age are more shrewd in relation to their own kind than the sons of light.

9 "And I say to you, make friends for yourselves by means of the mammon of unrighteousness; that when it fails, they may receive you into the eternal dwellings.

10 "He who is faithful in a very little thing is faithful also in much; and he who is unrighteous in a very little thing is unrighteous also in much.

11 "If therefore you have not been faithful in the *use of* unrighteous mammon, who will entrust the true *riches* to you?

12 "And if you have not been faithful in *the use of* that which is another's, who will give you that which is your own?

13 "No servant can serve two masters; for either he will hate the one, and love the other, or else he will hold to one, and despise the other. You cannot serve God and mammon."

14 Now the Pharisees, who were lovers of money, were listening to all these things, and they were scoffing at Him.

15 And He said to them, "You are those who justify yourselves in the sight of men, but God knows your hearts; for that which is highly esteemed among men is detestable in the sight of God.

16 "The Law and the Prophets *were* proclaimed until John; since then the gospel of the kingdom of God is preached, and every one is forcing his way into it.

17 "But it is easier for heaven and earth to pass away than for one stroke of a letter of the Law to fail.

18 "Every one who divorces his wife and marries another commits adultery; and he who marries one who is divorced from a husband commits adultery.

19 "Now there was a certain rich man, and he habitually dressed in purple and fine linen, gaily living in splendor every day.

20 "And a certain poor man named Lazarus was laid at his gate, covered with sores,

21 and longing to be fed with the *crumbs* which were falling from the rich man's table; besides, even the dogs were coming and licking his sores.

22 "Now it came about that the poor man died and he was carried away by the angels to Abraham's bosom; and the rich man also died and was buried.

23 "And in Hades he lifted up his eyes, being in torment, and *saw Abraham far away, and Lazarus in his bosom.

24 "And he cried out and said, 'Father Abraham, have mercy on me, and send Lazarus, that he may dip the tip of his finger in water and cool off my tongue; for I am in agony in this flame.'

25 "But Abraham said, 'Child, remember that during your life you received your good things, and likewise

Lazarus bad things; but now he is being comforted here, and you are in agony.

26 'And besides all this, between us and you there is a great chasm fixed, in order that those who wish to come over from here to you may not be able, and *that* none may cross over from there to us.'

27 "And he said, 'Then I beg you, Father, that you send him to my father's house —

28 for I have five brothers — that he may warn them, lest they also come to this place of torment.'

29 "But Abraham *said, 'They have Moses and the Prophets; let them hear them.'

30 "But he said, 'No, Father Abraham, but if someone goes to them from the dead, they will repent!'

31 "But he said to him, 'If they do not listen to Moses and the Prophets, neither will they be persuaded if someone rises from the dead.' "

CHAPTER 17

AND He said to His disciples, "It is inevitable that stumbling blocks should come, but woe to him through whom they come!

2 "It would be better for him if a millstone were hung around his neck and he were thrown into the sea, than that he should cause one of these little ones to stumble.

3 "Be on your guard! If your brother sins, rebuke him; and if he repents, forgive him.

4 "And if he sins against you seven times a day, and returns to you seven times, saying, 'I repent,' forgive him."

5 And the apostles said to the Lord, "Increase our faith!"

6 And the Lord said, "If you had faith like a mustard seed, you would say to this mulberry tree, 'Be uprooted and be planted in the sea'; and it would obey you.

7 "But which of you, having a slave plowing or tending sheep, will say to him when he has come in from the field, 'Come immediately and sit down to eat'?

8 "But will he not say to him, 'Prepare something for me to eat, and *properly* clothe yourself and serve me until I have eaten and drunk; and afterward you will eat and drink'?

9 "He does not thank the slave because he did the things which were commanded, does he?

10 "So you too, when you do all the things which are commanded you, say, 'We are unworthy slaves; we have done *only* that which we ought to have done.' "

11 And it came about while He was on the way to Jerusalem, that He was passing between Samaria and Galilee.

12 And as He entered a certain village, there met Him ten leprous men, who stood at a distance;

13 and they raised their voices, saying, "Jesus, Master, have mercy on us!"

14 And when He saw them, He said to them, "Go and show yourselves to the priests." And it came about that as they were going, they were cleansed.

15 Now one of them, when he saw that he had been healed, turned back, glorifying God with a loud voice,

16 and he fell on his face at His feet, giving thanks to Him. And he was a Samaritan.

17 And Jesus answered and said, "Were there not ten cleansed? But the nine — where are they?

18 "Were none found who turned back to give glory to God, except this foreigner?"

19 And He said to him, "Rise, and go your way; your faith has made you well."

20 Now having been questioned

by the Pharisees as to when the kingdom of God was coming, He answered them and said, "The kingdom of God is not coming with signs to be observed;

21 nor will they say, 'Look, here *it is!*' or, 'There *it is!*' For behold, the kingdom of God is in your midst."

22 And He said to the disciples, "The days shall come when you will long to see one of the days of the Son of Man, and you will not see it.

23 "And they will say to you, 'Look there! Look here!' Do not go away, and do not run after *them.*

24 "For just as the lightning, when it flashes out of one part of the sky, shines to the other part of the sky, so will the Son of Man be in His day.

25 "But first He must suffer many things and be rejected by this generation.

26 "And just as it happened in the days of Noah, so it shall be also in the days of the Son of Man:

27 they were eating, they were drinking, they were marrying, they were being given in marriage, until the day that Noah entered the ark, and the flood came and destroyed them all.

28 "It was the same as happened in the days of Lot: they were eating, they were drinking, they were buying, they were selling, they were planting, they were building;

29 but on the day that Lot went out from Sodom it rained fire and brimstone from heaven and destroyed them all.

30 "It will be just the same on the day that the Son of Man is revealed.

31 "On that day, let not the one who is on the housetop and whose goods are in the house go down to take them away; and likewise let not the one who is in the field turn back.

32 "Remember Lot's wife.

33 "Whoever seeks to keep his life shall lose it, and whoever loses *his life* shall preserve it alive.

34 "I tell you, on that night there will be two men in one bed; one will be taken, and the other will be left.

35 "There will be two women grinding at the same place; one will be taken, and the other will be left."

36 (See footnote (1))

37 And answering they *said to Him, "Where, Lord?" And He said to them, "Where the body *is,* there also will the vultures be gathered."

CHAPTER 18

NOW He was telling them a parable to show that at all times they ought to pray and not to lose heart,

2 saying, "There was in a certain city a judge who did not fear God, and did not respect man.

3 "And there was a widow in that city, and she kept coming to him, saying, 'Give me legal protection from my opponent.'

4 "And for a while he was unwilling; but afterward he said to himself, 'Even though I do not fear God nor respect man,

5 yet because this widow bothers me, I will give her legal protection, lest by continually coming she wear me out.'"

6 And the Lord said, "Hear what the unrighteous judge *said;

7 now shall not God bring about justice for His elect, who cry to Him day and night, and will He delay long over them?

8 "I tell you that He will bring about justice for them speedily. However, when the Son of Man comes, will He find faith on the earth?"

---

(1) Some mss. add verse 36, *Two men will be in the field; one will be taken and the other will be left.* cf. Matt. 24:40

9 And He also told this parable to certain ones who trusted in themselves that they were righteous, and viewed others with contempt: (r1)

10 "Two men went up into the temple to pray, one a Pharisee, and the other a tax-gatherer. (a)

11 "The Pharisee stood and was praying thus to himself, 'God, I thank Thee that I am not like other people: swindlers, unjust, adulterers, or even like this tax-gatherer.

12 'I fast twice a week; I pay tithes of all that I get.' (b)

13 "But the tax-gatherer, standing some distance away, was even unwilling to lift up his eyes to heaven, but was beating his breast, saying, 'God, be merciful to me, the sinner!' (c)

14 "I tell you, this man went down to his house justified rather than the other; for every one who exalts himself shall be humbled, but he who humbles himself shall be exalted." (d)

15 And they were bringing even their babies to Him, in order that He might touch them, but when the disciples saw it, they *began* rebuking them.

16 But Jesus called for them, saying, "Permit the children to come to Me, and stop hindering them, for the kingdom of God belongs to such as these.

17 "Truly I say to you, whoever does not receive the kingdom of God like a child shall not enter it *at all.*"

18 And a certain ruler questioned Him, saying, "Good Teacher, what shall I do to obtain eternal life?"

19 And Jesus said to him, "Why do you call Me good? No one is good except God alone.

20 "You know the commandments, 'DO NOT COMMIT ADULTERY, DO NOT MURDER, DO NOT STEAL, DO NOT BEAR FALSE WITNESS, HONOR YOUR FATHER AND MOTHER.' "

21 And he said, "All these things I have kept from *my* youth."

22 And when Jesus heard *this*, He said to him, "One thing you still lack; sell all that you possess, and distribute it to the poor, and you shall have treasure in heaven; and come, follow Me."

23 But when he had heard these things, he became very sad; for he was extremely rich.

24 And Jesus looked at him and

(r1) PARABLE ON PRAYER. Concerning prayer Jesus teaches of:

(a) The Applicants—One was a self-righteous pharisee, and the other a sin ruined tax gatherer.

(b) The Attitudes—The pharisee was proud, and the tax gatherer was humble.

(c) The Approach to God—The pharisee stood and in thirty-three words boasted, "I am not like other people." He offered self praise, "I fast twice in the week, I give tithes of all I get." The tax gatherer bowed, "unwilling to lift up his eyes to heaven." He begged from a contrite heart, "God be merciful to me the sinner," praying only seven words.

The pharisee came proudly to God upon his merit. The tax gatherer approached God reverently seeking mercy.

(d) The Answer—The humble man was heard. He "went down to his house justified, which means, just as if I had never sinned. He was forgiven and exalted to fellowship with God.

The proud pharisee went home denied. He was judged unworthy.

Will God listen when you pray? Learn the lesson. Seek the Lord with a contrite heart, humble yourself. Confess you are a sinner. Ask God for mercy.

Turn to page 219, read Rom. 10:9-14, then read Reference No. 6, Sec. 1 and pray the prayer suggested there.

said, "How hard it is for those who are wealthy to enter the kingdom of God!

25 "For it is easier for a camel to go through the eye of a needle, than for a rich man to enter the kingdom of God."

26 And they who heard it said, "Then who can be saved?"

27 But He said, "The things impossible with men are possible with God."

28 And Peter said, "Behold, we have left our own *homes*, and followed You."

29 And He said to them, "Truly I say to you, there is no one who has left house or wife or brothers or parents or children, for the sake of the kingdom of God,

30 who shall not receive many times as much at this time and in the age to come, eternal life."

31 And He took the twelve aside and said to them, "Behold, we are going up to Jerusalem, and all things which are written through the prophets about the Son of Man will be accomplished.

32 "For He will be delivered up to the Gentiles, and will be mocked and mistreated and spit upon,

33 and after they have scourged Him, they will kill Him; and the third day He will rise again."

34 And they understood none of these things, and this saying was hidden from them, and they did not comprehend the things that were said.

35 And it came about that as He was approaching Jericho, a certain blind man was sitting by the road, begging.

36 Now hearing a multitude going by, he *began* to inquire what this might be.

37 And they told him that Jesus of Nazareth was passing by.

38 And he called out, saying, "Jesus, Son of David, have mercy on me!"

39 And those who led the way were sternly telling him to be quiet; but he kept crying out all the more, "Son of David, have mercy on me!"

40 And Jesus stopped and commanded that he be brought to Him; and when he had come near, He questioned him,

41 "What do you want Me to do for you?" And he said, "Lord, *I want* to receive my sight!"

42 And Jesus said to him, "Receive your sight; your faith has made you well."

43 And immediately he received his sight, and *began* following Him, glorifying God; and when all the people saw it, they gave praise to God.

Chapter 19

AND He entered and was passing through Jericho.

2 And behold, there was a man called by the name of Zaccheus; and he was a chief tax-gatherer, and he was rich.

3 And he was trying to see who Jesus was, and he was unable because of the crowd, for he was small in stature.

4 And he ran on ahead and climbed up into a sycamore tree in order to see Him, for He was about to pass through that way.

5 And when Jesus came to the place, He looked up and said to him, "Zaccheus, hurry and come down, for today I must stay at your house."

6 And he hurried and came down, and received Him gladly.

7 And when they saw it, they all *began* to grumble, saying, "He has gone to be the guest of a man who is a sinner."

8 And Zaccheus stopped and said to the Lord, "Behold, Lord, half of my possessions I will give to the poor, and if I have defrauded anyone of

anything, I will give back four times as much."

9 And Jesus said to him, "Today salvation has come to this house, because he, too, is a son of Abraham.

10 "For the Son of Man has come to seek and to save that which was lost."

11 And while they were listening to these things, He went on to tell a parable, because He was near Jerusalem, and they supposed that the kingdom of God was going to appear immediately.

12 He said therefore, "A certain nobleman went to a distant country to receive a kingdom for himself, and *then* return.

13 "And he called ten of his slaves, and gave them ten minas, and said to them, 'Do business *with this* until I come *back.*'

14 "But his citizens hated him, and sent a delegation after him, saying, 'We do not want this man to reign over us.'

15 "And it came about that when he returned, after receiving the kingdom, he ordered that these slaves, to whom he had given the money, be called to him in order that he might know what business they had done.

16 "And the first appeared, saying, 'Master, your mina has made ten minas more.'

17 "And he said to him, 'Well done, good slave, because you have been faithful in a very little thing, be in authority over ten cities.'

18 "And the second came, saying, 'Your mina, master, has made five minas.'

19 "And he said to him also, 'And you are to be over five cities.'

20 "And another came, saying, 'Master, behold your mina, which I kept put away in a handkerchief;

21 for I was afraid of you, because you are an exacting man; you take up what you did not lay down, and reap what you did not sow.'

22 "He *said to him, 'By your own words I will judge you, you worthless slave. Did you know that I am an exacting man, taking up what I did not lay down, and reaping what I did not sow?

23 'Then why did you not put the money in the bank, and having come, I would have collected it with interest?'

24 "And he said to the bystanders, 'Take the mina away from him, and give it to the one who has the ten minas.'

25 "And they said to him, 'Master, he has ten minas *already.*'

26 "I tell you, that to everyone who has shall *more* be given, but from the one who does not have, even what he does have shall be taken away.

27 "But these enemies of mine, who did not want me to reign over them, bring them here, and slay them in my presence."

28 And after He had said these things, He was going on ahead, ascending to Jerusalem.

29 And it came about that when He approached Bethphage and Bethany, near the mount that is called Olivet, He sent two of the disciples,

30 saying, "Go into the village opposite *you*, in which as you enter you will find a colt tied, on which no one yet has ever sat; untie it, and bring it *here.*

31 "And if anyone asks you, 'Why are you untying it?' thus shall you speak, 'The Lord has need of it.' "

32 And those who were sent went away and found it just as He had told them.

33 And as they were untying the colt, its owners said to them, "Why are you untying the colt?"

34 And they said, "The Lord has need of it."

35 And they brought it to Jesus, and they threw their garments on the colt, and put Jesus *on it.*

36 And as He was going, they were spreading their garments in the road.

37 And as He was now approaching, near the descent of the Mount of Olives, the whole multitude of the disciples began to praise God joyfully with a loud voice for all the miracles which they had seen,

38 saying,

"BLESSED IS THE King WHO COMES IN THE NAME OF THE LORD;

Peace in heaven and glory in the highest!"

39 And some of the Pharisees in the multitude said to Him, "Teacher, rebuke Your disciples."

40 And He answered and said, "I tell you, if these become silent, the stones will cry out!"

41 And when He approached, He saw the city and wept over it,

42 saying, "If you had known in this day, even you, the things which make for peace! But now they have been hidden from your eyes.

43 "For the days shall come upon you when your enemies will throw up a bank before you, and surround you, and hem you in on every side,

44 and will level you to the ground and your children within you, and they will not leave in you one stone upon another, because you did not recognize the time of your visitation."

45 And He entered the temple and began to cast out those who were selling,

46 saying to them, "It is written, 'AND MY HOUSE SHALL BE A HOUSE OF PRAYER,' but you have made it a robbers' den."

47 And He was teaching daily in the temple; but the chief priests and the scribes and the leading men among the people were trying to destroy Him,

48 and they could not find anything that they might do, for all the people were hanging upon His words.

CHAPTER 20

AND it came about on one of the days while He was teaching the people in the temple and preaching the gospel, that the chief priests and the scribes with the elders confronted *Him*,

2 and they spoke, saying to Him, "Tell us by what authority You are doing these things, or who is the one who gave You this authority?"

3 And He answered and said to them, "I shall also ask you a question, and you tell Me:

4 "Was the baptism of John from heaven or from men?"

5 And they reasoned among themselves, saying, "If we say, 'From heaven,' He will say, 'Why did you not believe him?'

6 "But if we say, 'From men,' all the people will stone us to death, for they are convinced that John was a prophet."

7 And they answered that they did not know where *it came* from.

8 And Jesus said to them, "Neither will I tell you by what authority I am doing these things."

9 And He began to tell the people this parable: "A man planted a vineyard and rented it out to vine-growers, and went on a journey for a long time.

10 "And at the *harvest* time he sent a slave to the vine-growers, in order that they might give him *some* of the produce of the vineyard; but the vine-growers beat him and sent him away empty-handed.

11 "And he proceeded to send another slave; and they beat him also and treated him shamefully, and sent him away empty-handed.

12 "And he proceeded to send a third; and this one also they wounded and cast out.

13 "And the owner of the vineyard said, 'What shall I do? I will send my

beloved son; perhaps they will respect him.'

14 "But when the vine-growers saw him, they reasoned with one another, saying, 'This is the heir; let us kill him that the inheritance may be ours.'

15 "And they cast him out of the vineyard and killed him. What, therefore, will the owner of the vineyard do to them?

16 "He will come and destroy these vine-growers and will give the vineyard to others." And when they heard it, they said, "May it never be!"

17 But He looked at them and said, "What then is this that is written,

'The STONE WHICH THE BUILDERS REJECTED,
THIS BECAME THE CHIEF CORNER *stone*'?

18 "Every one who falls on that stone will be broken to pieces; but on whomever it falls, it will scatter him like dust."

19 And the scribes and the chief priests tried to lay hands on Him that very hour, and they feared the people; for they understood that He spoke this parable against them.

20 And they watched Him, and sent spies who pretended to be righteous, in order that they might catch Him in some statement, so as to deliver Him up to the rule and the authority of the governor.

21 And they questioned Him, saying, "Teacher, we know that You speak and teach correctly, and You are not partial to any, but teach the way of God in truth.

22 "Is it lawful for us to pay taxes to Caesar, or not?"

23 But He detected their trickery and said to them,

24 "Show Me a denarius. Whose head and inscription does it have?" And they said, "Caesar's."

25 And He said to them, "Then render to Caesar the things that are Caesar's, and to God the things that are God's."

26 And they were unable to catch Him in a saying in the presence of the people; and marveling at His answer, they became silent.

27 Now there came to Him some of the Sadducees (who say that there is no resurrection),

28 and they questioned Him, saying, "Teacher, Moses wrote us that IF A MAN'S BROTHER DIES, having a wife, AND HE IS CHILDLESS, HIS BROTHER SHOULD TAKE THE WIFE AND RAISE UP OFFSPRING TO HIS BROTHER.

29 "Now there were seven brothers; and the first took a wife, and died childless;

30 and the second

31 and the third took her; and in the same way the seven also died, leaving no children.

32 "Finally the woman died also.

33 "In the resurrection therefore, which one's wife will the woman be? For the seven had her as wife."

34 And Jesus said to them, "The sons of this age marry and are given in marriage,

35 but those who are considered worthy to attain to that age and the resurrection from the dead, neither marry, nor are given in marriage;

36 for neither can they die any more, for they are like angels, and are sons of God, being sons of the resurrection.

37 "But that the dead are raised, even Moses showed, in the *passage about the burning* bush, where he calls the Lord THE GOD OF ABRAHAM, AND THE GOD OF ISAAC, AND THE GOD OF JACOB.

38 "Now He is not the God of the dead, but of the living; for all live to Him."

39 And some of the scribes answered and said, "Teacher, You have spoken well."

40 For they did not have courage to question Him any longer about anything.

41 And He said to them, "How *is it that* they say the Christ is David's son?

42 "For David himself says in the book of Psalms,

'THE LORD SAID TO MY LORD,
"SIT AT MY RIGHT HAND,

43   UNTIL I MAKE THINE ENEMIES
      A FOOTSTOOL FOR THY
      FEET." '

44 "David therefore calls Him 'Lord,' and how is He his son?"

45 And while all the people were listening, He said to the disciples,

46 "Beware of the scribes, who like to walk around in long robes, and love respectful greetings in the market places, and chief seats in the synagogues, and places of honor at banquets,

47 who devour widows' houses, and for appearance's sake offer long prayers; these will receive greater condemnation."

CHAPTER 21

AND He looked up and saw the rich putting their gifts into the treasury.

2 And He saw a certain poor widow putting in two small copper coins.

3 And He said, "Truly I say to you, this poor widow put in more than all *of them;*

4 for they all out of their surplus put into the offering; but she out of her poverty put in all that she had to live on."

5 And while some were talking about the temple, that it was adorned with beautiful stones and votive gifts, He said,

6 "*As for* these things which you are looking at, the days will come in which there will not be left one stone upon another which will not be torn down."

7 And they questioned Him, saying, "Teacher, when therefore will these things be? And what *will be* the sign when these things are about to take place?"

8 And He said, "Take heed that you be not misled; for many will come in My name, saying, 'I am *He,*' and, 'The time is at hand'; do not go after them.

9 "And when you hear of wars and disturbances, do not be terrified; for these things must take place first, but the end *does* not *follow* immediately."

10 Then He continued by saying to them, "Nation will rise against nation, and kingdom against kingdom,

11 and there will be great earthquakes, and in various places plagues and famines; and there will be terrors and great signs from heaven.

12 "But before all these things, they will lay their hands on you and will persecute you, delivering you to the synagogues and prisons, bringing you before kings and governors for My name's sake.

13 "It will lead to an opportunity for your testimony.

14 "So make up your minds not to prepare beforehand to defend yourselves;

15 for I will give you utterance and wisdom which none of your opponents will be able to resist or refute.

16 "But you will be betrayed even by parents and brothers and relatives and friends, and they will put *some* of you to death,

17 and you will be hated by all on account of My name.

18 "Yet not a hair of your head will perish.

19 "By your perseverance you will win your souls.

20 "But when you see Jerusalem

surrounded by armies, then recognize that her desolation is at hand.

21 "Then let those who are in Judea flee to the mountains, and let those who are in the midst of the city depart, and let not those who are in the country enter the city;

22 because these are days of vengeance, in order that all things which are written may be fulfilled.

23 "Woe to those who are with child and to those who nurse babes in those days; for there will be great distress upon the land, and wrath to this people,

24 and they will fall by the edge of the sword, and will be led captive into all the nations; and Jerusalem will be trampled underfoot by the Gentiles until the times of the Gentiles be fulfilled.

25 "And there will be signs in sun and moon and stars, and upon the earth dismay among nations, in perplexity at the roaring of the sea and the waves,

26 men fainting from fear and the expectation of the things which are coming upon the world; for the powers of the heavens will be shaken.

27 "And then will they see THE SON OF MAN COMING IN A CLOUD with power and great glory.

28 "But when these things begin to take place, straighten up and lift up your heads, because your redemption is drawing near."

29 And He told them a parable: "Behold the fig tree, and all the trees;

30 as soon as they put forth *leaves*, you see it and know for yourselves that the summer is now near.

31 "Even so you, too, when you see these things happening, recognize that the kingdom of God is near.

32 "Truly I say to you, this generation will not pass away until all things take place.

33 "Heaven and earth will pass away, but My words will not pass away.

34 "Be on guard, that your hearts may not be weighted down with dissipation and drunkenness and the worries of life, and that day come on you suddenly like a trap;

35 for it will come upon all those who dwell on the face of all the earth.

36 "But keep on the alert at all times, praying in order that you may have strength to escape all these things that are about to take place, and to stand before the Son of Man."

37 Now during the day He was teaching in the temple, but at evening He would go out and spend the night on the mount that is called Olivet.

38 And all the people would get up early in the morning *to come* to Him in the temple to listen to Him.

CHAPTER 22

NOW the Feast of Unleavened Bread, which is called the Passover, was approaching.

2 And the chief priests and the scribes were seeking how they might put Him to death; for they were afraid of the people.

3 And Satan entered into Judas who was called Iscariot, belonging to the number of the twelve.

4 And he went away and discussed with the chief priests and officers how he might betray Him to them.

5 And they were delighted, and agreed to give him money.

6 And he consented, and *began* seeking a good opportunity to betray Him to them apart from the multitude.

7 Then came the day of Unleavened Bread on which the Passover *lamb* had to be sacrificed.

8 And He sent Peter and John,

saying, "Go and prepare the Passover for us, that we may eat it."

9 And they said to Him, "Where do You want us to prepare it?"

10 And He said to them, "Behold, when you have entered the city, a man will meet you carrying a pitcher of water; follow him into the house that he enters.

11 "And you shall say to the owner of the house, 'The Teacher says to you, "Where is the guest room in which I may eat the Passover with My disciples?"'

12 "And he will show you a large, furnished, upper room; prepare it there."

13 And they departed and found *everything* just as He had told them; and they prepared the Passover.

14 And when the hour had come He reclined *at table*, and the apostles with Him.

15 And He said to them, "I have earnestly desired to eat this Passover with you before I suffer;

16 for I say to you, I shall never again eat it until it is fulfilled in the kingdom of God."

17 And having taken a cup, when He had given thanks, He said, "Take this and share it among yourselves;

18 for I say to you, I will not drink of the fruit of the vine from now on until the kingdom of God comes."

19 And having taken *some* bread, when He had given thanks, He broke *it*, and gave *it* to them, saying, "This is My body which is given for you; do this in remembrance of Me."

20 And in the same way *He took* the cup after they had eaten, saying, "This cup which is poured out for you is the new covenant in My blood.

21 "But behold, the hand of the one betraying Me is with Me on the table.

22 "For indeed, the Son of Man is going as it has been determined; but woe to that man through whom He is betrayed!"

23 And they began to discuss among themselves which one of them it might be who was going to do this thing.

24 And there arose also a dispute among them *as to* which one of them was regarded to be greatest.

25 And He said to them, "The kings of the Gentiles lord it over them; and those who have authority over them are called 'Benefactors.'

26 "But not so with you, but let him who is the greatest among you become as the youngest, and the leader as the servant.

27 "For who is greater, the one who reclines *at table*, or the one who serves? Is it not the one who reclines *at table?* But I am among you as the one who serves.

28 "And you are those who have stood by Me in My trials;

29 and just as My Father has granted Me a kingdom, I grant you

30 that you may eat and drink at My table in My kingdom, and you will sit on thrones judging the twelve tribes of Israel.

31 "Simon, Simon, behold, Satan has demanded *permission* to sift you like wheat;

32 but I have prayed for you, that your faith may not fail; and you, when once you have turned again, strengthen your brothers."

33 And he said to Him, "Lord, with You I am ready to go both to prison and to death!"

34 And He said, "I tell you, Peter, the cock will not crow today until you have denied three times that you know Me."

35 And He said to them, "When I sent you out without purse and bag and sandals, you did not lack anything, did you?" And they said, "No, nothing."

36 And He said to them, "But now, let him who has a purse take it along, likewise also a bag, and let him

who has no sword sell his robe and buy one.

37 "For I tell you, that this which is written must be fulfilled in Me, 'AND HE WAS CLASSED AMONG CRIMINALS'; for that which refers to Me has *its* fulfillment."

38 And they said, "Lord, look, here are two swords." And He said to them, "It is enough."

39 And He came out and proceeded as was His custom to the Mount of Olives; and the disciples also followed Him.

40 And when He arrived at the place, He said to them, "Pray that you may not enter into temptation."

41 And He withdrew from them about a stone's throw, and He knelt down and *began* to pray,

42 saying, "Father, if Thou art willing, remove this cup from Me; yet not My will, but Thine be done."

43 Now an angel from heaven appeared to Him, strengthening Him.

44 And being in agony He was praying very fervently; and His sweat became like drops of blood, falling down upon the ground.

45 And when He rose from prayer, He came to His disciples and found them sleeping from sorrow,

46 and said to them, "Why are you sleeping? Rise and pray that you may not enter into temptation."

47 While He was still speaking, behold, a multitude *came*, and the one called Judas, one of the twelve, was preceding them; and he approached Jesus to kiss Him.

48 But Jesus said to him, "Judas, are you betraying the Son of Man with a kiss?"

49 And when those who were around Him saw what was going to happen, they said, "Lord, shall we strike with the sword?"

50 And a certain one of them struck the slave of the high priest and cut off his right ear.

51 But Jesus answered and said,

"Stop! No more of this." And He touched his ear and healed him.

52 And Jesus said to the chief priests and officers of the temple and elders who had come against Him, "Have you come out with swords and clubs as against a robber?

53 "While I was with you daily in the temple, you did not lay hands on Me; but this hour and the power of darkness are yours."

54 And having arrested Him, they led Him *away*, and brought Him to the house of the high priest; but Peter was following at a distance.

55 And after they had kindled a fire in the middle of the courtyard and had sat down together, Peter was sitting among them.

56 And a certain servant-girl, seeing him as he sat in the firelight, and looking intently at him, said, "This man was with Him too."

57 But he denied *it*, saying, "Woman, I do not know Him."

58 And a little later, another saw him and said, "You are *one* of them too!" But Peter said, "Man, I am not!"

59 And after about an hour had passed, another man *began* to insist, saying, "Certainly this man also was with Him, for he is a Galilean too."

60 But Peter said, "Man, I do not know what you are talking about." And immediately, while he was still speaking, a cock crowed.

61 And the Lord turned and looked at Peter. And Peter remembered the word of the Lord, how He had told him, "Before a cock crows today, you will deny Me three times."

62 And he went outside and wept bitterly.

63 And the men who were holding Jesus in custody were mocking Him, and beating Him,

64 and they blindfolded Him and were asking Him, saying, "Prophesy, who is the one who hit You?"

65 And they were saying many other things against Him, blaspheming.

66 And when it was day, the Council of Elders of the people assembled, both chief priests and scribes, and they led Him away to their council *chamber*, saying,

67 "If You are the Christ, tell us." But He said to them, "If I tell you, you will not believe;

68 and if I ask a question, you will not answer.

69 "But from now on THE SON OF MAN WILL BE SEATED AT THE RIGHT HAND of the power OF GOD."

70 And they all said, "Are You the Son of God, then?" And He said to them, "Yes, I am."

71 And they said, "What further need do we have of testimony? For we have heard it ourselves from His own mouth."

CHAPTER 23

THEN the whole body of them arose and brought Him before Pilate.

2 And they began to accuse Him, saying, "We found this man misleading our nation and forbidding to pay taxes to Caesar, and saying that He Himself is Christ, a King."

3 And Pilate asked Him, saying, "Are You the King of the Jews?" And He answered him and said, "*It is as you say.*"

4 And Pilate said to the chief priests and the multitudes, "I find no guilt in this man."

5 But they kept on insisting, saying, "He stirs up the people, teaching all over Judea, starting from Galilee, even as far as this place."

6 But when Pilate heard it, he asked whether the man were a Galilean.

7 And when he learned that He belonged to Herod's jurisdiction, he sent Him to Herod, who himself also was in Jerusalem at that time.

8 Now Herod was very glad when he saw Jesus; for he had wanted to see Him for a long time, because he had been hearing about Him and was hoping to see some sign performed by Him.

9 And he questioned Him at some length; but He answered him nothing.

10 And the chief priests and the scribes were standing there, accusing Him vehemently.

11 And Herod with his soldiers, after treating Him with contempt and mocking Him, dressed Him in a gorgeous robe and sent Him back to Pilate.

12 Now Herod and Pilate became friends with one another that very day; for before they had been at enmity with each other.

13 And Pilate summoned the chief priests and the rulers and the people,

14 and said to them, "You brought this man to me as one who incites the people to rebellion, and behold, having examined Him before you, I have found no guilt in this man regarding the charges which you make against Him.

15 "No, nor has Herod, for he sent Him back to us; and behold, nothing deserving death has been done by Him.

16 "I will therefore punish Him and release Him."

17 (See footnote.)

18 But they cried out all together, saying, "Away with this man, and release for us Barabbas!"

19 (He was one who had been thrown in prison for a certain insur-

---

Some mss. insert verse 17, *Now he was obliged to release to them at the feast one prisoner.*

rection made in the city, and for murder.)

20 And Pilate, wanting to release Jesus, addressed them again,

21 but they kept on calling out, saying, "Crucify, crucify Him!"

22 And he said to them the third time, "Why, what evil has this man done? I have found in Him no guilt *demanding* death; I will therefore punish Him and release Him."

23 But they were insistent, with loud voices asking that He be crucified. And their voices *began* to prevail.

24 And Pilate pronounced sentence that their demand should be granted.

25 And he released the man they were asking for who had been thrown into prison for insurrection and murder, but he turned Jesus over to their will.

26 And when they led Him away, they laid hold of one Simon, a Cyrenian, coming in from the country, and placed on him the cross to carry behind Jesus.

27 And there were following Him a great multitude of the people, and of women who were mourning and lamenting Him.

28 But Jesus turning to them said, "Daughters of Jerusalem, stop weeping for Me, but weep for yourselves and for your children.

29 "For behold, the days are coming when they will say, 'Blessed are the barren, and the wombs that never bore, and the breasts that never nursed.'

30 "Then they will begin TO SAY TO THE MOUNTAINS, 'FALL ON US,' AND TO THE HILLS, 'COVER US.'

31 "For if they do these things in the green tree, what will happen in the dry?"

32 And two others also, who were criminals, were being led away to be put to death with Him.

33 And when they came to the place called The Skull, there they crucified Him and the criminals, one on the right and the other on the left.

34 But Jesus was saying, "Father forgive them; for they do not know what they are doing." AND THEY CAST LOTS, DIVIDING UP HIS GARMENTS AMONG THEMSELVES.

35 And the people stood by, looking on. And even the rulers were sneering at Him, saying, "He saved others; let Him save Himself if this is the Christ of God, His Chosen One."

36 And the soldiers also mocked Him, coming up to Him, offering Him sour wine,

37 and saying, "If You are the King of the Jews, save Yourself!"

38 Now there was also an inscription above Him, "THIS IS THE KING OF THE JEWS."

39 And one of the criminals who were hanged *there* was hurling abuse at Him, saying, "Are You not the Christ? Save Yourself and us!"

40 But the other answered, and rebuking him said, "Do you not even fear God, since you are under the same sentence of condemnation?

41 "And we indeed justly, for we are receiving what we deserve for our deeds; but this man has done nothing wrong."

42 And he was saying, "Jesus, remember me when You come in Your kingdom!"

43 And He said to him, "Truly I say to you, today you shall be with Me in Paradise."

44 And it was now about the sixth hour, and darkness fell over the whole land until the ninth hour,

45 the sun being obscured; and the veil of the temple was torn in two.

46 And Jesus, crying out with a loud voice, said, "Father, INTO THY HANDS I COMMIT MY SPIRIT." And having said this, He breathed His last.

47 Now when the centurion saw

what had happened, he *began* praising God, saying, "Certainly this man was innocent."

48 And all the multitudes who came together for this spectacle, when they observed what had happened, *began* to return, beating their breasts.

49 And all His acquaintances and the women who accompanied Him from Galilee, were standing at a distance, seeing these things.

50 And behold, a man named Joseph, who was a member of the Council, a good and righteous man

51 (he had not consented to their plan and action), *a man* from Arimathea, a city of the Jews, who was waiting for the kingdom of God;

52 this man went to Pilate and asked for the body of Jesus.

53 And he took it down and wrapped it in a linen cloth, and laid Him in a tomb cut into the rock, where no one had ever lain.

54 And it was the preparation day, and the Sabbath was about to begin.

55 Now the women who had come with Him out of Galilee followed after, and saw the tomb and how His body was laid.

56 And they returned and prepared spices and perfumes.

And on the Sabbath they rested according to the commandment.

Chapter 24

BUT on the first day of the week, at early dawn, they came to the tomb, bringing the spices which they had prepared.

2 And they found the stone rolled away from the tomb,

3 but when they entered, they did not find the body of the Lord Jesus.

4 And it happened that while they were perplexed about this, behold, two men suddenly stood near them in dazzling apparel;

5 and as *the women* were terrified and bowed their faces to the ground, *the men* said to them, "Why do you seek the living One among the dead?

6 "He is not here, but He has risen. Remember how He spoke to you while He was still in Galilee,

7 saying that the Son of Man must be delivered into the hands of sinful men, and be crucified, and the third day rise again."

8 And they remembered His words,

9 and returned from the tomb and reported all these things to the eleven and to all the rest.

10 Now they were Mary Magdalene and Joanna and Mary the *mother* of James; also the other women with them were telling these things to the apostles.

11 And these words appeared to them as nonsense, and they would not believe them.

12 [But Peter arose and ran to the tomb; stooping and looking in, he *saw the linen wrappings only; and he went away to his home, marveling at that which had happened.]

13 And behold, two of them were going that very day to a village named Emmaus, which was about seven miles from Jerusalem.

14 And they were conversing with each other about all these things which had taken place.

15 And it came about that while they were conversing and discussing, Jesus Himself approached, and *began* traveling with them.

16 But their eyes were prevented from recognizing Him.

17 And He said to them, "What are these words that you are exchanging with one another as you are walking?" And they stood still, looking sad.

18 And one of them, named Cleopas, answered and said to Him, "Are You the only one visiting Jerusalem and unaware of the things which have happened here in these days?"

19 And He said to them, "What things?" And they said to Him, "The things about Jesus the Nazarene, who was a prophet mighty in deed and word in the sight of God and all the people,

20 and how the chief priests and our rulers delivered Him up to the sentence of death, and crucified Him.

21 "But we were hoping that it was He who was going to redeem Israel. Indeed, besides all this, it is the third day since these things happened.

22 "But also some women among us amazed us. When they were at the tomb early in the morning,

23 and did not find His body, they came, saying that they had also seen a vision of angels, who said that He was alive.

24 "And some of those who were with us went to the tomb and found it just exactly as the women also had said; but Him they did not see."

25 And He said to them, "O foolish men and slow of heart to believe in all that the prophets have spoken!

26 "Was it not necessary for the Christ to suffer these things and to enter into His glory?"

27 And beginning with Moses and with all the prophets, He explained to them the things concerning Himself in all the Scriptures.

28 And they approached the village where they were going, and He acted as though He would go farther.

29 And they urged Him, saying, "Stay with us, for it is *getting* toward evening, and the day is now nearly over." And He went in to stay with them.

30 And it came about that when He had reclined *at table* with them, He took the bread and blessed *it,* and breaking *it,* He *began* giving *it* to them.

31 And their eyes were opened and they recognized Him; and He vanished from their sight.

32 And they said to one another, "Were not our hearts burning within us while He was speaking to us on the road, while He was explaining the Scriptures to us?"

33 And they arose that very hour and returned to Jerusalem, and found gathered together the eleven and those who were with them,

34 saying, "The Lord has really risen, and has appeared to Simon."

35 And they *began* to relate their experiences on the road and how He was recognized by them in the breaking of the bread.

36 And while they were telling these things, He Himself stood in their midst.

37 But they were startled and frightened and thought that they were seeing a spirit.

38 And He said to them, "Why are you troubled, and why do doubts arise in your hearts?

39 "See My hands and My feet, that it is I Myself; touch Me and see, for a spirit does not have flesh and bones as you see that I have."

40 (See footnote.)

41 And while they still could not believe *it* for joy and were marveling, He said to them, "Have you anything here to eat?"

42 And they gave Him a piece of a broiled fish;

43 and He took it and ate *it* in their sight.

44 Now He said to them, "These are My words which I spoke to you

---

Some mss. add verse 40, *And when He had said this, He showed them His hands and His feet.*

while I was still with you, that all things which are written about Me in the Law of Moses and the Prophets and the Psalms must be fulfilled."

45 Then He opened their minds to understand the Scriptures,

46 and He said to them, "Thus it is written, that the Christ should suffer and rise again from the dead the third day;

47 and that repentance for forgiveness of sins should be proclaimed in His name to all the nations beginning from Jerusalem.

48 "You are witnesses of these things.

49 "And behold, I am sending forth the promise of My Father upon you; but you are to stay in the city until you are clothed with power from on high."

50 And He led them out as far as Bethany, and He lifted up His hands and blessed them.

51 And it came about that while He was blessing them, He parted from them.

52 And they returned to Jerusalem with great joy,

53 and were continually in the temple, praising God.

THE GOSPEL

ACCORDING TO

JOHN

IN the beginning was the Word, and the Word was with God, and the Word was God.

2 He was in the beginning with God.

3 All things came into being through Him; and apart from Him nothing came into being that has come into being.

4 In Him was life; and the life was the light of men.

5 And the light shines in the darkness; and the darkness did not comprehend it.

6 There came a man, sent from God, whose name was John.

7 He came for a witness, that he might bear witness of the light, that all might believe through him.

8 He was not the light, but *came* that he might bear witness of the light.

9 There was the true light which, coming into the world, enlightens every man.

10 He was in the world, and the world was made through Him, and the world did not know Him.

11 He came to His own, and those who were His own did not receive Him.

12 But as many as received Him, to them He gave the right to become children of God, *even* to those who believe in His name,

13 who were born not of blood, nor of the will of the flesh, nor of the will of man, but of God.

14 And the Word became flesh, and dwelt among us, and we beheld His glory, glory as of the only begotten from the Father, full of grace and truth.

15 John *bore witness of Him, and cried out, saying, "This was He of whom I said, 'He who comes after me has a higher rank than I, for He existed before me.' "

16 For of His fulness we have all received, and grace upon grace.

17 For the law was given through Moses; grace and truth were realized through Jesus Christ.

18 No man has seen God at any time; the only begotten God, who is in the bosom of the Father, He has explained *Him*.

19 And this is the witness of John, when the Jews sent to him priests and Levites from Jerusalem to ask him, "Who are you?"

20 And he confessed, and did not deny, and he confessed, "I am not the Christ."

21 And they asked him, "What then? Are you Elijah?" And he *said, "I am not." "Are you the Prophet?" And he answered, "No."

22 They said then to him, "Who are you, so that we may give an answer to those who sent us? What do you say about yourself?"

23 He said, "I am a voice of one crying in the wilderness, 'MAKE STRAIGHT THE WAY OF THE LORD,' as Isaiah the prophet said."

24 Now they had been sent from the Pharisees.

25 And they asked him, and said to him, "Why then are you baptizing, if you are not the Christ, nor Elijah, nor the Prophet?"

26 John answered them saying, "I baptize in water, *but* among you stands One whom you do not know.

27 "*It is* He who comes after me, the thong of whose sandal I am not worthy to untie."

28 These things took place in Bethany beyond the Jordan, where John was baptizing.

29 The next day he *saw Jesus coming to him, and *said, "Behold, the Lamb of God who takes away the sin of the world!

30 "This is He on behalf of whom I said, 'After me comes a Man who has a higher rank than I, for He existed before me.'

31 "And I did not recognize Him, but in order that He might be manifested to Israel, I came baptizing in water."

32 And John bore witness saying, "I have beheld the Spirit descending as a dove out of heaven; and He remained upon Him.

33 "And I did not recognize Him, but He who sent me to baptize in water said to me, 'He upon whom you see the Spirit descending and remaining upon Him, this is the one who baptizes in the Holy Spirit.'

34 "And I have seen, and have borne witness that this is the Son of God."

35 Again the next day John was standing, and two of his disciples;

36 and he looked upon Jesus as He walked, and *said, "Behold, the Lamb of God!"

37 And the two disciples heard him speak, and they followed Jesus.

38 And Jesus turned, and beheld them following, and *said to them, "What do you seek?" And they said to Him, "Rabbi (which translated means Teacher), where are You staying?"

39 He *said to them, "Come, and you will see." They came therefore and saw where He was staying; and they stayed with Him that day, for it was about the tenth hour.

40 One of the two who heard John *speak*, and followed Him, was Andrew, Simon Peter's brother.

41 He *found first his own brother Simon, and *said to him, "We have found the Messiah" (which translated means Christ).

42 He brought him to Jesus. Jesus looked at him, and said, "You are Simon the son of John; you shall be called Cephas" (which translated means Peter).

43 The next day *He* purposed to go forth into Galilee, and He *found Philip, and Jesus *said to him, "Follow Me."

44 Now Philip was from Bethsaida, of the city of Andrew and Peter.

45 Philip *found Nathanael, and *said to him, "We have found Him, of whom Moses in the Law and also the Prophets wrote, Jesus of Nazareth, the son of Joseph."

46 And Nathanael *said to him, "Can any good thing come out of Nazareth?" Philip *said to him, "Come and see."

47 Jesus saw Nathanael coming to Him, and *said of him, "Behold, an Israelite indeed, in whom is no guile!"

48 Nathanael *said to Him, "How do You know me?" Jesus answered and said to him, "Before Philip called you, when you were under the fig tree, I saw you."

49 Nathanael answered Him, "Rabbi, You are the Son of God; You are the King of Israel."

50 Jesus answered and said to him, "Because I said to you that I saw you under the fig tree, do you believe? You shall see greater things than these."

51 And He *said to him, "Truly, truly, I say to you, you shall see the heavens opened, and the angels of God ascending and descending upon the Son of Man."

CHAPTER 2

AND on the third day there was a wedding in Cana of Galilee; and the mother of Jesus was there;

2 and Jesus also was invited, and His disciples, to the wedding.

3 And when the wine gave out, the mother of Jesus *said to Him, "They have no wine."

4 And Jesus *said to her, "Woman, what do I have to do with you? My hour has not yet come."

5 His mother *said to the servants, "Whatever He says to you, do it."

6 Now there were six stone waterpots set there for the Jewish custom of purification, containing twenty or thirty gallons each.

7 Jesus *said to them, "Fill the waterpots with water." And they filled them up to the brim.

8 And He *said to them, "Draw *some* out now, and take it to the headwaiter." And they took it *to him.*

9 And when the headwaiter tasted the water which had become wine, and did not know where it came from (but the servants who had drawn the water knew), the headwaiter *called the bridegroom,

10 and *said to him, "Every man serves the good wine first, and when *men* have drunk freely, *then* that which is poorer; you have kept the good wine until now."

11 This beginning of *His* signs Jesus did in Cana of Galilee, and manifested His glory, and His disciples believed in Him.

12 After this He went down to Capernaum, He and His mother, and *His* brothers, and His disciples; and there they stayed a few days.

13 And the Passover of the Jews was at hand, and Jesus went up to Jerusalem.

14 And He found in the temple those who were selling oxen and sheep and doves, and the moneychangers seated.

15 And He made a scourge of cords, and drove *them* all out of the temple, with the sheep and the oxen; and He poured out the coins of the moneychangers, and overturned their tables;

16 and to those who were selling the doves He said, "Take these things away; stop making My Father s house a house of merchandise."

17 His disciples remembered that it was written, "ZEAL FOR THY HOUSE WILL CONSUME ME."

18 The Jews therefore answered

and said to Him, "What sign do You show to us, seeing that You do these things?"

19 Jesus answered and said to them, "Destroy this temple, and in three days I will raise it up."

20 The Jews therefore said, "It took forty-six years to build this temple, and will You raise it up in three days?"

21 But He was speaking of the temple of His body.

22 When therefore He was raised from the dead, His disciples remembered that He said this; and they believed the Scripture, and the word which Jesus had spoken.

23 Now when He was in Jerusalem at the Passover, during the feast, many believed in His name, beholding His signs which He was doing.

24 But Jesus, on His part, was not entrusting Himself to them, for He knew all men,

25 and because He did not need any one to bear witness concerning man for He Himself knew what was in man.

CHAPTER 3

NOW there was a man of the Pharisees, named Nicodemus, a ruler of the Jews;

2 this man came to Him by night, and said to Him, "Rabbi, we know that You have come from God *as* a teacher; for no one can do these signs that You do unless God is with him."

3 Jesus answered and said to him, "Truly, truly, I say to you, unless one is born again, he cannot see the kingdom of God."

4 Nicodemus *said to Him, "How can a man be born when he is old? He cannot enter a second time into his mother's womb and be born, can he?"

5 Jesus answered, "Truly, truly, I say to you, unless one is born of water and the Spirit, he cannot enter into the kingdom of God.

6 "That which is born of the flesh is flesh; and that which is born of the Spirit is spirit.

7 "Do not marvel that I said to you, 'You must be born again.'

8 "The wind blows where it wishes and you hear the sound of it, but do not know where it comes from and where it is going; so is every one who is born of the Spirit."

9 Nicodemus answered and said to Him, "How can these things be?"

10 Jesus answered and said to him, "Are you the teacher of Israel, and do not understand these things?

11 "Truly, truly, I say to you, we speak that which we know, and bear witness of that which we have seen; and you do not receive our witness.

12 "If I told you earthly things and you do not believe, how shall you believe if I tell you heavenly things?

13 "And no one has ascended into heaven, but He who descended from heaven, *even* the Son of Man.

14 "And as Moses lifted up the serpent in the wilderness, even so must the Son of Man be lifted up;

15 that whoever believes may in Him have eternal life.

16 "For God so loved the world, that He gave His only begotten Son, that whoever believes in Him should not perish, but have eternal life. (a)

(a) THE SWEETEST STORY EVER TOLD.

First the Source of our salvation is God's love. "God so loved," that "He first loved us," I John 4:19, Love is the cause of the forgiveness He provides. Page 325.

Second, the sacrifice for our salvation is the death of His Son. "He gave His only begotten Son" as a substitute to die for our sins. The cost He paid "demonstrates His own love toward us." Rom. 5:8, page 211.

(Turn to next page.)

17 "For God did not send the Son into the world to judge the world; but that the world should be saved through Him.

18 "He who believes in Him is not judged; he who does not believe has been judged already, because he has not believed in the name of the only begotten Son of God.

19 "And this is the judgment, that the light is come into the world, and men loved the darkness rather than the light; for their deeds were evil.

20 "For everyone who does evil hates the light, and does not come to the light, lest his deeds should be exposed.

21 "But he who practices the truth comes to the light, that his deeds may be manifested as having been wrought in God."

22 After these things Jesus and His disciples came into the land of Judea; and there He was spending time with them, and baptizing.

23 And John also was baptizing in Aenon near Salim, because there was much water there; and they were coming, and were being baptized.

24 For John had not yet been thrown into prison.

25 There arose therefore a discussion on the part of John's disciples with a Jew about purification.

26 And they came to John, and said to him, "Rabbi, He who was with you beyond the Jordan, to whom you have borne witness, behold, He is baptizing, and all are coming to Him."

27 John answered and said, "A man can receive nothing, unless it has been given him from heaven.

28 "You yourselves bear me witness, that I said, 'I am not the Christ', but, 'I have been sent before Him.'

29 "He who has the bride is the bridegroom; but the friend of the bridegroom, who stands and hears him, rejoices greatly because of the bridegroom's voice. And so this joy of mine has been made full.

30 "He must increase, but I must decrease.

31 "He who comes from above is above all, he who is of the earth is from the earth and speaks of the earth. He who comes from heaven is above all.

32 "What He has seen and heard, of that He bears witness; and no man receives His witness.

33 "He who has received His witness has set his seal to *this*, that God is true.

34 "For He whom God has sent speaks the words of God; for He gives the Spirit without measure.

35 "The Father loves the Son, and has given all things into His hand.

36 "He who believes in the Son has eternal life; but he who does not obey the Son shall not see life, but the wrath of God abides on him."

(Continued from page 125.)

Third, the scope of our salvation includes "whoever believes in Him." The only condition for anyone to meet is to believe that Christ was given to "taste death for everyone." Heb. 2:9, page 296.

Fourth, the Security of our salvation is shown in that every believer "should not perish but have eternal life." We are safe because Jesus said "no one shall snatch them out of my hand," John 10:28, page 140. Therefore the believer "does not come into judgment, but has passed out of death into life." John 5:24, page 130.

Be sure you have accepted God's Love. Put your trust in His death, burial and resurrection. Make the commitment of yourself to His keeping. To do this read Rom. 10:9-14 and Reference No. 6, Sec. 1, page 219. Then pray the prayer suggested there.

CHAPTER 4

WHEN therefore the Lord knew that the Pharisees had heard that Jesus was making and baptizing more disciples than John

2 (although Jesus Himself was not baptizing, but His disciples were),

3 He left Judea, and departed again into Galilee.

4 And He had to pass through Samaria.

5 So He *came to a city of Samaria, called Sychar, near the parcel of ground that Jacob gave to his son Joseph;

6 and Jacob's well was there. Jesus therefore, being wearied from His journey, was sitting thus by the well. It was about the sixth hour.

7 There *came a woman of Samaria to draw water. Jesus *said to her, "Give Me a drink."

8 For His disciples had gone away into the city to buy food.

9 The Samaritan woman therefore *said to Him, "How is it that You, being a Jew, ask me for a drink since I am a Samaritan woman?" (For Jews have no dealings with Samaritans.)

10 Jesus answered and said to her, "If you knew the gift of God, and who it is who says to you, 'Give Me a drink,' you would have asked Him, and He would have given you living water."

11 She *said to Him, "Sir, You have nothing to draw with and the well is deep; where then do You get that living water?

12 "You are not greater than our father Jacob, are You, who gave us the well, and drank of it himself, and his sons, and his cattle?"

13 Jesus answered and said to her, "Everyone who drinks of this water shall thirst again;

14 but whoever drinks of the water that I shall give him shall never thirst; but the water that I shall give him shall become in him a well of water springing up to eternal life."

15 The woman *said to Him, "Sir, give me this water, so I will not be thirsty, nor come all the way here to draw."

16 He *said to her, "Go, call your husband, and come here."

17 The woman answered and said, "I have no husband." Jesus *said to her, "You have well said, 'I have no husband';

18 for you have had five husbands; and the one whom you now have is not your husband; this you have said truly."

19 The woman *said to Him, "Sir, I perceive that You are a prophet.

20 "Our fathers worshiped in this mountain; and you *people* say that in Jerusalem is the place where men ought to worship."

21 Jesus *said to her, "Woman, believe Me, an hour is coming when neither in this mountain, nor in Jerusalem, shall you worship the Father.

22 "You worship that which you do not know; we worship that which we know; for salvation is from the Jews.

23 "But an hour is coming, and now is, when the true worshipers shall worship the Father in spirit and truth; for such people the Father seeks to be His worshipers.

24 "God is spirit; and those who worship Him must worship in spirit and truth."

25 The woman *said to Him, "I know that Messiah is coming (He who is called Christ); when that One comes, He will declare all things to us."

26 Jesus *said to her, "I who speak to you am *He*."

27 And at this point His disciples came, and they marveled that He had been speaking with a woman; yet no

one said, "What do You seek?" or, "Why do You speak with her?"

28 So the woman left her waterpot, and went into the city, and *said to the men,

29 "Come, see a man who told me all the things that I *have* done; this is not the Christ, is it?"

30 They went out of the city, and were coming to Him.

31 In the meanwhile the disciples were requesting Him, saying, "Rabbi, eat."

32 But He said to them, "I have food to eat that you do not know about."

33 The disciples therefore were saying to one another, "No one brought Him *anything* to eat, did he?"

34 Jesus *said to them, "My food is to do the will of Him who sent Me, and to accomplish His work.

35 "Do you not say, 'There are yet four months, and *then* comes the harvest'? Behold, I say to you, lift up your eyes, and look on the fields, that they are white for harvest.

36 "Already he who reaps is receiving wages, and is gathering fruit for life eternal; that he who sows and he who reaps may rejoice together.

37 "For in this *case* the saying is true, 'One sows, and another reaps.'

38 "I sent you to reap that for which you have not labored; others have labored, and you have entered into their labor."

39 And from that city many of the Samaritans believed in Him because of the word of the woman who testified, "He told me all the things that I *have* done."

40 So when the Samaritans came to Him, they were asking Him to stay with them; and He stayed there two days.

41 And many more believed because of His word;

42 and they were saying to the woman, "It is no longer because of what you said that we believe, for we have heard for ourselves and know that this One is indeed the Savior of the world."

43 And after the two days He went forth from there into Galilee.

44 For Jesus Himself testified that a prophet has no honor in his own country.

45 So when He came to Galilee, the Galileans received Him, having seen all the things that He did in Jerusalem at the feast; for they themselves also went to the feast.

46 He came therefore again to Cana of Galilee where He had made the water wine. And there was a certain royal official, whose son was sick at Capernaum.

47 When he heard that Jesus had come out of Judea into Galilee, he went to Him, and was requesting *Him* to come down and heal his son; for he was at the point of death.

48 Jesus therefore said to him, "Unless you *people* see signs and wonders, you *simply* will not believe."

49 The royal official *said to Him, "Sir, come down before my child dies."

50 Jesus *said to him, "Go your way; your son lives." The man believed the word that Jesus spoke to him, and he started off.

51 And as he was now going down, *his* slaves met him, saying that his son was living.

52 So he inquired of them the hour when he began to get better. They said therefore to him, "Yesterday at the seventh hour the fever left him."

53 So the father knew that *it was* at that hour in which Jesus said to him, "Your son lives;" and he himself believed, and his whole household.

54 This is again a second sign that Jesus performed, when He had come out of Judea into Galilee.

CHAPTER 5

AFTER these things there was a feast of the Jews; and Jesus went up to Jerusalem.

2 Now there is in Jerusalem by the sheep *gate* a pool, which is called in Hebrew Bethesda, having five porticoes.

3 In these lay a multitude of those who were sick, blind, lame, withered.

4 (See footnote.)

5 And a certain man was there, who had been thirty-eight years in his sickness.

6 When Jesus saw him lying there, and knew that he had already been a long time *in that condition*, He *said to him, "Do you wish to get well?"

7 The sick man answered Him, "Sir, I have no man to put me into the pool when the water is stirred up, but while I am coming, another steps down before me."

8 Jesus *said to him, "Arise, take up your pallet, and walk."

9 And immediately the man became well, and took up his pallet and *began* to walk.

Now it was the Sabbath on that day.

10 Therefore the Jews were saying to him who was cured, "It is the Sabbath, and it is not permissible for you to carry your pallet."

11 But he answered them, "He who made me well was the one who said to me, 'Take up your pallet and walk.'"

12 They asked him, "Who is the man who said to you, 'Take up *your* pallet, and walk'?"

13 But he who was healed did not know who it was; for Jesus had slipped away while there was a crowd in *that* place.

14 Afterward Jesus *found him in the temple, and said to him, "Behold, you have become well; do not sin any more, so that nothing worse may befall you."

15 The man went away, and told the Jews that it was Jesus who had made him well.

16 And for this reason the Jews were persecuting Jesus, because He was doing these things on the Sabbath.

17 But He answered them, "My Father is working until now, and I Myself am working."

18 For this cause therefore the Jews were seeking all the more to kill Him, because He not only was breaking the Sabbath, but also was calling God His own Father, making Himself equal with God.

19 Jesus therefore answered and was saying to them, "Truly, truly, I say to you, the Son can do nothing of Himself, unless *it is* something He sees the Father doing; for whatever *the Father* does, these things the Son also does in like manner.

20 "For the Father loves the Son, and shows Him all things that He Himself is doing; and greater works than these will He show Him, that you may marvel.

21 "For just as the Father raises the dead and gives them life, even so the Son also gives life to whom He wishes.

22 "For not even the Father judges any one, but He has given all judgment to the Son,

23 in order that all may honor the Son, even as they honor the Father.

---

(1) Many authorities insert, wholly or in part, *waiting for the moving of the waters;* V.4 *for an angel of the Lord went down at certain seasons into the pool, and stirred up the water: whoever then first after the stirring up of the water stepped in was made well from whatever disease with which he was afflicted.*

He who does not honor the Son does not honor the Father who sent Him.

24 "Truly, truly, I say to you, he who hears My word, and believes Him who sent Me, has eternal life, and does not come into judgment, but has passed out of death into life.

25 "Truly, truly, I say to you, an hour is coming and now is, when the dead shall hear the voice of the Son of God; and those who hear shall live.

26 "For just as the Father has life in Himself, even so He gave to the Son also to have life in Himself;

27 and He gave Him authority to execute judgment, because He is *the* Son of Man.

28 "Do not marvel at this; for an hour is coming, in which all who are in the tombs shall hear His voice,

29 and shall come forth; those who did the good *deeds*, to a resurrection of life, those who committed the evil *deeds* to a resurrection of judgment.

30 "I can do nothing on My own initiative. As I hear, I judge; and My judgment is just, because I do not seek My own will, but the will of Him who sent Me.

31 "If I *alone* bear witness of Myself, My testimony is not true.

32 "There is another who bears witness of Me; and I know that the testimony which He bears of Me is true.

33 "You have sent to John, and he has borne witness to the truth.

34 "But the witness which I receive is not from man; but I say these things, that you may be saved.

35 "He was the lamp that was burning and was shining and you were willing to rejoice for a while in his light.

36 "But the witness which I have is greater than *that of* John; for the works which the Father has given Me to accomplish, the very works that I do, bear witness of Me, that the Father has sent Me.

37 "And the Father who sent Me, He has borne witness of Me. You have neither heard His voice at any time, nor seen His form.

38 "And you do not have His word abiding in you, for you do not believe Him whom He sent.

39 "You search the Scriptures, because you think that in them you have eternal life; and it is these that bear witness of Me;

40 and you are unwilling to come to Me, that you may have life.

41 "I do not receive glory from men;

42 but I know you, that you do not have the love of God in yourselves.

43 "I have come in My Father's name, and you do not receive Me; if another shall come in his own name, you will receive him.

44 "How can you believe, when you receive glory from one another, and you do not seek the glory that is from the *one and* only God?

45 "Do not think that I will accuse you before the Father; the one who accuses you is Moses, in whom you have set your hope.

46 "For if you believed Moses, you would believe Me; for he wrote of Me.

47 "But if you do not believe his writings, how will you believe My words?"

Chapter 6

AFTER these things Jesus went away to the other side of the sea of Galilee (or Tiberias).

2 And a great multitude was following Him, because they were seeing the signs which He was performing on those who were sick.

3 And Jesus went up on the mountain, and there He sat with His disciples.

4 Now the Passover, the feast of the Jews, was at hand.

5 Jesus therefore lifting up His eyes, and seeing that a great multitude was coming to Him, *said to Philip, "Where are we to buy bread, that these may eat?"

6 And this He was saying to test him; for He Himself knew what He was intending to do.

7 Philip answered Him, "Two hundred denarii worth of bread is not sufficient for them, for every one to receive a little."

8 One of His disciples, Andrew, Simon Peter's brother, *said to Him,

9 "There is a lad here, who has five barley loaves, and two fish; but what are these for so many people?"

10 Jesus said, "Have the people sit down." Now there was much grass in the place. So the men sat down, in number about five thousand.

11 Jesus therefore took the loaves; and having given thanks, He distributed to those who were seated; likewise also of the fish as much as they wanted.

12 And when they were filled, He *said to His disciples, "Gather up the leftover fragments that nothing may be lost."

13 And so they gathered them up, and filled twelve baskets with fragments from the five barley loaves, which were left over by those who had eaten.

14 When therefore the people saw the sign which He had performed, they said, "This is of a truth the Prophet who is to come into the world."

15 Jesus therefore perceiving that they were intending to come and take Him by force, to make Him king, withdrew again to the mountain by Himself alone.

16 Now when evening came, His disciples went down to the sea,

17 and after getting into a boat, they *started to* cross the sea to Caper-

naum. And it had already become dark, and Jesus had not yet come to them.

18 And the sea *began* to be stirred up because a strong wind was blowing.

19 When therefore they had rowed about three or four miles, they *beheld Jesus walking on the sea and drawing near to the boat; and they were frightened.

20 But He *said to them, "It is I; do not be afraid."

21 They were willing therefore to receive Him into the boat; and immediately the boat was at the land to which they were going.

22 The next day the multitude that stood on the other side of the sea saw that there was no other small boat there, except one, and that Jesus had not entered with His disciples into the boat, but *that* His disciples had gone away alone.

23 There came other small boats from Tiberias near to the place where they ate the bread after the Lord had given thanks.

24 When the multitude therefore saw that Jesus was not there, nor His disciples, they themselves got into the small boats, and came to Capernaum, seeking Jesus.

25 And when they found Him on the other side of the sea, they said to Him, "Rabbi, when did You get here?"

26 Jesus answered them and said, "Truly, truly, I say to you, you seek Me, not because you saw signs, but because you ate of the loaves, and were filled.

27 "Do not work for the food which perishes, but for the food which endures to eternal life, which the Son of Man shall give to you, for on Him the Father, *even* God, has set His seal."

28 They said therefore to Him, "What shall we do, that we may work the works of God?"

29 Jesus answered and said to them, "This is the work of God, that you believe in Him whom He has sent."

30 They said therefore to Him, "What then do You do for a sign, that we may see, and believe You? What work do You perform?

31 "Our fathers ate the manna in the wilderness; as it is written, 'HE GAVE THEM BREAD OUT OF HEAVEN TO EAT.'"

32 Jesus therefore said to them, "Truly, truly, I say to you, it is not Moses who has given you the bread out of heaven, but it is My Father who gives you the true bread out of heaven.

33 "For the bread of God is that which comes down out of heaven, and gives life to the world."

34 They said therefore to Him, "Lord, evermore give us this bread."

35 Jesus said to them, "I am the bread of life; he who comes to Me shall not hunger, and he who believes in Me shall never thirst.

36 "But I said to you, that you have seen Me, and yet do not believe.

37 "All that the Father gives Me shall come to Me; and the one who comes to Me I will certainly not cast out.

38 "For I have come down from heaven, not to do My own will, but the will of Him who sent Me.

39 "And this is the will of Him who sent Me, that of all that He has given Me I lose nothing, but raise it up on the last day.

40 "For this is the will of My Father, that every one who beholds the Son, and believes in Him, may have eternal life; and I Myself will raise him up on the last day."

41 The Jews therefore were grumbling about Him, because He said, "I am the bread that came down out of heaven."

42 And they were saying, "Is not this Jesus, the son of Joseph, whose father and mother we know? How does He now say, 'I have come down out of heaven'?"

43 Jesus answered and said to them, "Do not grumble among yourselves.

44 "No one can come to Me, unless the Father who sent Me draws him; and I will raise him up on the last day.

45 "It is written in the prophets, 'AND THEY SHALL ALL BE TAUGHT OF GOD.' Every one who has heard and learned from the Father, comes to Me.

46 "Not that any man has seen the Father, except the One who is from God; He has seen the Father.

47 "Truly, truly, I say to you, he who believes has eternal life.

48 "I am the bread of life.

49 "Your fathers ate the manna in the wilderness, and they died.

50 "This is the bread which comes down out of heaven, so that one may eat of it and not die.

51 "I am the living bread that came down out of heaven; if any one eats of this bread, he shall live forever; and the bread also which I shall give for the life of the world is My flesh."

52 The Jews therefore *began* to argue with one another, saying, "How can this man give us *His* flesh to eat?"

53 Jesus therefore said to them, "Truly, truly, I say to you, unless you eat the flesh of the Son of Man and drink His blood, you have no life in yourselves.

54 "He who eats My flesh and drinks My blood has eternal life; and I will raise him up on the last day.

55 "For My flesh is true food, and My blood is true drink.

56 "He who eats My flesh and drinks My blood abides in Me, and I in him.

57 "As the living Father sent Me, and I live because of the Father; so he

who eats Me, he also shall live because of Me.

58 "This is the bread which came down out of heaven; not as the fathers ate, and died, he who eats this bread shall live forever."

59 These things He said in the synagogue, as He taught in Capernaum.

60 Many therefore of His disciples, when they heard *this* said, "This is a difficult statement; who can listen to it?"

61 But Jesus, conscious that His disciples grumbled at this, said to them, "Does this cause you to stumble?

62 "*What* then if you should behold the Son of Man ascending where He was before?

63 "It is the Spirit who gives life; the flesh profits nothing; the words that I have spoken to you are spirit and are life.

64 "But there are some of you who do not believe." For Jesus knew from the beginning who they were who did not believe, and who it was that would betray Him.

65 And He was saying, "For this reason I have said to you, that no one can come to Me, unless it has been granted him from the Father."

66 As a result of this many of His disciples withdrew, and were not walking with Him any more.

67 Jesus said therefore to the twelve, "You do not want to go away also, do you?"

68 Simon Peter answered Him, "Lord, to whom shall we go? You have words of eternal life.

69 "And we have believed and have come to know that You are the Holy One of God."

70 Jesus answered them, "Did I Myself not choose you, the twelve, and *yet* one of you is a devil?"

71 Now He meant Judas *the son* of Simon Iscariot, for he, one of the twelve, was going to betray Him.

CHAPTER 7

AND after these things Jesus was walking in Galilee; for He was unwilling to walk in Judea, because the Jews were seeking to kill Him.

2 Now the feast of the Jews, the Feast of Tabernacles, was at hand.

3 His brothers therefore said to Him, "Depart from here, and go into Judea, that Your disciples also may behold Your works which You are doing.

4 "For no one does anything in secret, when he himself seeks to be *known* publicly. If You do these things, show Yourself to the world."

5 For not even His brothers were believing in Him.

6 Jesus therefore *said to them, "My time is not yet at hand; but your time is always opportune.

7 "The world cannot hate you; but it hates Me, because I testify of it, that its deeds are evil.

8 "Go up to the feast yourselves; I do not go up to this feast because My time has not yet fully come."

9 And having said these things to them, He stayed in Galilee.

10 But when His brothers had gone up to the feast, then He Himself also went up, not publicly, but as it were, in secret.

11 The Jews therefore were seeking Him at the feast, and were saying, "Where is He?"

12 And there was much grumbling among the multitudes concerning Him; some were saying, "He is a good man;" others were saying, "No, on the contrary, He leads the multitude astray."

13 Yet no one was speaking openly of Him for fear of the Jews.

14 But when it was now the midst of the feast Jesus went up into the temple, and *began to* teach.

15 The Jews therefore were marveling, saying, "How has this man

become learned, having never been educated?"

16 Jesus therefore answered them, and said, "My teaching is not Mine, but His who sent Me.

17 "If any man is willing to do His will, he shall know of the teaching, whether it is of God, or *whether* I speak from Myself.

18 "He who speaks from himself seeks his own glory; but He who is seeking the glory of the one who sent Him, He is true, and there is no unrighteousness in Him.

19 "Did not Moses give you the law, and *yet* none of you carries out the law? Why do you seek to kill Me?"

20 The multitude answered, "You have a demon! Who seeks to kill You?"

21 Jesus answered and said to them, "I did one deed, and you all marvel.

22 "On this account Moses has given you circumcision (not because it is from Moses, but from the fathers); and on *the* Sabbath you circumcise a man.

23 "If a man receives circumcision on *the* Sabbath that the Law of Moses may not be broken, are you angry with Me because I made an entire man well on *the* Sabbath?

24 "Do not judge according to appearance, but judge with righteous judgment."

25 Therefore some of the people of Jerusalem were saying, "Is this not the man whom they are seeking to kill?

26 "And look, He is speaking publicly, and they are saying nothing to Him. The rulers do not really know that this is the Christ, do they?

27 "However we know where this man is from; but whenever the Christ may come, no one knows where He is from."

28 Jesus therefore cried out in the temple, teaching and saying, "You both know Me, and know where I am from; and I have not come of Myself, but He who sent Me is true, whom you do not know.

29 "I know Him; because I am from Him, and He sent Me."

30 They were seeking therefore to seize Him; and no man laid his hand on Him, because His hour had not yet come.

31 But many of the multitude believed in Him; and they were saying, "When the Christ shall come, He will not perform more signs than those which this man has, will He?"

32 The Pharisees heard the multitude muttering these things about Him; and the chief priests and the Pharisees sent officers to seize Him.

33 Jesus therefore said, "For a little while longer I am with you, then I go to Him who sent Me.

34 "You shall seek Me, and shall not find Me; and where I am, you cannot come."

35 The Jews therefore said to one another, "Where does this man intend to go that we shall not find Him? He is not intending to go to the Dispersion among the Greeks, and teach the Greeks, is He?

36 "What is this statement that He said, 'You will seek Me, and will not find Me; and where I am, you cannot come'?"

37 Now on the last day, the great *day* of the feast, Jesus stood and cried out, saying, "If any man is thirsty, let him come to Me and drink.

38 "He who believes in Me, as the Scripture said, 'From his innermost being shall flow rivers of living water.'"

39 But this He spoke of the Spirit, whom those who believed in Him were to receive; for the Spirit was not yet *given*, because Jesus was not yet glorified.

40 *Some* of the multitude there-

fore, when they heard these words, were saying, "This certainly is the Prophet."

41 Others were saying, "This is the Christ." Still others were saying, "Surely the Christ is not going to come from Galilee, is He?

42 "Has not the Scripture said that THE CHRIST COMES FROM THE OFF-SPRING OF DAVID, AND FROM BETHLE-HEM, the village where David was?"

43 So there arose a division in the multitude because of Him.

44 And some of them wanted to seize Him, but no one laid hands on Him.

45 The officers therefore came to the chief priests and Pharisees, and they said to them, "Why did you not bring Him?"

46 The officers answered, "Never did a man speak the way this man speaks."

47 The Pharisees therefore answered them, "You have not also been led astray, have you?

48 "No one of the rulers or Pharisees has believed in Him, has he?

49 "But this multitude which does not know the Law is accursed."

50 Nicodemus *said to them (he who came to Him before, being one of them),

51 "Our Law does not judge a man, unless it first hears from him and knows what he is doing, does it?"

52 They answered and said to him, "You are not also from Galilee, are you? Search, and see that no prophet arises out of Galilee."

53 [And everyone went to his home.

CHAPTER 8

BUT Jesus went to the Mount of Olives.

2 And early in the morning He came again into the temple, and all the people were coming to Him; and He sat down and *began* to teach them.

3 And the scribes and the Pharisees *brought a woman caught in adultery, and having set her in the midst,

4 they *said to Him, "Teacher, this woman has been caught in adultery, in the very act.

5 "Now in the Law Moses commanded us to stone such women; what then do You say?"

6 And they were saying this, testing Him, in order that they might have grounds for accusing Him. But Jesus stooped down, and with His finger wrote on the ground.

7 But when they persisted in asking Him, He straightened up, and said to them, "He who is without sin among you, let him *be the* first to throw a stone at her."

8 And again He stooped down, and wrote on the ground.

9 And when they heard it, they *began* to go out one by one, beginning with the older ones, and He was left alone, and the woman, *where she had been*, in the midst.

10 And straightening up, Jesus said to her, "Woman, where are they? Did no one condemn you?"

11 And she said, "No one, Lord." And Jesus said, "Neither do I condemn you; go your way; from now on sin no more."]

12 Again therefore Jesus spoke to them, saying, "I am the light of the world; he who follows Me shall not walk in the darkness, but shall have the light of life."

13 The Pharisees therefore said to Him, "You are bearing witness of Yourself; Your witness is not true."

14 Jesus answered and said to them, "Even if I bear witness of Myself, My witness is true; for I know where I came from, and where I am going; but you do not know where I come from, or where I am going.

15 "You people judge according to the flesh; I am not judging any one.

16 "But even if I do judge, My judgment is true; for I am not alone *in it*, but I and He who sent Me.

17 "Even in your law it has been written, that the testimony of two men is true.

18 "I am He who bears witness of Myself, and the Father who sent Me bears witness of Me."

19 And so they were saying to Him, "Where is Your Father?" Jesus answered, "You know neither Me, nor My Father; if you knew Me, you would know My Father also."

20 These words He spoke in the treasury, as He taught in the temple; and no one seized Him, because His hour had not yet come.

21 He said therefore again to them, "I go away, and you shall seek Me, and shall die in your sin; where I am going, you cannot come."

22 Therefore the Jews were saying, "Surely He will not kill Himself, will He, since He says, 'Where I am going, you cannot come'?"

23 And He was saying to them, "You are from below, I am from above; you are of this world; I am not of this world.

24 "I said therefore to you, that you shall die in your sins; for unless you believe that I am *He*, you shall die in your sins."

25 And so they were saying to Him, "Who are You?" Jesus said to them, "What have I been saying to you *from* the beginning?

26 "I have many things to speak and to judge concerning you, but He who sent Me is true; and the things which I heard from Him, these I speak to the world."

27 They did not realize that He had been speaking to them about the Father.

28 Jesus therefore said, "When you lift up the Son of Man, then you will know that I am *He*, and I do nothing on My own initiative, but I speak these things as the Father taught Me.

29 "And He who sent Me is with Me; He has not left Me alone, for I always do the things that are pleasing to Him."

30 As He spoke these things, many came to believe in Him.

31 Jesus therefore was saying to those Jews who had believed Him, "If you abide in My word, *then* you are truly disciples of Mine;

32 and you shall know the truth, and the truth shall make you free."

33 They answered Him, "We are Abraham's offspring, and have never yet been enslaved to anyone; how is it that You say, 'You shall become free'?"

34 Jesus answered them, "Truly, truly, I say to you, every one who commits sin is the slave of sin.

35 "And the slave does not remain in the house forever; the son does remain forever.

36 "If therefore the Son shall make you free, you shall be free indeed.

37 "I know that you are Abraham's offspring; yet you seek to kill Me, because My word has no place in you.

38 "I speak the things which I have seen with *My* Father; therefore you also do the things which you heard from *your* father."

39 They answered and said to Him, "Abraham is our father." Jesus *said to them, "If you are Abraham's children, do the deeds of Abraham.

40 "But as it is, you are seeking to kill Me, a man who has told you the truth, which I heard from God; this Abraham did not do.

41 "You are doing the deeds of your father." They said to Him, "We were not born of fornication; we have one Father, *even* God."

42 Jesus said to them, "If God were your Father, you would love Me; for I proceeded forth and have come

from God, for I have not even come on My own initiative, but He sent Me.

43 "Why do you not understand what I am saying? *It is* because you cannot hear My word.

44 "You are of *your* father the devil, and you want to do the desires of your father. He was a murderer from the beginning, and does not stand in the truth, because there is no truth in him. Whenever he speaks a lie, he speaks from his own *nature*; for he is a liar, and the father of lies.

45 "But because I speak the truth, you do not believe Me.

46 "Which one of you convicts Me of sin? If I speak truth, why do you not believe Me?

47 "He who is of God hears the words of God; for this reason you do not hear *them,* because you are not of God."

48 The Jews answered and said to Him, "Do we not say rightly that You are a Samaritan and have a demon?"

49 Jesus answered, "I do not have a demon; but I honor My Father, and you dishonor Me.

50 "But I do not seek My glory; there is One who seeks and judges.

51 "Truly, truly, I say to you, if anyone keeps My word he shall never see death."

52 The Jews said to Him, "Now we know that You have a demon. Abraham died, and the prophets *also*; and You say, 'If anyone keeps My word, he shall never taste of death.'

53 "Surely You are not greater than our father Abraham, who died? The prophets died too; whom do You make Yourself out *to be?*"

54 Jesus answered, "If I glorify Myself, My glory is nothing; it is My Father who glorifies Me, of whom you say, 'He is our God;'

55 and you have not come to know Him, but I know Him; and if I say

that I do not know Him, I shall be a liar like you, but I do know Him, and keep His word.

56 "Your father Abraham rejoiced to see My day; and he saw *it,* and was glad."

57 The Jews therefore said to Him, "You are not yet fifty years old, and have You seen Abraham?"

58 Jesus said to them, "Truly, truly, I say to you, before Abraham was born, I AM."

59 Therefore they picked up stones to throw at Him; but Jesus hid Himself, and went out of the temple.

CHAPTER 9

AND as He passed by, He saw a man blind from birth.

2 And His disciples asked Him, saying, "Rabbi, who sinned, this man or his parents, that he should be born blind?"

3 Jesus answered, "*It was* neither *that* this man sinned, nor his parents; but *it was* in order that the works of God might be displayed in him.

4 "We must work the works of Him who sent Me, as long as it is day; night is coming, when no man can work.

5 "While I am in the world, I am the light of the world."

6 When He had said this, He spat on the ground, and made clay of the spittle, and applied the clay to his eyes,

7 and said to him, "Go, wash in the pool of Siloam" (which is translated, Sent). And so he went away and washed, and came *back* seeing.

8 The neighbors therefore, and those who previously saw him as a beggar, were saying, "Is not this the one who used to sit and beg?"

9 Others were saying, "This is he," *still* others were saying, "No, but he is like him." He kept saying, "I am the one."

10 Therefore they were saying to

him, "How then were your eyes opened?"

11 He answered, "The man who is called Jesus made clay, and anointed my eyes, and said to me, 'Go to Siloam, and wash'; so I went away and washed, and I received sight."

12 And they said to him, "Where is He?" He *said, "I do not know."

13 They *brought to the Pharisees him who was formerly blind.

14 Now it was a Sabbath on the day when Jesus made the clay, and opened his eyes.

15 Again, therefore, the Pharisees also were asking him how he received his sight. And he said to them, "He applied clay to my eyes, and I washed, and I see."

16 Therefore some of the Pharisees were saying, "This man is not from God, because he does not keep the Sabbath." But others were saying, "How can a man who is a sinner perform such signs?" And there was a division among them.

17 They *said therefore to the blind man again, "What do you say about Him, since He opened your eyes?" And he said, "He is a prophet."

18 The Jews therefore did not believe it of him, that he had been blind, and had received sight, until they called the parents of the very one who had received his sight,

19 and questioned them, saying, "Is this your son, who you say was born blind? Then how does he now see?"

20 His parents answered then, and said, "We know that this is our son, and that he was born blind;

21 but how he now sees, we do not know; or who opened his eyes, we do not know. Ask him; he is of age, he shall speak for himself."

22 His parents said this because they were afraid of the Jews; for the Jews had already agreed, that if any one should confess Him to be Christ, he should be put out of the synagogue.

23 For this reason his parents said, "He is of age; ask him."

24 So a second time they called the man who had been blind, and said to him, "Give glory to God; we know that this man is a sinner."

25 He therefore answered, "Whether He is a sinner, I do not know; one thing I do know, that, whereas I was blind, now I see."

26 They said therefore to him, "What did He do to you? How did He open your eyes?"

27 He answered them, "I told you already, and you did not listen; why do you want to hear it again? You do not want to become His disciples too, do you?"

28 And they reviled him, and said, "You are His disciple; but we are disciples of Moses.

29 "We know that God has spoken to Moses; but as for this man, we do not know where He is from."

30 The man answered and said to them, "Well, here is an amazing thing, that you do not know where He is from, and yet He opened my eyes.

31 "We know that God does not hear sinners; but if any one is Godfearing, and does His will, He hears him.

32 "Since the beginning of time it has never been heard that any one opened the eyes of a person born blind.

33 "If this man were not from God, He could do nothing."

34 They answered and said to him, "You were born entirely in sins, and are you teaching us?" And they put him out.

35 Jesus heard that they had put him out; and finding him, He said, "Do you believe in the Son of Man?"

36 He answered and said, "And who is He, Lord, that I may believe in Him?"

37 Jesus said to him, "You have both seen Him, and He is the one who is talking with you."

38 And he said, "Lord, I believe." And he worshiped Him.

39 And Jesus said, "For judgment I came into this world, that those who do not see may see; and that those who see may become blind."

40 Those of the Pharisees who were with Him heard these things, and said to Him, "We are not blind too, are we?"

41 Jesus said to them, "If you were blind, you would have no sin; but now you say, 'We see;' your sin remains.

CHAPTER 10

"TRULY, truly, I say to you, he who does not enter by the door into the fold of the sheep, but climbs up some other way, he is a thief and a robber.

2 "But he who enters by the door is a shepherd of the sheep.

3 "To him the doorkeeper opens, and the sheep hear his voice, and he calls his own sheep by name, and leads them out.

4 "When he puts forth all his own, he goes before them, and the sheep follow him because they know his voice.

5 "And a stranger they simply will not follow, but will flee from him, because they do not know the voice of strangers."

6 This figure of speech Jesus spoke to them, but they did not understand what those things were which He had been saying to them.

7 Jesus therefore said to them again, "Truly, truly, I say to you, I am the door of the sheep.

8 "All who came before Me are thieves and robbers; but the sheep did not hear them.

9 "I am the door; if anyone enters through Me, he shall be saved, and shall go in and out, and find pasture.

10 "The thief comes only to steal, and kill, and destroy; I came that they might have life, and might have *it* abundantly.

11 "I am the good shepherd; the good shepherd lays down His life for the sheep.

12 "He who is a hireling, and not a shepherd, who is not the owner of the sheep, beholds the wolf coming, and leaves the sheep, and flees, and the wolf snatches them, and scatters *them.*

13 *"He flees* because he is a hireling, and is not concerned about the sheep.

14 "I am the good shepherd; and I know My own, and My own know Me,

15 even as the Father knows Me and I know the Father; and I lay down My life for the sheep.

16 "And I have other sheep, which are not of this fold; I must bring them also, and they shall hear My voice; and they shall become one flock *with* one shepherd.

17 "For this reason the Father loves Me, because I lay down My life that I may take it again.

18 "No one has taken it away from Me, but I lay it down on My own initiative. I have authority to lay it down, and I have authority to take it up again. This commandment I received from My Father."

19 There arose a division again among the Jews because of these words.

20 And many of them were saying, "He has a demon, and is insane; why do you listen to Him?"

21 Others were saying, "These are not the sayings of one demon-possessed. A demon cannot open the eyes of the blind, can he?"

22 At that time the Feast of the Dedication took place at Jerusalem;

23 it was winter, and Jesus was

walking in the temple in the portico of Solomon.

24 The Jews therefore gathered around Him, and were saying to Him, "How long will You keep us in suspense? If You are the Christ, tell us plainly."

25 Jesus answered them, "I told you, and you do not believe; the works that I do in My Father's name, these bear witness of Me.

26 "But you do not believe, because you are not of My sheep.

27 "My sheep hear My voice, and I know them, and they follow Me;

28 <u>and I give eternal life to them, and they shall never perish; and no one shall snatch them out of My hand.</u>

29 <u>"My Father, who has given *them* to Me, is greater than all; and no one is able to snatch *them* out of the Father's hand.</u>

30 "I and the Father are one."

31 The Jews took up stones again to stone Him.

32 Jesus answered them, "I showed you many good works from the Father; for which of them are you stoning Me?"

33 The Jews answered Him, "For a good work we do not stone You, but for blasphemy; and because You, being a man, make Yourself out *to be* God."

34 Jesus answered them, "Has it not been written in your Law, 'I said, you are gods'?

35 "If he called them gods, to whom the word of God came (and the Scripture cannot be broken),

36 do you say of Him, whom the Father sanctified and sent into the world, 'You are blaspheming,' because I said, 'I am the Son of God'?

37 "If I do not do the works of My Father, do not believe Me;

38 but if I do them, though you do not believe Me, believe the works, that you may know and understand

that the Father is in Me, and I in the Father."

39 Therefore they were seeking again to seize Him; and He eluded their grasp.

40 And He went away again beyond the Jordan to the place where John was first baptizing; and He was staying there.

41 And many came to Him; and they were saying, "While John performed no sign, yet everything John said about this man was true."

42 And many believed in Him there.

CHAPTER 11

NOW a certain man was sick, Lazarus of Bethany, of the village of Mary and her sister Martha.

2 And it was the Mary who anointed the Lord with ointment, and wiped His feet with her hair, whose brother Lazarus was sick.

3 The sisters therefore sent to Him, saying, "Lord, behold, he whom You love is sick."

4 But when Jesus heard it, He said, "This sickness is not unto death, but for the glory of God, that the Son of God may be glorified by it."

5 Now Jesus loved Martha, and her sister, and Lazarus.

6 When therefore He heard that he was sick, He stayed then two days *longer* in the place where He was.

7 Then after this He *said to the disciples, "Let us go to Judea again."

8 The disciples *said to Him, "Rabbi, the Jews were just now seeking to stone You; and are You going there again?"

9 Jesus answered, "Are there not twelve hours in the day? If anyone walks in the day, he does not stumble, because he sees the light of this world.

10 "But if anyone walks in the night, he stumbles, because the light is not in him."

11 This He said, and after that He *said to them, "Our friend Lazarus has fallen asleep; but I go, that I may awaken him out of sleep."

12 The disciples therefore said to Him, "Lord, if he has fallen asleep, he will recover."

13 Now Jesus had spoken of his death; but they thought that He was speaking of literal sleep.

14 Then Jesus therefore said to them plainly, "Lazarus is dead,

15 and I am glad for your sakes that I was not there, so that you may believe; but let us go to him."

16 Thomas therefore, who is called Didymus, said to *his* fellow disciples, "Let us also go, that we may die with Him."

17 So when Jesus came, He found that he had already been in the tomb four days.

18 Now Bethany was near Jerusalem, about two miles off;

19 and many of the Jews had come to Martha and Mary, to console them concerning *their* brother.

20 Martha therefore, when she heard that Jesus was coming, went to meet Him; but Mary still sat in the house.

21 Martha therefore said to Jesus, "Lord, if You had been here, my brother would not have died.

22 "Even now I know that whatever You ask of God, God will give You."

23 Jesus *said to her, "Your brother shall rise again."

24 Martha *said to Him, "I know that he will rise again in the resurrection on the last day."

25 Jesus said to her, "I am the resurrection and the life; he who believes in Me shall live even if he dies,

26 and everyone who lives and believes in Me shall never die. Do you believe this?"

27 She *said to Him, "Yes, Lord; I have believed that You are the Christ, the Son of God, *even* He who comes into the world."

28 And when she had said this, she went away, and called Mary her sister, saying secretly, "The Teacher is here, and is calling for you."

29 And when she heard it, she *arose quickly, and was coming to Him.

30 Now Jesus had not yet come into the village, but was still in the place where Martha met Him.

31 The Jews then who were with her in the house, and consoling her, when they saw that Mary rose up quickly and went out, followed her, supposing that she was going to the tomb to weep there.

32 Therefore, when Mary came where Jesus was, she saw Him, and fell at His feet, saying to Him, "Lord, if You had been here, my brother would not have died."

33 When Jesus therefore saw her weeping, and the Jews who came with her, *also* weeping, He was deeply moved in spirit, and was troubled,

34 and said, "Where have you laid him?" They *said to Him, "Lord, come and see."

35 Jesus wept.

36 And so the Jews were saying, "Behold how He loved him!"

37 But some of them said, "Could not this man, who opened the eyes of him who was blind, have kept this man also from dying?"

38 Jesus therefore again being deeply moved within, *came to the tomb. Now it was a cave, and a stone was lying against it.

39 Jesus *said, "Remove the stone." Martha, the sister of the deceased, *said to Him, "Lord, by this time there is a stench; for he *has been dead* four days."

40 Jesus *said to her, "Did I not say to you, if you believe, you will see the glory of God?"

41 And so they removed the stone.

And Jesus raised His eyes, and said, "Father, I thank Thee that Thou heardest Me.

42 "And I knew that Thou hearest Me always; but because of the people standing around I said it, that they may believe that Thou didst send Me."

43 And when He had said these things, He cried out with a loud voice, "Lazarus, come forth."

44 He who had died came forth, bound hand and foot with wrappings; and his face was wrapped around with a cloth. Jesus *said to them, "Unbind him, and let him go."

45 Many therefore of the Jews, who had come to Mary and beheld what He had done, believed in Him.

46 But some of them went away to the Pharisees, and told them the things which Jesus had done.

47 Therefore the chief priests and the Pharisees convened a council, and were saying, "What are we doing? For this man is performing many signs.

48 "If we let Him go on like this, all men will believe in Him, and the Romans will come and take away both our place and our nation."

49 But a certain one of them, Caiaphas, who was high priest that year, said to them, "You know nothing at all,

50 nor do you take into account that it is expedient for you that one man should die for the people, and that the whole nation should not perish."

51 Now this he did not say on his own initiative; but being high priest that year, he prophesied that Jesus was going to die for the nation;

52 and not for the nation only, but that He might also gather together into one the children of God who are scattered abroad.

53 So from that day on they planned together to kill Him.

54 Jesus therefore no longer continued to walk publicly among the Jews, but went away from there to the country near the wilderness, into a city called Ephraim; and there He stayed with the disciples.

55 Now the Passover of the Jews was at hand, and many went up to Jerusalem out of the country before the Passover, to purify themselves.

56 Therefore they were seeking for Jesus, and were saying to one another, as they stood in the temple, "What do you think; that He will not come to the feast at all?"

57 Now the chief priests and the Pharisees had given orders that if any one knew where He was, he should report it, that they might seize Him.

CHAPTER 12

JESUS, therefore, six days before the Passover, came to Bethany where Lazarus was, whom Jesus had raised from the dead.

2 So they made Him a supper there; and Martha was serving; but Lazarus was one of those reclining *at the table* with Him.

3 Mary therefore took a pound of very costly, genuine spikenard ointment, and anointed the feet of Jesus, and wiped His feet with her hair; and the house was filled with the fragrance of the ointment.

4 But Judas Iscariot, one of His disciples, who was intending to betray Him, *said,

5 "Why was this ointment not sold for three hundred denarii, and given to poor *people?*"

6 Now he said this, not because he was concerned about the poor, but because he was a thief, and as he had the money box, he used to pilfer what was put into it.

7 Jesus therefore said, "Let her alone, in order that she may keep it for the day of My burial.

8 "For the poor you always have

with you; but you do not always have Me."

9 The great multitude therefore of the Jews learned that He was there; and they came, not for Jesus' sake only, but that they might also see Lazarus, whom He raised from the dead.

10 But the chief priests took counsel that they might put Lazarus to death also;

11 because on account of him many of the Jews were going away, and were believing in Jesus.

12 On the next day the great multitude who had come to the feast, when they heard that Jesus was coming to Jerusalem,

13 took the branches of the palm trees, and went out to meet Him, and *began* to cry out, "Hosanna! BLESSED *is* HE WHO COMES IN THE NAME OF THE LORD, even the King of Israel."

14 And Jesus, finding a young donkey, sat on it; as it is written,

15 "FEAR NOT, DAUGHTER OF ZION; BEHOLD, YOUR KING COMES SITTING ON A DONKEY'S COLT."

16 These things His disciples did not understand at the first; but when Jesus was glorified, then they remembered that these things were written of Him, and that they had done these things to Him.

17 And so the multitude who were with Him when He called Lazarus out of the tomb, and raised him from the dead, were bearing Him witness.

18 For this cause also the multitude went and met Him, because they heard that He had performed this sign.

19 The Pharisees therefore said to one another, "You see that you are not doing any good; look, the world has gone after Him."

20 Now there were certain Greeks among those who were going up to worship at the feast;

21 these therefore came to Philip, who was from Bethsaida of Galilee,

and *began to* ask him, saying, "Sir, we wish to see Jesus."

22 Philip *came and *told Andrew; Andrew and Philip *came, and they *told Jesus.

23 And Jesus *answered them, saying, "The hour has come for the Son of Man to be glorified.

24 "Truly, truly, I say to you, unless a grain of wheat falls into the earth and dies, it remains by itself alone; but if it dies, it bears much fruit.

25 "He who loves his life loses it; and he who hates his life in this world shall keep it to life eternal.

26 "If any one serves Me, let him follow Me; and where I am, there shall My servant also be; if any one serves Me, the Father will honor him.

27 "Now My soul has become troubled; and what shall I say, 'Father, save Me from this hour'? But for this purpose I came to this hour.

28 "Father, glorify Thy name." There came therefore a voice out of heaven: "I have both glorified it, and will glorify it again."

29 The multitude therefore, who stood by and heard it, were saying that it had thundered; others were saying, "An angel has spoken to Him."

30 Jesus answered and said, "This voice has not come for My sake, but for your sakes.

31 "Now judgment is upon this world; now the ruler of this world shall be cast out.

32 "And I, if I be lifted up from the earth, will draw all men to Myself."

33 But He was saying this to indicate the kind of death by which He was to die.

34 The multitude therefore answered Him, "We have heard out of the Law that the Christ is to remain forever; and how can You say, 'The Son of Man must be lifted up'? Who is this Son of Man?"

35 Jesus therefore said to them, "For a little while longer the light is among you. Walk while you have the light, that darkness may not overtake you; he who walks in the darkness does not know where he goes.

36 "While you have the light, believe in the light, in order that you may become sons of light."

These things Jesus spoke, and He departed and hid Himself from them.

37 But though He had performed so many signs before them, *yet* they were not believing in Him;

38 that the word of Isaiah the prophet might be fulfilled, which he spoke, "LORD, WHO HAS BELIEVED OUR REPORT? AND TO WHOM HAS THE ARM OF THE LORD BEEN REVEALED?"

39 For this cause they could not believe, for Isaiah said again,

40 "HE HAS BLINDED THEIR EYES, AND HE HARDENED THEIR HEART; LEST THEY SEE WITH THEIR EYES, AND PERCEIVE WITH THEIR HEART, AND BE CONVERTED, AND I HEAL THEM."

41 These things Isaiah said, because he saw His glory, and he spoke of Him.

42 Nevertheless many even of the rulers believed in Him, but because of the Pharisees they were not confessing *Him*, lest they should be put out of the synagogue;

43 for they loved the approval of men rather than the approval of God.

44 And Jesus cried out and said, "He who believes in Me does not believe in Me, but in Him who sent Me.

45 "And he who beholds Me beholds the One who sent Me.

46 "I have come *as* light into the world, that everyone who believes in Me may not remain in darkness.

47 "And if any one hears My sayings, and does not keep them, I do not judge him; for I did not come to judge the world, but to save the world.

48 "He who rejects Me, and does not receive My sayings, has one who judges him; the word I spoke is what will judge him at the last day.

49 "For I did not speak on My own initiative, but the Father Himself who sent Me has given Me commandment, what to say, and what to speak.

50 "And I know that His commandment is eternal life; therefore the things I speak, I speak just as the Father has told Me."

CHAPTER 13

NOW before the Feast of the Passover, Jesus knowing that His hour had come that He should depart out of this world to the Father, having loved His own who were in the world, He loved them to the end.

2 And during supper, the devil having already put into the heart of Judas Iscariot, *the son* of Simon, to betray Him,

3 *Jesus*, knowing that the Father had given all things into His hands, and that He had come forth from God, and was going back to God,

4 *rose from supper, and *laid aside His garments; and taking a towel, girded Himself about.

5 Then He *poured water into the basin, and began to wash the disciples' feet, and to wipe them with the towel with which He was girded.

6 And so He *came to Simon Peter. He *said to Him, "Lord, do You wash my feet?"

7 Jesus answered and said to him, "What I do you do not realize now; but you shall understand hereafter."

8 Peter *said to Him, "Never shall You wash my feet!" Jesus answered him, "If I do not wash you, you have no part with Me."

9 Simon Peter *said to Him, "Lord, not my feet only, but also my hands and my head."

10 Jesus *said to him, "He who has

bathed needs only to wash his feet, but is completely clean; and you are clean, but not all *of you.*"

11 For He knew the one who was betraying Him; for this reason He said, "Not all of you are clean."

12 And so when He had washed their feet, and taken His garments, and reclined *at table* again, He said to them, "Do you know what I have done to you?

13 "You call Me Teacher, and Lord; and you are right; for *so* I am.

14 "If I then, the Lord and the Teacher, washed your feet, you also ought to wash one another's feet.

15 "For I gave you an example that you also should do as I did to you.

16 "Truly, truly, I say to you, a slave is not greater than his master; neither one who is sent greater than the one who sent him.

17 "If you know these things, you are blessed if you do them.

18 "I do not speak of all of you. I know the ones I have chosen; but *it is* that the Scripture may be fulfilled, 'HE WHO EATS MY BREAD HAS LIFTED UP HIS HEEL AGAINST ME.'

19 "From now on I am telling you before *it* comes to pass, so that when it does occur, you may believe that I am *He*.

20 "Truly, truly, I say to you, he who receives whomever I send receives Me; and he who receives Me receives Him who sent Me."

21 When Jesus had said this, He became troubled in spirit, and testified, and said, "Truly, truly, I say to you, that one of you will betray Me."

22 The disciples *began* looking at one another, at a loss *to know* of which one He was speaking.

23 There was reclining on Jesus' breast one of His disciples, whom Jesus loved.

24 Simon Peter therefore *gestured to him, and *said to him, "Tell *us* who it is of whom He is speaking."

25 He, leaning back thus on Jesus' breast, *said to Him, "Lord, who is it?"

26 Jesus therefore *answered, "That is the one for whom I shall dip the morsel and give it to him." So when He had dipped the morsel, He *took and *gave it to Judas, *the son* of Simon Iscariot.

27 And after the morsel, Satan then entered into him. Jesus therefore *said to him, "What you do, do quickly."

28 Now no one of those reclining *at table* knew for what purpose He had said this to him.

29 For some were supposing, because Judas had the money box, that Jesus was saying to him, "Buy the things we have need of for the feast"; or else, that he should give something to the poor.

30 And so after receiving the morsel he went out immediately; and it was night.

31 When therefore he had gone out, Jesus *said, "Now is the Son of Man glorified, and God is glorified in Him;

32 if God is glorified in Him, God will also glorify Him in Himself, and will glorify Him immediately.

33 "Little children, I am with you a little while longer. You shall seek Me; and as I said to the Jews, 'Where I am going, you cannot come', now I say to you also.

34 "A new commandment I give to you, that you love one another, even as I have loved you, that you also love one another.

35 "By this all men will know that you are My disciples, if you have love for one another." (a)

(a) The Highest Duty and Greatest Obligation of the Believer.
"If you have love for one another" is the means Christ has chosen to

(Turn to next page.)

36 Simon Peter *said to Him, "Lord, where are You going?" Jesus answered, "Where I go, you cannot follow Me now; but you shall follow later."

37 Peter *said to Him, "Lord, why can I not follow You right now? I will lay down my life for You."

38 Jesus *answered, "Will you lay down your life for Me? Truly, truly, I say to you, a cock shall not crow, until you deny Me three times.

CHAPTER 14

"LET not your heart be troubled; believe in God, believe also in Me.

2 "In My Father's house are many dwelling places; if it were not so, I would have told you; for I go to prepare a place for you.

3 "And if I go and prepare a place for you, I will come again, and receive you to Myself; that where I am, *there* you may be also.

4 "And you know the way where I am going."

5 Thomas *said to Him, "Lord, we do not know where You are going; how do we know the way?"

6 Jesus *said to him, "I am the way, and the truth, and the life; no one comes to the Father, but through Me.

7 "If you had known Me, you would have known My Father also; from now on you know Him, and have seen Him."

8 Philip *said to Him, "Lord, show us the Father, and it is enough for us."

9 Jesus *said to him, "Have I been so long with you, and *yet* you have not come to know Me, Philip? He who has seen Me has seen the Father; how do you say, 'Show us the Father'?

10 "Do you not believe that I am in the Father, and the Father is in Me? The words that I say to you I do not speak on My own initiative, but the Father abiding in Me does His works.

11 "Believe Me that I am in the Father, and the Father in Me; otherwise believe on account of the works themselves.

12 "Truly, truly, I say to you, he who believes in Me, the works that I do shall he do also; and greater *works* than these shall he do; because I go to the Father.

13 "And whatever you ask in My name, that will I do, that the Father may be glorified in the Son.

14 "If you ask Me anything in My name, I will do *it*.

15 "If you love Me, you will keep My commandments.

16 "And I will ask the Father, and He will give you another Helper, that He may be with you forever;

17 *that is* the Spirit of truth, whom

(Continued from page 145.)

Manifest His disciples to the world. To know love is to know God, for "God is love." "Love is from God, everyone who loves is born of God." God's family is identified by love. God knows "we love because He first loved us." His

Motive is that He wants all men to know that you are his disciple. Jesus said "If you love me, you will keep my commandments." He taught that the first commandment is to "love God . . . and your neighbor as yourself." The

Message of the disciple of Christ is love. To love the brethren is to "know that we have passed out of death into life." "Whoever loves the Father loves the child born of Him." The message of love is given not "with word or with tongue, but in deed and truth."

Do you have love for God and your neighbor? Your highest duty is to love God. Your greatest obligation is to love your neighbor as yourself. Love that you may show, and others may know, you are the disciple of Jesus Christ our Lord and, "To God be the glory!"

the world cannot receive, because it does not behold Him or know Him, *but* you know Him because He abides with you, and will be in you.

18 "I will not leave you as orphans; I will come to you.

19 "After a little while the world will behold Me no more; but you *will* behold Me; because I live, you shall live also.

20 "In that day you shall know that I am in My Father, and you in Me, and I in you.

21 "He who has My commandments and keeps them, he it is who loves Me; and he who loves Me shall be loved by My Father, and I will love him, and will disclose Myself to him."

22 Judas (not Iscariot) *said to Him, "Lord, what then has happened that You are going to disclose Yourself to us, and not to the world?"

23 Jesus answered and said to him, "If anyone loves Me, he will keep My word; and My Father will love him, and We will come to him, and make Our abode with him.

24 "He who does not love Me does not keep My words; and the word which you hear is not Mine, but the Father's who sent Me.

25 "These things I have spoken to you, while abiding with you.

26 "But the Helper, the Holy Spirit, whom the Father will send in My name, He will teach you all things, and bring to your remembrance all that I said to you.

27 "Peace I leave with you; My peace I give to you; not as the world gives, do I give to you. Let not your heart be troubled, nor let it be fearful.

28 "You heard that I said to you, 'I go away, and I will come to you.' If you loved Me, you would have rejoiced, because I go to the Father; for the Father is greater than I.

29 "And now I have told you before it comes to pass, that when it comes to pass, you may believe.

30 "I will not speak much more with you, for the ruler of the world is coming, and he has nothing in Me;

31 but that the world may know that I love the Father, and as the Father gave Me commandment, even so I do. Arise, let us go from here.

Chapter 15

"I AM the true vine, and My Father is the vinedresser.

2 "Every branch in Me that does not bear fruit, He takes away; and every *branch* that bears fruit, He prunes it, that it may bear more fruit.

3 "You are already clean because of the word which I have spoken to you.

4 "Abide in Me, and I in you. As the branch cannot bear fruit of itself, unless it abides in the vine, so neither *can* you, unless you abide in Me.

5 "I am the vine, you are the branches; he who abides in Me, and I in him, he bears much fruit; for apart from Me you can do nothing.

6 "If anyone does not abide in Me, he is thrown away as a branch, and dries up; and they gather them, and cast them into the fire, and they are burned.

7 "If you abide in Me, and My words abide in you, ask whatever you wish, and it shall be done for you.

8 "By this is My Father glorified, that you bear much fruit, and *so* prove to be My disciples.

9 "Just as the Father has loved Me, I have also loved you; abide in My love.

10 "If you keep My commandments, you will abide in My love; just as I have kept My Father's commandments, and abide in His love.

11 "These things I have spoken to you, that My joy may be in you, and *that* your joy may be made full.

12 "This is My commandment, that you love one another, just as I have loved you.

13 "Greater love has no one than this, that one lay down his life for his friends.

14 "You are My friends, if you do what I command you.

15 "No longer do I call you slaves; for the slave does not know what his master is doing; but I have called you friends, for all things that I have heard from My Father I have made known to you.

16 "You did not choose Me, but I chose you, and appointed you, that you should go and bear fruit, and *that* your fruit should remain, that whatever you ask of the Father in My name, He may give to you.

17 "This I command you, that you love one another.

18 "If the world hates you, you know that it has hated Me before *it* hated you.

19 "If you were of the world, the world would love its own; but because you are not of the world, but I chose you out of the world, therefore the world hates you.

20 "Remember the word that I said to you, 'A slave is not greater than his master.' If they persecuted Me, they will also persecute you; if they kept My word, they will keep yours also.

21 "But all these things they will do to you for My name's sake, because they do not know the One who sent Me.

22 "If I had not come and spoken to them, they would not have sin, but now they have no excuse for their sin.

23 "He who hates Me hates My Father also.

24 "If I had not done among them the works which no one else did, they would not have sin; but now they have both seen and hated Me and My Father as well.

25 "But *they have done this* in order that the word may be fulfilled that is written in their Law, 'THEY HATED ME WITHOUT A CAUSE.'

SCRIPTURE NO. 3, SEC. 4

26 "When the Helper comes, whom I will send to you from the Father, *that is* the Spirit of truth, who proceeds from the Father, He will bear witness of Me,

27 and you *will* bear witness also, because you have been with Me from the beginning. (r3)

(r3) REFERENCE NO. 3, SEC. 4—
WHAT YOU SHOULD KNOW ABOUT THE HOLY SPIRIT.
"The Spirit of truth, who proceeds from the Father"
is the Holy Spirit and is called "the Helper." He is one with God the Father and God the Son. Jesus told His disciples to baptize "in the name of the Father and the Son and the Holy Spirit."

The unsaved or "natural man does not accept the things of the Spirit of God." And "the thoughts of God no one knows except the Spirit of God." Through God's word He speaks to the unsaved—"to give the light of the Knowledge of the glory of God."

Jesus said, "I will send Him to you" and "He will bear witness of Me." "He shall glorify Me; for He shall take of Mine and shall disclose it to you." "He will guide you into all the truth." "And He ... will convict the world concerning sin, and righteousness, and judgment." He convicts of sin "because they do not believe in Jesus." When you believe in Christ as your Lord and Savior He makes you "alive together with Christ." "It is the Spirit who gives life."

Jesus said, "repent and believe in the gospel." When you do "you shall receive the gift of the Holy Spirit ... whom God has given to those who obey Him." Jesus

(Continued on next page.)

CHAPTER 16

"THESE things I have spoken to you, that you may be kept from stumbling.

2 "They will make you outcasts from the synagogue; but an hour is coming for everyone who kills you to think that he is offering service to God.

3 "And these things they will do, because they have not known the Father, or Me.

4 "But these things I have spoken to you, that when their hour comes, you may remember that I told you of them. And these things I did not say to you at the beginning, because I was with you.

5 "But now I am going to Him who sent Me; and none of you asks Me, 'Where are You going?'

6 "But because I have said these things to you, sorrow has filled your heart.

7 "But I tell you the truth, it is to your advantage that I go away; for if I do not go away, the Helper shall not come to you; but if I go, I will send Him to you.

8 "And He, when He comes, will convict the world concerning sin, and righteousness, and judgment;

9 concerning sin, because they do not believe in Me;

10 and concerning righteousness, because I go to the Father, and you no longer behold Me;

11 and concerning judgment, because the ruler of this world has been judged.

12 "I have many more things to say to you, but you cannot bear *them* now.

13 "But when He, the Spirit of truth, comes, He will guide you into all the truth; for He will not speak on His own initiative, but whatever He hears, He will speak; and He will disclose to you what is to come.

14 "He shall glorify Me; for He shall take of Mine, and shall disclose *it* to you.

15 "All things that the Father has are Mine; therefore I said, that He takes of Mine, and will disclose *it* to you.

16 "A little while, and you *will* no longer behold Me; and again a little while, and you will see Me."

17 *Some* of His disciples therefore said to one another, "What is this thing He is telling us, 'A little while, and you *will* not behold Me; and again a little while, and you will see Me'; and, 'Because I go to the Father'?"

18 And so they were saying, "What is this that He says, 'A little while'? We do not know what He is talking about."

19 Jesus knew that they wished to question Him, and He said to them, "Are you deliberating together about this, that I said, 'A little while, and you *will* not behold Me, and again a little while, and you *will* see Me'?

20 "Truly, truly, I say to you, that you will weep and lament, but the world will rejoice; you will be sorrowful, but your sorrow will be turned to joy.

(Continued from page 148.)

promised the Holy Spirit "will be in you . . . that He may be with you forever." In this way "the love of God has been poured out within our hearts through the Holy Spirit who was given to us." "All who are being led by the Spirit of God, these are sons of God."

Do you desire the Holy Spirit to "guide you into all truth" . . . "teach you all things" and make you "alive together with Christ?" If so, say:

"I desire the Holy Spirit to guide me into all truth and teach me the things of Christ."

Now turn to page 278, Scripture No. 4, Sec. 4, 1 Thess. 2:13.

21 "Whenever a woman is in travail she has sorrow, because her hour has come; but when she gives birth to the child, she remembers the anguish no more, for joy that a child has been born into the world.

22 "Therefore you, too, now have sorrow; but I will see you again, and your heart will rejoice, and no one takes your joy away from you.

23 "And in that day you will ask Me no question. Truly, truly, I say to you, if you shall ask the Father for anything, He will give it to you in My name.

24 "Until now you have asked for nothing in My name; ask, and you will receive, that your joy may be made full.

25 "These things I have spoken to you in figurative language; an hour is coming, when I will speak no more to you in figurative language, but will tell you plainly of the Father.

26 "In that day you will ask in My name; and I do not say to you that I will request the Father on your behalf;

27 for the Father Himself loves you, because you have loved Me, and have believed that I came forth from the Father.

28 "I came forth from the Father, and have come into the world; I am leaving the world again, and going to the Father."

29 His disciples *said, "Lo, now

You are speaking plainly, and are not using a figure of speech.

30 "Now we know that You know all things, and have no need for anyone to question You; by this we believe that You came from God."

31 Jesus answered them, "Do you now believe?

32 "Behold, an hour is coming, and has *already* come, for you to be scattered, each to his own *home,* and to leave Me alone; and *yet* I am not alone, because the Father is with Me.

33 "These things I have spoken to you, that in Me you may have peace. In the world you have tribulation, but take courage; I have overcome the world."

CHAPTER 17

THESE things Jesus spoke; and lifting up His eyes to heaven, He said, "Father, the hour has come; glorify Thy Son, that the Son may glorify Thee,

2 even as Thou gavest Him authority over all mankind, that to all whom Thou hast given Him, He may give eternal life.

SCRIPTURE NO. 1, SEC. 4

3 "And this is eternal life, that they may know Thee, the only true God, and Jesus Christ whom Thou hast sent. (r1)

This is the first of four references concerning scriptures showing
"What you should know to be saved."

(r1) REFERENCE NO. 1, SEC. 4—
   WHAT YOU SHOULD KNOW ABOUT THE ONLY TRUE GOD.

The Lord Jesus Christ prayed *"that they may know Thee the only true God."* He included you in this prayer. God wants you to know Him. You can know Him by faith. He says, "he who comes to God must believe that He is, and that He is a rewarder of those who seek Him."

"The living Jesus" is the "Father of our Lord Jesus Christ." He is the Creator "who made the heavens and the earth and the sea, and all that is in them." He "does not dwell in temples made with hands."

Jesus said, "the Father has life in Himself." "The True God and Father Himself gives

(Continued on next page.)

4 "I glorified Thee on the earth, having accomplished the work which Thou hast given Me to do.

5 "And now, glorify Thou Me together with Thyself, Father, with the glory which I ever had with Thee before the world was.

6 "I manifested Thy name to the men whom Thou gavest Me out of the world; Thine they were, and Thou gavest them to Me, and they have kept Thy word.

7 "Now they have come to know that everything Thou hast given Me is from Thee;

8 for the words which Thou gavest Me I have given to them; and they received *them*, and truly understood that I came forth from Thee, and they believed that Thou didst send Me.

9 "I ask on their behalf; I do not ask on behalf of the world, but of those whom Thou hast given Me; for they are Thine;

10 and all things that are Mine are Thine, and Thine are Mine; and I have been glorified in them.

11 "And I am no more in the world; and *yet* they themselves are in the world, and I come to Thee. Holy Father, keep them in Thy name, *the name* which Thou hast given Me, that they may be one, even as We *are*.

12 "While I was with them, I was keeping them in Thy name which Thou hast given Me; and I guarded them, and not one of them perished but the son of perdition, that the Scripture might be fulfilled.

13 "But now I come to Thee; and these things I speak in the world, that they may have My joy made full in themselves.

14 "I have given them Thy word; and the world has hated them, because they are not of the world, even as I am not of the world.

15 "I do not ask Thee to take them out of the world, but to keep them from the evil *one*.

16 "They are not of the world, even as I am not of the world.

17 "Sanctify them in the truth; Thy word is truth.

18 "As Thou didst send Me into the world, I also have sent them into the world.

19 "And for their sakes I sanctify Myself, that they themselves also may be sanctified in truth.

20 "I do not ask in behalf of these alone, but for those also who believe in Me through their word;

21 that they may all be one; even as Thou, Father, *art* in Me, and I in Thee, that they also may be in Us; that the world may believe that Thou didst send Me.

(Continued from page 150.)

to all life and breath and all things." "For in Him we live and move and exist." He is not "an image formed by the art and thought of man" because "God is spirit." Therefore "we ought not to think that the Divine Nature is like gold or silver or stone."

"God is light, and in Him there is no darkness at all." He is called "the Father of lights." He wants you "to turn from darkness to light" and see "the light of the world" or "the glory of God in the face of Christ." Jesus Christ, whom God sent, is "the true light which, coming into the world, enlightens every man."

"God is love". He "so loved" you, "that He gave His only begotten Son, that whoever believes in Him should not perish, but have eternal life."

Do you now understand that God loves you and offers you eternal life? If so, say: "I now understand the true God offers me the free gift of eternal life in Jesus Christ."

Now turn to page 23, Scripture No. 2, Sec. 4, Matt. 16:16. After reading this underlined scripture, please read Reference No. 2 at the bottom of the page. Then continue through the chain of numbered scriptures and references until completed.

22 "And the glory which Thou hast given Me I have given to them; that they may be one, just as We are one;

23 I in them, and Thou in Me, that they may be perfected in unity, that the world may know that Thou didst send Me, and didst love them, even as Thou didst love Me.

24 "Father, I desire that they also, whom Thou hast given Me, be with Me where I am, in order that they may behold My glory, which Thou hast given Me; for Thou didst love Me before the foundation of the world.

25 "O righteous Father, although the world has not known Thee, yet I have known Thee; and these have known that Thou didst send Me;

26 and I have made Thy name known to them, and will make it known; that the love wherewith Thou didst love Me may be in them, and I in them."

CHAPTER 18

W HEN Jesus had spoken these words, He went forth with His disciples over the ravine of the Kidron, where there was a garden, into which He Himself entered, and His disciples.

2 Now Judas also, who was betraying Him, knew the place; for Jesus had often met there with His disciples.

3 Judas then, having received the *Roman* cohort, and officers from the chief priests and the Pharisees, *came there with lanterns and torches and weapons.

4 Jesus therefore, knowing all the things that were coming upon Him, went forth, and *said to them, "Whom do you seek?"

5 They answered Him, "Jesus the Nazarene." He *said to them, "I am *He.*" And Judas also who was betraying Him, was standing with them.

6 When therefore He said to them, "I am *He*", they drew back, and fell to the ground.

7 Again therefore He asked them, "Whom do you seek?" And they said, "Jesus the Nazarene."

8 Jesus answered, "I told you that I am *He*; if therefore you seek Me, let these go their way,"

9 that the word might be fulfilled which He spoke, "Of those whom Thou hast given Me I lost not one."

10 Simon Peter therefore having a sword, drew it, and struck the high priest's slave, and cut off his right ear; and the slave's name was Malchus.

11 Jesus therefore said to Peter, "Put the sword into the sheath; the cup which the Father has given Me, shall I not drink it?"

12 So the *Roman* cohort and the commander, and the officers of the Jews, arrested Jesus and bound Him,

13 and led Him to Annas first; for he was father-in-law of Caiaphas, who was high priest that year.

14 Now Caiaphas was the one who had advised the Jews that it was expedient for one man to die on behalf of the people.

15 And Simon Peter was following Jesus, and *so was* another disciple. Now that disciple was known to the high priest, and entered with Jesus into the court of the high priest,

16 but Peter was standing at the door outside. So the other disciple, who was known to the high priest, went out and spoke to the door-keeper, and brought in Peter.

17 The slave-girl therefore who kept the door *said to Peter, "You are not also *one* of this man's disciples, are you?" He *said, "I am not."

18 Now the slaves and the officers were standing *there*, having made a charcoal fire, for it was cold and they were warming themselves; and Peter also was with them, standing and warming himself.

19 The high priest therefore questioned Jesus about His disciples, and about His teaching.

20 Jesus answered him, "I have spoken openly to the world; I always taught in synagogues, and in the temple, where all the Jews come together; and I spoke nothing in secret.

21 "Why do you question Me? Question those who have heard what I spoke to them; behold, these know what I said."

22 And when He had said this, one of the officers standing by gave Jesus a blow, saying, "Is that the way You answer the high priest?"

23 Jesus answered him, "If I have spoken wrongly, bear witness of the wrong; but if rightly, why do you strike Me?"

24 Annas therefore sent Him bound to Caiaphas the high priest.

25 Now Simon Peter was standing and warming himself. They said therefore to him, "You are not also *one* of His disciples, are you?" He denied *it*, and said, "I am not."

26 One of the slaves of the high priest, being a relative of the one whose ear Peter cut off, *said, "Did I not see you in the garden with Him?"

27 Peter therefore denied *it* again; and immediately a cock crowed.

28 They *led Jesus therefore from Caiaphas into the Praetorium; and it was early; and they themselves did not enter into the Praetorium in order that they might not be defiled, but might eat the Passover.

29 Pilate therefore went out to them, and *said, "What accusation do you bring against this Man?"

30 They answered and said to him, "If this Man were not an evildoer, we would not have delivered Him up to you."

31 Pilate therefore said to them, "Take Him yourselves, and judge Him according to your law." The Jews said to him, "We are not permitted to put any one to death,"

32 that the word of Jesus might be fulfilled, which He spoke, signifying by what kind of death He was about to die.

33 Pilate therefore entered again into the Praetorium, and summoned Jesus, and said to Him, "You are the King of the Jews?"

34 Jesus answered, "Are you saying this on your own initiative, or did others tell you about Me?"

35 Pilate answered, "I am not a Jew, am I? Your own nation and the chief priests delivered You up to me; what have You done?"

36 Jesus answered, "My kingdom is not of this world. If My kingdom were of this world, then My servants would be fighting, that I might not be delivered up to the Jews; but as it is, My kingdom is not of this realm."

37 Pilate therefore said to Him, "So You are a king?" Jesus answered, "You say *correctly* that I am a king. For this I have been born, and for this I have come into the world, to bear witness to the truth. Every one who is of the truth hears My voice."

38 Pilate *said to Him, "What is truth?"

And when he had said this, he went out again to the Jews, and *said to them, "I find no guilt in Him.

39 "But you have a custom, that I should release someone for you at the Passover; do you wish then that I release for you the King of the Jews?"

40 Therefore they cried out again, saying, "Not this Man, but Barabbas." Now Barabbas was a robber.

CHAPTER 19

THEN Pilate therefore took Jesus, and scourged Him.

2 And the soldiers wove a crown of thorns and put it on His head, and arrayed Him in a purple robe;

3 and they *began* to come up to Him, and say, "Hail, King of the Jews!" and to give Him blows in the face.

4 And Pilate came out again, and *said to them, "Behold, I am bringing Him out to you, that you may know that I find no guilt in Him."

5 Jesus therefore came out, wearing the crown of thorns and the purple robe. And *Pilate* *said to them, "Behold, the Man!"

6 When therefore the chief priests and the officers saw Him, they cried out, saying, "Crucify, crucify!" Pilate *said to them, "Take Him yourselves, and crucify Him, for I find no guilt in Him."

7 The Jews answered him, "We have a law, and by that law He ought to die because He made Himself out *to be* the Son of God."

8 When Pilate therefore heard this statement, he was the more afraid;

9 and he entered into the Praetorium again, and *said to Jesus, "Where are You from?" But Jesus gave him no answer.

10 Pilate therefore *said to Him, "You do not speak to me? Do You not know that I have authority to release You, and I have authority to crucify You?"

11 Jesus answered, "You would have no authority over Me, unless it had been given you from above; for this reason he who delivered Me up to you has *the* greater sin."

12 As a result of this Pilate made efforts to release Him, but the Jews cried out, saying, "If you release this Man, you are no friend of Caesar; every one who makes himself out *to be* a king opposes Caesar."

13 When Pilate therefore heard these words, he brought Jesus out, and sat down on the judgment seat at a place called The Pavement, but in Hebrew, Gabbatha.

14 Now it was the day of preparation for the Passover; it was about the sixth hour. And he *said to the Jews, "Behold, your King!"

15 They therefore cried out, "Away with *Him*, away with *Him*, crucify Him!" Pilate *said to them, "Shall I crucify your King?" The chief priests answered, "We have no king but Caesar."

16 And so he then delivered Him up to them to be crucified.

17 They took Jesus therefore; and He went out, bearing His own cross, to the place called the Place of a Skull, which is called in Hebrew Golgotha;

18 where they crucified Him, and with Him two other men, one on either side, and Jesus in between.

19 And Pilate wrote an inscription also, and put it on the cross. And it was written, "JESUS THE NAZARENE, THE KING OF THE JEWS."

20 Therefore this inscription many of the Jews read, for the place where Jesus was crucified was near the city; and it was written in Hebrew, Latin, *and* in Greek.

21 And so the chief priests of the Jews were saying to Pilate, "Do not write, 'The King of the Jews'; but that He said, 'I am King of the Jews.'"

22 Pilate answered, "What I have written I have written."

23 The soldiers therefore, when they had crucified Jesus, took His outer garments and made four parts, a part to every soldier and *also* the tunic; now the tunic was seamless, woven in one piece.

24 They said therefore to one another, "Let us not tear it, but cast lots for it, *to decide* whose it shall be;" that the Scripture might be fulfilled, "THEY DIVIDED MY OUTER GARMENTS AMONG THEM, AND FOR MY CLOTHING THEY CAST LOTS."

25 Therefore the soldiers did these things. But there were standing by the cross of Jesus His mother, and His mother's sister, Mary the *wife* of Clopas, and Mary Magdalene.

26 When Jesus therefore saw His mother, and the disciple whom He loved standing nearby, He *said to His mother, "Woman, behold, your son!"

27 Then He *said to the disciple, "Behold, your mother!" And from that hour the disciple took her into his own *household*.

28 After this, Jesus, knowing that all things had already been accomplished, in order that the Scripture might be fulfilled, *said, "I am thirsty."

29 A jar full of sour wine was standing there; so they put a sponge full of the sour wine upon *a branch of* hyssop, and brought it up to His mouth.

30 When Jesus therefore had received the sour wine, He said, "It is finished!" And He bowed His head, and gave up His spirit.

31 The Jews therefore, because it was the day of preparation, so that the bodies should not remain on the cross on the Sabbath (for that Sabbath was a high *day*), asked Pilate that their legs might be broken, and *that* they might be taken away.

32 The soldiers therefore came, and broke the legs of the first man, and of the other man who was crucified with Him;

33 but coming to Jesus, when they saw that He was already dead, they did not break His legs;

34 but one of the soldiers pierced His side with a spear, and immediately there came out blood and water.

35 And he who has seen has borne witness, and his witness is true; and he knows that he is telling the truth, so that you also may believe.

36 For these things came to pass, that the Scripture might be fulfilled, "NOT A BONE OF HIM SHALL BE BROKEN."

37 And again another Scripture says, "THEY SHALL LOOK ON HIM WHOM THEY PIERCED."

38 And after these things Joseph of Arimathea, being a disciple of Jesus, but a secret *one*, for fear of the Jews, asked Pilate that he might take away the body of Jesus; and Pilate granted permission. He came therefore, and took away His body.

39 And Nicodemus came also, who had first come to Him by night; bringing a mixture of myrrh and aloes, about a hundred pounds *weight*.

40 And so they took the body of Jesus, and bound it in linen wrappings with the spices, as is the burial custom of the Jews.

41 Now in the place where He was crucified there was a garden; and in the garden a new tomb, in which no one had yet been laid.

42 Therefore on account of the Jewish day of preparation, because the tomb was nearby, they laid Jesus there.

CHAPTER 20

NOW on the first *day* of the week Mary Magdalene *came early to the tomb, while it *was still dark, and *saw the stone *already* taken away from the tomb.

2 And so she *ran and *came to Simon Peter, and to the other disciple whom Jesus loved, and *said to them, "They have taken away the Lord out of the tomb, and we do not know where they have laid Him."

3 Peter therefore went forth, and the other disciple, and they were going to the tomb.

4 And the two were running together; and the other disciple ran ahead faster than Peter, and came to the tomb first;

5 and stooping and looking in, he *saw the linen wrappings lying *there*; but he did not go in.

6 Simon Peter therefore also *came, following him, and entered the tomb; and he *beheld the linen wrappings lying *there*,

7 and the face-cloth, which had been on His head, not lying with the linen wrappings, but rolled up in a place by itself.

8 Then entered in therefore the other disciple also, who had first come to the tomb, and he saw, and believed.

9 For as yet they did not understand the Scripture, that He must rise again from the dead.

10 So the disciples went away again to their own homes.

11 But Mary was standing outside the tomb weeping; and so, as she wept, she stooped and looked into the tomb;

12 and she *beheld two angels in white sitting, one at the head, and one at the feet, where the body of Jesus had been lying.

13 And they *said to her, "Woman, why are you weeping?" She *said to them, "Because they have taken away my Lord, and I do not know where they have laid Him."

14 When she had said this, she turned around, and *beheld Jesus standing *there*, and did not know that it was Jesus.

15 Jesus *said to her, "Woman, why are you weeping? Whom are you seeking?" Supposing Him to be the gardener, she *said to Him, "Sir, if you have carried Him away, tell me where you have laid Him, and I will take Him away."

16 Jesus *said to her, "Mary!" She *turned and *said to Him in Hebrew, "Rabboni!" (which means, Teacher).

17 Jesus *said to her, "Stop clinging to Me; for I have not yet ascended to the Father; but go to My brethren, and say to them, 'I ascend to My Father and your Father, and My God and your God.'"

18 Mary Magdalene *came, announcing to the disciples, "I have seen the Lord," and *that He had said these things to her.

19 When therefore it was evening, on that day, the first *day of the week, and when the doors were shut where the disciples were, for fear of the Jews, Jesus came and stood in their midst, and *said to them, "Peace *be with you."

20 And when He had said this, He showed them both His hands and His side. The disciples therefore rejoiced when they saw the Lord.

21 Jesus therefore said to them again, "Peace *be with you; as the Father has sent Me, I also send you."

22 And when He had said this, He breathed on them, and *said to them, "Receive the Holy Spirit. (a)

Have you read Reference No. 3, Sec. 4, page 148, "What You Should Know About the Holy Spirit."?

(a) **The gift of the person of the Holy Spirit, His power and His purpose.**
The sequence of the gift of the person of the Holy Spirit and the clothing of the power of the Holy Spirit is very clear in the scriptures. Jesus made two definite promises concerning the Holy Spirit and accordingly made two provisions to fulfill them. The first brought peace synonymous with salvation; the second brought power which was for service.

Promise of the person of the Holy Spirit was given by Jesus in John 14:16, 17, page 146, when he said, "I will ask the Father and He will give you another helper, that He may be with you forever . . . You know Him because He abides with you, and will be in you." The Holy Spirit was to become resident in the believers. Jesus keeping His promise of John 14:16, 17, page 146.

Provided the gift of the person of the Holy Spirit in John 20:21, 22, page 156, on the night of the resurrection. There Jesus said, "Peace be with you . . . when He had

(Continued on next page.)

23 "If you forgive the sins of any, *their sins* have been forgiven them; if you retain the *sins* of any, they have been retained."

24 But Thomas, one of the twelve, called Didymus, was not with them when Jesus came.

25 The other disciples therefore were saying to him, "We have seen the Lord!" But he said to them, "Unless I shall see in His hands the imprint of the nails, and put my finger into the place of the nails, and put my hand into His side, I will not believe."

26 And after eight days again His disciples were inside, and Thomas with them. Jesus *came, the doors having been shut, and stood in their midst, and said, "Peace *be* with you."

27 Then He *said to Thomas, "Reach here your finger, and see My hands; and reach here your hand, and put it into My side; and be not unbelieving, but believing."

28 Thomas answered and said to Him, "My Lord and my God!"

29 Jesus *said to him, "Because you have seen Me, have you believed? Blessed *are* they who did not see, and *yet* believed."

30 Many other signs therefore Jesus also performed in the presence of the disciples, which are not written in this book;

31 but these have been written that you may believe that Jesus is the Christ, the Son of God; and that believing you may have life in His name.

CHAPTER 21

AFTER these things Jesus manifested Himself again to the disciples

---

(Continued from page 156.)

said this, He breathed on them, and said to them, 'receive the Holy Spirit'." They received the Holy Spirit and He became resident. It is similar today for He is received by a believer "hearing with faith," Gal. 3:2, page 258, and dwells in your body which "is a temple of the Holy Spirit," (I Cor. 6:19) page 232. To the disciples in whom the Holy Spirit was resident Jesus

Promised the power of the Holy Spirit almost seven weeks after He became resident in the disciples. At the scene of His ascension He said in Luke 24:49, page 122, "and behold I am sending forth the promise of My Father upon you; but you are to stay in the City until you are clothed with power from on High." This is the same promise recorded in Acts 1:8, page 159, "You shall receive power when the Holy Spirit has come upon you," which likewise was made at the time of the ascension.

Provided the Power. Jesus as He had promised sent forth the power of the Holy Spirit on the day of Pentecost. The record is given in Acts 2:3, 4, page 161. The Holy Spirit sat on or, "rested on each of them and they were all filled with the Holy Spirit and began to speak with other tongues, as the Spirit was giving them utterance." This glorious power to those who possessed the Holy Spirit was given for the

Purpose of communicating the gospel and glorifying Christ Jesus. The hearers said "We hear them in our own tongues speaking of the mighty deed of God," Acts 2:11, page 161. Jesus said, "He shall glorify Me, for He shall take of mine, and shall disclose it to you." "So then tongues are for a sign, not to those who believe, but to unbelievers" I Cor. 14:22, page 241. The public display of the power of the Holy Spirit is to communicate the gospel of Jesus Christ, and not to work confusion. "For God is not a God of confusion but of peace," I Cor. 14:33, page 241. Therefore "let all things be done properly and in an orderly manner," I Cor. 14:40, page 242.

Let it be known that if the power confuses it is counterfeit. To be of God the power must communicate Christ and glorify Him so His divine purpose may be accomplished.

at the sea of Tiberias; and He manifested *Himself* in this way.

2 There were together Simon Peter, and Thomas called Didymus, and Nathanael of Cana in Galilee, and the *sons* of Zebedee, and two others of His disciples.

3 Simon Peter *said to them, "I am going fishing." They *said to him, "We will also come with you." They went out, and got into the boat; and that night they caught nothing.

4 But when the day was now breaking, Jesus stood on the beach; yet the disciples did not know that it was Jesus.

5 Jesus therefore *said to them, "Children, you do not have any fish, do you?" They answered Him, "No."

6 And He said to them, "Cast the net on the right-hand side of the boat, and you will find *a catch.*" They cast therefore, and then they were not able to haul it in because of the great number of fish.

7 That disciple therefore whom Jesus loved *said to Peter, "It is the Lord." And so when Simon Peter heard that it was the Lord, he put his outer garment on (for he was stripped *for work*), and threw himself into the sea.

8 But the other disciples came in the little boat, for they were not far from the land, but about one hundred yards away, dragging the net *full of* fish.

9 And so when they got out upon the land, they *saw a charcoal fire *already* laid, and fish placed on it, and bread.

10 Jesus *said to them, "Bring some of the fish which you have now caught."

11 Simon Peter went up, and drew the net to land, full of large fish, a hundred and fifty-three; and although there were so many, the net was not torn.

12 Jesus *said to them, "Come

and have breakfast." None of the disciples ventured to question Him, "Who are You?" knowing that it was the Lord.

13 Jesus *came and *took the bread, and *gave them, and the fish likewise.

14 This is now the third time that Jesus was manifested to the disciples, after He was raised from the dead.

15 So when they had finished breakfast, Jesus *said to Simon Peter, "Simon, *son* of John, do you love Me more than these?" He *said to Him, "Yes, Lord; You know that I love You." He *said to him, "Tend My lambs."

16 He *said to him again a second time, "Simon, *son* of John, do you love Me?" He *said to Him, "Yes, Lord; You know that I love You." He *said to him, "Shepherd My sheep."

17 He *said to him the third time, "Simon, *son* of John, do you love Me?" Peter was grieved because He said to him the third time, "Do you love Me?" And he said to Him, "Lord, You know all things; You know that I love You." Jesus *said to him, "Tend My sheep.

18 "Truly, truly, I say to you, when you were younger, you used to gird yourself, and walk wherever you wished; but when you grow old, you will stretch out your hands, and someone else will gird you, and bring you where you do not wish to *go.*"

19 Now this He said, signifying by what kind of death he would glorify God. And when He had spoken this, He *said to him, "Follow Me!"

20 Peter, turning around, *saw the disciple whom Jesus loved following *them*; the one who also had leaned back on His breast at the supper, and said, "Lord, who is the one who betrays You?"

21 Peter therefore seeing him *said to Jesus, "Lord, and what about this man?"

22 Jesus *said to him, "If I want him to remain until I come, what *is that* to you? You follow Me!"

23 This saying therefore went out among the brethren that that disciple would not die; yet Jesus did not say to him that he would not die, but *only*, "If I want him to remain until I come, what *is that* to you?"

24 This is the disciple who bears witness of these things, and wrote these things; and we know that his witness is true.

25 And there are also many other things which Jesus did, which if they *were written in detail, I suppose that even the world itself *would not contain the books which *were written.

THE ACTS

OF THE APOSTLES

THE first account I composed, Theophilus, about all that Jesus began to do and teach,

2 until the day when He was taken up, after He had by the Holy Spirit given orders to the apostles whom He had chosen.

3 To these He also presented Himself alive, after His suffering, by many convincing proofs, appearing to them over *a period of* forty days, and speaking of the things concerning the kingdom of God.

4 And gathering them together, He commanded them not to leave Jerusalem, but to wait for what the Father had promised, "Which," *He said,* "you heard of from Me;

5 for John baptized with water,

but you shall be baptized with the Holy Spirit not many days from now."

6 And so when they had come together, they were asking Him, saying, "Lord, is it at this time You are restoring the kingdom to Israel?"

7 He said to them, "It is not for you to know times or epochs which the Father has fixed by His own authority;

SCRIPTURE NO. 4, SEC. 2

8 but you shall receive power when the Holy Spirit has come upon you; and you shall be My witnesses both in Jerusalem, and in all Judea and Samaria, and even to the remotest part of the earth." (r4)

(r4) REFERENCE NO. 4, SEC. 2—
WITNESSING FOR CHRIST SHOWS SALVATION.
"You shall be My witnesses"

These are among the last audible words of Jesus on earth. It is His commission to all who know and love Him.

As a believer you are God's "workmanship, created in Christ Jesus for good works." When you witness for Christ "it is God who is at work in you." "By the power of the Holy Spirit," you give forth "God's Message": "that Christ died for our sins . . . was buried, and that He was raised on the third day according to the Scriptures." And

(Turn to next page.)

9 And after He had said these things, He was lifted up while they were looking on, and a cloud received Him out of their sight.

10 And as they were gazing intently into the sky while He was departing, behold, two men in white clothing stood beside them;

11 and they also said, "Men of Galilee, why do you stand looking into the sky? This Jesus, who has been taken up from you into heaven, will come in just the same way as you have watched Him go into heaven."

12 Then they returned to Jerusalem from the mount called Olivet, which is near Jerusalem, a Sabbath day's journey away.

13 And when they had entered, they went up to the upper room, where they were staying; that is, Peter and John and James and Andrew, Philip and Thomas, Bartholomew and Matthew, James *the son* of Alphaeus, and Simon the Zealot, and Judas *the son* of James.

14 These all with one mind were continually devoting themselves to prayer, along with *the* women, and Mary the mother of Jesus, and with His brothers.

15 And at this time Peter stood up in the midst of the brethren (a gathering of about one hundred and twenty persons was there together), and said,

16 "Brethren, the Scripture had to be fulfilled, which the Holy Spirit foretold by the mouth of David concerning Judas, who became a guide to those who arrested Jesus.

17 "For he was counted among us, and received his portion in this ministry."

18 (Now this man acquired a field with the price of his wickedness; and falling headlong, he burst open in the middle and all his bowels gushed out.

19 And it became known to all who were living in Jerusalem; so that

---

(Continued from page 159.)

"that through His name everyone who believes in Him has received forgiveness of sins."

As you obey the Lord "you should go and bear fruit," for He "is able to do exceeding abundantly beyond all that we ask or think, according to the power that works within us."

Begin witnessing like Andrew who "found first his own brother Simon . . . and he brought him to Jesus."

Go obediently like Philip whom God told to "arise and go" and "he arose and went." He met an unsaved man from Ethiopia. He "opened his mouth, and . . . preached Jesus to him."

"And this gospel of the Kingdom shall be preached in the whole world for a witness to all nations."

Do you see you are to witness and the Holy Spirit is the source of your power to tell others of Jesus? If so, say:

"I will obey Christ's command to witness depending on power by the Holy Spirit."

As God directs you, begin your ministry for maturity (page xiii and page 370).

ASSIGNMENT TO WITNESS. Now take your Soul Winner's New Testament to the unsaved person to whom God leads you. Read with him the scriptures and six references beginning on page 186, Acts 16:30–34. Invite the one to whom you witness to be your guest in church or a gospel meeting. Pray that he will confess Christ publicly, be baptized, and serve God giving Him "glory in the church." Your witness is not complete until the one you win becomes a witness for Christ.

in their own language that field was called Hakeldama, that is, Field of Blood).

20 "For it is written in the book of Psalms,

'LET HIS HOMESTEAD BE MADE
    DESOLATE,
AND LET NO MAN DWELL IN IT';
and,
'HIS OFFICE LET ANOTHER MAN
    TAKE.'

21 "It is therefore necessary that of the men who have accompanied us all the time that the Lord Jesus went in and out among us—

22 beginning with the baptism of John, until the day that He was taken up from us—one of these should become a witness with us of His resurrection."

23 And they put forward two men, Joseph called Barsabbas (who was also called Justus), and Matthias.

24 And they prayed, and said, "Thou, Lord, who knowest the hearts of all men, show which one of these two Thou hast chosen

25 to occupy this ministry and apostleship from which Judas turned aside to go to his own place."

26 And they drew lots for them, and the lot fell to Matthias; and he was numbered with the eleven apostles.

CHAPTER 2

AND when the day of Pentecost had come, they were all together in one place.

2 And suddenly there came from heaven a noise like a violent, rushing wind, and it filled the whole house where they were sitting.

3 And there appeared to them tongues as of fire distributing themselves, and they rested on each one of them.

4 And they were all filled with the Holy Spirit and began to speak with other tongues, as the Spirit was giving them utterance.

5 Now there were Jews living in Jerusalem, devout men, from every nation under heaven.

6 And when this sound occurred, the multitude came together, and were bewildered, because they were each one hearing them speak in his own language.

7 And they were amazed and marveled, saying, "Why, are not all these who are speaking Galileans?

8 "And how is it that we each hear *them* in our own language to which we were born?

9 "Parthians and Medes and Elamites, and residents of Mesopotamia, Judea and Cappadocia, Pontus and Asia,

10 Phrygia and Pamphylia, Egypt and the districts of Libya around Cyrene, and visitors from Rome, both Jews and proselytes,

11 Cretans and Arabs—we hear them in our *own* tongues speaking of the mighty deeds of God."

12 And they continued in amazement and great perplexity, saying to one another, "What does this mean?"

13 But others were mocking and saying, "They are full of sweet wine."

14 But Peter, taking his stand with the eleven, raised his voice and declared to them: "Men of Judea, and all you who live in Jerusalem, let this be known to you, and give heed to my words.

15 "For these men are not drunk, as you suppose, for it is *only* the third hour of the day;

16 but this is what was spoken of through the prophet Joel:

17   'AND IT SHALL BE IN THE LAST
        DAYS,' GOD SAYS,
        'THAT I WILL POUR FORTH OF
        MY SPIRIT UPON ALL MAN-
        KIND;

AND YOUR SONS AND YOUR DAUGHTERS SHALL PROPHESY,

AND YOUR YOUNG MEN SHALL SEE VISIONS,

AND YOUR OLD MEN SHALL DREAM DREAMS;

18 EVEN UPON MY BONDSLAVES, BOTH MEN AND WOMEN,

I WILL IN THOSE DAYS POUR FORTH OF MY SPIRIT

And they shall prophesy.

19 'AND I WILL GRANT WONDERS IN THE SKY ABOVE,

AND SIGNS ON THE EARTH BENEATH,

BLOOD, AND FIRE, AND VAPOR OF SMOKE.

20 'THE SUN SHALL BE TURNED INTO DARKNESS,

AND THE MOON INTO BLOOD, BEFORE THE GREAT AND GLORIOUS DAY OF THE LORD SHALL COME.

21 'AND IT SHALL BE, THAT EVERY ONE WHO CALLS ON THE NAME OF THE LORD SHALL BE SAVED.'

22 "Men of Israel, listen to these words: Jesus the Nazarene, a man attested to you by God with miracles and wonders and signs which God performed through Him in your midst, just as you yourselves know—

23 this *Man*, delivered up by the predetermined plan and foreknowledge of God, you nailed to a cross by the hands of godless men and put *Him* to death.

24 "And God raised Him up again, putting an end to the agony of death, since it was impossible for Him to be held in its power.

25 "For David says of Him,

'I WAS ALWAYS BEHOLDING THE LORD IN MY PRESENCE;

FOR HE IS AT MY RIGHT HAND, THAT I MAY NOT BE SHAKEN.

26 'THEREFORE MY HEART WAS GLAD AND MY TONGUE EXULTED;

MOREOVER MY FLESH ALSO WILL ABIDE IN HOPE;

27 BECAUSE THOU WILT NOT ABANDON MY SOUL TO HADES, NOR ALLOW THY HOLY ONE TO UNDERGO DECAY.

28 'THOU HAST MADE KNOWN TO ME THE WAYS OF LIFE;

THOU WILT MAKE ME FULL OF GLADNESS WITH THY PRESENCE.'

29 "Brethren, I may confidently say to you regarding the patriarch David that he both died and was buried, and his tomb is with us to this day.

30 "And so, because he was a prophet, and knew that God had sworn to him with an oath to seat *one* of his descendants upon his throne,

31 he looked ahead and spoke of the resurrection of the Christ, that He was neither abandoned to Hades, nor did His flesh suffer decay.

32 "This Jesus God raised up again, to which we are all witnesses.

33 "Therefore having been exalted to the right hand of God, and having received from the Father the promise of the Holy Spirit, He has poured forth this which you both see and hear.

34 "For it was not David who ascended into heaven, but he himself says:

'THE LORD SAID TO MY LORD, "SIT AT MY RIGHT HAND,

35 UNTIL I MAKE THINE ENEMIES A FOOTSTOOL FOR THY FEET." '

36 "Therefore let all the house of Israel know for certain that God has made Him both Lord and Christ— this Jesus whom you crucified."

37 Now when they heard *this*, they were pierced to the heart, and said to Peter and the rest of the apostles, "Brethren, what shall we do?"

38 And Peter *said* to them, "Repent, and let each of you be baptized in the name of Jesus Christ for the forgiveness of your sins; and you shall receive the gift of the Holy Spirit.

39 "For the promise is for you and your children, and for all who are far off, as many as the Lord our God shall call to Himself."

40 And with many other words he solemnly testified and kept on exhorting them, saying, "Be saved from this perverse generation!"

41 So then, those who had received his word were baptized; and there were added that day about three thousand souls.

42 And they were continually devoting themselves to the apostles' teaching and to fellowship, to the breaking of bread and to prayer.

43 And everyone kept feeling a sense of awe; and many wonders and signs were taking place through the apostles.

44 And all those who had believed were together, and had all things in common;

45 and they *began* selling their property and possessions, and were sharing them with all, as anyone might have need.

46 And day by day continuing with one mind in the temple, and breaking bread from house to house, they were taking their meals together with gladness and sincerity of heart,

47 praising God, and having favor with all the people. And the Lord was adding to their number day by day those who were being saved.

CHAPTER 3

NOW Peter and John were going up to the temple at the ninth *hour,* the hour of prayer.

2 And a certain man who had been lame from his mother's womb was being carried along, whom they used to set down every day at the gate of the temple which is called Beautiful, in order to beg alms of those who were entering the temple.

3 And when he saw Peter and John about to go into the temple, he *began* asking to receive alms.

4 And Peter, along with John, fixed his gaze upon him and said, "Look at us!"

5 And he *began* to give them his attention, expecting to receive something from them.

6 But Peter said, "I do not possess silver and gold, but what I do have I give to you: In the name of Jesus Christ the Nazarene—walk!"

7 And seizing him by the right hand, he raised him up; and immediately his feet and his ankles were strengthened.

8 And with a leap, he stood upright and *began* to walk; and he entered the temple with them, walking and leaping and praising God.

9 And all the people saw him walking and praising God;

10 and they were taking note of him as being the one who used to sit at the Beautiful Gate of the temple to *beg* alms, and they were filled with wonder and amazement at what had happened to him.

11 And while he was clinging to Peter and John, all the people ran together to them at the so-called portico of Solomon, full of amazement.

12 But when Peter saw *this,* he replied to the people, "Men of Israel, why do you marvel at this, or why do you gaze at us, as if by our own power or piety we had made him walk?

13 "The God of Abraham, Isaac, and Jacob, the God of our fathers, has glorified His Servant Jesus, *the one* whom you delivered up, and disowned in the presence of Pilate, when he had decided to release Him.

14 "But you disowned the Holy and Righteous One, and asked for a murderer to be granted to you,

15 but put to death the Prince of life, *the one* whom God raised from the dead,—*a fact* to which we are witnesses.

16 "And on the basis of faith in His name, *it is* the name of Jesus which has strengthened this man whom you see and know; and the faith which *comes* through Him has given him this perfect health in the presence of you all.

17 "And now, brethren, I know that you acted in ignorance, just as your rulers did also.

18 "But the things which God announced beforehand by the mouth of all the prophets, that His Christ should suffer, He has thus fulfilled.

19 "Repent therefore and return, that your sins may be wiped away, in order that times of refreshing may come from the presence of the Lord;

20 and that He may send Jesus, the Christ appointed for you,

21 whom heaven must receive until *the* period of restoration of all things about which God spoke by the mouth of His holy prophets from ancient time.

22 "Moses said, 'THE LORD GOD SHALL RAISE UP FOR YOU A PROPHET LIKE ME FROM YOUR BRETHREN; TO HIM YOU SHALL GIVE HEED IN EVERYTHING HE SAYS TO YOU.

23 'AND IT SHALL BE THAT EVERY SOUL THAT DOES NOT HEED THAT PROPHET SHALL BE UTTERLY DE-STROYED FROM AMONG THE PEOPLE.'

24 "And likewise, all the prophets who have spoken, from Samuel and *his* successors onward, also announced these days.

25 "It is you who are the sons of the prophets, and of the covenant which God made with your fathers, saying to Abraham, 'AND IN YOUR SEED ALL THE FAMILIES OF THE EARTH SHALL BE BLESSED.'

26 "For you first, God raised up His Servant, and sent Him to bless you by

turning every one *of you* from your wicked ways."

CHAPTER 4

AND as they were speaking to the people, the priests and the captain of the temple *guard*, and the Sadducees, came upon them,

2 being greatly disturbed because they were teaching the people and proclaiming in Jesus the resurrection from the dead.

3 And they laid hands on them, and put them in jail until the next day, for it was already evening.

4 But many of those who had heard the message believed; and the number of the men came to be about five thousand.

5 And it came about on the next day, that their rulers and elders and scribes were gathered together in Jerusalem;

6 and Annas the high priest *was there*, and Caiaphas and John and Alexander, and all who were of high-priestly descent.

7 And when they had placed them in the center, they *began to* inquire, "By what power, or in what name, have you done this?"

8 Then Peter, filled with the Holy Spirit, said to them, "Rulers and elders of the people,

9 if we are on trial today for a benefit done to a sick man, as to how this man has been made well,

10 let it be known to all of you, and to all the people of Israel, that by the name of Jesus Christ the Nazarene, whom you crucified, whom God raised from the dead,—by this *name* this man stands here before you in good health.

11 "He is the STONE WHICH WAS RE-JECTED by you, THE BUILDERS, *but* WHICH BECAME THE VERY CORNER *stone*.

12 "And there is salvation in no one else; for there is no other name under heaven that has been given among men, by which we must be saved."

13 Now as they observed the confidence of Peter and John, and understood that they were uneducated and untrained men, they were marveling, and *began* to recognize them as having been with Jesus.

14 And seeing the man who had been healed standing with them, they had nothing to say in reply.

15 But when they had ordered them to go aside out of the Council, they *began* to confer with one another,

16 saying, "What shall we do with these men? For the fact that a noteworthy miracle has taken place through them is apparent to all who live in Jerusalem, and we cannot deny it.

17 "But in order that it may not spread any further among the people, let us warn them to speak no more to any man in this name."

18 And when they had summoned them, they commanded them not to speak or teach at all in the name of Jesus.

19 But Peter and John answered and said to them, "Whether it is right in the sight of God to give heed to you rather than to God, you be the judge;

20 for we cannot stop speaking what we have seen and heard."

21 And when they had threatened them further, they let them go (finding no basis on which they might punish them) on account of the people, because they were all glorifying God for what had happened;

22 for the man was more than forty years old on whom this miracle of healing had been performed.

23 And when they had been released, they went to their own *companions*, and reported all that the chief priests and the elders had said to them.

24 And when they heard *this*, they lifted their voices to God with one accord and said, "O Lord, it is Thou who DIDST MAKE THE HEAVEN AND THE EARTH AND THE SEA, AND ALL THAT IS IN THEM,

25 who by the Holy Spirit, *through* the mouth of our father David Thy servant, didst say,

'WHY DID THE GENTILES RAGE,
AND THE PEOPLES DEVISE FUTILE THINGS?

26 'THE KINGS OF THE EARTH TOOK THEIR STAND,
AND THE RULERS WERE GATHERED TOGETHER
AGAINST THE LORD, AND AGAINST HIS CHRIST.'

27 "For truly in this city there were gathered together against Thy holy Servant Jesus, whom Thou didst anoint, both Herod and Pontius Pilate, along with the Gentiles and the peoples of Israel,

28 to do whatever Thy hand and Thy purpose predestined to occur.

29 "And now, Lord, take note of their threats, and grant that Thy bond-servants may speak Thy word with all confidence,

30 while Thou dost extend Thy hand to heal, and signs and wonders take place through the name of Thy holy Servant Jesus."

31 And when they had prayed, the place where they had gathered together was shaken, and they were all filled with the Holy Spirit, and *began* to speak the word of God with boldness.

32 And the congregation of those who believed were of one heart and soul; and not one *of them* claimed that anything belonging to him was his own; but all things were common property to them.

33 And with great power the apostles were giving witness to the resur-

rection of the Lord Jesus, and abundant grace was upon them all.

34 For there was not a needy person among them, for all who were owners of land or houses would sell them and bring the proceeds of the sales,

35 and lay them at the apostles' feet; and they would be distributed to each, as any had need.

36 And Joseph, a Levite of Cyprian birth, who was also called Barnabas by the apostles (which translated means, Son of Encouragement),

37 and who owned a tract of land, sold it and brought the money and laid it at the apostles' feet.

BUT a certain man named Ananias, with his wife Sapphira, sold a piece of property,

2 and kept back *some* of the price for himself, with his wife's full knowledge, and bringing a portion of it, he laid it at the apostles' feet.

3 But Peter said, "Ananias, why has Satan filled your heart to lie to the Holy Spirit, and to keep back *some* of the price of the land?

4 "While it remained *unsold*, did it not remain your own? And after it was sold, was it not under your control? Why is it that you have conceived this deed in your heart? You have not lied to men, but to God."

5 And as he heard these words, Ananias fell down and breathed his last; and great fear came upon all who heard of it.

6 And the young men arose and covered him up, and after carrying him out, they buried him.

7 Now there elapsed an interval of about three hours, and his wife came in, not knowing what had happened.

8 And Peter responded to her, "Tell me whether you sold the land for such and such a price?" And she said, "Yes, that was the price."

9 Then Peter *said* to her, "Why is it that you have agreed together to put the Spirit of the Lord to the test? Behold, the feet of those who have buried your husband are at the door, and they shall carry you out *as well*."

10 And she fell immediately at his feet, and breathed her last; and the young men came in and found her dead, and they carried her out and buried her beside her husband.

11 And great fear came upon the whole church, and upon all who heard of these things.

12 And at the hands of the apostles many signs and wonders were taking place among the people; and they were all with one accord in Solomon's portico.

13 But none of the rest dared to associate with them; however, the people held them in high esteem.

14 And all the more believers in the Lord, multitudes of men and women, were constantly added to *their number;*

15 to such an extent that they even carried the sick out into the streets, and laid them on cots and pallets, so that when Peter came by, at least his shadow might fall on any one of them.

16 And also the people from the cities in the vicinity of Jerusalem were coming together, bringing people who were sick or afflicted with unclean spirits; and they were all being healed.

17 But the high priest rose up, along with all his associates (that is the sect of the Sadducees), and they were filled with jealousy;

18 and they laid hands on the apostles, and put them in a public jail.

19 But an angel of the Lord during the night opened the gates of the prison, and taking them out he said,

20 "Go your way, stand and speak

to the people in the temple the whole message of this Life."

21 And upon hearing *this*, they entered into the temple about daybreak, and *began* to teach. Now when the high priest and his associates had come, they called the Council together, even all the Senate of the sons of Israel, and sent *orders* to the prison house for them to be brought.

22 But the officers who came did not find them in the prison; and they returned, and reported back,

23 saying, "We found the prison house locked quite securely and the guards standing at the doors; but when we had opened up, we found no one inside."

24 Now when the captain of the temple *guard* and the chief priests heard these words, they were greatly perplexed about them as to what would come of this.

25 But someone came and reported to them, "Behold, the men whom you put in prison are standing in the temple and teaching the people!"

26 Then the captain went along with the officers and *proceeded* to bring them *back* without violence; (for they were afraid of the people, lest they should be stoned).

27 And when they had brought them, they stood them before the Council. And the high priest questioned them,

28 saying, "We gave you strict orders not to continue teaching in this name, and behold, you have filled Jerusalem with your teaching, and intend to bring this man's blood upon us."

29 But Peter and the apostles answered and said, "We must obey God rather than men.

30 "The God of our fathers raised up Jesus, whom you had put to death by hanging Him on a cross.

31 "He is the one whom God exalted to His right hand as a Prince and

a Savior, to grant repentance to Israel, and forgiveness of sins.

32 "And we are witnesses of these things; and *so is* the Holy Spirit, whom God has given to those who obey Him."

33 But when they heard this, they were cut to the quick and were intending to slay them.

34 But a certain Pharisee named Gamaliel, a teacher of the Law, respected by all the people, stood up in the Council and gave orders to put the men outside for a short time.

35 And he said to them, "Men of Israel, take care what you propose to do with these men.

36 "For sometime ago Theudas rose up, claiming to be somebody; and a group of about four hundred men joined up with him. And he was slain; and all who followed him were dispersed and came to nothing.

37 "After this man Judas of Galilee rose up in the days of the census, and drew away *some* people after him, he too perished, and all those who followed him were scattered.

38 "And so in the present case, I say to you, stay away from these men and let them alone, for if this plan or action should be of men, it will be overthrown;

39 but if it is of God, you will not be able to overthrow them; or else you may even be found fighting against God."

40 And they took his advice; and after calling the apostles in, they flogged them and ordered them to speak no more in the name of Jesus, and *then* released them.

41 So they went on their way from the presence of the Council, rejoicing that they had been considered worthy to suffer shame for *His* name.

42 And every day, in the temple and from house to house, they kept right on teaching and preaching Jesus *as* the Christ.

CHAPTER 6

NOW at this time while the disciples were increasing *in number,* a complaint arose on the part of the Hellenistic *Jews* against the *native* Hebrews, because their widows were being overlooked in the daily serving *of food.*

2 And the twelve summoned the congregation of the disciples and said, "It is not desirable for us to neglect the word of God in order to serve tables.

3 "But select from among you, brethren, seven men of good reputation, full of the Spirit and of wisdom, whom we may put in charge of this task.

4 "But we will devote ourselves to prayer, and to the ministry of the word."

5 And the statement found approval with the whole congregation; and they chose Stephen, a man full of faith and of the Holy Spirit, and Philip, Prochorus, Nicanor, Timon, Parmenas and Nicolas, a proselyte from Antioch.

6 And these they brought before the apostles; and after praying, they laid their hands on them.

7 And the word of God kept on spreading; and the number of the disciples continued to increase greatly in Jerusalem, and a great many of the priests were becoming obedient to the faith.

8 And Stephen, full of grace and power, was performing great wonders and signs among the people.

9 But some men from what was called the Synagogue of the Freedmen, *including* both Cyrenians and Alexandrians, and some from Cilicia and Asia, rose up and argued with Stephen.

10 And *yet* they were unable to cope with the wisdom and the Spirit with which he was speaking.

11 Then they secretly induced men to say, "We have heard him speak blasphemous words against Moses and *against* God."

12 And they stirred up the people, the elders and the scribes, and they came upon him and dragged him away, and brought him before the Council.

13 And they put forward false witnesses who said, "This man incessantly speaks against this holy place, and the Law;

14 for we have heard him say that this Nazarene, Jesus, will destroy this place and alter the customs which Moses handed down to us."

15 And fixing their gaze on him, all who were sitting in the Council saw his face like the face of an angel.

CHAPTER 7

AND the high priest said, "Are these things so?"

2 And he said, "Hear me, brethren and fathers! The God of glory appeared to our father Abraham when he was in Mesopotamia, before he lived in Haran,

3 AND SAID TO HIM, 'DEPART FROM YOUR COUNTRY AND YOUR RELATIVES, AND COME INTO THE LAND THAT I WILL SHOW YOU.'

4 "Then he departed from the land of the Chaldeans, and settled in Haran. And from there, after his father died, God removed him into this country in which you are now living.

5 "And He gave him no inheritance in it, not even a foot of ground; and *yet,* even when he had no child, He promised that HE WOULD GIVE IT TO HIM AS A POSSESSION, AND TO HIS OFFSPRING AFTER HIM.

6 "But God spoke to this effect, that HIS OFFSPRING WOULD BE ALIENS IN A FOREIGN LAND, AND THAT THEY WOULD BE ENSLAVED AND MISTREATED FOR FOUR HUNDRED YEARS.

7 " 'AND WHATEVER NATION TO WHICH THEY SHALL BE IN BONDAGE I

MYSELF WILL JUDGE,' said God, 'AND AFTER THAT THEY WILL COME OUT AND SERVE ME IN THIS PLACE.'

8 "And He gave him the covenant of circumcision; and so *Abraham* became the father of Isaac, and circumcised him on the eighth day; and Isaac *became the father of* Jacob, and Jacob *of* the twelve patriarchs.

9 "And the patriarchs BECAME JEALOUS OF JOSEPH AND SOLD HIM INTO EGYPT. And *yet* God WAS WITH HIM,

10 and rescued him from all his afflictions, and GRANTED HIM FAVOR and wisdom IN THE SIGHT OF PHARAOH, KING OF EGYPT; AND HE MADE HIM GOVERNOR OVER EGYPT AND ALL HIS HOUSEHOLD.

11 "Now A FAMINE CAME OVER ALL EGYPT AND CANAAN, and great affliction *with it*; and our fathers could find no food.

12 "But WHEN JACOB HEARD THAT THERE WAS GRAIN IN EGYPT, he sent our fathers *there* the first time.

13 "And on the second *visit* Joseph made himself known to his brothers, and Joseph's family was disclosed to Pharaoh.

14 "And Joseph sent *word* and invited Jacob his father and all his relatives to come to him, seventy-five persons *in all*.

15 "And Jacob WENT DOWN TO EGYPT AND *there* PASSED AWAY, he and our fathers.

16 "And *from there* they were removed to Shechem, and laid in the tomb which Abraham had purchased for a sum of money from the sons of Hamor in Shechem.

17 "But as the time of the promise was approaching which God had assured to Abraham, the people increased and multiplied in Egypt,

18 until THERE AROSE ANOTHER KING OVER EGYPT WHO KNEW NOTHING ABOUT JOSEPH.

19 "It was he who took shrewd advantage of our race, and mistreated our fathers so that they would expose their infants and they would not survive.

20 "And it was at this time that Moses was born; and he was lovely in the sight of God; and he was nurtured three months in his father's home.

21 "And after he had been exposed, Pharaoh's daughter took him away, and nurtured him as her own son.

22 "And Moses was educated in all the learning of the Egyptians, and he was a man of power in words and deeds.

23 "But when he was approaching the age of forty, it entered his mind to visit his brethren, the sons of Israel.

24 "And when he saw one *of them* being treated unjustly, he defended him and took vengeance for the oppressed by striking down the Egyptian.

25 "And he supposed that his brethren understood that God was granting them deliverance through him; but they did not understand.

26 "And on the following day he appeared to them as they were fighting together, and he tried to reconcile them in peace, saying, 'Men, you are brethren, why do you injure one another?'

27 "BUT THE ONE WHO WAS INJURING HIS NEIGHBOR pushed him away, saying, 'WHO MADE YOU A RULER AND JUDGE OVER US?

28 'YOU DO NOT MEAN TO KILL ME AS YOU KILLED THE EGYPTIAN YESTERDAY, DO YOU?'

29 "AND AT THIS REMARK MOSES FLED, AND BECAME AN ALIEN IN THE LAND OF MIDIAN, where he became the father of two sons.

30 "And after forty years had passed, AN ANGEL APPEARED TO HIM IN THE WILDERNESS OF MOUNT Sinai, IN THE FLAME OF A BURNING THORN BUSH.

31 "And when Moses saw it, he *began* to marvel at the sight; and as he

approached to look *more* closely, there came the voice of the Lord:

32 'I AM THE GOD OF YOUR FATHERS, THE GOD OF ABRAHAM AND ISAAC AND JACOB.' And Moses shook *with fear* and would not venture to look.

33 "BUT THE LORD SAID TO HIM, 'TAKE OFF THE SANDALS FROM YOUR FEET, FOR THE PLACE ON WHICH YOU ARE STANDING IS HOLY GROUND.

34 'I HAVE CERTAINLY SEEN THE OPPRESSION OF MY PEOPLE IN EGYPT, AND HAVE HEARD THEIR GROANS, AND I HAVE COME DOWN TO DELIVER THEM; COME NOW, AND I WILL SEND YOU TO EGYPT.'

35 "This Moses whom they disowned, saying, 'WHO MADE YOU A RULER AND A JUDGE?' is the one whom God sent *to be* both a ruler and a deliverer with the help of the angel who appeared to him in the thorn bush.

36 "This man led them out, performing wonders and signs in the land of Egypt and in the Red Sea and in the wilderness for forty years.

37 "This is the Moses who said to the sons of Israel, 'GOD SHALL RAISE UP FOR YOU A PROPHET LIKE ME FROM YOUR BRETHREN.'

38 "This is the one who was in the congregation in the wilderness together with the angel who was speaking to him in Mount Sinai, and *who was* with our fathers; and he received living oracles to pass on to you.

39 "And our fathers were unwilling to be obedient to him, but repudiated him and in their hearts turned back to Egypt,

40 SAYING TO AARON, 'MAKE FOR US GODS WHO WILL GO BEFORE US; FOR THIS MOSES WHO LED US OUT OF THE LAND OF EGYPT—WE DO NOT KNOW WHAT HAPPENED TO HIM.'

41 "And at that time they made a calf and brought a sacrifice to the idol, and were rejoicing in the works of their hands.

42 "But God turned away and delivered them up to serve the host of heaven; as it is written in the book of the prophets, 'IT WAS NOT TO ME THAT YOU OFFERED VICTIMS AND SACRIFICES FORTY YEARS IN THE WILDERNESS, WAS IT, O HOUSE OF ISRAEL?

43 'YOU ALSO TOOK ALONG THE TABERNACLE OF MOLOCH AND THE STAR OF THE GOD ROMPHA, THE IMAGES WHICH YOU MADE TO WORSHIP THEM. I ALSO WILL REMOVE YOU BEYOND BABYLON.'

44 "Our fathers had the tabernacle of testimony in the wilderness, just as He who spoke to Moses directed *him* to make it according to the pattern which he had seen.

45 "And having received it in their turn, our fathers brought it in with Joshua upon dispossessing the nations whom God drove out before our fathers, until the time of David.

46 "And *David* found favor in God's sight, and asked that he might find a dwelling place for the God of Jacob.

47 "But it was Solomon who built a house for Him.

48 "However, the Most High does not dwell in *houses* made by *human* hands; as the prophet says:

49   'HEAVEN IS MY THRONE,
        AND EARTH IS THE FOOTSTOOL
            OF MY FEET;
        WHAT KIND OF HOUSE WILL
            YOU BUILD FOR ME?' says the
            Lord;
        'OR WHAT PLACE IS THERE FOR
            MY REPOSE?

50   'WAS IT NOT MY HAND WHICH
            MADE ALL THESE THINGS?'

51 "You men who are stiff-necked and uncircumcised in heart and ears are always resisting the Holy Spirit; you are doing just as your fathers did.

52 "Which one of the prophets did your fathers not persecute? And they killed those who had previously announced the coming of the Righteous

One, whose betrayers and murderers you have now become;

53 you who received the law as ordained by angels, and *yet* did not keep it."

54 Now when they heard this, they were cut to the quick, and they *began* gnashing their teeth at him.

55 But being full of the Holy Spirit, he gazed intently into heaven and saw the glory of God, and Jesus standing at the right hand of God;

56 and he said, "Behold, I see the heavens opened up and the Son of Man standing at the right hand of God."

57 But they cried out with a loud voice, and covered their ears, and they rushed upon him with one impulse.

58 And when they had driven him out of the city, they *began* stoning *him*, and the witnesses laid aside their robes at the feet of a young man named Saul.

59 And they went on stoning Stephen as he called upon *the Lord* and said, "Lord Jesus, receive my spirit!"

60 And falling on his knees, he cried out with a loud voice, "Lord, do not hold this sin against them!" And having said this, he fell asleep.

CHAPTER 8

AND Saul was in hearty agreement with putting him to death.

And on that day a great persecution arose against the church in Jerusalem; and they were all scattered throughout the regions of Judea and Samaria, except the apostles.

2 And *some* devout men buried Stephen, and made loud lamentation over him.

3 But Saul *began* ravaging the church, entering house after house; and dragging off men and women, he would put them in prison.

4 Therefore, those who had been scattered went about preaching the word.

5 And Philip went down to the city of Samaria and *began* proclaiming Christ to them.

6 And the multitudes with one accord were giving attention to what was said by Philip, as they heard and saw the signs which he was performing.

7 For *in the case of* many who had unclean spirits, they were coming out *of them* shouting with a loud voice; and many who had been paralyzed and lame were healed.

8 And there was much rejoicing in that city.

9 Now there was a certain man named Simon, who formerly was practicing magic in the city, and astonishing the people of Samaria, claiming to be someone great;

10 and they all, from smallest to greatest, were giving attention to him, saying, "This man is what is called the Great Power of God."

11 And they were giving him attention because he had for a long time astonished them with his magic arts.

12 But when they believed Philip preaching the good news about the kingdom of God and the name of Jesus Christ, they were being baptized, men and women alike.

13 And even Simon himself believed; and after being baptized, he continued on with Philip; and as he observed signs and great miracles taking place, he was constantly amazed.

14 Now when the apostles in Jerusalem heard that Samaria had received the word of God, they sent them Peter and John,

15 who came down and prayed for them, that they might receive the Holy Spirit.

16 For He had not yet fallen upon any of them; they had simply been

baptized in the name of the Lord Jesus.

17 Then they *began* laying their hands on them, and they were receiving the Holy Spirit.

18 Now when Simon saw that the Spirit was bestowed through the laying on of the apostles' hands, he offered them money,

19 saying, "Give this authority to me as well, so that everyone on whom I lay my hands may receive the Holy Spirit."

20 But Peter said to him, "May your silver perish with you, because you thought you could obtain the gift of God with money!

21 "You have no part or portion in this matter, for your heart is not right before God.

22 "Therefore repent of this wickedness of yours, and pray the Lord that if possible, the intention of your heart may be forgiven you.

23 "For I see that you are in the gall of bitterness and in the bondage of iniquity."

24 But Simon answered and said, "Pray to the Lord for me yourselves, so that nothing of what you have said may come upon me."

25 And so, when they had solemnly testified and spoken the word of the Lord, they started back to Jerusalem, and were preaching the gospel to many villages of the Samaritans.

26 But an angel of the Lord spoke to Philip saying, "Arise and go south to the road that descends from Jerusalem to Gaza." (This is a desert *road.*)

27 And he arose and went; and behold, there was an Ethiopian eunuch, a court official of Candace, queen of the Ethiopians, who was in charge of all her treasure; and he had come to Jerusalem to worship.

28 And he was returning and sitting in his chariot, and was reading the prophet Isaiah.

29 And the Spirit said to Philip, "Go up and join this chariot."

30 And when Philip had run up, he heard him reading Isaiah the prophet, and said, "Do you understand what you are reading?"

31 And he said, "Well, how could I, unless someone guides me?" And he invited Philip to come up and sit with him.

32 Now the passage of Scripture which he was reading was this:

"HE WAS LED AS A SHEEP TO
   SLAUGHTER;
AND AS A LAMB BEFORE ITS
   SHEARER IS SILENT,
SO HE DOES NOT OPEN HIS
   MOUTH.

33 "IN HUMILIATION HIS JUDG-
   MENT WAS TAKEN AWAY;
WHO SHALL RELATE HIS GEN-
   ERATION?
FOR HIS LIFE IS REMOVED FROM
   THE EARTH."

34 And the eunuch answered Philip and said, "Please *tell me,* of whom does the prophet say this? Of himself, or of someone else?"

35 And Philip opened his mouth, and beginning from this Scripture he preached Jesus to him.

36 And as they went along the road they came to some water; and the eunuch *said, "Look! Water! What prevents me from being baptized?"

37 [*And Philip said, "If you believe with all your heart, you may." And he answered and said, "I believe that Jesus Christ is the son of God."*] (1)

38 And he ordered the chariot to stop; and they both went down into the water, Philip as well as the eunuch; and he baptized him.

39 And when they came up out of

---

(1) Late mss. insert verse 37.

the water, the Spirit of the Lord snatched Philip away; and the eunuch saw him no more, but went on his way rejoicing.

40 But Philip found himself at Azotus; and as he passed through he kept preaching the gospel to all the cities, until he came to Caesarea.

CHAPTER 9

NOW Saul, still breathing threats and murder against the disciples of the Lord, went to the high priest,

2 and asked for letters from him to the synagogues at Damascus, so that if he found any belonging to the Way, both men and women, he might bring them bound to Jerusalem.

3 And it came about that as he journeyed, he was approaching Damascus, and suddenly a light from heaven flashed around him;

4 and he fell to the ground, and heard a voice saying to him, "Saul, Saul, why are you persecuting Me?"

5 And he said, "Who art Thou, Lord?" And He *said*, "I am Jesus whom you are persecuting,

6 but rise, and enter the city, and it shall be told you what you must do."

7 And the men who traveled with him stood speechless, hearing the voice, but seeing no one.

8 And Saul got up from the ground, and though his eyes were open, he could see nothing; and leading him by the hand, they brought him into Damascus.

9 And he was three days without sight, and neither ate nor drank.

10 Now there was a certain disciple at Damascus, named Ananias; and the Lord said to him in a vision, "Ananias." And he said, "Behold, *here am* I, Lord."

11 And the Lord *said* to him, "Arise and go to the street called Straight, and inquire at the house of Judas for a man from Tarsus named Saul, for behold, he is praying,

12 and he has seen in a vision a man named Ananias come in and lay his hands on him, so that he might regain his sight."

13 But Ananias answered, "Lord, I have heard from many about this man, how much harm he did to Thy saints at Jerusalem;

14 and here he has authority from the chief priests to bind all who call upon Thy name."

15 But the Lord said to him, "Go, for he is a chosen instrument of Mine, to bear My name before the Gentiles and kings and the sons of Israel;

16 for I will show him how much he must suffer for My name's sake."

17 And Ananias departed and entered the house, and after laying his hands on him said, "Brother Saul, the Lord Jesus, who appeared to you on the road by which you were coming, has sent me so that you may regain your sight, and be filled with the Holy Spirit."

18 And immediately there fell from his eyes something like scales, and he regained his sight, and he arose and was baptized;

19 and he took food and was strengthened.

Now for several days he was with the disciples who were at Damascus,

20 and immediately he *began* to proclaim Jesus in the synagogues, saying, "He is the Son of God."

21 And all those hearing him continued to be amazed, and were saying, "Is this not he who in Jerusalem destroyed those who called on this name, and *who* had come here for the purpose of bringing them bound before the chief priests?"

22 But Saul kept increasing in strength and confounding the Jews who lived at Damascus by proving that this *Jesus* is the Christ.

23 And when many days had

elapsed, the Jews plotted together to do away with him,

24 but their plot became known to Saul. And they were also watching the gates day and night so that they might put him to death;

25 but his disciples took him by night, and let him down through *an opening in* the wall, lowering him in a basket.

26 And when he had come to Jerusalem, he was trying to associate with the disciples; and they were all afraid of him, not believing that he was a disciple.

27 But Barnabas took hold of him and brought him to the apostles and described to them how he had seen the Lord on the road, and that He had talked to him, and how at Damascus he had spoken out boldly in the name of Jesus.

28 And he was with them moving about freely in Jerusalem, speaking out boldly in the name of the Lord.

29 And he was talking and arguing with the Hellenistic *Jews*; but they were attempting to put him to death.

30 But when the brethren learned *of it*, they brought him down to Caesarea and sent him away to Tarsus.

31 So the church throughout all Judea and Galilee and Samaria enjoyed peace, being built up; and, going on in the fear of the Lord and in the comfort of the Holy Spirit, it continued to increase.

32 Now it came about that as Peter was traveling through all *those parts*, he came down also to the saints who lived at Lydda.

33 And there he found a certain man named Aeneas, who had been bedridden eight years, for he was paralyzed.

34 And Peter said to him, "Aeneas, Jesus Christ heals you; arise, and make your bed." And immediately he arose.

35 And all who lived at Lydda and Sharon saw him, and they turned to the Lord.

36 Now in Joppa there was a certain disciple named Tabitha (which translated *in Greek* is called Dorcas); this woman was abounding with deeds of kindness and charity, which she continually did.

37 And it came about at that time that she fell sick and died; and when they had washed her body, they laid it in an upper room.

38 And since Lydda was near Joppa, the disciples, having heard that Peter was there, sent two men to him, entreating him, "Do not delay to come to us."

39 And Peter arose and went with them. And when he had come, they brought him into the upper room; and all the widows stood beside him weeping, and showing all the tunics and garments that Dorcas used to make while she was with them.

40 But Peter sent them all out and knelt down and prayed, and turning to the body, he said, "Tabitha, arise." And she opened her eyes, and when she saw Peter, she sat up.

41 And he gave her his hand and raised her up; and calling the saints and widows, he presented her alive.

42 And it became known all over Joppa, and many believed in the Lord.

43 And it came about that he stayed many days in Joppa with a certain tanner, Simon.

Chapter 10

NOW *there was* a certain man at Caesarea named Cornelius, a centurion of what was called the Italian cohort,

2 a devout man, and one who feared God with all his household, and gave many alms to the *Jewish* people, and prayed to God continually.

3 About the ninth hour of the day he clearly saw in a vision an angel of God who had *just* come in to him, and said to him, "Cornelius!"

4 And fixing his gaze upon him and being much alarmed, he said, "What is it, Lord?" And he said to him, "Your prayers and alms have ascended as a memorial before God.

5 "And now dispatch *some* men to Joppa, and send for a man *named* Simon, who is also called Peter;

6 he is staying with a certain tanner *named* Simon, whose house is by the sea."

7 And when the angel who was speaking to him had departed, he summoned two of his servants and a devout soldier of those who were in constant attendance upon him,

8 and after he had explained everything to them, he sent them to Joppa.

9 And on the next day, as they were on their way, and approaching the city, Peter went up on the housetop about the sixth hour to pray.

10 And he became hungry, and was desiring to eat; but while they were making preparations, he fell into a trance;

11 and he *beheld the sky opened up, and a certain object like a great sheet coming down, lowered by four corners to the ground,

12 and there were in it all *kinds of* four-footed animals and crawling creatures of the earth and birds of the air.

13 And a voice came to him, "Arise, Peter, kill and eat!"

14 But Peter said, "By no means, Lord, for I have never eaten anything unholy and unclean."

15 And again a voice *came* to him a second time, "What God has cleansed, no *longer* consider unholy."

16 And this happened three times; and immediately the object was taken up into the sky.

17 Now while Peter was greatly perplexed in mind as to what the vision which he had seen might be, behold, the men who had been sent by Cornelius, having asked directions for Simon's house, appeared at the gate;

18 and calling out, they were asking whether Simon, who was also called Peter, was staying there.

19 And while Peter was reflecting on the vision, the Spirit said to him, "Behold, three men are looking for you.

20 "But arise, go downstairs, and accompany them without misgivings; for I have sent them Myself."

21 And Peter went down to the men and said, "Behold, I am the one you are looking for; what is the reason for which you have come?"

22 And they said, "Cornelius, a centurion, a righteous and God-fearing man well spoken of by the entire nation of the Jews, was *divinely* directed by a holy angel to send for you *to come* to his house and hear a message from you."

23 And so he invited them in and gave them lodging.

And on the next day he arose and went away with them, and some of the brethren from Joppa accompanied him.

24 And on the following day he entered Caesarea. Now Cornelius was waiting for them, and had called together his relatives and close friends.

25 And when it came about that Peter entered, Cornelius met him, and fell at his feet and worshiped *him.*

26 But Peter raised him up, saying, "Stand up; I too am *just* a man."

27 And as he talked with him, he entered, and found many people assembled.

28 And he said to them, "You yourselves know how unlawful it is for a man who is a Jew to associate with a foreigner or to visit him; and *yet* God has shown me that I should not call any man unholy or unclean.

29 "That is why I came without even raising any objection when I was sent for. And so I ask for what reason you have sent for me."

30 And Cornelius said, "Four days ago to this hour, I was praying in my house during the ninth hour; and behold, a man stood before me in shining garments,

31 and he *said, 'Cornelius, your prayer has been heard and your alms have been remembered before God.

32 'Send therefore to Joppa and invite Simon, who is also called Peter, to come to you; he is staying at the house of Simon *the* tanner by the sea.'

33 "And so I sent to you immediately, and you have been kind enough to come. Now then, we are all here present before God to hear all that you have been commanded by the Lord."

34 And opening his mouth, Peter said: (r1)

"I most certainly understand *now* that God is not one to show partiality,

35 but in every nation the man who fears Him and does what is right, is welcome to Him.

36 "The word which He sent to the sons of Israel, preaching peace through Jesus Christ (He is Lord of all) —

37 you yourselves know the thing which took place throughout all Judea, starting from Galilee, after the baptism which John proclaimed.

38 "*You know of* Jesus of Nazareth, how God anointed Him with the Holy Spirit and with power, and *how* He went about doing good, and healing all who were oppressed by the devil; for God was with Him. (a)

39 "And we are witnesses of all the things He did both in the land of the Jews and in Jerusalem. And they also put Him to death by hanging Him on a cross. (b)

40 "God raised Him up on the third day, and granted that He should become visible,

41 not to all the people, but to witnesses who were chosen beforehand by God, *that is,* to us, who ate and drank with Him after He arose from the dead. (c)

42 "And He ordered us to preach to the people, and solemnly to testify that this is the One who has been appointed by God as Judge of the living and the dead.

43 "Of Him all the prophets bear witness that through His name every one who believes in Him has received forgiveness of sins." (d)

44 While Peter was still speaking these words, the Holy Spirit fell upon all those who were listening to the message.

45 And all the circumcised believers who had come with Peter were amazed, because the gift of the Holy

---

(r1) CONVERSION OF CORNELIUS. Peter preached in the power of the Holy Spirit to those in the house of Cornelius. His sermon:

(a) Communicated Christ Jesus, His person and work; "Jesus of Nazareth . . . anointed with power . . . went about doing good, and healing;"

(b) Concerned His crucifixion, "They . . . put Him to death by hanging Him on a Cross;" See page 242.

(c) Conveyed convincing proofs of His resurrection, "God raised Him up . . . that He should become visible . . . to us, who ate and drank with Him after He arose from the dead";

(d) Convinced Cornelius that the condition of forgiveness of sin is faith in Christ's Name, "Everyone who believes in Him has received forgiveness of sins."

Refer to page 177, see results.

Spirit had been poured out upon the Gentiles also. (r1)

46 For they were hearing them speaking with tongues and exalting God. Then Peter answered, (a)

47 Surely no one can refuse the water for these to be baptized who have received the Holy Spirit just as we *did*, can he?" (b)

48 And he ordered them to be baptized in the name of Jesus Christ. Then they asked him to stay on for a few days. (c)

CHAPTER 11

NOW the apostles and the brethren who were throughout Judea heard that the Gentiles also had received the word of God.

2 And when Peter came up to Jerusalem, those who were circumcised took issue with him,

3 saying, "You went to uncircumcised men and ate with them."

4 But Peter began *speaking* and *proceeded* to explain to them in orderly sequence, saying,

5 "I was in the city of Joppa praying; and in a trance I saw a vision, a certain object coming down like a great sheet lowered by four corners from the sky; and it came right down to me,

6 and when I had fixed my gaze upon it and was observing it I saw the four-footed animals of the earth and the wild beasts and the crawling creatures and the birds of the air.

7 "And I also heard a voice saying to me, 'Arise, Peter; kill and eat.'

8 "But I said, 'By no means, Lord, for nothing unholy or unclean has ever entered my mouth.'

9 "But a voice from heaven answered a second time, 'What God has cleansed, no longer consider unholy.'

10 "And this happened three times, and everything was drawn back up into the sky.

11 "And behold, at that moment three men appeared before the house in which we were *staying*, having been sent to me from Caesarea.

12 "And the Spirit told me to go with them without misgivings. And these six brethren also went with me, and we entered the man's house.

13 "And he reported to us how he had seen the angel standing in his house, and saying, 'Send to Joppa, and have Simon, who is also called Peter, brought here;

14 and he shall speak words to you by which you will be saved, you and all your household.'

15 "And as I began to speak, the Holy Spirit fell upon them, just as *He did* upon us at the beginning.

16 "And I remembered the word of the Lord, how He used to say, 'John baptized with water, but you shall be baptized with the Holy Spirit.'

17 "If God therefore gave to them the same gift as *He gave* to us also after believing in the Lord Jesus Christ, who was I that I could stand in God's way?"

18 And when they heard this, they quieted down, and glorified God, say-

---

(r1) THE RESULTS OF PETER'S SERMON

(a) Confession of Christ by the converts—"They were hearing them speaking . . . and exalting God."

(b) Convinced the church members—"The circumcised believers . . . were amazed . . . Surely no one can refuse the water for these to be baptized who have received the Holy Spirit."

(c) Command to be baptized—"He ordered them to be baptized." Have you heard the gospel and believed? If so, you are to confess Christ and obey the command to be baptized, see page 45, Scripture No. 1, Sec. 2, Matt. 28:18–20 and Reference No. 1, Sec. 2 and do as Christ commanded you.

ing, "Well then, God has granted to the Gentiles also the repentance *that leads* to life."

19 So then those who were scattered because of the persecution that arose in connection with Stephen made their way to Phoenicia and Cyprus and Antioch, speaking the word to no one except to Jews alone.

20 But there were some of them, men of Cyprus and Cyrene, who came to Antioch and *began* speaking to the Greeks also, preaching the Lord Jesus.

21 And the hand of the Lord was with them, and a large number who believed turned to the Lord.

22 And the news about them reached the ears of the church at Jerusalem, and they sent Barnabas off to Antioch.

23 Then when he had come and witnessed the grace of God, he rejoiced and *began* to encourage them all with resolute heart to remain *true* to the Lord;

24 for he was a good man, and full of the Holy Spirit and of faith. And considerable numbers were brought to the Lord.

25 And he left for Tarsus to look for Saul;

26 and when he had found him, he brought him to Antioch. And it came about that for an entire year they met with the church, and taught considerable numbers; and the disciples were first called Christians in Antioch.

27 Now at this time some prophets came down from Jerusalem to Antioch.

28 And one of them named Agabus stood up and *began* to indicate by the Spirit that there would certainly be a great famine all over the world. And this took place in the *reign* of Claudius.

29 And in the proportion that any of the disciples had means, each of them determined to send *a contribu-*tion for the relief of the brethren living in Judea.

30 And this they did, sending it in charge of Barnabas and Saul to the elders.

Chapter 12

NOW about that time Herod the king laid hands on some who belonged to the church, in order to mistreat them.

2 And he had James the brother of John put to death with a sword.

3 And when he saw that it pleased the Jews, he proceeded to arrest Peter also. Now it was during the days of *the Feast of* Unleavened Bread.

4 And when he had seized him, he put him in prison, delivering him to four squads of soldiers to guard him, intending after the Passover to bring him out before the people.

5 So Peter was kept in the prison, but prayer for him was being made fervently by the church to God.

6 And on the very night when Herod was about to bring him forward, Peter was sleeping between two soldiers, bound with two chains; and guards in front of the door were watching over the prison.

7 And behold, an angel of the Lord suddenly appeared, and a light shone in the cell; and he struck Peter's side and roused him, saying, "Get up quickly." And his chains fell off his hands.

8 And the angel said to him, "Gird yourself and put on your sandals." And he did so. And he *said to him, "Wrap your cloak around you and follow me."

9 And he went out and continued to follow, and he did not know that what was being done by the angel was real, but thought he was seeing a vision.

10 And when they had passed the first and second guard, they came to the iron gate that leads into the city, which opened for them by itself; and they went out and went along one street; and immediately the angel departed from him.

11 And when Peter came to himself, he said, "Now I know for sure that the Lord has sent forth His angel and rescued me from the hand of Herod and from all that the Jewish people were expecting."

12 And when he realized *this*, he went to the house of Mary, the mother of John who was also called Mark, where many were gathered together and were praying.

13 And when he knocked at the door of the gate, a servant-girl named Rhoda came to answer.

14 And when she recognized Peter's voice, because of her joy she did not open the gate, but ran in and announced that Peter was standing in front of the gate.

15 And they said to her, "You are out of your mind!" But she kept insisting that it was so. And they kept saying, "It is his angel."

16 But Peter continued knocking; and when they had opened, they saw him and were amazed.

17 But motioning to them with his hand to be silent, he described to them how the Lord had led him out of the prison. And he said, "Report these things to James and the brethren." And he departed and went to another place.

18 Now when day came, there was no small disturbance among the soldiers *as to* what could have become of Peter.

19 And when Herod had searched for him and had not found him, he examined the guards and ordered that they be led away *to execution.* And he went down from Judea to Caesarea and was spending time there.

20 Now he was very angry with the people of Tyre and Sidon; and with one accord they came to him, and having won over Blastus the king's chamberlain, they were asking for peace, because their country was fed by the king's country.

21 And on an appointed day Herod, having put on his royal apparel, took his seat on the rostrum and *began* delivering an address to them.

22 And the people kept crying out, "The voice of a god and not of a man!"

23 And immediately an angel of the Lord struck him because he did not give God the glory, and he was eaten by worms and died.

24 But the word of the Lord continued to grow and to be multiplied.

25 And Barnabas and Saul returned from Jerusalem when they had fulfilled their mission, taking along with *them* John, who was also called Mark.

CHAPTER 13

Now there were at Antioch, in the church that was *there*, prophets and teachers: Barnabas, and Simeon who was called Niger, and Lucius of Cyrene, and Manaen who had been brought up with Herod the tetrarch, and Saul.

2 And while they were ministering to the Lord and fasting, the Holy Spirit said, "Set apart for Me Barnabas and Saul for the work to which I have called them."

3 Then, when they had fasted and prayed and laid their hands on them, they sent them away.

4 So, being sent out by the Holy Spirit, they went down to Seleucia and from there they sailed to Cyprus.

5 And when they reached Salamis, they *began* to proclaim the word of God in the synagogues of the Jews; and they also had John as their helper.

6 And when they had gone through the whole island as far as

Paphos, they found a certain magician, a Jewish false prophet whose name was Bar-Jesus,

7 who was with the proconsul, Sergius Paulus, a man of intelligence. This man summoned Barnabas and Saul and sought to hear the word of God.

8 But Elymas the magician (for thus his name is translated) was opposing them, seeking to turn the proconsul away from the faith.

9 But Saul, who was also *known as* Paul, filled with the Holy Spirit, fixed his gaze upon him,

10 and said, "You who are full of all deceit and fraud, you son of the devil, you enemy of all righteousness, will you not cease to make crooked the straight ways of the Lord?

11 "And now, behold, the hand of the Lord is upon you, and you will be blind and not see the sun for a time." And immediately a mist and a darkness fell upon him, and he went about seeking those who would lead him by the hand.

12 Then the proconsul believed when he saw what had happened, being amazed at the teaching of the Lord.

13 Now Paul and his companions put out to sea from Paphos and came to Perga in Pamphylia; and John left them and returned to Jerusalem.

14 But going on from Perga, they arrived at Pisidian Antioch, and on the Sabbath day they went into the synagogue and sat down.

15 And after the reading of the Law and the Prophets the synagogue officials sent to them, saying, "Brethren, if you have any word of exhortation for the people, say it."

16 And Paul stood up, and motioning with his hand, he said,

"**M**en of Israel, and you who fear God, listen:

17 "The God of this people Israel chose our fathers, and made the people great during their stay in the land of Egypt, and with an uplifted arm He led them out from it.

18 "And for about a period of forty years He put up with them in the wilderness.

19 "And when He had destroyed seven nations in the land of Canaan, He distributed their land as an inheritance—*all of which took* about four hundred and fifty years.

20 "And after these things He gave *them* judges until Samuel the prophet.

21 "And then they asked for a king, and God gave them Saul the son of Kish, a man of the tribe of Benjamin, for forty years.

22 "And after He had removed him, He raised up David to be their king, concerning whom He also testified and said, 'I have found David the son of Jesse, a man after My heart, who will do all My will.'

23 "From the offspring of this man, according to promise, God has brought to Israel a Savior, Jesus,

24 after John had proclaimed before His coming a baptism of repentance to all the people of Israel.

25 "And while John was completing his course, he kept saying, 'What do you suppose that I am? I am not *He.* But behold, one is coming after me the sandals of whose feet I am not worthy to untie.'

26 "Brethren, sons of Abraham's family, and those among you who fear God, to us the word of this salvation is sent out.

27 "For those who live in Jerusalem, and their rulers, recognizing neither Him nor the utterances of the prophets which are read every Sabbath, fulfilled *these* by condemning *Him.*

28 "And though they found no ground for *putting Him to* death, they asked Pilate that He be executed.

29 "And when they had carried out all that was written concerning Him,

they took Him down from the cross and laid Him in a tomb.

30 "But God raised Him from the dead;

31 and for many days He appeared to those who came up with Him from Galilee to Jerusalem, the very ones who are now His witnesses to the people.

32 "And we preach to you the good news of the promise made to the fathers,

33 that God has fulfilled this *promise* to our children in that He raised up Jesus, as it is also written in the second Psalm, 'THOU ART MY SON; TODAY I HAVE BEGOTTEN THEE.'

34 "*And as for the fact* that He raised Him up from the dead, no more to return to decay, He has spoken in this way: 'I WILL GIVE YOU THE HOLY *and* SURE *blessings* OF DAVID.'

35 "Therefore He also says in another *Psalm,* 'THOU WILT NOT ALLOW THY HOLY ONE TO UNDERGO DECAY.'

36 "For David, after he had served the purpose of God in his own generation, fell asleep, and was laid among his fathers, and underwent decay;

37 but He whom God raised did not undergo decay.

38 "Therefore let it be known to you, brethren, that through Him forgiveness of sins is proclaimed to you,

39 and through Him everyone who believes is freed from all things, from which you could not be freed through the Law of Moses.

40 "Take heed therefore, so that the thing spoken of in the Prophets may not come upon *you:*

41 'BEHOLD, YOU SCOFFERS, AND MARVEL, AND PERISH;

FOR I AM ACCOMPLISHING A WORK IN YOUR DAYS,

A WORK WHICH YOU WILL NEVER BELIEVE, THOUGH SOMEONE SHOULD DESCRIBE IT TO YOU.' "

42 And as Paul and Barnabas were going out, the people kept begging that these things might be spoken to them the next Sabbath.

43 Now when *the meeting of* the synagogue had broken up, many of the Jews and of the God-fearing proselytes followed Paul and Barnabas, who, speaking to them, were urging them to continue in the grace of God.

44 And the next Sabbath nearly the whole city assembled to hear the word of God.

45 But when the Jews saw the crowds, they were filled with jealousy, and *began* contradicting the things spoken by Paul, and were blaspheming.

46 And Paul and Barnabas spoke out boldly and said, "It was necessary that the word of God should be spoken to you first; since you repudiate it, and judge yourselves unworthy of eternal life, behold, we are turning to the Gentiles.

47 "For thus the Lord has commanded us,

'I HAVE PLACED YOU AS A LIGHT FOR THE GENTILES,

THAT YOU SHOULD BRING SALVATION TO THE END OF THE EARTH.' "

48 And when the Gentiles heard this, they *began* rejoicing and glorifying the word of the Lord; and as many as had been appointed to eternal life believed.

49 And the word of the Lord was being spread through the whole region.

50 But the Jews aroused the devout women of prominence and the leading men of the city, and instigated a persecution against Paul and Barnabas, and drove them out of their district.

51 But they shook off the dust of their feet *in protest* against them and went to Iconium.

52 And the disciples were continu-

ally filled with joy and with the Holy Spirit.

Chapter 14

AND it came about that in Iconium they entered the synagogue of the Jews together, and spoke in such a manner that a great multitude believed, both of Jews and of Greeks.

2 But the Jews who disbelieved stirred up the minds of the Gentiles, and embittered them against the brethren.

3 Therefore they spent a long time *there* speaking boldly *with reliance* upon the Lord, who was bearing witness to the word of His grace, granting that signs and wonders be done by their hands.

4 But the multitude of the city was divided; and some sided with the Jews, and some with the apostles.

5 And when an attempt was made by both the Gentiles and the Jews with their rulers, to mistreat and to stone them,

6 they became aware of it and fled to the cities of Lycaonia, Lystra and Derbe, and the surrounding region;

7 and there they continued to preach the gospel.

8 And at Lystra there was sitting a certain man, without strength in his feet, lame from his mother's womb, who had never walked.

9 This man was listening to Paul as he spoke, who, when he had fixed his gaze upon him, and had seen that he had faith to be made well,

10 said with a loud voice, "Stand upright on your feet." And he leaped up and *began* to walk.

11 And when the multitudes saw what Paul had done, they raised their voice, saying in the Lycaonian language, "The gods have become like men and have come down to us."

12 And they *began* calling Barnabas, Zeus, and Paul, Hermes, because he was the chief speaker.

13 And the priest of Zeus, whose *temple* was just outside the city, brought oxen and garlands to the gates, and wanted to offer sacrifice with the crowds.

14 But when the apostles, Barnabas and Paul, heard of it, they tore their robes and rushed out into the crowd, crying out

15 and saying, "Men, why are you doing these things? We are also men of the same nature as you, and preach the gospel to you in order that you should turn from these vain things to a living God, WHO MADE THE HEAVEN AND THE EARTH AND THE SEA, AND ALL THAT IS IN THEM.

16 "And in the generations gone by He permitted all the nations to go their own ways;

17 and yet He did not leave Himself without witness, in that He did good and gave you rains from heaven and fruitful seasons, satisfying your hearts with food and gladness."

18 And *even* saying these things, they with difficulty restrained the crowds from offering sacrifice to them.

19 But Jews came from Antioch and Iconium, and having won over the multitudes, they stoned Paul and dragged him out of the city, supposing him to be dead.

20 But while the disciples stood around him, he arose and entered the city. And the next day he went away with Barnabas to Derbe.

21 And after they had preached the gospel to that city and had made many disciples, they returned to Lystra and to Iconium and to Antioch,

22 strengthening the souls of the disciples, encouraging them to continue in the faith, and *saying*, "Through many tribulations we must enter the kingdom of God."

23 And when they had appointed elders for them in every church, hav-

ing prayed with fasting, they commended them to the Lord in whom they had believed.

24 And they passed through Pisidia and came into Pamphylia.

25 And when they had spoken the word in Perga, they went down to Attalia;

26 and from there they sailed to Antioch, from which they had been commended to the grace of God for the work that they had accomplished.

27 And when they had arrived and gathered the church together, they *began* to report all things that God had done with them and how He had opened a door of faith to the Gentiles.

28 And they spent a long time with the disciples.

Chapter 15

AND some men came down from Judea and *began* teaching the brethren, "Unless you are circumcised according to the custom of Moses, you cannot be saved."

2 And when Paul and Barnabas had great dissension and debate with them, *the brethren* determined that Paul and Barnabas and certain others of them, should go up to Jerusalem to the apostles and elders concerning this issue.

3 Therefore, being sent on their way by the church, they were passing through both Phoenicia and Samaria, describing in detail the conversion of the Gentiles, and were bringing great joy to all the brethren.

4 And when they arrived at Jerusalem, they were received by the church and the apostles and the elders, and they reported all that God had done with them.

5 But certain ones of the sect of the Pharisees who had believed, stood up, saying, "It is necessary to circumcise them, and to direct them to observe the Law of Moses."

6 And the apostles and the elders came together to look into this matter.

7 And after there had been much debate, Peter stood up and said to them, "Brethren, you know that in the early days God made a choice among you, that by my mouth the Gentiles should hear the word of the gospel and believe.

8 "And God, who knows the heart, bore witness to them, giving them the Holy Spirit, just as He also did to us;

9 and He made no distinction between us and them, cleansing their hearts by faith.

10 "Now therefore why do you put God to the test by placing upon the neck of the disciples a yoke which neither our fathers nor we have been able to bear?

11 "But we believe that we are saved through the grace of the Lord Jesus, in the same way as they also are."

12 And all the multitude kept silent, and they were listening to Barnabas and Paul as they were relating what signs and wonders God had done through them among the Gentiles.

13 And after they had stopped speaking, James answered, saying, "Brethren, listen to me.

14 "Simeon has related how God first concerned Himself about taking from among the Gentiles a people for His name.

15 "And with this the words of the Prophets agree, just as it is written,

16 'AFTER THESE THINGS I WILL RETURN,
   AND I WILL REBUILD THE TABERNACLE OF DAVID WHICH HAS FALLEN,
   AND I WILL REBUILD ITS RUINS,
   AND I WILL RESTORE IT,

17   IN ORDER THAT THE REST OF
        MANKIND MAY SEEK THE
        LORD,
        AND ALL THE GENTILES WHO
        ARE CALLED BY MY NAME,
18   SAYS THE LORD, WHO MAKES
        THESE THINGS KNOWN FROM
        OF OLD.'

19 "Therefore it is my judgment
that we do not trouble those who are
turning to God from among the Gentiles,

20 but that we write to them that
they abstain from things contaminated by idols and from fornication
and from what is strangled and from
blood.

21 "For Moses from ancient generations has in every city those who
preach him, since he is read in the
synagogues every Sabbath."

22 Then it seemed good to the
apostles and the elders, with the
whole church, to choose men from
among them to send to Antioch with
Paul and Barnabas—Judas called Barsabbas, and Silas, leading men among
the brethren,

23 and they sent this letter by
them,

        "The apostles and the
        brethren who are elders,
        to the brethren in Antioch and Syria and Cilicia
        who are from the Gentiles, greetings.
24   "Since we have heard that
        some of our number to
        whom we gave no instruction have disturbed
        you with *their* words, unsettling your souls,
25   it seemed good to us,
        having become of one
        mind, to select men to
        send to you with our beloved Barnabas and Paul,
26   men who have risked

their lives for the name
of our Lord Jesus Christ.

27 "Therefore we have sent
Judas and Silas, who
themselves will also report the same things by
word *of mouth.*

28 "For it seemed good to
the Holy Spirit and to us
to lay upon you no
greater burden than
these essentials:

29 that you abstain from
things sacrificed to idols
and from blood and from
things strangled and
from fornication; if you
keep yourselves free
from such things, you
will do well. Farewell."

30 So, when they were sent away,
they went down to Antioch; and having gathered the congregation together, they delivered the letter.

31 And when they had read it, they
rejoiced because of its encouragement.

32 And Judas and Silas, also being
prophets themselves, encouraged and
strengthened the brethren with a
lengthy message.

33 And after they had spent time
there, they were sent away from the
brethren in peace to those who had
sent them out.

34 (See footnote.)

35 But Paul and Barnabas stayed
in Antioch, teaching and preaching,
with many others also, the word of the
Lord.

36 And after some days Paul said
to Barnabas, "Let us return and visit
the brethren in every city in which we
proclaimed the word of the Lord, *and
see* how they are."

37 And Barnabas was desirous of
taking John, called Mark, along with
them also.

Some mss. add verse 34, *But it seemed good to Silas to remain there.*

38 But Paul kept insisting that they should not take him along who had deserted them in Pamphylia and had not gone with them to the work.

39 And there arose such a sharp disagreement that they separated from one another, and Barnabas took Mark with him and sailed away to Cyprus.

40 But Paul chose Silas and departed, being committed by the brethren to the grace of the Lord.

41 And he was traveling through Syria and Cilicia, strengthening the churches.

CHAPTER 16

AND he came also to Derbe and to Lystra. And behold, a certain disciple was there, named Timothy, the son of a Jewish woman who was a believer, but his father was a Greek,

2 and he was well spoken of by the brethren who were in Lystra and Iconium.

3 Paul wanted this man to go with him; and he took him and circumcised him because of the Jews who were in those parts, for they all knew that his father was a Greek.

4 Now while they were passing through the cities, they were delivering the decrees, which had been decided upon by the apostles and elders who were in Jerusalem, for them to observe.

5 So the churches were being strengthened in the faith, and were increasing in number daily.

6 And they passed through the Phrygian and Galatian region, having been forbidden by the Holy Spirit to speak the word in Asia;

7 and when they had come to Mysia, they were trying to go into Bithynia, and the Spirit of Jesus did not permit them;

8 and passing by Mysia, they came down to Troas.

9 And a vision appeared to Paul in the night: a certain man of Macedonia was standing and appealing to him, and saying, "Come over to Macedonia and help us."

10 And when he had seen the vision, immediately we sought to go into Macedonia, concluding that God had called us to preach the gospel to them.

11 Therefore putting out to sea from Troas, we ran a straight course to Samothrace, and on the day following to Neapolis;

12 and from there to Philippi, which is a leading city of the district of Macedonia, a Roman colony; and we were staying in this city for some days.

13 And on the Sabbath day we went outside the gate to a riverside, where we were supposing that there would be a place of prayer; and we sat down and began speaking to the women who had assembled.

14 And a certain woman named Lydia, from the city of Thyatira, a seller of purple fabrics, a worshiper of God, was listening; and the Lord opened her heart to respond to the things spoken by Paul.

15 And when she and her household had been baptized, she urged us, saying, "If you have judged me to be faithful to the Lord, come into my house and stay." And she prevailed upon us.

16 And it happened that as we were going to the place of prayer, a certain slave-girl having a spirit of divination met us, who was bringing her masters much profit by fortunetelling.

17 Following after Paul and us, she kept crying out, saying, "These men are bond-servants of the Most High God, who are proclaiming to you the way of salvation."

18 And she continued doing this for many days. But Paul was greatly annoyed, and turned and said to the

spirit, "I command you in the name of Jesus Christ to come out of her!" And it came out at that very moment.

19 But when her masters saw that their hope of profit was gone, they seized Paul and Silas, and dragged them into the market place before the authorities,

20 and when they had brought them to the chief magistrates, they said, "These men are throwing our city into confusion, being Jews,

21 and are proclaiming customs which it is not lawful for us to accept or to observe, being Romans."

22 And the crowd rose up together against them, and the chief magistrates tore their robes off them, and proceeded to order *them* to be beaten with rods.

23 And when they had inflicted many blows upon them, they threw them into prison, commanding the jailer to guard them securely;

24 and he, having received such a command, threw them into the inner prison, and fastened their feet in the stocks.

25 But about midnight Paul and Silas were praying and singing hymns of praise to God, and the prisoners were listening to them;

26 and suddenly there came a great earthquake, so that the foundations of the prison-house were shaken;

and immediately all the doors were opened, and everyone's chains were unfastened.

27 And when the jailer had been roused out of sleep and had seen the prison doors opened, he drew his sword and was about to kill himself, supposing that the prisoners had escaped.

28 But Paul cried out with a loud voice, saying, "Do yourself no harm, for we are all here!"

29 And he called for lights and rushed in and, trembling with fear, he fell down before Paul and Silas,

SCRIPTURE NO. 1, SEC. 1

30 and after he brought them out, he said, "Sirs, what must I do to be saved?"

31 And they said, "Believe in the Lord Jesus, and you shall be saved, you and your household."

32 And they spoke the word of the Lord to him together with all who were in his house.

33 And he took them that *very* hour of the night and washed their wounds, and immediately he was baptized, he and all his *household*.

34 And he brought them into his house and set food before them, and rejoiced greatly, having believed in God with his whole household. (r1)

(r1) REFERENCE NO. 1, SEC. 1—WHAT YOU MUST DO TO BE SAVED.

"What must I do to be saved?" This is your greatest question.

"Believe in the Lord Jesus, and you shall be saved," is God's answer.

In these verses a man realized his need for "repentance toward God and faith in our Lord Jesus Christ." "They spoke the word of the Lord to him." He learned that the Lord Jesus "to all those who obey Him became the source of eternal salvation." He "turned to God from idols to serve a living and true God."

He was saved. He showed it by his changed life, when he "washed their wounds . . . was baptized ∴ . . . set food before them and rejoiced greatly."

You, too, need to "repent and turn to God" from sin. "Believe in the Lord Jesus" and confess Him "before men." You can show your salvation by being baptized." Then you, too, will rejoice. Will you admit you need to be saved? If so, say: "I need to be saved."

Now turn to page 209, Scripture No. 2, Sec. 1, Rom. 3:23.

35 Now when day came, the chief magistrates sent their policemen, saying, "Release those men."

36 And the jailer reported these words to Paul, *saying*, "The chief magistrates have sent to release you. Now therefore come out and go in peace."

37 But Paul said to them, "They have beaten us in public without trial, men who are Romans, and have thrown us into prison; and now are they sending us away secretly? No indeed! But let them come themselves and bring us out."

38 And the policemen reported these words to the chief magistrates. And they were afraid when they heard that they were Romans,

39 and they came and appealed to them, and when they had brought them out, they kept begging them to leave the city.

40 And they went out of the prison and entered *the house of* Lydia, and when they saw the brethren, they encouraged them and departed.

CHAPTER 17

NOW when they had traveled through Amphipolis and Apollonia, they came to Thessalonica, where there was a synagogue of the Jews.

2 And according to Paul's custom, he went to them, and for three Sabbaths reasoned with them from the Scriptures,

3 explaining and giving evidence that the Christ had to suffer and rise again from the dead, and *saying*, "This Jesus whom I am proclaiming to you is the Christ."

4 And some of them were persuaded and joined Paul and Silas, along with a great multitude of the God-fearing Greeks and a number of the leading women.

5 But the Jews, becoming jealous and taking along some wicked men from the market place, formed a mob and set the city in an uproar; and coming upon the house of Jason, they were seeking to bring them out to the people.

6 And when they did not find them, they *began* dragging Jason and some brethren before the city authorities, shouting, "These men who have upset the world have come here also;

7 and Jason has welcomed them, and they all act contrary to the decrees of Caesar, saying that there is another king, Jesus."

8 And they stirred up the crowd and the city authorities who heard these things.

9 And when they had received a pledge from Jason and the others, they released them.

10 And the brethren immediately sent Paul and Silas away by night to Berea; and when they arrived, they went into the synagogue of the Jews.

11 Now these were more noble-minded than those in Thessalonica, for they received the word with great eagerness, examining the Scriptures daily, *to see* whether these things were so.

12 Many of them therefore believed, along with a number of prominent Greek women and men.

13 But when the Jews of Thessalonica found out that the word of God had been proclaimed by Paul in Berea also, they came there likewise, agitating and stirring up the crowds.

14 And then immediately the brethren sent Paul out to go as far as the sea; and Silas and Timothy remained there.

15 Now those who conducted Paul brought him as far as Athens; and receiving a command for Silas and Timothy to come to him as soon as possible, they departed.

16 Now while Paul was waiting for them at Athens, his spirit was being provoked within him as he was beholding the city full of idols.

17 So he was reasoning in the synagogue with the Jews and the God-fearing *Gentiles*, and in the market place every day with those who happened to be present.

18 And also some of the Epicurean and Stoic philosophers were conversing with him. And some were saying, "What would this idle babbler wish to say?" Others, "He seems to be a proclaimer of strange deities,"—because he was preaching Jesus and the resurrection.

19 And they took him and brought him to the Areopagus, saying, "May we know what this new teaching is which you are proclaiming?

20 "For you are bringing some strange things to our ears; we want to know therefore what these things mean."

21 (Now all the Athenians and the strangers visiting there used to spend their time in nothing other than telling or hearing something new.)

22 And Paul stood in the midst of the Areopagus and said, "Men of Athens, I observe that you are very religious in all respects.

23 "For while I was passing through and examining the objects of your worship, I also found an altar with this inscription, 'TO AN UNKNOWN GOD.' What therefore you worship in ignorance, this I proclaim to you.

24 "The God who made the world and all things in it, since He is Lord of heaven and earth, does not dwell in temples made with hands;

25 neither is He served by human hands, as though He needed anything, since He Himself gives to all life and breath and all things;

26 and He made from one, every nation of mankind to live on all the face of the earth, having determined *their* appointed times, and the boundaries of their habitation,

27 that they should seek God, if perhaps they might grope for Him and find Him, though He is not far from each one of us;

28 for in Him we live and move and exist, as even some of your own poets have said, 'For we also are His offspring.'

29 "Being then the offspring of God, we ought not to think that the Divine Nature is like gold or silver or stone, an image formed by the art and thought of man.

30 "Therefore having overlooked the times of ignorance, God is now declaring to men that all everywhere should repent, (a)

31 because He has fixed a day in which He will judge the world in righteousness through a Man whom He has appointed, having furnished proof to all men by raising Him from the dead."

32 Now when they heard of the resurrection of the dead, some *began* to sneer, but others said, "We shall hear you again concerning this."

33 So Paul went out of their midst.

34 But some men joined him and believed, among whom also was Dionysius the Areopagite and a woman named Damaris and others with them.

(a) Repentance is:
Imperative—God commands that you repent; and it is
Inclusive—"All everywhere" includes and applies to you; and most
Important—"Unless you repent you will . . . perish", Luke 13:5, page 101.

CHAPTER 18

AFTER these things he left Athens and went to Corinth.

2 And he found a certain Jew named Aquila, a native of Pontus, having recently come from Italy with his wife Priscilla, because Claudius had commanded all the Jews to leave Rome. He came to them,

3 and because he was of the same trade, he stayed with them and they were working; for by trade they were tent-makers.

4 And he was reasoning in the synagogue every Sabbath and trying to persuade Jews and Greeks.

5 But when Silas and Timothy came down from Macedonia, Paul *began* devoting himself completely to the word, solemnly testifying to the Jews that Jesus was the Christ.

6 And when they resisted and blasphemed, he shook out his garments and said to them, "Your blood *be* upon your own heads! I am clean. From now on I shall go to the Gentiles."

7 And he departed from there and went to the house of a certain man named Titius Justus, a worshiper of God, whose house was next to the synagogue.

8 And Crispus, the leader of the synagogue, believed in the Lord with all his household, and many of the Corinthians when they heard were believing and being baptized.

9 And the Lord said to Paul in the night by a vision, "Do not be afraid *any longer*, but go on speaking and do not be silent;

10 for I am with you, and no man will attack you in order to harm you, for I have many people in this city."

11 And he settled *there* a year and six months, teaching the word of God among them.

12 But while Gallio was proconsul of Achaia, the Jews with one accord rose up against Paul and brought him before the judgment seat,

13 saying, "This man persuades men to worship God contrary to the law."

14 But when Paul was about to open his mouth, Gallio said to the Jews, "If it were a matter of wrong or of vicious crime, O Jews, it would be reasonable for me to put up with you;

15 but if there are questions about words and names and your own law, look after it yourselves; I am unwilling to be a judge of these matters."

16 And he drove them away from the judgment seat.

17 And they all took hold of Sosthenes, the leader of the synagogue, and *began* beating him in front of the judgment seat. And Gallio was not concerned about any of these things.

18 And Paul, having remained many days longer, took leave of the brethren and put out to sea for Syria, and with him were Priscilla and Aquila. In Cenchrea he had his hair cut, for he was keeping a vow.

19 And they came to Ephesus, and he left them there. Now he himself entered the synagogue and reasoned with the Jews.

20 And when they asked him to stay for a longer time, he did not consent,

21 but taking leave of them and saying, "I will return to you again if God wills," he set sail from Ephesus.

22 And when he had landed at Caesarea, he went up and greeted the church, and went down to Antioch.

23 And having spent some time *there*, he departed and passed successively through the Galatian region and Phrygia, strengthening all the disciples.

24 Now a certain Jew named Apollos, an Alexandrian by birth, an eloquent man, came to Ephesus; and he was mighty in the Scriptures.

25 This man had been instructed in the way of the Lord; and being fervent in spirit, he was speaking and teaching accurately the things concerning Jesus, being acquainted only with the baptism of John;

26 and he began to speak out boldly in the synagogue. But when Priscilla and Aquila heard him, they took him aside and explained to him the way of God more accurately.

27 And when he wanted to go across to Achaia, the brethren encouraged him and wrote to the disciples to welcome him; and when he had arrived, he helped greatly those who had believed through grace;

28 for he powerfully refuted the Jews in public, demonstrating by the Scriptures that Jesus was the Christ.

CHAPTER 19

AND it came about that while Apollos was at Corinth, Paul having passed through the upper country came to Ephesus, and found some disciples,

2 and he said to them, "Did you receive the Holy Spirit when you believed?" And they *said* to him, "No, we have not even heard whether there is a Holy Spirit."

3 And he said, "Into what then were you baptized?" And they said, "Into John's baptism."

4 And Paul said, "John baptized with the baptism of repentance, telling the people to believe in Him who was coming after him, that is, in Jesus."

5 And when they heard this, they were baptized in the name of the Lord Jesus.

6 And when Paul had laid his hands upon them, the Holy Spirit came on them, and they *began* speaking with tongues and prophesying.

7 And there were in all about twelve men.

8 And he entered the synagogue and continued speaking out boldly for three months, reasoning and persuading *them* about the kingdom of God.

9 But when some were becoming hardened and disobedient, speaking evil of the Way before the multitude, he withdrew from them and took away the disciples, reasoning daily in the school of Tyrannus.

10 And this took place for two years, so that all who lived in Asia heard the word of the Lord, both Jews and Greeks.

11 And God was performing extraordinary miracles by the hands of Paul,

12 so that handkerchiefs or aprons were even carried from his body to the sick, and the diseases left them and the evil spirits went out.

13 But also some of the Jewish exorcists, who went from place to place, attempted to name over those who had the evil spirits the name of the Lord Jesus, saying, "I adjure you by Jesus whom Paul preaches."

14 And seven sons of one Sceva, a Jewish chief priest, were doing this.

15 And the evil spirit answered and said to them, "I recognize Jesus, and I know about Paul, but who are you?"

16 And the man, in whom was the evil spirit, leaped on them and subdued both of them and overpowered them, so that they fled out of that house naked and wounded.

17 And this became known to all, both Jews and Greeks, who lived in Ephesus; and fear fell upon them all and the name of the Lord Jesus was being magnified.

18 Many also of those who had believed kept coming, confessing and disclosing their practices.

19 And many of those who practiced magic brought their books together and *began* burning them in the sight of all; and they counted up the

price of them and found it fifty thousand pieces of silver.

20 So the word of the Lord was growing mightily and prevailing.

21 Now after these things were finished, Paul purposed in the spirit to go to Jerusalem after he had passed through Macedonia and Achaia, saying, "After I have been there, I must also see Rome."

22 And having sent into Macedonia two of those who ministered to him, Timothy and Erastus, he himself stayed in Asia for a while.

23 And about that time there arose no small disturbance concerning the Way.

24 For a certain man named Demetrius, a silversmith, who made silver shrines of Artemis, was bringing no little business to the craftsmen;

25 these he gathered together with the workmen of similar *trades,* and said, "Men, you know that our prosperity depends upon this business.

26 "And you see and hear that not only in Ephesus, but in almost all of Asia, this Paul has persuaded and turned away a considerable number of people, saying that gods made with hands are no gods *at all.*

27 "And not only is there danger that this trade of ours fall into disrepute, but also that the temple of the great goddess Artemis be regarded as worthless and that she whom all of Asia and the world worship should even be dethroned from her magnificence."

28 And when they heard *this* and were filled with rage, they *began* crying out, saying, "Great is Artemis of the Ephesians!"

29 And the city was filled with the confusion, and they rushed with one accord into the theater, dragging along Gaius and Aristarchus, Paul's traveling companions from Macedonia.

30 And when Paul wanted to go into the assembly, the disciples would not let him.

31 And also some of the Asiarchs who were friends of his sent to him and repeatedly urged him not to venture into the theater.

32 So then, some were shouting one thing and some another, for the assembly was in confusion, and the majority did not know for what cause they had come together.

33 And some of the crowd concluded *it was* Alexander, since the Jews had put him forward; and having motioned with his hand, Alexander was intending to make a defense to the assembly.

34 But when they recognized that he was a Jew, a single outcry arose from them all as they shouted for about two hours, "Great is Artemis of the Ephesians!"

35 And after quieting the multitude, the townclerk *said, "Men of Ephesus, what man is there after all who does not know that the city of the Ephesians is guardian of the temple of the great Artemis, and of the *image* which fell down from heaven?

36 "Since then these are undeniable facts, you ought to keep calm and to do nothing rash.

37 "For you have brought these men *here* who are neither robbers of temples nor blasphemers of our goddess.

38 "So then, if Demetrius and the craftsmen who are with him have a complaint against any man, the courts are in session and proconsuls are *available;* let them bring charges against one another.

39 "But if you want anything beyond this, it shall be settled in the lawful assembly.

40 "For indeed we are in danger of being accused of a riot in connection with today's affair, since there is no

real cause *for it;* and in this connection we shall be unable to account for this disorderly gathering."

41 And after saying this he dismissed the assembly.

CHAPTER 20

And after the uproar had ceased, Paul sent for the disciples and when he had exhorted them and taken his leave of them, he departed to go to Macedonia.

2 And when he had gone through those districts and had given them much exhortation, he came to Greece.

3 And *there* he spent three months, and when a plot was formed against him by the Jews as he was about to set sail for Syria, he determined to return through Macedonia.

4 And he was accompanied by Sopater of Berea, *the son* of Pyrrhus; and by Aristarchus and Secundus of the Thessalonians; and Gaius of Derbe, and Timothy; and Tychicus and Trophimus of Asia.

5 But these had gone on ahead and were waiting for us at Troas.

6 And we sailed from Philippi after the days of Unleavened Bread, and came to them at Troas within five days; and there we stayed seven days.

7 And on the first day of the week, when we were gathered together to break bread, Paul *began* talking to them, intending to depart the next day, and he prolonged his message until midnight.

8 And there were many lamps in the upper room where we were gathered together.

9 And there was a certain young man named Eutychus sitting on the window-sill, sinking into a deep sleep; and as Paul kept on talking, he was overcome by sleep and fell down from the third floor, and was picked up dead.

10 But Paul went down and fell upon him and after embracing him, he said, "Do not be troubled, for his life is in him."

11 And when he had gone *back* up, and had broken the bread and eaten, he talked with them a long while, until daybreak, and so departed.

12 And they took away the boy alive, and were greatly comforted.

13 But we, going ahead to the ship, set sail for Assos, intending from there to take Paul on board; for thus he had arranged it, intending himself to go by land.

14 And when he met us at Assos, we took him on board and came to Mitylene.

15 And sailing from there, we arrived the following day opposite Chios; and the next day we crossed over to Samos; and the day following we came to Miletus.

16 For Paul had decided to sail past Ephesus in order that he might not have to spend time in Asia; for he was hurrying to be in Jerusalem, if possible, on the day of Pentecost.

17 And from Miletus he sent to Ephesus and called to him the elders of the church.

18 And when they had come to him, he said to them,

"You yourselves know, from the first day that I set foot in Asia, how I was with you the whole time,

19 serving the Lord with all humility and with tears and with trials which came upon me through the plots of the Jews;

20 how I did not shrink from declaring to you anything that was profitable, and teaching you publicly and from house to house,

21 solemnly testifying to both Jews and Greeks of repentance toward God and faith in our Lord Jesus Christ.

22 "And now, behold, bound in spirit, I am on my way to Jerusalem,

not knowing what will happen to me there,

23 except that the Holy Spirit solemnly testifies to me in every city, saying that bonds and afflictions await me.

24 "But I do not consider my life of any account as dear to myself, in order that I may finish my course, and the ministry which I received from the Lord Jesus, to testify solemnly of the gospel of the grace of God.

25 "And now, behold, I know that you all, among whom I went about preaching the kingdom, will see my face no more.

26 "Therefore I testify to you this day, that I am innocent of the blood of all men.

27 "For I did not shrink from declaring to you the whole purpose of God.

28 "Be on guard for yourselves and for all the flock, among which the Holy Spirit has made you overseers, to shepherd the church of God which He purchased with His own blood.

29 "I know that after my departure savage wolves will come in among you, not sparing the flock;

30 and from among your own selves men will arise, speaking perverse things, to draw away the disciples after them.

31 "Therefore be on the alert, remembering that night and day for a period of three years I did not cease to admonish each one with tears.

32 "And now I commend you to God and to the word of His grace, which is able to build *you* up and to give *you* the inheritance among all those who are sanctified.

33 "I have coveted no one's silver or gold or clothes.

34 "You yourselves know that these hands ministered to my *own* needs and to the men who were with me.

35 "In every thing I showed you that by working hard in this manner you must help the weak and remember the words of the Lord Jesus, that He Himself said, 'It is more blessed to give than to receive.' "

36 And when he had said these things, he knelt down and prayed with them all.

37 And they *began* to weep aloud and embraced Paul, and repeatedly kissed him,

38 grieving especially over the word which he had spoken, that they should see his face no more. And they were accompanying him to the ship.

CHAPTER 21

AND when it came about that we had parted from them and had set sail, we ran a straight course to Cos and the next day to Rhodes and from there to Patara;

2 and having found a ship crossing over to Phoenicia, we went aboard and set sail.

3 And when we had come in sight of Cyprus, leaving it on the left, we kept sailing to Syria and landed at Tyre; for there the ship was to unload its cargo.

4 And after looking up the disciples, we stayed there seven days; and they kept telling Paul through the Spirit not to set foot in Jerusalem.

5 And when it came about that our days there were ended, we departed and started on our journey, while they all, with wives and children, escorted us until *we were* out of the city. And after kneeling down on the beach and praying, we said farewell to one another.

6 Then we went on board the ship, and they returned home again.

7 And when we had finished the voyage from Tyre, we arrived at Ptolemais; and after greeting the brethren, we stayed with them for a day.

8 And on the next day we departed and came to Caesarea; and

entering the house of Philip the evangelist, who was one of the seven, we stayed with him.

9 Now this man had four virgin daughters who were prophetesses.

10 And as we were staying there for some days, a certain prophet named Agabus came down from Judea.

11 And coming to us, he took Paul's belt and bound his own feet and hands, and said, "This is what the Holy Spirit says: 'In this way the Jews at Jerusalem will bind the man who owns this belt and deliver him into the hands of the Gentiles.' "

12 And when we had heard this, we as well as the local residents *began* begging him not to go up to Jerusalem.

13 Then Paul answered, "What are you doing, weeping and breaking my heart? For I am ready not only to be bound, but even to die at Jerusalem for the name of the Lord Jesus."

14 And since he would not be persuaded, we fell silent, remarking, "The will of the Lord be done!"

15 And after these days we got ready and started on our way up to Jerusalem.

16 And *some* of the disciples from Caesarea also came with us, taking us to Mnason of Cyprus, a disciple of long standing with whom we were to lodge.

17 And when we had come to Jerusalem, the brethren received us gladly.

18 And now the following day Paul went in with us to James, and all the elders were present.

19 And after he had greeted them, he *began* to relate one by one the things which God had done among the Gentiles through his ministry.

20 And when they heard it they *began* glorifying God; and they said to him, "You see, brother, how many thousands there are among the Jews

of those who have believed, and they are all zealous for the Law;

21 and they have been told about you, that you are teaching all the Jews who are among the Gentiles to forsake Moses, telling them not to circumcise their children nor to walk according to the customs.

22 "What, then, is *to be done?* They will certainly hear that you have come.

23 "Therefore do this that we tell you. We have four men who are under a vow;

24 take them and purify yourself along with them, and pay their expenses in order that they may shave their heads; and all will know that there is nothing to the things which they have been told about you, but that you yourself also walk orderly, keeping the Law.

25 "But concerning the Gentiles who have believed, we wrote, having decided that they should abstain from meat sacrificed to idols and from blood and from what is strangled and from fornication."

26 Then Paul took the men, and the next day, purifying himself along with them, went into the temple, giving notice of the completion of the days of purification, until the sacrifice was offered for each one of them.

27 And when the seven days were almost over, the Jews from Asia, upon seeing him in the temple, *began* to stir up all the multitude and laid hands on him,

28 crying out, "Men of Israel, come to our aid! This is the man who preaches to all men everywhere against our people, and the Law, and this place; and besides he has even brought Greeks into the temple and has defiled this holy place."

29 For they had previously seen Trophimus the Ephesian in the city with him, and they supposed that

Paul had brought him into the temple.

30 And all the city was aroused, and the people rushed together; and taking hold of Paul, they dragged him out of the temple; and immediately the doors were shut.

31 And while they were seeking to kill him, a report came up to the commander of the *Roman* cohort that all Jerusalem was in confusion.

32 And at once he took along *some* soldiers and centurions, and ran down to them; and when they saw the commander and the soldiers, they stopped beating Paul.

33 Then the commander came up and took hold of him, and ordered him to be bound with two chains; and he *began* asking who he was and what he had done.

34 But among the crowd some were shouting one thing *and* some another, and when he could not find out the facts on account of the uproar, he ordered him to be brought into the barracks.

35 And when he got to the stairs, it so happened that he was carried by the soldiers because of the violence of the mob;

36 for the multitude of the people kept following behind, crying out, "Away with him!"

37 And as Paul was about to be brought into the barracks, he said to the commander, "May I say something to you?" And he *said, "Do you know Greek?

38 "Then you are not the Egyptian who some time ago stirred up a revolt and led the four thousand men of the Assassins out into the wilderness?"

39 But Paul said, "I am a Jew of Tarsus in Cilicia, a citizen of no insignificant city; and I beg you, allow me to speak to the people."

40 And when he had given him permission, Paul, standing on the stairs, motioned to the people with his hand; and when there was a great hush, he spoke to them in the Hebrew dialect, saying,

CHAPTER 22

"BRETHREN and fathers, hear my defense which I now *offer* to you."

2 And when they heard that he was addressing them in the Hebrew dialect, they became even more quiet; and he *said,

3 "I am a Jew, born in Tarsus of Cilicia, but brought up in this city, educated under Gamaliel, strictly according to the law of our fathers, being zealous for God, just as you all are today.

4 "And I persecuted this Way to the death, binding and putting both men and women into prisons,

5 as also the high priest and all the Council of the elders can testify. From them I also received letters to the brethren, and started off for Damascus in order to bring even those who were there to Jerusalem as prisoners to be punished.

6 "And it came about that as I was on my way, approaching Damascus about noontime, a very bright light suddenly flashed from heaven all around me,

7 and I fell to the ground and heard a voice saying to me, 'Saul, Saul, why are you persecuting Me?'

8 "And I answered, 'Who art Thou, Lord?' And He said to me, 'I am Jesus the Nazarene, whom you are persecuting.'

9 "And those who were with me beheld the light, to be sure, but did not understand the voice of the One who was speaking to me.

10 "And I said, 'What shall I do, Lord?' And the Lord said to me, 'Arise and go on into Damascus; and there you will be told of all that has been appointed for you to do.'

11 "But since I could not see because of the brightness of that light, I

was led by the hand by those who were with me, and came into Damascus.

12 "And a certain Ananias, a man who was devout by the standard of the Law, *and* well spoken of by all the Jews who lived there,

13 came to me, and standing near said to me, 'Brother Saul, receive your sight!' And at that very time I looked up at him.

14 "And he said, 'The God of our fathers has appointed you to know His will, and to see the Righteous One, and to hear an utterance from His mouth.

15 'For you will be a witness for Him to all men of what you have seen and heard.

16 'And now why do you delay? Arise, and be baptized, and wash away your sins, calling on His name.'

17 "And it came about when I returned to Jerusalem and was praying in the temple, that I fell into a trance,

18 and I saw Him saying to me, 'Make haste, and get out of Jerusalem quickly, because they will not accept your testimony about Me.'

19 "And I said, 'Lord, they themselves understand that in one synagogue after another I used to imprison and beat those who believed in Thee.

20 'And when the blood of Thy witness Stephen was being shed, I also was standing by approving, and watching out for the cloaks of those who were slaying him.'

21 "And He said to me, 'Go! For I will send you far away to the Gentiles.'"

22 And they listened to him up to this statement, and *then* they raised their voices and said, "Away with such a fellow from the earth, for he should not be allowed to live!"

23 And as they were crying out and throwing off their cloaks and tossing dust into the air,

24 the commander ordered him to be brought into the barracks, stating that he should be examined by scourging so that he might find out the reason why they were shouting against him that way.

25 And when they stretched him out with thongs, Paul said to the centurion who was standing by, "Is it lawful for you to scourge a man who is a Roman and uncondemned?"

26 And when the centurion heard *this,* he went to the commander and told him, saying, "What are you about to do? For this man is a Roman."

27 And the commander came and said to him, "Tell me, are you a Roman?" And he said, "Yes."

28 And the commander answered, "I acquired this citizenship with a large sum of money." And Paul said, "But I was actually born *a citizen.*"

29 Therefore those who were about to examine him immediately let go of him; and the commander also was afraid when he found out that he was a Roman, and because he had put him in chains.

30 But on the next day, wishing to know for certain why he had been accused by the Jews, he released him and ordered the chief priests and all the Council to assemble, and brought Paul down and set him before them.

CHAPTER 23

AND Paul, looking intently at the Council, said, "Brethren, I have lived my life with a perfectly good conscience before God up to this day."

2 And the high priest Ananias commanded those standing beside him to strike him on the mouth.

3 Then Paul said to him, "God is going to strike you, you white-washed wall! And do you sit to try me according to the Law, and in violation of the Law order me to be struck?"

4 But the bystanders said, "Do you revile God's high priest?"

5 And Paul said, "I was not aware, brethren, that he was high priest; for it is written, 'YOU SHALL NOT SPEAK EVIL OF A RULER OF YOUR PEOPLE.'"

6 But perceiving that one part were Sadducees and the other Pharisees, Paul *began* crying out in the Council, "Brethren, I am a Pharisee, a son of Pharisees; I am on trial for the hope and resurrection of the dead!"

7 And as he said this, there arose a dissension between the Pharisees and Sadducees; and the assembly was divided.

8 For the Sadducees say that there is no resurrection, nor an angel, nor a spirit; but the Pharisees acknowledge them all.

9 And there arose a great uproar; and some of the scribes of the Pharisaic party stood up and *began* to argue heatedly, saying, "We find nothing wrong with this man; suppose a spirit or an angel has spoken to him?"

10 And as a great dissension was developing, the commander was afraid Paul would be torn to pieces by them and ordered the troops to go down and take him away from them by force, and bring him into the barracks.

11 But on the night *immediately* following, the Lord stood at his side and said, "Take courage; for as you have solemnly witnessed to My cause at Jerusalem, so you must witness at Rome also."

12 And when it was day, the Jews formed a conspiracy and bound themselves under an oath, saying that they would neither eat nor drink until they had killed Paul.

13 And there were more than forty who formed this plot.

14 And they came to the chief priests and the elders, and said, "We have bound ourselves under a solemn oath to taste nothing until we have killed Paul.

15 "Now, therefore, you and the Council notify the commander to bring him down to you, as though you were going to determine his case by a more thorough investigation; and we for our part are ready to slay him before he comes near *the place.*"

16 But the son of Paul's sister heard of their ambush, and he came and entered the barracks and told Paul.

17 And Paul called one of the centurions to him and said, "Lead this young man to the commander, for he has something to report to him."

18 So he took him and led him to the commander and *said, "Paul the prisoner called me to him and asked me to lead this young man to you since he has something to tell you."

19 And the commander took him by the hand and stepping aside, *began* to inquire of him privately, "What is it that you have to report to me?"

20 And he said, "The Jews have agreed to ask you to bring Paul down tomorrow to the Council, as though they were going to inquire somewhat more thoroughly about him.

21 "So do not listen to them, for more than forty of them are lying in wait for him who have bound themselves under a curse not to eat or drink until they slay him; and now they are ready and waiting for the promise from you."

22 Therefore the commander let the young man go, instructing him, "Tell no one that you have notified me of these things."

23 And he called to him two of the centurions, and said, "Get two hundred soldiers ready by the third hour of the night to proceed to Caesarea, with seventy horsemen and two hundred spearmen."

24 *They were* also to provide mounts to put Paul on and bring him safely to Felix the governor.

25 And he wrote a letter having this form:

26 "Claudius Lysias, to the most excellent governor Felix, greetings.

27 "When this man was arrested by the Jews and was about to be slain by them, I came upon them with the troops and rescued him, having learned that he was a Roman.

28 "And wanting to ascertain the charge for which they were accusing him, I brought him down to their Council;

29 and I found him to be accused over questions about their Law, but under no accusation deserving death or imprisonment.

30 "And when I was informed that there would be a plot against the man, I sent him to you at once, also instructing his accusers to bring charges against him before you."

31 So the soldiers, in accordance with their orders, took Paul and brought him by night to Antipatris.

32 But the next day, leaving the horsemen to go on with him, they returned to the barracks.

33 And when these had come to Caesarea and delivered the letter to the governor, they also presented Paul to him.

34 And when he had read it, he asked from what province he was; and when he learned that he was from Cilicia,

35 he said, "I will give you a hearing after your accusers arrive also," giving orders for him to be kept in Herod's Praetorium.

AND after five days the high priest Ananias came down with some elders, with a certain attorney *named* Tertullus; and they brought charges to the governor against Paul.

2 And after *Paul* had been summoned, Tertullus began to accuse him, saying *to the governor*,

"Since we have through you attained much peace, and since by your providence reforms are being carried out for this nation,

3 we acknowledge *this* in every way and everywhere, most excellent Felix, with all thankfulness.

4 "But, that I may not weary you any further, I beg you to grant us, by your kindness, a brief hearing.

5 "For we have found this man a real pest and a fellow who stirs up dissension among all the Jews throughout the world, and a ringleader of the sect of the Nazarenes.

6 "And he even tried to desecrate the temple; and then we arrested him.

7 (See footnote.)

8 "And by examining him yourself concerning all these matters, you will be able to ascertain the things of which we accuse him."

9 And the Jews also joined in the attack, asserting that these things were so.

10 And when the governor had nodded for him to speak, Paul responded:

"Knowing that for many years you have been a judge to this nation, I cheerfully make my defense,

11 since you can take note of the fact that no more than twelve days ago I went up to Jerusalem to worship.

12 "And neither in the temple, nor

Some later mss. add [*And we wanted to judge him according to our own Law. 7 "But Lysias the commander came along, and with much violence took him out of our hands, 8 ordering his accusers to come before you.*]

in the synagogues, nor in the city *itself* did they find me carrying on a discussion with anyone or causing a riot.

13 "Nor can they prove to you the charges of which they now accuse me.

14 "But this I admit to you, that according to the Way which they call a sect I do serve the God of our fathers, believing everything that is in accordance with the Law, and that is written in the Prophets;

15 having a hope in God, which these men cherish themselves, that there shall certainly be a resurrection of both the righteous and the wicked.

16 "In view of this, I also do my best to maintain always a blameless conscience *both* before God and before men.

17 "Now after several years I came to bring alms to my nation and to present offerings;

18 in which they found me *occupied* in the temple, having been purified, without *any* crowd or uproar. But *there were* certain Jews from Asia—

19 who ought to have been present before you, and to make accusation, if they should have anything against me.

20 "Or else let these men themselves tell what misdeed they found when I stood before the Council,

21 other than for this one statement which I shouted out while standing among them, 'For the resurrection of the dead I am on trial before you today.'"

22 But Felix, having a more exact knowledge about the Way, put them off, saying, "When Lysias the commander comes down, I will decide your case."

23 And he gave orders to the centurion for him to be kept in custody and *yet* have *some* freedom, and not to prevent any of his friends from ministering to him.

24 But some days later, Felix arrived with Drusilla, his wife who was a Jewess, and sent for Paul, and heard him *speak* about faith in Christ Jesus.

25 And as he was discussing righteousness, self-control and the judgment to come, Felix became frightened and said, "Go away for the present, and when I find time, I will summon you."

26 At the same time too, he was hoping that money would be given him by Paul; therefore he also used to send for him quite often and converse with him.

27 But after two years had passed, Felix was succeeded by Porcius Festus; and wishing to do the Jews a favor, Felix left Paul imprisoned.

CHAPTER 25

FESTUS therefore, having arrived in the province, three days later went up to Jerusalem from Caesarea.

2 And the chief priests and the leading men of the Jews brought charges against Paul; and they were urging him,

3 requesting a concession against Paul, that he might have him brought to Jerusalem, (*at the same time*, setting an ambush to kill him on the way).

4 Festus then answered that Paul was being kept in custody at Caesarea and that he himself was about to leave shortly.

5 "Therefore," he *said, "let the influential men among you go there with me, and if there is anything wrong about the man, let them prosecute him."

6 And after he had spent not more than eight or ten days among them, he went down to Caesarea; and on the next day he took his seat on the tribunal and ordered Paul to be brought.

7 And after he had arrived, the Jews who had come down from Jeru-

salem stood around him, bringing many and serious charges against him which they could not prove;

8 while Paul said in his own defense, "I have committed no offense either against the Law of the Jews or against the temple or against Caesar."

9 But Festus, wishing to do the Jews a favor, answered Paul and said, "Are you willing to go up to Jerusalem and stand trial before me on these charges?"

10 But Paul said, "I am standing before Caesar's tribunal, where I ought to be tried. I have done no wrong to the Jews, as you also very well know.

11 "If then I am a wrongdoer, and have committed anything worthy of death, I do not refuse to die; but if none of those things is true of which these men accuse me, no one can hand me over to them. I appeal to Caesar."

12 Then when Festus had conferred with his council, he answered, "You have appealed to Caesar, to Caesar you shall go."

13 Now when several days had elapsed, King Agrippa and Bernice arrived at Caesarea, and paid their respects to Festus.

14 And while they were spending many days there, Festus laid Paul's case before the king, saying, "There is a certain man left a prisoner by Felix;

15 and when I was at Jerusalem, the chief priests and the elders of the Jews brought charges against him, asking for a sentence of condemnation upon him.

16 "And I answered them that it is not the custom of the Romans to hand over any man before the accused meets his accusers face to face, and has an opportunity to make his defense against the charges.

17 "And so after they had assembled here, I made no delay, but on the next day took my seat on the tribunal, and ordered the man to be brought.

18 "And when the accusers stood up, they began bringing charges against him not of such crimes as I was expecting;

19 but they simply had some points of disagreement with him about their own religion and about a certain dead man, Jesus, whom Paul asserted to be alive.

20 "And being at a loss how to investigate such matters, I asked whether he was willing to go to Jerusalem and there stand trial on these matters.

21 "But when Paul appealed to be held in custody for the Emperor's decision, I ordered him to be kept in custody until I send him to Caesar."

22 And Agrippa said to Festus, "I also would like to hear the man myself." "Tomorrow," he *said, "you shall hear him."

23 And so, on the next day when Agrippa had come together with Bernice, amid great pomp, and had entered the auditorium accompanied by the commanders and the prominent men of the city, at the command of Festus, Paul was brought in.

24 And Festus *said, "King Agrippa, and all you gentlemen here present with us, you behold this man about whom all the people of the Jews appealed to me, both at Jerusalem and here, loudly declaring that he ought not to live any longer.

25 "But I found that he had committed nothing worthy of death; and since he himself appealed to the Emperor, I decided to send him.

26 "Yet I have nothing definite about him to write to my lord. Therefore I have brought him before you all and especially before you, King Agrippa, so that after the investigation has taken place, I may have something to write.

27 "For it seems absurd to me in

sending a prisoner, not to indicate also the charges against him."

CHAPTER 26

AND Agrippa said to Paul, "You are permitted to speak for yourself." Then Paul stretched out his hand and *proceeded* to make his defense:

2 "In regard to all the things of which I am accused by the Jews, I consider myself fortunate, King Agrippa, that I am about to make my defense before you today;

3 especially because you are an expert in all customs and questions among *the* Jews; therefore I beg you to listen to me patiently.

4 "So then, all Jews know my manner of life from my youth up, which from the beginning was spent among my *own* nation and at Jerusalem;

5 since they have known about me for a long time previously, if they are willing to testify, that I lived *as* a Pharisee according to the strictest sect of our religion.

6 "And now I am standing trial for the hope of the promise made by God to our fathers;

7 *the promise* to which our twelve tribes hope to attain, as they earnestly serve God night and day. And for this hope, O King, I am being accused by Jews.

8 "Why is it considered incredible among you *people* if God does raise the dead?

9 "So then, I thought to myself that I had to do many things hostile to the name of Jesus of Nazareth.

10 "And this is just what I did in Jerusalem; not only did I lock up many of the saints in prisons, having received authority from the chief priests, but also when they were being put to death I cast my vote against them.

11 "And as I punished them often in all the synagogues, I tried to force them to blaspheme; and being furiously enraged at them, I kept pursuing them even to foreign cities.

12 "While thus engaged as I was journeying to Damascus with the authority and commission of the chief priests,

13 at midday, O King, I saw on the way a light from heaven, brighter than the sun, shining all around me and those who were journeying with me.

14 "And when we had all fallen to the ground, I heard a voice saying to me in the Hebrew dialect, 'Saul, Saul, why are you persecuting Me? It is hard for you to kick against the goads.'

15 "And I said, 'Who art Thou, Lord?' And the Lord said, 'I am Jesus whom you are persecuting.

16 'But arise, and stand on your feet; for this purpose I have appeared to you, to appoint you a minister and a witness not only to the things which you have seen, but also to the things in which I will appear to you;

17 delivering you from the *Jewish* people and from the Gentiles, to whom I am sending you,

18 to open their eyes so that they may turn from darkness to light and from the dominion of Satan to God, in order that they may receive forgiveness of sins and an inheritance among those who have been sanctified by faith in Me.'

19 "Consequently, King Agrippa, I did not prove disobedient to the heavenly vision,

20 but *kept* declaring both to those of Damascus first, and *also* at Jerusalem and *then* throughout all the region of Judea, and *even* to the Gentiles, that they should repent and turn to God, performing deeds appropriate to repentance.

21 "For this reason *some* Jews seized me in the temple and tried to put me to death.

22 "And so, having obtained help

from God, I stand to this day testifying both to small and great, stating nothing but what the Prophets and Moses said was going to take place;

23 that the Christ was to suffer, *and* that by reason of *His* resurrection from the dead He should be the first to proclaim light both to the *Jewish* people and to the Gentiles."

24 And while *Paul* was saying this in his defense, Festus *said in a loud voice, "Paul, you are out of your mind! *Your* great learning is driving you mad."

25 But Paul *said, "I am not out of my mind, most excellent Festus, but I utter words of sober truth.

26 "For the king knows about these matters, and I speak to him also with confidence, since I am persuaded that none of these things escape his notice; for this has not been done in a corner.

27 "King Agrippa, do you believe the Prophets? I know that you do."

28 And Agrippa *replied* to Paul, "In a short time you will persuade me to become a Christian."

29 And Paul *said,* "I would to God, that whether in a short or long time, not only you, but also all who hear me this day, might become such as I am, except for these chains."

.30 And the king arose and the governor and Bernice, and those who were sitting with them,

31 and when they had drawn aside, they *began* talking to one another, saying, "This man is not doing anything worthy of death or imprisonment."

32 And Agrippa said to Festus, "This man might have been set free if he had not appealed to Caesar."

Chapter 27

AND when it was decided that we should sail for Italy, they proceeded to deliver Paul and some other prisoners to a centurion of the Augustan cohort named Julius.

2 And embarking in an Adramyttium ship, which was about to sail to the regions along the coast of Asia, we put out to sea, accompanied by Aristarchus, a Macedonian of Thessalonica.

3 And the next day we put in at Sidon; and Julius treated Paul with consideration and allowed him to go to his friends and receive care.

4 And from there we put out to sea and sailed under the shelter of Cyprus because the winds were contrary.

5 And when we had sailed through the sea along the coast of Cilicia and Pamphylia, we landed at Myra in Lycia.

6 And there the centurion found an Alexandrian ship sailing for Italy, and he put us aboard it.

7 And when we had sailed slowly for a good many days, and with difficulty had arrived off Cnidus, since the wind did not permit us *to go* farther, we sailed under the shelter of Crete, off Salmone;

8 and with difficulty sailing past it we came to a certain place called Fair Havens, near which was the city of Lasea.

9 And when considerable time had passed and the voyage was now dangerous, since even the fast was already over, Paul *began* to admonish them,

10 and said to them, "Men, I perceive that the voyage will certainly be *attended* with damage and great loss, not only of the cargo and the ship, but also of our lives."

11 But the centurion was more persuaded by the pilot and the captain of the ship, than by what was being said by Paul.

12 And because the harbor was not suitable for wintering, the majority reached a decision to put out to sea from there, if somehow they could

reach Phoenix, a harbor of Crete, facing northeast and southeast, and spend the winter *there*.

13 And when a moderate south wind came up, supposing that they had gained their purpose, they weighed anchor and *began* sailing along Crete, close *inshore*.

14 But before very long there rushed down from the land a violent wind, called Euraquilo;

15 and when the ship was caught *in it*, and could not face the wind, we gave way *to it*, and let ourselves be driven along.

16 And running under the shelter of a small island called Clauda, we were scarcely able to get the *ship's* boat under control.

17 And after they had hoisted it up, they used supporting cables in undergirding the ship; and fearing that they might run aground on *the shallows* of Syrtis, they let down the sea anchor, and so let themselves be driven along.

18 The next day as we were being violently storm-tossed, they began to jettison the cargo;

19 and on the third day they threw the ship's tackle overboard with their own hands.

20 And since neither sun nor stars appeared for many days, and no small storm was assailing *us*, from then on all hope of our being saved was gradually abandoned.

21 And when they had gone a long time without food, then Paul stood up in their midst and said, "Men, you ought to have followed my advice and not to have set sail from Crete, and incurred this damage and loss.

22 "And *yet* now I urge you to keep up your courage, for there shall be no loss of life among you, but *only* of the ship.

23 "For this very night an angel of the God to whom I belong and whom I serve stood before me,

24 saying, 'Do not be afraid, Paul;

you must stand before Caesar; and behold, God has granted you all those who are sailing with you.'

25 "Therefore, keep up your courage, men, for I believe God, that it will turn out exactly as I have been told.

26 "But we must run aground on a certain island."

27 But when the fourteenth night had come, as we were being driven about in the Adriatic Sea, about midnight the sailors *began* to surmise that they were approaching some land.

28 And they took soundings, and found *it to be* twenty fathoms; and a little farther on they took another sounding and found *it to be* fifteen fathoms.

29 And fearing that we might run aground somewhere on the rocks, they cast four anchors from the stern and wished for daybreak.

30 And as the sailors were trying to escape from the ship, and had let down the *ship's* boat into the sea, on the pretense of intending to lay out anchors from the bow,

31 Paul said to the centurion and to the soldiers, "Unless these men remain in the ship, you yourselves cannot be saved."

32 Then the soldiers cut away the ropes of the *ship's* boat, and let it fall away.

33 And until the day was about to dawn, Paul was encouraging them all to take some food, saying, "Today is the fourteenth day that you have been constantly watching and going without eating, having taken nothing.

34 "Therefore I encourage you to take some food, for this is for your preservation; for not a hair from the head of any of you shall perish."

35 And having said this, he took bread and gave thanks to God in the presence of all; and he broke it and began to eat.

36 And all of them were encour-

aged, and they themselves also took food.

37 And all of us in the ship were two hundred and seventy-six persons.

38 And when they had eaten enough, they *began* to lighten the ship by throwing out the wheat into the sea.

39 And when day came, they could not recognize the land; but they did observe a certain bay with a beach, and they resolved to drive the ship onto it if they could.

40 And casting off the anchors, they left them in the sea while at the same time they were loosening the ropes of the rudders, and hoisting the foresail to the wind, they were heading for the beach.

41 But striking a reef where two seas met, they ran the vessel aground; and the prow stuck fast and remained immovable, but the stern *began* to be broken up by the force *of the waves.*

42 And the soldiers' plan was to kill the prisoners, that none *of them* should swim away and escape;

43 but the centurion, wanting to bring Paul safely through, kept them from their intention, and commanded that those who could swim should jump overboard first and get to land,

44 and the rest *should follow*, some on planks, and others on various things from the ship. And thus it happened that they all were brought safely to land.

CHAPTER 28

AND when they had been brought safely through, then we found out that the island was called Malta.

2 And the natives showed us extraordinary kindness; for because of the rain that had set in and because of the cold, they kindled a fire and received us all.

3 But when Paul had gathered a bundle of sticks and laid them on the fire, a viper came out because of the heat, and fastened on his hand.

4 And when the natives saw the creature hanging from his hand, they *began* saying to one another, "Undoubtedly this man is a murderer, and though he has been saved from the sea, justice has not allowed him to live."

5 However he shook the creature off into the fire and suffered no harm.

6 But they were expecting that he was about to swell up or suddenly fall down dead. But after they had waited a long time and had seen nothing unusual happen to him, they changed their minds and *began* to say that he was a god.

7 Now in the neighborhood of that place were lands belonging to the leading man of the island, named Publius, who welcomed us and entertained us courteously three days.

8 And it came about that the father of Publius was lying *in bed* afflicted with *recurrent* fever and dysentery; and Paul went in *to see* him and after he had prayed, he laid his hands on him and healed him.

9 And after this had happened, the rest of the people on the island who had diseases were coming to him and getting cured.

10 And they also honored us with many marks of respect; and when we were setting sail, they supplied *us* with all we needed.

11 And at the end of three months we set sail on an Alexandrian ship which had wintered at the island, and which had the Twin Brothers for its figurehead.

12 And after we put in at Syracuse, we stayed there for three days.

13 And from there we sailed around and arrived at Rhegium, and a day later a south wind sprang up, and on the second day we came to Puteoli.

14 There we found *some* brethren, and were invited to stay with them for seven days; and thus we came to Rome.

15 And the brethren, when they heard about us, came from there as far as the Market of Appius and Three Inns to meet us; and when Paul saw them, he thanked God and took courage.

16 And when we entered Rome, Paul was allowed to stay by himself, with the soldier who was guarding him.

17 And it happened that after three days he called together those who were the leading men of the Jews, and when they had come together, he *began* saying to them, "Brethren, though I had done nothing against our people, or the customs of our fathers, yet I was delivered prisoner from Jerusalem into the hands of the Romans.

18 "And when they had examined me, they were willing to release me because there was no ground for putting me to death.

19 "But when the Jews objected, I was forced to appeal to Caesar; not that I had any accusation against my nation.

20 "For this reason therefore, I requested to see you and to speak with you, for I am wearing this chain for the sake of the hope of Israel."

21 And they said to him, "We have neither received letters from Judea concerning you, nor have any of the brethren come here and reported or spoken anything bad about you.

22 "But we desire to hear from you what your views are; for concerning this sect, it is known to us that it is spoken against everywhere."

23 And when they had set a day for him, they came to him at his lodging in large numbers; and he was explaining to them by solemnly testifying about the kingdom of God, and trying to persuade them concerning Jesus, from both the Law of Moses and from the Prophets, from morning until evening.

24 And some were being persuaded by the things spoken, but others would not believe.

25 And when they did not agree with one another, they *began* leaving after Paul had spoken one parting word, "The Holy Spirit rightly spoke through Isaiah the prophet to your fathers,

26 saying,

'GO TO THIS PEOPLE AND SAY,
"YOU WILL KEEP ON HEARING,
    BUT WILL NOT UNDERSTAND;
AND YOU WILL KEEP ON SEEING,
    BUT WILL NOT PERCEIVE;

27 FOR THE HEART OF THIS PEOPLE
    HAS BECOME DULL,
AND WITH THEIR EARS THEY
    SCARCELY HEAR,
AND THEY HAVE CLOSED THEIR
    EYES;
LEST THEY SHOULD SEE WITH
    THEIR EYES,
AND HEAR WITH THEIR EARS,
AND UNDERSTAND WITH THEIR
    HEART AND TURN AGAIN,
AND I SHOULD HEAL THEM." '

28 "Let it be known to you therefore, that this salvation of God has been sent to the Gentiles; they will also listen."

29 (See footnote.)

30 And he stayed two full years in his own rented quarters, and was welcoming all who came to him,

31 preaching the kingdom of God, and teaching concerning the Lord Jesus Christ with all openness, unhindered.

Some mss. add vs. 29, *And when he had spoken these words, the Jews departed, having a great dispute among themselves.*

PAUL, a bond-servant of Christ Jesus, called *as* an apostle, set apart for the gospel of God,

2 which He promised beforehand through His prophets in the holy Scriptures,

3 concerning His Son, who was born of the seed of David according to the flesh,

4 who was declared with power *to be* the Son of God by the resurrection from the dead, according to the Spirit of holiness, Jesus Christ our Lord,

5 through whom we have received grace and apostleship to bring about *the* obedience of faith among all the Gentiles, for His name's sake,

6 among whom you also are the called of Jesus Christ;

7 to all who are beloved of God in Rome, called *as* saints: Grace to you and peace from God our Father and the Lord Jesus Christ.

8 First, I thank my God through Jesus Christ for you all, because your faith is being proclaimed throughout the whole world.

9 For God, whom I serve in my spirit in the *preaching of the* gospel of His Son, is my witness *as to* how unceasingly I make mention of you,

10 always in my prayers making request, if perhaps now at last by the will of God I may succeed in coming to you.

11 For I long to see you in order that I may impart some spiritual gift to you, that you may be established;

12 that is, that I may be encouraged together with you *while* among you, each of us by the other's faith, both yours and mine.

13 And I do not want you to be unaware, brethren, that often I have planned to come to you (and have been prevented thus far) in order that I might obtain some fruit among you also, even as among the rest of the Gentiles.

14 I am under obligation both to Greeks and to barbarians, both to the wise and to the foolish.

15 Thus, for my part, I am eager to preach the gospel to you also who are in Rome.

16 For I am not ashamed of the gospel, for it is the power of God for salvation to every one who believes, to the Jew first and also to the Greek.

17 For in it *the* righteousness of God is revealed from faith to faith; as it is written, "BUT THE RIGHTEOUS *man* SHALL LIVE BY FAITH."

18 For the wrath of God is revealed from heaven against all ungodliness and unrighteousness of men, who suppress the truth in unrighteousness,

19 because that which is known about God is evident within them; for God made it evident to them.

20 For since the creation of the world His invisible attributes, His eternal power and divine nature, have been clearly seen, being understood through what has been made, so that they are without excuse.

21 For even though they knew God, they did not honor Him as God, or give thanks; but they became futile in their speculations, and their foolish heart was darkened.

22 Professing to be wise, they became fools,

23 and exchanged the glory of the incorruptible God for an image in the form of corruptible man and of birds and four-footed animals and crawling creatures.

24 Therefore God gave them over in the lusts of their hearts to impurity,

that their bodies might be dishonored among them.

25 For they exchanged the truth of God for a lie, and worshiped and served the creature rather than the Creator, who is blessed forever. Amen.

26 For this reason God gave them over to degrading passions; for their women exchanged the natural function for that which is unnatural,

27 and in the same way also the men abandoned the natural function of the woman and burned in their desire towards one another, men with men committing indecent acts and receiving in their own persons the due penalty of their error.

28 And just as they did not see fit to acknowledge God any longer, God gave them over to a depraved mind, to do those things which are not proper,

29 being filled with all unrighteousness, wickedness, greed, malice; full of envy, murder, strife, deceit, malice; *they are* gossips,

30 slanderers, haters of God, insolent, arrogant, boastful, inventors of evil, disobedient to parents,

31 without understanding, untrustworthy, unloving, unmerciful;

32 and, although they know the ordinance of God, that those who practice such things are worthy of death, they not only do the same, but also give hearty approval to those who practice them.

CHAPTER 2

THEREFORE you are without excuse, every man *of you* who passes judgment, for in that you judge another, you condemn yourself; for you who judge practice the same things.

2 And we know that the judgment of God rightly falls upon those who practice such things.

3 And do you suppose this, O man, when you pass judgment upon those who practice such things and do the same *yourself*, that you will escape the judgment of God?

SCRIPTURE NO. 5, SEC. 1

4 Or do you think lightly of the riches of His kindness and forbearance and patience, not knowing that the kindness of God leads you to repentance? (r5)

5 But because of your stubbornness and unrepentant heart you are storing up wrath for yourself in the day of wrath and revelation of the righteous judgment of God,

6 who WILL RENDER TO EVERY MAN ACCORDING TO HIS DEEDS:

(r5) REFERENCE NO. 5, SEC. 1—
WHAT GOD'S KINDNESS OR LOVE SHOULD LEAD YOU TO DO.
"The kindness of God leads you to repentance."

Repentance is a change of mind, heart, and direction. It is shown in a "sorrow according to the will of God," which leads you to "turn to God from idols to serve a living and true God." You make an about face from sin "without regret leading to salvation."

Jesus warns, "unless you repent, you will all likewise perish."

Remember, "God is now declaring to men that all everywhere should repent."

Obey God's command now. "Repent therefore and return, that your sins may be wiped away." This shows you "The Lord . . . is not wishing for any to perish but for all to come to repentance."

"Are you sorry for your sins and willing to repent?" If so, say:

"I am sorry for my sins. I see that the kindness or love of God leads me to repent."

Now turn to page 219, Scripture No. 6, Sec. 1, Rom. 10:9-14.

7 to those who by perseverance in doing good seek for glory and honor and immortality, eternal life;

8 but to those who are selfishly ambitious and do not obey the truth, but obey unrighteousness, wrath and indignation.

9 *There will be* tribulation and distress for every soul of man who does evil, of the Jew first and also of the Greek,

10 but glory and honor and peace to every man who does good, to the Jew first and also to the Greek.

11 For there is no partiality with God.

12 For all who have sinned without the Law will also perish without the Law; and all who have sinned under the Law will be judged by the Law;

13 for not the hearers of the Law are just before God, but the doers of the Law will be justified.

14 For when Gentiles who do not have the Law do instinctively the things of the Law, these, not having the Law, are a law to themselves,

15 in that they show the work of the Law written in their hearts, their conscience bearing witness, and their thoughts alternately accusing or else defending them,

16 on the day when, according to my gospel, God will judge the secrets of men through Christ Jesus.

17 But if you bear the name 'Jew,' and rely upon the Law, and boast in God,

18 and know *His* will, and approve the things that are essential, being instructed out of the Law,

19 and are confident that you yourself are a guide to the blind, a light to those who are in darkness,

20 a corrector of the foolish, a teacher of the immature, having in the Law the embodiment of knowledge and of the truth,

21 you, therefore, who teach another, do you not teach yourself? You who preach that one should not steal, do you steal?

22 You who say that one should not commit adultery, do you commit adultery? You who abhor idols, do you rob temples?

23 You who boast in the Law, through your breaking the Law, do you dishonor God?

24 For "THE NAME OF GOD IS BLASPHEMED AMONG THE GENTILES BECAUSE OF YOU," just as it is written.

25 For indeed circumcision is of value, if you practice the Law; but if you are a transgressor of the Law, your circumcision has become uncircumcision.

26 If therefore the uncircumcised man keeps the requirements of the Law, will not his uncircumcision be regarded as circumcision?

27 And will not he who is physically uncircumcised, if he keeps the Law, will he not judge you who though having the letter *of the Law* and circumcision are a transgressor of the Law?

28 For he is not a Jew who is one outwardly; neither is circumcision that which is outward in the flesh.

29 But he is a Jew who is one inwardly; and circumcision is that which is of the heart, by the Spirit, not by the letter; and his praise is not from men, but from God.

CHAPTER 3

THEN what advantage has the Jew? Or what is the benefit of circumcision?

2 Great in every respect. First of all, that they were entrusted with the oracles of God.

3 What then? If some did not believe, their unbelief will not nullify the faithfulness of God, will it?

4 May it never be! Rather, let God be found true, though every man *be found* a liar, as it is written,

"THAT THOU MIGHTEST BE JUS-
TIFIED IN THY WORDS,
AND MIGHTEST PREVAIL WHEN
THOU ART JUDGED."

5 But if our unrighteousness demonstrates the righteousness of God, what shall we say? The God who inflicts wrath is not unrighteous, is He? (I am speaking in human terms.)

6 May it never be! For otherwise how will God judge the world?

7 But if through my lie the truth of God abounded to His glory, why am I also still being judged as a sinner?

8 And why not *say* (as we are slanderously reported and as some affirm that we say), "Let us do evil that good may come"? Their condemnation is just.

9 What then? Are we better than they? Not at all; for we have already charged that both Jews and Greeks are all under sin;

10 as it is written,

"THERE IS NONE RIGHTEOUS,
NOT EVEN ONE;

11 THERE IS NONE WHO UNDER-
STANDS,
THERE IS NONE WHO SEEKS FOR
GOD;

12 ALL HAVE TURNED ASIDE, TO-
GETHER THEY HAVE BECOME
USELESS;
THERE IS NONE WHO DOES
GOOD,
THERE IS NOT EVEN ONE."

13 "THEIR THROAT IS AN OPEN
GRAVE,
WITH THEIR TONGUES THEY
KEEP DECEIVING,"
"THE POISON OF ASPS IS UNDER
THEIR LIPS;"

14 "WHOSE MOUTH IS FULL OF
CURSING AND BITTERNESS;"

15 "THEIR FEET ARE SWIFT TO SHED
BLOOD,

16 DESTRUCTION AND MISERY ARE
IN THEIR PATHS,

17 AND THE PATH OF PEACE HAVE
THEY NOT KNOWN."

18 "THERE IS NO FEAR OF GOD BE-
FORE THEIR EYES."

19 Now we know that whatever the Law says, it speaks to those who are under the Law, that every mouth may be closed, and all the world may become accountable to God;

20 because by the works of the Law no flesh will be justified in His sight; for through the Law *comes* the knowledge of sin.

21 But now apart from the Law *the* righteousness of God has been manifested, being witnessed by the Law and the Prophets,

22 even *the* righteousness of God through faith in Jesus Christ for all those who believe; for there is no distinction;

SCRIPTURE NO. 2, SEC. 1

23 for all have sinned and fall short of the glory of God, (r2)

(r2) REFERENCE NO. 2, SEC. 1—THE FACT OF SIN.

"All have sinned" includes you, me, and everyone.

What is sin? God answers, "All unrighteousness is sin." That is, all wrong or evil is sin. "Whatever is not from faith is sin," and the "one who knows the right thing to do and does not do it, to him it is sin."

"If we say that we have no sin, we are deceiving ourselves . . . if we say we have not sinned, we make Him a liar, and His word is not in us."

Because you have sinned you are "accountable to God." That is why you need to be forgiven and saved.

Will you admit you are a sinner? If so, say:

"I have sinned and fallen short of the glory of God."

Now turn to page 214, Scripture No. 3, Sec. 1, Rom. 6:23.

24 being justified as a gift by His grace through the redemption which is in Christ Jesus;

25 whom God displayed publicly as a propitiation in His blood through faith. *This was* to demonstrate His righteousness, because in the forbearance of God He passed over the sins previously committed;

26 for the demonstration, *I say,* of His righteousness at the present time, that He might be just and the justifier of the one who has faith in Jesus.

27 Where then is boasting? It is excluded. By what kind of law? Of works? No, but by a law of faith.

28 For we maintain that a man is justified by faith apart from works of the Law.

29 Or is God *the God* of Jews only? Is He not *the God* of Gentiles also? Yes, of Gentiles also—

30 if indeed God is one—and He will justify the circumcised by faith and the uncircumcised through faith.

31 Do we then nullify the Law through faith? May it never be! On the contrary, we establish the Law.

CHAPTER 4

WHAT then shall we say that Abraham, our forefather according to the flesh, has found?

2 For if Abraham was justified by works, he has something to boast about; but not before God.

3 For what does the Scripture say? "AND ABRAHAM BELIEVED GOD, AND IT WAS RECKONED TO HIM AS RIGHTEOUSNESS."

4 Now to the one who works, his wage is not reckoned as a favor but as what is due.

5 But to the one who does not work, but believes in Him who justifies the ungodly, his faith is reckoned as righteousness,

6 just as David also speaks of the blessing upon the man to whom God reckons righteousness apart from works:

7 "BLESSED ARE THOSE WHOSE LAWLESS DEEDS HAVE BEEN FORGIVEN,
AND WHOSE SINS HAVE BEEN COVERED.

8 "BLESSED IS THE MAN WHOSE SIN THE LORD WILL NOT TAKE INTO ACCOUNT."

9 Is this blessing then upon the circumcised, or upon the uncircumcised also? For we say, "FAITH WAS RECKONED TO ABRAHAM AS RIGHTEOUSNESS."

10 How then was it reckoned? While he was circumcised, or uncircumcised? Not while circumcised, but while uncircumcised;

11 and he received the sign of circumcision, a seal of the righteousness of the faith which he had while uncircumcised, that he might be the father of all who believe without being circumcised, that righteousness might be reckoned to them,

12 and the father of circumcision to those who not only are of the circumcision, but who also follow in the steps of the faith of our father Abraham which he had while uncircumcised.

13 For the promise to Abraham or to his descendants that he would be heir of the world was not through the Law, but through the righteousness of faith.

14 For if those who are of the Law are heirs, faith is made void and the promise is nullified;

15 for the Law brings about wrath, but where there is no law, neither is there violation.

16 For this reason *it is* by faith, that *it might be* in accordance with grace, in order that the promise may be certain to all the descendants, not only to those who are of the Law, but also to those who are of the faith of Abraham, who is the father of us all,

17 (as it is written, "A FATHER OF

MANY NATIONS HAVE I MADE YOU") in the sight of Him whom he believed, *even* God, who gives life to the dead and calls into being that which does not exist.

18 In hope against hope he believed, in order that he might become a father of many nations, according to that which had been spoken, "So SHALL YOUR DESCENDANTS BE."

19 And without becoming weak in faith he contemplated his own body, now as good as dead since he was about a hundred years old, and the deadness of Sarah's womb;

20 yet, with respect to the promise of God, he did not waver in unbelief, but grew strong in faith, giving glory to God,

21 and being fully assured that what He had promised, He was able also to perform.

22 Therefore also IT WAS RECKONED TO HIM AS RIGHTEOUSNESS.

23 Now not for his sake only was it written, that "IT WAS RECKONED TO HIM,"

24 but for our sake also, to whom it will be reckoned, as those who believe in Him who raised Jesus our Lord from the dead,

25 *He* who was delivered up because of our transgressions, and was raised because of our justification.

CHAPTER 5

THEREFORE having been justified by faith, we have peace with God through our Lord Jesus Christ,

2 through whom also we have obtained our introduction by faith into this grace in which we stand; and we exult in hope of the glory of God.

3 And not only this, but we also exult in our tribulations, knowing that tribulation brings about perseverance;

4 and perseverance, proven character; and proven character, hope;

5 and hope does not disappoint, because the love of God has been poured out within our hearts through the Holy Spirit who was given to us.

6 For while we were still helpless, at the right time Christ died for the ungodly.

7 For one will hardly die for a righteous man; though perhaps for the good man someone would dare even to die.

SCRIPTURE No. 4, SEC. 1

8 But God demonstrates His own love toward us, in that while we were yet sinners, Christ died for us. (r4)

9 Much more then, having now been justified by His blood, we shall be saved from the wrath *of God* through Him.

10 For if while we were enemies, we were reconciled to God through the death of His Son, much more, having been reconciled, we shall be saved by His life.

11 And not only this, but we also exult in God through our Lord Jesus

---

(r4) REFERENCE NO. 4, SEC. 1—PAYMENT GOD MADE FOR YOUR SIN.
"While we were yet sinners, Christ died for us."
Christ paid the penalty for your sin. Because the wages of your sin is death, He died for you.
On the cross, Jesus poured out His "blood on behalf of many for forgiveness of sins." He did this so "that by the grace of God He might taste death for everyone." In this way, "God demonstrates His own love toward us."
Do you believe God made payment for your sins in Christ's death for you on the cross? If so, say:
"I believe Christ died for my sins."
Now turn to page 207, Scripture No. 5, Sec. 1, Rom. 2:4.

Christ, through whom we have now received the reconciliation.

12 Therefore, just as through one man sin entered into the world, and death through sin, and so death spread to all men, because all sinned—

13 for until the Law sin was in the world; but sin is not imputed when there is no law.

14 Nevertheless death reigned from Adam until Moses, even over those who had not sinned in the likeness of Adam's offense, who is a type of Him who was to come.

15 But the free gift is not like the transgression. For if by the transgression of the one the many died, much more did the grace of God and the gift by the grace of the one Man, Jesus Christ, abound to the many.

16 And the gift is not like *that which came* through the one who sinned; for on the one hand the judgment *arose* from one *transgression* resulting in condemnation, but on the other hand the free gift *arose* from many transgressions resulting in justification.

17 For if by the transgression of the one, death reigned through one, much more those who receive the abundance of grace and of the gift of righteousness will reign in life through the One, Jesus Christ.

18 So then as through one transgression there resulted condemnation to all men, even so through one act of righteousness there resulted justification of life to all men.

19 For as through the one man's disobedience the many were made sinners, even so through the obedience of the One the many will be made righteous.

20 And the Law came in that the transgression might increase; but where sin increased, grace abounded all the more,

21 that, as sin reigned in death, even so grace might reign through righteousness to eternal life through Jesus Christ our Lord.

Chapter 6

WHAT shall we say then? Are we to continue in sin that grace might increase?

2 May it never be! How shall we who died to sin still live in it?

3 Or do you not know that all of us who have been baptized into Christ Jesus have been baptized into His death? (a)

4 Therefore we have been buried with Him through baptism into death, in order that as Christ was raised from the dead through the glory of the Father, so we too might walk in newness of life. (b)

THE SYMBOL THAT SHOWS SALVATION.

(a) Spiritual Death to Sin—"All of us who have been baptized into Christ Jesus have been baptized into His death." The believer has "been crucified with Christ," Gal. 2:20, page 258. By faith he considers himself "to be dead to sin, but alive to God in Christ Jesus," Rom. 6:11, page 213. "For by one spirit we were all baptized into one body," I Cor. 12:13, p. 239. This is experienced by "repentance toward God and faith in Our Lord Jesus Christ." "For you have died and your life is hidden with Christ in God," Col. 3:3, page 275. Jesus commanded his disciples to baptize all believers in water and they obeyed Him for they "ordered them to be baptized", Act 10:48, page 177. Water baptism is an expression of the experience of salvation. It is a picture or

(b) Symbol of the Gospel, "Christ died for our sins . . . He was buried . . . He was raised on the third day," I Cor. 15:3-4, page 242. By water baptism "therefore we have been buried with Him . . . in order that as Christ was raised up from the dead . . . we too might walk in newness of life." The believer's baptism also is a

(Continued on next page.)

5 For if we have become united with *Him* in the likeness of His death, certainly we shall be also *in the likeness* of His resurrection, (c)

6 knowing this, that our old self was crucified with *Him*, that our body of sin might be done away with, that we should no longer be slaves to sin;

7 for he who has died is freed from sin.

8 Now if we have died with Christ, we believe that we shall also live with Him,

9 knowing that Christ, having been raised from the dead, is never to die again; death no longer is master over Him.

10 For the death that He died, He died to sin, once for all; but the life that He lives, He lives to God.

11 Even so consider yourselves to be dead to sin, but alive to God in Christ Jesus. (c)

12 Therefore do not let sin reign in your mortal body that you should obey its lusts,

13 and do not go on presenting the members of your body to sin *as* instruments of unrighteousness; but present yourselves to God as those alive from the dead, and your members *as* instruments of righteousness to God.

14 For sin shall not be master over you, for you are not under law, but under grace.

15 What then? Shall we sin because we are not under law but under grace? May it never be!

16 Do you not know that when you present yourselves to someone *as* slaves for obedience, you are slaves of the one whom you obey, either of sin resulting in death, or of obedience resulting in righteousness?

17 But thanks be to God that though you were slaves of sin, you became obedient from the heart to that form of teaching to which you were committed,

18 and having been freed from sin, you became slaves of righteousness.

19 I am speaking in human terms because of the weakness of your flesh. For just as you presented your members *as* slaves to impurity and to lawlessness, resulting in *further* lawlessness, so now present your members *as* slaves to righteousness, resulting in sanctification.

(Continued from page 212.)

(c) Symbol of the Resurrection—At Christ's Second Coming "He who raised the Lord Jesus will raise us also" and "will transform the body of our humble state into conformity with the body of His glory". "Certainly we shall be also in the likeness of His resurrection." "For the Lord Himself will descend from heaven . . . and the dead in Christ shall rise first," 1 Thes. 4:16 page 280. Therefore the symbol of baptism shows the believer's faith in three tenses: (1) Past, "Christ died, . . . He was buried, . . . He was raised on the third day," 1 Cor. 15:3, 4 page 242. (2) Present, The believer portrays himself to be "crucified with Christ," and raised "to walk in newness of life," that is, "dead to sin, but alive to God in Christ Jesus." (3) Future, As baptism portrays the resurrection of Christ, even so it pictures the believer's hope of his bodily resurrection at the return of Jesus. "Certainly we shall be also in the likeness of His resurrection." II Cor. 4:14, page 247, Phil. 3:21, page 272.

20 For when you were slaves of sin, you were free in regard to righteousness.

21 Therefore what benefit were you then deriving from the things of which you are now ashamed? For the outcome of those things is death.

22 But now having been freed from sin and enslaved to God, you derive your benefit, resulting in sanctification, and the outcome, eternal life.

SCRIPTURE NO. 3, SEC. 1

23 <u>For the wages of sin is death, but the free gift of God is eternal life in Christ Jesus our Lord</u>. (r3)

CHAPTER 7

OR do you not know, brethren (for I am speaking to those who know the law), that the law has jurisdiction over a person as long as he lives?

2 For the married woman is bound by law to her husband while he is living; but if her husband dies, she is released from the law concerning the husband.

3 So then if, while her husband is living, she is joined to another man, she shall be called an adulteress; but if her husband dies, she is free from the law, so that she is not an adulteress, though she is joined to another man.

4 Therefore, my brethren, you also were made to die to the Law through the body of Christ, that you might be joined to another, to Him who was raised from the dead, that we might bear fruit for God.

5 For while we were in the flesh, the sinful passions, which were *aroused* by the Law, were at work in the members of our body to bear fruit for death.

6 But now we have been released from the Law, having died to that by which we were bound, so that we serve

---

(r3) REFERENCE NO. 3, SEC. 1—THE PENALTY OF SIN.
"The wages of sin is death."

Wages are the pay you get for work. Death is "the pay you get for sin." Death means separation or to be "cut off" from God. The penalty of "death spread to all men, because all sinned." Since you are not saved, God says you are spiritually dead. That is, you are "dead in your trespasses and sins." This is your state of <u>Present Death</u> as a lost person. You too face <u>physical</u> death. "For the body without the spirit is dead." God says of physical death, "It is appointed for men to die once." This can happen to you at anytime. Also there is <u>permanent</u> death if you suffer <u>physical</u> death while "dead in your trespasses and sins," then at God's Judgment you will experience "the second death." That is, you will be with those who have "their part . . . in the lake that burns with fire and brimstone, which is the second death." This is the threefold death or wages your sin pays. How terrible!

You do not have to die like that and be "cut off," or separated, from God forever. God wants you to be saved from eternal death. He offers you the gift of eternal life. This is the "free gift of God, . . . in Christ Jesus our Lord." Jesus said, "He who hears My word and believes Him who sent Me, has eternal life, and does not come into judgment." Since eternal life is a gift it can not be obtained by "works, that no one should boast" "For by grace are you saved through faith; and that not of yourselves, it is the gift of God." God now offers you eternal life. Jesus Christ died and paid the debt for your sin. To be saved you must, by faith, accept this payment.

Do you want eternal life instead of eternal death? If so, say:

"The wages of my sin is death. But I see now God offers to give me eternal life in Jesus Christ."

Now turn to page 211, Scripture No. 4, Sec. 1, Rom. 5:8.

in newness of the Spirit and not in oldness of the letter.

7 What shall we say then? Is the Law sin? May it never be! On the contrary, I would not have come to know sin except through the Law; for I would not have known about coveting if the Law had not said, "YOU SHALL NOT COVET."

8 But sin, taking opportunity through the commandment, produced in me coveting of every kind; for apart from the Law sin *is* dead.

9 And I was once alive apart from the Law; but when the commandment came, sin became alive, and I died;

10 and this commandment, which was to result in life, proved to result in death for me;

11 for sin, taking opportunity through the commandment, deceived me, and through it killed me.

12 So then, the Law is holy, and the commandment is holy and righteous and good.

13 Therefore did that which is good become *a cause of* death for me? May it never be! Rather it was sin, in order that it might be shown to be sin by effecting my death through that which is good, that through the commandment sin might become utterly sinful.

14 For we know that the Law is spiritual; but I am of flesh, sold into bondage to sin.

15 For that which I am doing, I do not understand; for I am not practicing what I *would* like to *do,* but I am doing the very thing I hate.

16 But if I do the very thing I do not wish *to do,* I agree with the Law, *confessing* that it is good.

17 So now, no longer am I the one doing it, but sin which indwells me.

18 For I know that nothing good dwells in me, that is, in my flesh; for the wishing is present in me, but the doing of the good *is* not.

19 For the good that I wish, I do not do; but I practice the very evil that I do not wish.

20 But if I am doing the very thing I do not wish, I am no longer the one doing it, but sin which dwells in me.

21 I find then the principle that evil is present in me, the one who wishes to do good.

22 For I joyfully concur with the law of God in the inner man,

23 but I see a different law in the members of my body, waging war against the law of my mind, and making me a prisoner of the law of sin which is in my members.

24 Wretched man that I am! Who will set me free from the body of this death?

25 Thanks be to God through Jesus Christ our Lord! So then, on the one hand I myself with my mind am serving the law of God, but on the other, with my flesh the law of sin.

CHAPTER 8

THERE is therefore now no condemnation for those who are in Christ Jesus.

2 For the law of the Spirit of life in Christ Jesus has set you free from the law of sin and of death.

3 For what the Law could not do, weak as it was through the flesh, God *did:* sending His own Son in the likeness of sinful flesh and *as an offering* for sin, He condemned sin in the flesh,

4 in order that the requirement of the Law might be fulfilled in us, who do not walk according to the flesh, but according to the Spirit.

5 For those who are according to the flesh set their minds on the things of the flesh, but those who are according to the Spirit, the things of the Spirit.

6 For the mind set on the flesh is death, but the mind set on the Spirit is life and peace,

7 because the mind set on the flesh is hostile toward God; for it does not subject itself to the law of God, for it is not even able *to do so;*

8 and those who are in the flesh cannot please God.

9 However you are not in the flesh but in the Spirit, if indeed the Spirit of God dwells in you. But if anyone does not have the Spirit of Christ, he does not belong to Him.

10 And if Christ is in you, though the body is dead because of sin, yet the spirit is alive because of righteousness.

11 But if the Spirit of Him who raised Jesus from the dead dwells in you, He who raised Christ Jesus from the dead will also give life to your mortal bodies through His Spirit who indwells you.

12 So then, brethren, we are under obligation, not to the flesh, to live according to the flesh—

13 for if you are living according to the flesh, you must die; but if by the Spirit you are putting to death the deeds of the body, you will live.

14 For all who are being led by the Spirit of God, these are sons of God.

15 For you have not received a spirit of slavery leading to fear again, but you have received a spirit of adoption as sons by which we cry out, "Abba! Father!"

16 The Spirit Himself bears witness with our spirit that we are children of God,

17 and if children, heirs also, heirs of God and fellow-heirs with Christ, if indeed we suffer with *Him* in order that we may also be glorified with *Him.*

18 For I consider that the sufferings of this present time are not worthy to be compared with the glory that is to be revealed to us.

19 For the anxious longing of the creation waits eagerly for the revealing of the sons of God.

20 For the creation was subjected to futility, not of its own will, but because of Him who subjected it, in hope

21 that the creation itself also will be set free from its slavery to corruption into the freedom of the glory of the children of God.

22 For we know that the whole creation groans and suffers the pains of childbirth together until now.

23 And not only this, but also we ourselves, having the first fruits of the Spirit, even we ourselves groan within ourselves, waiting eagerly for *our* adoption as sons, the redemption of our body.

24 For in hope we have been saved, but hope that is seen is not hope; for why does one also hope for what he sees?

25 But if we hope for what we do not see, with perseverance we wait eagerly for it.

26 And in the same way the Spirit also helps our weakness; for we do not know how to pray as we should, but the Spirit Himself intercedes for *us* with groanings too deep for words;

27 and He who searches the hearts knows what the mind of the Spirit is, because He intercedes for the saints according to *the will of* God.

28 And we know that God causes all things to work together for good to those who love God, to those who are called according to *His* purpose.

29 For whom He foreknew, He also predestined *to become* conformed to the image of His Son, that He might be the first-born among many brethren;

30 and whom He predestined, these He also called; and whom He called, these He also justified; and whom He justified, these He also glorified.

31 What then shall we say to these things? If God *is* for us, who *is* against us?

32 He who did not spare His own Son, but delivered Him up for us all, how will He not also with Him freely give us all things?

33 Who will bring a charge against God's elect? God is the one who justifies;

34 who is the one who condemns? Christ Jesus is He who died, yes, rather who was raised, who is at the right hand of God, who also intercedes for us.

35 Who shall separate us from the love of Christ? Shall tribulation, or distress, or persecution, or famine, or nakedness, or peril, or sword?

36 Just as it is written,
"FOR THY SAKE WE ARE BEING
    PUT TO DEATH ALL DAY LONG;
    WE WERE CONSIDERED AS
        SHEEP TO BE SLAUGHTERED."

37 But in all these things we overwhelmingly conquer through Him who loved us.

38 For I am convinced that neither death, nor life, nor angels, nor principalities, nor things present, nor things to come, nor powers,

39 nor height, nor depth, nor any other created thing, shall be able to separate us from the love of God, which is in Christ Jesus our Lord.

CHAPTER 9

I AM telling the truth in Christ, I am not lying, my conscience bearing me witness in the Holy Spirit,

2 that I have great sorrow and unceasing grief in my heart.

3 For I could wish that I myself were accursed, *separated* from Christ for the sake of my brethren, my kinsmen according to the flesh,

4 who are Israelites, to whom belongs the adoption as sons and the glory and the covenants and the giving of the Law and the *temple* service and the promises,

5 whose are the fathers, and from whom is the Christ according to the flesh, who is over all, God blessed forever. Amen.

6 But *it is* not as though the word of God has failed. For they are not all Israel who are *descended* from Israel;

7 neither are they all children because they are Abraham's descendants, but: "THROUGH ISAAC YOUR DESCENDANTS WILL BE NAMED."

8 That is, it is not the children of the flesh who are children of God, but the children of the promise are regarded as descendants.

9 For this is a word of promise: "AT THIS TIME I WILL COME, AND SARAH SHALL HAVE A SON."

10 And not only this, but there was Rebekah also, when she had conceived *twins* by one man, our father Isaac;

11 for though *the twins* were not yet born, and had not done anything good or bad, in order that God's purpose according to *His* choice might stand, not because of works, but because of Him who calls,

12 it was said to her, "THE OLDER WILL SERVE THE YOUNGER."

13 Just as it is written, "JACOB I LOVED, BUT ESAU I HATED."

14 What shall we say then? There is no injustice with God, is there? May it never be!

15 For He says to Moses, "I WILL HAVE MERCY ON WHOM I HAVE MERCY, AND I WILL HAVE COMPASSION ON WHOM I HAVE COMPASSION."

16 So then it *does* not *depend* on the man who wills or the man who runs, but on God who has mercy.

17 For the Scripture says to Pharaoh, "FOR THIS VERY PURPOSE I RAISED

YOU UP, TO DEMONSTRATE MY POWER IN YOU, AND THAT MY NAME MIGHT BE PROCLAIMED THROUGHOUT THE WHOLE EARTH."

18 So then He has mercy on whom He desires, and He hardens whom He desires.

19 You will say to me then, "Why does He still find fault? For who resists His will?"

20 On the contrary, who are you, O man, who answers back to God? The thing molded will not say to the molder, "Why did you make me like this," will it?

21 Or does not the potter have a right over the clay, to make from the same lump one vessel for honorable use, and another for common use?

22 What if God, although willing to demonstrate His wrath and to make His power known, endured with much patience vessels of wrath prepared for destruction?

23 And *He did so* in order that He might make known the riches of His glory upon vessels of mercy, which He prepared beforehand for glory,

24 *even* us, whom He also called, not from among Jews only, but also from among Gentiles.

25 As He says also in Hosea,
"I WILL CALL THOSE WHO WERE NOT MY PEOPLE, 'MY PEOPLE,'
AND HER WHO WAS NOT BELOVED, 'BELOVED.' "

26 "AND IT SHALL BE THAT IN THE PLACE WHERE IT WAS SAID TO THEM, 'YOU ARE NOT MY PEOPLE,'
THERE THEY SHALL BE CALLED SONS OF THE LIVING GOD."

27 And Isaiah cries out concerning Israel, "THOUGH THE NUMBER OF THE SONS OF ISRAEL BE AS THE SAND OF THE SEA, IT IS THE REMNANT THAT WILL BE SAVED;

28 FOR THE LORD WILL EXECUTE HIS WORD UPON THE EARTH, THOROUGHLY AND QUICKLY."

29 And just as Isaiah foretold,
"EXCEPT THE LORD OF SABAOTH HAD LEFT TO US A POSTERITY,
WE WOULD HAVE BECOME AS SODOM, AND WOULD HAVE RESEMBLED GOMORRAH."

30 What shall we say then? That Gentiles, who did not pursue righteousness, attained righteousness, even the righteousness which is by faith;

31 but Israel, pursuing a law of righteousness, did not arrive at *that* law.

32 Why? Because *they did* not *pursue it* by faith, but as though *it were* by works. They stumbled over THE STUMBLING STONE,

33 just as it is written,
"BEHOLD, I LAY IN ZION A STONE OF STUMBLING AND A ROCK OF OFFENSE,
AND HE WHO BELIEVES IN HIM WILL NOT BE DISAPPOINTED."

CHAPTER 10

BRETHREN, my heart's desire and my prayer to God for them is for *their* salvation.

2 For I bear them witness that they have a zeal for God, but not in accordance with knowledge.

3 For not knowing about God's righteousness, and seeking to establish their own, they did not subject themselves to the righteousness of God.

4 For Christ is the end of the law for righteousness to everyone who believes.

5 For Moses writes that the man who practices the righteousness which is based on law shall live by that righteousness.

6 But the righteousness based on faith speaks thus, "DO NOT SAY IN YOUR HEART, 'WHO WILL ASCEND INTO HEAVEN?' (that is, to bring Christ down),

7 or 'WHO WILL DESCEND INTO THE ABYSS?' (that is, to bring Christ up from the dead)."

8 But what does it say? "THE WORD IS NEAR YOU, IN YOUR MOUTH AND IN YOUR HEART"—that is, the word of faith which we are preaching,

SCRIPTURE NO. 6, SEC. 1

9 that if you confess with your mouth Jesus *as* Lord, and believe in your heart that God raised Him from the dead, you shall be saved;

10 for with the heart man believes, resulting in righteousness, and with the mouth he confesses, resulting in salvation.

11 For the Scripture says, "WHOEVER BELIEVES IN HIM WILL NOT BE DISAPPOINTED."

12 For there is no distinction between Jew and Greek; for the same *Lord* is Lord of all, abounding in riches for all who call upon Him;

13 for "WHOEVER WILL CALL UPON THE NAME OF THE LORD WILL BE SAVED."

14 How then shall they call upon Him in whom they have not believed? And how shall they believe in Him whom they have not heard? And how shall they hear without a preacher? (r6)

(r6) REFERENCE NO. 6, SEC. 1—CONFESSION OF CHRIST.

When "you confess with your mouth Jesus as Lord, and believe in your heart that God raised Him from the dead, you shall be saved."

God makes it simple. You trust with your heart and tell with your mouth, and this results in righteousness.

"Whoever will call upon the name of the Lord will be saved." You express your faith by calling in prayer. In this way you invite Jesus into your heart. He promises "if anyone hears my voice and opens the door, I will come in to him."

Jesus told how one man was saved when he spoke from his heart only seven words: "God be merciful to me, a sinner."

When should you "call upon the name of the Lord?" God says, "At the acceptable time I listened to you . . . behold, now is the acceptable time, behold now is the day of salvation."

Believe Jesus died for your sin and "God raised Him from the dead." "Call upon the name of the Lord" and "confess with your mouth Jesus Christ as Lord." He promises "everyone therefore who confesses Me before men, I will also confess him before my Father who is in heaven." When you do this you know that you are saved.

Will you call upon the Lord to come into your heart and save you now? If so, say: "I will call upon the Lord inviting Him to come into my heart and save me now." So do it now. Pray this simple prayer:

"Lord, I have sinned. I'm sorry for my sins. I now give my life to You. I accept You as my Lord and Savior. I ask You to save me and live in my life. God be merciful to me a sinner. In Jesus name I pray, Amen."

If you believe God has saved you now, turn to page 45, Scripture No. 1, Sec. 2, Matt. 28:18-20.

Begin a new set of scriptures and references; read Scripture No. 1, Sec. 2, Matt. 28:18-20, the verses which are underlined. Then Read Reference No. 1, entitled: "How you show you are saved." Continue to read the chain of scriptures and references as instructed at the bottom of each page.

15 And how shall they preach unless they are sent? Just as it is written, "HOW BEAUTIFUL ARE THE FEET OF THOSE WHO BRING GLAD TIDINGS OF GOOD THINGS!"

16 However, they did not all heed the glad tidings; for Isaiah says, "LORD, WHO HAS BELIEVED OUR REPORT?"

17 So faith *comes* from hearing, and hearing by the word of Christ. (a)

18 But I say, surely they have never heard, have they? Indeed they have:

"THEIR VOICE HAS GONE OUT
    INTO ALL THE EARTH,
AND THEIR WORDS TO THE ENDS
    OF THE WORLD."

19 But I say, surely Israel did not know, did they? At the first Moses says,

"I WILL MAKE YOU JEALOUS BY
    THAT WHICH IS NOT A NATION,
BY A NATION WITHOUT UNDERSTANDING WILL I ANGER
    YOU."

20 And Isaiah is very bold and says,

"I WAS FOUND BY THOSE WHO
    SOUGHT ME NOT,
I BECAME MANIFEST TO THOSE
    WHO DID NOT ASK FOR ME."

21 But as for Israel He says, "ALL THE DAY LONG I HAVE STRETCHED OUT MY HANDS TO A DISOBEDIENT AND OBSTINATE PEOPLE."

CHAPTER 11

I SAY then, God has not rejected His people, has He? May it never be! For I too am an Israelite, a descendant of Abraham, of the tribe of Benjamin.

2 God has not rejected His people whom He foreknew. Or do you not know what the Scripture says in *the passage about* Elijah, how he pleads with God against Israel?

3 "Lord, THEY HAVE KILLED THY PROPHETS, THEY HAVE TORN DOWN THINE ALTARS, AND I ALONE AM LEFT, AND THEY ARE SEEKING MY LIFE."

4 But what is the divine response to him? "I HAVE KEPT for Myself SEVEN THOUSAND MEN WHO HAVE NOT BOWED THE KNEE TO BAAL."

5 In the same way then, there has also come to be at the present time a remnant according to God's gracious choice.

6 But if it is by grace, it is no longer on the basis of works, otherwise grace is no longer grace.

7 What then? That which Israel is seeking for, it has not obtained, but

---

(a) "The Way of Faith"

(1) Word of Faith—"So faith comes from hearing, and hearing by the Word of Christ, Rom. 10:17, page 220.
    It was said Peter would preach "and he shall speak words to you by which you will be saved," Acts 11:14, page 177.

(2) Work of Faith—God "has granted to us His precious and magnificent promises, in order that by them you might become partakers of the divine nature", II Pet. 1:4, page 319. "In the exercise of His will He brought us forth by the word of truth, so we might be as it were the first fruits among His creatures", James 1:18, page 309. "For by grace you have been saved through faith," Eph. 2:8, page 263.

(3) Way of Faith—"For we walk by faith," II Cor. 5:7, page 248. The word of faith does the work of faith in the heart and the new life of the new creature becomes the Way of Faith ... "the righteous man shall live by faith", Rom. 1:17, page 206.

those who were chosen obtained it, and the rest were hardened;

8 just as it is written,

"GOD GAVE THEM A SPIRIT OF STUPOR,

EYES TO SEE NOT AND EARS TO HEAR NOT,

DOWN TO THIS VERY DAY."

9 And David says,

"LET THEIR TABLE BECOME A SNARE AND A TRAP,

AND A STUMBLING BLOCK AND A RETRIBUTION TO THEM.

10 "LET THEIR EYES BE DARKENED TO SEE NOT,

AND BEND THEIR BACKS FOREVER."

11 I say then, they did not stumble so as to fall, did they? May it never be! But by their transgression salvation *has come* to the Gentiles, to make them jealous.

12 Now if their transgression be riches for the world and their failure be riches for the Gentiles, how much more will their fulfillment be!

13 But I am speaking to you who are Gentiles. Inasmuch then as I am an apostle of Gentiles, I magnify my ministry,

14 if somehow I might move to jealousy my fellow-countrymen and save some of them.

15 For if their rejection be the reconciliation of the world, what will *their* acceptance be but life from the dead?

16 And if the first piece *of dough* be holy, the lump is also; and if the root be holy, the branches are too.

17 But if some of the branches were broken off, and you, being a wild olive, were grafted in among them and became partaker with them of the rich root of the olive tree,

18 do not be arrogant toward the branches; but if you are arrogant, *remember that* it is not you who supports the root, but the root *supports* you.

19 You will say then, "Branches were broken off so that I might be grafted in."

20 Quite right, they were broken off for their unbelief, and you stand *only* by your faith. Do not be conceited, but fear;

21 for if God did not spare the natural branches, neither will He spare you.

22 Behold then the kindness and severity of God; to those who fell, severity, but to you, God's kindness, if you continue in His kindness; otherwise you also will be cut off.

23 And they also, if they do not continue in their unbelief, will be grafted in; for God is able to graft them in again.

24 For if you were cut off from what is by nature a wild olive tree, and were grafted contrary to nature into a cultivated olive tree, how much more shall these who are the natural *branches* be grafted into their own olive tree?

25 For I do not want you, brethren, to be uninformed of this mystery, lest you be wise in your own estimation, that a partial hardening has happened to Israel until the fulness of the Gentiles has come in;

26 and thus all Israel will be saved; just as it is written,

"THE DELIVERER WILL COME FROM ZION,

HE WILL REMOVE UNGODLINESS FROM JACOB."

27 "AND THIS IS MY COVENANT WITH THEM,

WHEN I TAKE AWAY THEIR SINS."

28 From the standpoint of the gospel they are enemies for your sake, but from the standpoint of *God's* choice they are beloved for the sake of the fathers;

29 for the gifts and the calling of God are irrevocable.

30 For just as you once were dis-

obedient to God but now have been shown mercy because of their disobedience,

31 so these also now have been disobedient, in order that because of the mercy shown to you they also may now be shown mercy.

32 For God has shut up all in disobedience that He might show mercy to all.

33 Oh, the depth of the riches both of the wisdom and knowledge of God! How unsearchable are His judgments and unfathomable His ways!

34 FOR WHO HAS KNOWN THE MIND OF THE LORD, OR WHO BECAME HIS COUNSELOR?

35 OR WHO HAS FIRST GIVEN TO HIM THAT IT MIGHT BE PAID BACK TO HIM AGAIN?

36 For from Him and through Him and to Him are all things. To Him *be* the glory forever. Amen.

CHAPTER 12

I URGE you therefore, brethren, by the mercies of God, to present your bodies a living and holy sacrifice, acceptable to God, *which is* your spiritual service of worship.

2 And do not be conformed to this world, but be transformed by the renewing of your mind, that you may prove what the will of God is, that which is good and acceptable and perfect.

3 For through the grace given to me I say to every man among you not to think more highly of himself than he ought to think; but to think so as to have sound judgment, as God has allotted to each a measure of faith.

4 For just as we have many members in one body and all the members do not have the same function,

5 so we, who are many, are one body in Christ, and individually members one of another.

6 And since we have gifts that differ according to the grace given to us, *let each exercise them accordingly*: if prophecy, according to the proportion of his faith;

7 if service, in his serving; or he who teaches, in his teaching;

8 or he who exhorts, in his exhortation; he who gives, with liberality; he who leads, with diligence; he who shows mercy, with cheerfulness.

9 Let love be without hypocrisy. Abhor what is evil; cling to what is good.

10 Be devoted to one another in brotherly love; give preference to one another in honor;

11 not lagging behind in diligence, fervent in spirit, serving the Lord;

12 rejoicing in hope, persevering in tribulation, devoted to prayer,

13 contributing to the needs of the saints, practicing hospitality.

14 Bless those who persecute you; bless and curse not.

15 Rejoice with those who rejoice, and weep with those who weep.

16 Be of the same mind toward one another; do not be haughty in mind, but associate with the lowly. Do not be wise in your own estimation.

17 Never pay back evil for evil to anyone. Respect what is right in the sight of all men.

18 If possible, so far as it depends on you, be at peace with all men.

19 Never take your own revenge, beloved, but leave room for the wrath *of God,* for it is written, "VENGEANCE IS MINE, I WILL REPAY, SAYS THE LORD."

20 "BUT IF YOUR ENEMY IS HUNGRY, FEED HIM, AND IF HE IS THIRSTY, GIVE HIM A DRINK; FOR IN SO DOING YOU WILL HEAP BURNING COALS UPON HIS HEAD."

21 Do not be overcome by evil, but overcome evil with good.

Chapter 13

LET every person be in subjection to the governing authorities. For there is no authority except from God, and those which exist are established by God.

2 Therefore he who resists authority has opposed the ordinance of God; and they who have opposed will receive condemnation upon themselves.

3 For rulers are not a cause of fear for good behavior, but for evil. Do you want to have no fear of authority? Do what is good, and you will have praise from the same;

4 for it is a minister of God to you for good. But if you do what is evil, be afraid; for it does not bear the sword for nothing; for it is a minister of God, an avenger who brings wrath upon the one who practices evil.

5 Wherefore it is necessary to be in subjection, not only because of wrath, but also for conscience' sake.

6 For because of this you also pay taxes, for *rulers* are servants of God, devoting themselves to this very thing.

7 Render to all what is due them: tax to whom tax *is due*; custom to whom custom; fear to whom fear; honor to whom honor.

8 Owe nothing to anyone except to love one another; for he who loves his neighbor has fulfilled *the* law.

9 For this, "YOU SHALL NOT COMMIT ADULTERY, YOU SHALL NOT MURDER, YOU SHALL NOT STEAL, YOU SHALL NOT COVET," and if there is any other commandment, it is summed up in this saying, "YOU SHALL LOVE YOUR NEIGHBOR AS YOURSELF."

10 Love does no wrong to a neighbor; love therefore is the fulfillment of *the* law.

11 And this *do*, knowing the time, that it is already the hour for you to awaken from sleep; for now salvation is nearer to us than when we believed.

12 The night is almost gone, and the day is at hand. Let us therefore lay aside the deeds of darkness and put on the armor of light.

13 Let us behave properly as in the day, not in carousing and drunkenness, not in sexual promiscuity and sensuality, not in strife and jealousy.

14 But put on the Lord Jesus Christ, and make no provision for the flesh in regard to *its* lusts.

Chapter 14

NOW accept the one who is weak in faith, *but* not for *the purpose of* passing judgment on his opinions.

2 One man has faith that he may eat all things, but he who is weak eats vegetables *only*.

3 Let not him who eats regard with contempt him who does not eat, and let not him who does not eat judge him who eats, for God has accepted him.

4 Who are you to judge the servant of another? To his own master he stands or falls; and stand he will, for the Lord is able to make him stand.

5 One man regards one day above another, another regards every day *alike*. Let each man be fully convinced in his own mind.

6 He who observes the day, observes it for the Lord, and he who eats, does so for the Lord, for he gives thanks to God; and he who eats not, for the Lord he does not eat, and gives thanks to God.

7 For not one of us lives for himself, and not one dies for himself;

8 for if we live, we live for the Lord, or if we die, we die for the Lord; therefore whether we live or die, we are the Lord's.

9 For to this end Christ died and

lived *again*, that He might be Lord both of the dead and of the living.

10 But you, why do you judge your brother? Or you again, why do you regard your brother with contempt? For we shall all stand before the judgment seat of God.

11 For it is written,

"AS I LIVE, SAYS THE LORD, EVERY KNEE SHALL BOW TO ME, AND EVERY TONGUE SHALL GIVE PRAISE TO GOD."

12 So then each one of us shall give account of himself to God.

13 Therefore let us not judge one another any more, but rather determine this — not to put an obstacle or a stumbling block in a brother's way.

14 I know and am convinced in the Lord Jesus that nothing is unclean in itself; but to him who thinks anything to be unclean, to him it is unclean.

15 For if because of food your brother is hurt, you are no longer walking according to love. Do not destroy with your food him for whom Christ died.

16 Therefore do not let what is for you a good thing be spoken of as evil;

17 for the kingdom of God is not eating and drinking, but righteousness and peace and joy in the Holy Spirit.

18 For he who in this *way* serves Christ is acceptable to God and approved by men.

19 So then let us pursue the things which make for peace and the building up of one another.

20 Do not tear down the work of God for the sake of food. All things indeed are clean, but they are evil for the man who eats and gives offense.

21 It is good not to eat meat or to drink wine, or *to do anything* by which your brother stumbles.

22 The faith which you have, have as your own conviction before God. Happy is he who does not condemn himself in what he approves.

23 But he who doubts is condemned if he eats, because *his eating is* not from faith; and whatever is not from faith is sin.

CHAPTER 15

NOW we who are strong ought to bear the weaknesses of those without strength and not *just* please ourselves.

2 Let each of us please his neighbor for his good, to his edification.

3 For even Christ did not please Himself; but as it is written, "THE REPROACHES OF THOSE WHO REPROACHED THEE FELL UPON ME."

4 For whatever was written in earlier times was written for our instruction, that through perseverance and the encouragement of the Scriptures we might have hope.

5 Now may the God who gives perseverance and encouragement grant you to be of the same mind with one another according to Christ Jesus;

6 that with one accord you may with one voice glorify the God and Father of our Lord Jesus Christ.

7 Wherefore, accept one another, just as Christ also accepted us to the glory of God.

8 For I say that Christ has become a servant to the circumcision on behalf of the truth of God to confirm the promises *given* to the fathers,

9 and for the Gentiles to glorify God for His mercy; as it is written,

"THEREFORE I WILL GIVE PRAISE TO THEE AMONG THE GENTILES,

AND I WILL SING TO THY NAME."

10 And again he says,

"REJOICE, O GENTILES, WITH HIS PEOPLE."

11 And again,

"PRAISE THE LORD ALL YOU GENTILES,

And let all the peoples praise Him."

12 And again Isaiah says,

"There shall come the root of Jesse,
And He who arises to rule over the Gentiles,
In Him shall the Gentiles hope."

13 Now may the God of hope fill you with all joy and peace in believing, that you may abound in hope by the power of the Holy Spirit.

14 And concerning you, my brethren, I myself also am convinced that you yourselves are full of goodness, filled with all knowledge, and able also to admonish one another.

15 But I have written very boldly to you on some points, so as to remind you again, because of the grace that was given me from God,

16 to be a minister of Christ Jesus to the Gentiles, ministering as a priest the gospel of God, that *my* offering of the Gentiles might become acceptable, sanctified by the Holy Spirit.

17 Therefore in Christ Jesus I have found reason for boasting in things pertaining to God.

18 For I will not presume to speak of anything except what Christ has accomplished through me, resulting in the obedience of the Gentiles by word and deed,

19 in the power of signs and wonders, in the power of the Spirit; so that from Jerusalem and round about as far as Illyricum I have fully preached the gospel of Christ.

20 And thus I aspired to preach the gospel, not where Christ was *already* named, that I might not build upon another man's foundation;

21 but as it is written,

"They who had no news of Him shall see,
And they who have not heard shall understand."

22 For this reason I have often been hindered from coming to you;

23 but now, with no further place for me in these regions, and since I have had for many years a longing to come to you

24 whenever I go to Spain — for I hope to see you in passing, and to be helped on my way there by you, when I have first enjoyed your company for awhile —

25 but now, I am going to Jerusalem serving the saints.

26 For Macedonia and Achaia have been pleased to make a contribution for the poor among the saints in Jerusalem.

27 Yes, they were pleased *to do so,* and they are indebted to them. For if the Gentiles have shared in their spiritual things, they are indebted to minister to them also in material things.

28 Therefore, when I have finished this, and have put my seal on this fruit of theirs, I will go on by way of you to Spain.

29 And I know that when I come to you, I will come in the fulness of the blessing of Christ.

30 Now I urge you, brethren, by our Lord Jesus Christ and by the love of the Spirit, to strive together with me in your prayers to God for me,

31 that I may be delivered from those who are disobedient in Judea, and *that* my service for Jerusalem may prove acceptable to the saints;

32 so that I may come to you in joy by the will of God and find *refreshing* rest in your company.

33 Now the God of peace be with you all. Amen.

Chapter 16

I COMMEND to you our sister Phoebe, who is a servant of the church which is at Cenchrea;

2 that you receive her in the Lord in a manner worthy of the saints, and that you help her in whatever matter she may have need of you; for she herself has also been a helper of many, and of myself as well.

3 Greet Prisca and Aquila, my fellow-workers in Christ Jesus,

4 who for my life risked their own necks, to whom not only do I give thanks, but also all the churches of the Gentiles;

5 also *greet* the church that is in their house. Greet Epaenetus, my beloved, who is the first convert to Christ from Asia.

6 Greet Mary, who has worked hard for you.

7 Greet Andronicus and Junias, my kinsmen, and my fellow-prisoners, who are outstanding among the apostles, who also were in Christ before me.

8 Greet Ampliatus, my beloved in the Lord.

9 Greet Urbanus, our fellow-worker in Christ, and Stachys my beloved.

10 Greet Apelles, the approved in Christ. Greet those who are of the *household* of Aristobulus.

11 Greet Herodion, my kinsman. Greet those of the *household* of Narcissus, who are in the Lord.

12 Greet Tryphaena and Tryphosa, workers in the Lord. Greet Persis the beloved, who has worked hard in the Lord.

13 Greet Rufus, a choice man in the Lord, also his mother and mine.

14 Greet Asyncritus, Phlegon, Hermes, Patrobas, Hermas and the brethren with them.

15 Greet Philologus and Julia, Nereus and his sister, and Olympas, and all the saints who are with them.

16 Greet one another with a holy kiss. All the churches of Christ greet you.

17 Now I urge you, brethren, keep your eye on those who cause dissensions and hindrances contrary to the teaching which you learned, and turn away from them.

18 For such men are slaves not of our Lord Christ but of their own appetites; and by their smooth and flattering speech they deceive the hearts of the unsuspecting.

19 For the report of your obedience has reached to all; therefore I am rejoicing over you, but I want you to be wise in what is good, and innocent in what is evil.

20 And the God of peace will soon crush Satan under your feet.

The grace of our Lord Jesus be with you.

21 Timothy my fellow-worker greets you; and *so do* Lucius and Jason and Sosipater, my kinsmen.

22 I, Tertius, who write this letter, greet you in the Lord.

23 Gaius, host to me and to the whole church, greets you. Erastus, the city treasurer greets you, and Quartus, the brother.

24 (See footnote.)

25 Now to Him who is able to establish you according to my gospel and the preaching of Jesus Christ, according to the revelation of the mystery which has been kept secret for long ages past,

26 but now is manifested, and by the Scriptures of the prophets, according to the commandment of the

---

eternal God, has been made known to all the nations, *leading* to obedience of faith;

27 to the only wise God, through Jesus Christ, be the glory forever. Amen.

THE FIRST EPISTLE OF PAUL TO THE
CORINTHIANS

PAUL, called *as* an apostle of Jesus Christ by the will of God, and Sosthenes our brother,

2 to the church of God which is at Corinth, to those who have been sanctified in Christ Jesus, saints by calling, with all who in every place call upon the name of our Lord Jesus Christ, their *Lord* and ours:

3 Grace to you and peace from God our Father and the Lord Jesus Christ.

4 I thank my God always concerning you, for the grace of God which was given you in Christ Jesus,

5 that in everything you were enriched in Him, in all speech and all knowledge,

6 even as the testimony concerning Christ was confirmed in you,

7 so that you are not lacking in any gift, awaiting eagerly the revelation of our Lord Jesus Christ,

8 who shall also confirm you to the end, blameless in the day of our Lord Jesus Christ.

9 God is faithful, through whom you were called into fellowship with His Son, Jesus Christ our Lord.

10 Now I exhort you, brethren, by the name of our Lord Jesus Christ, that you all agree, and there be no divisions among you, but you be made complete in the same mind and in the same judgment.

11 For I have been informed concerning you, my brethren, by Chloe's *people,* that there are quarrels among you.

12 Now I mean this, that each one of you is saying, "I am of Paul," and "I of Apollos," and "I of Cephas," and "I of Christ."

13 Has Christ been divided? Paul was not crucified for you, was he? Or were you baptized in the name of Paul?

14 I thank God that I baptized none of you except Crispus and Gaius,

15 that no man should say you were baptized in my name.

16 Now I did baptize also the household of Stephanas; beyond that, I do not know whether I baptized any other.

17 For Christ did not send me to baptize, but to preach the gospel, not in cleverness of speech, that the cross of Christ should not be made void.

18 For the word of the cross is to those who are perishing foolishness, but to us who are being saved it is the power of God.

19 For it is written,

"I will destroy the wisdom of the wise,

And the cleverness of the clever I will set aside."

20 Where is the wise man? Where is the scribe? Where is the debater of this age? Has not God made foolish the wisdom of the world?

21 For since in the wisdom of God

the world through its wisdom did not *come to* know God, God was well pleased through the foolishness of the message preached to save those who believe.

22 For indeed Jews ask for signs, and Greeks search for wisdom;

23 but we preach Christ crucified, to Jews a stumbling block, and to Gentiles foolishness,

24 but to those who are the called, both Jews and Greeks, Christ the power of God and the wisdom of God.

25 Because the foolishness of God is wiser than men, and the weakness of God is stronger than men.

26 For consider your calling, brethren, that there were not many wise according to the flesh, not many mighty, not many noble;

27 but God has chosen the foolish things of the world to shame the wise, and God has chosen the weak things of the world to shame the things which are strong,

28 and the base things of the world and the despised, God has chosen, the things that are not, that He might nullify the things that are,

29 that no man should boast before God.

30 But by His doing you are in Christ Jesus, who became to us wisdom from God, and righteousness and sanctification, and redemption,

31 that, just as it is written, "LET HIM WHO BOASTS, BOAST IN THE LORD."

CHAPTER 2

AND when I came to you, brethren, I did not come with superiority of speech or of wisdom, proclaiming to you the testimony of God.

2 For I determined to know nothing among you except Jesus Christ, and Him crucified.

3 And I was with you in weakness and in fear and in much trembling.

4 And my message and my preaching were not in persuasive words of wisdom, but in demonstration of the Spirit and of power,

5 that your faith should not rest on the wisdom of men, but on the power of God.

6 Yet we do speak wisdom among those who are mature; a wisdom, however, not of this age, nor of the rulers of this age, who are passing away;

7 but we speak God's wisdom in a mystery, the hidden *wisdom*, which God predestined before the ages to our glory;

8 *the wisdom* which none of the rulers of this age has understood; for if they had understood it, they would not have crucified the Lord of glory;

9 but just as it is written,

"THINGS WHICH EYE HAS NOT SEEN AND EAR HAS NOT HEARD,

AND *which* HAVE NOT ENTERED THE HEART OF MAN,

ALL THAT GOD HAS PREPARED FOR THOSE WHO LOVE HIM."

10 For to us God revealed *them* through the Spirit; for the Spirit searches all things, even the depths of God.

11 For who among men knows the *thoughts* of a man except the spirit of the man, which is in him? Even so the *thoughts* of God no one knows except the Spirit of God.

12 Now we have received, not the spirit of the world, but the Spirit who is from God, that we might know the things freely given to us by God,

13 which things we also speak, not in words taught by human wisdom, but in those taught by the Spirit, combining spiritual *thoughts* with spiritual *words*.

14 But a natural man does not accept the things of the Spirit of God; for they are foolishness to him, and he cannot understand them, because they are spiritually appraised.

15 But he who is spiritual appraises all things, yet he himself is appraised by no man.

16 For WHO HAS KNOWN THE MIND OF THE LORD, THAT HE SHOULD INSTRUCT HIM? But we have the mind of Christ.

CHAPTER 3

AND I, brethren, could not speak to you as to spiritual men, but as to men of flesh, as to babes in Christ.

2 I gave you milk to drink, not solid food; for you were not yet able *to receive it*. Indeed, even now you are not yet able,

3 for you are still fleshly. For since there is jealousy and strife among you, are you not fleshly, and are you not walking like mere men?

4 For when one says, "I am of Paul," and another, "I am of Apollos," are you not *mere* men?

5 What then is Apollos? And what is Paul? Servants through whom you believed, even as the Lord gave *opportunity* to each one.

6 I planted, Apollos watered, but God was causing the growth.

7 So then neither the one who plants nor the one who waters is anything, but God who causes the growth.

8 Now he who plants and he who waters are one; but each will receive his own reward according to his own labor.

9 For we are God's fellow-workers; you are God's field, God's building.

10 According to the grace of God which was given to me, as a wise master builder I laid a foundation, and another is building upon it. But let each man be careful how he builds upon it.

11 For no man can lay a foundation other than the one which is laid, which is Jesus Christ.

12 Now if any man builds upon the foundation with gold, silver, precious stones, wood, hay, straw,

13 each man's work will become evident; for the day will show it, because it is *to be* revealed with fire; and the fire itself will test the quality of each man's work.

14 If any man's work which he has built upon it remains, he shall receive a reward.

15 If any man's work is burned up, he shall suffer loss; but he himself shall be saved, yet so as through fire.

16 Do you not know that you are a temple of God, and *that* the Spirit of God dwells in you?

17 If any man destroys the temple of God, God will destroy him, for the temple of God is holy, and that is what you are.

18 Let no man deceive himself. If any man among you thinks that he is wise in this age, let him become foolish that he may become wise.

19 For the wisdom of this world is foolishness before God. For it is written, "*He is* THE ONE WHO CATCHES THE WISE IN THEIR CRAFTINESS";

20 and again, "THE LORD KNOWS THE REASONINGS of the wise, THAT THEY ARE USELESS."

21 So then let no one boast in men. For all things belong to you,

22 whether Paul or Apollos or Cephas or the world or life or death or things present or things to come; all things belong to you,

23 and you belong to Christ; and Christ belongs to God.

CHAPTER 4

LET a man regard us in this manner, as servants of Christ, and stewards of the mysteries of God.

2 In this case, moreover, it is required of stewards that one be found trustworthy.

3 But to me it is a very small thing that I should be examined by you, or

by *any* human court; in fact, I do not even examine myself.

4 I am conscious of nothing against myself, yet I am not by this acquitted; but the one who examines me is the Lord.

5 Therefore do not go on passing judgment before the time, *but wait* until the Lord comes who will both bring to light the things hidden in the darkness and disclose the motives of *men's* hearts; and then each man's praise will come to him from God.

6 Now these things, brethren, I have figuratively applied to myself and Apollos for your sakes, that in us you might learn not to exceed what is written, in order that no one of you might become arrogant in behalf of one against the other.

7 For who regards you as superior? And what do you have that you did not receive? But if you did receive it, why do you boast as if you had not received it?

8 You are already filled, you have already become rich, you have become kings without us; and *I* would indeed that you had become kings so that we also might reign with you.

9 For, I think, God has exhibited us apostles last of all, as men condemned to death; because we have become a spectacle to the world, both to angels and to men.

10 We are fools for Christ's sake, but you are prudent in Christ; we are weak, but you are strong; you are distinguished, but we are without honor.

11 To this present hour we are both hungry and thirsty, and are poorly clothed, and are roughly treated, and are homeless;

12 and we toil, working with our own hands; when we are reviled, we bless; when we are persecuted, we endure;

13 when we are slandered, we try to conciliate; we have become as the scum of the world, the dregs of all things, *even* until now.

14 I do not write these things to shame you, but to admonish you as my beloved children.

15 For if you were to have countless tutors in Christ, yet *you would* not *have* many fathers; for in Christ Jesus I became your father through the gospel.

16 I exhort you therefore, be imitators of me.

17 For this reason I have sent to you Timothy, who is my beloved and faithful child in the Lord, and he will remind you of my ways which are in Christ, just as I teach everywhere in every church.

18 Now some have become arrogant, as though I were not coming to you.

19 But I will come to you soon, if the Lord wills, and I shall find out, not the words of those who are arrogant, but their power.

20 For the kingdom of God does not consist in words, but in power.

21 What do you desire? Shall I come to you with a rod or with love and a spirit of gentleness?

CHAPTER 5

IT is actually reported that there is immorality among you, and immorality of such a kind as does not exist even among the Gentiles, that someone has his father's wife.

2 And you have become arrogant, and have not mourned instead, in order that the one who had done this deed might be removed from your midst.

3 For I, on my part, though absent in body but present in spirit, have already judged him who has so committed this, as though I were present.

4 In the name of our Lord Jesus, when you are assembled, and I with

you in spirit, with the power of our Lord Jesus,

5 *I have decided* to deliver such a one to Satan for the destruction of his flesh, that his spirit may be saved in the day of the Lord Jesus.

6 Your boasting is not good. Do you not know that a little leaven leavens the whole lump *of dough?*

7 Clean out the old leaven, that you may be a new lump, just as you are *in fact* unleavened. For Christ our Passover also has been sacrificed.

8 Let us therefore celebrate the feast, not with old leaven, nor with the leaven of malice and wickedness, but with the unleavened bread of sincerity and truth.

9 I wrote you in my letter not to associate with immoral people;

10 I *did* not at all *mean* with the immoral people of this world, or with the covetous and swindlers, or with idolaters; for then you would have to go out of the world.

11 But actually, I wrote to you not to associate with any so-called brother if he should be an immoral person, or covetous, or an idolater, or a reviler, or a drunkard, or a swindler—not even to eat with such a one.

12 For what have I to do with judging outsiders? Do you not judge those who are within *the church?*

13 But those who are outside, God judges. Remove the wicked man from among yourselves.

Chapter 6

DOES any one of you, when he has a case against his neighbor, dare to go to law before the unrighteous, and not before the saints?

2 Or do you not know that the saints will judge the world? And if the world is judged by you, are you not competent *to constitute* the smallest law courts?

3 Do you not know that we shall judge angels? How much more, matters of this life?

4 If then you have law courts dealing with matters of this life, do you appoint them as judges who are of no account in the church?

5 I say *this* to your shame. *Is it* so, *that* there is not among you one wise man who will be able to decide between his brethren,

6 but brother goes to law with brother, and that before unbelievers?

7 Actually, then, it is already a defeat for you, that you have lawsuits with one another. Why not rather be wronged? Why not rather be defrauded?

8 On the contrary, you yourselves wrong and defraud, and that *your* brethren.

9 Or do you not know that the unrighteous shall not inherit the kingdom of God? Do not be deceived; neither fornicators, nor idolaters, nor adulterers, nor effeminate, nor homosexuals,

10 nor thieves, nor covetous, nor drunkards, nor revilers, nor swindlers, shall inherit the kingdom of God.

11 And such were some of you; but you were washed, but you were sanctified, but you were justified in the name of the Lord Jesus Christ, and in the Spirit of our God.

12 All things are lawful for me, but not all things are profitable. All things are lawful for me, but I will not be mastered by anything.

13 Food is for the stomach, and the stomach is for food; but God will do away with both of them. Yet the body is not for immorality, but for the Lord; and the Lord is for the body.

14 Now God has not only raised the Lord, but will also raise us up through His power.

15 Do you not know that your bodies are members of Christ? Shall I then take away the members of Christ

and make them members of a harlot? May it never be!

16 Or do you not know that the one who joins himself to a harlot is one body *with her?* For He says, "THE TWO WILL BECOME ONE FLESH."

17 But the one who joins himself to the Lord is one spirit *with Him.*

18 Flee immorality. Every *other* sin that a man commits is outside the body, but the immoral man sins against his own body.

19 Or do you not know that your body is a temple of the Holy Spirit who is in you, whom you have from God, and that you are not your own?

20 For you have been bought with a price: therefore glorify God in your body.

CHAPTER 7

NOW concerning the things about which you wrote, it is good for a man not to touch a woman.

2 But because of immoralities, let each man have his own wife, and let each woman have her own husband.

3 Let the husband fulfill his duty to his wife, and likewise also the wife to her husband.

4 The wife does not have authority over her own body, but the husband *does;* and likewise also the husband does not have authority over his own body, but the wife *does.*

5 Stop depriving one another, except by agreement for a time that you may devote yourselves to prayer, and come together again lest Satan tempt you because of your lack of self-control.

6 But this I say by way of concession, not of command.

7 Yet I wish that all men were even as I myself am. However, each man has his own gift from God, one in this manner, and another in that.

8 But I say to the unmarried and to widows that it is good for them if they remain even as I.

9 But if they do not have self-control, let them marry; for it is better to marry than to burn.

10 But to the married I give instructions, not I, but the Lord, that the wife should not leave her husband

11 (but if she does leave, let her remain unmarried, or else be reconciled to her husband), and that the husband should not send his wife away.

12 But to the rest I say, not the Lord, that if any brother has a wife who is an unbeliever, and she consents to live with him, let him not send her away.

13 And a woman who has an unbelieving husband, and he consents to live with her, let her not send her husband away.

14 For the unbelieving husband is sanctified through his wife, and the unbelieving wife is sanctified through her believing husband; for otherwise your children are unclean, but now they are holy.

15 Yet if the unbelieving one leaves, let him leave; the brother or the sister is not under bondage in such *cases,* but God has called us to peace.

16 For how do you know, O wife, whether you will save your husband? Or how do you know, O husband, whether you will save your wife?

17 Only, as the Lord has assigned to each one, as God has called each, in this manner let him walk. And thus I direct in all the churches.

18 Was any man called *already* circumcised? Let him not become uncircumcised. Has anyone been called in uncircumcision? Let him not be circumcised.

19 Circumcision is nothing, and uncircumcision is nothing, but *what matters is* the keeping of the commandments of God.

20 Let each man remain in that condition in which he was called.

21 Were you called while a slave? Do not worry about it; but if you are able also to become free, rather do that.

22 For he who was called in the Lord while a slave, is the Lord's freedman; likewise he who was called while free, is Christ's slave.

23 You were bought with a price; do not become slaves of men.

24 Brethren, let each man remain with God in that *condition* in which he was called.

25 Now concerning virgins I have no command of the Lord, but I give an opinion as one who by the mercy of the Lord is trustworthy.

26 I think then that this is good in view of the present distress, that it is good for a man to remain as he is.

27 Are you bound to a wife? Do not seek to be released. Are you released from a wife? Do not seek a wife.

28 But if you should marry, you have not sinned; and if a virgin should marry, she has not sinned. Yet such will have trouble in this life, and I am trying to spare you.

29 But this I say, brethren, the time has been shortened, so that from now on both those who have wives should be as though they had none;

30 and those who weep, as though they did not weep; and those who rejoice, as though they did not rejoice; and those who buy, as though they did not possess;

31 and those who use the world, as though they did not make full use of it; for the form of this world is passing away.

32 But I want you to be free from concern. One who is unmarried is concerned about the things of the Lord, how he may please the Lord;

33 but one who is married is concerned about the things of the world, how he may please his wife,

34 and *his interests* are divided. And the woman who is unmarried, and the virgin, is concerned about the things of the Lord, that she may be holy both in body and spirit; but one who is married is concerned about the things of the world, how she may please her husband.

35 And this I say for your own benefit; not to put a restraint upon you, but to promote what is seemly, and *to secure* undistracted devotion to the Lord.

36 But if any man thinks that he is acting unbecomingly toward his virgin *daughter*, if she should be of full age, and if it must be so, let him do what he wishes, he does not sin; let her marry.

37 But he who stands firm in his heart, being under no constraint, but has authority over his own will, and has decided this in his own heart, to keep his own virgin *daughter*, he will do well.

38 So then both he who gives his own virgin *daughter* in marriage does well, and he who does not give her in marriage will do better.

39 A wife is bound as long as her husband lives; but if her husband is dead, she is free to be married to whom she wishes, only in the Lord.

40 But in my opinion she is happier if she remains as she is; and I think that I also have the Spirit of God.

CHAPTER 8

NOW concerning things sacrificed to idols, we know that we all have knowledge. Knowledge makes arrogant, but love edifies.

2 If any one supposes that he knows anything, he has not yet known as he ought to know;

3 but if any one loves God, he is known by Him.

4 Therefore concerning the eating of things sacrificed to idols, we know that there is no such thing as an idol in the world, and that there is no God but one.

5 For even if there are so-called gods whether in heaven or on earth, as indeed there are many gods and many lords,

6 yet for us there is *but* one God, the Father, from whom are all things, and we *exist* for Him; and one Lord, Jesus Christ, through whom are all things, and we *exist* through Him.

7 However not all men have this knowledge; but some, being accustomed to the idol until now, eat food as if it were sacrificed to an idol; and their conscience being weak is defiled.

8 But food will not commend us to God; we are neither the worse if we do not eat, nor the better if we do eat.

9 But take care lest this liberty of yours somehow become a stumbling block to the weak.

10 For if someone sees you, who have knowledge, dining in an idol's temple, will not his conscience, if he is weak, be strengthened to eat things sacrificed to idols?

11 For through your knowledge he who is weak is ruined, the brother for whose sake Christ died.

12 And thus, by sinning against the brethren and wounding their conscience when it is weak, you sin against Christ.

13 Therefore, if food causes my brother to stumble, I will never eat meat again, that I might not cause my brother to stumble.

CHAPTER 9

AM I not free? Am I not an apostle? Have I not seen Jesus our Lord? Are you not my work in the Lord?

2 If to others I am not an apostle, at least I am to you; for you are the seal of my apostleship in the Lord.

3 My defense to those who examine me is this:

4 Do we not have a right to eat and drink?

5 Do we not have a right to take along a believing wife, even as the rest of the apostles, and the brothers of the Lord, and Cephas?

6 Or do only Barnabas and I not have a right to refrain from working?

7 Who at any time serves as a soldier at his own expense? Who plants a vineyard, and does not eat the fruit of it? Or who tends a flock and does not use the milk of the flock?

8 I am not speaking these things according to human judgment, am I? Or does not the Law also say these things?

9 For it is written in the Law of Moses, "YOU SHALL NOT MUZZLE THE OX WHILE HE IS THRESHING." God is not concerned about oxen, is He?

10 Or is He speaking altogether for our sake? Yes, for our sake it was written, because the plowman ought to plow in hope, and the thresher *to thresh* in hope of sharing *the crops*.

11 If we sowed spiritual things in you, is it too much if we should reap material things from you?

12 If others share the right over you, do we not more? Nevertheless, we did not use this right, but we endure all things, that we may cause no hindrance to the gospel of Christ.

13 Do you not know that those who perform sacred services eat the *food* of the temple, *and* those who attend regularly to the altar have their share with the altar?

14 So also the Lord directed those who proclaim the gospel to get their living from the gospel.

15 But I have used none of these things. And I am not writing these

things that it may be done so in my case; for it would be better for me to die than have any man make my boast an empty one.

16 For if I preach the gospel, I have nothing to boast of, for I am under compulsion; for woe is me if I do not preach the gospel.

17 For if I do this voluntarily, I have a reward; but if against my will, I have a stewardship entrusted to me.

18 What then is my reward? That, when I preach the gospel, I may offer the gospel without charge, so as not to make full use of my right in the gospel.

19 For though I am free from all *men*, I have made myself a slave to all, that I might win the more.

20 And to the Jews I became as a Jew, that I might win Jews; to those who are under the Law, as under the Law, though not being myself under the Law, that I might win those who are under the Law;

21 to those who are without law, as without law, though not being without the law of God but under the law of Christ, that I might win those who are without law.

22 To the weak I became weak, that I might win the weak; I have become all things to all men, that I may by all means save some.

23 And I do all things for the sake of the gospel, that I may become a fellow-partaker of it.

24 Do you not know that those who run in a race all run, but *only* one receives the prize? Run in such a way that you may win.

25 And everyone who competes in the games exercises self-control in all things. They then *do it* to receive a perishable wreath, but we an imperishable.

26 Therefore I run in such a way, as not without aim; I box in such a way, as not beating the air;

27 but I buffet my body and make it my slave, lest possibly, after I have preached to others, I myself should be disqualified.

CHAPTER 10

FOR I do not want you to be unaware, brethren, that our fathers were all under the cloud, and all passed through the sea;

2 and all were baptized into Moses in the cloud and in the sea;

3 and all ate the same spiritual food;

4 and all drank the same spiritual drink, for they were drinking from a spiritual rock which followed them; and the rock was Christ.

5 Nevertheless, with most of them God was not well-pleased; for they were laid low in the wilderness.

6 Now these things happened as examples for us, that we should not crave evil things, as they also craved.

7 And do not be idolaters, as some of them were; as it is written, "THE PEOPLE SAT DOWN TO EAT AND DRINK, AND STOOD UP TO PLAY."

8 Nor let us act immorally, as some of them did, and twenty-three thousand fell in one day.

9 Nor let us try the Lord, as some of them did, and were destroyed by the serpents.

10 Nor grumble, as some of them did, and were destroyed by the destroyer.

11 Now these things happened to them as an example, and they were written for our instruction, upon whom the ends of the ages have come.

12 Therefore let him who thinks he stands take heed lest he fall.

13 No temptation has overtaken you but such as is common to man; and God is faithful, who will not allow you to be tempted beyond what you

are able, but with the temptation will provide the way of escape also, that you may be able to endure it. (a)

14 Therefore, my beloved, flee from idolatry.

15 I speak as to wise men; you judge what I say.

16 Is not the cup of blessing which we bless a sharing in the blood of Christ? Is not the bread which we break a sharing in the body of Christ?

17 Since there is one bread, we who are many are one body; for we all partake of the one bread.

18 Look at the nation Israel; are not those who eat the sacrifices sharers in the altar?

19 What do I mean then? That a thing sacrificed to idols is anything, or that an idol is anything?

20 No, but *I say* that the things which the Gentiles sacrifice, they sacrifice to demons, and not to God; and I do not want you to become sharers in demons.

21 You cannot drink the cup of the Lord and the cup of demons; you cannot partake of the table of the Lord and the table of demons.

22 Or do we provoke the Lord to jealousy? We are not stronger than He, are we?

23 All things are lawful, but not all things are profitable. All things are lawful, but not all things edify.

24 Let no one seek his own *good*, but that of his neighbor.

25 Eat anything that is sold in the meat market, without asking questions for conscience' sake;

26 FOR THE EARTH IS THE LORD'S, AND ALL IT CONTAINS.

27 If one of the unbelievers invites you, and you wish to go, eat anything that is set before you, without asking questions for conscience' sake.

28 But if anyone should say to you, "This is meat sacrificed to idols," do not eat *it*, for the sake of the one who informed *you*, and for conscience' sake;

(a) TRIUMPH OVER TEMPTATION. "Temptation has overtaken you." Believers in Christ Jesus are tempted. It is

COMMON TO MAN—"But each one is tempted when he is carried away and enticed by his own lust," James 1:14, page 309. The tempter may try, test, and tempt you but you can have

CONFIDENCE IN VICTORY—"God is faithful, who will not allow you to be tempted beyond what you are able." Jesus taught His disciples to pray, "Do not lead us into temptation, but deliver us from evil." Matt. 6:13, page 7. "This is the victory that has overcome the world—our faith," I John 5:4, page 325. The believer is promised strength to

CONQUER TEMPTATION—"God is faithful" and "with the temptation will provide the way of escape." For "in all these things we overwhelmingly conquer through Him who loved us," Rom. 8:37, page 217. By faith he can say, "I can do all things through Him who strengthens me," Phil. 4:13, page 273. The believer is "protected by the power of God through faith," I Peter 1:5, page 313. Christ Jesus "is able to save forever those who draw near to God through Him, since He always lives to make intercession for them," Heb. 7:25, page 300. Therefore yield your mind and body to

CHRIST'S CONTROL—Claim His strength. You will "be able to endure" temptation. You will be victorious for "God shall supply all your needs," Phil. 4:19, page 273. Remember Jesus said, "My grace is sufficient for you, for power is perfected in weakness," II Cor. 12:9, page 254. "Press on to maturity," Heb. 6:1, page 298. Then you can say "I know whom I have believed and I am convinced that He is able to guard what I have entrusted to Him until that day," II Tim. 1:12, page 289.

29 I mean not your own conscience, but the other *man's*; for why is my freedom judged by another's conscience?

30 If I partake with thankfulness, why am I slandered concerning that for which I give thanks?

31 Whether, then, you eat or drink or whatever you do, do all to the glory of God.

32 Give no offense either to Jews or to Greeks or to the church of God;

33 just as I also please all men in all things, not seeking my own profit, but the *profit* of the many, that they may be saved.

Chapter 11

B E imitators of me, just as I also am of Christ.

2 Now I praise you because you remember me in everything, and hold firmly to the traditions, just as I delivered them to you.

3 But I want you to understand that Christ is the head of every man, and the man is the head of a woman, and God is the head of Christ.

4 Every man who has *something* on his head while praying or prophesying, disgraces his head.

5 But every woman who has her head uncovered while praying or prophesying, disgraces her head; for she is one and the same with her whose head is shaved.

6 For if a woman does not cover her head, let her also have her hair cut off; but if it is disgraceful for a woman to have her hair cut off or her head shaved, let her cover her head.

7 For a man ought not to have his head covered, since he is the image and glory of God; but the woman is the glory of man.

8 For man does not originate from woman, but woman from man;

9 for indeed man was not created

for the woman's sake, but woman for the man's sake.

10 Therefore the woman ought to have *a symbol of* authority on her head, because of the angels.

11 However, in the Lord, neither is woman independent of man, nor is man independent of woman.

12 For as the woman originates from the man, so also the man has his birth through the woman; and all things originate from God.

13 Judge for yourselves: is it proper for a woman to pray to God *with head* uncovered?

14 Does not even nature itself teach you that if a man has long hair, it is a dishonor to him,

15 but if a woman has long hair, it is a glory to her? For her hair is given to her for a covering.

16 But if one is inclined to be contentious, we have no other practice, nor have the churches of God.

17 But in giving this instruction, I do not praise you, because you come together not for the better but for the worse.

18 For, in the first place, when you come together as a church, I hear that divisions exist among you; and in part, I believe it.

19 For there must also be factions among you, in order that those who are approved may have become evident among you.

20 Therefore when you meet together, it is not to eat the Lord's Supper,

21 for in your eating each one takes his own supper first; and one is hungry and another is drunk.

22 What! Do you not have houses in which to eat and drink? Or do you despise the church of God, and shame those who have nothing? What shall I say to you? Shall I praise you? In this I will not praise you.

23 For I received from the Lord that which I also delivered to you,

that the Lord Jesus in the night in which He was betrayed took bread;

24 and when He had given thanks, He broke it, and said, "This is My body, which is for you; do this in remembrance of Me."

25 In the same way *He took* the cup also, after supper, saying, "This cup is the new covenant in My blood; do this, as often as you drink *it*, in remembrance of Me."

26 For as often as you eat this bread and drink the cup, you proclaim the Lord's death until He comes.

27 Therefore whoever eats the bread or drinks the cup of the Lord in an unworthy manner, shall be guilty of the body and the blood of the Lord.

28 But let a man examine himself, and so let him eat of the bread and drink of the cup.

29 For he who eats and drinks, eats and drinks judgment to himself, if he does not judge the body rightly.

30 For this reason many among you are weak and sick, and a number sleep. (a)

31 But if we judged ourselves rightly, we should not be judged. (b)

32 But when we are judged, we are disciplined by the Lord in order that we may not be condemned along with the world. (c)

33 So then, my brethren, when you come together to eat, wait for one another.

34 If anyone is hungry, let him eat at home, so that you may not come together for judgment. And the remaining matters I shall arrange when I come.

CHAPTER 12

NOW concerning spiritual *gifts*, brethren, I do not want you to be unaware.

2 You know that when you were pagans, *you were* led astray to the dumb idols, however you were led.

3 Therefore I make known to you, that no one speaking by the

DISCIPLINE OF DISCIPLES.

(a) Cause of Discipline—Sin is the reason for discipline or chastening. "If we say that we have no sin, we are deceiving ourselves, and the truth is not in us," I John 1:8, page 322. "For those whom the Lord loves He disciplines and he scourges every son whom he receives," Heb. 12:6, page 306.

(b) Cleansing and Rebound back into fellowship with God. Every believer is to judge himself by confession of each sin by name to God. "If we confess our sins, He is faithful and righteous to forgive us our sins and to cleanse us from all unrighteousness." Confess, claim forgiveness, and experience the cleansing, I John ,1:9, p. 322.

(c) Compensation of Discipline—When we are judged, we are disciplined by the Lord. "He disciplines us for our good that we may share His Holiness . . . to those who have been trained by it, afterward it yields the peaceful fruit of righteousness," Heb. 12:10-11, page 306.

Consider the Consequence—"Many among you are weak, sick and a number sleep." "Shall we not much rather be subject to the Father of Spirits and live?" Heb. 12:9, page 306. "There is a sin leading to death," I John 5:16, page 326. What a warning! The discipline of one believer was "to deliver such a one to Satan for the destruction of his flesh, that his spirit may be saved in the day of the Lord Jesus," I Cor. 5:5, page 231. Therefore take heed, "If any man's work is burned up, he shall suffer loss, but he himself shall be saved, yet so as through fire," I Cor. 3:15, page 229. "For we must all appear before the judgment seat of Christ," II Cor. 5:10, page 248.

How will you appear—Judge yourself now that you may not be judged.

Spirit of God says, "Jesus is accursed"; and no one can say, "Jesus is Lord," except by the Holy Spirit.

4 Now there are varieties of gifts, but the same Spirit.

5 And there are varieties of ministries, and the same Lord.

6 And there are varieties of effects, but the same God who works all things in all *persons.*

7 But to each one is given the manifestation of the Spirit for the common good.

8 For to one is given the word of wisdom through the Spirit, and to another the word of knowledge according to the same Spirit;

9 to another faith by the same Spirit, and to another gifts of healing by the one Spirit,

10 and to another the effecting of miracles, and to another prophecy, and to another the distinguishing of spirits, to another *various* kinds of tongues, and to another the interpretation of tongues.

11 But one and the same Spirit works all these things, distributing to each one individually just as He wills.

12 For even as the body is one and *yet* has many members, and all the members of the body, though they are many, are one body, so also is Christ.

13 For by one Spirit we were all baptized into one body, whether Jews or Greeks, whether slaves or free, and we were all made to drink of one Spirit.

14 For the body is not one member, but many.

15 If the foot should say, "Because I am not a hand, I am not *a part* of the body," it is not for this reason any the less *a part* of the body.

16 And if the ear should say, "Because I am not an eye, I am not *a part* of the body," it is not for this reason any the less *a part* of the body.

17 If the whole body were an eye, where would the hearing be? If the whole were hearing, where would the sense of smell be?

18 But now God has placed the members, each one of them, in the body, just as He desired.

19 And if they were all one member, where would the body be?

20 But now there are many members, but one body.

21 And the eye cannot say to the hand, "I have no need of you"; or again the head to the feet, "I have no need of you."

22 On the contrary, it is much truer that the members of the body which seem to be weaker are necessary;

23 and those *members* of the body, which we deem less honorable, on these we bestow more abundant honor, and our unseemly *members come to* have more abundant seemliness,

24 whereas our seemly *members* have no need *of it.* But God has *so* composed the body, giving more abundant honor to that *member* which lacked,

25 that there should be no division in the body, but *that* the members should have the same care for one another.

26 And if one member suffers, all the members suffer with it; if *one* member is honored, all the members rejoice with it.

27 Now you are Christ's body, and individually members of it.

28 And God has appointed in the church, first apostles, second prophets, third teachers, then miracles, then gifts of healings, helps, administrations, *various* kinds of tongues.

29 All are not apostles, are they? All are not prophets, are they? All are not teachers, are they? All are not *workers of* miracles, are they?

30 All do not have gifts of healings, do they? All do not speak with tongues, do they? All do not interpret, do they?

31 But earnestly desire the greater gifts.

And I show you a still more excellent way.

CHAPTER 13

IF I speak with the tongues of men and of angels, but do not have love, I have become a noisy gong or a clanging cymbal.

2 And if I have *the gift of* prophecy, and know all mysteries and all knowledge; and if I have all faith, so as to remove mountains, but do not have love, I am nothing.

3 And if I give all my possessions to feed *the poor*, and if I deliver my body to be burned, but do not have love, it profits me nothing.

4 Love is patient, love is kind, *and* is not jealous; love does not brag *and* is not arrogant,

5 does not act unbecomingly; it does not seek its own, is not provoked, does not take into account a wrong *suffered*,

6 does not rejoice in unrighteousness, but rejoices with the truth;

7 bears all things, believes all things, hopes all things, endures all things.

8 Love never fails; but if *there are* gifts of prophecy, they will be done away; if *there are* tongues, they will cease; if *there is* knowledge, it will be done away.

9 For we know in part, and we prophesy in part;

10 but when the perfect comes, the partial will be done away.

11 When I was a child, I used to speak as a child, think as a child, reason as a child; when I became a man, I did away with childish things.

12 For now we see in a mirror dimly, but then face to face; now I know in part, but then I shall know

fully just as I also have been fully known.

13 But now abide faith, hope, love, these three; but the greatest of these is love.

CHAPTER 14

PURSUE love, yet desire earnestly spiritual *gifts*, but especially that you may prophesy.

2 For one who speaks in a tongue does not speak to men, but to God; for no one understands, but in *his* spirit he speaks mysteries.

3 But one who prophesies speaks to men for edification and exhortation and consolation.

4 One who speaks in a tongue edifies himself; but one who prophesies edifies the church.

5 Now I wish that you all spoke in tongues, but *even* more that you would prophesy; and greater is one who prophesies than one who speaks in tongues, unless he interprets, so that the church may receive edifying.

6 But now, brethren, if I come to you speaking in tongues, what shall I profit you, unless I speak to you either by way of revelation or of knowledge or of prophecy or of teaching?

7 Yet *even* lifeless things, either flute or harp, in producing a sound, if they do not produce a distinction in the tones, how will it be known what is played on the flute or on the harp?

8 For if the bugle produces an indistinct sound, who will prepare himself for battle?

9 So also you, unless you utter by the tongue speech that is clear, how will it be known what is spoken? For you will be speaking into the air.

10 There are, perhaps, a great many kinds of languages in the world, and no *kind* is without meaning.

11 If then I do not know the meaning of the language, I shall be to the

one who speaks a barbarian, and the one who speaks will be a barbarian to me.

12 So also you, since you are zealous of spiritual *gifts*, seek to abound for the edification of the church.

13 Therefore let one who speaks in a tongue pray that he may interpret.

14 For if I pray in a tongue, my spirit prays, but my mind is unfruitful.

15 What is *the outcome* then? I shall pray with the spirit and I shall pray with the mind also; I shall sing with the spirit and I shall sing with the mind also.

16 Otherwise if you bless in the spirit *only*, how will the one who fills the place of the ungifted say the "Amen" at your giving of thanks, since he does not know what you are saying?

17 For you are giving thanks well enough, but the other man is not edified.

18 I thank God, I speak in tongues more than you all;

19 however, in the church I desire to speak five words with my mind, that I may instruct others also, rather than ten thousand words in a tongue.

20 Brethren, do not be children in your thinking; yet in evil be babes, but in your thinking be mature.

21 In the Law it is written, "BY MEN OF STRANGE TONGUES AND BY THE LIPS OF STRANGERS I WILL SPEAK TO THIS PEOPLE, AND EVEN SO THEY WILL NOT LISTEN TO ME," says the Lord.

22 So then tongues are for a sign, not to those who believe, but to unbelievers; but prophecy *is for a sign*, not to unbelievers, but to those who believe.

23 If therefore the whole church should assemble together and all speak in tongues, and ungifted men or unbelievers enter, will they not say that you are mad?

24 But if all prophesy, and an un-

believer or an ungifted man enters, he is convicted by all, he is called to account by all;

25 the secrets of his heart are disclosed; and so he will fall on his face and worship God, declaring that God is certainly among you.

26 What is *the outcome* then, brethren? When you assemble, each one has a psalm, has a teaching, has a revelation, has a tongue, has an interpretation. Let all things be done for edification.

27 If any one speaks in a tongue, *it should be* by two or at the most three, and *each* in turn, and let one interpret;

28 but if there is no interpreter, let him keep silent in the church; and let him speak to himself and to God.

29 And let two or three prophets speak, and let the others pass judgment.

30 But if a revelation is made to another who is seated, let the first keep silent.

31 For you can all prophesy one by one, so that all may learn and all may be exhorted;

32 and the spirits of prophets are subject to prophets;

33 for God is not *a God* of confusion but of peace, as in all the churches of the saints.

34 Let the women keep silent in the churches; for they are not permitted to speak, but let them subject themselves, just as the Law also says.

35 And if they desire to learn anything, let them ask their own husbands at home; for it is improper for a woman to speak in church.

36 Was it from you that the word of God *first* went forth? Or has it come to you only?

37 If any one thinks he is a prophet or spiritual, let him recognize that the things which I write to you are the Lord's commandment.

38 But if any one does not recognize *this*, he is not recognized.

39 Therefore, my brethren, desire earnestly to prophesy, and do not forbid to speak in tongues.

40 But let all things be done properly and in an orderly manner.

CHAPTER 15

NOW I make known to you, brethren, the gospel which I preached to you, which also you received, in which also you stand,

2 by which also you are saved, if you hold fast the word which I preached to you, unless you believed in vain.

3 For I delivered to you as of first importance what I also received, that Christ died for our sins according to the Scriptures,

4 and that He was buried, and that He was raised on the third day according to the Scriptures, (a)

5 and that He appeared to Cephas, then to the twelve.

6 After that He appeared to more than five hundred brethren at one time, most of whom remain until now, but some have fallen asleep;

7 then He appeared to James, then to all the apostles;

8 and last of all, as it were to one untimely born, He appeared to me also.·

9 For I am the least of the apostles, who am not fit to be called an apostle, because I persecuted the church of God.

10 But by the grace of God I am what I am, and His grace toward me did not prove vain; but I labored even more than all of them, yet not I, but the grace of God with me.

11 Whether then *it was* I or they, so we preach and so you believed.

12 Now if Christ is preached, that He has been raised from the dead, how do some among you say that there is no resurrection of the dead?

13 But if there is no resurrection of the dead, not even Christ has been raised;

14 and if Christ has not been raised, then our preaching is vain, your faith also is vain.

15 Moreover we are even found *to be* false witnesses of God, because we witnessed against God that He raised Christ, whom He did not raise, if in fact the dead are not raised.

16 For if the dead are not raised, not even Christ has been raised;

17 and if Christ has not been raised, your faith is worthless; you are still in your sins.

18 Then those also who have fallen asleep in Christ have perished.

19 If we have only hoped in Christ in this life, we are of all men most to be pitied.

20 But now Christ has been raised from the dead, the first fruits of those who are asleep.

21 For since by a man *came* death, by a man also *came* the resurrection of the dead.

22 For as in Adam all die, so also in Christ all shall be made alive.

23 But each in his own order: Christ the first fruits, after that those who are Christ's at His coming,

24 then *comes* the end, when He delivers up the kingdom to the God and Father, when He has abolished all rule and all authority and power.

25 For He must reign until He has put all His enemies under His feet.

26 The last enemy that will be abolished is death.

27 For HE HAS PUT ALL THINGS IN SUBJECTION UNDER HIS FEET. But when He says, "All things are put in subjection," it is evident that He is excepted

---

(a) The gospel defined: "Christ died for our sins . . . He was buried, and that He was raised on the third day."

who put all things in subjection to Him.

28 And when all things are subjected to Him, then the Son Himself also will be subjected to the One who subjected all things to Him, that God may be all in all.

29 Otherwise, what will those do who are baptized for the dead? If the dead are not raised at all, why then are they baptized for them?

30 Why are we also in danger every hour?

31 I protest, brethren, by the boasting in you, which I have in Christ Jesus our Lord, I die daily.

32 If from human motives I fought with wild beasts at Ephesus, what does it profit me? If the dead are not raised, LET US EAT AND DRINK, FOR TOMORROW WE DIE.

33 Do not be deceived: "Bad company corrupts good morals."

34 Become sober-minded as you ought, and stop sinning; for some have no knowledge of God. I speak *this* to your shame.

35 But some one will say, "How are the dead raised? And with what kind of body do they come?"

36 You fool! That which you sow does not come to life unless it dies;

37 and that which you sow, you do not sow the body which is to be, but a bare grain, perhaps of wheat or of something else.

38 But God gives it a body just as He wished, and to each of the seeds a body of its own.

39 All flesh is not the same flesh, but there is *one flesh* of men, and another flesh of beasts, and another flesh of birds, and another of fish.

40 There are also heavenly bodies and earthly bodies, but the glory of the heavenly is one, and the *glory* of the earthly is another.

41 There is one glory of the sun, and another glory of the moon, and another glory of the stars; for star differs from star in glory.

42 So also is the resurrection of the dead. It is sown a perishable *body*, it is raised an imperishable *body*;

43 it is sown in dishonor, it is raised in glory; it is sown in weakness, it is raised in power;

44 it is sown a natural body, it is raised a spiritual body. If there is a natural body, there is also a spiritual *body*.

45 So also it is written, "The first MAN, Adam, BECAME A LIVING SOUL." The last Adam *became* a life-giving spirit.

46 However, the spiritual is not first, but the natural; then the spiritual.

47 The first man is from the earth, earthy; the second man is from heaven.

48 As is the earthy, so also are those who are earthy; and as is the heavenly, so also are those who are heavenly.

49 And just as we have borne the image of the earthy, we shall also bear the image of the heavenly.

50 Now I say this, brethren, that flesh and blood cannot inherit the kingdom of God; nor does the perishable inherit the imperishable.

51 Behold, I tell you a mystery; we shall not all sleep, but we shall all be changed,

52 in a moment, in the twinkling of an eye, at the last trumpet; for the trumpet will sound, and the dead will be raised imperishable, and we shall be changed.

53 For this perishable must put on the imperishable, and this mortal must put on immortality.

54 But when this perishable will have put on the imperishable, and this mortal will have put on immortality, then will come about the saying that is written, "DEATH IS SWALLOWED UP IN VICTORY.

55 "O DEATH, WHERE IS YOUR VIC-

TORY? O DEATH, WHERE IS YOUR STING?"

56 The sting of death is sin, and the power of sin is the law;

57 but thanks be to God, who gives us the victory through our Lord Jesus Christ.

58 Therefore, my beloved brethren, be steadfast, immovable, always abounding in the work of the Lord, knowing that your toil is not *in* vain in the Lord.

CHAPTER 16

NOW concerning the collection for the saints, as I directed the churches of Galatia, so do you also.

2 On the first day of every week let each one of you put aside and save, as he may prosper, that no collections be made when I come.

3 And when I arrive, whomever you may approve, I shall send them with letters to carry your gift to Jerusalem;

4 and if it is fitting for me to go also, they will go with me.

5 But I shall come to you after I go through Macedonia, for I am going through Macedonia;

6 and perhaps I shall stay with you, or even spend the winter, that you may send me on my way wherever I may go.

7 For I do not wish to see you now *just* in passing; for I hope to remain with you for some time, if the Lord permits.

8 But I shall remain in Ephesus until Pentecost;

9 for a wide door for effective *service* has opened to me, and there are many adversaries.

10 Now if Timothy comes, see that he is with you without cause to be afraid; for he is doing the Lord's work, as I also am.

11 Let no one therefore despise him. But send him on his way in peace, so that he may come to me; for I expect him with the brethren.

12 But concerning Apollos our brother, I encouraged him greatly to come to you with the brethren; and it was not at all *his* desire to come now, but he will come when he has opportunity.

13 Be on the alert, stand firm in the faith, act like men, be strong.

14 Let all that you do be done in love.

15 Now I urge you, brethren (you know the household of Stephanas, that they were the first fruits of Achaia, and that they have devoted themselves for ministry to the saints),

16 that you also be in subjection to such men and to everyone who helps in the work and labors.

17 And I rejoice over the coming of Stephanas and Fortunatus and Achaicus; because they have supplied what was lacking on your part.

18 For they have refreshed my spirit and yours. Therefore acknowledge such men.

19 The churches of Asia greet you. Aquila and Prisca greet you heartily in the Lord, with the church that is in their house.

20 All the brethren greet you. Greet one another with a holy kiss.

21 The greeting is in my own hand—Paul.

22 If any one does not love the Lord, let him be accursed. Maranatha.

23 The grace of the Lord Jesus be with you.

24 My love be with you all in Christ Jesus. Amen.

Paul, an apostle of Christ Jesus by the will of God, and Timothy *our* brother, to the church of God which is at Corinth with all the saints who are throughout Achaia:

2 Grace to you and peace from God our Father and the Lord Jesus Christ.

3 Blessed *be* the God and Father of our Lord Jesus Christ, the Father of mercies and God of all comfort;

4 who comforts us in all our affliction so that we may be able to comfort those who are in any affliction with the comfort with which we ourselves are comforted by God.

5 For just as the sufferings of Christ are ours in abundance, so also our comfort is abundant through Christ.

6 But if we are afflicted, it is for your comfort and salvation; or if we are comforted, it is for your comfort, which is effective in the patient enduring of the same sufferings which we also suffer;

7 and our hope for you is firmly grounded, knowing that as you are sharers of our sufferings, so also you are *sharers* of our comfort.

8 For we do not want you to be unaware, brethren, of our affliction which came *to us* in Asia, that we were burdened excessively, beyond our strength, so that we despaired even of life;

9 indeed, we had the sentence of death within ourselves in order that we should not trust in ourselves, but in God who raises the dead;

10 who delivered us from so great a *peril of* death, and will deliver *us*, He on whom we have set our hope. And He will yet deliver us,

11 you also joining in helping us through your prayers, that thanks may be given by many persons on our behalf for the favor bestowed upon us through *the prayers of* many.

12 For our proud confidence is this, the testimony of our conscience, that in holiness and godly sincerity, not in fleshly wisdom but in the grace of God, we have conducted ourselves in the world, and especially toward you.

13 For we write nothing else to you than what you read and understand, and I hope you will understand until the end;

14 just as you also partially did understand us, that we are your reason to be proud as you also are ours, in the day of our Lord Jesus.

15 And in this confidence I intended at first to come to you, that you might twice receive a blessing;

16 that is, to pass your way into Macedonia, and again from Macedonia to come to you, and by you to be helped on my journey to Judea.

17 Therefore, I was not vacillating when I intended to do this, was I? Or that which I purpose, do I purpose according to the flesh, that with me there should be yes, yes and no, no *at the same time?*

18 But as God is faithful, our word to you is not yes and no.

19 For the Son of God, Christ Jesus, who was preached among you by us,—by me and Silvanus and Timothy—was not yes and no, but is yes in Him.

20 For as many as may be the promises of God, in Him they are yes; wherefore also by Him is our Amen to the glory of God through us.

21 Now He who establishes us with you in Christ and anointed us is God,

22 who also sealed us and gave *us* the Spirit in our hearts as a pledge.

23 But I call God as witness to my soul, that to spare you I came no more to Corinth.

24 Not that we lord it over your faith, but are workers with you for your joy; for in your faith you are standing firm.

Chapter 2

BUT I determined this for my own sake, that I would not come to you in sorrow again.

2 For if I cause you sorrow, who then makes me glad but the one whom I made sorrowful?

3 And this is the very thing I wrote you, lest, when I came, I should have sorrow from those who ought to make me rejoice; having confidence in you all, that my joy would be *the joy* of you all.

4 For out of much affliction and anguish of heart I wrote to you with many tears; not that you should be made sorrowful, but that you might know the love which I have especially for you.

5 But if any has caused sorrow, he has caused sorrow not to me, but in some degree—in order not to say too much—to all of you.

6 Sufficient for such a one is this punishment which was *inflicted by* the majority,

7 so that on the contrary you should rather forgive and comfort *him*, lest somehow such a one be overwhelmed by excessive sorrow.

8 Wherefore I urge you to reaffirm *your* love for him.

9 For to this end also I wrote that I might put you to the test, whether you are obedient in all things.

10 But whom you forgive anything, I *forgive* also; for indeed what I have forgiven, if I have forgiven anything, I *did it* for your sakes in the presence of Christ,

11 in order that no advantage be taken of us by Satan; for we are not ignorant of his schemes.

12 Now when I came to Troas for the gospel of Christ and when a door was opened for me in the Lord,

13 I had no rest for my spirit, not finding Titus my brother; but taking my leave of them, I went on to Macedonia.

14 But thanks be to God, who always leads us in His triumph in Christ, and manifests through us the sweet aroma of the knowledge of Him in every place.

15 For we are a fragrance of Christ to God among those who are being saved and among those who are perishing;

16 to the one an aroma from death to death, to the other an aroma from life to life. And who is adequate for these things?

17 For we are not like many, peddling the word of God, but as from sincerity, but as from God, we speak in Christ in the sight of God.

Chapter 3

ARE we beginning to commend ourselves again? Or do we need, as some, letters of commendation to you or from you?

2 You are our letter, written in our hearts, known and read by all men;

3 being manifested that you are a letter of Christ, cared for by us, written not with ink, but with the Spirit of the living God, not on tablets of stone, but on tablets of human hearts.

4 And such confidence we have through Christ toward God.

5 Not that we are adequate in ourselves to consider anything as *coming* from ourselves, but our adequacy is from God,

6 who also made us adequate *as* servants of a new covenant, not of the letter, but of the Spirit; for the letter kills, but the Spirit gives life.

7 But if the ministry of death, in letters engraved on stones, came with glory, so that the sons of Israel could not look intently at the face of Moses because of the glory of his face, fading *as* it was,

8 how shall the ministry of the Spirit fail to be even more with glory?

9 For if the ministry of condemnation has glory, much more does the ministry of righteousness abound in glory.

10 For indeed what had glory, in this case has no glory on account of the glory that surpasses *it.*

11 For if that which fades away *was* with glory, much more that which remains *is* in glory.

12 Having therefore such a hope, we use great boldness in *our* speech,

13 and *are* not as Moses, *who* used to put a veil over his face that the sons of Israel might not look intently at the end of what was fading away.

14 But their minds were hardened; for until this very day at the reading of the old covenant the same veil remains unlifted, because it is removed in Christ.

15 But to this day whenever Moses is read, a veil lies over their heart;

16 BUT WHENEVER A MAN TURNS TO THE LORD, THE VEIL IS TAKEN AWAY.

17 Now the Lord is the Spirit; and where the Spirit of the Lord is, *there* is liberty.

18 But we all, with unveiled face beholding as in a mirror the glory of the Lord, are being transformed into the same image from glory to glory, just as from the Lord, the Spirit.

CHAPTER 4

THEREFORE, since we have this ministry, as we received mercy, we do not lose heart,

2 but we have renounced the things hidden because of shame, not walking in craftiness or adulterating the word of God, but by the manifestation of truth commending ourselves to every man's conscience in the sight of God.

3 And even if our gospel is veiled, it is veiled to those who are perishing,

4 in whose case the god of this world has blinded the minds of the unbelieving, that they might not see the light of the gospel of the glory of Christ, who is the image of God.

5 For we do not preach ourselves but Christ Jesus as Lord, and ourselves as your bond-servants for Jesus' sake.

6 For God, who said, "Light shall shine out of darkness," is the One who has shone in our hearts to give the light of the knowledge of the glory of God in the face of Christ.

7 But we have this treasure in earthen vessels, that the surpassing greatness of the power may be of God and not from ourselves;

8 *we are* afflicted in every way, but not crushed; perplexed, but not despairing;

9 persecuted, but not forsaken; struck down, but not destroyed;

10 always carrying about in the body the dying of Jesus, that the life of Jesus also may be manifested in our body.

11 For we who live are constantly being delivered over to death for Jesus' sake, that the life of Jesus also may be manifested in our mortal flesh.

12 So death works in us, but life in you.

13 But having the same spirit of faith, according to what is written, "I BELIEVED, THEREFORE I SPOKE," we also believe, therefore also we speak;

14 knowing that He who raised the Lord Jesus will raise us also with Jesus and will present us with you.

15 For all things *are* for your sakes,

that the grace which is spreading to more and more people may cause the giving of thanks to abound to the glory of God.

16 Therefore we do not lose heart, but though our outer man is decaying, yet our inner man is being renewed day by day.

17 For momentary, light affliction is producing for us an eternal weight of glory far beyond all comparison,

18 while we look not at the things which are seen, but at the things which are not seen; for the things which are seen are temporal, but the things which are not seen are eternal.

CHAPTER 5

FOR we know that if the earthly tent which is our house is torn down, we have a building from God, a house not made with hands, eternal in the heavens.

2 For indeed in this *house* we groan, longing to be clothed with our dwelling from heaven;

3 inasmuch as we, having put it on, shall not be found naked.

4 For indeed while we are in this tent, we groan, being burdened, because we do not want to be unclothed, but to be clothed, in order that what is mortal may be swallowed up by life.

5 Now He who prepared us for this very purpose is God, who gave to us the Spirit as a pledge.

6 Therefore, being always of good courage, and knowing that while we are at home in the body we are absent from the Lord—

7 for we walk by faith, not by sight—

8 we are of good courage, I say, and prefer rather to be absent from the body and to be at home with the Lord.

9 Therefore also we have as our ambition, whether at home or absent, to be pleasing to Him.

10 For we must all appear before the judgment seat of Christ, that each one may be recompensed for his deeds in the body, according to what he has done, whether good or bad.

11 Therefore knowing the fear of the Lord, we persuade men, but we are made manifest to God; and I hope that we are made manifest also in your consciences.

12 We are not again commending ourselves to you but *are* giving you an occasion to be proud of us, that you may have *an answer* for those who take pride in appearance, and not in heart.

13 For if we are beside ourselves, it is for God; if we are of sound mind, it is for you.

14 For the love of Christ controls us, having concluded this, that one died for all, therefore all died;

15 and He died for all, that they who live should no longer live for themselves, but for Him who died and rose again on their behalf.

16 Therefore from now on we recognize no man according to the flesh; even though we have known Christ according to the flesh, yet now we know *Him thus* no longer.

17 Therefore if any man is in Christ, *he is* a new creature; the old things passed away; behold, new things have come.

18 Now all *these* things are from God, who reconciled us to Himself through Christ, and gave us the ministry of reconciliation,

19 namely, that God was in Christ reconciling the world to Himself, not counting their trespasses against them, and He has committed to us the word of reconciliation.

20 Therefore, we are ambassadors for Christ, as though God were entreating through us; we beg you on behalf of Christ, be reconciled to God.

21 He made Him who knew no sin *to be* sin on our behalf, that we might become the righteousness of God in Him.

CHAPTER 6

AND working together *with Him,* we also urge you not to receive the grace of God in vain—

2 for He says,

"AT THE ACCEPTABLE TIME I LIS-
TENED TO YOU,
AND ON THE DAY OF SALVATION
I HELPED YOU";

behold, now is "THE ACCEPTABLE TIME," behold, now is "THE DAY OF SALVATION"— (a)

3 giving no cause for offense in anything, in order that the ministry be not discredited,

4 but in everything commending ourselves as servants of God, in much endurance, in afflictions, in hardships, in distresses,

5 in beatings, in imprisonments, in tumults, in labors, in sleeplessness, in hunger,

6 in purity, in knowledge, in patience, in kindness, in the Holy Spirit, in genuine love,

7 in the word of truth, in the power of God; by the weapons of righteousness for the right hand and the left,

8 by glory and dishonor, by evil report and good report; *regarded* as deceivers and yet true;

9 as unknown yet well-known, as dying yet behold, we live; as punished yet not put to death,

10 as sorrowful yet always rejoicing, as poor yet making many rich, as having nothing yet possessing all things.

11 Our mouth has spoken freely to you, O Corinthians, our heart is opened wide.

12 You are not restrained by us, but you are restrained in your own affections.

13 Now in a like exchange—I speak as to children,—open wide *to us* also.

14 Do not be bound together with unbelievers; for what partnership have righteousness and lawlessness, or what fellowship has light with darkness?

15 Or what harmony has Christ with Belial, or what has a believer in common with an unbeliever?

16 Or what agreement has the temple of God with idols? For we are the temple of the living God; just as God said,

"I WILL DWELL IN THEM AND
WALK AMONG THEM;
AND I WILL BE THEIR GOD,
AND THEY SHALL BE MY PEO-
PLE.

17 "Therefore, COME OUT FROM THEIR MIDST AND BE SEPA-RATE," says the Lord.

(a) Assurance God Answers Prayer.

HEARS—God Hears Your Prayer. "At the acceptable time I listened to you . . . now is the acceptable time." God hears you the moment you repent and cry to Him "the prayer offered in faith." So now "Call upon the name of the Lord" Rom. 10:13, page 219.

HELPS—God hurries to help—"and on the day of salvation, I helped you." When the repenting sinner "got up and came to his father, while he was still a long way off, his father saw him, and felt compassion for him, and ran and embraced him," Luke 15:20, page 105. God not only listens but looks for you to come to Him.

HOPE—God offers salvation NOW—"Now is the day of Salvation." The question is, "how shall we escape if we neglect so great a salvation?" Heb. 2:3, page 295. So repent and come with a contrite heart and call on the name of the Lord now. Turn to page 219. Read Rom. 10:9–14 and Reference No. 6, Sec. 1. And pray the prayer suggested there.

"AND DO NOT TOUCH WHAT IS
UNCLEAN;
AND I WILL WELCOME YOU.

18 "AND I WILL BE A FATHER TO
YOU,
AND YOU SHALL BE SONS and
daughters TO ME,
SAYS THE LORD ALMIGHTY."

CHAPTER 7

THEREFORE, having these promises, beloved, let us cleanse ourselves
from all defilement of flesh and spirit,
perfecting holiness in the fear of God.

2 Make room for us *in your
hearts;* we wronged no one, we corrupted no one, we took advantage of
no one.

3 I do not speak to condemn you;
for I have said before that you are in
our hearts to die together and to live
together.

4 Great is my confidence in you,
great is my boasting on your behalf; I
am filled with comfort. I am overflowing with joy in all our affliction.

5 For even when we came into
Macedonia our flesh had no rest, but
we were afflicted on every side: conflicts without, fears within.

6 But God, who comforts the de-
pressed, comforted us by the coming
of Titus;

7 and not only by his coming, but
also by the comfort with which he was
comforted in you, as he reported to us
your longing, your mourning, your
zeal for me; so that I rejoiced even
more.

8 For though I caused you sorrow
by my letter, I do not regret it; though
I did regret it,—*for* I see that that
letter caused you sorrow, though only
for a while—

9 I now rejoice, not that you were
made sorrowful, but that you were
made sorrowful to *the point of* repentance; for you were made sorrowful
according to *the will of* God, in order

that you might not suffer loss in anything through us.

10 For the sorrow that is according
to *the will of* God produces a repentance without regret, *leading* to salvation; but the sorrow of the world produces death.

11 For behold what earnestness
this very thing, this godly sorrow, has
produced in you: what vindication of
yourselves, what indignation, what
fear, what longing, what zeal, what
avenging of wrong! In everything you
demonstrated yourselves to be innocent in the matter.

12 So although I wrote to you *it
was* not for the sake of the offender,
nor for the sake of the one offended,
but that your earnestness on our behalf might be made known to you in
the sight of God.

13 For this reason we have been
comforted.

And besides our comfort, we rejoiced even much more for the joy of
Titus, because his spirit has been refreshed by you all.

14 For if in anything I have
boasted to him about you, I was not
put to shame; but as we spoke all
things to you in truth, so also our
boasting before Titus proved to be
the truth.

15 And his affection abounds all
the more toward you, as he remembers the obedience of you all, how
you received him with fear and trembling.

16 I rejoice that in everything I
have confidence in you.

CHAPTER 8

NOW, brethren, we *wish* to make
known to you the grace of God which
has been given in the churches of
Macedonia,

2 that in a great ordeal of affliction their abundance of joy and their
deep poverty overflowed in the wealth
of their liberality.

3 For I testify that according to their ability, and beyond their ability *they gave* of their own accord,

4 begging us with much entreaty for the favor of participation in the support of the saints,

5 and *this*, not as we had expected, but they first gave themselves to the Lord and to us by the will of God.

6 Consequently we urged Titus that as he had previously made a beginning, so he would also complete in you this gracious work as well.

7 But just as you abound in everything, in faith and utterance and knowledge and in all earnestness and in the love we inspired in you, *see* that you abound in this gracious work also.

8 I am not speaking *this* as a command, but as proving through the earnestness of others the sincerity of your love also.

9 For you know the grace of our Lord Jesus Christ, that though He was rich, yet for your sake He became poor, that you through His poverty might become rich.

10 And I give *my* opinion in this matter, for this is to your advantage, who were the first to begin a year ago not only to do *this*, but also to desire *to do it*.

11 But now finish doing it also; that just as *there was* the readiness to desire it, so *there may be* also the completion of it by your ability.

12 For if the readiness is present, it is acceptable according to what *a man* has, not according to what he does not have.

13 For *this* is not for the ease of others *and* for your affliction, but by way of equality—

14 at this present time your abundance *being a supply* for their want, that their abundance also may become *a supply* for your want, that there may be equality;

15 as it is written, "HE WHO gath-ered MUCH DID NOT HAVE TOO MUCH, AND HE WHO *gathered* LITTLE HAD NO LACK."

16 But thanks be to God, who puts the same earnestness on your behalf in the heart of Titus.

17 For he not only accepted our appeal, but being himself very earnest, he has gone to you of his own accord.

18 And we have sent along with him the brother whose fame in *the things of* the gospel *has spread* through all the churches;

19 and not only *this*, but he has also been appointed by the churches to travel with us in this gracious work, which is being administered by us for the glory of the Lord Himself, and *to show* our readiness,

20 taking precaution that no one should discredit us in our administration of this generous gift;

21 for we have regard for what is honorable, not only in the sight of the Lord, but also in the sight of men.

22 And we have sent with them our brother, whom we have often tested and found diligent in many things, but now even more diligent, because of *his* great confidence in you.

23 As for Titus, *he is* my partner and fellow-worker among you; as for our brethren, *they are* messengers of the churches, a glory to Christ.

24 Therefore openly before the churches show them the proof of your love and of our reason for boasting about you.

CHAPTER 9

FOR it is superfluous for me to write to you about this ministry to the saints;

2 for I know your readiness, of which I boast about you to the Macedonians, *namely*, that Achaia has been prepared since last year, and

your zeal has stirred up most of them.

3 But I have sent the brethren, that our boasting about you may not be made empty in this case, that, as I was saying, you may be prepared;

4 lest if any Macedonians come with me and find you unprepared, we (not to speak of you) should be put to shame by this confidence.

5 So I thought it necessary to urge the brethren that they would go on ahead to you and arrange beforehand your previously promised bountiful gift, that the same might be ready as a bountiful gift, and not affected by covetousness.

6 Now this I say, he who sows sparingly shall also reap sparingly; and he who sows bountifully shall also reap bountifully.

7 Let each one do just as he has purposed in his heart; not grudgingly or under compulsion; for God loves a cheerful giver.

8 And God is able to make all grace abound to you, that always having all sufficiency in everything, you may have an abundance for every good deed;

9 as it is written,
"HE SCATTERED ABROAD, HE GAVE TO THE POOR,
HIS RIGHTEOUSNESS ABIDES FOREVER."

10 Now He who supplies seed to the sower and bread for food, will supply and multiply your seed for sowing and increase the harvest of your righteousness;

11 you will be enriched in everything for all liberality, which through us is producing thanksgiving to God.

12 For the ministry of this service is not only fully supplying the needs of the saints, but is also overflowing through many thanksgivings to God.

13 Because of the proof given by this ministry they will glorify God for your obedience to your confession of the gospel of Christ, and for the liberality of your contribution to them and to all,

14 while they also, by prayer on your behalf, yearn for you because of the surpassing grace of God in you.

15 Thanks be to God for His indescribable gift!

CHAPTER 10

NOW I Paul myself urge you by the meekness and gentleness of Christ,—I who am meek when face to face with you, but bold toward you when absent!

2 I ask that when I am present I may not be bold with the confidence with which I propose to be courageous against some, who regard us as if we walked according to the flesh.

3 For though we walk in the flesh, we do not war according to the flesh,

4 for the weapons of our warfare are not of the flesh, but divinely powerful for the destruction of fortresses.

5 We are destroying speculations and every lofty thing raised up against the knowledge of God, and we are taking every thought captive to the obedience of Christ,

6 and we are ready to punish all disobedience, whenever your obedience is complete.

7 You are looking at things as they are outwardly. If any one is confident in himself that he is Christ's, let him consider this again within himself, that just as he is Christ's, so also are we.

8 For even if I should boast somewhat further about our authority, which the Lord gave for building you up and not for destroying you, I shall not be put to shame,

9 for I do not wish to seem as if I would terrify you by my letters.

10 For they say, "His letters are weighty and strong, but his personal

presence is unimpressive, and his speech contemptible."

11 Let such a person consider this, that what we are in word by letters when absent, such persons *we are* also in deed when present.

12 For we are not bold to class or compare ourselves with some of those who commend themselves; but when they measure themselves by themselves, and compare themselves with themselves, they are without understanding.

13 But we will not boast beyond *our* measure, but within the measure of the sphere which God apportioned to us as a measure, to reach even as far as you.

14 For we are not overextending ourselves, as if we did not reach to you, for we were the first to come even as far as you in the gospel of Christ;

15 not boasting beyond *our* measure, *that is,* in other men's labors, but with the hope that as your faith grows, we shall be, within our sphere, enlarged even more by you,

16 so as to preach the gospel even to the regions beyond you, *and* not to boast in what has been accomplished in the sphere of another.

17 But HE WHO BOASTS, LET HIM BOAST IN THE LORD.

18 For not he who commends himself is approved, but whom the Lord commends.

CHAPTER 11

I WISH that you would bear with me in a little foolishness; but indeed you are bearing with me.

2 For I am jealous for you with a godly jealousy; for I betrothed you to one husband, that to Christ I might present you *as* a pure virgin.

3 But I am afraid, lest as the serpent deceived Eve by his craftiness, your minds should be led astray from the simplicity and purity *of devotion* to Christ.

4 For if one comes and preaches another Jesus whom we have not preached, or you receive a different spirit which you have not received, or a different gospel which you have not accepted, you bear *this* beautifully.

5 For I consider myself not in the least inferior to the most eminent apostles.

6 But even if I am unskilled in speech, yet I am not *so* in knowledge; in fact, in every way we have made *this* evident to you in all things.

7 Or did I commit a sin in humbling myself that you might be exalted, because I preached the gospel of God to you without charge?

8 I robbed other churches, taking wages *from them* to serve you;

9 and when I was present with you and was in need, I was not a burden to anyone; for when the brethren came from Macedonia, they fully supplied my need, and in everything I kept myself from being a burden to you, and will continue to do so.

10 As the truth of Christ is in me, this boasting of mine will not be stopped in the regions of Achaia.

11 Why? Because I do not love you? God knows *I do!*

12 But what I am doing, I will continue to do, that I may cut off opportunity from those who desire an opportunity to be regarded just as we are in the matter about which they are boasting.

13 For such men are false apostles, deceitful workers, disguising themselves as apostles of Christ.

14 And no wonder, for even Satan disguises himself as an angel of light.

15 Therefore it is not surprising if his servants also disguise themselves as servants of righteousness; whose end shall be according to their deeds.

16 Again I say, let no one think me foolish; but if *you do*, receive me even

as foolish, that I also may boast a little.

17 That which I am speaking, I am not speaking as the Lord would, but as in foolishness, in this confidence of boasting.

18 Since many boast according to the flesh, I will boast also.

19 For you, being *so* wise, bear with the foolish gladly.

20 For you bear with anyone if he enslaves you, if he devours you, if he takes advantage of you, if he exalts himself, if he hits you in the face.

21 To *my* shame I *must* say that we have been weak *by comparison.* But in whatever respect anyone *else* is bold (I speak in foolishness), I am just as bold myself.

22 Are they Hebrews? So am I. Are they Israelites? So am I. Are they descendants of Abraham? So am I.

23 Are they servants of Christ? (I speak as if insane) I more so; in far more labors, in far more imprisonments, beaten times without number, often in danger of death.

24 Five times I received from the Jews thirty-nine *lashes.*

25 Three times I was beaten with rods, once I was stoned, three times I was shipwrecked, a night and a day I have spent in the deep.

26 *I have been* on frequent journeys, in dangers from rivers, dangers from robbers, dangers from *my* countrymen, dangers from the Gentiles, dangers in the city, dangers in the wilderness, dangers on the sea, dangers among false brethren;

27 *I have been* in labor and hardship, through many sleepless nights, in hunger and thirst, often without food, in cold and exposure.

28 Apart from *such* external things, there is the daily pressure upon me *of* concern for all the churches.

29 Who is weak without my being weak? Who is led into sin without my intense concern?

30 If I have to boast, I will boast of what pertains to my weakness.

31 The God and Father of the Lord Jesus, He who is blessed forever, knows that I am not lying.

32 In Damascus the ethnarch under Aretas the king was guarding the city of the Damascenes in order to seize me,

33 and I was let down in a basket through a window in the wall, and *so* escaped his hands.

CHAPTER 12

BOASTING is necessary, though it is not profitable; but I will go on to visions and revelations of the Lord.

2 I know a man in Christ who fourteen years ago—whether in the body I do not know, or out of the body I do not know, God knows—such a man was caught up to the third heaven.

3 And I know how such a man—whether in the body or apart from the body I do not know, God knows—

4 was caught up into Paradise, and heard inexpressible words, which a man is not permitted to speak.

5 On behalf of such a man will I boast; but on my own behalf I will not boast, except in regard to *my* weaknesses.

6 For if I do wish to boast I shall not be foolish, for I shall be speaking the truth; but I refrain *from this,* so that no one may credit me with more than he sees *in* me or hears from me.

7 And because of the surpassing greatness of the revelations, for this reason, to keep me from exalting myself, there was given me a thorn in the flesh, a messenger of Satan to buffet me—to keep me from exalting myself!

8 Concerning this I entreated the Lord three times that it might depart from me.

9 And He has said to me, "My

grace is sufficient for you, for power is perfected in weakness." Most gladly, therefore, I will rather boast about my weaknesses, that the power of Christ may dwell in me.

10 Therefore I am well content with weaknesses, with insults, with distresses, with persecutions, with difficulties, for Christ's sake; for when I am weak, then I am strong.

11 I have become foolish; you yourselves compelled me. Actually I should have been commended by you, for in no respect was I inferior to the most eminent apostles, even though I am a nobody.

12 The signs of a true apostle were performed among you with all perseverance, by signs and wonders and miracles.

13 For in what respect were you treated as inferior to the rest of the churches, except that I myself did not become a burden to you? Forgive me this wrong!

14 Here for this third time I am ready to come to you, and I will not be a burden to you; for I do not seek what is yours, but you; for children are not responsible to save up for *their* parents, but parents for *their* children.

15 And I will most gladly spend and be expended for your souls. If I love you the more, am I to be loved the less?

16 But be that as it may, I did not burden you myself; nevertheless, crafty fellow that I am, I took you in by deceit.

17 Certainly I have not taken advantage of you through any of those whom I have sent to you, have I?

18 I urged Titus *to go,* and sent the brother with him. Titus did not take any advantage of you, did he? Did we not conduct ourselves in the same spirit *and walk* in the same steps?

19 All this time you have been thinking that we are defending ourselves to you. *Actually,* it is in the sight of God that we have been speaking in Christ; and all for your upbuilding, beloved.

20 For I am afraid that perhaps when I come I may find you to be not what I wish and may be found by you to be not what you wish; that perhaps *there may be* strife, jealousy, angry tempers, disputes, slanders, gossip, arrogance, disturbances;

21 I am afraid that when I come again my God may humiliate me before you, and I may mourn over many of those who have sinned in the past and not repented of the impurity, immorality and sensuality which they have practiced.

CHAPTER 13

THIS is the third time I am coming to you. EVERY FACT IS TO BE CONFIRMED BY THE TESTIMONY OF TWO OR THREE WITNESSES.

2 I have previously said when present the second time, and though now absent I say in advance to those who have sinned in the past and to all the rest as well, that if I come again, I will not spare *anyone,*

3 since you are seeking for proof of the Christ who speaks in me, and who is not weak toward you, but mighty in you.

4 For indeed He was crucified because of weakness, yet He lives because of the power of God. For we also are weak in Him, yet we shall live with Him because of the power of God *directed* toward you.

5 Test yourselves *to see* if you are in the faith; examine yourselves! Or do you not recognize this about yourselves, that Jesus Christ is in you—unless indeed you fail the test?

6 But I trust that you will realize that we ourselves do not fail the test.

7 Now we pray to God that you

do no wrong; not that we ourselves may appear approved, but that you may do what is right, even though we should appear unapproved.

8 For we can do nothing against the truth, but *only* for the truth.

9 For we rejoice when we ourselves are weak but you are strong; this we also pray for, that you be made complete.

10 For this reason I am writing these things while absent, in order that when present I may not use severity, in accordance with the authority which the Lord gave me, for building up and not for tearing down.

11 Finally, brethren, rejoice, be made complete, be comforted, be like-minded, live in peace; and the God of love and peace shall be with you.

12 Greet one another with a holy kiss.

13 All the saints greet you.

14 The grace of the Lord Jesus Christ, and the love of God, and the fellowship of the Holy Spirit, be with you all.

THE EPISTLE OF PAUL TO THE

GALATIANS

PAUL, an apostle (not *sent* from men, nor through the agency of man, but through Jesus Christ, and God the Father, who raised Him from the dead),

2 and all the brethren who are with me, to the churches of Galatia:

3 Grace to you and peace from God our Father, and the Lord Jesus Christ,

4 who gave Himself for our sins, that He might deliver us out of this present evil age, according to the will of our God and Father,

5 to whom *be* the glory forevermore. Amen.

6 I am amazed that you are so quickly deserting Him who called you by the grace of Christ, for a different gospel;

7 which is *really* not another; only there are some who are disturbing you, and want to distort the gospel of Christ.

8 But even though we, or an angel from heaven, should preach to you a gospel contrary to that which we have preached to you, let him be accursed.

9 As we have said before, so I say again now, if any man is preaching to you a gospel contrary to that which you received, let him be accursed.

10 For am I now seeking the favor of men, or of God? Or am I striving to please men? If I were still trying to please men, I would not be a bond-servant of Christ.

11 For I would have you know, brethren, that the gospel which was preached by me is not according to man.

12 For I neither received it from man, nor was I taught it, but *I received it* through a revelation of Jesus Christ.

13 For you have heard of my former manner of life in Judaism, how I used to persecute the church of God beyond measure, and tried to destroy it;

14 and I was advancing in Judaism beyond many of my contemporaries among my countrymen, being more extremely zealous for my ancestral traditions.

15 But when He who had set me apart, *even* from my mother's womb, and called me through His grace, was pleased

16 to reveal His Son in me, that I might preach Him among the Gentiles, I did not immediately consult with flesh and blood,

17 nor did I go up to Jerusalem to those who were apostles before me; but I went away to Arabia, and returned once more to Damascus.

18 Then three years later I went up to Jerusalem to become acquainted with Cephas, and stayed with him fifteen days.

19 But I did not see any other of the apostles except James the Lord's brother.

20 (Now in what I am writing to you, I assure you before God *that* I am not lying.)

21 Then I went into the regions of Syria and Cilicia.

22 And I was *still* unknown by sight to the churches of Judea which were in Christ;

23 but only, they kept hearing, "He who once persecuted us is now preaching the faith which he once *tried to* destroy."

24 And they were glorifying God because of me.

CHAPTER 2

THEN after an interval of fourteen years I went up again to Jerusalem with Barnabas, taking Titus along also.

2 And it was because of a revelation that I went up; and I submitted to them the gospel which I preach among the Gentiles, but I did so in private to those who were of reputation, for fear that I might be running, or had run, in vain.

3 But not even Titus who was with me, though he was a Greek, was compelled to be circumcised.

4 But *it was* because of the false brethren who had sneaked in to spy out our liberty which we have in Christ Jesus, in order to bring us into bondage.

5 But we did not yield in subjection to them for even an hour, so that the truth of the gospel might remain with you.

6 But from those who were of high reputation (what they were makes no difference to me; God shows no partiality)—well, those who were of reputation contributed nothing to me.

7 But on the contrary, seeing that I had been entrusted with the gospel to the uncircumcised, just as Peter with *the gospel* to the circumcised

8 (for He who effectually worked for Peter in *his* apostleship to the circumcised effectually worked for me also to the Gentiles),

9 and recognizing the grace that had been given to me, James and Cephas and John, who were reputed to be pillars, gave to me and Barnabas the right hand of fellowship, that we might go to the Gentiles, and they to the circumcised.

10 *They* only *asked* us to remember the poor—the very thing I also was eager to do.

11 But when Cephas came to Antioch, I opposed him to his face, because he stood condemned.

12 For prior to the coming of certain men from James, he used to eat with the Gentiles; but when they came, he *began* to withdraw and hold himself aloof, fearing the party of the circumcision.

13 And the rest of the Jews joined him in hypocrisy, with the result that even Barnabas was carried away by their hypocrisy.

14 But when I saw that they were not straightforward about the truth of the gospel, I said to Cephas in the presence of all, "If you, being a Jew, live like the Gentiles and not like the Jews, how *is it that* you compel the Gentiles to live like Jews?

15 "We *are* Jews by nature, and not sinners from among the Gentiles;

16 nevertheless knowing that a man is not justified by the works of the Law but through faith in Christ Jesus, even we have believed in Christ Jesus, that we may be justified by faith in Christ, and not by the works of the Law; since by the works of the Law shall no flesh be justified.

17 "But if, while seeking to be justified in Christ, we ourselves have also been found sinners, is Christ then a minister of sin? May it never be!

18 "For if I rebuild what I have *once* destroyed, I prove myself to be a transgressor.

19 "For through the Law I died to the Law, that I might live to God.

20 "I have been crucified with Christ; and it is no longer I who live, but Christ lives in me; and the *life* which I now live in the flesh I live by faith in the Son of God, who loved me, and delivered Himself up for me.

21 "I do not nullify the grace of God; for if righteousness *comes* through the Law, then Christ died needlessly."

CHAPTER 3

YOU foolish Galatians, who has bewitched you, before whose eyes Jesus Christ was publicly portrayed *as* crucified?

2 This is the only thing I want to find out from you: did you receive the Spirit by the works of the Law, or by hearing with faith?

3 Are you so foolish? Having begun by the Spirit, are you now being perfected by the flesh?

4 Did you suffer so many things in vain—if indeed it was in vain?

5 Does He then who provides you with the Spirit and works miracles among you, do it by the works of the Law, or by hearing with faith?

6 Even so Abraham BELIEVED GOD, AND IT WAS RECKONED TO HIM AS RIGHTEOUSNESS.

7 Therefore, be sure that it is those who are of faith that are sons of Abraham.

8 And the Scripture, foreseeing that God would justify the Gentiles by faith, preached the gospel beforehand to Abraham, *saying*, "ALL THE NATIONS SHALL BE BLESSED IN YOU."

9 So then those who are of faith are blessed with Abraham, the believer.

10 For as many as are of the works of the Law are under a curse; for it is written, "CURSED IS EVERY ONE WHO DOES NOT ABIDE BY ALL THINGS WRITTEN IN THE BOOK OF THE LAW, TO PERFORM THEM."

11 Now that no one is justified by the Law before God is evident; for, "THE RIGHTEOUS MAN SHALL LIVE BY FAITH."

12 However, the Law is not of faith; on the contrary, "HE WHO PRACTICES THEM SHALL LIVE BY THEM."

13 Christ redeemed us from the curse of the Law, having become a curse for us—for it is written, "CURSED IS EVERY ONE WHO HANGS ON A TREE"—

14 in order that in Christ Jesus the blessing of Abraham might come to the Gentiles, so that we might receive the promise of the Spirit through faith.

15 Brethren, I speak in terms of human relations: even though it is *only* a man's covenant, yet when it has been ratified, no one sets it aside or adds conditions to it.

16 Now the promises were spoken to Abraham and to his seed. He does not say, "AND TO SEEDS," as *referring* to many, but *rather* to one, "AND TO YOUR SEED," that is, Christ.

17 What I am saying is this: the Law, which came four hundred and thirty years later, does not invalidate a covenant previously ratified by God, so as to nullify the promise.

18 For if the inheritance is based on law, it is no longer based on a

promise; but God has granted it to Abraham by means of a promise.

19 Why the Law then? It was added because of transgressions, having been ordained through angels by the agency of a mediator, until the seed should come to whom the promise had been made.

20 Now a mediator is not for one *party only;* whereas God is *only* one.

21 Is the Law then contrary to the promises of God? May it never be! For if a law had been given which was able to impart life, then righteousness would indeed have been based on law.

22 But the Scripture has shut up all men under sin, that the promise by faith in Jesus Christ might be given to those who believe.

23 But before faith came, we were kept in custody under the law, being shut up to the faith which was later to be revealed.

24 Therefore the Law has become our tutor *to lead us* to Christ, that we may be justified by faith.

25 But now that faith has come, we are no longer under a tutor.

26 For you are all sons of God through faith in Christ Jesus.

27 For all of you who were baptized into Christ have clothed yourselves with Christ.

28 There is neither Jew nor Greek, there is neither slave nor free man, there is neither male nor female; for you are all one in Christ Jesus.

29 And if you belong to Christ, then you are Abraham's offspring, heirs according to promise.

CHAPTER 4

NOW I say, as long as the heir is a child, he does not differ at all from a slave although he is owner of everything,

2 but he is under guardians and managers until the date set by the father.

3 So also we, while we were children, were held in bondage under the elemental things of the world.

4 But when the fulness of the time came, God sent forth His Son, born of a woman, born under the Law,

5 in order that He might redeem those who were under the Law, that we might receive the adoption as sons.

6 And because you are sons, God has sent forth the Spirit of His Son into our hearts, crying, "Abba! Father!"

7 Therefore you are no longer a slave, but a son; and if a son, then an heir through God.

8 However at that time, when you did not know God, you were slaves to those which by nature are no gods.

9 But now that you have come to know God, or rather to be known by God, how is it that you turn back again to the weak and worthless elemental things, to which you desire to be enslaved all over again?

10 You observe days and months and seasons and years.

11 I fear for you, that perhaps I have labored over you in vain.

12 I beg of you, brethren, become as *I am,* for I also *have become* as you *are.* You have done me no wrong;

13 but you know that it was because of a bodily illness that I preached the gospel to you the first time;

14 and that which was a trial to you in my bodily condition you did not despise or loathe, but you received me as an angel of God, as Christ Jesus *Himself.*

15 Where then is that sense of blessing you had? For I bear you witness, that if possible, you would have plucked out your eyes and given them to me.

16 Have I therefore become your enemy by telling you the truth?

17 They eagerly seek you, not commendably, but they wish to shut you out, in order that you may seek them.

18 But it is good always to be eagerly sought in a commendable manner, and not only when I am present with you.

19 My children, with whom I am again in labor until Christ is formed in you —

20 but I could wish to be present with you now and to change my tone, for I am perplexed about you.

21 Tell me, you who want to be under law, do you not listen to the law?

22 For it is written that Abraham had two sons, one by the bondwoman and one by the free woman.

23 But the son by the bondwoman was born according to the flesh, and the son by the free woman through the promise.

24 This contains an allegory: for these *women* are two covenants, one *proceeding* from Mount Sinai bearing children who are to be slaves; she is Hagar.

25 Now this Hagar is Mount Sinai in Arabia, and corresponds to the present Jerusalem, for she is in slavery with her children.

26 But the Jerusalem above is free; she is our mother.

27 For it is written,

> "REJOICE, BARREN WOMAN WHO
>   DOES NOT BEAR;
> BREAK FORTH AND SHOUT, YOU
>   WHO ARE NOT IN LABOR;
> FOR MORE ARE THE CHILDREN
>   OF THE DESOLATE
> THAN OF THE ONE WHO HAS A
>   HUSBAND."

28 And you brethren, like Isaac, are children of promise.

29 But as at that time he who was born according to the flesh persecuted him *who was born* according to the Spirit, so it is now also.

30 But what does the Scripture say?

> "CAST OUT THE BONDWOMAN
>   AND HER SON,
> FOR THE SON OF THE BOND-
>   WOMAN SHALL NOT BE AN
>   HEIR WITH THE SON OF THE
>   FREE WOMAN."

31 So then, brethren, we are not children of a bondwoman, but of the free woman.

CHAPTER 5

IT was for freedom that Christ set us free; therefore keep standing firm and do not be subject again to a yoke of slavery.

2 Behold I, Paul, say to you that if you receive circumcision, Christ will be of no benefit to you.

3 And I testify again to every man who receives circumcision, that he is under obligation to keep the whole Law.

4 You have been severed from Christ, you who are seeking to be justified by law; you have fallen from grace.

5 For we through the Spirit, by faith, are waiting for the hope of righteousness.

6 For in Christ Jesus neither circumcision nor uncircumcision means anything, but faith working through love.

7 You were running well; who hindered you from obeying the truth?

8 This persuasion *did* not *come* from Him who calls you.

9 A little leaven leavens the whole lump *of dough.*

10 I have confidence in you in the Lord, that you will adopt no other view; but the one who is disturbing you shall bear his judgment, whoever he is.

11 But I, brethren, if I still preach circumcision, why am I still persecuted? Then the stumbling block of the cross has been abolished.

12 Would that those who are troubling you would even mutilate themselves.

13 For you were called to freedom, brethren; only *do* not *turn* your freedom into an opportunity for the flesh, but through love serve one another.

14 For the whole Law is fulfilled in one word, in the *statement*, "You shall love your neighbor as yourself."

15 But if you bite and devour one another, take care lest you be consumed by one another.

16 But I say, walk by the Spirit, and you will not carry out the desire of the flesh.

17 For the flesh sets its desire against the Spirit, and the Spirit against the flesh; for these are in opposition to one another, so that you may not do the things that you please.

18 But if you are led by the Spirit, you are not under the Law.

19 Now the deeds of the flesh are evident, which are: immorality, impurity, sensuality,

20 idolatry, sorcery, enmities, strife, jealousy, outbursts of anger, disputes, dissensions, factions,

21 envyings, drunkenness, carousings, and things like these, of which I forewarn you just as I have forewarned you that those who practice such things shall not inherit the kingdom of God.

22 But the fruit of the Spirit is love, joy, peace, patience, kindness, goodness, faithfulness,

23 gentleness, self-control; against such things there is no law.

24 Now those who belong to Christ Jesus have crucified the flesh with its passions and desires.

25 If we live by the Spirit, let us also walk by the Spirit.

26 Let us not become boastful, challenging one another, envying one another.

Chapter 6

Brethren, even if a man is caught in any trespass, you who are spiritual, restore such a one in a spirit of gentleness; looking to yourselves, lest you too be tempted.

2 Bear one another's burdens, and thus fulfill the law of Christ.

3 For if anyone thinks he is something when he is nothing, he deceives himself.

4 But let each one examine his own work, and then he will have *reason for* boasting in regard to himself alone, and not in regard to another.

5 For each one shall bear his own load.

6 And let the one who is taught the word share all good things with him who teaches.

7 Do not be deceived, God is not mocked; for whatever a man sows, this he will also reap.

8 For the one who sows to his own flesh shall from the flesh reap corruption, but the one who sows to the Spirit shall from the Spirit reap eternal life.

9 And let us not lose heart in doing good, for in due time we shall reap if we do not grow weary.

10 So then, while we have opportunity, let us do good to all men, and especially to those who are of the household of the faith.

11 See with what large letters I am writing to you with my own hand.

12 Those who desire to make a good showing in the flesh try to compel you to be circumcised, simply that they may not be persecuted for the cross of Christ.

13 For those who are circumcised do not even keep the Law themselves, but they desire to have you circumcised, that they may boast in your flesh.

14 But may it never be that I should boast, except in the cross of our Lord Jesus Christ, through which the world has been crucified to me, and I to the world.

15 For neither is circumcision any-thing, nor uncircumcision, but a new creation.

16 And those who will walk by this rule, peace and mercy *be* upon them, and upon the Israel of God.

17 From now on let no one cause trouble for me, for I bear on my body the brand-marks of Jesus.

18 The grace of our Lord Jesus Christ be with your spirit, brethren. Amen.

THE EPISTLE OF PAUL TO THE

EPHESIANS

Paul, an apostle of Christ Jesus by the will of God, to the saints who are at Ephesus, and *who are* faithful in Christ Jesus:

2 Grace to you and peace from God our Father and the Lord Jesus Christ.

3 Blessed *be* the God and Father of our Lord Jesus Christ, who has blessed us with every spiritual blessing in the heavenly *places* in Christ,

4 just as He chose us in Him before the foundation of the world, that we should be holy and blameless before Him. In love

5 He predestined us to adoption as sons through Jesus Christ to Himself, according to the kind intention of His will,

6 to the praise of the glory of His grace, which He freely bestowed on us in the Beloved.

7 In Him we have redemption through His blood, the forgiveness of our trespasses, according to the riches of His grace,

8 which He lavished upon us. In all wisdom and insight

9 He made known to us the mystery of His will, according to His kind intention which He purposed in Him

10 with a view to an administration suitable to the fulness of the times, *that is,* the summing up of all things in Christ, things in the heavens and things upon the earth. In Him

11 also we have obtained an inheritance, having been predestined according to His purpose who works all things after the counsel of His will,

12 to the end that we who were the first to hope in Christ should be to the praise of His glory.

13 In Him, you also, after listening to the message of truth, the gospel of your salvation—having also believed, you were sealed in Him with the Holy Spirit of promise,

14 who is given as a pledge of our inheritance, with a view to the redemption of *God's own* possession, to the praise of His glory.

15 For this reason I too, having heard of the faith in the Lord Jesus which *exists* among you, and your love for all the saints,

16 do not cease giving thanks for you, while making mention *of you* in my prayers;

17 that the God of our Lord Jesus Christ, the Father of glory, may give to you a spirit of wisdom and of revelation in the knowledge of Him.

18 *I pray that* the eyes of your heart may be enlightened, so that you may know what is the hope of His

calling, what are the riches of the glory of His inheritance in the saints,

19 and what is the surpassing greatness of His power toward us who believe. *These are* in accordance with the working of the strength of His might

20 which He brought about in Christ, when He raised Him from the dead, and seated Him at His right hand in the heavenly *places,*

21 far above all rule and authority and power and dominion, and every name that is named, not only in this age, but also in the one to come.

22 And He put all things in subjection under His feet, and gave Him as head over all things to the church,

23 which is His body, the fulness of Him who fills all in all.

CHAPTER 2

And you were dead in your trespasses and sins,

2 in which you formerly walked according to the course of this world, according to the prince of the power of the air, of the spirit that is now working in the sons of disobedience.

3 Among them we too all formerly lived in the lusts of our flesh, indulging the desires of the flesh and of the mind, and were by nature children of wrath, even as the rest.

4 But God, being rich in mercy, because of His great love with which He loved us,

5 even when we were dead in our transgressions, made us alive together with Christ (by grace you have been saved),

6 and raised us up with Him, and seated us with Him in the heavenly *places,* in Christ Jesus,

7 in order that in the ages to come He might show the surpassing riches of His grace in kindness toward us in Christ Jesus.

8 For by grace you have been saved through faith; and that not of yourselves, *it is* the gift of God;

9 not as a result of works, that no one should boast.

10 For we are His workmanship, created in Christ Jesus for good works, which God prepared beforehand, that we should walk in them.

11 Therefore remember, that formerly you, the Gentiles in the flesh, who are called "Uncircumcision" by the so-called "Circumcision," *which is* performed in the flesh by human hands—

12 *remember* that you were at that time separate from Christ, excluded from the commonwealth of Israel, and strangers to the covenants of promise, having no hope and without God in the world.

13 But now in Christ Jesus you who formerly were far off have been brought near by the blood of Christ.

14 For He Himself is our peace, who made both *groups into* one, and broke down the barrier of the dividing wall,

15 by abolishing in His flesh the enmity, *which is* the Law of commandments *contained* in ordinances, that in Himself He might make the two into one new man, *thus* establishing peace,

16 and might reconcile them both in one body to God through the cross, by it having put to death the enmity.

17 AND HE CAME AND PREACHED PEACE TO YOU WHO WERE FAR AWAY, AND PEACE TO THOSE WHO WERE NEAR;

18 for through Him we both have our access in one Spirit to the Father.

19 So then you are no longer strangers and aliens, but you are fellow-citizens with the saints, and are of God's household,

20 having been built upon the foundation of the apostles and prophets, Christ Jesus Himself being the corner *stone,*

21 in whom the whole building, being fitted together is growing into a holy temple in the Lord;

22 in whom you also are being built together into a dwelling of God in the Spirit.

Chapter 3

F OR this reason I, Paul, the prisoner of Christ Jesus for the sake of you Gentiles—

2 if indeed you have heard of the stewardship of God's grace which was given to me for you;

3 that by revelation there was made known to me the mystery, as I wrote before in brief.

4 And by referring to this, when you read you can understand my insight into the mystery of Christ,

5 which in other generations was not made known to the sons of men, as it has now been revealed to His holy apostles and prophets in the Spirit;

6 *to be specific,* that the Gentiles are fellow-heirs and fellow-members of the body, and fellow-partakers of the promise in Christ Jesus through the gospel,

7 of which I was made a minister, according to the gift of God's grace which was given to me according to the working of His power.

8 To me, the very least of all saints, this grace was given, to preach to the Gentiles the unfathomable riches of Christ,

9 and to bring to light what is the administration of the mystery which for ages has been hidden in God, who created all things;

10 in order that the manifold wisdom of God might now be made known through the church to the rulers and the authorities in the heavenly *places.*

11 *This was* in accordance with the eternal purpose which He carried out in Christ Jesus our Lord,

12 in whom we have boldness and confident access through faith in Him.

13 Therefore I ask you not to lose heart at my tribulations on your behalf, for they are your glory.

14 For this reason, I bow my knees before the Father,

15 from whom every family in heaven and on earth derives its name,

16 that He would grant you, according to the riches of His glory, to be strengthened with power through His Spirit in the inner man;

17 so that Christ may dwell in your hearts through faith; *and* that you, being rooted and grounded in love,

18 may be able to comprehend with all the saints what is the breadth and length and height and depth,

19 and to know the love of Christ which surpasses knowledge, that you may be filled up to all the fulness of God.

Scripture No. 2, Sec. 2

20 Now to Him who is able to do exceeding abundantly beyond all that we ask or think, according to the power that works within us,

21 to Him *be* the glory in the church and in Christ Jesus to all generations forever and ever. Amen. (r2)

(r2) REFERENCE NO. 2, SEC. 2—
      CHURCH MEMBERSHIP OF BELIEVERS SHOWS SALVATION.
    "To Him be the glory in the church and in Christ Jesus to all generations."
    When you receive Christ, you are "born into His body which is the Church." That is "the church of the first born who are enrolled in heaven," His spiritual body. It is made up of all who are saved.

(Continued on next page.)

CHAPTER 4

I, THEREFORE, the prisoner of the Lord, entreat you to walk in a manner worthy of the calling with which you have been called,

2 with all humility and gentleness, with patience, showing forbearance to one another in love,

3 being diligent to preserve the unity of the Spirit in the bond of peace.

4 *There is* one body and one Spirit, just as also you were called in one hope of your calling;

5 one Lord, one faith, one baptism,

6 one God and Father of all who is over all and through all and in all.

7 But to each one of us grace was given according to the measure of Christ's gift.

8 Therefore it says,

"WHEN HE ASCENDED ON HIGH,
HE LED CAPTIVE A HOST OF CAPTIVES,
AND HE GAVE GIFTS TO MEN."

9 (Now this *expression*, "He ascended," what does it mean except that He also had descended into the lower parts of the earth?

10 He who descended is Himself also He who ascended far above all the heavens, that He might fill all things.)

11 And He gave some *as* apostles, and some *as* prophets, and some *as* evangelists, and some *as* pastors and teachers,

12 for the equipping of the saints for the work of service, to the building up of the body of Christ;

13 until we all attain to the unity of the faith, and of the knowledge of the Son of God, to a mature man, to the measure of the stature which belongs to the fulness of Christ.

14 As a result, we are no longer to be children, tossed here and there by waves, and carried about by every wind of doctrine, by the trickery of men, by craftiness in deceitful scheming;

(Continued from page 264.)

Usually in the New Testament the word "church" refers to a local church. It is made up of local believers who have received Christ as Savior. The church is not a building but people like those meeting in the house of Philemon, to whom Paul sent greetings, "to the church in your house."

You give to Him "glory in the church" when you obey Christ who said, "Confess Me before men." So when you are baptized, you are like "those who had received His word; and there were added that day about three thousand souls." And you give glory to Him.

Like the members of that first century church, you should come together "on the first day of the week . . . to break bread," and "proclaim the Lord's death until He comes." You are "to stimulate one another to love and good deeds, not forsaking our own assembling together."

"On the first day of the week let each one of you put aside and save as He may prosper" to provide for the work of the local church.

Also prayer is to be made in the church. When "Peter was kept in the prison" . . . "prayer for him was being made fervently by the church to God."

The church sends out teachers and missionaries. "It seemed good to . . . the whole church, to choose men from among them to send to Antioch . . . leading men from among them to instruct and encourage the congregation."

Do you see that your Savior the Lord Jesus wants you to be an active member of the local church, supporting it and the work of Christ? If so, say:

"I will join, attend, support and serve the Lord through a local church."

Now turn to page 314, Scripture No. 3, Sec. 2, I Peter 2:2.

15 but speaking the truth in love, we are to grow up in all *aspects* into Him, who is the head, *even* Christ,

16 from whom the whole body, being fitted and held together by that which every joint supplies, according to the proper working of each individual part, causes the growth of the body for the building up of itself in love.

17 This I say therefore, and affirm together with the Lord, that you walk no longer just as the Gentiles also walk, in the futility of their mind,

18 being darkened in their understanding, excluded from the life of God, because of the ignorance that is in them, because of the hardness of their heart;

19 and they, having become callous, have given themselves over to sensuality, for the practice of every kind of impurity with greediness.

20 But you did not learn Christ in this way,

21 if indeed you have heard Him and have been taught in Him, just as truth is in Jesus,

22 that, in reference to your former manner of life, you lay aside the old self, which is being corrupted in accordance with the lusts of deceit,

23 and that you be renewed in the spirit of your mind,

24 and put on the new self, which in *the likeness of* God has been created in righteousness and holiness of the truth.

25 Therefore, laying aside falsehood, SPEAK TRUTH, EACH ONE *of you*, WITH HIS NEIGHBOR, for we are members of one another.

26 BE ANGRY, AND *yet* DO NOT SIN; do not let the sun go down on your anger,

27 and do not give the devil an opportunity.

28 Let him who steals steal no longer; but rather let him labor, performing with his own hands what is good, in order that he may have *something* to share with him who has need.

29 Let no unwholesome word proceed from your mouth, but only such *a word* as is good for edification according to the need *of the moment*, that it may give grace to those who hear.

30 And do not grieve the Holy Spirit of God, by whom you were sealed for the day of redemption.

31 Let all bitterness and wrath and anger and clamor and slander be put away from you, along with all malice.

32 And be kind to one another, tender-hearted, forgiving each other, just as God in Christ also has forgiven you.

CHAPTER 5

THEREFORE be imitators of God, as beloved children;

2 and walk in love, just as Christ also loved you, and gave Himself up for us, an offering and a sacrifice to God as a fragrant aroma.

3 But do not let immorality or any impurity or greed even be named among you, as is proper among saints;

4 and *there must be no* filthiness and silly talk, or coarse jesting, which are not fitting, but rather giving of thanks.

5 For this you know with certainty, that no immoral or impure person or covetous man, who is an idolater, has an inheritance in the kingdom of Christ and God.

6 Let no one deceive you with empty words, for because of these things the wrath of God comes upon the sons of disobedience.

7 Therefore do not be partakers with them;

8 for you were formerly darkness, but now you are light in the Lord; walk as children of light

9 (for the fruit of the light con-

sists in all goodness and righteousness and truth),

10 trying to learn what is pleasing to the Lord.

11 And do not participate in the unfruitful deeds of darkness, but instead even expose them;

12 for it is disgraceful even to speak of the things which are done by them in secret.

13 But all things become visible when they are exposed by the light, for everything that becomes visible is light.

14 For this reason it says,
"AWAKE, SLEEPER,
AND ARISE FROM THE DEAD,
AND CHRIST WILL SHINE ON
YOU."

15 Therefore be careful how you walk, not as unwise men, but as wise,

16 making the most of your time, because the days are evil.

17 So then do not be foolish, but understand what the will of the Lord is.

18 And do not get drunk with wine, for that is dissipation, but be filled with the Spirit,

19 speaking to one another in psalms and hymns and spiritual songs, singing and making melody with your heart to the Lord;

20 always giving thanks for all things in the name of our Lord Jesus Christ to God, even the Father;

21 and be subject to one another in the fear of Christ.

22 Wives, *be subject* to your own husbands, as to the Lord.

23 For the husband is the head of the wife, as Christ also is the head of the church, He Himself *being* the Savior of the body.

24 But as the church is subject to Christ, so also the wives *ought to be* to their husbands in everything.

25 Husbands, love your wives, just as Christ also loved the church and gave Himself up for her;

26 that He might sanctify her, having cleansed her by the washing of water with the word,

27 that He might present to Himself the church in all her glory, having no spot or wrinkle or any such thing; but that she should be holy and blameless.

28 So husbands ought also to love their own wives as their own bodies. He who loves his own wife loves himself;

29 for no one ever hated his own flesh, but nourishes and cherishes it, just as Christ also *does* the church,

30 because we are members of His body.

31 FOR THIS CAUSE A MAN SHALL LEAVE HIS FATHER AND MOTHER, AND SHALL CLEAVE TO HIS WIFE; AND THE TWO SHALL BECOME ONE FLESH.

32 This mystery is great; but I am speaking with reference to Christ and the church.

33 Nevertheless let each individual among you also love his own wife even as himself; and *let* the wife *see to it* that she respect her husband.

CHAPTER 6

CHILDREN, obey your parents in the Lord, for this is right.

2 HONOR YOUR FATHER AND MOTHER (which is the first commandment with a promise),

3 THAT IT MAY BE WELL WITH YOU, AND THAT YOU MAY LIVE LONG ON THE EARTH.

4 And, fathers, do not provoke your children to anger; but bring them up in the discipline and instruction of the Lord.

5 Slaves, be obedient to those who are your masters according to the flesh, with fear and trembling, in the sincerity of your heart, as to Christ;

6 not by way of eyeservice, as men-pleasers, but as slaves of Christ, doing the will of God from the heart.

7 With good will render service, as to the Lord, and not to men,

8 knowing that whatever good thing each one does, this he will receive back from the Lord, whether slave or free.

9 And, masters, do the same things to them, and give up threatening, knowing that both their Master and yours is in heaven, and there is no partiality with Him.

10 Finally, be strong in the Lord, and in the strength of His might.

11 Put on the full armor of God, that you may be able to stand firm against the schemes of the devil.

12 For our struggle is not against flesh and blood, but against the rulers, against the powers, against the world-forces of this darkness, against the spiritual *forces* of wickedness in the heavenly *places*.

13 Therefore, take up the full armor of God, that you may be able to resist in the evil day, and having done everything, to stand firm.

14 Stand firm therefore, HAVING GIRDED YOUR LOINS WITH TRUTH, and HAVING PUT ON THE BREASTPLATE OF RIGHTEOUSNESS,

15 and having shod YOUR FEET WITH THE PREPARATION OF THE GOSPEL OF PEACE;

16 in addition to all, taking up the shield of faith with which you will be able to extinguish all the flaming missiles of the evil *one.*

17 And take the helmet of salvation, and the sword of the Spirit, which is the word of God.

18 With all prayer and petition pray at all times in the Spirit, and with this in view, be on the alert with all perseverance and petition for all the saints,

19 and *pray* on my behalf, that utterance may be given to me in the opening of my mouth, to make known with boldness the mystery of the gospel,

20 for which I am an ambassador in chains; that in *proclaiming* it I may speak boldly, as I ought to speak.

21 But that you also may know about my circumstances, how I am doing, Tychicus, the beloved brother and faithful minister in the Lord, will make everything known to you.

22 And I have sent him to you for this very purpose, so that you may know about us, and that he may comfort your hearts.

23 Peace be to the brethren, and love with faith, from God the Father and the Lord Jesus Christ.

24 Grace be with all those who love our Lord Jesus Christ with *a love* incorruptible.

THE EPISTLE OF PAUL TO THE
PHILIPPIANS

Paul and Timothy, bond-servants of Christ Jesus, to all the saints in Christ Jesus who are in Philippi, including the overseers and deacons:

2 Grace to you and peace from God our Father and the Lord Jesus Christ.

3 I thank my God in all my remembrance of you,

4 always offering prayer with joy in my every prayer for you all,

5 in view of your participation in the gospel from the first day until now.

6 *For I am* confident of this very thing, that He who began a good work in you will perfect it until the day of Christ Jesus.

7 For it is only right for me to feel this way about you all, because I have you in my heart, since both in my imprisonment and in the defense and confirmation of the gospel, you all are partakers of grace with me.

8 For God is my witness, how I long for you all with the affection of Christ Jesus.

9 And this I pray, that your love may abound still more and more in real knowledge and all discernment,

10 so that you may approve the things that are excellent, in order to be sincere and blameless until the day of Christ;

11 having been filled with the fruit of righteousness which *comes* through Jesus Christ, to the glory and praise of God.

12 Now I want you to know, brethren, that my circumstances have turned out for the greater progress of the gospel,

13 so that my imprisonment in *the cause of* Christ has become well-known throughout the whole praetorian guard and to everyone else,

14 and that most of the brethren, trusting in the Lord because of my imprisonment, have far more courage to speak the word of God without fear.

15 Some, to be sure, are preaching Christ even from envy and strife, but some also from good will;

16 the latter *do it* out of love, knowing that I am appointed for the defense of the gospel;

17 the former proclaim Christ out of selfish ambition, rather than from pure motives, thinking to cause me distress in my imprisonment.

18 What then? Only that in every way, whether in pretense or in truth, Christ is proclaimed; and in this I rejoice, yes, and I will rejoice.

19 For I know that this shall turn out for my deliverance through your prayers and the provision of the Spirit of Jesus Christ,

20 according to my earnest expectation and hope, that I shall not be put to shame in anything, but *that* with all boldness, Christ shall even now, as always, be exalted in my body, whether by life or by death.

21 For to me, to live is Christ, and to die is gain.

22 But if *I am* to live *on* in the flesh, this *will mean* fruitful labor for me; and I do not know which to choose.

23 But I am hard pressed from both *directions*, having the desire to depart and be with Christ, for *that* is very much better;

24 yet to remain on in the flesh is more necessary for your sake.

25 And convinced of this, I know that I shall remain and continue with you all for your progress and joy in the faith,

26 so that your proud confidence in me may abound in Christ Jesus through my coming to you again.

27 Only conduct yourselves in a manner worthy of the gospel of Christ; so that whether I come and see you or remain absent, I may hear of you that you are standing firm in one spirit, with one mind striving together for the faith of the gospel;

28 in no way alarmed by *your* opponents—which is a sign of destruction for them, but of salvation for you, and that *too*, from God.

29 For to you it has been granted for Christ's sake, not only to believe in Him, but also to suffer for His sake,

30 experiencing the same conflict which you saw in me, and now hear *to be* in me.

Chapter 2

IF therefore there is any encouragement in Christ, if there is any consolation of love, if there is any fellowship of the Spirit, if any affection and compassion,

2 make my joy complete by being of the same mind, maintaining the same love, united in spirit, intent on one purpose.

3 Do nothing from selfishness or empty conceit, but with humility of mind let each of you regard one another as more important than himself;

4 do not *merely* look out for your own personal interests, but also for the interests of others.

5 Have this attitude in yourselves which was also in Christ Jesus,

6 who, although He existed in the form of God, did not regard equality with God a thing to be grasped,

7 but emptied Himself, taking the form of a bond-servant, *and* being made in the likeness of men.

8 And being found in appearance as a man, He humbled Himself by becoming obedient to the point of death, even death on a cross.

SCRIPTURE NO. 1, SEC. 3

9 Therefore also God highly exalted Him, and bestowed on Him the name which is above every name,

10 that at the name of Jesus every knee should bow, of those who are in heaven, and on earth, and under the earth,

11 and that every tongue should confess that Jesus Christ is Lord, to the glory of God the Father. (r1)

12 So then, my beloved, just as you have always obeyed, not as in my presence only, but now much more in my absence, work out your salvation with fear and trembling;

13 for it is God who is at work in you, both to will and to work for *His* good pleasure.

14 Do all things without grumbling or disputing;

Have you read the chain of six scriptures and references of section one on "What you must do to be saved" *beginning on page 186 and the chain of four references in Section 2 on* "How I can show others I am saved" *beginning on page 45? It is suggested that you read these ten scriptures and references* before *you read the following seven references.*

This is the first of seven (7) references concerning scriptures answering the question: "Is your name written in Heaven?" and showing how God's word gives assurance that "you can know your name is written in Heaven."

(r1) REFERENCE NO. 1, SEC. 3—
    GOD'S DEMAND THAT YOU DECLARE YOUR FAITH

"God highly exalted Him, and bestowed on Him a name which is above every name . . . that every tongue should confess that Jesus Christ is Lord."

Jesus was "obedient to the point of death, even death on a cross." It was God's will that He "taste death for everyone," so He "was delivered up because of our transgressions."

Now God desires everyone to "confess with your mouth Jesus as Lord, and believe in your heart God raised Him from the dead." This means that you acknowledge the payment Christ made for your sins on the cross.

Do you see that God requires you to humble yourself and confess Jesus Christ as Lord? If so, say:

"I acknowledge that God requires me to confess Jesus Christ as Lord to the glory of God the Father."

Now turn to page 13, Scripture No. 2, Sec. 3, Matt. 10:32,33.

15 that you may prove yourselves to be blameless and innocent, children of God above reproach in the midst of a crooked and perverse generation, among whom you appear as lights in the world,

16 holding fast the word of life, so that in the day of Christ I may have cause to glory because I did not run in vain nor toil in vain.

17 But even if I am being poured out as a drink offering upon the sacrifice and service of your faith, I rejoice and share my joy with you all.

18 And you too, *I urge you*, rejoice in the same way and share your joy with me.

19 But I hope in the Lord Jesus to send Timothy to you shortly, so that I also may be encouraged when I learn of your condition.

20 For I have no one *else* of kindred spirit who will genuinely be concerned for your welfare.

21 For they all seek after their own interests, not those of Christ Jesus.

22 But you know of his proven worth that he served with me in the furtherance of the gospel like a child *serving* his father.

23 Therefore I hope to send him immediately, as soon as I see how things *go* with me;

24 and I trust in the Lord that I myself also shall be coming shortly.

25 But I thought it necessary to send to you Epaphroditus, my brother and fellow-worker and fellow-soldier, who is also your messenger and minister to my need;

26 because he was longing for you all and was distressed because you had heard that he was sick.

27 For indeed he was sick to the point of death, but God had mercy on him, and not on him only but also on me, lest I should have sorrow upon sorrow.

28 Therefore I have sent him all the more eagerly in order that when you see him again you may rejoice and I may be less concerned *about you.*

29 Therefore receive him in the Lord with all joy, and hold men like him in high regard;

30 because he came close to death for the work of Christ, risking his life to complete what was deficient in your service to me.

Chapter 3

F INALLY, my brethren, rejoice in the Lord. To write the same things *again* is no trouble to me, and it is a safeguard for you.

2 Beware of the dogs, beware of the evil workers, beware of the false circumcision;

3 for we are the *true* circumcision, who worship in the Spirit of God and glory in Christ Jesus and put no confidence in the flesh,

4 although I myself might have confidence even in the flesh. If anyone else has a mind to put confidence in the flesh, I far more:

5 circumcised the eighth day, of the nation of Israel, of the tribe of Benjamin, a Hebrew of Hebrews; as to the Law, a Pharisee;

6 as to zeal, a persecutor of the church; as to the righteousness which is in the Law, found blameless.

7 But whatever things *were* gain to me, those things I have counted as loss for the sake of Christ.

8 More than that, I count all things to be loss in view of the surpassing value of knowing Christ Jesus my Lord, for whom I have suffered the loss of all things, and count them but rubbish in order that I may gain Christ,

9 and may be found in Him, not having a righteousness of my own derived from *the* Law, but that which is

through faith in Christ, the righteousness which *comes* from God on the basis of faith,

10 that I may know Him, and the power of His resurrection and the fellowship of His sufferings, being conformed to His death;

11 in order that I may attain to the resurrection from the dead.

12 Not that I have already obtained *it*, or have already become perfect, but I press on in order that I may lay hold of that for which also I was laid hold of by Christ Jesus.

13 Brethren, I do not regard myself as having laid hold of *it* yet; but one thing *I do*: forgetting what *lies* behind and reaching forward to what *lies* ahead,

14 I press on toward the goal for the prize of the upward call of God in Christ Jesus.

15 Let us therefore, as many as are perfect, have this attitude; and if in anything you have a different attitude, God will reveal that also to you;

16 however, let us keep living by that same *standard* to which we have attained.

17 Brethren, join in following my example, and observe those who walk according to the pattern you have in us.

18 For many walk, of whom I often told you, and now tell you even weeping, *that they are* enemies of the cross of Christ,

19 whose end is destruction, whose god is *their* appetite, and *whose* glory is in their shame, who set their minds on earthly things.

20 For our citizenship is in heaven, from which also we eagerly wait for a Savior, the Lord Jesus Christ;

21 who will transform the body of our humble state into conformity with the body of His glory, by the exertion of the power that He has even to subject all things to Himself.

CHAPTER 4

THEREFORE, my beloved brethren whom I long *to see*, my joy and crown, so stand firm in the Lord, my beloved.

2 I urge Euodia and I urge Syntyche to live in harmony in the Lord.

3 Indeed, true comrade, I ask you also to help these women who have shared my struggle in *the cause of* the gospel, together with Clement also, and the rest of my fellow-workers, whose names are in the book of life.

4 Rejoice in the Lord always; again I will say, rejoice!

5 Let your forbearing *spirit* be known to all men. The Lord is near.

6 Be anxious for nothing, but in everything by prayer and supplication with thanksgiving let your requests be made known to God.

7 And the peace of God, which surpasses all comprehension, shall guard your hearts and your minds in Christ Jesus.

8 Finally, brethren, whatever is true, whatever is honorable, whatever is right, whatever is pure, whatever is lovely, whatever is of good repute, if there is any excellence and if anything worthy of praise, let your mind dwell on these things.

9 The things you have learned and received and heard and seen in me, practice these things; and the God of peace shall be with you.

10 But I rejoiced in the Lord greatly, that now at last you have revived your concern for me; indeed, you were concerned *before*, but you lacked opportunity.

11 Not that I speak from want; for I have learned to be content in whatever circumstances I am.

12 I know how to get along with humble means, and I also know how to live in prosperity; in any and every circumstance I have learned the se-

cret of being filled and going hungry, both of having abundance and suffering need.

13 I can do all things through Him who strengthens me.

14 Nevertheless, you have done well to share *with me* in my affliction.

15 And you yourselves also know, Philippians, that at the first preaching of the gospel, after I departed from Macedonia, no church shared with me in the matter of giving and receiving but you alone;

16 for even in Thessalonica you sent *a gift* more than once for my needs.

17 Not that I seek the gift itself, but I seek for the profit which increases to your account.

18 But I have received everything in full, and have an abundance; I am amply supplied, having received from Epaphroditus what you have sent, a fragrant aroma, an acceptable sacrifice, well-pleasing to God.

19 And my God shall supply all your needs according to His riches in glory in Christ Jesus.

20 Now to our God and Father *be* the glory forever and ever. Amen.

21 Greet every saint in Christ Jesus. The brethren who are with me greet you.

22 All the saints greet you, especially those of Caesar's household.

23 The grace of the Lord Jesus Christ be with your spirit.

THE EPISTLE OF PAUL TO THE
COLOSSIANS

PAUL, an apostle of Jesus Christ by the will of God, and Timothy our brother,

2 to the saints and faithful brethren in Christ *who are* at Colossae: Grace to you and peace from God our Father.

3 We give thanks to God, the Father of our Lord Jesus Christ, praying always for you,

4 since we heard of your faith in Christ Jesus and the love which you have for all the saints;

5 because of the hope laid up for you in heaven, of which you previously heard in the word of truth, the gospel,

6 which has come to you, just as in all the world also it is constantly bearing fruit and increasing, even as *it has been doing* in you also since the day you heard *of it* and understood the grace of God in truth;

7 just as you learned *it* from Epa-

phras, our beloved fellow bond-servant, who is a faithful servant of Christ on our behalf,

8 and he also informed us of your love in the Spirit.

9 For this reason also, since the day we heard *of it*, we have not ceased to pray for you and to ask that you may be filled with the knowledge of His will in all spiritual wisdom and understanding,

10 so that you may walk in a manner worthy of the Lord, to please *Him* in all respects, bearing fruit in every good work and increasing in the knowledge of God;

11 strengthened with all power, according to His glorious might, for the attaining of all steadfastness and patience; joyously

12 giving thanks to the Father, who has qualified us to share in the inheritance of the saints in light.

13 For He delivered us from the

domain of darkness, and transferred us to the kingdom of His beloved Son,

14 in whom we have redemption, the forgiveness of sins.

15 And He is the image of the invisible God, the first-born of all creation.

16 For in Him all things were created, *both* in the heavens and on earth, visible and invisible, whether thrones or dominions or rulers or authorities—all things have been created through Him and for Him.

17 And He is before all things, and in Him all things hold together.

18 He is also head of the body, the church; and He is the beginning, the first-born from the dead; so that He Himself might come to have first place in everything.

19 For it was the *Father's* good pleasure for all the fulness to dwell in Him,

20 and through Him to reconcile all things to Himself, having made peace through the blood of His cross; through Him, *I say*, whether things on earth or things in heaven.

21 And although you were formerly alienated and hostile in mind, *engaged* in evil deeds,

22 yet He has now reconciled you in His fleshly body through death, in order to present you before Him holy and blameless and beyond reproach—

23 if indeed you continue in the faith firmly established and steadfast, and not moved away from the hope of the gospel that you have heard, which was proclaimed in all creation under heaven, and of which I, Paul, was made a minister.

24 Now I rejoice in my sufferings for your sake, and in my flesh I do my share on behalf of His body (which is the church) in filling up that which is lacking in Christ's afflictions.

25 Of *this church* I was made a minister according to the stewardship from God bestowed on me for your benefit, that I might fully carry out the *preaching of* the word of God,

26 *that is*, the mystery which has been hidden from the *past* ages and generations; but has now been manifested to His saints,

27 to whom God willed to make known what is the riches of the glory of this mystery among the Gentiles, which is Christ in you, the hope of glory.

28 And we proclaim Him, admonishing every man and teaching every man with all wisdom, that we may present every man complete in Christ.

29 And for this purpose also I labor, striving according to His power, which mightily works within me.

CHAPTER 2

FOR I want you to know how great a struggle I have on your behalf, and for those who are at Laodicea, and for all those who have not personally seen my face,

2 that their hearts may be encouraged, having been knit together in love, and *attaining* to all the wealth that comes from the full assurance of understanding, *resulting* in a true knowledge of God's mystery, *that is*, Christ *Himself*,

3 in whom are hidden all the treasures of wisdom and knowledge.

4 I say this in order that no one may delude you with persuasive argument.

5 For even though I am absent in body, nevertheless I am with you in spirit, rejoicing to see your good discipline and the stability of your faith in Christ.

6 As you therefore have received Christ Jesus the Lord, *so* walk in Him,

7 having been firmly rooted *and now* being built up in Him and established in your faith, just as you were instructed, *and* overflowing with gratitude.

8 See to it that no one takes you captive through philosophy and empty deception, according to the tradition of men, according to the elementary principles of the world, rather than according to Christ.

9 For in Him all the fulness of Deity dwells in bodily form,

10 and in Him you have been made complete, and He is the head over all rule and authority;

11 and in Him you were also circumcised with a circumcision made without hands, in the removal of the body of the flesh by the circumcision of Christ;

12 having been buried with Him in baptism, in which you were also raised up with Him through faith in the working of God, who raised Him from the dead.

13 And when you were dead in your transgressions and the uncircumcision of your flesh, He made you alive together with Him, having forgiven us all our transgressions,

14 having cancelled out the certificate of debt consisting of decrees against us *and* which was hostile to us; and He has taken it out of the way, having nailed it to the cross.

15 When He had disarmed the rulers and authorities, He made a public display of them, having triumphed over them through Him.

16 Therefore let no one act as your judge in regard to food or drink or in respect to a festival or a new moon or a Sabbath day—

17 things which are a *mere* shadow of what is to come; but the substance belongs to Christ.

18 Let no one keep defrauding you of your prize by delighting in self-abasement and the worship of the angels, taking his stand on *visions* he

has seen, inflated without cause by his fleshly mind,

19 and not holding fast to the head, from whom the entire body, being supplied and held together by the joints and ligaments, grows with a growth which is from God.

20 If you have died with Christ to the elementary principles of the world, why, as if you were living in the world, do you submit yourself to decrees, such as,

21 "Do not handle, do not taste, do not touch!"

22 (which all *refer to* things destined to perish with the using)—in accordance with the commandments and teachings of men?

23 These are matters which have, to be sure, the appearance of wisdom in self-made religion and self-abasement and severe treatment of the body, *but are* of no value against fleshly indulgence.

CHAPTER 3

IF then you have been raised up with Christ, keep seeking the things above, where Christ is, seated at the right hand of God.

2 Set your mind on the things above, not on the things that are on earth.

3 For you have died and your life is hidden with Christ in God.

4 When Christ, who is our life, is revealed, then you also will be revealed with Him in glory.

5 Therefore consider the members of your earthly body as dead to immorality, impurity, passion, evil desire, and greed, which amounts to idolatry.

6 For it is on account of these things that the wrath of God will come,

7 and in them you also once walked, when you were living in them.

8 But now you also, put them all

aside: anger, wrath, malice, slander, *and* abusive speech from your mouth.

9 Do not lie to one another, since you laid aside the old self with its *evil* practices,

10 and have put on the new self who is being renewed to a true knowledge according to the image of the One who created him,

11 —a *renewal* in which there is no *distinction between* Greek and Jew, circumcised and uncircumcised, barbarian, Scythian, slave and freeman, but Christ is all, and in all.

12 And so, as those who have been chosen of God, holy and beloved, put on a heart of compassion, kindness, humility, gentleness and patience;

13 bearing with one another, and forgiving each other, whoever has a complaint against any one; just as the Lord forgave you, so also should you.

14 And beyond all these things *put on* love, which is the perfect bond of unity.

15 And let the peace of Christ rule in your hearts, to which indeed you were called in one body; and be thankful.

16 Let the word of Christ richly dwell within you, with all wisdom teaching and admonishing one another with psalms *and* hymns *and* spiritual songs, singing with thankfulness in your hearts to God.

17 And whatever you do in word or deed, *do* all in the name of the Lord Jesus, giving thanks through Him to God the Father.

18 Wives, be subject to your husbands, as is fitting in the Lord.

19 Husbands, love your wives, and do not be embittered against them.

20 Children, be obedient to your parents in all things, for this is well-pleasing to the Lord.

21 Fathers, do not exasperate your children, that they may not lose heart.

22 Slaves, in all things obey those who are your masters on earth, not with external service, as those who *merely* please men, but with sincerity of heart, fearing the Lord.

23 Whatever you do, do your work heartily, as for the Lord rather than for men;

24 knowing that from the Lord you will receive the reward of the inheritance. It is the Lord Christ whom you serve.

25 For he who does wrong will receive the consequences of the wrong which he has done, and that without partiality.

CHAPTER 4

Masters, grant to your slaves justice and fairness, knowing that you too have a Master in heaven.

2 Devote yourselves to prayer, keeping alert in it with *an attitude of* thanksgiving;

3 praying at the same time for us as well, that God may open up to us a door for the word, so that we may speak forth the mystery of Christ, for which I have also been imprisoned;

4 in order that I may make it clear in the way I ought to speak.

5 Conduct yourselves with wisdom toward outsiders, making the most of the opportunity.

6 Let your speech always be with grace, seasoned, *as it were*, with salt, so that you may know how you should respond to each person.

7 As to all my affairs, Tychicus, *our* beloved brother and faithful servant and fellow-bondslave in the Lord, will bring you information.

8 For I have sent him to you for this very purpose, that you may know *about* our circumstances and that he may encourage your hearts;

9 and with him Onesimus, *our* faithful and beloved brother, who is one of your *number*. They will inform

you about the whole situation here.

10 Aristarchus, my fellow prisoner, sends you his greetings; and *also* Barnabas' cousin Mark (about whom you received instructions: if he comes to you, welcome him);

11 and *also* Jesus who is called Justus; these are the only fellow-workers for the kingdom of God who are from the circumcision; and they have proved to be an encouragement to me.

12 Epaphras, who is one of your number, a bondslave of Jesus Christ, sends you his greetings, always laboring earnestly for you in his prayers, that you may stand perfect and fully assured in all the will of God.

13 For I bear him witness that he has a deep concern for you and for those who are in Laodicea and Hierapolis.

14 Luke, the beloved physician, sends you his greetings, and *also* Demas.

15 Greet the brethren who are in Laodicea and also Nympha and the church that is in her house.

16 And when this letter is read among you, have it also read in the church of the Laodiceans; and you, for your part read my letter *that is coming* from Laodicea.

17 And say to Archippus, "Take heed to the ministry which you have received in the Lord, that you may fulfill it."

18 I, Paul, write this greeting with my own hand. Remember my imprisonment. Grace be with you.

THE FIRST EPISTLE OF PAUL TO THE

THESSALONIANS

PAUL and Silvanus and Timothy to the church of the Thessalonians in God the Father and the Lord Jesus Christ: Grace to you and peace.

2 We give thanks to God always for all of you, making mention *of you* in our prayers;

3 constantly bearing in mind your work of faith and labor of love and steadfastness of hope in our Lord Jesus Christ in the presence of our God and Father,

4 knowing, brethren beloved by God, *His* choice of you;

5 for our gospel did not come to you in word only, but also in power and in the Holy Spirit and with full conviction; just as you know what kind of men we proved to be among you for your sake.

6 You also became imitators of us and of the Lord, having received the word in much tribulation with the joy of the Holy Spirit,

7 so that you became an example to all the believers in Macedonia and in Achaia.

8 For the word of the Lord has sounded forth from you, not only in Macedonia and Achaia, but also in every place your faith toward God has gone forth, so that we have no need to say anything.

9 For they themselves report about us what kind of a reception we had with you, and how you turned to God from idols to serve a living and true God,

10 and to wait for His Son from heaven, whom He raised from the dead, *that is* Jesus, who delivers us from the wrath to come.

CHAPTER 2

FOR you yourselves know, brethren, that our coming to you was not in vain,

2 but after we had already suffered and been mistreated in Philippi, as you know, we had the boldness in our God to speak to you the gospel of God amid much opposition.

3 For our exhortation does not *come* from error or impurity or by way of deceit;

4 but just as we have been approved by God to be entrusted with the gospel, so we speak, not as pleasing men but God, who examines our hearts.

5 For we never came with flattering speech, as you know, nor with a pretext for greed—God is witness —

6 nor did we seek glory from men, either from you or from others, even though as apostles of Christ we might have asserted our authority.

7 But we proved to be gentle among you, as a nursing *mother* tenderly cares for her own children.

8 Having thus a fond affection for you, we were well pleased to impart to you not only the gospel but also our own lives, because you had become very dear to us.

9 For you recall, brethren, our labor and hardship, *how* working night and day so as not to be a burden to any of you, we proclaimed to you the gospel of God.

10 You are witnesses, and *so is* God, how devoutly and uprightly and blamelessly we behaved toward you believers;

11 just as you know how we *were* exhorting and encouraging and imploring each one of you as a father *would* his own children,

12 so that you may walk in a manner worthy of the God who calls you into His own kingdom and glory.

SCRIPTURE NO. 4, SEC. 4

13 And for this reason we also constantly thank God that when you received from us the word of God's message, you accepted *it* not *as the* word of men, but *for* what it really is, the word of God, which also performs its work in you who believe. (r4)

14 For you, brethren, became imi-

(r4) REFERENCE NO. 4, SEC. 4—
WHAT YOU SHOULD KNOW ABOUT GOD'S WORD.

"The word of God . . . performs its work in you who believe." This work is "salvation through faith which is in Christ Jesus."

God gave His word when "men moved by the Holy Spirit spoke from God." So "all scripture is inspired by God." God speaks His "words to you by which you will be saved." You are only "saved by faith, . . . it is the gift of God." And "faith comes by hearing" God's word.

The word of God's message "is a light." The message is "able to give you the wisdom that leads to salvation through faith which is in Christ Jesus."

The entire Bible can be understood only by those saved or "born of the Spirit." The unsaved "man does not accept the things of the Spirit of God . . . He cannot understand them . . . they are spiritually appraised."

For His disciples, Jesus "opened their minds to understand the scriptures." When you become His disciple, you will be like "the man who hears the word and understands it." You begin by being saved or "born again . . . through the living and abiding word of God."

Receive "God's message for what it really is, the word of God."

(Continued on next page.)

tators of the churches of God in Christ Jesus that are in Judea, for you also endured the same sufferings at the hands of your own countrymen, even as they *did* from the Jews,

15 who both killed the Lord Jesus and the prophets, and drove us out. They are not pleasing to God, but hostile to all men,

16 hindering us from speaking to the Gentiles that they might be saved; with the result that they always fill up the measure of their sins. But wrath has come upon them to the utmost.

17 But we, brethren, having been bereft of you for a short while—in person, not in spirit—were all the more eager with great desire to see your face.

18 For we wanted to come to you—I, Paul, more than once—and *yet* Satan thwarted us.

19 For who is our hope or joy or crown of exultation? Is it not even you, in the presence of our Lord Jesus at His coming?

20 For you are our glory and joy.

Chapter 3

THEREFORE when we could endure *it* no longer, we thought it best to be left behind at Athens alone;

2 and we sent Timothy, our brother and God's fellow-worker in the gospel of Christ, to strengthen and encourage you as to your faith;

3 so that no man may be disturbed by these afflictions; for you yourselves know that we have been destined for this.

4 For indeed when we were with you, we *kept* telling you in advance that we were going to suffer affliction; and so it came to pass, as you know.

5 For this reason, when I could endure *it* no longer, I also sent to find out about your faith, for fear that the tempter might have tempted you, and our labor should be in vain.

6 But now that Timothy has come to us from you, and has brought us good news of your faith and love, and that you always think kindly of us, longing to see us just as we also long to see you,

7 for this reason, brethren, in all our distress and affliction we were comforted about you through your faith;

8 for now we *really* live, if you stand firm in the Lord.

9 For what thanks can we render to God for you in return for all the joy with which we rejoice before our God on your account,

10 as we night and day keep praying most earnestly that we may see your face, and may complete what is lacking in your faith?

11 Now may our God and Father Himself and Jesus our Lord direct our way to you;

12 and may the Lord cause you to increase and abound in love for one another, and for all men, just as we also *do* for you;

13 so that He may establish your hearts unblamable in holiness before

---

(Continued from page 278.)

Do you understand that the scriptures are God's Word? If so, say:

"I receive God's message for what it really is, the word of God."

If you have not already confessed Christ as your personal savior, and you desire God to speak to you through His word, turn to page 186. Begin a new set of scriptures and references; read Scripture No. 1, Sec. 1, Acts 16:30-34, the verses which are underlined. Then read Reference No. 1, entitled: "What you must do to be saved." Continue to read the chain of scriptures and references as instructed at the bottom of each page.

our God and Father at the coming of our Lord Jesus with all His saints.

CHAPTER 4

FINALLY then, brethren, we request and exhort you in the Lord Jesus that, as you received from us *instruction* as to how you ought to walk and please God (just as you actually do walk), that you may excel still more.

2 For you know what commandments we gave you by *the authority of* the Lord Jesus.

3 For this is the will of God, your sanctification; *that is,* that you abstain from sexual immorality;

4 that each of you know how to possess his own vessel in sanctification and honor,

5 not in lustful passion, like the Gentiles who do not know God;

6 *and* that no man transgress and defraud his brother in the matter because the Lord is *the* avenger in all these things, just as we also told you before and solemnly warned *you.*

7 For God has not called us for the purpose of impurity, but in sanctification.

8 Consequently, he who rejects *this* is not rejecting man but the God who gives His Holy Spirit to you.

9 Now as to the love of the brethren, you have no need for *any one* to write to you, for you yourselves are taught by God to love one another;

10 for indeed you do practice it toward all the brethren who are in all Macedonia. But we urge you, brethren, to excel still more,

11 and to make it your ambition to lead a quiet life and attend to your own business and work with your hands, just as we commanded you;

12 so that you may behave properly toward outsiders and not be in any need.

13 But we do not want you to be uninformed, brethren, about those who are asleep, that you may not grieve, as do the rest who have no hope.

14 For if we believe that Jesus died and rose again, even so God will bring with Him those who have fallen asleep in Jesus.

15 For this we say to you by the word of the Lord, that we who are alive, and remain until the coming of the Lord, shall not precede those who have fallen asleep.

16 For the Lord Himself will descend from heaven with a shout, with the voice of *the* archangel, and with the trumpet of God; and the dead in Christ shall rise first.

17 Then we who are alive and remain shall be caught up together with them in the clouds to meet the Lord in the air, and thus we shall always be with the Lord.

18 Therefore comfort one another with these words.

CHAPTER 5

NOW as to the times and the epochs, brethren, you have no need of anything to be written to you.

2 For you yourselves know full well that the day of the Lord will come just like a thief in the night.

3 While they are saying, "Peace and safety!" then destruction will come upon them suddenly like birth pangs upon a woman with child; and they shall not escape.

4 But you, brethren, are not in darkness, that the day should overtake you like a thief;

5 for you are all sons of light and sons of day. We are not of night nor of darkness;

6 so then let us not sleep as others do, but let us be alert and sober.

7 For those who sleep do their sleeping at night, and those who get drunk get drunk at night.

8 But since we are of *the* day, let

us be sober, having put on the breastplate of faith and love, and as a helmet, the hope of salvation.

9 For God has not destined us for wrath, but for obtaining salvation through our Lord Jesus Christ,

10 who died for us, that whether we are awake or asleep, we may live together with Him.

11 Therefore encourage one another, and build up one another, just as you also are doing.

12 But we request of you, brethren, that you appreciate those who diligently labor among you, and have charge over you in the Lord and give you instruction,

13 and that you esteem them very highly in love because of their work. Live in peace with one another.

14 And we urge you, brethren, admonish the unruly, encourage the fainthearted, help the weak, be patient with all men.

15 See that no one repays another with evil for evil, but always seek after that which is good for one another and for all men.

16 Rejoice always;

17 pray without ceasing;

18 in everything give thanks; for this is God's will for you in Christ Jesus.

19 Do not quench the Spirit;

20 do not despise prophetic utterances.

21 But examine everything *carefully;* hold fast to that which is good;

22 abstain from every form of evil.

23 Now may the God of peace Himself sanctify you entirely; and may your spirit and soul and body be preserved complete, without blame at the coming of our Lord Jesus Christ.

24 Faithful is He who calls you, and He also will bring it to pass.

25 Brethren, pray for us.

26 Greet all the brethren with a holy kiss.

27 I adjure you by the Lord to have this letter read to all the brethren.

28 The grace of our Lord Jesus Christ be with you.

THE SECOND EPISTLE OF PAUL TO THE
THESSALONIANS

P AUL and Silvanus and Timothy to the church of the Thessalonians in God our Father and the Lord Jesus Christ:

2 Grace to you and peace from God the Father and the Lord Jesus Christ.

3 We ought always to give thanks to God for you, brethren, as is *only* fitting, because your faith is greatly enlarged, and the love of each one of you all toward one another grows *ever* greater;

4 therefore, we ourselves speak proudly of you among the churches of God for your perseverance and faith in the midst of all your persecutions and afflictions which you endure.

5 *This is* a plain indication of God's righteous judgment so that you may be considered worthy of the kingdom of God, for which indeed you are suffering.

6 For after all it is *only* just for God to repay with affliction those who afflict you,

7 and *to give* relief to you who are afflicted and to us as well when the

Lord Jesus shall be revealed from heaven with His mighty angels in flaming fire,

8 dealing out retribution to those who do not know God and to those who do not obey the gospel of our Lord Jesus.

9 And these will pay the penalty of eternal destruction, away from the presence of the Lord and from the glory of His power,

10 when He comes to be glorified in His saints on that day, and to be marveled at among all who have believed—for our testimony to you was believed.

11 To this end also we pray for you always that our God may count you worthy of your calling, and fulfill every desire for goodness and the work of faith with power;

12 in order that the name of our Lord Jesus may be glorified in you, and you in Him, according to the grace of our God and the Lord Jesus Christ.

CHAPTER 2

NOW we request you, brethren, with regard to the coming of our Lord Jesus Christ, and our gathering together to Him,

2 that you may not be quickly shaken from your composure or be disturbed either by a spirit or a message or a letter as if from us, to the effect that the day of the Lord has come.

3 Let no one in any way deceive you, for it will not come unless the apostasy comes first, and the man of lawlessness is revealed, the son of destruction,

4 who opposes and exalts himself above every so-called god or object of worship, so that he takes his seat in the temple of God, displaying himself as being God.

5 Do you not remember that while I was still with you, I was telling you these things?

6 And you know what restrains him now, so that in his time he may be revealed.

7 For the mystery of lawlessness is already at work; only he who now restrains will do so until he is taken out of the way.

8 And then that lawless one will be revealed whom the Lord will slay with the breath of His mouth and bring to an end by the appearance of His coming;

9 that is, the one whose coming is in accord with the activity of Satan, with all power and signs and false wonders,

10 and with all the deception of wickedness for those who perish, because they did not receive the love of the truth so as to be saved.

11 And for this reason God will send upon them a deluding influence so that they might believe what is false,

12 in order that they all may be judged who did not believe the truth, but took pleasure in wickedness.

13 But we should always give thanks to God for you, brethren beloved by the Lord, because God has chosen you from the beginning for salvation through sanctification by the Spirit and faith in the truth.

14 And it was for this He called you through our gospel, that you may gain the glory of our Lord Jesus Christ.

15 So then, brethren, stand firm and hold to the traditions which you were taught, whether by word of mouth or by letter from us.

16 Now may our Lord Jesus Christ Himself and God our Father, who has loved us and given us eternal comfort and good hope by grace,

17 comfort and strengthen your hearts in every good work and word.

CHAPTER 3

Finally, brethren, pray for us that the word of the Lord may spread rapidly and be glorified, just as *it did* also with you;

2 and that we may be delivered from perverse and evil men; for not all have faith.

3 But the Lord is faithful, and He will strengthen and protect you from the evil *one.*

4 And we have confidence in the Lord concerning you, that you are doing and will continue to do what we command.

5 And may the Lord direct your hearts into the love of God and into the steadfastness of Christ.

6 Now we command you, brethren, in the name of our Lord Jesus Christ, that you keep aloof from every brother who leads an unruly life and not according to the tradition which you received from us.

7 For you yourselves know how you ought to follow our example, because we did not act in an undisciplined manner among you,

8 nor did we eat anyone's bread without paying for it, but with labor and hardship we *kept* working night and day so that we might not be a burden to any of you;

9 not because we do not have the right *to this,* but in order to offer ourselves as a model for you, that you might follow our example.

10 For even when we were with you, we used to give you this order: If anyone will not work, neither let him eat.

11 For we hear that some among you are leading an undisciplined life, doing no work at all, but acting like busybodies.

12 Now such persons we command and exhort in the Lord Jesus Christ to work in quiet fashion and eat their own bread.

13 But as for you, brethren, do not grow weary of doing good.

14 And if anyone does not obey our instruction in this letter, take special note of that man and do not associate with him, so that he may be put to shame.

15 And *yet* do not regard him as an enemy, but admonish him as a brother.

16 Now may the Lord of peace Himself continually grant you peace in every circumstance. The Lord be with you all!

17 I, Paul, write this greeting with my own hand, and this is a distinguishing mark in every letter; this is the way I write.

18 The grace of our Lord Jesus Christ be with you all.

THE FIRST EPISTLE OF PAUL TO

TIMOTHY

Paul, an apostle of Christ Jesus according to the commandment of God our Savior, and of Christ Jesus, *who is* our hope;

2 to Timothy, *my* true child in *the* faith: Grace, mercy *and* peace from God the Father and Christ Jesus our Lord.

3 As I urged you upon my departure for Macedonia, remain on at Ephesus, in order that you may instruct certain men not to teach strange doctrines,

4 nor to pay attention to myths and endless genealogies, which give rise to mere speculation rather than

furthering the administration of God which is by faith.

5 But the goal of our instruction is love from a pure heart and a good conscience and a sincere faith.

6 For some men, straying from these things, have turned aside to fruitless discussion,

7 wanting to be teachers of the Law, even though they do not understand either what they are saying or the matters about which they make confident assertions.

8 But we know that the Law is good, if one uses it lawfully,

9 realizing the fact that law is not made for a righteous man, but for those who are lawless and rebellious, for the ungodly and sinners, for the unholy and profane, for those who kill their fathers or mothers, for murderers

10 and immoral men and homosexuals and kidnappers and liars and perjurers, and whatever else is contrary to sound teaching,

11 according to the glorious gospel of the blessed God, with which I have been entrusted.

12 I thank Christ Jesus our Lord, who has strengthened me, because He considered me faithful, putting me into service;

13 even though I was formerly a blasphemer and a persecutor and a violent aggressor. And yet I was shown mercy, because I acted ignorantly in unbelief;

14 and the grace of our Lord was more than abundant, with the faith and love which are *found* in Christ Jesus.

15 It is a trustworthy statement, deserving full acceptance, that Christ Jesus came into the world to save sinners, among whom I am foremost *of all.*

16 And yet for this reason I found mercy, in order that in me as the foremost, Jesus Christ might demonstrate His perfect patience, as an ex-

ample for those who would believe in Him for eternal life.

17 Now to the King eternal, immortal, invisible, the only God, *be* honor and glory forever and ever. Amen.

18 This command I entrust to you, Timothy, my son, in accordance with the prophecies previously made concerning you, that by them you may fight the good fight,

19 keeping faith and a good conscience, which some have rejected and suffered shipwreck in regard to their faith.

20 Among these are Hymenaeus and Alexander, whom I have delivered over to Satan, so that they may be taught not to blaspheme.

Chapter 2

FIRST of all, then, I urge that entreaties *and* prayers, petitions *and* thanksgivings, be made on behalf of all men,

2 for kings and all who are in authority, in order that we may lead a tranquil and quiet life in all godliness and dignity.

3 This is good and acceptable in the sight of God our Savior,

4 who desires all men to be saved and to come to the knowledge of the truth.

5 For there is one God, *and* one mediator also between God and men, *the* man Christ Jesus,

6 who gave Himself as a ransom for all, the testimony *borne* at the proper time.

7 And for this I was appointed a preacher and an apostle (I am telling the truth, I am not lying) as a teacher of the Gentiles in faith and truth.

8 Therefore I want the men in every place to pray, lifting up holy hands, without wrath and dissension.

9 Likewise, *I want* women to adorn themselves with proper clothing, modestly and discreetly, not with

braided hair and gold or pearls or costly garments;

10 but rather by means of good works, as befits women making a claim to godliness.

11 Let a woman quietly receive instruction with entire submissiveness.

12 But I do not allow a woman to teach or exercise authority over a man, but to remain quiet.

13 For it was Adam who was first created, *and* then Eve.

14 And *it was* not Adam *who* was deceived, but the woman being quite deceived, fell into transgression.

15 But women shall be preserved through the bearing of children if *they* continue in faith and love and sanctity with self-restraint.

CHAPTER 3

IT is a trustworthy statement; if any man aspires to the office of overseer, it is a fine work he desires *to do.*

2 An overseer, then, must be above reproach, the husband of one wife, temperate, prudent, respectable, hospitable, able to teach,

3 not addicted to wine or pugnacious, but gentle, uncontentious, free from the love of money.

4 *He must be* one who manages his own household well, keeping his children under control with all dignity

5 (but if a man does not know how to manage his own household, how will he take care of the church of God?);

6 *and* not a new convert, lest he become conceited and fall into the condemnation incurred by the devil.

7 And he must have a good reputation with those outside *the church,* so that he may not fall into reproach and the snare of the devil.

8 Deacons likewise *must be* men of dignity, not double-tongued, or ad-

dicted to much wine or fond of sordid gain,

9 *but* holding to the mystery of the faith with a clear conscience.

10 And let these also first be tested; then let them serve as deacons if they are beyond reproach.

11 Women *must* likewise *be* dignified, not malicious gossips, but temperate, faithful in all things.

12 Let deacons be husbands of *only* one wife, *and* good managers of *their* children and their own households.

13 For those who have served well as deacons obtain for themselves a high standing and great confidence in the faith that is in Christ Jesus.

14 I am writing these things to you, hoping to come to you before long;

15 but in case I am delayed, *I write* so that you may know how one ought to conduct himself in the household of God, which is the church of the living God, the pillar and support of the truth.

16 And by common confession great is the mystery of godliness:

He who was revealed in the flesh,
Was vindicated in the Spirit,
Beheld by angels,
Proclaimed among the nations,
Believed on in the world,
Taken up in glory.

CHAPTER 4

BUT the Spirit explicitly says that in later times some will fall away from the faith, paying attention to deceitful spirits and doctrines of demons,

2 by means of the hypocrisy of liars seared in their own conscience as with a branding iron,

3 *men* who forbid marriage *and advocate* abstaining from foods, which God has created to be grate-

fully shared in by those who believe and know the truth.

4 For everything created by God is good, and nothing is to be rejected, if it is received with gratitude;

5 for it is sanctified by means of the word of God and prayer.

6 In pointing out these things to the brethren, you will be a good servant of Christ Jesus, *constantly* nourished on the words of the faith and of the sound doctrine which you have been following.

7 But have nothing to do with worldly fables fit only for old women. On the other hand, discipline yourself for the purpose of godliness;

8 for bodily discipline is only of little profit, but godliness is profitable for all things, since it holds promise for the present life and *also* for the *life* to come.

9 It is a trustworthy statement deserving full acceptance.

10 For it is for this we labor and strive, because we have fixed our hope on the living God, who is the Savior of all men, especially of believers.

11 Prescribe and teach these things.

12 Let no one look down on your youthfulness, but *rather* in speech, conduct, love, faith *and* purity, show yourself an example of those who believe.

13 Until I come, give attention to the *public* reading of *Scripture*, to exhortation and teaching.

14 Do not neglect the spiritual gift within you, which was bestowed upon you through prophetic utterance with the laying on of hands by the presbytery.

15 Take pains with these things; be *absorbed* in them, so that your progress may be evident to all.

16 Pay close attention to yourself and to your teaching; persevere in these things; for as you do this you will insure salvation both for yourself and for those who hear you.

Chapter 5

Do not sharply rebuke an older man, *but rather* appeal to him as a father, to the younger men as brothers,

2 the older women as mothers, *and* the younger women as sisters, in all purity.

3 Honor widows who are widows indeed;

4 but if any widow has children or grandchildren, let them first learn to practice piety in regard to their own family, and to make some return to their parents; for this is acceptable in the sight of God.

5 Now she who is a widow, indeed, and who has been left alone has fixed her hope on God, and continues in entreaties and prayers night and day.

6 But she who gives herself to wanton pleasure is dead even while she lives.

7 Prescribe these things as well, so that they may be above reproach.

8 But if any one does not provide for his own, and especially for those of his household, he has denied the faith, and is worse than an unbeliever.

9 Let a widow be put on the list only if she is not less than sixty years old, *having been* the wife of one man,

10 having a reputation for good works; *and* if she has brought up children, if she has shown hospitality to strangers, if she has washed the saints' feet, if she has assisted those in distress, *and* if she has devoted herself to every good work.

11 But refuse *to put* younger widows *on the list*, for when they feel sensual desires in disregard of Christ, they want to get married,

12 *thus* incurring condemnation,

because they have set aside their previous pledge.

13 And at the same time they also learn *to be* idle, as they go around from house to house; and not merely idle, but also gossips and busybodies, talking about things not proper *to mention.*

14 Therefore, I want younger *widows* to get married, bear children, keep house, *and* give the enemy no occasion for reproach;

15 for some have already turned aside to follow Satan.

16 If any woman who is a believer has *dependent* widows, let her assist them, and let not the church be burdened, so that it may assist those who are widows indeed.

17 Let the elders who rule well be considered worthy of double honor, especially those who work hard at preaching and teaching.

18 For the Scripture says, "YOU SHALL NOT MUZZLE THE OX WHILE HE IS THRESHING," and "The laborer is worthy of his wages."

19 Do not receive an accusation against an elder except on the basis of two or three witnesses.

20 Those who continue in sin, rebuke in the presence of all, so that the rest also may be fearful *of sinning.*

21 I solemnly charge you in the presence of God and of Christ Jesus and of *His* chosen angels, to maintain these *principles* without bias, doing nothing in a *spirit of* partiality.

22 Do not lay hands upon any one *too* hastily and thus share *responsibility for* the sins of others; keep yourself free from sin.

23 No longer drink water *exclusively,* but use a little wine for the sake of your stomach and your frequent ailments.

24 The sins of some men are quite evident, going before them to judgment; for others, their *sins* follow after.

25 Likewise also, deeds that are good are quite evident, and those which are otherwise cannot be concealed.

CHAPTER 6

LET all who are under the yoke as slaves regard their own masters as worthy of all honor so that the name of God and *our* doctrine may not be spoken against.

2 And let those who have believers as their masters not be disrespectful to them because they are brethren, but let them serve them all the more, because those who partake of the benefit are believers and beloved. Teach and preach these *principles.*

3 If any one advocates a different doctrine, and does not agree with sound words, those of our Lord Jesus Christ, and with the doctrine conforming to godliness,

4 he is conceited *and* understands nothing; but he has a morbid interest in controversial questions and disputes about words, out of which arise envy, strife, abusive language, evil suspicions,

5 and constant friction between men of depraved mind and deprived of the truth, who suppose that godliness is a means of gain.

6 But godliness *actually* is a means of great gain, when accompanied by contentment.

7 For we have brought nothing into the world, so we cannot take anything out of it either.

8 And if we have food and covering, with these we shall be content.

9 But those who want to get rich fall into temptation and a snare and many foolish and harmful desires which plunge men into ruin and destruction.

10 For the love of money is a root of all sorts of evil, and some by longing for it have wandered away from

the faith, and pierced themselves with many a pang.

11 But flee from these things, you man of God; and pursue righteousness, godliness, faith, love, perseverance *and* gentleness.

12 Fight the good fight of faith; take hold of the eternal life to which you were called, and you made the good confession in the presence of many witnesses.

13 I charge you in the presence of God, who gives life to all things, and of Christ Jesus, who testified the good confession before Pontius Pilate,

14 that you keep the commandment without stain or reproach, until the appearing of our Lord Jesus Christ,

15 which He will bring about at the proper time—He who is the blessed and only Sovereign, the King of kings and Lord of lords;

16 who alone possesses immortality and dwells in unapproachable light; whom no man has seen or can see. To Him *be* honor and eternal dominion! Amen.

17 Instruct those who are rich in this present world not to be conceited or to fix their hope on the uncertainty of riches, but on God, who richly supplies us with all things to enjoy.

18 *Instruct them* to do good, to be rich in good works, to be generous and ready to share,

19 storing up for themselves the treasure of a good foundation for the future, so that they may take hold of that which is life indeed.

20 O Timothy, guard what has been entrusted to you, avoiding worldly *and* empty chatter *and* the opposing arguments of what is falsely called "knowledge"—

21 which some have professed and thus gone astray from the faith.

Grace be with you.

THE SECOND EPISTLE OF PAUL TO
TIMOTHY

PAUL, an apostle of Christ Jesus by the will of God, according to the promise of life in Christ Jesus,

2 to Timothy, my beloved son: Grace, mercy *and* peace from God the Father and Christ Jesus our Lord.

3 I thank God, whom I serve with a clear conscience the way my forefathers did, as I constantly remember you in my prayers night and day,

4 longing to see you, even as I recall your tears, so that I may be filled with joy.

5 For I am mindful of the sincere faith within you, which first dwelt in your grandmother Lois, and your mother Eunice, and I am sure that *it is* in you as well.

6 And for this reason I remind you to kindle afresh the gift of God which is in you through the laying on of my hands.

7 For God has not given us a spirit of timidity, but of power and love and discipline.

8 Therefore do not be ashamed of the testimony of our Lord, or of me His prisoner; but join with *me* in suffering for the gospel according to the power of God;

9 who has saved us, and called us with a holy calling, not according to our works, but according to His own purpose and grace which was granted us in Christ Jesus from all eternity,

10 but now has been revealed by the appearing of our Savior Christ Jesus, who abolished death, and brought life and immortality to light through the gospel,

11 for which I was appointed a preacher and an apostle and a teacher.

12 For this reason I also suffer these things, but I am not ashamed; for I know whom I have believed and I am convinced that He is able to guard what I have entrusted to Him until that day.

13 Retain the standard of sound words which you have heard from me, in the faith and love which are in Christ Jesus.

14 Guard through the Holy Spirit who dwells in us, the treasure which has been entrusted to *you.*

15 You are aware of the fact that all who are in Asia turned away from me, among whom are Phygelus and Hermogenes.

16 The Lord grant mercy to the house of Onesiphorus for he often refreshed me, and was not ashamed of my chains;

17 but when he was in Rome, he eagerly searched for me, and found me—

18 the Lord grant to him to find mercy from the Lord on that day— and you know very well what services he rendered at Ephesus.

CHAPTER 2

Y OU therefore, my son, be strong in the grace that is in Christ Jesus.

2 And the things which you have heard from me in the presence of many witnesses, these entrust to faithful men, who will be able to teach others also.

3 Suffer hardship with *me,* as a good soldier of Christ Jesus.

4 No soldier in active service entangles himself in the affairs of everyday life, so that he may please the one who enlisted him as a soldier.

5 And also if any one competes as an athlete, he does not win the prize unless he competes according to the rules.

6 The hard-working farmer ought to be the first to receive his share of the crops.

7 Consider what I say, for the Lord will give you understanding in everything.

8 Remember Jesus Christ, risen from the dead, descendant of David, according to my gospel,

9 for which I suffer hardship even to imprisonment as a criminal; but the word of God is not imprisoned.

10 For this reason I endure all things for the sake of those who are chosen, that they also may obtain the salvation which is in Christ Jesus *and* with *it* eternal glory.

11 It is a trustworthy statement:
For if we died with Him, we shall also live with Him;

12 If we endure, we shall also reign with Him;
If we deny Him, He also will deny us;

13 If we are faithless, He remains faithful; for He cannot deny Himself.

14 Remind *them* of these things, and solemnly charge *them* in the presence of God not to wrangle about words, which is useless, *and leads* to the ruin of the hearers.

15 Be diligent to present yourself approved to God as a workman who does not need to be ashamed, handling accurately the word of truth.

16 But avoid worldly *and* empty chatter, for it will lead to further ungodliness,

17 and their talk will spread like gangrene. Among them are Hymenaeus and Philetus,

18 *men* who have gone astray from

the truth saying that the resurrection has already taken place, and thus they upset the faith of some.

19 Nevertheless, the firm foundation of God stands, having this seal, "The Lord knows those who are His," and, "Let every one who names the name of the Lord abstain from wickedness."

20 Now in a large house there are not only gold and silver vessels, but also vessels of wood and of earthenware, and some to honor and some to dishonor.

21 Therefore, if a man cleanses himself from these *things,* he will be a vessel for honor, sanctified, useful to the Master, prepared for every good work.

22 Now flee from youthful lusts, and pursue righteousness, faith, love *and* peace, with those who call on the Lord from a pure heart.

23 But refuse foolish and ignorant speculations, knowing that they produce quarrels.

24 And the Lord's bond-servant must not be quarrelsome, but be kind to all, able to teach, patient when wronged,

25 with gentleness correcting those who are in opposition, if perhaps God may grant them repentance leading to the knowledge of the truth,

26 and they may come to their senses *and escape* from the snare of the devil, having been held captive by him to do his will.

CHAPTER 3

BUT realize this, that in the last days difficult times will come.

2 For men will be lovers of self, lovers of money, boastful, arrogant, revilers, disobedient to parents, ungrateful, unholy,

3 unloving, irreconcilable, malicious gossips, without self-control, brutal, haters of good,

4 treacherous, reckless, conceited, lovers of pleasure rather than lovers of God;

5 holding to a form of godliness, although they have denied its power; and avoid such men as these.

6 For among them are those who enter into households and captivate weak women weighed down with sins, led on by various impulses,

7 always learning and never able to come to the knowledge of the truth.

8 And just as Jannes and Jambres opposed Moses, so these *men* also oppose the truth, men of depraved mind, rejected as regards the faith.

9 But they will not make further progress; for their folly will be obvious to all, as also that of those *two* came to be.

10 But you followed my teaching, conduct, purpose, faith, patience, love, perseverance,

11 persecutions, sufferings, such as happened to me at Antioch, at Iconium *and* at Lystra; what persecutions I endured, and out of them all the Lord delivered me!

12 And indeed, all who desire to live godly in Christ Jesus will be persecuted.

13 But evil men and impostors will proceed *from bad* to worse, deceiving and being deceived.

14 You, however, continue in the things you have learned and become convinced of, knowing from whom you have learned *them;*

15 and that from childhood you have known the sacred writings which are able to give you the wisdom that leads to salvation through faith which is in Christ Jesus.

16 All Scripture is inspired by God and profitable for teaching, for reproof, for correction, for training in righteousness;

17 that the man of God may be adequate, equipped for every good work.

CHAPTER 4

I SOLEMNLY charge *you* in the presence of God and of Christ Jesus, who is to judge the living and the dead, and by His appearing and His kingdom:

2 preach the word; be ready in season *and* out of season; reprove, rebuke, exhort, with great patience and instruction.

3 For the time will come when they will not endure sound doctrine; but *wanting* to have their ears tickled, they will accumulate for themselves teachers in accordance to their own desires;

4 and will turn away their ears from the truth, and will turn aside to myths.

5 But you, be sober in all things, endure hardship, do the work of an evangelist, fulfill your ministry.

6 For I am already being poured out as a drink offering, and the time of my departure has come.

7 I have fought the good fight, I have finished the course, I have kept the faith;

8 in the future there is laid up for me the crown of righteousness, which the Lord, the righteous Judge, will award to me on that day; and not only to me, but also to all who have loved His appearing.

9 Make every effort to come to me soon;

10 for Demas, having loved this present world, has deserted me and gone to Thessalonica; Crescens *has* gone to Galatia, Titus to Dalmatia.

11 Only Luke is with me. Pick up Mark and bring him with you, for he is useful to me for service.

12 But Tychicus I have sent to Ephesus.

13 When you come bring the cloak which I left at Troas with Carpus, and the books, especially the parchments.

14 Alexander the coppersmith did me much harm; the Lord will repay him according to his deeds.

15 Be on guard against him yourself, for he vigorously opposed our teaching.

16 At my first defense no one supported me, but all deserted me; may it not be counted against them.

17 But the Lord stood with me, and strengthened me, in order that through me the proclamation might be fully accomplished, and that all the Gentiles might hear; and I was delivered out of the lion's mouth.

18 The Lord will deliver me from every evil deed, and will bring me safely to His heavenly kingdom; to Him *be* the glory forever and ever. Amen.

19 Greet Prisca and Aquila, and the household of Onesiphorus.

20 Erastus remained at Corinth, but Trophimus I left sick at Miletus.

21 Make every effort to come before winter. Eubulus greets you, also Pudens and Linus and Claudia and all the brethren.

22 The Lord be with your spirit. Grace be with you.

TITUS

PAUL, a bond-servant of God, and an apostle of Jesus Christ, for the faith of those chosen of God and the knowledge of the truth which is according to godliness,

2 in the hope of eternal life, which God, who cannot lie, promised long ages ago,

3 but at the proper time manifested, *even* His word, in the proclamation with which I was entrusted according to the commandment of God our Savior;

4 to Titus, my true child in a common faith: Grace and peace from God the Father and Christ Jesus our Savior.

5 For this reason I left you in Crete, that you might set in order what remains, and appoint elders in every city as I directed you,

6 namely, if any man be above reproach, the husband of one wife, having children who believe, not accused of dissipation or rebellion.

7 For the overseer must be above reproach as God's steward, not self-willed, not quick-tempered, not addicted to wine, not pugnacious, not fond of sordid gain,

'8 but hospitable, loving what is good, sensible, just, devout, self-controlled,

9 holding fast the faithful word which is in accordance with the teaching, that he may be able both to exhort in sound doctrine and to refute those who contradict.

10 For there are many rebellious men, empty talkers and deceivers, especially those of the circumcision,

11 who must be silenced because they are upsetting whole families, teaching things they should not *teach*, for the sake of sordid gain.

12 One of themselves, a prophet of their own, said, "Cretans are always liars, evil beasts, lazy gluttons."

13 This testimony is true. For this cause reprove them severely that they may be sound in the faith,

14 not paying attention to Jewish myths and commandments of men who turn away from the truth.

15 To the pure, all things are pure; but to those who are defiled and unbelieving, nothing is pure, but both their mind and their conscience are defiled.

16 They profess to know God, but by *their* deeds they deny *Him*, being detestable and disobedient, and worthless for any good deed.

CHAPTER 2

BUT as for you, speak the things which are fitting for sound doctrine.

2 Older men are to be temperate, dignified, sensible, sound in faith, in love, in perseverance.

3 Older women likewise are to be reverent in their behavior, not malicious gossips, nor enslaved to much wine, teaching what is good,

4 that they may encourage the young women to love their husbands, to love their children,

5 *to be* sensible, pure, workers at home, kind, being subject to their own husbands, that the word of God may not be dishonored.

6 Likewise urge the young men to be sensible;

7 in all things show yourself to be an example of good deeds, *with* purity in doctrine, dignified,

8 sound *in* speech which is beyond reproach, in order that the opponent may be put to shame, having nothing bad to say about us.

9 Urge bondslaves to be subject

to their own masters in everything, to be well-pleasing, not argumentative,

10 not pilfering, but showing all good faith that they may adorn the doctrine of God our Savior in every respect.

11 For the grace of God has appeared, bringing salvation to all men,

12 instructing us to deny ungodliness and worldly desires and to live sensibly, righteously and godly in the present age,

13 looking for the blessed hope and the appearing of the glory of our great God and Savior, Christ Jesus;

14 who gave Himself for us, that HE MIGHT REDEEM US FROM EVERY LAWLESS DEED and PURIFY FOR HIMSELF A PEOPLE FOR HIS OWN POSSESSION, zealous for good deeds.

15 These things speak and exhort and reprove with all authority. Let no one disregard you.

CHAPTER 3

REMIND them to be subject to rulers, to authorities, to be obedient, to be ready for every good deed,

2 to malign no one, to be uncontentious, gentle, showing every consideration for all men.

3 For we also once were foolish ourselves, disobedient, deceived, enslaved to various lusts and pleasures, spending our life in malice and envy, hateful, hating one another.

4 But when the kindness of God our Savior and *His* love for mankind appeared,

5 He saved us, not on the basis of deeds which we have done in righteousness, but according to His mercy, by the washing of regeneration and renewing by the Holy Spirit,

6 whom He poured out upon us richly through Jesus Christ our Savior,

7 that being justified by His grace we might be made heirs according to *the* hope of eternal life.

8 This is a trustworthy statement; and concerning these things I want you to speak confidently, so that those who have believed God may be careful to engage in good deeds. These things are good and profitable for men.

9 But shun foolish controversies and genealogies and strife and disputes about the Law; for they are unprofitable and worthless.

10 Reject a factious man after a first and second warning,

11 knowing that such a man is perverted and is sinning, being self-condemned.

12 When I send Artemas or Tychicus to you, make every effort to come to me at Nicopolis, for I have decided to spend the winter there.

13 Diligently help Zenas the lawyer and Apollos on their way so that nothing is lacking for them.

14 And let our *people* also learn to engage in good deeds to meet pressing needs, that they may not be unfruitful.

15 All who are with me greet you. Greet those who love us in *the* faith. Grace be with you all.

THE EPISTLE OF PAUL TO
PHILEMON

PAUL, a prisoner of Christ Jesus, and Timothy our brother, to Philemon our beloved *brother* and fellow-worker,

2 and to Apphia our sister, and to Archippus our fellow-soldier, and to the church in your house:

3 Grace to you and peace from God our Father and the Lord Jesus Christ.

4 I thank my God always, making mention of you in my prayers,

5 because I hear of your love, and of the faith which you have toward the Lord Jesus, and toward all the saints;

6 *and I pray* that the fellowship of your faith may become effective through the knowledge of every good thing which is in you for Christ's sake.

7 For I have come to have much joy and comfort in your love, because the hearts of the saints have been refreshed through you, brother.

8 Therefore, though I have enough confidence in Christ to order you *to do* that which is proper,

9 yet for love's sake I rather appeal *to you*—since I am such a person as Paul, the aged, and now also a prisoner of Christ Jesus—

10 I appeal to you for my child, whom I have begotten in my imprisonment, Onesimus,

11 who formerly was useless to you, but now is useful both to you and to me.

12 And I have sent him back to you in person, that is, *sending* my very heart,

13 whom I wished to keep with me, that in your behalf he might minister to me in my imprisonment for the gospel;

14 but without your consent I did not want to do anything, that your goodness should not be as it were by compulsion, but of your own free will.

15 For perhaps he was for this reason parted *from you* for a while, that you should have him back forever,

16 no longer as a slave, but more than a slave, a beloved brother, especially to me, but how much more to you, both in the flesh and in the Lord.

17 If then you regard me a partner, accept him as *you would* me.

18 But if he has wronged you in any way, or owes you anything, charge that to my account;

19 I, Paul, am writing this with my own hand, I will repay it (lest I should mention to you that you owe to me even your own self as well).

20 Yes, brother, let me benefit from you in the Lord; refresh my heart in Christ.

21 Having confidence in your obedience, I write to you, since I know that you will do even more than what I say.

22 And at the same time also prepare me a lodging; for I hope that through your prayers I shall be given to you.

23 Epaphras, my fellow-prisoner in Christ Jesus, greets you,

24 *as do* Mark, Aristarchus, Demas, Luke, my fellow-workers.

25 The grace of the Lord Jesus Christ be with your spirit.

THE EPISTLE TO THE

HEBREWS

G OD, after He spoke long ago to the fathers in the prophets in many portions and in many ways,

2 in these last days has spoken to us in *His* Son, whom He appointed heir of all things, through whom also He made the world.

3 And He is the radiance of His glory and the exact representation of His nature, and upholds all things by the word of His power. When He had made purification of sins, He sat down at the right hand of the Majesty on high;

4 having become as much better than the angels, as He has inherited a more excellent name than they.

5 For to which of the angels did He ever say,

"THOU ART MY SON,
TODAY I HAVE BEGOTTEN THEE"?

And again,

"I WILL BE A FATHER TO HIM,
AND HE SHALL BE A SON TO ME"?

6 And when He again brings the first-born into the world, He says,

"AND LET ALL THE ANGELS OF GOD WORSHIP HIM."

7 And of the angels He says,

"WHO MAKES HIS ANGELS WINDS,
AND HIS MINISTERS A FLAME OF FIRE."

8 But of the Son *He says*,

"THY THRONE, O GOD, IS FOR-EVER AND EVER,
AND THE RIGHTEOUS SCEPTER IS THE SCEPTER OF HIS KING-DOM.

9 "THOU HAST LOVED RIGHTEOUS-NESS AND HATED LAWLESS-NESS;
THEREFORE GOD, THY GOD, HATH ANOINTED THEE

WITH THE OIL OF GLADNESS ABOVE THY COMPANIONS."

10 And,

"THOU, LORD, IN THE BEGIN-NING DIDST LAY THE FOUNDA-TION OF THE EARTH,
AND THE HEAVENS ARE THE WORKS OF THY HANDS;

11 THEY WILL PERISH, BUT THOU REMAINEST;
AND THEY ALL WILL BECOME OLD AS A GARMENT,

12 AND AS A MANTLE THOU WILT ROLL THEM UP;
AS A GARMENT THEY WILL ALSO BE CHANGED.
BUT THOU ART THE SAME,
AND THY YEARS WILL NOT COME TO AN END."

13 But to which of the angels has He ever said,

"SIT AT MY RIGHT HAND,
UNTIL I MAKE THINE ENEMIES A FOOTSTOOL FOR THY FEET"?

14 Are they not all ministering spirits, sent out to render service for the sake of those who will inherit salvation?

CHAPTER 2

F OR this reason we must pay much closer attention to what we have heard, lest we drift away *from it.*

2 For if the word spoken through angels proved unalterable, and every transgression and disobedience received a just recompense,

3 how shall we escape if we ne-glect so great a salvation? After it was at the first spoken through the Lord, it was confirmed to us by those who heard,

4 God also bearing witness with them, both by signs and wonders and

by various miracles and by gifts of the Holy Spirit according to His own will.

5 For He did not subject to angels the world to come, concerning which we are speaking.

6 But one has testified somewhere, saying,

"WHAT IS MAN, THAT THOU RE-MEMBEREST HIM?

OR THE SON OF MAN, THAT THOU ART CONCERNED ABOUT HIM?

7 "THOU HAST MADE HIM FOR A LITTLE WHILE LOWER THAN THE ANGELS;

THOU HAST CROWNED HIM WITH GLORY AND HONOR,

AND HAST APPOINTED HIM OVER THE WORKS OF THY HANDS;

8 THOU HAST PUT ALL THINGS IN SUBJECTION UNDER HIS FEET."

For in subjecting all things to him, He left nothing that is not subject to him. But now we do not yet see all things subjected to him.

9 But we do see Him who has been made for a little while lower than the angels, *namely*, Jesus, because of the suffering of death crowned with glory and honor, that by the grace of God He might taste death for every one.

10 For it was fitting for Him, for whom are all things, and through whom are all things, in bringing many sons to glory, to perfect the author of their salvation through sufferings.

11 For both He who sanctifies and those who are sanctified are all from one *Father*; for which reason He is not ashamed to call them brethren,

12 saying,

"I WILL PROCLAIM THY NAME TO MY BRETHREN,

IN THE MIDST OF THE CONGRE-GATION I WILL SING THY PRAISE."

13 And again,

"I WILL PUT MY TRUST IN HIM."

And again,

"BEHOLD, I AND THE CHILDREN WHOM GOD HAS GIVEN ME."

14 Since then the children share in flesh and blood, He Himself likewise also partook of the same, that through death He might render powerless him who had the power of death, that is, the devil;

15 and might deliver those who through fear of death were subject to slavery all their lives.

16 For assuredly He does not give help to angels, but He gives help to the seed of Abraham.

17 Therefore, He had to be made like His brethren in all things, that He might become a merciful and faithful high priest in things pertaining to God, to make propitiation for the sins of the people.

18 For since He Himself was tempted in that which He has suffered, He is able to come to the aid of those who are tempted.

CHAPTER 3

THEREFORE, holy brethren, partakers of a heavenly calling, consider Jesus, the Apostle and High Priest of our confession.

2 He was faithful to Him who appointed Him, as Moses also was in all His house.

3 For He has been counted worthy of more glory than Moses, by just so much as the builder of the house has more honor than the house.

4 For every house is built by someone, but the builder of all things is God.

5 Now Moses was faithful in all His house as a servant, for a testimony of those things which were to be spoken later;

6 but Christ *was faithful* as a Son over His house whose house we are, if we hold fast our confidence and the boast of our hope firm until the end.

7 Therefore, just as the Holy Spirit says,

"TODAY IF YOU HEAR HIS VOICE,
8   DO NOT HARDEN YOUR HEARTS AS WHEN THEY PROVOKED ME,
    AS IN THE DAY OF TRIAL IN THE WILDERNESS,
9   WHERE YOUR FATHERS TRIED ME BY TESTING ME,
    AND SAW MY WORKS FOR FORTY YEARS.
10 "THEREFORE I WAS ANGRY WITH THIS GENERATION,
    AND SAID, 'THEY ALWAYS GO ASTRAY IN THEIR HEART;
    AND THEY DID NOT KNOW MY WAYS';
11 AS I SWORE IN MY WRATH, 'THEY SHALL NOT ENTER MY REST.' "

12 Take care, brethren, lest there should be in any one of you an evil, unbelieving heart, in falling away from the living God.

13 But encourage one another day after day, as long as it is *still* called "Today," lest any one of you be hardened by the deceitfulness of sin.

14 For we have become partakers of Christ, if we hold fast the beginning of our assurance firm until the end;

15 while it is said,

"TODAY IF YOU HEAR HIS VOICE,
    DO NOT HARDEN YOUR HEARTS,
    AS WHEN THEY PROVOKED ME."

16 For who provoked *Him* when they had heard? Indeed, did not all those who came out of Egypt *led* by Moses?

17 And with whom was He angry for forty years? Was it not with those who sinned, whose bodies fell in the wilderness?

18 And to whom did He swear that they should not enter His rest, but to those who were disobedient?

19 And *so* we see that they were not able to enter because of unbelief.

CHAPTER 4

THEREFORE, let us fear lest, while a promise remains of entering His rest, any one of you should seem to have come short of it.

2 For indeed we have had good news preached to us, just as they also; but the word they heard did not profit them, because it was not united by faith in those who heard.

3 For we who have believed enter that rest, just as He has said,

"AS I SWORE IN MY WRATH,
    THEY SHALL NOT ENTER MY REST,"

although His works were finished from the foundation of the world.

4 For He has thus said somewhere concerning the seventh *day*, "AND GOD RESTED ON THE SEVENTH DAY FROM ALL HIS WORKS";

5 and again in this *passage*, "THEY SHALL NOT ENTER MY REST."

6 Since therefore it remains for some to enter it, and those who formerly had good news preached to them failed to enter because of disobedience,

7 He again fixes a certain day, "Today," saying through David after so long a time just as has been said before,

"TODAY IF YOU HEAR HIS VOICE,
    DO NOT HARDEN YOUR HEARTS."

8 For if Joshua had given them rest, He would not have spoken of another day after that.

9 There remains therefore a Sabbath rest for the people of God.

10 For the one who has entered His rest has himself also rested from his works, as God did from His.

11 Let us therefore be diligent to enter that rest, lest anyone fall

through *following* the same example of disobedience.

12 For the word of God is living and active and sharper than any two-edged sword, and piercing as far as the division of soul and spirit, of both joints and marrow, and able to judge the thoughts and intentions of the heart.

13 And there is no creature hidden from His sight, but all things are open and laid bare to the eyes of Him with whom we have to do.

14 Since then we have a great high priest who has passed through the heavens, Jesus the Son of God, let us hold fast our confession.

15 For we do not have a high priest who cannot sympathize with our weaknesses, but one who has been tempted in all things as *we are,* yet without sin.

16 Let us therefore draw near with confidence to the throne of grace, that we may receive mercy and may find grace to help in time of need.

CHAPTER 5

FOR every high priest taken from among men is appointed on behalf of men in things pertaining to God, in order to offer both gifts and sacrifices for sins;

2 he can deal gently with the ignorant and misguided, since he himself also is beset with weakness;

3 and because of it he is obligated to offer *sacrifices* for sins, as for the people, so also for himself.

4 And no one takes the honor to himself, but *receives it* when he is called by God, even as Aaron was.

5 So also Christ did not glorify Himself so as to become a high priest, but He who said to Him,

"Thou art My Son,
   Today I have begotten Thee";

6 just as He says also in another *passage,*

"Thou art a priest forever
   According to the order of
   Melchizedek."

7 In the days of His flesh, when He offered up both prayers and supplications with loud crying and tears to Him who was able to save Him from death, and who was heard because of His piety,

8 although He was a Son, He learned obedience from the things which He suffered;

9 and having been made perfect, He became to all those who obey Him the source of eternal salvation;

10 being designated by God as a high priest according to the order of Melchizedek.

11 Concerning him we have much to say, and *it is* hard to explain, since you have become dull of hearing.

12 For though by this time you ought to be teachers, you have need again for some one to teach you the elementary principles of the oracles of God, and you have come to need milk and not solid food.

13 For every one who partakes *only* of milk is not accustomed to the word of righteousness, for he is a babe.

14 But solid food is for the mature, who because of practice have their senses trained to discern good and evil.

CHAPTER 6

THEREFORE leaving the elementary teaching about the Christ, let us press on to maturity, not laying again a foundation of repentance from dead works and of faith toward God,

2 of instruction about washings, and laying on of hands, and the resurrection of the dead, and eternal judgment.

3 And this we shall do, if God permits.

4 For in the case of those who have once been enlightened and have tasted of the heavenly gift and have been made partakers of the Holy Spirit,

5 and have tasted the good word of God and the powers of the age to come,

6 and *then* have fallen away, it is impossible to renew them again to repentance, since they again crucify to themselves the Son of God, and put Him to open shame.

7 For ground that drinks the rain which often falls upon it and brings forth vegetation useful to those for whose sake it is also tilled, receives a blessing from God;

8 but if it yields thorns and thistles, it is worthless and close to being cursed, and it ends up being burned.

9 But, beloved, we are convinced of better things concerning you, and things that accompany salvation, though we are speaking in this way.

10 For God is not unjust so as to forget your work and the love which you have shown toward His name, in having ministered and in still ministering to the saints.

11 And we desire that each one of you show the same diligence so as to realize the full assurance of hope until the end,

12 that you may not be sluggish, but imitators of those who through faith and patience inherit the promises.

13 For when God made the promise to Abraham, since He could swear by no one greater, He swore by Himself,

14 saying, "I WILL SURELY BLESS YOU, AND I WILL SURELY MULTIPLY YOU."

15 And thus, having patiently waited, he obtained the promise.

16 For men swear by one greater than *themselves*, and with them an oath *given* as confirmation is an end of every dispute.

17 In the same way God, desiring even more to show to the heirs of the promise the unchangeableness of His purpose, interposed with an oath,

18 in order that by two unchangeable things, in which it is impossible for God to lie, we may have strong encouragement, we who have fled for refuge in laying hold of the hope set before us.

19 This hope we have as an anchor of the soul, a *hope* both sure and steadfast and one which enters within the veil,

20 where Jesus has entered as a forerunner for us, having become a high priest forever according to the order of Melchizedek.

CHAPTER 7

FOR this Melchizedek, king of Salem, priest of the Most High God, who met Abraham as he was returning from the slaughter of the kings and blessed him,

2 to whom also Abraham apportioned a tenth part of all *the spoils*, was first of all, by the translation *of his name*, king of righteousness, and then also king of Salem, which is king of peace.

3 Without father, without mother, without genealogy, having neither beginning of days nor end of life, but made like the Son of God, he abides a priest perpetually.

4 Now observe how great this man was to whom Abraham, the patriarch, gave a tenth of the choicest spoils.

5 And those indeed of the sons of Levi who receive the priest's office have commandment in the Law to collect a tenth from the people, that is, from their brethren, although these are descended from Abraham.

6 But the one whose genealogy is

not traced from them collected a tenth from Abraham, and blessed the one who had the promises.

7 But without any dispute the lesser is blessed by the greater.

8 And in this case mortal men receive tithes, but in that case one *receives them*, of whom it is witnessed that he lives on.

9 And, so to speak, through Abraham even Levi, who received tithes, paid tithes,

10 for he was still in the loins of his father when Melchizedek met him.

11 Now if perfection was through the Levitical priesthood (for on the basis of it the people received the Law), what further need *was there* for another priest to arise according to the order of Melchizedek, and not be designated according to the order of Aaron?

12 For when the priesthood is changed, of necessity there takes place a change of law also.

13 For the one concerning whom these things are spoken belongs to another tribe, from which no one has officiated at the altar.

14 For it is evident that our Lord was descended from Judah, a tribe with reference to which Moses spoke nothing concerning priests.

15 And this is clearer still, if another priest arises according to the likeness of Melchizedek,

16 who has become *such* not on the basis of a law of physical requirement, but according to the power of an indestructible life.

17 For it is witnessed *of Him,*
"Thou art a priest forever
According to the order of
Melchizedek."

18 For, on the one hand, there is a setting aside of a former commandment because of its weakness and uselessness

19 (for the Law made nothing perfect), and on the other hand there is

a bringing in of a better hope, through which we draw near to God.

20 And inasmuch as *it was* not without an oath

21 (for they indeed became priests without an oath, but He with an oath through the One who said to Him,
"The Lord has sworn
And will not change His
mind,
'Thou art a priest forever' ");

22 so much the more also Jesus has become the guarantee of a better covenant.

23 And the *former* priests, on the one hand, existed in greater numbers, because they were prevented by death from continuing,

24 but He, on the other hand, because He abides forever, holds His priesthood permanently.

25 Hence, also, He is able to save forever those who draw near to God through Him, since He always lives to make intercession for them.

26 For it was fitting that we should have such a high priest, holy, innocent, undefiled, separated from sinners and exalted above the heavens;

27 who does not need daily, like those high priests, to offer up sacrifices, first for His own sins, and then for the *sins* of the people, because this He did once for all when He offered up Himself.

28 For the Law appoints men as high priests who are weak, but the word of the oath, which came after the Law, *appoints* a Son, made perfect forever.

Chapter 8

Now the main point in what has been said *is this:* we have such a high priest, who has taken His seat at the right hand of the throne of the Majesty in the heavens,

2 a minister in the sanctuary, and

in the true tabernacle, which the Lord pitched, not man.

3 For every high priest is appointed to offer both gifts and sacrifices; hence it is necessary that this *high priest* also have something to offer.

4 Now if He were on earth, He would not be a priest at all, since there are those who offer the gifts according to the Law;

5 who serve a copy and shadow of the heavenly things, just as Moses was warned *by God* when he was about to erect the tabernacle; for, "SEE," He says, "THAT YOU MAKE ALL THINGS ACCORDING TO THE PATTERN WHICH WAS SHOWN YOU ON THE MOUNTAIN."

6 But now He has obtained a more excellent ministry, by as much as He is also the mediator of a better covenant, which has been enacted on better promises.

7 For if that first *covenant* had been faultless, there would have been no occasion sought for a second.

8 For finding fault with them, He says,

> "BEHOLD, DAYS ARE COMING, SAYS THE LORD,
> WHEN I WILL EFFECT A NEW COVENANT
> WITH THE HOUSE OF ISRAEL AND WITH THE HOUSE OF JUDAH;

9 NOT LIKE THE COVENANT WHICH I MADE WITH THEIR FATHERS
> ON THE DAY WHEN I TOOK THEM BY THE HAND
> TO LEAD THEM OUT OF THE LAND OF EGYPT;
> FOR THEY DID NOT CONTINUE IN MY COVENANT,
> AND I DID NOT CARE FOR THEM, SAYS THE LORD.

10 "FOR THIS IS THE COVENANT THAT I WILL MAKE WITH THE HOUSE OF ISRAEL
> AFTER THOSE DAYS, SAYS THE LORD:

> I WILL PUT MY LAWS INTO THEIR MINDS,
> AND I WILL WRITE THEM UPON THEIR HEARTS.
> AND I WILL BE THEIR GOD, AND THEY SHALL BE MY PEOPLE.

11 "AND THEY SHALL NOT TEACH EVERY ONE HIS FELLOW-CITIZEN,
> AND EVERY ONE HIS BROTHER, SAYING, 'KNOW THE LORD,'
> FOR ALL SHALL KNOW ME,
> FROM THE LEAST TO THE GREATEST OF THEM.

12 "FOR I WILL BE MERCIFUL TO THEIR INIQUITIES,
> AND I WILL REMEMBER THEIR SINS NO MORE."

13 When He said, "A new *covenant*," He has made the first obsolete. But whatever is becoming obsolete and growing old is ready to disappear.

CHAPTER 9

NOW even the first *covenant* had regulations of divine worship and the earthly sanctuary.

2 For there was a tabernacle prepared, the outer one, in which *were* the lampstand and the table and the sacred bread; this is called the holy place.

3 And behind the second veil, there was a tabernacle which is called the Holy of Holies,

4 having a golden altar of incense and the ark of the covenant covered on all sides with gold, in which *was* a golden jar holding the manna, and Aaron's rod which budded, and the tables of the covenant.

5 And above it *were* the cherubim of glory overshadowing the mercy seat; but of these things we cannot now speak in detail.

6 Now when these things have been thus prepared, the priests are

continually entering the outer tabernacle, performing the divine worship,

7 but into the second only the high priest *enters*, once a year, not without *taking* blood, which he offers for himself and for the sins of the people committed in ignorance.

8 The Holy Spirit *is* signifying this, that the way into the holy place has not yet been disclosed, while the outer tabernacle is still standing,

9 which *is* a symbol for the time *then* present, according to which both gifts and sacrifices are offered which cannot make the worshiper perfect in conscience,

10 since they *relate* only to food and drink and various washings, regulations for the body imposed until a time of reformation.

11 But when Christ appeared *as* a high priest of the good things to come, He *entered* through the greater and more perfect tabernacle, not made with hands, that is to say, not of this creation;

12 and not through the blood of goats and calves, but through His own blood, He entered the holy place once for all, having obtained eternal redemption.

13 For if the blood of goats and bulls and the ashes of a heifer sprinkling those who have been defiled, sanctify for the cleansing of the flesh,

14 how much more will the eternal Spirit offered Himself without blemish to God, cleanse your conscience from dead works to serve the living God?

15 And for this reason He is the mediator of a new covenant, in order that since a death has taken place for the redemption of the transgressions that were *committed* under the first covenant, those who have been called may receive the promise of the eternal inheritance.

16 For where a covenant is, there must of necessity be the death of the one who made it.

17 For a covenant is valid *only* when men are dead, for it is never in force while the one who made it lives.

18 Therefore even the first *covenant* was not inaugurated without blood.

19 For when every commandment had been spoken by Moses to all the people according to the Law, he took the blood of the calves and the goats, with water and scarlet wool and hyssop, and sprinkled both the book itself and all the people,

20 saying, "THIS IS THE BLOOD OF THE COVENANT WHICH GOD COMMANDED YOU."

21 And in the same way he sprinkled both the tabernacle and all the vessels of the ministry with the blood.

22 And according to the Law, *one may* almost *say*, all things are cleansed with blood, and without shedding of blood there is no forgiveness.

23 Therefore it was necessary for the copies of the things in the heavens to be cleansed with these, but the heavenly things themselves with better sacrifices than these.

24 For Christ did not enter a holy place made with hands, a *mere* copy of the true one, but into heaven itself, now to appear in the presence of God for us;

25 nor was it that He should offer Himself often, as the high priest enters the holy place year by year with blood not his own.

26 Otherwise, He would have needed to suffer often since the foundation of the world; but now once at the consummation He has been manifested to put away sin by the sacrifice of Himself.

27 And inasmuch as it is appointed for men to die once, and after this *comes* judgment;

28 so Christ also, having been of-

fered once to bear the sins of many, shall appear a second time, not to bear sin, to those who eagerly await Him, for salvation.

CHAPTER 10

For the Law, since it has *only* a shadow of the good things to come *and* not the very form of things, can never by the same sacrifices year by year, which they offer continually, make perfect those who draw near.

2 Otherwise, would they not have ceased to be offered, because the worshipers, having once been cleansed, would no longer have had consciousness of sins?

3 But in those *sacrifices* there is a reminder of sins year by year.

4 For it is impossible for the blood of bulls and goats to take away sins.

5 Therefore, when He comes into the world, He says,
"SACRIFICE AND OFFERING THOU HAST NOT DESIRED,
BUT A BODY THOU HAST PREPARED FOR ME;

6 IN WHOLE BURNT OFFERINGS AND *sacrifices* FOR SIN THOU HAST TAKEN NO PLEASURE.

7 "THEN I SAID, 'BEHOLD, I HAVE COME
(IN THE ROLL OF THE BOOK IT IS WRITTEN OF ME)
TO DO THY WILL, O GOD.' "

8 After saying above, "SACRIFICES AND OFFERINGS AND WHOLE BURNT OFFERINGS AND *sacrifices* FOR SIN THOU HAST NOT DESIRED, NOR HAST THOU TAKEN PLEASURE *in them*" (which are offered according to the Law),

9 then He said, "BEHOLD, I HAVE COME TO DO THY WILL." He takes away the first in order to establish the second.

10 By this will we have been sanctified through the offering of the body of Jesus Christ once for all.

11 And every priest stands daily ministering and offering time after time the same sacrifices, which can never take away sins;

12 but He, having offered one sacrifice for sins for all time, sat down at the right hand of God,

13 waiting from that time onward UNTIL HIS ENEMIES BE MADE A FOOTSTOOL FOR HIS FEET.

14 For by one offering He has perfected for all time those who are sanctified.

15 And the Holy Spirit also bears witness to us; for after saying,
16 "THIS IS THE COVENANT THAT I WILL MAKE WITH THEM
AFTER THOSE DAYS, SAYS THE LORD:
I WILL PUT MY LAWS UPON THEIR HEART,
AND UPON THEIR MIND I WILL WRITE THEM,"
He then says,
17 "AND THEIR SINS AND THEIR LAWLESS DEEDS
I WILL REMEMBER NO MORE."

18 Now where there is forgiveness of these things, there is no longer *any* offering for sin.

19 Since therefore, brethren, we have confidence to enter the holy place by the blood of Jesus,

20 by a new and living way which He inaugurated for us through the veil, that is, His flesh,

21 and since *we have* a great priest over the house of God,

22 let us draw near with a sincere heart in full assurance of faith, having our hearts sprinkled *clean* from an evil conscience and our body washed with pure water.

23 Let us hold fast the confession of our hope without wavering, for He who promised is faithful;

24 and let us consider how to stimulate one another to love and good deeds,

25 not forsaking our own assembling together, as is the habit of some,

but encouraging *one another*; and all the more, as you see the day drawing near.

26 For if we go on sinning willfully after receiving the knowledge of the truth, there no longer remains a sacrifice for sins,

27 but a certain terrifying expectation of judgment, and THE FURY OF A FIRE WHICH WILL CONSUME THE ADVERSARIES.

28 Anyone who has set aside the Law of Moses dies without mercy on *the testimony of* two or three witnesses.

29 How much severer punishment do you think he will deserve who has trampled under foot the Son of God, and has regarded as unclean the blood of the covenant by which he was sanctified, and has insulted the Spirit of grace?

30 For we know Him who said, "VENGEANCE IS MINE, I WILL REPAY." And again, "THE LORD WILL JUDGE HIS PEOPLE."

31 It is a terrifying thing to fall into the hands of the living God.

32 But remember the former days, when, after being enlightened, you endured a great conflict of sufferings,

33 partly, by being made a public spectacle through reproaches and tribulations, and partly by becoming sharers with those who were so treated.

34 For you showed sympathy to the prisoners, and accepted joyfully the seizure of your property, knowing that you have for yourselves a better possession and an abiding one.

35 Therefore, do not throw away your confidence, which has a great reward.

36 For you have need of endurance, so that when you have done the will of God, you may receive what was promised.

37   FOR YET IN A VERY LITTLE WHILE,

HE WHO IS COMING WILL COME, AND WILL NOT DELAY.

38   BUT MY RIGHTEOUS ONE SHALL LIVE BY FAITH;
AND IF HE SHRINKS BACK, MY SOUL HAS NO PLEASURE IN HIM.

39 But we are not of those who shrink back to destruction, but of those who have faith to the preserving of the soul.

CHAPTER 11

NOW faith is the assurance of *things* hoped for, the conviction of things not seen.

2 For by it the men of old gained approval.

3 By faith we understand that the worlds were prepared by the word of God, so that what is seen was not made out of things which are visible.

4 By faith Abel offered to God a better sacrifice than Cain, through which he obtained the testimony that he was righteous, God testifying about his gifts, and through faith, though he is dead, he still speaks.

5 By faith Enoch was taken up so that he should not see death; and he was not found because God took him up; for he obtained the witness that before his being taken up he was pleasing to God.

6 And without faith it is impossible to please *Him*, for he who comes to God must believe that He is, and *that* He is a rewarder of those who seek Him.

7 By faith Noah, being warned *by God* about things not yet seen, in reverence prepared an ark for the salvation of his household, by which he condemned the world, and became an heir of the righteousness which is according to faith.

8 By faith Abraham, when he was called, obeyed by going out to a place which he was to receive for an inheritance; and he went out, not knowing where he was going.

9 By faith he lived as an alien in the land of promise, as in a foreign *land*, dwelling in tents with Isaac and Jacob, fellow-heirs of the same promise;

10 for he was looking for the city which has foundations, whose architect and builder is God.

11 By faith even Sarah herself received ability to conceive, even beyond the proper time of life, since she considered Him faithful who had promised;

12 therefore, also, there was born of one man, and him as good as dead at that, *as many descendants* AS THE STARS OF HEAVEN IN NUMBER, AND INNUMERABLE AS THE SAND WHICH IS BY THE SEASHORE.

13 All these died in faith, without receiving the promises, but having seen them and having welcomed them from a distance, and having confessed that they were strangers and exiles on the earth.

14 For those who say such things make it clear that they are seeking a country of their own.

15 And indeed if they had been thinking of that *country* from which they went out, they would have had opportunity to return.

16 But as it is, they desire a better *country*, that is a heavenly one. Therefore God is not ashamed to be called their God; for He has prepared a city for them.

17 By faith Abraham, when he was tested, offered up Isaac; and he who had received the promises was offering up his only begotten *son*;

18 *it was he* to whom it was said, "IN ISAAC YOUR SEED SHALL BE CALLED."

19 He considered that God is able to raise *men* even from the dead; from which he also received him back as a type.

20 By faith Isaac blessed Jacob

and Esau, even regarding things to come.

21 By faith Jacob, as he was dying, blessed each of the sons of Joseph, and worshiped, *leaning* on the top of his staff.

22 By faith Joseph, when he was dying, made mention of the exodus of the sons of Israel, and gave orders concerning his bones.

23 By faith Moses, when he was born, was hidden for three months by his parents, because they saw he was a beautiful child; and they were not afraid of the king's edict.

24 By faith Moses, when he had grown up, refused to be called the son of Pharaoh's daughter;

25 choosing rather to endure ill-treatment with the people of God, than to enjoy the passing pleasures of sin;

26 considering the reproach of Christ greater riches than the treasures of Egypt; for he was looking to the reward.

27 By faith he left Egypt, not fearing the wrath of the king; for he endured, as seeing Him who is unseen.

28 By faith he kept the Passover and the sprinkling of the blood, so that he who destroyed the first-born might not touch them.

29 By faith they passed through the Red Sea as though *they were passing* through dry land; and the Egyptians, when they attempted it, were drowned.

30 By faith the walls of Jericho fell down, after they had been encircled for seven days.

31 By faith Rahab the harlot did not perish along with those who were disobedient, after she had welcomed the spies in peace.

32 And what more shall I say? For time will fail me if I tell of Gideon, Barak, Samson, Jephthah, of David and Samuel and the prophets,

33 who by faith conquered king-

doms, performed *acts of* righteousness, obtained promises, shut the mouths of lions,

34 quenched the power of fire, escaped the edge of the sword, from weakness were made strong, became mighty in war, put foreign armies to flight.

35 Women received *back* their dead by resurrection; and others were tortured, not accepting their release, in order that they might obtain a better resurrection;

36 and others experienced mockings and scourgings, yes, also chains and imprisonment.

37 They were stoned, they were sawn in two, they were tempted, they were put to death with the sword; they went about in sheepskins, in goatskins, being destitute, afflicted, ill-treated

38 (*men* of whom the world was not worthy), wandering in deserts and mountains and caves and holes in the ground.

39 And all these, having gained approval through their faith, did not receive what was promised,

40 because God had provided something better for us, so that apart from us they should not be made perfect.

CHAPTER 12

THEREFORE, since we have so great a cloud of witnesses surrounding us, let us also lay aside every encumbrance, and the sin which so easily entangles us, and let us run with endurance the race that is set before us,

2 fixing our eyes on Jesus, the author and perfecter of faith, who for the joy set before Him endured the cross, despising the shame, and has sat down at the right hand of the throne of God.

3 For consider Him who has endured such hostility by sinners against

Himself, so that you may not grow weary and lose heart.

4 You have not yet resisted to the point of shedding blood in your striving against sin;

5 and you have forgotten the exhortation which is addressed to you as sons,

"MY SON, DO NOT REGARD LIGHTLY THE DISCIPLINE OF THE LORD,

NOR FAINT WHEN YOU ARE REPROVED BY HIM;

6 FOR THOSE WHOM THE LORD LOVES HE DISCIPLINES,

AND HE SCOURGES EVERY SON WHOM HE RECEIVES."

7 It is for discipline that you endure; God deals with you as with sons; for what son is there whom *his* father does not discipline?

8 But if you are without discipline, of which all have become partakers, then you are illegitimate children and not sons.

9 Furthermore, we had earthly fathers to discipline us, and we respected them; shall we not much rather be subject to the Father of spirits, and live?

10 For they disciplined us for a short time as seemed best to them, but He disciplines us for *our* good, that we may share His holiness.

11 All discipline for the moment seems not to be joyful, but sorrowful; yet to those who have been trained by it, afterwards it yields the peaceful fruit of righteousness.

12 Therefore, strengthen the hands that are weak and the knees that are feeble,

13 and make straight paths for your feet, so that *the limb* which is lame may not be put out of joint, but rather be healed.

14 Pursue peace with all men, and the sanctification without which no one will see the Lord.

15 See to it that no one comes short of the grace of God; that no root of bitterness springing up causes trouble, and by it many be defiled;

16 that *there be* no immoral or godless person like Esau, who sold his own birthright for a single meal.

17 For you know that even afterwards, when he desired to inherit the blessing, he was rejected, for he found no place for repentance, though he sought for it with tears.

18 For you have not come to *a mountain* that may be touched and to a blazing fire, and to darkness and gloom and whirlwind,

19 and to the blast of a trumpet and the sound of words which *sound was such that* those who heard begged that no further word should be spoken to them.

20 For they could not bear the command, "IF EVEN A BEAST TOUCHES THE MOUNTAIN, IT WILL BE STONED."

21 And so terrible was the sight, *that* Moses said, "I AM FULL OF FEAR AND TREMBLING."

22 But you have come to Mount Zion and to the city of the living God, the heavenly Jerusalem, and to myriads of angels,

SCRIPTURE No. 5, SEC. 3

23 to the general assembly and church of the first-born who are enrolled in heaven, and to God, the judge of all, and to the spirits of righteous men made perfect, (r5)

24 and to Jesus, the mediator of a new covenant, and to the sprinkled blood, which speaks better than *the blood* of Abel.

25 See to it that you do not refuse Him who is speaking. For if those did not escape when they refused him who warned *them* on earth, much less *shall* we *escape* who turn away from Him who *warns* from heaven.

26 And His voice shook the earth then, but now He has promised, saying, "YET ONCE MORE I WILL SHAKE NOT ONLY THE EARTH, BUT ALSO THE HEAVEN."

27 And this *expression*, "Yet once more," denotes the removing of those things which can be shaken, as of created things, in order that those things which cannot be shaken may remain.

28 Therefore, since we receive a kingdom which cannot be shaken, let us show gratitude, by which we may offer to God an acceptable service with reverence and awe;

29 for our God is a consuming fire.

CHAPTER 13

LET love of the brethren continue.

2 Do not neglect to show hospitality to strangers, for by this some have entertained angels without knowing it.

3 Remember the prisoners, as

(r5) REFERENCE NO. 5, SEC. 3—
WHO ARE THE PEOPLE WHOSE NAMES ARE WRITTEN IN HEAVEN?

"The general assembly and church of the first-born who are enrolled in heaven."

It is by faith in Christ Jesus you become a member of the family of the "first born."

"That which is born of the Spirit is spirit" and "you are all sons of God through faith in Christ Jesus." When you receive Him you will be "born of the Spirit." You can only say, "Jesus is Lord" . . . "by the Holy Spirit." Then and only then Jesus confesses you, and your name is enrolled in Heaven.

Do you see your relationship in the family of God would assure you that your name would be enrolled in Heaven? If so, say:

"I acknowledge that I must be born of the Holy Spirit to be a member of God's family and then I will know my name is enrolled in heaven."

Now turn to page 349, Scripture No. 6, Sec. 3, Rev. 21:27.

though in prison with them, and those who are ill-treated, since you yourselves also are in the body.

4 *Let* marriage *be held* in honor among all, and let the *marriage* bed *be* undefiled; for fornicators and adulterers God will judge.

5 Let your way of life be free from the love of money, being content with what you have; for He Himself has said, "I WILL NEVER DESERT YOU, NOR WILL I EVER FORSAKE YOU,"

6 so that we confidently say,

"THE LORD IS MY HELPER, I WILL NOT BE AFRAID.

WHAT SHALL MAN DO TO ME?"

7 Remember those who led you, who spoke the word of God to you; and considering the outcome of their way of life, imitate their faith.

8 Jesus Christ *is* the same yesterday and today, *yes* and forever.

9 Do not be carried away by varied and strange teachings; for it is good for the heart to be strengthened by grace, not by foods, through which those who were thus occupied were not benefited.

10 We have an altar, from which those who serve the tabernacle have no right to eat.

11 For the bodies of those animals whose blood is brought into the holy place by the high priest *as an offering* for sin, are burned outside the camp.

12 Therefore Jesus also, that He might sanctify the people through His own blood, suffered outside the gate.

13 Hence, let us go out to Him outside the camp, bearing His reproach.

14 For here we do not have a lasting city, but we are seeking *the city* which is to come.

15 Through Him, then let us continually offer up a sacrifice of praise to God, that is, the fruit of lips that give thanks to His name.

16 And do not neglect doing good and sharing; for with such sacrifices God is pleased.

17 Obey your leaders, and submit *to them*; for they keep watch over your souls, as those who will give an account. Let them do this with joy and not with grief, for this would be unprofitable for you.

18 Pray for us, for we are sure that we have a good conscience, desiring to conduct ourselves honorably in all things.

19 And I urge *you* all the more to do this, that I may be restored to you the sooner.

20 Now the God of peace, who brought up from the dead the great Shepherd of the sheep through the blood of the eternal covenant, *even* Jesus our Lord,

21 equip you in every good thing to do His will, working in us that which is pleasing in His sight, through Jesus Christ, to whom *be* the glory forever and ever. Amen.

22 But I urge you, brethren, bear with this word of exhortation, for I have written to you briefly.

23 Take notice that our brother Timothy has been released, with whom, if he comes soon, I shall see you.

24 Greet all of your leaders and all the saints. Those from Italy greet you.

25 Grace be with you all.

THE EPISTLE OF
JAMES

JAMES, a bond-servant of God and of the Lord Jesus Christ, to the twelve tribes who are dispersed abroad, greetings.

2 Consider it all joy, my brethren, when you encounter various trials,

3 knowing that the testing of your faith produces endurance.

4 And let endurance have *its* perfect result, that you may be perfect and complete, lacking in nothing.

5 But if any of you lacks wisdom, let him ask of God, who gives to all men generously and without reproach, and it will be given to him.

6 But let him ask in faith without any doubting, for the one who doubts is like the surf of the sea driven and tossed by the wind.

7 For let not that man expect that he will receive anything from the Lord,

8 *being* a double-minded man, unstable in all his ways.

9 But let the brother of humble circumstances glory in his high position;

10 and *let* the rich man *glory* in his humiliation, because like flowering grass he will pass away.

11 For the sun rises with a scorching wind, and withers the grass; and its flower falls off, and the beauty of its appearance is destroyed; so too the rich man in the midst of his pursuits will fade away.

12 Blessed is a man who perseveres under trial; for once he has been approved, he will receive the crown of life, which *the Lord* has promised to those who love Him.

13 Let no one say when he is tempted, "I am being tempted by God"; for God cannot be tempted by evil, and He Himself does not tempt any one.

14 But each one is tempted when he is carried away and enticed by his own lust.

15 Then when lust has conceived, it gives birth to sin; and when sin is accomplished, it brings forth death.

16 Do not be deceived, my beloved brethren.

17 Every good thing bestowed and every perfect gift is from above, coming down from the Father of lights, with whom there is no variation, or shifting shadow.

18 In the exercise of His will He brought us forth by the word of truth, so that we might be, as it were, the first fruits among His creatures.

19 *This* you know, my beloved brethren. But let every one be quick to hear, slow to speak *and* slow to anger;

20 for the anger of man does not achieve the righteousness of God.

21 Therefore putting aside all filthiness and *all* that remains of wickedness, in humility receive the word implanted, which is able to save your souls.

22 But prove yourselves doers of the word, and not merely hearers who delude themselves.

23 For if any one is a hearer of the word and not a doer, he is like a man who looks at his natural face in a mirror;

24 for *once* he has looked at himself and gone away, he has immediately forgotten what kind of person he was.

25 But one who looks intently at the perfect law, the *law* of liberty, and abides by it, not having become a forgetful hearer but an effectual doer, this man shall be blessed in what he does.

26 If any one thinks himself to be religious, and yet does not bridle his tongue but deceives his *own* heart, this man's religion is worthless.

27 This is pure and undefiled religion in the sight of *our* God and Father, to visit orphans and widows in their distress, *and* to keep oneself unstained by the world.

CHAPTER 2

MY brethren, do not hold your faith in our glorious Lord Jesus Christ with *an attitude of* personal favoritism.

2 For if a man comes into your assembly with a gold ring and dressed in fine clothes, and there also comes in a poor man in dirty clothes,

3 and you pay special attention to the one who is wearing the fine clothes, and say, "You sit here in a good place," and you say to the poor man, "You stand over there, or sit down by my footstool,"

4 have you not made distinctions among yourselves, and become judges with evil motives?

5 Listen, my beloved brethren: did not God choose the poor of this world *to be* rich in faith and heirs of the kingdom which He promised to those who love Him?

6 But you have dishonored the poor man. Is it not the rich who oppress you and personally drag you into court?

7 Do they not blaspheme the fair name by which you have been called?

8 If, however, you are fulfilling the royal law, according to the Scripture, "YOU SHALL LOVE YOUR NEIGHBOR AS YOURSELF," you are doing well.

9 But if you show partiality, you are committing sin *and* are convicted by the law as transgressors.

10 For whoever keeps the whole law and yet stumbles in one *point*, he has become guilty of all.

11 For He who said, "DO NOT COMMIT ADULTERY," also said, "DO NOT COMMIT MURDER." Now if you do not commit adultery, but do commit murder, you have become a transgressor of the law.

12 So speak and so act, as those who are to be judged by *the* law of liberty.

13 For judgment *will be* merciless to one who has shown no mercy; mercy triumphs over judgment.

14 What use is it, my brethren, if a man says he has faith, but he has no works? Can that faith save him?

15 If a brother or sister is without clothing and in need of daily food,

16 and one of you says to them, "Go in peace, be warmed and be filled," and yet you do not give them what is necessary for *their* body, what use is that?

17 Even so faith, if it has no works, is dead, *being* by itself.

18 But someone may *well* say, "You have faith, and I have works; show me your faith without the works, and I will show you my faith by my works."

19 You believe that God is one. You do well; the demons also believe, and shudder.

20 But are you willing to recognize, you foolish fellow, that faith without works is useless?

21 Was not Abraham our father justified by works, when he offered up Isaac his son on the altar?

22 You see that faith was working with his works, and as a result of the works, faith was perfected;

23 and the Scripture was fulfilled which says, "AND ABRAHAM BELIEVED GOD, AND IT WAS RECKONED TO HIM AS RIGHTEOUSNESS," and he was called the friend of God.

24 You see that a man is justified by works, and not by faith alone.

25 And in the same way was not

Rahab the harlot also justified by works, when she received the messengers and sent them out by another way?

26 For just as the body without *the* spirit is dead, so also faith without works is dead.

CHAPTER 3

LET not many *of you* become teachers, my brethren, knowing that as such we shall incur a stricter judgment.

2 For we all stumble in many *ways*. If any one does not stumble in what he says, he is a perfect man, able to bridle the whole body as well.

3 Now if we put the bits into the horses' mouths so that they may obey us, we direct their entire body as well.

4 Behold, the ships also, though they are so great and are driven by strong winds, are still directed by a very small rudder, wherever the inclination of the pilot desires.

5 So also the tongue is a small part of the body, and *yet* it boasts of great things. Behold, how great a forest is set aflame by such a small fire!

6 And the tongue is a fire, the *very* world of iniquity; the tongue is set among our members as that which defiles the entire body, and sets on fire the course of *our* life, and is set on fire by hell.

7 For every species of beasts and birds, of reptiles and creatures of the sea, is tamed, and has been tamed by the human race.

8 But no one can tame the tongue; *it is* a restless evil *and* full of deadly poison.

9 With it we bless *our* Lord and Father; and with it we curse men, who have been made in the likeness of God;

10 from the same mouth come *both* blessing and cursing. My brethren, these things ought not to be this way.

11 Does a fountain send out from the same opening *both* fresh and bitter *water?*

12 Can a fig tree, my brethren, produce olives, or a vine produce figs? Neither *can* salt water produce fresh.

13 Who among you is wise and understanding? Let him show by his good behavior his deeds in the gentleness of wisdom.

14 But if you have bitter jealousy and selfish ambition in your heart, do not be arrogant and *so* lie against the truth.

15 This wisdom is not that which comes down from above, but is earthly, natural, demonic.

16 For where jealousy and selfish ambition exist, there is disorder and every evil thing.

17 But the wisdom from above is first pure, then peaceable, gentle, reasonable, full of mercy and good fruits, unwavering, without hypocrisy.

18 And the seed whose fruit is righteousness is sown in peace by those who make peace.

CHAPTER 4

WHAT is the source of quarrels and conflicts among you? Is not the source your pleasures that wage war in your members?

2 You lust and do not have; *so* you commit murder. And you are envious and cannot obtain; *so* you fight and quarrel. You do not have because you do not ask.

3 You ask and do not receive, because you ask with wrong motives, so that you may spend *it* on your pleasures.

4 You adulteresses, do you not know that friendship with the world is hostility toward God? Therefore whoever wishes to be a friend of the world makes himself an enemy of God.

5 Or do you think that the Scripture speaks to no purpose: "He jealously desires the spirit which He has made to dwell in us"?

6 But He gives a greater grace. Therefore *it* says, "GOD IS OPPOSED TO THE PROUD, BUT GIVES GRACE TO THE HUMBLE."

7 Submit therefore to God. Resist the devil and he will flee from you.

8 Draw near to God and He will draw near to you. Cleanse your hands, you sinners; and purify your hearts, you double-minded.

9 Be miserable and mourn and weep; let your laughter be turned into mourning, and your joy to gloom.

10 Humble yourselves in the presence of the Lord, and He will exalt you.

11 Do not speak against one another, brethren. He who speaks against a brother, or judges his brother, speaks against the law, and judges the law; but if you judge the law, you are not a doer of the law, but a judge *of it*.

12 There is *only* one Lawgiver and Judge, the One who is able to save and to destroy; but who are you who judge your neighbor?

13 Come now, you who say, "Today or tomorrow, we shall go to such and such a city, and spend a year there and engage in business and make a profit."

14 Yet you do not know what your life will be like tomorrow. You are *just* a vapor that appears for a little while and then vanishes away.

15 Instead, *you* ought to say, "If the Lord wills, we shall live and also do this or that."

16 But as it is, you boast in your arrogance; all such boasting is evil.

17 Therefore, to one who knows *the* right thing to do, and does not do it, to him it is sin.

CHAPTER 5

COME now, you rich, weep and howl for your miseries which are coming upon you.

2 Your riches have rotted and your garments have become motheaten.

3 Your gold and your silver have rusted; and their rust will be a witness against you and will consume your flesh like fire. It is in the last days that you have stored up your treasure!

4 Behold, the pay of the laborers who mowed your fields, *and* which has been withheld by you, cries out *against you*; and the outcry of those who did the harvesting has reached the ears of the Lord of Sabaoth.

5 You have lived luxuriously on the earth and led a life of wanton pleasure; you have fattened your hearts in a day of slaughter.

6 You have condemned and put to death the righteous *man*; he does not resist you.

7 Be patient, therefore, brethren, until the coming of the Lord. Behold, the farmer waits for the precious produce of the soil, being patient about it, until it gets the early and late rains.

8 You too be patient; strengthen your hearts, for the coming of the Lord is at hand.

9 Do not complain, brethren, against one another, that you yourselves may not be judged; behold, the Judge is standing right at the door.

10 As an example, brethren, of suffering and patience, take the prophets who spoke in the name of the Lord.

11 Behold, we count those blessed who endured. You have heard of the endurance of Job and have seen the outcome of the Lord's dealings, that the Lord is full of compassion and *is* merciful.

12 But above all, my brethren, do not swear, either by heaven or by

earth or with any other oath; but let your yes be yes, and your no, no; so that you may not fall under judgment.

13 Is anyone among you suffering? Let him pray. Is anyone cheerful? Let him sing praises.

14 Is anyone among you sick? Let him call for the elders of the church, and let them pray over him, anointing him with oil in the name of the Lord;

15 and the prayer offered in faith will restore the one who is sick, and the Lord will raise him up, and if he has committed sins, they will be forgiven him.

16 Therefore, confess your sins to one another, and pray for one another, so that you may be healed. The effective prayer of a righteous man can accomplish much.

17 Elijah was a man with a nature like ours, and he prayed earnestly that it might not rain; and it did not rain on the earth for three years and six months.

18 And he prayed again, and the sky poured rain, and the earth produced its fruit.

19 My brethren, if any among you strays from the truth, and one turns him back,

20 let him know that he who turns a sinner from the error of his way will save his soul from death, and will cover a multitude of sins.

THE FIRST EPISTLE OF

PETER

P ETER, an apostle of Jesus Christ, to those who reside as aliens, scattered throughout Pontus, Galatia, Cappadocia, Asia, and Bithynia, who are chosen

2 according to the foreknowledge of God the Father, by the sanctifying work of the Spirit, that you may obey Jesus Christ and be sprinkled with His blood: May grace and peace be yours in fullest measure.

3 Blessed be the God and Father of our Lord Jesus Christ, who according to His great mercy has caused us to be born again to a living hope through the resurrection of Jesus Christ from the dead,

4 to *obtain* an inheritance *which is* imperishable and undefiled and will not fade away, reserved in heaven for you,

5 who are protected by the power of God through faith for a salvation ready to be revealed in the last time.

6 In this you greatly rejoice, even though now for a little while, if necessary, you have been distressed by various trials,

7 that the proof of your faith, *being* more precious than gold which is perishable, even though tested by fire, may be found to result in praise and glory and honor at the revelation of Jesus Christ;

8 and though you have not seen Him, you love Him, and though you do not see Him now, but believe in Him, you greatly rejoice with joy inexpressible and full of glory,

9 obtaining as the outcome of your faith the salvation of your souls.

10 As to this salvation, the prophets who prophesied of the grace that *would come* to you made careful search and inquiry,

11 seeking to know what person or time the Spirit of Christ within them was indicating as He predicted the sufferings of Christ and the glories to follow.

12 It was revealed to them that they were not serving themselves, but you, in these things which now have been announced to you through those who preached the gospel to you by the Holy Spirit sent from heaven—things into which angels long to look.

13 Therefore, gird your minds for action, keep sober *in spirit*, fix your hope completely on the grace to be brought to you at the revelation of Jesus Christ.

14 As obedient children, do not be conformed to the former lusts *which were yours* in your ignorance,

15 but like the Holy One who called you, be holy yourselves also in all *your* behavior;

16 because it is written, "You SHALL BE HOLY, FOR I AM HOLY."

17 And if you address as Father the One who impartially judges according to each man's work, conduct yourselves in fear during the time of your stay *upon earth;*

18 knowing that you were not redeemed with perishable things like silver or gold from your futile way of life inherited from your forefathers,

19 but with precious blood, as of a lamb unblemished and spotless, *the blood* of Christ.

20 For He was foreknown before the foundation of the world, but has appeared in these last times for the sake of you

21 who through Him are believers in God, who raised Him from the dead and gave Him glory, so that your faith and hope are in God.

22 Since you have in obedience to the truth purified your souls for a sincere love of the brethren, fervently love one another from the heart,

23 for you have been born again not of seed which is perishable but imperishable, *that is*, through the living and abiding word of God.

24 For,

"ALL FLESH IS LIKE GRASS,
AND ALL ITS GLORY LIKE THE
  FLOWER OF GRASS.
THE GRASS WITHERS,
AND THE FLOWER FALLS OFF,
25 BUT THE WORD OF THE LORD
  ABIDES FOREVER."

And this is the word which was preached to you.

CHAPTER 2

THEREFORE, putting aside all malice and all guile and hypocrisy and envy and all slander,

SCRIPTURE NO. 3, SEC. 2

2 like newborn babes, long for the pure milk of the word, that by it you may grow in respect to salvation, (r3)

3 if you have tasted the kindness of the Lord.

(r3) REFERENCE NO. 3, SEC. 2—
HOW GROWTH IN GRACE AS A BELIEVER SHOWS SALVATION.
"Like newborn babes grow in respect to salvation."

Your salvation, in point of time, is an event. It is past as it relates to your spiritual birth into the family of God. "For you have been born again, not of seed which is perishable but imperishable, that is, through the living and abiding word of God." You begin the Christian life as a babe when you are saved.

Your new life in Christ becomes an experience as you "grow in grace and knowledge of our Lord and Savior Jesus Christ." The Holy Spirit led you to believe "His precious and magnificent promises in order that by them you might be partakers

(Continued on next page.)

4 And coming to Him as to a living stone, rejected by men, but choice and precious in the sight of God,

5 you also, as living stones, are being built up as a spiritual house for a holy priesthood, to offer up spiritual sacrifices acceptable to God through Jesus Christ.

6 For *this* is contained in Scripture:

> "BEHOLD I LAY IN ZION A CHOICE STONE, A PRECIOUS CORNER *stone*,
> AND HE WHO BELIEVES IN HIM SHALL NOT BE DISAPPOINTED."

7 This precious value, then, is for you who believe, but for those who disbelieve,

> "THE STONE WHICH THE BUILDERS REJECTED,
> THIS BECAME THE VERY CORNER *stone*."

8 and,

> "A STONE OF STUMBLING AND A ROCK OF OFFENSE";

for they stumble because they are disobedient to the word, and to this *doom* they were also appointed.

9 But you are A CHOSEN RACE, A ROYAL PRIESTHOOD, A HOLY NATION, A PEOPLE FOR *God's* OWN POSSESSION, that you may proclaim the excellencies of Him who has called you out of darkness into His marvelous light;

10 for you once were NOT A PEOPLE, but now you are THE PEOPLE OF GOD; you had NOT RECEIVED MERCY, but now you have RECEIVED MERCY.

11 Beloved, I urge you as aliens and strangers to abstain from fleshly lusts, which wage war against the soul.

12 Keep your behavior excellent

(Continued from page 314.)

of the divine nature." This new nature in you needs spiritual nourishment. As your physical body desires food, your new spirit should "long for the pure milk of the word."

"We are to grow up in all aspects of Him." This means giving daily "attention to the reading of scripture." "Be diligent . . . handling accurately the word of truth."

You also have a new command from God. You "ought to pray." Start the day with prayer. The Bible says, "My voice shalt thou hear in the morning, O Lord; in the morning will I direct my prayer unto thee, and will look up." Then you are to "pray at all times in the Spirit," that is, "pray without ceasing."

Your salvation includes and requires you to make a dedication of your body to Him. That is "present your bodies a living and holy sacrifice acceptable to God, which is your spiritual service of worship. And do not be conformed to this world, but be transformed by the renewing of your mind, that you may prove what the will of God is." It is God's will, that, "in speech, conduct, love, faith and purity show yourself an example of those who believe." So, "whether then, you eat or drink or whatever you do, do all to the glory of God." "Examine everything carefully; hold fast to that which is good; abstain from every form of evil."

If you sin, confess it so you can rebound back into fellowship with Christ. "If we confess our sins, He is faithful and righteous to forgive us our sins and to cleanse us from all unrighteousness."

The goal in your salvation is to be "conformed to the image of His Son." That is, "grow in grace" and "press on to maturity" as one in Christ.

Do you desire to grow to maturity in Christ? If so, say:

"I now commit myself to daily read God's word, pray, and witness for Jesus, dedicating myself to assure my constant growth in grace and communion with Christ."

Now turn to page 159, Scripture No. 4, Sec. 2, Acts 1:8.

among the Gentiles, so that in the thing in which they slander you as evildoers, they may on account of your good deeds, as they observe *them*, glorify God in the day of visitation.

13 Submit yourselves for the Lord's sake to every human institution, whether to a king as the one in authority,

14 or to governors as sent by him for the punishment of evildoers and the praise of those who do right.

15 For such is the will of God that by doing right you may silence the ignorance of foolish men.

16 *Act* as free men, and do not use your freedom as a covering for evil, but *use it* as bondslaves of God.

17 Honor all men; love the brotherhood, fear God, honor the king.

18 Servants, be submissive to your masters with all respect, not only to those who are good and gentle, but also to those who are unreasonable.

19 For this *finds* favor, if for the sake of conscience toward God a man bears up under sorrows when suffering unjustly.

20 For what credit is there if, when you sin and are harshly treated, you endure it with patience? But if when you do what is right and suffer *for it* you patiently endure it, this *finds* favor with God.

21 For you have been called for this purpose, since Christ also suffered for you, leaving you an example for you to follow in His steps,

22 WHO COMMITTED NO SIN, NOR WAS ANY DECEIT FOUND IN HIS MOUTH;

23 and while being reviled, He did not revile in return; while suffering, He uttered no threats, but kept entrusting *Himself* to Him who judges righteously;

24 and He Himself bore our sins in His body on the cross, that we might die to sin and live to righteousness; for by His wounds you were healed.

25 For you were continually straying like sheep, but now you have returned to the Shepherd and Guardian of your souls.

CHAPTER 3

IN the same way, you wives, be submissive to your own husbands so that even if any *of them* are disobedient to the word, they may be won without a word by the behavior of their wives,

2 as they observe your chaste and respectful behavior.

3 And let not your adornment be external *only*—braiding the hair, and wearing gold jewelry, and putting on dresses;

4 but *let it be* the hidden person of the heart, with the imperishable quality of a gentle and quiet spirit, which is precious in the sight of God.

5 For in this way in former times the holy women also, who hoped in God, used to adorn themselves, being submissive to their own husbands.

6 Thus Sarah obeyed Abraham, calling him lord, and you have become her children if you do what is right without being frightened by any fear.

7 You husbands likewise, live with your wives in an understanding way, as with a weaker vessel, since she is a woman; and grant her honor as a fellow-heir of the grace of life, so that your prayers may not be hindered.

8 To sum up, let all be harmonious, sympathetic, brotherly, kindhearted, and humble in spirit;

9 not returning evil for evil, or insult for insult, but giving a blessing instead; for you were called for the very purpose that you might inherit a blessing.

10 For

"LET HIM WHO MEANS TO LOVE LIFE AND SEE GOOD DAYS

REFRAIN HIS TONGUE FROM EVIL AND HIS LIPS FROM SPEAKING GUILE.

11 "AND LET HIM TURN AWAY FROM EVIL AND DO GOOD; LET HIM SEEK PEACE AND PURSUE IT.

12 "FOR THE EYES OF THE LORD ARE UPON THE RIGHTEOUS, AND HIS EARS ATTEND TO THEIR PRAYER, BUT THE FACE OF THE LORD IS AGAINST THOSE WHO DO EVIL."

13 And who is there to harm you if you prove zealous for what is good?

14 But even if you should suffer for the sake of righteousness, *you are* blessed. AND DO NOT FEAR THEIR INTIMIDATION, AND DO NOT BE TROUBLED,

15 but SANCTIFY Christ as Lord in your hearts, always *being* ready to make a defense to every one who asks you to give an account for the hope that is in you, yet with gentleness and reverence;

16 and keep a good conscience so that in the thing in which you are slandered, those who revile your good behavior in Christ may be put to shame.

17 For it is better, if God should will it so, that you suffer for doing what is right rather than for doing what is wrong.

18 For Christ also died for sins once for all, *the* just for *the* unjust, in order that He might bring us to God, having been put to death in the flesh, but made alive in the spirit;

19 in which also He went and made proclamation to the spirits *now* in prison,

20 who once were disobedient, when the patience of God kept waiting in the days of Noah, during the construction of the ark, in which a few, that is, eight persons, were brought safely through *the* water.

21 And corresponding to that, baptism now saves you—not the removal of dirt from the flesh, but an appeal to God for a good conscience—through the resurrection of Jesus Christ,

22 who is at the right hand of God, having gone into heaven, after angels and authorities and powers had been subjected to Him.

CHAPTER 4

THEREFORE, since Christ has suffered in the flesh, arm yourselves also with the same purpose, because he who has suffered in the flesh has ceased from sin,

2 so as to live the rest of the time in the flesh no longer for the lusts of men, but for the will of God.

3 For the time already past is sufficient *for you* to have carried out the desire of the Gentiles, having pursued a course of sensuality, lusts, drunkenness, carousals, drinking parties and abominable idolatries.

4 And in *all* this, they are surprised that you do not run with *them* into the same excess of dissipation, and they malign *you;*

5 but they shall give account to Him who is ready to judge the living and the dead.

6 For the gospel has for this purpose been preached even to those who are dead, that though they are judged in the flesh as men, they may live in the spirit according to *the will of* God.

7 The end of all things is at hand; therefore, be of sound judgment and sober *spirit* for the purpose of prayer.

8 Above all, keep fervent in your love for one another, because love covers a multitude of sins.

9 Be hospitable to one another without complaint.

10 As each one has received a *special* gift, employ it in serving one another, as good stewards of the manifold grace of God.

11 Whoever speaks, *let him speak,*

as it were, the utterances of God; whoever serves, *let him do so* as by the strength which God supplies; so that in all things God may be glorified through Jesus Christ, to whom belongs the glory and dominion forever and ever. Amen.

12 Beloved, do not be surprised at the fiery ordeal among you, which comes upon you for your testing, as though some strange thing were happening to you;

13 but to the degree that you share the sufferings of Christ, keep on rejoicing; so that also at the revelation of His glory, you may rejoice with exultation.

14 If you are reviled for the name of Christ, you are blessed, because the Spirit of glory and of God rests upon you.

15 By no means let any of you suffer as a murderer, or thief, or evildoer, or a troublesome meddler;

16 but if *anyone suffers* as a Christian, let him not feel ashamed, but in that name let him glorify God.

17 For *it is* time for judgment to begin with the household of God; and if *it begins* with us first, what *will be* the outcome for those who do not obey the gospel of God?

18 AND IF IT IS WITH DIFFICULTY THAT THE RIGHTEOUS IS SAVED, WHAT WILL BECOME OF THE GODLESS MAN AND THE SINNER?

19 Therefore, let those also who suffer according to the will of God entrust their souls to a faithful Creator in doing what is right.

CHAPTER 5

T HEREFORE, I exhort the elders among you, as *your* fellow-elder and witness of the sufferings of Christ, and a partaker also of the glory that is to be revealed:

2 shepherd the flock of God among you, not under compulsion, but voluntarily, according to *the will of* God; and not for sordid gain, but with eagerness;

3 nor yet as lording it over those allotted to your charge, but proving to be examples to the flock.

4 And when the Chief Shepherd appears, you will receive the unfading crown of glory.

5 You younger men, likewise, be subject to your elders; and all of you, clothe yourselves with humility toward one another, for GOD IS OPPOSED TO THE PROUD, BUT GIVES GRACE TO THE HUMBLE.

6 Humble yourselves, therefore, under the mighty hand of God, that He may exalt you at the proper time,

7 casting all your anxiety upon Him, because He cares for you.

8 Be of sober *spirit*, be on the alert. Your adversary, the devil, prowls about like a roaring lion, seeking someone to devour.

9 But resist him, firm in *your* faith, knowing that the same experiences of suffering are being accomplished by your brethren who are in the world.

10 And after you have suffered for a little, the God of all grace, who called you to His eternal glory in Christ, will Himself perfect, confirm, strengthen *and* establish you.

11 To Him *be* dominion forever and ever. Amen.

12 Through Silvanus, our faithful brother (for so I regard *him*), I have written to you briefly, exhorting and testifying that this is the true grace of God. Stand firm in it!

13 She who is in Babylon, chosen together with you, sends you greetings, and *so does* my son, Mark.

14 Greet one another with a kiss of love.

Peace be to you all who are in Christ.

THE SECOND EPISTLE OF

PETER

SIMON PETER, a bond-servant and apostle of Jesus Christ, to those who have received a faith of the same kind as ours, by the righteousness of our God and Savior, Jesus Christ:

2 Grace and peace be multiplied to you in the knowledge of God and of Jesus our Lord;

3 seeing that His divine power has granted to us everything pertaining to life and godliness, through the true knowledge of Him who called us by His own glory and excellence.

4 For by these He has granted to us His precious and magnificent promises, in order that by them you might become partakers of *the* divine nature, having escaped the corruption that is in the world by lust.

5 Now for this very reason also, applying all diligence, in your faith supply moral excellence, and in *your* moral excellence, knowledge;

6 and in *your* knowledge, self-control, and in *your* self-control, perseverance, and in *your* perseverance, godliness;

7 and in *your* godliness, brotherly kindness, and in *your* brotherly kindness, *Christian* love.

8 For if these *qualities* are yours and are increasing, they render you neither useless nor unfruitful in the true knowledge of our Lord Jesus Christ.

9 For he who lacks these *qualities* is blind *or* short-sighted, having forgotten *his* purification from his former sins.

10 Therefore, brethren, be all the more diligent to make certain about His calling and choosing you; for as long as you practice these things, you will never stumble;

11 for in this way the entrance into the eternal kingdom of our Lord and Savior Jesus Christ will be abundantly supplied to you.

12 Therefore, I shall always be ready to remind you of these things, even though you *already* know *them,* and have been established in the truth which is present with *you.*

13 And I consider it right, as long as I am in this *earthly* dwelling, to stir you up by way of reminder,

14 knowing that the laying aside of my *earthly* dwelling is imminent, as also our Lord Jesus Christ has made clear to me.

15 And I will also be diligent that at any time after my departure you may be able to call these things to mind.

16 For we did not follow cleverly devised tales when we made known to you the power and coming of our Lord Jesus Christ, but we were eyewitnesses of His majesty.

17 For when He received honor and glory from God the Father, such an utterance as this was made to Him by the Majestic Glory, "This is My beloved Son with whom I am well-pleased"—

18 and we ourselves heard this utterance made from heaven when we were with Him on the holy mountain.

19 And *so* we have the prophetic word *made* more sure, to which you do well to pay attention as to a lamp shining in a dark place, until the day dawns and the morning star arises in your hearts.

20 But know this first of all, that no prophecy of Scripture is *a matter* of one's own interpretation,

21 for no prophecy was ever made by an act of human will, but men moved by the Holy Spirit spoke from God.

CHAPTER 2

BUT false prophets also arose among the people, just as there will also be false teachers among you, who will secretly introduce destructive heresies, even denying the Master who bought them, bringing swift destruction upon themselves.

2 And many will follow their sensuality, and because of them the way of the truth will be maligned;

3 and in *their* greed they will exploit you with false words; their judgment from long ago is not idle, and their destruction is not asleep.

4 For if God did not spare angels when they sinned, but cast them into hell and committed them to pits of darkness, reserved for judgment;

5 and did not spare the ancient world, but preserved Noah, a preacher of righteousness, with seven others, when He brought a flood upon the world of the ungodly;

6 and *if* He condemned the cities of Sodom and Gomorrah to destruction by reducing *them* to ashes, having made them an example to those who would live ungodly thereafter;

7 and if He rescued righteous Lot, oppressed by the sensual conduct of unprincipled men

8 (for by what he saw and heard *that* righteous man, while living among them, felt *his* righteous soul tormented day after day with *their* lawless deeds),

9 *then* the Lord knows how to rescue the godly from temptation, and to keep the unrighteous under punishment for the day of judgment,

10 and especially those who indulge the flesh in *its* corrupt desires and despise authority. Daring, self-willed, they do not tremble when they revile angelic majesties,

11 whereas angels who are greater in might and power do not bring a reviling judgment against them before the Lord.

12 But these, like unreasoning animals, born as creatures of instinct to be captured and killed, reviling where they have no knowledge, will in the destruction of those creatures also be destroyed,

13 suffering wrong as the wages of doing wrong. They count it a pleasure to revel in the daytime. They are stains and blemishes, reveling in their deceptions, as they carouse with you;

14 having eyes full of adultery and that never cease from sin; enticing unstable souls, having a heart trained in greed, accursed children;

15 forsaking the right way they have gone astray, having followed the way of Balaam, the *son* of Beor, who loved the wages of unrighteousness,

16 but he received a rebuke for his own transgression; *for* a dumb donkey, speaking with a voice of a man, restrained the madness of the prophet.

17 These are springs without water, and mists driven by a storm, for whom the black darkness has been reserved.

18 For speaking out arrogant *words* of vanity they entice by fleshly desires, by sensuality, those who barely escape from the ones who live in error,

19 promising them freedom while they themselves are slaves of corruption; for by what a man is overcome, by this he is enslaved.

20 For if after they have escaped the defilements of the world by the knowledge of the Lord and Savior Jesus Christ, they are again entangled in them and are overcome, the last state has become worse for them than the first.

21 For it would be better for them not to have known the way of righteousness, than having known it, to turn away from the holy commandment delivered to them.

22 It has happened to them according to the true proverb, "A DOG

RETURNS TO ITS OWN VOMIT," and, "A sow, after washing, *returns* to wallowing in the mire."

CHAPTER 3

THIS is now, beloved, the second letter I am writing to you in which I am stirring up your sincere mind by way of reminder,

2 that you should remember the words spoken beforehand by the holy prophets and the commandment of the Lord and Savior *spoken* by your apostles.

3 Know this first of all, that in the last days mockers will come with *their* mocking, following after their own lusts,

4 and saying, "Where is the promise of His coming? For *ever* since the fathers fell asleep, all continues just as it was from the beginning of creation."

5 For when they maintain this, it escapes their notice that by the word of God *the* heavens existed long ago and *the* earth was formed out of water and by water,

6 through which the world at that time was destroyed, being flooded with water.

7 But the present heavens and earth by His word are being reserved for fire, kept for the day of judgment and destruction of ungodly men.

8 But do not let this one *fact* escape your notice, beloved, that with the Lord one day is as a thousand years, and a thousand years as one day.

9 The Lord is not slow about His promise, as some count slowness, but is patient toward you, not wishing for any to perish but for all to come to repentance.

10 But the day of the Lord will come like a thief, in which the heavens will pass away with a roar and the elements will be destroyed with intense heat, and the earth and its works will be burned up.

11 Since all these things are to be destroyed in this way, what sort of people ought you to be in holy conduct and godliness,

12 looking for and hastening the coming of the day of God, on account of which the heavens will be destroyed by burning, and the elements will melt with intense heat!

13 But according to His promise we are looking for new heavens and a new earth, in which righteousness dwells.

14 Therefore, beloved, since you look for these things, be diligent to be found by Him in peace, spotless and blameless,

15 and regard the patience of our Lord *to be* salvation; just as also our beloved brother Paul, according to the wisdom given him, wrote to you,

16 as also in all *his* letters, speaking in them of these things, in which are some things hard to understand, which the untaught and unstable distort, as *they do* also the rest of the Scriptures, to their own destruction.

17 You therefore, beloved, knowing this beforehand, be on your guard lest, being carried away by the error of unprincipled men, you fall from your own steadfastness,

18 but grow in the grace and knowledge of our Lord and Savior Jesus Christ. To Him *be* the glory, both now and to the day of eternity. Amen.

THE FIRST EPISTLE OF
JOHN

WHAT was from the beginning, what we have heard, what we have seen with our eyes, what we beheld and our hands handled, concerning the Word of Life—

2 and the life was manifested, and we have seen and bear witness and proclaim to you the eternal life, which was with the Father and was manifested to us—

3 what we have seen and heard we proclaim to you also, that you also may have fellowship with us; and indeed our fellowship is with the Father, and with His Son Jesus Christ.

4 And these things we write, so that our joy may be made complete.

5 And this is the message we have heard from Him and announce to you, that God is light, and in Him there is no darkness at all.

6 If we say that we have fellowship with Him and yet walk in the darkness, we lie and do not practice the truth;

7 but if we walk in the light as He Himself is in the light, we have fellowship with one another, and the blood of Jesus His Son cleanses us from all sin.

8 If we say that we have no sin, we are deceiving ourselves, and the truth is not in us.

9 If we confess our sins, He is faithful and righteous to forgive us our sins and to cleanse us from all unrighteousness.

10 If we say that we have not sinned, we make Him a liar, and His word is not in us.

CHAPTER 2

MY little children, I am writing these things to you that you may not sin. And if anyone sins, we have an Advocate with the Father, Jesus Christ the righteous;

2 and He Himself is the propitiation for our sins; and not for ours only, but also for *those of* the whole world.

3 And by this we know that we have come to know Him, if we keep His commandments.

4 The one who says, "I have come to know Him," and does not keep His commandments, is a liar, and the truth is not in him;

5 but whoever keeps His word, in him the love of God has truly been perfected. By this we know that we are in Him:

6 the one who says he abides in Him ought himself to walk in the same manner as He walked.

7 Beloved, I am not writing a new commandment to you, but an old commandment which you have had from the beginning; the old commandment is the word which you have heard.

8 On the other hand, I am writing a new commandment to you, which is true in Him and in you, because the darkness is passing away, and the true light is already shining.

9 The one who says he is in the light and yet hates his brother is in the darkness until now.

10 The one who loves his brother abides in the light and there is no cause for stumbling in him.

11 But the one who hates his brother is in the darkness and walks in the darkness, and does not know where he is going because the darkness has blinded his eyes.

12 I am writing to you, little children, because your sins are forgiven you for His name's sake.

13 I am writing to you, fathers,

because you know Him who has been from the beginning. I am writing to you, young men, because you have overcome the evil one. I have written to you, children, because you know the Father.

14 I have written to you, fathers, because you know Him who has been from the beginning. I have written to you, young men, because you are strong, and the word of God abides in you, and you have overcome the evil one.

15 Do not love the world, nor the things in the world. If any one loves the world, the love of the Father is not in him.

16 For all that is in the world, the lust of the flesh and the lust of the eyes and the boastful pride of life, is not from the Father, but is from the world.

17 And the world is passing away, and *also* its lusts; but the one who does the will of God abides forever.

18 Children, it is the last hour; and just as you heard that antichrist is coming, even now many antichrists have arisen; from this we know that it is the last hour.

19 They went out from us, but they were not *really* of us; for if they had been of us, they would have remained with us; but *they went out*, in order that it might be shown that they all are not of us.

20 But you have an anointing from the Holy One, and you all know.

21 I have not written to you because you do not know the truth, but because you do know it, and because no lie is of the truth.

22 Who is the liar but the one who denies that Jesus is the Christ? This is the antichrist, the one who denies the Father and the Son.

23 Whoever denies the Son does not have the Father; the one who confesses the Son has the Father also.

24 As for you, let that abide in you which you heard from the beginning. If what you heard from the beginning abides in you, you also will abide in the Son and in the Father.

25 And this is the promise which He Himself made to us: eternal life.

26 These things I have written to you concerning those who are trying to deceive you.

27 And as for you, the anointing which you received from Him abides in you, and you have no need for any one to teach you; but as His anointing teaches you about all things, and is true and is not a lie, and just as it has taught you, you abide in Him.

28 And now, little children, abide in Him, so that when He appears, we may have confidence and not shrink away from Him in shame at His coming.

29 If you know that He is righteous, you know that every one also who practices righteousness is born of Him.

CHAPTER 3

SEE how great a love the Father has bestowed upon us, that we should be called children of God; and *such* we are. For this reason the world does not know us, because it did not know Him.

2 Beloved, now we are children of God, and it has not appeared as yet what we shall be. We know that, when He appears, we shall be like Him, because we shall see Him just as He is.

3 And every one who has this hope *fixed* on Him purifies himself, just as He is pure.

4 Every one who practices sin also practices lawlessness; and sin is lawlessness.

5 And you know that He appeared in order to take away sins; and in Him there is no sin.

6 No one who abides in Him sins; no one who sins has seen Him or knows Him.

7 Little children, let no one deceive you; the one who practices righteousness is righteous, just as He is righteous;

8 the one who practices sin is of the devil; for the devil has sinned from the beginning. The Son of God appeared for this purpose, that He might destroy the works of the devil.

9 No one who is born of God practices sin, because His seed abides in him; and he cannot sin, because he is born of God.

10 By this the children of God and the children of the devil are obvious: any one who does not practice righteousness is not of God, nor the one who does not love his brother.

11 For this is the message which you have heard from the beginning, that we should love one another;

12 not as Cain, *who* was of the evil one, and slew his brother. And for what reason did he slay him? Because his deeds were evil, and his brother's were righteous.

13 Do not marvel, brethren, if the world hates you.

14 We know that we have passed out of death into life, because we love the brethren. He who does not love abides in death.

15 Every one who hates his brother is a murderer; and you know that no murderer has eternal life abiding in him.

16 We know love by this, that He laid down His life for us; and we ought to lay down our lives for the brethren.

17 But whoever has the world's goods, and beholds his brother in need and closes his heart against him, how does the love of God abide in him?

18 Little children, let us not love with word or with tongue, but in deed and truth.

19 We shall know by this that we are of the truth, and shall assure our heart before Him,

20 in whatever our heart condemns us; for God is greater than our heart, and knows all things.

21 Beloved, if our heart does not condemn us, we have confidence before God;

22 and whatever we ask we receive from Him, because we keep His commandments and do the things that are pleasing in His sight.

23 And this is His commandment, that we believe in the name of His Son Jesus Christ, and love one another, just as He commanded us.

24 And the one who keeps His commandments abides in Him, and He in him. And we know by this that He abides in us, by the Spirit which He has given us.

CHAPTER 4

BELOVED, do not believe every spirit, but test the spirits to see whether they are from God; because many false prophets have gone out into the world.

2 By this you know the Spirit of God: every spirit that confesses that Jesus Christ has come in the flesh is from God;

3 and every spirit that does not confess Jesus is not from God; and this is the *spirit* of the antichrist, of which you have heard that it is coming, and now it is already in the world.

4 You are from God, little children, and have overcome them; because greater is He who is in you than he who is in the world.

5 They are from the world; therefore they speak *as* from the world, and the world listens to them.

6 We are from God; he who knows God listens to us; he who is not from God does not listen to us. By

this we know the spirit of truth and the spirit of error.

7 Beloved, let us love one another, for love is from God; and every one who loves is born of God and knows God.

8 The one who does not love does not know God, for God is love.

9 By this the love of God was manifested in us, that God has sent His only begotten Son into the world so that we might live through Him.

10 In this is love, not that we loved God, but that He loved us and sent His Son *to be* the propitiation for our sins.

11 Beloved, if God so loved us, we also ought to love one another.

12 No one has beheld God at any time; if we love one another, God abides in us, and His love is perfected in us.

13 By this we know that we abide in Him and He in us, because He has given us of His Spirit.

14 And we have beheld and bear witness that the Father has sent the Son *to be* the Savior of the world.

15 Whoever confesses that Jesus is the Son of God, God abides in him, and he in God.

16 And we have come to know and have believed the love which God has for us. God is love, and the one who abides in love abides in God, and God abides in him.

17 By this, love is perfected with us, that we may have confidence in the day of judgment; because as He is, so also are we in this world.

18 There is no fear in love; but perfect love casts out fear, because fear involves punishment, and the one who fears is not perfected in love.

19 We love, because He first loved us.

20 If some one says, "I love God," and hates his brother, he is a liar; for the one who does not love his brother whom he has seen, cannot love God whom he has not seen.

21 And this commandment we have from Him, that the one who loves God should love his brother also.

CHAPTER 5

WHOEVER believes that Jesus is the Christ is born of God; and whoever loves the Father loves the *child* born of Him.

2 By this we know that we love the children of God, when we love God and observe His commandments.

3 For this is the love of God, that we keep His commandments; and His commandments are not burdensome.

4 For whatever is born of God overcomes the world; and this is the victory that has overcome the world—our faith.

5 And who is the one who overcomes the world, but he who believes that Jesus is the Son of God?

6 This is the one who came by water and blood, Jesus Christ; not with the water only, but with the water and with the blood.

7 And it is the Spirit who bears witness, because the Spirit is the truth.

8 For there are three that bear witness, the Spirit and the water and the blood; and the three are in agreement.

9 If we receive the witness of men, the witness of God is greater; for the witness of God is this, that He has borne witness concerning His Son.

10 The one who believes in the Son of God has the witness in himself; the one who does not believe God has made Him a liar, because he has not believed in the witness that God has borne concerning His Son.

11 And the witness is this, that

God has given us eternal life, and this life is in His Son.

12　He who has the Son has the life; he who does not have the Son of God does not have the life.

13　These things I have written to you who believe in the name of the Son of God, in order that you may know that you have eternal life.

14　And this is the confidence which we have before Him, that, if we ask anything according to His will, He hears us.

15　And if we know that He hears us *in* whatever we ask, we know that we have the requests which we have asked from Him.

16　If any one sees his brother committing a sin not *leading* to death, he shall ask and God will for him give life to those who commit sin not *leading*

to death. There is a sin *leading* to death; I do not say that he should make request for this.

17　All unrighteousness is sin, and there is a sin not *leading* to death.

18　We know that no one who is born of God sins; but He who was born of God keeps him and the evil one does not touch him.

19　We know that we are of God, and the whole world lies in *the power of* the evil one.

20　And we know that the Son of God has come, and has given us understanding, in order that we might know Him who is true, and we are in Him who is true, in His Son Jesus Christ. This is the true God and eternal life.

21　Little children, guard yourselves from idols.

THE SECOND EPISTLE OF

JOHN

THE elder to the chosen lady and her children, whom I love in truth; and not only I, but also all who know the truth,

2　for the sake of the truth which abides in us and will be with us forever:

3　Grace, mercy *and* peace will be with us, from God the Father and from Jesus Christ, the Son of the Father, in truth and love.

4　I was very glad to find *some* of your children walking in truth, just as we have received commandment *to do* from the Father.

5　And now I ask you, lady, not as writing to you a new commandment, but the one which we have had from the beginning, that we love one another.

6　And this is love, that we walk according to His commandments. This is the commandment, just as you have heard from the beginning, that you should walk in it.

7　For many deceivers have gone out into the world, those who do not acknowledge Jesus Christ *as* coming in the flesh. This is the deceiver and the antichrist.

8　Watch yourselves, that you might not lose what we have accomplished, but that you may receive a full reward.

9　Any one who goes too far and does not abide in the teaching of Christ, does not have God; the one who abides in the teaching, he has both the Father and the Son.

10　If any one comes to you and

does not bring this teaching, do not receive him into *your* house, and do not give him a greeting;

11 for the one who gives him a greeting participates in his evil deeds.

12 Having many things to write to you, I do not want to *do so* with paper and ink; but I hope to come to you and speak face to face, that your joy may be made full.

13 The children of your chosen sister greet you.

THE THIRD EPISTLE OF
JOHN

THE elder to the beloved Gaius, whom I love in truth.

2 Beloved, I pray that in all respects you may prosper and be in good health, just as your soul prospers.

3 For I was very glad when brethren came and bore witness to your truth, *that is*, how you are walking in truth.

4 I have no greater joy than this, to hear of my children walking in the truth.

5 Beloved, you are acting faithfully in whatever you accomplish for the brethren, and especially *when they are* strangers;

6 and they bear witness to your love before the church; and you will do well to send them on their way in a manner worthy of God.

7 For they went out for the sake of the Name, accepting nothing from the Gentiles.

8 Therefore we ought to support such men, that we may be fellow-workers with the truth.

9 I wrote something to the church; but Diotrephes, who loves to be first among them, does not accept what we say.

10 For this reason, if I come, I will call attention to his deeds which he does, unjustly accusing us with wicked words; and not satisfied with this, neither does he himself receive the brethren, and he forbids those who desire *to do so*, and puts *them* out of the church.

11 Beloved, do not imitate what is evil, but what is good. The one who does good is of God; the one who does evil has not seen God.

12 Demetrius has received a good testimony from everyone, and from the truth itself; and we also bear witness, and you know that our witness is true.

13 I had many things to write to you, but I am not willing to write *them* to you with pen and ink;

14 but I hope to see you shortly, and we shall speak face to face. Peace *be* to you. The friends greet you. Greet the friends by name.

THE EPISTLE OF

JUDE

JUDE, a bond-servant of Jesus Christ, and brother of James, to those who are the called, beloved in God the Father, and kept for Jesus Christ:

2 May mercy and peace and love be multiplied to you.

3 Beloved, while I was making every effort to write you about our common salvation, I felt the necessity to write to you appealing that you contend earnestly for the faith which was once for all delivered to the saints.

4 For certain persons have crept in unnoticed, those who were long beforehand marked out for this condemnation, ungodly persons who turn the grace of our God into licentiousness and deny our only Master and Lord, Jesus Christ.

5 Now I desire to remind you, though you know all things once for all, that the Lord, after saving a people out of the land of Egypt, subsequently destroyed those who did not believe.

6 And angels who did not keep their own domain, but abandoned their proper abode, He has kept in eternal bonds under darkness for the judgment of the great day.

7 Just as Sodom and Gomorrah and the cities around them, since they in the same way as these indulged in gross immorality and went after strange flesh, are exhibited as an example, in undergoing the punishment of eternal fire.

8 Yet in the same manner these men, also by dreaming, defile the flesh, and reject authority, and revile angelic majesties.

9 But Michael the archangel, when he disputed with the devil and argued about the body of Moses, did not dare pronounce against him a railing judgment, but said, "THE LORD REBUKE YOU."

10 But these men revile the things which they do not understand; and the things which they know by instinct, like unreasoning animals, by these things they are destroyed.

11 Woe to them! For they have gone the way of Cain, and for pay they have rushed headlong into the error of Balaam, and perished in the rebellion of Korah.

12 These men are those who are hidden reefs in your love-feasts when they feast with you without fear, caring for themselves; clouds without water, carried along by winds; autumn trees without fruit, doubly dead, uprooted;

13 wild waves of the sea, casting up their own shame like foam; wandering stars, for whom the black darkness has been reserved forever.

14 And about these also Enoch, *in* the seventh *generation* from Adam, prophesied, saying, "Behold, the Lord came with many thousands of His holy ones,

15 to execute judgment upon all, and to convict all the ungodly of all their ungodly deeds which they have done in an ungodly way, and of all the harsh things which ungodly sinners have spoken against Him."

16 These are grumblers, finding fault, following after their *own* lusts; they speak arrogantly, flattering people for the sake of *gaining an* advantage.

17 But you, beloved, ought to remember the words that were spoken beforehand by the apostles of our Lord Jesus Christ,

18 that they were saying to you, "In the last time there shall be mock-

ers, following after their own ungodly lusts."

19 These are the ones who cause divisions, worldly-minded, devoid of the Spirit.

20 But you, beloved, building yourselves up on your most holy faith; praying in the Holy Spirit;

21 keep yourselves in the love of God, waiting anxiously for the mercy of our Lord Jesus Christ to eternal life.

22 And have mercy on some, who are doubting;

23 save others, snatching them out of the fire; and on some have mercy with fear, hating even the garment polluted by the flesh.

24 Now to Him who is able to keep you from stumbling, and to make you stand in the presence of His glory blameless with great joy,

25 to the only God our Savior, through Jesus Christ our Lord, *be* glory, majesty, dominion and authority, before all time and now and forever. Amen.

THE REVELATION OF JOHN

The Revelation of Jesus Christ, which God gave Him to show to His bond-servants, the things which must shortly take place; and He sent and communicated *it* by His angel to His bond-servant John,

2 who bore witness to the word of God and to the testimony of Jesus Christ, *even* to all that he saw.

3 Blessed is he who reads and those who hear the words of the prophecy, and heed the things which are written in it; for the time is near.

4 John to the seven churches that are in Asia: Grace to you and peace, from Him who is and who was and who is to come; and from the seven Spirits who are before His throne;

5 and from Jesus Christ, the faithful witness, the first-born of the dead, and the ruler of the kings of the earth. To Him who loves us, and released us from our sins by His blood,

6 and He has made us *to be* a kingdom, priests to His God and Father; to Him *be* the glory and the dominion forever and ever. Amen.

7 BEHOLD, HE IS COMING WITH THE CLOUDS, and EVERY EYE WILL SEE HIM, EVEN THOSE WHO PIERCED HIM; AND ALL THE TRIBES OF THE EARTH WILL MOURN OVER HIM. Even so. Amen.

8 "I am the Alpha and the Omega," says the Lord God, "who is and who was and who is to come, the Almighty."

9 I, John, your brother and fellow-partaker in the tribulation and kingdom and perseverance *which are* in Jesus, was on the island called Patmos, because of the word of God and the testimony of Jesus.

10 I was in the Spirit on the Lord's day, and I heard behind me a loud voice like *the sound* of a trumpet,

11 saying, "Write in a book what you see, and send *it* to the seven churches: to Ephesus and to Smyrna and to Pergamum and to Thyatira and to Sardis and to Philadelphia and to Laodicea."

12 And I turned to see the voice that was speaking with me. And having turned I saw seven golden lampstands;

13 and in the middle of the lampstands one like a son of man, clothed in a robe reaching to the feet, and girded across His breast with a golden girdle.

14 And His head and His hair were white like white wool, like snow; and His eyes were like a flame of fire;

15 and His feet *were* like burnished bronze, when it has been caused to glow in a furnace, and His voice *was* like the sound of many waters.

16 And in His right hand He held seven stars; and out of His mouth came a sharp two-edged sword; and His face was like the sun shining in its strength.

17 And when I saw Him, I fell at His feet as a dead man. And He laid His right hand upon me, saying, "Do not be afraid; I am the first and the last,

18 and the living One; and I was dead, and behold, I am alive forevermore, and I have the keys of death and of Hades.

19 "Write therefore the things which you have seen, and the things which are, and the things which shall take place after these things.

20 "As for the mystery of the seven stars which you saw in My right hand, and the seven golden lampstands: the seven stars are the angels of the seven churches, and the seven lampstands are the seven churches.

CHAPTER 2

"TO the angel of the church in Ephesus write:

The One who holds the seven stars in His right hand, the One who walks among the seven golden lampstands, says this:

2 'I know your deeds and your toil and perseverance, and that you cannot endure evil men, and you put to the test those who call themselves apostles, and they are not, and you found them *to be* false;

3 and you have perseverance and

have endured for My name's sake, and have not grown weary.

4 'But I have *this* against you, that you have left your first love.

5 'Remember therefore from where you have fallen, and repent and do the deeds you did at first; or else I am coming to you, and will remove your lampstand out of its place — unless you repent.

6 'Yet this you do have, that you hate the deeds of the Nicolaitans, which I also hate.

7 'He who has an ear, let him hear what the Spirit says to the churches. To him who overcomes, I will grant to eat of the tree of life, which is in the Paradise of God.'

8 "And to the angel of the church in Smyrna write:

The first and the last, who was dead, and has come to life, says this:

9 'I know your tribulation and your poverty (but you are rich), and the blasphemy by those who say they are Jews and are not, but are a synagogue of Satan.

10 'Do not fear what you are about to suffer. Behold, the devil is about to cast some of you into prison, that you may be tested, and you will have tribulation ten days. Be faithful until death, and I will give you the crown of life.

11 'He who has an ear, let him hear what the Spirit says to the churches. He who overcomes shall not be hurt by the second death.'

12 "And to the angel of the church in Pergamum write:

The One who has the sharp two-edged sword says this:

13 'I know where you dwell, where Satan's throne is; and you hold fast My name, and did not deny My faith, even in the days of Antipas, My witness, My faithful one, who was killed among you, where Satan dwells.

14 'But I have a few things against you, because you have there some who hold the teaching of Balaam, who kept teaching Balak to put a stumbling block before the sons of Israel, to eat things sacrificed to idols, and to commit *acts of* immorality.

15 'Thus you also have some who in the same way hold the teaching of the Nicolaitans.

16 'Repent therefore; or else I am coming to you quickly, and I will make war against them with the sword of My mouth.

17 'He who has an ear, let him hear what the Spirit says to the churches. To him who overcomes, to him I will give *some* of the hidden manna, and I will give him a white stone, and a new name written on the stone which no one knows but he who receives it.'

18 "And to the angel of the church in Thyatira write:

The Son of God, who has eyes like a flame of fire, and His feet are like burnished bronze, says this:

19 'I know your deeds, and your love and faith and service and perseverance, and that your deeds of late are greater than at first.

20 'But I have *this* against you, that you tolerate the woman Jezebel, who calls herself a prophetess, and she teaches and leads My bond-servants astray, so that they commit *acts of* immorality and eat things sacrificed to idols.

21 'And I gave her time to repent; and she does not want to repent of her immorality.

22 'Behold, I will cast her upon a bed *of sickness*, and those who commit adultery with her into great tribulation, unless they repent of her deeds.

23 'And I will kill her children with pestilence; and all the churches will know that I am He who searches the minds and hearts; and I will give to each one of you according to your deeds.

24 'But I say to you, the rest who are in Thyatira, who do not hold this teaching, who have not known the deep things of Satan, as they call them — I place no other burden on you.

25 'Nevertheless what you have, hold fast until I come.

26 'And he who overcomes, and he who keeps My deeds until the end, TO HIM I WILL GIVE AUTHORITY OVER THE NATIONS;

27 AND HE SHALL RULE THEM WITH A ROD OF IRON, AS THE VESSELS OF THE POTTER ARE BROKEN TO PIECES, as I also have received *authority* from My Father;

28 and I will give him the morning star.

29 'He who has an ear, let him hear what the Spirit says to the churches.'

CHAPTER 3

"AND to the angel of the church in Sardis write:

He who has the seven Spirits of God, and the seven stars, says this: I know your deeds, that you have a name that you are alive, and you are dead.

2 'Wake up, and strengthen the things that remain, which were about to die; for I have not found your deeds completed in the sight of My God.

3 'Remember therefore what you have received and heard; and keep *it*, and repent. If therefore you will not wake up, I will come like a thief, and you will not know at what hour I will come upon you.

4 'But you have a few people in Sardis who have not soiled their garments; and they will walk with Me in white; for they are worthy.

5 'He who overcomes shall thus be clothed in white garments; and I will not erase his name from the book of life, and I will confess his name

before My Father, and before His angels.

6 'He who has an ear, let him hear what the Spirit says to the churches.'

7 "And to the angel of the church in Philadelphia write:

He who is holy, who is true, who has the key of David, who opens and no one will shut, and who shuts and no one opens, says this:

8 'I know your deeds. Behold, I have put before you an open door which no one can shut, because you have a little power, and have kept My word, and have not denied My name.

9 'Behold, I will cause *those* of the synagogue of Satan, who say that they are Jews, and are not, but lie — behold, I will make them to come and bow down at your feet, and to know that I have loved you.

10 'Because you have kept the word of My perseverance, I also will keep you from the hour of testing, that *hour* which is about to come upon the whole world, to test those who dwell upon the earth.

11 'I am coming quickly; hold fast what you have, in order that no one take your crown.

12 'He who overcomes, I will make him a pillar in the temple of My God, and he will not go out from it any more; and I will write upon him the name of My God, and the name of the city of My God, the new Jerusalem, which comes down out of heaven from My God, and My new name.

13 'He who has an ear, let him hear what the Spirit says to the churches.'

14 "And to the angel of the church in Laodicea write:

The Amen, the faithful and true Witness, the Beginning of the creation of God, says this:

15 'I know your deeds, that you are neither cold nor hot; I would that you were cold or hot.

16 'So because you are lukewarm, and neither hot nor cold, I will spit you out of My mouth.

17 'Because you say, "I am rich, and have become wealthy, and have need of nothing," and you do not know that you are wretched and miserable and poor and blind and naked,

18 'I advise you to buy from Me gold refined by fire, that you may become rich, and white garments, that you may clothe yourself, and *that* the shame of your nakedness may not be revealed; and eyesalve to anoint your eyes, that you may see.

19 'Those whom I love, I reprove and discipline; be zealous therefore, and repent.

20 'Behold, I stand at the door and knock; if any one hears My voice and opens the door, I will come in to him, and will dine with him, and he with Me.

21 'He who overcomes, I will grant to him to sit down with Me on My throne, as I also overcame and sat down with My Father on His throne.

22 'He who has an ear, let him hear what the Spirit says to the churches.' "

CHAPTER 4

AFTER these things I looked, and behold, a door *standing* open in heaven, and the first voice which I had heard, like *the sound* of a trumpet speaking with me, said, "Come up here, and I will show you what must take place after these things."

2 Immediately I was in the spirit; and behold, a throne was standing in heaven, and One sitting on the throne.

3 And He who was sitting *was* like a jasper stone and a sardius in appearance; and *there was* a rainbow around the throne, like an emerald in appearance.

4 And around the throne *were* twenty-four thrones; and upon the

thrones *I saw* twenty-four elders sitting, clothed in white garments, and golden crowns on their heads.

5 And from the throne proceed flashes of lightning and sounds and peals of thunder. And *there were* seven lamps of fire burning before the throne, which are the seven Spirits of God;

6 and before the throne *there was*, as it were, a sea of glass like crystal; and in the center and around the throne, four living creatures full of eyes in front and behind.

7 And the first creature *was* like a lion, and the second creature like a calf, and the third creature had a face like that of a man, and the fourth creature *was* like a flying eagle.

8 And the four living creatures, each one of them having six wings, are full of eyes around and within; and day and night they do not cease to say,

> "HOLY, HOLY, HOLY, *is* THE LORD GOD, THE ALMIGHTY, who was and who is and who is to come."

9 And when the living creatures give glory and honor and thanks to Him who sits on the throne, to Him who lives forever and ever,

10 the twenty-four elders will fall down before Him who sits on the throne, and will worship Him who lives forever and ever, and will cast their crowns before the throne, saying,

11 "Worthy art Thou, our Lord and our God, to receive glory and honor and power; for Thou didst create all things, and because of Thy will they existed, and were created."

CHAPTER 5

A ND I saw in the right hand of Him who sat on the throne a book written inside and on the back, sealed up with seven seals.

2 And I saw a strong angel proclaiming with a loud voice, "Who is worthy to open the book and to break its seals?"

3 And no one in heaven, or on the earth, or under the earth, was able to open the book, or to look into it.

4 And I *began* to weep greatly, because no one was found worthy to open the book, or to look into it;

5 and one of the elders *said to me, "Stop weeping; behold, the Lion that is from the tribe of Judah, the Root of David, has overcome so as to open the book and its seven seals."

6 And I saw between the throne (with the four living creatures) and the elders a Lamb standing, as if slain, having seven horns and seven eyes, which are the seven Spirits of God, sent out into all the earth.

7 And He came, and He took *it* out of the right hand of Him who sat on the throne.

8 And when He had taken the book, the four living creatures and the twenty-four elders fell down before the Lamb, having each one a harp, and golden bowls full of incense, which are the prayers of the saints.

9 And they *sang a new song, saying,

> "Worthy art Thou to take the book, and to break its seals; for Thou wast slain, and didst purchase for God with Thy blood *men* from every tribe and tongue and people and nation.

10 "And Thou hast made them *to be* a kingdom and priests to our God; and they will reign upon the earth."

11 And I looked, and I heard the voice of many angels around the throne and the living creatures and the elders; and the number of them

was myriads of myriads, and thousands of thousands,

12 saying with a loud voice,

> "Worthy is the Lamb that was
> slain to receive power and
> riches and wisdom and might
> and honor and glory and
> blessing."

13 And every created thing which is in heaven and on the earth and under the earth and on the sea, and all things in them, I heard saying,

> "To Him who sits on the
> throne, and to the Lamb,
> *be* blessing and honor and
> glory and dominion forever
> and ever."

14 And the four living creatures kept saying, "Amen." And the elders fell down and worshiped.

CHAPTER 6

AND I saw when the Lamb broke one of the seven seals, and I heard one of the four living creatures saying as with a voice of thunder, "Come."

2 And I looked, and behold, a white horse, and he who sat on it had a bow; and a crown was given to him; and he went out conquering, and to conquer.

3 And when He broke the second seal, I heard the second living creature saying, "Come."

4 And another, a red horse, went out; and to him who sat on it, it was granted to take peace from the earth, and that *men* should slay one another; and a great sword was given to him.

5 And when He broke the third seal, I heard the third living creature saying, "Come." And I looked, and behold, a black horse; and he who sat on it had a pair of scales in his hand.

6 And I heard as it were a voice in the center of the four living creatures saying, "A quart of wheat for a denarius, and three quarts of barley for a denarius; and do not harm the oil and the wine."

7 And when He broke the fourth seal, I heard the voice of the fourth living creature saying, "Come."

8 And I looked, and behold, an ashen horse; and he who sat on it had the name "Death"; and Hades was following with him. And authority was given to them over a fourth of the earth, TO KILL WITH SWORD AND WITH FAMINE AND WITH PESTILENCE AND BY THE WILD BEASTS OF THE EARTH.

9 And when He broke the fifth seal, I saw underneath the altar the souls of those who had been slain because of the word of God, and because of the testimony which they had maintained;

10 and they cried out with a loud voice, saying, "How long, O Lord, holy and true, wilt Thou refrain from judging and avenging our blood on those who dwell on the earth?"

11 And there was given to each of them a white robe; and they were told that they should rest for a little while longer, until *the number of* their fellow-servants and their brethren who were to be killed even as they had been, should be completed also.

12 And I looked when He broke the sixth seal, and there was a great earthquake; and the sun became black as sackcloth *made* of hair, and the whole moon became like blood;

13 and the stars of the sky fell to the earth, as a fig tree casts its unripe figs when shaken by a great wind.

14 And the sky was split apart like a scroll when it is rolled up; and every mountain and island were moved out of their places.

15 And the kings of the earth and the great men and the commanders and the rich and the strong and every slave and free man, hid themselves in the caves and among the rocks of the mountains;

16 and they *said to the mountains and to the rocks, "Fall on us and hide us from the presence of Him who sits on the throne, and from the wrath of the Lamb;

17 for the great day of their wrath has come; and who is able to stand?"

Chapter 7

AFTER this I saw four angels standing at the four corners of the earth, holding back the four winds of the earth, so that no wind should blow on the earth or on the sea or on any tree.

2 And I saw another angel ascending from the rising of the sun, having the seal of the living God; and he cried out with a loud voice to the four angels to whom it was granted to harm the earth and the sea,

3 saying, "Do not harm the earth or the sea or the trees, until we have sealed the bond-servants of our God on their foreheads."

4 And I heard the number of those who were sealed, one hundred and forty-four thousand sealed from every tribe of the sons of Israel:

5 from the tribe of Judah, twelve thousand *were* sealed, from the tribe of Reuben twelve thousand, from the tribe of Gad twelve thousand,

6 from the tribe of Asher twelve thousand, from the tribe of Naphtali twelve thousand, from the tribe of Manasseh twelve thousand,

7 from the tribe of Simeon twelve thousand, from the tribe of Levi twelve thousand, from the tribe of Issachar twelve thousand,

8 from the tribe of Zebulun twelve thousand, from the tribe of Joseph twelve thousand, from the tribe of Benjamin, twelve thousand *were* sealed.

9 After these things I looked, and behold, a great multitude, which no one could count, from every nation and *all* tribes and peoples and tongues, standing before the throne and before the Lamb, clothed in white robes, and palm branches *were* in their hands;

10 and they cry out with a loud voice, saying,

"**S**alvation to our God who sits on the throne, and to the Lamb."

11 And all the angels were standing around the throne and *around* the elders and the four living creatures; and they fell on their faces before the throne and worshiped God,

12 saying,

"**A**men, blessing and glory and wisdom and thanksgiving and honor and power and might, *be* to our God forever and ever. Amen."

13 And one of the elders answered, saying to me, "These who are clothed in the white robes, who are they, and from where have they come?"

14 And I said to him, "My lord, you know." And he said to me, "These are the ones who come out of the great tribulation, and they have washed their robes and made them white in the blood of the Lamb.

15 "For this reason, they are before the throne of God; and they serve Him day and night in His temple; and He who sits on the throne shall spread His tabernacle over them.

16 "They shall hunger no more, neither thirst any more; neither shall the sun beat down on them, nor any heat;

17 for the Lamb in the center of the throne shall be their shepherd, and shall guide them to springs of the water of life; and God shall wipe every tear from their eyes."

Chapter 8

AND when He broke the seventh seal, there was silence in heaven for about half an hour.

2 And I saw the seven angels who stand before God; and seven trumpets were given to them.

3 And another angel came and stood at the altar, holding a golden censer; and much incense was given to him, that he might add it to the prayers of all the saints upon the golden altar which was before the throne.

4 And the smoke of the incense, with the prayers of the saints, went up before God out of the angel's hand.

5 And the angel took the censer; and he filled it with the fire of the altar and threw it to the earth; and there followed peals of thunder and sounds and flashes of lightning and an earthquake.

6 And the seven angels who had the seven trumpets prepared themselves to sound them.

7 And the first sounded, and there came hail and fire, mixed with blood, and they were thrown to the earth; and a third of the earth was burnt up, and a third of the trees were burnt up, and all the green grass was burnt up.

8 And the second angel sounded, and *something* like a great mountain burning with fire was thrown into the sea; and a third of the sea became blood;

9 and a third of the creatures, which were in the sea and had life, died; and a third of the ships were destroyed.

10 And the third angel sounded, and a great star fell from heaven, burning like a torch, and it fell on a third of the rivers and on the springs of waters;

11 and the name of the star is called Wormwood; and a third of the waters became wormwood; and many men died from the waters, because they were made bitter.

12 And the fourth angel sounded, and a third of the sun and a third of the moon and a third of the stars were smitten, so that a third of them might be darkened and the day might not shine for a third of it, and the night in the same way.

13 And I looked, and I heard an eagle flying in midheaven, saying with a loud voice, "Woe, woe, woe, to those who dwell on the earth, because of the remaining blasts of the trumpet of the three angels who are about to sound!"

CHAPTER 9

AND the fifth angel sounded, and I saw a star from heaven which had fallen to the earth; and the key of the bottomless pit was given to him.

2 And he opened the bottomless pit; and smoke went up out of the pit, like the smoke of a great furnace; and the sun and the air were darkened by the smoke of the pit.

3 And out of the smoke came forth locusts upon the earth; and power was given them, as the scorpions of the earth have power.

4 And they were told that they should not hurt the grass of the earth, nor any green thing, nor any tree, but only the men who do not have the seal of God on their foreheads.

5 And they were not permitted to kill anyone, but to torment for five months; and their torment was like the torment of a scorpion when it stings a man.

6 And in those days men will seek death and will not find it; and they will long to die and death flees from them.

7 And the appearance of the locusts was like horses prepared for battle; and on their heads, as it were, crowns like gold, and their faces were like the faces of men.

8 And they had hair like the hair of women, and their teeth were like *the teeth* of lions.

9 And they had breastplates like breastplates of iron; and the sound of their wings was like the sound of chariots, of many horses rushing to battle.

10 And they have tails like scorpions, and stings; and in their tails is their power to hurt men for five months.

11 They have as king over them, the angel of the abyss; his name in Hebrew is Abaddon, and in the Greek he has the name Apollyon.

12 The first woe is past; behold, two woes are still coming after these things.

13 And the sixth angel sounded, and I heard a voice from the four horns of the golden altar which is before God,

14 one saying to the sixth angel who had the trumpet, "Release the four angels who are bound at the great river Euphrates."

15 And the four angels, who had been prepared for the hour and day and month and year, were released, so that they might kill a third of mankind.

16 And the number of the armies of the horsemen was two hundred million; I heard the number of them.

17 And this is how I saw in the vision the horses and those who sat on them: *the riders* had breastplates *the color* of fire and of hyacinth and of brimstone; and the heads of the horses are like the heads of lions; and out of their mouths proceed fire and smoke and brimstone.

18 A third of mankind was killed by these three plagues, by the fire and the smoke and the brimstone, which proceeded out of their mouths.

19 For the power of the horses is in their mouth and in their tails; for their tails are like serpents and have heads; and with them they do harm.

20 And the rest of mankind, who were not killed by these plagues, did not repent of THE WORKS OF THEIR HANDS, so as not to worship DEMONS, AND THE IDOLS OF GOLD AND OF SILVER AND OF BRASS AND OF STONE AND OF WOOD, WHICH CAN NEITHER SEE NOR HEAR NOR WALK;

21 and they did not repent of their murders nor of their sorceries nor of their immorality nor of their thefts.

CHAPTER 10

AND I saw another strong angel coming down out of heaven, clothed with a cloud; and the rainbow was upon his head, and his face was like the sun, and his feet like pillars of fire;

2 and he had in his hand a little book which was open. And he placed his right foot on the sea and his left on the land;

3 and he cried out with a loud voice, as when a lion roars; and when he had cried out, the seven peals of thunder uttered their voices.

4 And when the seven peals of thunder had spoken, I was about to write; and I heard a voice from heaven saying, "Seal up the things which the seven peals of thunder have spoken, and do not write them."

5 And the angel whom I saw standing on the sea and on the land LIFTED UP HIS RIGHT HAND TO HEAVEN,

6 AND SWORE BY HIM WHO LIVES FOREVER AND EVER, WHO CREATED HEAVEN AND THE THINGS IN IT, AND THE EARTH AND THE THINGS IN IT, AND THE SEA AND THE THINGS IN IT, that there shall be delay no longer,

7 but in the days of the voice of the seventh angel, when he is about to sound, then the mystery of God is finished, as He preached to His servants the prophets.

8 And the voice which I heard from heaven, *I heard* again speaking with me, and saying, "Go, take the book which is open in the hand of the

angel who stands on the sea and on the land."

9 And I went to the angel, telling him to give me the little book. And he *said to me, "Take it, and eat it; and it will make your stomach bitter, but in your mouth it will be sweet as honey."

10 And I took the little book out of the angel's hand and ate it, and it was in my mouth sweet as honey; and when I had eaten it, my stomach was made bitter.

11 And they *said to me, "You must prophesy again concerning many peoples and nations and tongues and kings."

CHAPTER 11

AND there was given me a measuring rod like a staff; and someone said, "Rise and measure the temple of God, and the altar, and those who worship in it.

2 "And leave out the court which is outside the temple, and do not measure it, for it has been given to the nations; and they will tread under foot the holy city for forty-two months.

3 "And I will grant *authority* to my .two witnesses, and they will prophesy for twelve hundred and sixty days, clothed in sackcloth."

4 These are the two olive trees and the two lampstands that stand before the Lord of the earth.

5 And if any one desires to harm them, fire proceeds out of their mouth and devours their enemies; and if any one would desire to harm them, in this manner he must be killed.

6 These have the power to shut up the sky, in order that rain may not fall during the days of their prophesying; and they have power over the waters to turn them into blood, and to smite the earth with every plague, as often as they desire.

7 And when they have finished their testimony, the beast that comes up out of the abyss will make war with them, and overcome them and kill them.

8 And their dead bodies *will lie* in the street of the great city which mystically is called Sodom and Egypt, where also their Lord was crucified.

9 And those from the peoples and tribes and tongues and nations *will* look at their dead bodies for three days and a half, and will not permit their dead bodies to be laid in a tomb.

10 And those who dwell on the earth *will* rejoice over them and make merry; and they will send gifts to one another, because these two prophets tormented those who dwell on the earth.

11 And after the three days and a half the breath of life from God came into them, and they stood on their feet; and great fear fell upon those who were beholding them.

12 And they heard a loud voice from heaven saying to them, "Come up here." And they went up into heaven in the cloud, and their enemies beheld them.

13 And in that hour there was a great earthquake, and a tenth of the city fell; and seven thousand people were killed in the earthquake, and the rest were terrified and gave glory to the God of heaven.

14 The second woe is past; behold, the third woe is coming quickly.

15 And the seventh angel sounded; and there arose loud voices in heaven, saying,

"The kingdom of the world has become *the kingdom* of our Lord, and of His Christ; and He will reign forever and ever."

16 And the twenty-four elders, who sit on their thrones before God, fell on their faces and worshiped God,

17 saying,

"**W**e give Thee thanks, O Lord God, the Almighty, who art and who wast, because Thou hast taken Thy great power and hast begun to reign.

18 "And the nations were enraged, and Thy wrath came, and the time *came* for the dead to be judged, and *the time* to give their reward to Thy bond-servants the prophets and to the saints and to those who fear Thy name, the small and the great, and to destroy those who destroy the earth."

19 And the temple of God which is in heaven was opened; and the ark of His covenant appeared in His temple, and there were flashes of lightning and sounds and peals of thunder and an earthquake and a great hailstorm.

CHAPTER 12

AND a great sign appeared in heaven: a woman clothed with the sun, and the moon under her feet, and on her head a crown of twelve stars;

2 and she was with child; and she *cried out, being in labor and in pain to give birth.

3 And another sign appeared in heaven: and behold, a great red dragon having seven heads and ten horns, and on his heads *were* seven diadems.

4 And his tail *swept away a third of the stars of heaven, and threw them to the earth. And the dragon stood before the woman who was about to give birth, so that when she gave birth he might devour her child.

5 And she gave birth to a son, a male *child*, who is to rule all the nations with a rod of iron; and her child was caught up to God and to His throne.

6 And the woman fled into the wilderness where she *had a place prepared by God, so that there she

might be nourished for one thousand two hundred and sixty days.

7 And there was war in heaven, Michael and his angels waging war with the dragon. And the dragon and his angels waged war,

8 and they were not strong enough, and there was no longer a place found for them in heaven.

9 And the great dragon was thrown down, the serpent of old who is called the devil and Satan, who deceives the whole world; he was thrown down to the earth, and his angels were thrown down with him.

10 And I heard a loud voice in heaven, saying,

"**N**ow the salvation, and the power, and the kingdom of our God and the authority of His Christ have come, for the accuser of our brethren has been thrown down, who accuses them before our God day and night.

11 "And they overcame him because of the blood of the Lamb and because of the word of their testimony, and they did not love their life even to death.

12 "For this reason, rejoice, O heavens and you who dwell in them. Woe to the earth and the sea; because the devil has come down to you, having great wrath, knowing that he has *only* a short time."

13 And when the dragon saw that he was thrown down to the earth, he persecuted the woman who gave birth to the male *child*.

14 And the two wings of the great eagle were given to the woman, in order that she might fly into the wilderness to her place, where she *was nourished for a time and times and half a time, from the presence of the serpent.

15 And the serpent poured water like a river out of his mouth after the woman, so that he might cause her to be swept away with the flood.

16 And the earth helped the

woman, and the earth opened its mouth and drank up the river which the dragon poured out of his mouth.

17 And the dragon was enraged with the woman, and went off to make war with the rest of her offspring, who keep the commandments of God and hold to the testimony of Jesus.

Chapter 13

AND he stood on the sand of the seashore.

And I saw a beast coming up out of the sea, having ten horns and seven heads, and on his horns *were* ten diadems, and on his heads *were* blasphemous names.

2 And the beast which I saw was like a leopard, and his feet were *like those* of a bear, and his mouth like the mouth of a lion. And the dragon gave him his power and his throne and great authority.

3 And *I saw* one of his heads as if it had been slain, and his fatal wound was healed. And the whole earth was amazed *and followed* after the beast;

4 and they worshiped the dragon, because he gave his authority to the beast; and they worshiped the beast, saying, "Who is like the beast, and who is able to wage war with him?"

5 And there was given to him a mouth speaking arrogant words and blasphemies; and authority to act for forty-two months was given to him.

6 And he opened his mouth in blasphemies against God, to blaspheme His name and His tabernacle, *that is,* those who dwell in heaven.

7 And it was given to him to make war with the saints and to overcome them; and authority over every tribe and people and tongue and nation was given to him.

8 And all who dwell on the earth will worship him, *every one* whose name has not been written from the foundation of the world in the book of life of the Lamb who has been slain.

9 If any one has an ear, let him hear.

10 If any one *is destined* for captivity, to captivity he goes; if any one kills with the sword, with the sword he must be killed. Here is the perseverance and the faith of the saints.

11 And I saw another beast coming up out of the earth; and he had two horns like a lamb, and he spoke as a dragon.

12 And he exercises all the authority of the first beast in his presence. And he makes the earth and those who dwell in it to worship the first beast, whose fatal wound was healed.

13 And he performs great signs, so that he even makes fire come down out of heaven to the earth in the presence of men.

14 And he deceives those who dwell on the earth because of the signs which it was given him to perform in the presence of the beast, telling those who dwell on the earth to make an image to the beast who *had the wound of the sword and has come to life.

15 And there was given to him to give breath to the image of the beast, that the image of the beast might even speak and cause as many as do not worship the image of the beast to be killed.

16 And he causes all, the small and the great, and the rich and the poor, and the free men and the slaves, to be given a mark on their right hand, or on their forehead,

17 and *he provides* that no one should be able to buy or to sell, except the one who has the mark, *either* the name of the beast or the number of his name.

18 Here is wisdom. Let him who has understanding calculate the number of the beast, for the number is that of a man; and his number is six hundred and sixty-six.

CHAPTER 14

AND I looked, and behold, the Lamb *was* standing on Mount Zion, and with Him one hundred and forty-four thousand, having His name and the name of His Father written on their foreheads.

2 And I heard a voice from heaven, like the sound of many waters and like the sound of loud thunder, and the voice which I heard *was* like *the sound* of harpists playing on their harps.

3 And they *sang a new song before the throne and before the four living creatures and the elders; and no one could learn the song except the one hundred and forty-four thousand who had been purchased from the earth.

4 These are the ones who have not been defiled with women, for they are celibates. These *are* the ones who follow the Lamb wherever He goes. These have been purchased from among men as first fruits to God and to the Lamb.

5 And no lie was found in their mouth; they are blameless.

6 And I saw another angel flying in midheaven, having an eternal gospel to preach to those who live on the earth, and to every nation and tribe and tongue and people;

7 and he said with a loud voice, "Fear God, and give Him glory, because the hour of His judgment has come; and worship Him who made the heaven and the earth and sea and springs of waters."

8 And another angel, a second one, followed, saying, "Fallen, fallen is Babylon the great, she who has made all the nations drink of the wine of the passion of her immorality."

9 And another angel, a third one, followed them, saying with a loud voice, "If any one worships the beast and his image, and receives a mark on his forehead or upon his hand,

10 he also will drink of the wine of the wrath of God, which is mixed in full strength in the cup of His anger; and he will be tormented with fire and brimstone in the presence of the holy angels and in the presence of the Lamb.

11 "And the smoke of their torment goes up forever and ever; and they have no rest day and night, those who worship the beast and his image, and whoever receives the mark of his name."

12 Here is the perseverance of the saints who keep the commandments of God and their faith in Jesus.

13 And I heard a voice from heaven, saying, "Write, 'Blessed are the dead who die in the Lord from now on!'" "Yes," says the Spirit, "that they may rest from their labors, for their deeds follow with them."

14 And I looked, and behold, a white cloud, and sitting on the cloud *was* one like a son of man, having a golden crown on His head, and a sharp sickle in His hand.

15 And another angel came out of the temple, crying out with a loud voice to Him who sat on the cloud, "Put in your sickle and reap, because the hour to reap has come, because the harvest of the earth is ripe."

16 And He who sat on the cloud swung His sickle over the earth; and the earth was reaped.

17 And another angel came out of the temple which is in heaven, and he also had a sharp sickle.

18 And another angel, the one who has power over fire, came out from the altar; and he called with a loud voice to him who had the sharp sickle, saying, "Put in your sharp sickle, and gather the clusters from the vine of the earth, because her grapes are ripe."

19 And the angel swung his sickle

to the earth, and gathered *the clusters from* the vine of the earth, and threw them into the great wine press of the wrath of God.

20   And the wine press was trodden outside the city, and blood came out from the wine press, up to the horses' bridles, for a distance of two hundred miles.

Chapter 15

AND I saw another sign in heaven, great and marvelous, seven angels who had seven plagues, *which are* the last, because in them the wrath of God is finished.

2   And I saw, as it were, a sea of glass mixed with fire, and those who had come off victorious from the beast and from his image and from the number of his name, standing on the sea of glass, holding harps of God.

3   And they *sang the song of Moses the bond-servant of God and the song of the Lamb, saying,

"GREAT AND MARVELOUS ARE
    THY WORKS,
O LORD GOD, THE ALMIGHTY;
RIGHTEOUS AND TRUE ARE THY
    WAYS,
THOU KING OF THE NATIONS.
4   "WHO WILL NOT FEAR, O LORD,
    AND GLORIFY THY NAME?
FOR THOU ALONE ART HOLY;
FOR ALL THE NATIONS WILL
    COME AND WORSHIP BEFORE
    THEE,
For Thy righteous acts have
    been revealed."

5   After these things I looked, and the temple of the tabernacle of testimony in heaven was opened,

6   and the seven angels who had the seven plagues came out of the temple, clothed in linen, clean *and* bright, and girded around their breasts with golden girdles.

7   And one of the four living creatures gave to the seven angels seven golden bowls full of the wrath of God, who lives forever and ever.

8   And the temple was filled with smoke from the glory of God and from His power; and no one was able to enter the temple until the seven plagues of the seven angels were finished.

Chapter 16

AND I heard a loud voice from the temple, saying to the seven angels, "Go and pour out the seven bowls of the wrath of God into the earth."

2   And the first *angel* went and poured out his bowl into the earth; and it became a loathsome and malignant sore upon the men who had the mark of the beast and who worshiped his image.

3   And the second *angel* poured out his bowl into the sea, and it became blood like *that* of a dead man; and every living thing in the sea died.

4   And the third *angel* poured out his bowl into the rivers and the springs of waters; and they became blood.

5   And I heard the angel of the waters saying, "Righteous art Thou, who art and who wast, O Holy One, because Thou didst judge these things;

6   for they poured out the blood of saints and prophets, and Thou hast given them blood to drink. They deserve it."

7   And I heard the altar saying, "Yes, O Lord God, the Almighty, true and righteous are Thy judgments."

8   And the fourth *angel* poured out his bowl upon the sun; and it was given to it to scorch men with fire.

9   And men were scorched with fierce heat; and they blasphemed the name of God who has the power over these plagues; and they did not repent, so as to give Him glory.

10 And the fifth *angel* poured out his bowl upon the throne of the beast; and his kingdom became darkened; and they gnawed their tongues because of pain,

11 and they blasphemed the God of heaven because of their pains and their sores; and they did not repent of their deeds.

12 And the sixth *angel* poured out his bowl upon the great river, the Euphrates; and its water was dried up, that the way might be prepared for the kings from the east.

13 And I saw *coming* out of the mouth of the dragon and out of the mouth of the beast and out of the mouth of the false prophet, three unclean spirits like frogs;

14 for they are spirits of demons, performing signs, which go out to the kings of the whole world, to gather them together for the war of the great day of God, the Almighty.

15 (Behold, I am coming like a thief. Blessed is the one who stays awake and keeps his garments, lest he walk about naked and men see his shame.)

16 And they gathered them together to the place which in Hebrew is called Har-Magedon.

17 And the seventh *angel* poured out his bowl upon the air; and a loud voice came out of the temple from the throne, saying, "It is done."

18 And there were flashes of lightning and sounds and peals of thunder; and there was a great earthquake, such as there had not been since man came to be upon the earth, so great an earthquake *was it, and* so mighty.

19 And the great city was split into three parts, and the cities of the nations fell. And Babylon the great was remembered before God, to give her the cup of the wine of His fierce wrath.

20 And every island fled away, and the mountains were not found.

21 And huge hailstones, about one hundred pounds each, *came down from heaven upon men; and men blasphemed God because of the plague of the hail, because its plague *was extremely severe.

CHAPTER 17

AND one of the seven angels who had the seven bowls came and spoke with me, saying, "Come here, I shall show you the judgment of the great harlot who sits on many waters,

2 with whom the kings of the earth committed *acts of* immorality, and those who dwell on the earth were made drunk with the wine of her immorality."

3 And he carried me away in the Spirit into a wilderness; and I saw a woman sitting on a scarlet beast, full of blasphemous names, having seven heads and ten horns.

4 And the woman was clothed in purple and scarlet, and adorned with gold and precious stones and pearls, having in her hand a gold cup full of abominations and of the unclean things of her immorality,

5 and upon her forehead a name *was* written, a mystery, "BABYLON THE GREAT, THE MOTHER OF HARLOTS AND OF THE ABOMINATIONS OF THE EARTH."

6 And I saw the woman drunk with the blood of the saints, and with the blood of the witnesses of Jesus. And when I saw her, I wondered greatly.

7 And the angel said to me, "Why do you wonder? I shall tell you the mystery of the woman and of the beast that carries her, which has the seven heads and the ten horns.

8 "The beast that you saw was and is not, and is about to come up out of the abyss and to go to destruction. And those who dwell on the earth will wonder, whose name has not been written in the book of life from the foundation of the world, when they see the beast, that he was and is not and will come.

9 "Here is the mind which has wisdom. The seven heads are seven mountains on which the woman sits,

10 and they are seven kings; five have fallen, one is, the other has not yet come; and when he comes, he must remain a little while.

11 "And the beast which was and is not, is himself also an eighth, and is *one* of the seven, and he goes to destruction.

12 "And the ten horns which you saw are ten kings, who have not yet received a kingdom, but they receive authority as kings with the beast for one hour.

13 "These have one purpose and they give their power and authority to the beast.

14 "These will wage war against the Lamb, and the Lamb will overcome them, because He is Lord of lords and King of kings, and those who are with Him *are the* called and chosen and faithful."

15 And he *said to me, "The waters which you saw where the harlot sits, are peoples and multitudes and nations and tongues.

16 "And the ten horns which you saw, and the beast, these will hate the harlot and will make her desolate and naked, and will eat her flesh and will burn her up with fire.

17 "For God has put it in their hearts to execute His purpose by having a common purpose, and by giving their kingdom to the beast, until the words of God should be fulfilled.

18 "And the woman whom you saw is the great city, which reigns over the kings of the earth."

Chapter 18

After these things I saw another angel coming down from heaven, hav-

ing great authority, and the earth was illumined with his glory.

2 And he cried out with a mighty voice, saying, "Fallen, fallen is Babylon the great! And she has become a dwelling place of demons and a prison of every unclean spirit, and a prison of every unclean and hateful bird.

3 "For all the nations have drunk of the wine of the passion of her immorality, and the kings of the earth have committed *acts of* immorality with her, and the merchants of the earth have become rich by the wealth of her sensuality."

4 And I heard another voice from heaven, saying, "Come out of her, my people, that you may not participate in her sins and that you may not receive of her plagues;

5 for her sins have piled up as high as heaven, and God has remembered her iniquities.

6 "Pay her back even as she has paid, and give back *to her* double according to her deeds; in the cup which she has mixed, mix twice as much for her.

7 "To the degree that she glorified herself and lived sensuously, to the same degree give her torment and mourning; for she says in her heart, 'I sit *as* a queen and I am not a widow, and will never see mourning.'

8 "For this reason in one day her plagues will come, pestilence and mourning and famine, and she will be burned up with fire; for the Lord God who judges her is strong.

9 "And the kings of the earth, who committed *acts of* immorality and lived sensuously with her, will weep and lament over her when they see the smoke of her burning,

10 standing at a distance because of the fear of her torment, saying, 'Woe, woe, the great city, Babylon, the strong city! For in one hour your judgment has come.'

11 "And the merchants of the earth

weep and mourn over her, because no one buys their cargoes any more;

12 cargoes of gold and silver and precious stones and pearls and fine linen and purple and silk and scarlet, and every *kind of* citron wood and every article of ivory and every article *made* from very costly wood and bronze and iron and marble,

13 and cinnamon and spice and incense and perfume and frankincense and wine and olive oil and fine flour and wheat and cattle and sheep, and *cargoes* of horses and chariots and slaves and human lives.

14 "And the fruit you long for has gone from you, and all things that were luxurious and splendid have passed away from you and *men* will no longer find them.

15 "The merchants of these things, who became rich from her, will stand at a distance because of the fear of her torment, weeping and mourning,

16 saying, 'Woe, woe, the great city, she who was clothed in fine linen and purple and scarlet, and adorned with gold and precious stones and pearls;

17 for in one hour such great wealth has been laid waste!' And every shipmaster and every passenger and sailor, and as many as make their living by the sea, stood at a distance,

18 and were crying out as they saw the smoke of her burning, saying, 'What *city* is like the great city?'

19 "And they threw dust on their heads and were crying out, weeping and mourning, saying, 'Woe, woe, the great city, in which all who had ships at sea became rich by her wealth, for in one hour she has been laid waste!'

20 "Rejoice over her, O heaven, and you saints and apostles and prophets, because God has pronounced judgment for you against her."

21 And a strong angel took up a stone like a great millstone and threw it into the sea, saying, "Thus will Babylon, the great city, be thrown down with violence, and will not be found any longer.

22 "And the sound of harpists and musicians and flute-players and trumpeters will not be heard in you any longer; and no craftsman of any craft will be found in you any longer; and the sound of a mill will not be heard in you any longer;

23 and the light of a lamp will not shine in you any longer; and the voice of the bridegroom and bride will not be heard in you any longer; for your merchants were the great men of the earth, because all the nations were deceived by your sorcery.

24 "And in her was found the blood of prophets and of saints and of all who have been slain on the earth."

CHAPTER 19

AFTER these things I heard, as it were, a loud voice of a great multitude in heaven, saying,

"Hallelujah! Salvation and glory and power belong to our God;

2 BECAUSE HIS JUDGMENTS ARE TRUE AND RIGHTEOUS; for He has judged the great harlot who was corrupting the earth with her immorality, and HE HAS AVENGED THE BLOOD OF HIS BOND-SERVANTS ON HER."

3 And a second time they said, "HALLELUJAH! HER SMOKE RISES UP FOREVER AND EVER."

4 And the twenty-four elders and the four living creatures fell down and worshiped God who sits on the throne saying, "Amen. Hallelujah!"

5 And a voice came from the throne, saying,

"GIVE PRAISE TO OUR GOD, ALL YOU HIS BOND-SERVANTS, YOU WHO FEAR HIM, THE SMALL AND THE GREAT."

6 And I heard, as it were, the voice of a great multitude and as the sound of many waters and as the

sound of mighty peals of thunder, saying,

"Hallelujah! For the Lord our God, the Almighty, reigns.

7 "Let us rejoice and be glad and give the glory to Him, for the marriage of the Lamb has come and His bride has made herself ready."

8 And it was given to her to clothe herself in fine linen, bright *and* clean; for the fine linen is the righteous acts of the saints.

9 And he *said to me, "Write, 'Blessed are those who are invited to the marriage supper of the Lamb.'" And he *said to me, "These are true words of God."

10 And I fell at his feet to worship him. And he *said to me, "Do not do that; I am a fellow-servant of yours and your brethren who hold the testimony of Jesus; worship God. For the testimony of Jesus is the spirit of prophecy."

11 And I saw heaven opened; and behold, a white horse, and He who sat upon it *is* called Faithful and True; and in righteousness He judges and wages war.

12 And His eyes *are* a flame of fire, and upon His head *are* many diadems; and He has a name written *upon Him* which no one knows except Himself.

13 And *He is* clothed with a robe dipped in blood; and His name is called The Word of God.

14 And the armies which are in heaven, clothed in fine linen, white *and* clean, were following Him on white horses.

15 And from His mouth comes a sharp sword, so that with it He may smite the nations; and He will rule them with a rod of iron; and He treads the wine press of the fierce wrath of God, the Almighty.

16 And on His robe and on His thigh He has a name written, "KING OF KINGS, AND LORD OF LORDS."

17 And I saw an angel standing in the sun; and he cried out with a loud voice, saying to all the birds which fly in midheaven, "Come, assemble for the great supper of God;

18 in order that you may eat the flesh of kings and the flesh of commanders and the flesh of mighty men and the flesh of horses and of those who sit on them and the flesh of all men, both free men and slaves, and small and great."

19 And I saw the beast and the kings of the earth and their armies, assembled to make war against Him who sat upon the horse, and against His army.

20 And the beast was seized, and with him the false prophet who performed the signs in his presence, by which he deceived those who had received the mark of the beast and those who worshiped his image; these two were thrown alive into the lake of fire which burns with brimstone.

21 And the rest were killed with the sword which came from the mouth of Him who sat upon the horse, and all the birds were filled with their flesh.

CHAPTER 20

AND I saw an angel coming down from heaven, having the key of the abyss and a great chain in his hand.

2 And he laid hold of the dragon, the serpent of old, who is the devil and Satan, and bound him for a thousand years,

3 and threw him into the abyss, and shut *it* and sealed *it* over him, so that he should not deceive the nations any longer, until the thousand years were completed; after these things he must be released for a short time.

4 And I saw thrones, and they sat upon them, and judgment was given to them. And I *saw* the souls of those who had been beheaded because of

the testimony of Jesus and because of the word of God, and those who had not worshiped the beast or his image, and had not received the mark upon their forehead and upon their hand; and they came to life and reigned with Christ for a thousand years.

5 The rest of the dead did not come to life until the thousand years were completed. This is the first resurrection.

6 Blessed and holy is the one who has a part in the first resurrection; over these the second death has no power, but they will be priests of God and of Christ and will reign with Him for a thousand years.

7 And when the thousand years are completed, Satan will be released from his prison,

8 and will come out to deceive the nations which are in the four corners of the earth, Gog and Magog, to gather them together for the war; the number of them is like the sand of the seashore.

9 And they came up on the broad plain of the earth and surrounded the camp of the saints and the beloved city, and fire came down from heaven and devoured them.

10 And the devil who deceived them was thrown into the lake of fire and brimstone, where the beast and the false prophet are also; and they will be tormented day and night forever and ever.

11 And I saw a great white throne and Him who sat upon it, from whose presence earth and heaven fled away, and no place was found for them.

12 And I saw the dead, the great and the small, standing before the throne, and books were opened; and another book was opened, which is *the book* of life; and the dead were judged from the things which were written in the books, according to their deeds.

13 And the sea gave up the dead which were in it, and death and Hades gave up the dead which were in them; and they were judged, every one *of them* according to their deeds.

14 And death and Hades were thrown into the lake of fire. This is the second death, the lake of fire.

SCRIPTURE No. 7, SEC. 3

15 And if anyone's name was not found written in the book of life, he was thrown into the lake of fire. (r7)

(r7) REFERENCE NO. 7, SEC. 3—YOUR NAME MUST BE RECORDED.

There is no escape from the "lake of fire" at God's Judgement at the "great white throne" if your name is "not found written in the book of life". You will be "thrown into the lake of fire." So you must have your name "recorded in heaven" in the book of life. To have your name recorded there you repent, believe on Jesus Christ, receive Him as Saviour, and confess Him before men. To repent is to change your mind, heart and direction. Express your repentance in prayer. Believe God will save you as you call on His name. Say this prayer:

"God, I am a sinner. I see I am lost. I cannot save myself for the wages of my sin is death. I believe Jesus Christ died for my sins. I trust Him now as my personal saviour. Come into my heart Lord Jesus. God be merciful to me a sinner. In Jesus name I pray."

God heard you the moment you prayed from your heart. Believe He now saves you. Confess Jesus Christ before men. He will confess you in heaven. As your name is called in heaven it is recorded in heaven.

For further study, see page 370 on Manifestations of Maturity.

CHAPTER 21

AND I saw a new heaven and a new earth; for the first heaven and the first earth passed away, and there is no longer *any* sea.

2 And I saw the holy city, new Jerusalem, coming down out of heaven from God, made ready as a bride adorned for her husband.

3 And I heard a loud voice from the throne, saying, "Behold, the tabernacle of God is among men, and He shall dwell among them, and they shall be His people, and God Himself shall be among them,

4 and He shall wipe away every tear from their eyes; and there shall no longer be *any* death; there shall no longer be *any* mourning, or crying, or pain; the first things have passed away."

5 And He who sits on the throne said, "Behold, I am making all things new." And He *said, "Write, for these words are faithful and true."

6 And He said to me, "It is done. I am the Alpha and the Omega, the beginning and the end. I will give to the one who thirsts from the spring of the water of life without cost.

7 "He who overcomes shall inherit these things, and I will be his God and he will be My son.

8 "But for the cowardly and unbelieving and abominable and murderers and immoral persons and sorcerers and idolaters and all liars, their part *will be* in the lake that burns with fire and brimstone, which is the second death."

9 And one of the seven angels who had the seven bowls full of the seven last plagues, came and spoke with me, saying, "Come here, I shall show you the bride, the wife of the Lamb."

10 And he carried me away in the Spirit to a great and high mountain, and showed me the holy city, Jerusalem, coming down out of heaven from God,

11 having the glory of God. Her brilliance was like a very costly stone, as a stone of crystal-clear jasper.

12 It had a great and high wall, with twelve gates, and at the gates twelve angels; and names *were* written on them, which are *those* of the twelve tribes of the sons of Israel.

13 *There were* three gates on the east and three gates on the north and three gates on the south and three gates on the west.

14 And the wall of the city had twelve foundation stones, and on them *were* the twelve names of the twelve apostles of the Lamb.

15 And the one who spoke with me had a gold measuring rod to measure the city, and its gates and its wall.

16 And the city is laid out as a square, and its length is as great as the width; and he measured the city with the rod, fifteen hundred miles; its length and width and height are equal.

17 And he measured its wall, seventy-two yards, *according to* human measurements, which are *also* angelic *measurements*.

18 And the material of the wall was jasper; and the city was pure gold, like clear glass.

19 The foundation stones of the city wall were adorned with every kind of precious stone. The first foundation stone was jasper; the second, sapphire; the third, chalcedony; the fourth, emerald;

20 the fifth, sardonyx; the sixth, sardius; the seventh, chrysolite; the eighth, beryl; the ninth, topaz; the tenth, chrysoprase; the eleventh, jacinth; the twelfth, amethyst.

21 And the twelve gates were twelve pearls; each one of the gates was a single pearl. And the street of the city was pure gold, like transparent glass.

22 And I saw no temple in it, for the Lord God, the Almighty, and the Lamb, are its temple.

23 And the city has no need of the sun or of the moon to shine upon it, for the glory of God has illumined it, and its lamp *is* the Lamb.

24 And the nations shall walk by its light, and the kings of the earth shall bring their glory into it.

25 And in the daytime (for there shall be no night there) its gates shall never be closed;

26 and they shall bring the glory and the honor of the nations into it;

Scripture No. 6, Sec. 3

27 and nothing unclean and no one who practices abomination and lying, shall ever come into it, but only those whose names are written in the Lamb's book of life. (r6)

Chapter 22

AND he showed me a river of the water of life, clear as crystal, coming from the throne of God and of the Lamb,

2 in the middle of its street. And on either side of the river was the tree of life, bearing twelve *kinds of* fruit, yielding its fruit every month; and the leaves of the tree were for the healing of the nations.

3 And there shall no longer be any curse; and the throne of God and of the Lamb shall be in it, and His bond-servants shall serve Him;

4 and they shall see His face, and His name *shall be* on their foreheads.

5 And there shall no longer be *any* night; and they shall not have need of the light of a lamp nor the light of the sun, because the Lord God shall illumine them; and they shall reign forever and ever.

6 And he said to me, "These words are faithful and true"; and the Lord, the God of the spirits of the prophets, sent His angel to show to His bond-servants the things which must shortly take place.

7 "And behold, I am coming quickly. Blessed is he who heeds the words of the prophecy of this book."

8 And I, John, am the one who heard and saw these things. And when I heard and saw, I fell down to worship at the feet of the angel who showed me these things.

9 And he *said to me, "Do not do that; I am a fellow-servant of yours and of your brethren the prophets

---

(r6) REFERENCE NO. 6, SEC. 3—
HOW YOU CAN KNOW YOU WILL ENTER HEAVEN.

No one "shall ever come into it, but only those whose names are written in the Lamb's book of life."

Entrance into heaven, the holy city, depends upon your name being written there. Jesus said, "I say to you, unless one is born again, he cannot see the Kingdom of God" and "he cannot enter into the Kingdom of God." To be "born again" requires "repentance toward God and faith in our Lord Jesus Christ." Therefore you must repent and trust Christ Jesus as Savior. Then as a son "of God through faith in Christ Jesus" your name will be recorded among the "first born." This will give you the right to enter heaven.

Do you want the assurance you have been born again, have eternal life and the right to enter heaven? If so, say:

"I desire to repent of my sins and receive Christ as savior so that I'll be sure to enter heaven."

Now turn to page 347, Scripture No. 7, Sec. 3, Rev. 20:15.

and of those who heed the words of this book; worship God."

10 And he *said to me, "Do not seal up the words of the prophecy of this book, for the time is near.

11 "Let the one who does wrong, still do wrong; and let the one who is filthy, still be filthy; and let the one who is righteous, still practice righteousness; and let the one who is holy, still keep himself holy."

12 "Behold, I am coming quickly, and My reward is with Me, to render to every man according to what he has done.

13 "I am the Alpha and the Omega, the first and the last, the beginning and the end."

14 Blessed are those who wash their robes, that they may have the right to the tree of life, and may enter by the gates into the city.

15 Outside are the dogs and the sorcerers and the immoral persons and the murderers and the idolaters, and everyone who loves and practices lying.

16 "I, Jesus, have sent My angel to testify to you these things for the churches. I am the root and the offspring of David, the bright morning star."

17 And the Spirit and the bride say, "Come." And let the one who hears say, "Come." And let the one who is thirsty come; let the one who wishes take the water of life without cost.

18 I testify to everyone who hears the words of the prophecy of this book: if anyone adds to them, God shall add to him the plagues which are written in this book;

19 and if anyone takes away from the words of the book of this prophecy, God shall take away his part from the tree of life and from the holy city, which are written in this book.

20 He who testifies to these things says, "Yes, I am coming quickly." Amen. Come, Lord Jesus. (a)

21 The grace of the Lord Jesus be with all. Amen.

(a) The Sudden Second Coming of Christ.

Jesus Christ will return to earth "just like a thief in the night". This inevitable event is:

CERTAIN—"For the Lord Himself shall descend from heaven with a shout," I Thes. 4:16, page 280. "Then He will sit on His glorious throne", Matt. 25:31, page 37. Then there will be the

CALL OF THE ARCHANGEL AT HIS COMING—"With the Voice of the Archangel . . . and the dead in Christ shall rise first." I Thes. 4:16. "All who are in the tombs shall hear his voice, and shall come forth," John 5:28, 29, page 130. And likewise there will be the

CATCHING AWAY OF THE SAVED TO BE WITH CHRIST—"Then we who are alive and remain shall be caught up together with them (the dead in Christ) to meet the Lord in the air, and thus we shall always be with the Lord." I Thes. 4:17, page 280. "We shall all be changed, in a moment, in the twinkling of an eye, at the last trumpet," I Cor. 15:51, 52, page 243. Then

CALAMITY BEFALLS THE LOST AT HIS COMING—"The Lord Jesus shall be revealed from heaven with His mighty angels in flaming fire, dealing out retribution to those who do not know God and to those who do not obey the gospel of our Lord Jesus," II Thes. 1:7, 10, pages 281, 282.

"For this reason you be ready too; for the Son of Man is coming at an hour when you do not think He will," Matt. 24:44, page 36.

So turn to page 219, study Reference No. 6, Sec. 1 and pray the prayer suggested there.

VISITATION EVANGELISM

How you and your church can use the Soul Winner's New American Standard New Testament in visitation and witnessing.

MISSION OF SOUL WINNING

The Soul Winner is called of God. He is privileged to perform a most sacred task. He is the human instrument the Holy Spirit uses to bring about the new birth of babes in Christ. So let us consider the Holy Spirit's method of using the Word of God, His message, the miracle He performs, and the maturity of newborn babes into men in Christ.

VOLUNTEERS TO VISIT

Enlisting volunteers to visit and witness with the Word is most difficult, since so many demands are made upon the people of God for their time. God can help you challenge them to arrange their priorities so that witnessing with the Word has its proper place in their lives. You will appeal to two groups:

First, you can with confidence assure the Christian who has never witnessed that he can now win a soul to Christ since he has a chain of references in the Soul Winner's New Testament providing him with all that he needs to say and all the scriptures he will need to use which are underlined and arranged numerically in a chain of references. He sees how easy it is with this soul-winning tool to witness as it becomes the source and the subject of the soul-winning conversation.

Second, the experienced Soul Winner who is open to innovation and is seeking ways to become more effective in witnessing. He will readily see that the Soul Winner's New Testament, as a gift to the new convert, will help him become established in the faith and active in the local church. The experienced Soul Winner heeds 2 John 8, page 326: "Watch yourselves, that you might not lose what we have accomplished, but that you may receive a full reward."

VICTORY—A MATURE MAN IN CHRIST

Maturity of the new Christian may be achieved by use of the section called "Maturing the New Man" (page 367) and the section entitled "Manifestation of Maturity" (page 370). Evangelism is not complete until the convert becomes an evangelist with the Word that won him. This New Testament should be used by the convert for continued study and growth.

VISIT IN TEAMS OF TWO

Remember Luke 10:1, page 94, says: "The Lord appointed seventy others, and sent them two and two ahead of Him." Let us follow this example. Experience proves you will obtain best results when you enlist your people in teams of two for study, practice of witnessing, and visitation. The husband-and-wife team has proven most effective for witnessing to the whole family. It is best that men witness in teams of two as they visit men and boys, and two women or young women visit women and girls.

VISITATION TEAMS CONVENED TOGETHER

Please assemble the visiting teams in a room adequate but not too large for the group. The spirit of togetherness and fellowship is lost when a small group meets in a large room. When they are assembled together, give each one two copies of the Soul Winner's New American Standard New Testament—one copy for the witness to make his own, in which he may write notes and the six headings on the six pages beginning on page 186; and one for the prospect he expects to visit. When the visiting teams are seated with two copies of the Soul Winner's New Testament and a ballpoint pen in hand, they should follow these instructions to become familiar with this soul-winning tool.

Open the Soul Winner's New Testament to page 148, John 15:16. These are the words of Jesus to you: "You did not choose Me, but I chose you, and appointed you, that you should go and bear fruit, and that your fruit should remain, that whatever you ask of the Father in My name, He may give to you."

Next, let us consider the method, message, miracle, and maturity of the man in Christ.

GOD'S METHOD

The visiting teams are men and women of wisdom, for Proverbs 11:30 says: "He who is wise wins souls." You have volunteered to witness because God has given you a vision, and victory shall be yours. You can witness effectively with the Word.

You will observe that this is an effort to train witnesses to use this tool.

God said to Moses in Exodus 4:2: "What is that in your hand?" And Moses found the rod was a source of miracles. Likewise, what you have in your hand can be used of God to work miracles—yes, miracles of the New Birth and transformed lives.

I know your burden is for those persons in your Sunday School, church, or study group who attend church at various intervals, have heard the Gospel at least once, and live in a community where there is a Christian witness, but yet have not confessed Christ or made a public profession of faith. These are the ones whom we will call "prospects," which your church has discovered. They need to be discipled, developed to a point of understanding, and brought to a decision for Christ. Let God lead.

GOD'S MESSAGE

First, turn to page 186. Observe that the words of Acts 16:30-34 are underlined and identified as Scripture No. 1, Sec. 1. Then at the end of verse 34 you find (r1), which refers you to Reference No. 1, Sec. 1, at the bottom of the page, entitled

"What you must do to be Saved"

You will see that the last line directs you to page 209. Now, you see how the chain works. You cannot go wrong if you follow the instructions at the bottom of the page.

This is the first of six scriptures and references using the familiar "Roman Road to Salvation." These six references, including the prayer on page 219, can be read aloud with a prospect in approximately 10 minutes. This is the section of scriptures of the Soul Winner's New Testament which you will use most frequently in witnessing. Later, we will show you how to find God's will concerning which section of this book to use first with a prospect.

MANIFESTATION OF THE MIRACLE

Now, second, let us turn to page 45. You will see that the words of Matthew 28:18-20, are underlined and identified as Scripture No. 1, Sec. 2. This section consists of four scriptures and references entitled

"How you can show others you are Saved."

This section is not to be read until after the prospect has been taught or discipled. Baptism of believers follows their decision for Christ. The prospect is "dipped" only when he is developed to the point of visually showing what he has voiced in his confession of faith. Faith is seen in the baptismal waters. The believer shows his faith in the vicarious death of Christ, His atonement for sin and burial in the grave, and His victorious Resurrection from the dead. It is pantomiming or re-enacting the Gospel.

You will observe that this section leads the one who decides for Christ into the church and into a place of service and usefulness in the Kingdom of God.

Third, turn to page 270. Here you find Philippians 2:9-11 underlined and identified as Scripture No. 1, Sec. 3. This is the first of seven references concerning Scriptures answering the question "Is your name written in Heaven?" and showing how God's Word gives assurance that

"you can know you are saved, and that your name is written in the Lamb's Book of Life."

This section of seven scriptures has been most helpful in bringing a person who has confessed faith in Christ privately in the home, to make his profession publicly in the church.

Often a person who has read the six scriptures on "What he must do to be Saved" during the first visit, but did not make his decision for Christ and pray the prayer of repentence (page 219) has been led by God to pray the prayer on page 347 after reading the seven references during a second visit.

Fourth, turn to page 150. Here you find John 17:3 underlined and identified as Scripture No. 1, Sec. 4. This section is most effective when used with a person who does not believe in God, doubts the Bible to be His Word, and does not attend church. College students have a lot of questions. They have inquiring minds. Many have been won with this New Testament when the witness begins with this section. You can think of other classes of people who need to read this section first. God may lead you to use it with someone whom I would never think to suggest. Now let us consider

GOD'S ANSWERS TO MAN'S EXCUSES

Here is an example. Many times a prospect states, "I cannot be saved now because I cannot overcome temptation and live the Christian life." If this excuse is used, then respond to the prospect by inviting him to read the six references beginning on page 186, and assuring him that when these references are completed you will then show him how, with God's strength in him, he can "triumph over temptation." Then show him 1 Cor. 10:13 on pages 235 and 236 and the explanation at the bottom of page 236.

Your prospect may say, "I don't believe in a God who makes people suffer" or "I'm not ready to make my decision because I don't feel like it." Whenever an effort is made to divert your soul-winning thrust, always read the plan of salvation, the six references beginning on page 186. Assure the prospect that you will try to answer his doubts after you read Section 1.

When you have become thoroughly familiar with the four chains of references, study the Table of Contents on page V. Look up each heading. These references will help you answer many of man's excuses.

THE PRIMACY OF PRAYER

Because prayer is the primary thing in soul winning it should be offered in faith believing the promises of God before every witness.

Now turn to page XIII and read God's Promise as recorded in Jeremiah 33:3: "Call to Me, and I will answer you, and I will tell you great and mighty things, which you do not know."

You make a SIMPLE request.
God promises a SURE reply,
revealing SUPERNATURAL revelations,
with SURPRISING results.

As we employ God's method and deliver His message we must expect Him to work a miracle. The birth of a soul into the family of God is the work of the Holy Spirit. Now turn to page 133 and read John 6:63: "It is the Spirit who gives life; the flesh profits nothing; the words that I have spoken to you are spirit and are life."

The Soul Winner is only an instrument in God's hand. As we use the tool of His Word the Holy Spirit does His work through the witness whom He controls. It is God at work in us. We see this as we turn to page 270. Let us read Phil. 2:13: "For it is God who is at work in you, both to will and to work for His good pleasure." Let us remember that when we see the miracle which He performs through us in saving a soul we must give Him all the glory. We learn this on page 228. Let us read 1 Cor. 1:29: "No man should boast before God."

In this spirit of humility and total dependence upon God, study, practice, and witness to win the lost to Christ.

The Soul Winner's method has been tried in the crucible of trial and error over a period or more than a quarter of a century of personal soul winning. This method has been engaged in continually and has proven most successful for beginners.

You will observe as you read the references following each of the scriptures that there has been a diligent effort to employ the scripture as found in its context in the Bible to explain the scripture. The Bible is the best commentary on the Bible. Now that we have looked at the tool in our hands, let us study:

THE METHOD OF WITNESSING WITH THE WORD

(a) <u>PREPARATION</u>: Thorough preparation must be made before you witness. You will need in your hand a ballpoint pen, paper for making notes or recording information, prospect cards revealing all known information about the prospect, Soul Winner's New Testaments for each prospect, a witnessing partner, and any other person who may be expected to take part in the reading of the scripture. It is important that the name of your church, the name of the pastor, and the address of the church, be stamped on the presentation page of each Soul Winner's New Testament. It is best to have a recent church bulletin or a brochure on the program and staff of the church, to leave in the home visited. It is good to have a calling card of the church or pastor, with a place for you to sign as visitor, and don't forget you need that something that will give you confidence that your breath will be sweet and not offensive when you talk to the prospect.

(b) <u>PRAYER</u>: Prayer should be offered by you and your partner before you leave the church or place where you accept the assignment to go witnessing with the Word. Each should pray that the Holy Spirit will take complete charge of you as you witness. Believe that as the Holy Spirit guided Philip to the Ethiopian, whose mind was being prepared by the scriptures, that He will likewise guide you and open the heart of the prospect to read the scriptures aloud with you. Turn to page 172. Let us read Acts 8:30, 31: "And when Philip had run up, <u>HE HEARD HIM READING ISAIAH, THE PROPHET</u>, and said, 'Do you understand what you are reading?' And he said, 'How could I unless someone guides me?' And he invited Philip to come up and sit with him."

Pray that the prospect will join you in reading aloud, as you invite him to employ the method of looking at the scriptures and listening at the same time. You will gain his participation in the reading of God's Word and overcome any preoccupation that may hinder his concentration on the scriptures.

Your soul-winning witness should not be the first visit from your church to the prospect. Possibly he has been visited before by someone who employed a completely different technique in order to obtain information and extend an invitation to your church. This is not a preliminary visit but one in which you expect to see the power of God produce results that glorify Christ. You pray with the knowledge gained from the prospect card or from a previous visit. You know that the prospect is not related to any local church, and possibly, has never professed faith in Christ. After the preliminary visit, the church has decided to invest the cost of the Soul Winner's New Testament in the prospect's spiritual life. Now, your soul-winning visit, to be successful, must go right to the point, and not follow the usual plan of a preliminary visit or a visit to a newcomer in the community. There is a time and a season for everything; a time to get acquainted and a time to find mutual interests or concerns. During such times of visitation we gain information which can be used in the soul-winning witness.

So pray for yourselves—that God will give you wisdom and pray for the prospect that God will open his heart and mind to receive the Word.

(c.) PROSPECT'S FIRST IMPRESSION MUST BE FAVORABLE: When you arrive at the prospect's residence, pause for a brief prayer with your partner before you leave the car. There may have been distractions on the way that have disrupted your spiritual attitude. Total dependence upon God is evident when expressed in prayer to God. Seek His direction and power as you approach the prospect.

After you knock on the door, step back two paces, so that the one answering the door might clearly see both members of your witnessing team. Hold your Soul Winner's New American Standard New Testament, in clear view, so that it can be easily seen, and immediately state to the one at the door,

"I am _____(your name). This is (pointing to your witnessing partner) _____(his name). We are from _____(name and address of your church and the name of your pastor). We are visiting the ones in whom our church has a special interest. (If the one answering the door is not your prospect, then continue and say): We would like to see _____(name of prospect). May we come in?"

You will observe that in the opening statement, you have told the one at the door who you are, who is with you, where you are from, why you are present, and the person whom you desire to see. This method of introduction of yourselves at the door should be practiced by each one who witnesses until it becomes "natural" for you to do it. Promise yourself you will practice before you present yourself to any prospect.

(d) <u>PRESENTATION OF THE GIFT</u>: Once you are inside the door, and while standing in the presence of the prospect (be sure you are inside the residence and still near the door), then speak directly to him. You will have in your hand the Soul Winner's New American Standard New Testament opened to page 186. Extending the gift copy of the New Testament, state:

"We have a gift for you. May we show you how helpful it is? It makes Bible study easy, with explanations, references, helps and notes, as seldom found in any Bible."

Ordinarily, the prospect will invite you to take a soft seat on the couch or in an easy chair. Therefore say, "May we sit at a table? We would like to write something in your gift copy. These notes will remind you what we did here as we study the Bible together." Now that the Soul Winner's New Testament has become the SOURCE of your conversation make the gift the SUBJECT and stay in command. When seated at the table say, "Your copy is open to the first of the six foundational truths of the Christian faith beginning here on page 186. Observe the underlined scripture Acts 16:30-34 in the righthand column identified as Scripture No. 1, and the reference found at the bottom of the page. I will ask you to read with (turning to your witnessing partner—call his name) the underlined scriptures, beginning with verse 30. When you finish verse 34, I will read the reference at the bottom of the page. I will ask you to follow as I read, and when I come to the words, "If so, say," I will pause, and we will all read together aloud the quotation at the bottom of the reference before we turn, as it instructs us to do, to Scripture No. 2. It ordinarily takes about 10 minutes to read these six foundational truths aloud in unison. But first let me write in your New Testament. May we begin?"

Before your partner reads with the prospect verses 30 through

34, you will write in the prospect's Soul Winner's New Testament, at the top of page 186 in the margin the words:

"SIX FOUNDATIONAL TRUTHS OF THE CHRISTIAN FAITH."

Above the words "Scripture No. 1, Sec. 1," write the words: "Start here." At the bottom line on the page under the words, "Now turn to page 209," write the words: "Let us do this."

Then your partner will read aloud the five verses with the prospect. If the prospect has not chosen to read or possibly cannot read, then your partner is to read just the same as if he was participating with him, and not draw any attention to the fact that he is not participating.

Immediately upon their conclusion of verse 34, you will please state: "Will you now follow me as I read Reference No. 1 at the bottom of the page, and join me in reading aloud when we come to the quotation at the end of the reference?" Then begin reading with the title of the reference; read it all down to the words, "If so, say." Pause and ask the prospect and your partner to join you in reading the quotation. You, as a skillful Soul Winner, have already placed your index finger in page 209. As you conclude the quotation, you immediately say, "Now let us turn to page 209 and read Romans 3:23." Directing yourself to the prospect say, "This passage of scripture shows

"WHY ALL OF US NEED TO BE SAVED."

You are to write these words at the top of page 209. You will have already written them in your personal New Testament and it will be easy for you to copy them in his book. Then say, "Will you join (call the partner's name) in reading verse 23, at the bottom of the righthand column?" Immediately upon the completion of their reading of the verse, you will read aloud Reference No. 2, asking them to follow you and join you in reading the quotation at the bottom of the reference. You will get use to practicing a pause at the end of the words "If so, say" and indicating to the prospect to join you in reading. After the reading of the quotation say, "Let us turn to page 214 and read Romans 6:23." Immediately say, "This Scripture shows

"WHAT SIN HAS DONE TO ALL OF US."

While your partner and the prospect are reading Romans 6:23, you will write these words at the top of the page. When they finish you will say, "Please follow me in reading the reference at the bottom of the page." As you finish, pause and ask them to join you in reading aloud the quotation. Immediately you will ask them to turn to page 211 and say, "Will both of you read Romans 5:8 in the righthand column, entitled Scripture No. 4?" While they are finding it you will state that this verse shows

"THE WAY JESUS PAID THE PRICE FOR OUR SINS."

As they finish the reading of verse 8 you will ask them to follow you as you read Reference No. 4. Make the usual pause at the words, "If so, say," and invite them to read the quotation. Then ask them to turn to page 207 and find Romans 2:4, and as they do state that this verse is in the form of a question. It is

GOD'S QUESTION AND YOUR INCENTIVE TO REPENT.

Before they read Romans 2:4, you will write at the top of page 207 the words above. When they finish reading verse 4, as you begin to read Reference No. 5, you may say the following: "If a person understands his spiritual need, why he has this need, what sin has done to him, then God's goodness and kindness are used by the Holy Spirit to lead him to a conviction of his sin and repentance toward God."

As you finish reading Reference No. 5, ask them to join you in reading the quotation. Then say, "Let us turn to page 219, Romans 10:9-14, for the last of these six references. Do you remember the man's question in the first verse you read on page 186: 'What must I do to be saved?' In Romans 10:9, you will see the answer.

TRUST AND TELL

Observe the two things you do to express your desire to repent: First, you confess; Second, you believe. Verse 10 tells you the order in which you do these two things to be saved. You believe with the heart first, that is, TRUST WITH THE HEART. Second, you confess with the mouth, that is, YOU TELL OF YOUR FAITH IN CHRIST JESUS AND HIS PAYMENT FOR YOUR SINS. Verse 13 is the means God gives for you to express your repentance. You tell God you accept His love and trust His Son to save you before you tell men. This is done in a simple prayer of faith. Now, will you please read together verses 9 through 14?"

As you explain in the words above, you will write in his copy at the top of page 219 the following:

"Two things you do to be saved—Verse 9."
"The order in which you do them—Verse 10."
"The way you express your repentance—Verse 13."

Since you have these lines written in your New Testament, it will be easy for you to copy them in your prospect's copy. The reading of the last reference is joined in by you when they have finished reading verse 14. You say, "Let all of us read aloud Reference No. 6 down through the prayer that is written there."

Immediately after finishing the prayer, make the statement, "This prayer is to be prayed when you feel the compulsion to pray in your heart. The desire to ask God for forgiveness comes from the heart, as you are moved by the Holy Spirit. That is why we do not ask you to pray this prayer, but we give you an opportunity to ask us to pray with you, as you voice this prayer to God."

PAUSE FOR PRAYER

This statement must be followed by a <u>pause</u> in which you are silently breathing a prayer for direction. If you ask the prospect to pray prematurely, the best you can expect is an abortive spiritual birth and not a newborn babe in Christ. Should your prospect pray, we suggest you follow the paragraph on assurance below. If your prospect is not ready to pray and the Holy Spirit impresses you to do so, stay in command of the conversation. Ask him to look at the first paragraph of the reference you have just read. Say, "I am underlining the words 'trust and tell' in your copy. Under this statement I am writing, 'See page 390.' There you will see the Cross and how Salvation is portrayed in the invisible Cross. First, your faith is Godward, as you pray and TRUST WITH YOUR HEART. Second, your faith is manward. That is, you tell with your mouth. The vertical faith of your heart reaches to Heaven. The horizontal faith of your heart reaches to man. Now turn back to page 219."

Then say, "There are two promises in this reference, which I want to draw to your attention. They are quoted from God's Word. Look at the second paragraph. In your copy I am underlining the word 'Promises' and under it I am writing 'See page 332.' Let us now turn to page 332. There let us read Revelation 3:20, which is underscored. Above this verse I am writing in your copy 'See page 219.'"

After reading Revelation 3:20, turn back to page 219. Ask the prospect to look at the last paragraph. Underscore the word "promises" in the fifth paragraph. Say to the prospect, "Do you notice that the statement following the word 'promises' is in quotation marks? This is quoted from Matthew 10:32. I am writing, 'See page 13' in your copy. Let us look at page 13. Now let us read Matthew 10:32, 33."

When you finish reading these two verses and before you read the reference at the bottom of page 13, you will say, "Romans 10:9 tells you to do two things: 'If you confess with your mouth Jesus as Lord, and believe in your heart that God raised Him from the dead, you shall be saved.' This passage of scripture is to show you where your confession is to be made. It must be public and not private. There are four things taught in these two verses: One, the PERSON whom you confess—the Savior who died for you. Two, the PUBLIC before whom you confess the Savior—that is, before men. Third, the PROMISE Jesus makes to confess you before the Father in Heaven when you confess Him before men on earth. The fourth and final thing is the awful fate and peril you face if you do not confess Christ before men in this life. Now, let us read this reference and see these four things."

After reading through the reference, invite your prospect to look at the paragraph that starts with the word "Second." Show him in the last word of the second line the word "six." Then say to him, "I am writing in your copy, 'See page 177.' Will you turn with me to page 177 and look in the righthand column and find Acts 11:12? I am putting a bracket around this verse relating to 'six brethren.' In New Testament times, the disciples took the church to the people that were to be saved. Now we go to the church building to hear preaching. Seven church members went to the house of Cornelius to preach to him. 'Cornelius was waiting for them, and had called together his relatives and close friends' (Acts 10:24, page 175). He was a centurion of what was called 'the Italian cohort" (Acts 10:1, page 174). These people were Italians, that is Romans; some were

Greeks and possibly other nationalities. Peter preached the Gospel to them: the death of Christ in verse 39 (page 176); His Resurrection in verse 40; the forgiveness of sins in verse 43. What glorious Good News! We know that the prayer of Cornelius was heard of God, and because of the powerful preaching of Peter under the anointing of the Holy Spirit, the hearers were saved while listening to the message. Three things resulted: verse 46—they confessed Christ before the church; verse 47—the church consented to the baptism of those who confessed Christ before the members; third—verse 48 tells of the command Peter gave to carry out the order of Jesus Christ to baptize the believers who had confessed their faith in the Lord. Let us read verses 46 through 48."

After reading the three verses, ask the prospect and your partner to join you in reading paragraphs a, b, and c at the bottom of the page. When the reading is completed, state that you are writing at the bottom of the page "Now turn back to page 13." As you do, ask the prospect to read verse 32 again with you. Then solemnly say, as you look at him, calling his name, "May I ask you a question?" When he consents, then say, "The question is printed as the title to Reference No. 2 on page 13. Let us read this question." Then pause and say, "Has Jesus confessed your name in Heaven? Have you done what the Bible says you must do in order to be sure your name is written in the Lamb's Book of Life?" HERE IS A STRATEGIC MOMENT. Pause, and let your prospect answer "Yes" or "No." If the answer is negative, then ask, "Do you know what to do to get your name confessed before your Father in Heaven by our Savior, the Lord Jesus, and get your name written in God's family book?" If your prospect's response is positive, then ask the Holy Spirit to lead you to turn back to page 219. State to your prospect: "Do you feel a desire in your heart to ask God to forgive you and save you for Jesus' sake?" If his answer is "Yes," draw his attention to the words of the prayer written there. The Holy Spirit will lead you as you ask the prospect to pray the prayer suggested in Reference No. 6, page 219. If your prospect receives Christ, then lead him to experience

ASSURANCE.

Assurance of salvation is most important to the new convert at this point. Immediately show him he has invited Christ to come into his heart and "live in my life." Ask him to turn to page 332;

show him Rev. 3:20: "If any one hears My voice and opens the door, I will come in to him." Then state: "Now when you ask Jesus to come into your heart He did what He promised." Show your convert 1 Thess. 5:24, page 281: "Faithful is He who calls you, and He also will bring it to pass." So ask him, "Where is Jesus now?" Wait a moment for the right answer; he should say, "In my heart." Lead him to find spiritual strength. Say, "Jesus enters your heart immediately upon your invitation. He empties out all sin, cleanses and forgives you, and enables you to live for Him. He strengthens you. Let us turn to page 273 and see the promises of Phil. 4:13: "I can do all things through Him who strengthens me."

Then say, "Now you will be kept by God's power. Turn to page 313 and read 1 Peter 1:5: "Who are protected through faith for a salvation ready to be revealed in the last time." You are now protected and guarded.

God will now protect and guard your soul. Let us read 2 Tim. 1:12 on page 289. Note the words,"I am convinced that He is able to guard what I have entrusted to Him until that day." If Paul was convinced God would guard what he entrusted to Him, can't you trust God too? Also you can be assured that this salvation is forever. Let us read Hebrews 7:25 on page 300: "Hence, also, He is able to save forever those who draw near to God through Him, since He always lives to make intercession for them."

Now that your convert is sure he is saved he is ready for his public profession of faith. This too gives assurance. Pray that your convert will understand and desire to comply with the requirement to confess Christ before men. Pray that he will be convinced that what he has done privately he must do publicly. Say, "Since you have now trusted Christ you can be sure that your name will be confessed before the Father in heaven when you confess Christ before men publicly. You will be introduced to the family of God assembled with the Lord. You will remember we read this in Matt. 10:32, page 13. Let us read it again: 'Everyone therefore who shall confess Me before men, I will also confess him before My Father who is in Heaven.'"

Explain to your convert that he confesses a person, the person of Christ. He confesses the Sin Bearer who died publicly, "before men." When this public confession of Christ's person before men is made, he can claim a promise. Christ promises to confess him before the Father in heaven. Then all the saints in heaven know he has repented and confessed faith in Jesus Christ as Savior. Help your convert see what "His precious and magnificent promises" will do for him. Let us read 2 Peter 1:4, page 319.

In the wisdom of God this horizontal relationship of your convert with the public is established by baptism and church membership. Salvation of the soul is instantaneous. "He who hears My word, and believes Him who sent Me, has eternal life, and does not come into judgment, but has passed out of death into life." (John 5:24, page 130) But salvation of the life is progressive. Your convert is to obey Christ's commands. Jesus said, "teaching them to observe all that I commanded you." (Matt. 28:20, page 45)

So to obey Christ, following his confession of faith, your prospect's next public act is to be baptized. Help your convert study the symbol that shows salvation at the bottom of pages 212, 213. Here you can articulate with confidence the importance of believer baptism as you instruct and teach your convert.

The Bible is very clear on the subject of when a convert should be baptized. There are four records of the time of baptism. These instances are (1) at once (Acts 8:36, page 172); (2) the very same hour (Acts 16:33, page 186); (3) the same day (Acts 2:41, page 163); and (4) three days after being saved (Acts 22:12, 13, 16, page 196). The Holy Spirit in recording these instances is teaching your convert that there should be no delay to declare his faith in this way.

The horizontal relationship of your convert to the Christian community is continued by Church membership. When a baby is born into this world God ordains that the child should have a home. And similarly the newborn babe in Christ should have a home and that home is the church. As the home protects, provides for, and grows the child so the church protects, and provides for the spiritual need and grows the newborn babe in Christ.

Show your convert that he "like newborn babes . . ." is to "grow in respect to salvation"; (1 Peter 2:2, page 314) that God wants him "in the church." (Eph. 3:21, page 264). Every human being wants to be a part, to belong. God made us that way. To meet this need Christ built the church. Lead your convert to be a part of and participate in the local church that believes the Bible and teaches atonement by the blood of Christ. As the health and growth of the human family depends upon environment, food, shelter, exercise and teaching even so it is true in God's family; the health and growth to maturity of the child of God depends upon the spiritual environment of the church; spiritual food in Bible study; prayer and fellowship with believers; exercise in witnessing and ministering; and helping others by extending God's Kingdom.

SECOND VISIT

If your prospect does not voluntarily pray and find Christ as Savior, then immediately seek an opportunity for a second visit. Make the time and place definite and certain.

In either case, whether there is a confession of faith or not, invite your prospect to accompany you to church. Make definite arrangements for him to attend. Ask permission to sit with him during the preaching service. Be sure he sits on the aisle, so he can easily go forward if the Holy Spirit draws him to confess Christ and make public his faith.

Since this is church-oriented Visitation Evangelism, we have learned that it is best to seek the will of the Lord concerning a second visit to the prospect who professes faith in Christ, to read with him Section No. 2 on church membership, beginning on page 45. This gives more depth and meaning to his experience. During revivals, we invite the prospect to come to the pastor's office or an inquirer's class before the preaching service to study this step of baptism. In this way your prospect can profess faith publicly and you can be confident that he is qualified to be presented for baptism.

Let us hasten to say that the Holy Spirit may direct you to read all four references of Section 2 with the prospect who confesses Christ in your presence during the <u>first visit.</u> Since you are walking with the Lord, He will guide you aright.

Sometimes, the second visit is used to read the seven references of Section 3, beginning at page 270. This will lead to a confession of faith, following the same procedure about the prayer recorded on page 347, as you did in the first visit when you read through the prayer on page 219. Remember your prospect must pray and make a definite decision from the heart without any compulsion from man before the subject of baptism is mentioned. After the prayer the Holy Spirit may lead you to turn to page 45, and read Matthew 28:18-20 and the reference.

The second visit to one who does not make a confession of faith may require that you start at Section 4, John 17:3, and read the four references beginning on page 150.

Bible study groups, Training Union Departments, and even Sunday School assemblies, have used this Soul Winner's New Testament to develop young Christians through the study of the outlines beginning on page 370 and ending on page 390. Many pastors have used the 21 numbered references, outlines, and helps in this book during new member orientation classes.

May I remind you of your responsibility, as the Soul Winner who has been used to win a person to Christ, is not complete until your convert grows in respect to salvation.

MATURING THE NEW MAN

Presenting the plan of salvation and seeing the birth of a new babe in Christ completes only the first phase of your witness with the Word. With the birth of the newborn babe in Christ comes the burden and responsibility of growing him to maturity.

You may minister to mature the new man in Christ by following the suggestions on page XIII. This is designed to help you to invite, instruct, and inspire him to be faithful. To establish him in the faith, help him study the seven manifestations of maturity on pages 370-373. This study could require more than one session. He must learn to rebound into fellowship with Christ when overtaken by sin. He should see his privileges and opportunities as a child of God, and he should be taught to accept his responsibilities, "That you might not lose what we have accomplished, but that you may receive a full reward" (2 John 8, p. 326).

May I, in closing, tell you a story? It is a true experience. I was in a revival in Norfolk, Virginia. I announced on Sunday that we would explain to the teachers and officers of the Sunday School, and to all who were interested in soul winning, the use of the Soul Winner's New Testament on Monday night following the service.

When we assembled we distributed the Soul Winner's New Testament to all adults present. We made a mistake. We overlooked an 11-year-old boy sitting beside his Sunday School teacher. She had led him to Christ during Vacation Bible School. He was eagerly learning all he could about the church, his Savior and his Bible. His father, a delinquent Catholic, would not allow him to be baptized.

I gave an abbreviated outline of everything which has been said here. Many made commitments and took assignments to witness with the Word.

The boy came forward and said to the pastor, "May I have one of those Soul Winner's New Testaments?" The pastor replied, "Why do you want it?" The boy said, "Preacher, you remember

Butch came with me to Vacation Bible School, and I was saved but he was not?" With a tear in his eye and a choke in his voice, he looked up in the pastor's face and continued "PREACHER, I DON'T WANT BUTCH TO GO TO HELL." As I looked at the pastor and the boy, I knew the pastor was praying for wisdom, as he felt the strong compassion in the heart of the youth for his friend who was lost. Then the pastor said, "I will give you this Soul Winner's New Testament for Butch, if you will have your father read these references with you twice before you go to bed, so you will be familiar with them as you read them with Butch tomorrow. I will also give you a Soul Winner's New Testament." The youth eagerly agreed to carry out the two commitments to have his father read these references to him and to read the references with Butch when he presented the gift.

The next night we learned what happened. We saw the youth who we learned was Butch sitting on the fifth row beside the youth and his father. He was right on the aisle. At the close of the sermon, and during the first moment of invitation, Butch walked forward holding the Soul Winner's New Testament in his hand. He told the pastor how his friend had used the book to lead him to Christ on the schoolground that day. After talking with the lad, the pastor stopped the invitation and told the congregation what had happened. He stated, "Any adult or Sunday School teacher can do what Butch's young friend did for him today. You, too, can win your friends and loved ones to Christ with this Soul Winner's New Testament." Then the pastor turned the invitation back to me. I called the young man to the front to tell how he did it. He explained how his father had read the references to him, and at the close of the reading, the father had asked him to let him keep the book as he went on to bed, with the assurance it would be on the table at breakfast time. He told of his witness and reading of the references. Then he turned to me and said, "Brother Clift, as I asked him to pray with me, and I saw the tear in his eye, I knew I had got him for God." I then asked him to sit by Butch on the front seat. As the invitation continued, on the very next verse of the song, the father began to make his way to the aisle, followed by his mother, an unenlisted Baptist. He had never been in church during the 11 years of his boy's life. As he reached the pastor, tears were in his eyes, and he told how he slipped down beside the table in his home after reading the references the third time and prayed the prayer and found forgiveness of his sins, and Salvation in Jesus

Christ. He then said to the pastor, "Preacher, I was wrong when I told you last summer that my boy did not know what he was doing. Last night I learned that he does know Christ, and this book showed me how to find Christ. I found forgiveness of sins and it says I should be baptized. Pastor, can't I be baptized with my boy? My wife and all of us want to join the church." Then all three of the family were heartily received along with Butch into the church.

Many people have won their first soul to Christ without any previous training by simply doing what this 11-year-old boy did. You, too, can win souls, as you witness with the Word. You have made a commitment. You can now gain COURAGE TO COMMENCE a witness by presenting a gift copy of the Soul Winner's New Testament to the prospect the Lord has laid on your heart. It is easy for you to start a conversation with the words "I have a gift for you."

As you study and read through these references at least twice with your witnessing partner, and practice going through a soul-winning witness, you will gain CONFIDENCE. Then you will know that you are able to COMMUNICATE CHRIST through use of the scriptures with your prospect.

Isn't it true that all we need, in addition to our COMMITMENT, COURAGE, and CONFIDENCE, is the God-given COMPASSION and CONCERN for the lost? Do you know someone who is in peril of dying without publicly confessing Christ? Do you feel a sense of responsibility to that person who you know is lost, and you have not witnessed to him with the Word? Cry out to God from your heart and ask Him to fill you with compassion for the lost. As God warms your heart, He will use you to win the lost to Christ.

In conclusion, let me ask you to pray for yourself, your church, your pastor, and the prospects on your outreach lists. Will you make time in your busy life to study these suggestions looking up the scriptures in your Soul Winner's New Testament? Will you write the words on each of the pages that assist you to move from one reference to another and help you command the conversation so that you will have great confidence in your ability to present the word with power? Will you please practice with a witnessing partner reading these references to each other at least twice before you go to witness? Will you prayerfully commit to memory what you will say to introduce yourself and your witnessing partner to the prospect? And finally, let me urge you to grow to maturity the fruit God gives to you as suggested herein. As you go, go with God.

MANIFESTATION OF MATURITY
A Mature Man

Scripture Eph. 4:3, Page 265, "until we all attain to the unity of the faith, and of the knowledge of the Son of God, to a Mature Man, to the measure of the stature which belongs to the fulness of Christ."

I.   CONSTANTLY ABIDE IN CHRIST. REBOUND INTO FELLOWSHIP.

Eph. 4:15, Page 266, "Grow up in all Aspects." When sin overtakes you, then as a believer, you are to rebound into fellowship with Christ. We are to claim the promises of I John 1:9, and believe I John 1:7 and I John 2:1, Page 322. Believe God and experience forgiveness and cleansing. God is ready to forgive. Psalms 86:5, "For thou Lord, art good and ready to forgive; and plenteous in mercy unto all them that call upon thee." We are also to forgive others and to ask them to forgive us, James 5:16, Page 313, Eph. 4:32, Page 266. We are to forgive as Christ forgave. Luke 23:34, Page 119. You who are Spiritual are to restore to fellowship those who sin, Gal. 6:1,2, Page 261.

II.   COMMUNION DAILY WITH GOD IN PRAYER.

I Cor. 2:6, Page 228, "We speak wisdom among those who are Mature." We learn that our voice heard daily in prayer brings victory over sin. Heb. 4:16, Page 298. We are to talk to God out of our hearts each day Psalms 5:3, Luke 18:1, Page 108, I Thes. 5:17, Page 281, Eph. 6:18, Page 268. God talks to us in daily Bible study; we talk to Him daily in prayer. Your daily devotion should be a dialogue.

III.   CONCENTRATE DAILY ON THE STUDY OF GOD'S WORD.

Heb. 5:14, Page 298, "Solid food is for the mature. God's word is food for our souls. We need a daily diet of the Bible to develop, I Pet. 2:2, Page 314. We are to allow God to talk to us out of His word by daily Bible study. II Tim. 2:15, Page 289.

IV. COMMUNICATE DAILY YOUR TESTIMONY TO OTHERS.

Heb. 6:1, Page 298, "Let us press on to <u>Maturity</u>." As exercise of muscles give physical strength even so exercise of our Spirit in witnessing gives strength. We are sent as Christ was sent to save the Lost and to reveal God to man, John 20:21, Page 156.

(a) God sent Jesus, John 3:17, Page 126. Jesus made manifest the Father. We are saved and sent to serve the Savior.

(b) Jesus sends all believers, John 13:16, Page 145; John 17:18, Page 151. Christ in the believer makes God known to men.

(c) We are to witness daily I Peter 3:15, Page 317. We grow by exercise, II Peter 3:18, Page 321; I Cor. 12:7, Page 239; I Peter 4:10, Page 317.

(d) We are to do good works for His glory, not our own, Eph. 2:10, Page 263; I Cor. 1:29, Page 228; Phil. 2:13, Page 270; James 2:17, Page 310. Our dedicated bodies are consecrated as we communicate Christ to those we contact. Consecration is expressed in service that bears the anointing of the Holy Spirit, Rom. 12:1,2, Page 222.

V. CONQUER TEMPTATION AND SIN.

I Cor. 14:20, Page 241, "In your thinking be <u>Mature</u>." You as a normal human being will be tempted, James 1:14, Page 309. But all believers are promised power to overcome temptation and sin, I Cor. 10:13, Page 235, (memorize this) Phil. 4:13, Page 273, (memorize this) James 4:7,8, Page 312; Rom. 6:11,14, Page 213; Heb. 7:25, Page 300; II Tim. 1:12, Page 289; I Peter 1:5, Page 313; Phil 1:6, Page 269.

VI. CHURCH MEMBERSHIP

Col. 1:28, Page 274, "We may present every <u>man complete</u> in Christ." There are four reasons why we should be members of a local church:1-2-3-4. Note

(1) PART OF THE CHURCH: We are to glorify God in the local church. Ninety-five out of one hundred and seventeen times the word "Church" appears in the New

Testament, it means a "local congregation", Eph. 3:21, Page 264, "to Him be the glory in the church and in Christ Jesus to all generations forever and ever. Amen."

(2) PRESENT AT THE CHURCH SERVICE: There is strength, enlightenment and encouragement in the association of the New Christian with other Christians, members of the family of God. Therefore, do not forsake the assembling of yourself with the Church. Heb. 10:25, Page 303.

(3) PARTICIPATE IN THE CHURCH LIFE: We are to give our lives to the church, living for its growth and development. Christ's love in us will love the church about us, Eph. 5:25, Page 267.

(4) PROMOTE THE KINGDOM OF GOD AS YOU PROVIDE FOR THE CHURCH: The church is Christ's means of manifesting His kingdom during this age. Our influence is to radiate through the church and we are to occupy until Christ comes, Luke 19:13, Page 111; Matt. 12:30, Page 16.

VII. CONTRIBUTE WEEKLY TO CHRIST'S CAUSE

I Cor. 13:11, Page 240, "When I became a man, I did away with childish things." The law did not inaugurate the tithe; neither did it terminate it.

(1) Sixteen out of the thirty-eight parables Jesus used were about stewardship.

(2) One out of every six verses in the New Testament mentions right or wrong use of possessions, man's relationship to material things.

(3) The tithe is to be paid weekly, I Cor. 16:2, Page 244.
   a. WHEN "on the first day of every week (Sunday)"
   b. WHO "Let each one of you"
   c. WHAT "Put aside and save"
   d. WAY "As he may prosper"
   e. WHY "That no collection be made when I come" see also II Cor. 9:6-8, Page 252, as to the manner in which the tithe is to be paid.

(4) Jesus believed in tithing, Matt. 23:23, Page 34; Lev. 27:30; Malachi 3:8-10.

(5) Christian workers are to live by the gospel and of the gospel, I Cor 9:14, Page 234.

CARDINAL RULE OF CHRISTIAN CONDUCT:

Give God the first part of every day. (My voice shalt thou hear in the morning, O Lord; in the morning will I direct my prayer unto thee, and will look up Psalm 5:3), the first day of every week, (And on the first day of the week, when we were gathered together to break bread, Paul began talking to them,) Acts. 20:7, Page 192; and, the first fruits of your increase "Honor the Lord with thy substance, and with the first fruits of all their increase: So shall thy barns be filled with plenty, and thy presses shall burst out with new wine," Prov. 3:9-10.

LIFE AFTER DEATH

<u>Lessons We Learn About Life After Death From Lazarus And The Rich Man.</u>

Scripture Lesson: Luke 16:19-31 Page 106

This story reveals the <u>certainty</u> of <u>Death</u>, the <u>consciousness</u> of the <u>Dead</u>, and the <u>choice</u> of <u>destiny</u> by every responsible human being. So study these scriptures. Let the Spirit of God speak to you and be your teacher.

I.   CERTAINTY OF DEATH.

Luke 16:22, Page 106, "Now it came about that the poor man died and he was carried away by the angels to Abraham's bosom; and the rich man also died and was buried."

(a) Source of death.

Rom. 5:12, Page 212, "Through one man sin entered into the world, and death through sin."

Heb. 2:14, Page 296, "Him who had the power of death, that is, the devil" This was done to Adam, the first man God created. The penalty of death for sin was declared by God to Adam. Gen. 2:17. Then Adam willfully disobeyed God. Gen. 3:6. He yielded to the tempter, the devil, and became the source of all death that results from sin. Gen. 5:5.

(b) Scope of death.

Rom. 5:12, Page 212, "So death spread to all men, because all sinned"

I Cor. 15:21, 22, Page 242, "For since by a man came death," "in Adam all die"

Rom. 5:15, Page 212, "For if by the transgression of the one the many died."

Heb. 9:27, Page 302, "And inasmuch as it is <u>appointed</u> for men to die once," So both Lazarus, representing the saved, and the Rich Man representing the lost, each died.

All die both saved and lost. The Psalmist asked the question Psalms 89:48, "What man can live and not see death?" My dear reader you have an inescapable appointment with death; and it could be

(c) Sudden death.

James 4:14, Page 312, "Yet you do not know what your life will be like tomorrow. You are just a vapor that appears for a little while and then vanishes away."

Psalms 102:11, "My days are like a lengthened shadow; And I wither away like grass."

Proverbs 27:1, "Do not boast about tomorrow. For you do not know what a day may bring forth." Note the warning in Proverbs. Jesus shows us you will be conscious for in this scripture He teaches the

II. CONSCIOUSNESS OF THE DEAD.

Luke 16:22, 25, Page 106-107, "the poor man died and he was carried away by the angels to Abraham's bosom;" "now he is being comforted here,"

(a) SEE   The dead see, they have eyes. The lost SEE after death. Luke 16:23, Page 106, "And in Hades he lifted up his eyes, being in torment and saw Abraham far away, and Lazarus in his bosom."

Matt. 5:29, Page 6, "And if your right eye makes you stumble, tear it out, and throw it from you; for it is better for you that one of the parts of your body perish, than for your whole body to be thrown into hell." Here is shown a "body" after death and the torment of the dead who are lost.

(b) SPEAK   The voice of the dead can be heard by others who are dead. His body was buried but he as spirit and soul remained conscious. Luke 16:22, Page 106, "and the rich man also died and was buried." You are a spirit, soul, and body. I Thes. 5:23, Page 281, "and may your spirit and soul and body be preserved complete." He remained alive after His body was buried, Luke 16:24, Page 106, "And he cried out and said, Father Abraham, have mercy on me, and send Lazarus, that he may dip the tip of his finger in water and cool off my tongue; for I am in agony in this flame." When denied, he further said, Luke 16:27, 28, Page 107, "And he said, Then I beg you Father, that you send him to my father's house for I have five brothers that he may warn them, lest they also come to this place of torment." and the dead who are lost

(c) SUFFER   Conscious torment is the agony of the lost. Luke 16:23, 24, Page 106, "being in torment" he said "I am in agony in this flame." He did not want his brothers to suffer for he desired that they be warned. Luke 16:28, Page 107, "for I have five brothers that he may warn them, lest they also come to this place of torment." The punishment is eternal, Matt. 25:31, 41, Pages 37, 38, "when the Son of Man comes in His glory" then he will say "Depart from Me, accursed ones, into the eternal fire which has been prepared for the devil and his angels."

II Thess. 1:7-9, Page 281, "The Lord Jesus shall be revealed from heaven with His mighty angels in flaming fire, dealing out retribution to those who do not know God and to those who do not obey the gospel of our Lord Jesus, And these will pay the penalty of eternal destruction." Rev. 19:20, Page 346, "And the beast was seized, and with him the false prophet . . . . these two were thrown alive into the lake of fire which burns with brimstone." Rev. 21:8, Page 348, "But for the cowardly and unbelieving and abominable and murderers and immoral persons and sorcerers and idolaters and all liars, their part will be in the lake that burns with fire and brimstone, which is the second death."

III. THE DEAD THAT ARE SAVED ARE CONSCIOUS.
They see, speak, and are satisfied.

(a) SEE   The dead that die in the Lord SEE, Jesus prayed, John 17:24, Page 152, "Father, I desire that they also whom Thou hast given Me <u>be with</u> Me where I am in order that they may <u>behold</u> My glory." This prayer of Jesus is answered for every Child of God. I Corn. 13:12, Page 240, "For now we see in a mirror dimly, but then face to face;" and then, I John 3:2, Page 323, "we shall see Him just as He is." Jesus said Abraham saw His Incarnation. John 8:56, Page 137, "Your father Abraham rejoiced to see My day; and he saw it, and was glad." Note, "<u>My Day</u>" (Incarnation). Matt 22:32, Page 32, "I am the God of Abraham, and the God of Isaac, and the God of Jacob, God is not the God of the dead but of the living." Heb. 12:1, Page 306, "Therefore, since we have so great a cloud of witnesses surrounding us, let us also lay aside every encumbrance, and the sin which so easily entangles us, and let us run with endurance the race that is set before us." The Child of God at the moment of the death of the body is transported into the Presence of Jesus up in Heaven. II Corn. 5:1, 6, 8, Page 248, "For we know that if the earthly tent which is our house is torn down, we have a building from God, a house not made with hands, eternal in the heavens . . . . and knowing that while we are at home in the body we are absent from the Lord . . . . . we are of good courage I say, and prefer rather to be absent from the body and to be at home with the Lord." Jesus who has been taken up into heaven, Acts 1:11, Page 160, "This Jesus who has been <u>taken up</u> from you into heaven," was seen by the first Martyr Stephen. Acts 7:55, Page 171, "he gazed intently into heaven and <u>saw</u> the glory of God, and Jesus standing at the right hand of God;" Paul who expresses this confidence had an experience in Heaven and was caught up to the third heaven. II Cor. 12:2, 3, 4, Page 254, "I know a man in Christ who fourteen years ago—whether in the body I do not know, or out of the body I do not know, God knows—such a man was caught up to the third heaven. And I know how such a man—whether in the body or apart from the body I do not know, God knows—was caught up into Paradise, and heard inexpressible words, which a man is not permitted to speak." Paul believed death to be "Gain" Phil 1:21-23, Page 269, "For to me, to live is Christ, and to die is gain. But if I am to live on in the flesh, this will mean fruitful labor for me; and I do not know which to choose. But I am hard pressed from both directions, having the desire to depart and be with Christ, for that is very much better." When he faced death at the close of his ministry he said, II Tim. 4:6, 8, Page 291, "and the time of my departure has come . . . . in the future there is laid up for me the crown of righteousness." Paul considered the body a tent or tabernacle where we live. He showed man consists of the three; Spirit, Soul and Body, I Thess. 5:23, Page 281, "Now may the God of Peace Himself sanctify you entirely; and may your spirit and soul and body be preserved complete, without blame at the coming of our Lord Jesus Christ." Peter considered death to be "the laying aside of my earthly dwelling" and said II Peter 1:14, 15, Page 319, "knowing that the laying aside of my earthly dwelling is imminent, as also our Lord Jesus Christ has made clear to me. And I will also be diligent that at any time after my departure (death) you may be able to call these things to mind."

(b) SPEAK   The saved that die SPEAK. Abraham spoke. Luke 16:25, Page 106, "But Abraham said, Child remember," Though dead, Moses talked to Jesus. Matt 17:3, Page 24, "And behold, Moses and Elijah appeared to them, talking with Him." Observe that they were "Talking with Him." Paul heard inexpressible words, II Corn. 12:4, Page 254, "and heard inexpressible words, which a man is not permitted to speak" In heaven the saved praise God. Rev. 7:9, 10, Page 335, "After these things I looked, and behold, a great multitude, which no one could count, from every nation and all tribes and peoples and tongues, standing before the throne and before the Lamb, clothed in white robes, and palm branches were in their hands; and they cry out with a loud voice, saying, 'Salvation to our God who sits on the throne, and to the Lamb.'

(c) THE DEAD WHO ARE SAVED ARE SATISFIED.
Heb. 4:9, Page 297, "There remains therefore a Sabbath rest for the people of God." They are at rest. Luke 16:25, Page 106-107, "But Abraham said, "Child, remember that during your life you received your good things, and likewise Lazarus bad things; but now he is being <u>comforted</u> here, and you are in agony." Lazarus was in <u>comfort</u>. The scene was a feast, in Abraham's bosom—reclining at the festive table. Rev. 14:13, Page 341, "And I heard a voice from heaven, saying, 'Write, Blessed are the dead who die in the Lord from now on! Yes says the Spirit, that they may rest from their labors, for their deeds follow with them.'" They rejoice when a sinner is saved, Luke 15:10, Page 104, "In the same way, I tell you, there is joy in the presence of the angels of God over one sinner who repents."

IV. CHOICE OF DESTINY

Each responsible individual chooses his destiny. You either <u>Receive</u> or <u>Reject</u> Jesus Christ as Lord. The rich man chose things, the Secular, Luke 16:25, Page 106, "you received your good things," The poor man chose the Spiritual. The Lost reject Jesus Christ as Lord, John 12:48, Page 144, "He who rejects Me, and does not receive My sayings, has one who judges him; the word I spoke is what will judge him at the last day."

Rejection of Christ as Lord is shown by:

(a) <u>Disbelief of Christ</u>. Mark 16:16, Page 74, "but he who has disbelieved shall be condemned." Refusal to obey, John 3:36, Page 126, "but he who does not obey the Son shall not see life, but the wrath of God abides on him."

(b) <u>Denying Christ</u>. Jude 4, Page 328, "ungodly persons who turn the grace of our God into licentiousness and deny our only Master and Lord, Jesus Christ." Matt. 10:33, Page 13, "But whoever shall <u>deny</u> Me before men, I will also deny him before My Father who is in heaven." It is shown by being ashamed of Christ,

Mark 8:38, Page 60, "For whoever is ashamed of Me and My words in this adulterous and sinful generation, the Son of Man will also be ashamed of him when He comes in the glory of His Father with the holy angels." II Tim. 2:12, Page 289, "If we endure, we shall also reign with Him; If we <u>deny</u> Him, He also will <u>deny</u> us." I John 2:22, Page 323, "Who is the liar but the one who <u>denies</u> that Jesus is the Christ."

I John 4:3, Page 324, "and every spirit that does not confess Jesus is not from God."

II John 7, Page 326, "For many deceivers have gone out into the world, those who do not acknowledge Jesus Christ as coming in the flesh. This is the deceiver and the antichrist."

The Saved <u>RECEIVE</u> Christ, John 1:12, Page 122, "But as many as received Him, to them He gave the right to become children of God, even to those who believe in His name." The saved invite Christ Jesus into the heart by repentance and faith, Rev. 3:20, Page 332, "Behold, I stand at the door and knock; if any one hears My voice and opens the door, I will <u>come in to him</u>, and will dine with him, and he with Me."

Eph. 3:17, Page 264, "so that Christ may dwell in your hearts through faith;"

John 14:23, Page 147, "Jesus answered and said to him, If anyone loves Me, he will keep My word; and My Father will love him, and We will <u>come to him</u>, and make Our <u>abode with him</u>"

You keep Christ Word by:

(a) COMING TO CHRIST   Matt. 11:28, Page 15, "Come to Me, all who are weary and heavy laden, and I will give you rest;"

(b)   CALLING ON THE NAME OF CHRIST
Rom. 10:13, Page 219, "For Whoever will call upon the Name of the Lord will be saved," and,

(c)   CONFESSING CHRIST BEFORE MEN
Rom. 10:9, Page 219, "That if you confess with your mouth Jesus as Lord, and believe in your heart that God raised Him from the dead, you shall be saved," Matt. 10:32, Page 13, "Every one therefore who shall confess Me before men, I will also confess him before My Father who is in heaven."

Express your choice. Place your confidence in Him—Believe. Come to Christ, Repent of your sins. Call on His name. Then confess Jesus as Lord and you will be sure that your destiny will be HEAVEN.

JUDGMENT

Lessons we learn from the Great White Throne Judgment.
Scripture Text: Rev. 20:11-15, Page 347

In this scripture we observe the Great White <u>Throne</u>, a place of Judgment; before it a <u>throng of people</u> great and small to be Judged; and throes of Judgment for those "<u>thrown</u> into the lake of fire."

The Holy scriptures teach: The <u>Appointment</u> before the Court is <u>Certain</u> (a day fixed); The <u>Appearance</u> for the reading of the <u>accusation</u> from the record (Books) is definite; and, the <u>Action</u> of the court determines the <u>destiny</u> of eternal doom for the accused who are unsaved, whose names are <u>not</u> written in the book of life.

I.   THRONE. APPOINTMENT BEFORE THE JUDGE.

<u>Appointed</u> . . . . a day certain and <u>Person</u> to Judge. Acts 17:31, Page 188, "because He has fixed a day in which He will judge the world in righteousness through a Man whom He has appointed, having furnished proof to all men by raising Him from the dead."

Rev. 20:11, Page 347, "And I saw a great white throne and Him who sat upon it, from whose presence earth and heaven fled away, and no place was found for them."

<u>Place</u> of the throne: Psalms 115:16, "The heaven, even the heavens, are the Lord's;" Psalms 11:4, "The Lord is in his holy temple, the Lord's <u>throne</u> is in <u>heaven</u>:"

The Judgment is <u>inescapable</u>. Hebrews 9:27, Page 302, "And inasmuch as it is appointed for men to die once, and after this comes Judgment."

II.   THRONG. APPEARANCE TO BE JUDGED.

<u>People</u> to be <u>Accused</u>, a throng.

Rev. 20:12, Page 347, "And I saw the dead, the great and the small, standing before the throne, and books were opened; and another book was opened, which is the book of life; and the

dead were <u>judged</u> from the things which were written in the books, according to their deeds."

APPEARANCE—An accusation to confront the Losts presented, "and books were opened;" The appearance is inevitable, Rom. 14:10, 11, 12, Page 224, "For we shall all stand before the judgment seat of God. For it is written, 'As I live, says the Lord, every knee shall bow to Me, and every tongue shall give praise to God.' So then <u>each one</u> of us <u>shall give account</u> of himself to God." II Peter 2:9, Page 320, "then the Lord knows how to rescue the godly from temptation, and to keep the unrighteous under punishment for the day of judgment."

III. THROWN. ACTION ON JUDGMENT OF THE COURT.

<u>Accused</u> are <u>Doomed</u>—<u>Condemnation</u>.

Rev. 20:14, Page 347, "And death and Hades were thrown into the lake of fire." Matt. 25:41, Page 38, "Then He will also say to those on His left, 'Depart from Me, accursed ones, into the eternal fire which has been prepared for the devil and his angels;" Who are included as accused ones? Rev. 20:15, Page 347, "And if <u>anyones's name</u> was <u>not found written</u> in the <u>book of life</u>, he was <u>thrown</u> into the lake of fire."

<u>What About</u> the <u>Saved</u>?

Do the ones whose names <u>are written</u> in the Book of Life give an <u>accounting</u> of their lives to God? II Cor. 5:10, Page 248, "For we must all appear before the judgment seat of Christ, that each one may be recompensed for his deeds in the body, according to what he has done, whether good or bad." I Cor. 3:9-15, Page 229, "For we are God's fellow-workers; you are God's field, God's building. According to the grace of God which was given to me, as a wise masterbuilder I laid a foundation, and another is building upon it. But let each man be careful how he builds upon it. For no man can lay a foundation other than the one which is laid, which is Jesus Christ. Now if any man builds upon the foundation with gold, silver, precious stones, wood, hay, straw, each man's work will become evident; for the day will show it, because it is to be revealed with fire; and the fire itself will test the quality of each man's work. If any man's work which he has built upon it remains he shall receive a reward."

There are Five Crowns of Grace for the saved I John 4:17, Page 325, "that we may have confidence in the day of judgment." they are:

(a) ACHIEVEMENT CROWN—INCORRUPTIBLE CROWN . . . . FOR DISCIPLINE.

I Cor. 9:24-27, Page 235, "Do you not know that those who run in a race all run, but only one receives the prize? Run in such a way that you may win. And everyone who competes in the games exercises self-control in all things. They then do it to receive a perishable wreath, but we an imperishable CROWN. Therefore I run in such a way, as not without aim; I box in such a way, as not beating the air; but I buffet my body and make it my slave, lest possibly, after I have preached to others, I myself should be disqualified."

(b) OVERCOMERS CROWN—"THE CROWN OF LIFE"

James 1:12, Page 309, "Blessed is a man who perseveres under trial; for once he has been approved, he will receive the crown of life, which the Lord has promised to those who love Him." The one who learns to Triumph over Temptation. I Cor. 10:13, Page 235, "No temptation has overtaken you but such as is common to man; and God is faithful who will not allow you to be tempted beyond what you are able; but with the temptation will provide the way of escape also, that you may be able to endure it." The one who learns to Triumph over temptation saves his life though he may lose it for Christ sake and the gospels, Mark 8:35, Page 60, "For whoever wishes to save his life shall lose it; and whoever loses his life for My sake and the gospel's shall save it."

(c) SOUL WINNER'S CROWN—EXULTATION.
I Thess. 2:19-20, Page 279, "For who is our hope or joy or crown of exultation? Is it not even you, in the presence of our Lord Jesus at His coming? For you are our glory and joy." John 4:36, Page 128, "that he who sows and he who reaps may rejoice together." Prov. 11:30, "and he who is wise wins souls."

(d) LOVER OF THE SECOND COMING CROWN—RIGHTEOUSNESS
II Tim. 4:7, 8, Page 291, "I have fought the good fight, I have finished the course, I have the faith; in the future there is laid up for me the crown of righteousness, which the Lord, the righteous Judge, will award to me on that day; and not only to me, but also to all who have loved His appearing."

(e) FLOCK FEEDERS—"CROWN OF GLORY"
I Peter 5:2-4, Page 318, "shepherd the flock of God among you, not under compulsion, but voluntarily, according to the will of God; and not for sordid gain, but with eagerness; not yet as lording it over those allotted to your charge, but proving to be examples to the flock. And when the Chief Shepherd appears, you will receive the unfading crown of glory."

Dear reader is your name in the Book of Life? If not, read the seven references of section 4. Begin with Phil. 2:9, Page 270. If you are sure your name is in the Book of Life will you be Crowned or a Castaway? "Run in such a way that you may Win." Study References 3 and 4 of Section 2; begin with I Peter 2:2, Page 314.

A B C's OF SALVATION

Scripture Reading: Romans 10:8-14, Page 219

STUDY PROCEDURE: Teacher requests that students read aloud in unison the outline, one paragraph at a time, stopping before the words, "will you say." Then open and read aloud together from the scriptures at least one reference; follow this by comments as the Holy Spirit leads before asking students to read quotations. Before reading Number 2, state: "Understand one is not saved simply by repeating words, but by personally believing and committing himself to Jesus Christ. The divine desire to speak must come from the heart. Conviction must come before confession. The printed quotations are to help the lost trust Christ."

I. A stands for ALL.

    1. ALL must acknowledge sin. Romans 3:23, Page 209.

        "Sin is lawlessness." I John 3:4, Page 323.

        "ALL unrighteousness is sin." I John 5:17, Page 326.

        "There is none righteous." Romans 3:10, Page 209.

        To sin is to do wrong and go against God. See Ten Commandments, Pages 391, 392.

    Will you say?

        a. "I have sinned and Fallen short of the glory of God."

    2. ALL sinners are ruined by sin. Romans 5:12, Page 212.

    Will you say?

        b. "I have been ruined by sin."

    3. ALL men (people) must repent of sin. Acts 17:30, Page 188.

        Change your mind, heart and direction.

        Turn from SIN and self to the SAVIOR.

        2 Corinthians 7:10, Page 250; Romans 2:4, Page 207; Luke 13:5, Page 101.

(DANGER OF HELL—AUTHORITY OF THE
SCRIPTURE—POWER OF GOD)

Will you say?

    c. "I now repent and turn from sin and self to God."

II.   B stands for BELIEVE.

   1.   To believe on Christ is to trust in, rely upon, depend on,
or cleave to Christ. Believing on Christ brings salvation
from sin. Saving faith involves the whole personality; the
head or mind; the heart or emotion; and the hand express-
ing the will or volition. All must act in union to express
belief. Acts. 16:31, Page 186; John 6:69, Page 133; Acts
8:37, Page 172; Romans 10:10, Page 219.

Will you now say?

    d. "I believe that Jesus Christ is the Son of God."

   2.   What is it to believe on Christ? Believe first that the wages
of sin is death. Romans 6:23, Page 214. Wages means the
pay you get for work. God says the pay you get for sin is
death; the penalty includes <u>present</u>, <u>physical</u> and <u>perma-
nent</u> death. Revelation 21:8, Page 348; Hebrews 9:22,
Page 302; James 1:15, Page 309; I Tim. 5:6, Page 286.

Will you say?

    e. "I now see that the wages of sin is death and that God
       offers me eternal life."

   3.   Then believe that Jesus died for your sins. I Corinthians
15:3, Page 242; Hebrews 2:9, Page 296; Romans 5:8, Page
211.

Will you say?

    f. "I now believe Christ died for my sins."

   4.   Believe that God raised Jesus from the dead. He is a living
Savior. I Corinthians 15:4, Page 242; Romans 10:9, Page
219. He lives to keep you saved; to keep what you commit
to Him; to intercede for you. Hebrews 7:25, Page 300.

Will you say?

    g. "I believe that God raised Jesus Christ from the dead."

III. C stands for COME.

    1. ALL must COME to Jesus to be saved. Accept HIS invitation. Matthew 11:28, Page 15. You must come or be lost forever. John 5:40, Page 130; John 6:37, Page 132.

Will you say?

    h. "I must come to Jesus Christ now."

    2. To come to Jesus Christ as Saviour is to call on His name in <u>Prayer</u> asking for the forgiveness of your sins. Romans 10:13-14, Page 219; Luke 18:13-14, Page 109; Luke 24:47, Page 122.

Then say:

    i. "I will now call on the name of the Lord Jesus Christ, asking God to Forgive my sins for Christ's sake."

    3. After you call on the name of the Lord and find forgiveness of sins, you are then required to confess Him publicly before men. Matthew 10:32-33, Page 13; Romans 10:9, Page 219.

Therefore will you say:

    j. "I will publicly confess the Lord Jesus Christ as my personal Savior now."

RESUME

Seven truths that lead to salvation. You must believe them and express them from your heart:

1. "I have sinned and fallen short of the glory of God." Romans 3:23, Page 209.
2. "I have been ruined by sin." Romans 5:12, Page 212.
3. "I now repent and turn from sin and self to God." Acts 17:30, Page 188.
4. "I believe that Jesus Christ is the Son of God." Acts 16:31, Page 186.
5. "I now see that the wages of sin is death and that God offers me eternal life." Romans 6:23, Page 214.
6. "I now believe that Jesus Christ died for my sins." Romans 5:8, Page 211.
7. "I believe that God raised Jesus Christ from the dead." I Corinthians 15:4, Page 242.

What you say you believe you must show. There are three things you do to show that you trust Jesus: they are:
(1) COME, (2) CALL, and (3) CONFESS. Then say:

1. "I must come to Jesus now." Matthew 11:28, Page 15.
2. "I will now call on the name of Jesus Christ, asking God to forgive my sins." Romans 10:13, Page 219.
3. "I will publicly confess the Lord Jesus Christ as my personal Saviour now."

SO COMMIT YOURSELF TO CHRIST NOW and pray, using the seven words of SALVATION:
"God be merciful to me the sinner." Luke 18:13, Page 109.

INVITATION:

(A) Acknowledge your sins to God.
(B) Believe on the Lord Jesus Christ, for God to forgive you of your sins now.
(C) Come to Christ now.

(D)   <u>Call</u> on the name of the Lord Jesus now to be saved.

(E)   <u>Commit</u> yourself to Christ by public confession of Jesus Christ as your personal Saviour before men and have your name confessed in Heaven by our Lord Jesus <u>Now</u>.

SALVATION PORTRAYED IN THE INVISIBLE CROSS IN YOUR LIFE

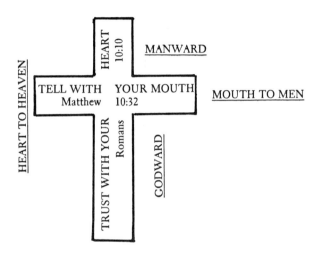

Let the cross be seen in your life. Look up to Jesus and as you TRUST HIM show the <u>vertical</u> faith that reaches from your heart to heaven (Godward). Step out before men and confess Christ and show the <u>horizontal</u> faith you have in Christ. It is from your mouth to men you tell that Christ saves you now (MANWARD).

As you TRUST with your HEART, it is VERTICAL faith (GODWARD). As you TELL with your MOUTH, it is HORIZONTAL faith (MANWARD).

NOW IS THE DAY OF SALVATION.

2 Corinthians 6:2, Page 249.

Matthew 18:3, Page 25   James 4:14, Page 312

THE TEN COMMANDMENTS

(Exodus 20:3-17)

3 You shall have no other gods before Me.

4 You shall not make for yourself an idol, or any likeness of what is in heaven above or on the earth beneath or in the water under the earth.

5 You shall not worship them or serve them; for I, the LORD your God, am a jealous God, visiting the iniquity of the fathers on the children, on the third and the fourth *generations* of those who hate Me, (Compare Eph. 6:1-3, Page 267)

6 but showing lovingkindness to thousands, to those who love Me and keep My commandments.

7 You shall not take the name of the LORD your God in vain, for the LORD will not leave him unpunished who takes His name in vain.

8 Remember the sabbath day, to keep it holy. (Compare Eph. 4:28, Page 266)

9 Six days you shall labor and do all your work,

10 but the seventh day is a sabbath of the LORD your God; *in it* you shall not do any work, you or your son or your daughter, your male servant or your female servant or your cattle or your sojourner who stays with you.

11 For in six days the LORD made the heavens and the earth, the sea and all that is in them, and rested on the seventh day; therefore the LORD blessed the sabbath day and made it holy.

12 Honor your father and your mother, that your days may be prolonged in the land which the LORD your God gives you.

13 You shall not murder.

14 You shall not commit adultery.

15 You shall not steal.

16 You shall not bear false witness against your neighbor. (Compare Col. 3:9, Page 276)

17 You shall not covet your neighbor's house; you shall not covet your neighbor's wife or his male servant or his female servant or his ox or his donkey or anything that belongs to your neighbor.

Now study I Cor. 6:8-10, Page 231.

BAPTISM
WHAT THE BIBLE
TEACHES ABOUT IMMERSION

To discover what the Bible teaches about baptism, first, let us see the scriptural <u>meaning</u> of the word baptize. Second, let us search to see if the SCRIPTURES show the <u>mode</u> by which baptism is administered. And thirdly, let us seek the <u>message</u> God intended to be conveyed by the ordinance of baptism.

The Meaning of the Word

Note the <u>meaning</u> of the word baptize. It is derived from the Greek word *baptizo.* You see this in the best classical Greek Lexicon by Liddell and Scott and the best New Testament Lexicon, Thayer's edition of Grimm. "These two dictionaries, which are regarded as the standards by the scholars of all denominations, should satisfy all honest inquirers. Liddell and Scott define *baptizo* "to dip in or under water." Thayer's definition of baptism is, "to dip repeatedly, to immerse, to submerge".[a]

The word baptize is the transliteration of the Greek word *"baptizo".* This verb is found 74 times in the New Testament and means to dip, put into, submerge or immerse. The word baptism is the transliteration of the Greek word *"baptisma".* This noun is found 22 times in the New Testament and means immersion, or the act of immersing.

"The Douay Bible with Haydocks notes has received the official indorsement of Pope Pius IX., and is therefore the highest possible Roman Catholic authority. This is the comment on Matthew 3:6: 'Baptized' the word baptism signifies a washing, particularly when it is done by <u>immersion</u> or by <u>dipping</u> or <u>plunging</u> a thing under water, which was formerly the ordinary way of administering the sacrament of baptism."[b]

[a]Pillars of Orthodoxy, or Defenders of the Faith, by Ben M. Bogard—Louisville, Ky. Baptist Book Concern. 1900—Page 387.
[b]Pillars of Orthodoxy, or Defenders of the Faith, by Ben M. Bogard—Louisville, Ky. Baptist Book Concern. 1900—Page 385.

The Mode of Baptism

The scriptural <u>mode</u> or method of baptism is explained by John Wesley, the eminent founder of the Methodist Church. In his Explanatory Notes upon the New Testament in two scriptures he says: "Romans 6:4, 'we are buried with him'—Alluding to the ancient manner of baptizing by <u>immersion</u>; that as Christ was raised from the dead by the glory—Glorious power, of the Father, so we also by the same power should rise again. And as he lives a new life in heaven, so we should walk in newness of life. This, says the apostle, our very baptism represents to us."[c] And, he further says in Colossians 2:12 "Buried with him in baptism! The ancient manner of baptizing by <u>immersion</u> is manifestly alluded to here, by which you are also risen with him—from the death of sin to the life of holiness. It does not appear, that in all this St. Paul speaks of justification at all, but of sanctification altogether."[d]

The historical practice of the Catholic Church during the early part of the Christian era was to administer baptism by immersion. With the permission of the publisher we quote from The Faith of Millions, "Credentials of the Catholic Religion" as follows: "The common method during the first twelve centuries was by <u>immersion</u>."[c]

Much of the confusion about the <u>mode</u> or method of baptism has grown out of the failure of the translators of the Bible to translate the Greek words *baptizo* and *baptisma*. The Church of England had practiced sprinkling as the mode of baptism before the Bible was translated in 1611 A.D. The translators were instructed by King James to retain and use only the old ecclesiastical words most commonly used at that time. To translate the Greek words *baptizo* and *baptisma* would have changed the doctrine of baptism from sprinkling to immersion. So the compromise to transliterate *baptizo* and *baptisma* seems to have changed the accepted meaning of the words

[c]Explanatory Notes Upon The New Testament by John Wesley, Published by Ezekiel Cooper and John Wilson, No. 249, 1806, New York, N. Y. Page 26.

[d]Same Volume, Pages 170 and 171.

[c]The Faith of Millions, Credentials of the Catholic Religion published by Our Sunday Visitor, Huntington, Indiana, 1938, Page 161.

in the mind of modern readers. Most Bibles printed since 1611 A.D. follow this error.

The Message of Immersion

The baptism of a believer by immersion tells the Good News, God's Message. The believer's experience is portrayed by baptism. "Anciently those who were baptized were immersed and buried in water to represent their death to sin, and then did rise up out of the water, to signify their entrance upon a new life, and to these customs the apostle alludes."[f] "In baptism, by a kind of analogy or resemblance, while our bodies are under the water we may be said to be buried with Him."[g]

Here we see the historical practice of baptism by immersion was based on scripture to show a picture of God's message of salvation. Now we ask the question, Do the inspired writings show·

How A Candidate Should Be Baptized?

Yes, the scriptural answer is by immersion. The scriptures show the amount of water required to baptize to be "much water". "And John also was baptizing in Aenon near Salim, because there was much water there, and they were coming, and were being baptized."[h] "And they were being baptized by him in the Jordan River . . ."[i]

Immersion requires that two go down into the water. "And the eunuch said, 'Look! Water! What prevents me from being baptized?'[j] And they both went down into the water, Philip as well as the eunuch; and he baptized him."[k]

[f]Archbishop Tillotson's works, Vol. 1, Page 179.

[g]Bishop Nicholson's Exposition of Church Catechism, Page 174, as quoted in The Converts Guide to First Principles of Evangelical Truth—Compiled by I. Roberds, New Haven, Conn. 1838, William Storer, Jun., Printer, Pages 165-166. Note—all scripture quotations are from the New American Standard Bible New Testament—Lockman Foundation, LaHabra, Calif.

[h]John 3:23, Page 126.

[i]Mark 1:5, Page 46.

[j]Acts 8:36, Page 172.

[k]Acts 8:38, Page 172.

Immersion requires the candidate to be buried in, and raised out of water. "Therefore we have been <u>buried</u> with him through baptism into death, in order that as Christ was <u>raised</u> from the dead through the glory of the Father, so we too might walk in newness of life."[1]

Likewise the Scriptures teach:

Who Is Qualified to Be Baptized?

The answer is only <u>a believer</u> in our Lord Jesus as Savior is qualified to be baptized or immersed. The Ethiopian asked Phillip, "what prevents me from being baptized?"[m] "And Phillip said, 'If you believe with all your heart you may' and he answered and said, 'I believe that Jesus Christ is the son of God.' "[n] Also the believers in the house of Cornelius had been converted and had received the Holy Spirit before they were baptized, "Surely no one can refuse water for these to be baptized who have received the Holy Spirit just as we did, can he?"[o]

The Scriptures also give the reason

Why Believers Should Be Immersed

The believer should be baptized to fulfill all righteousness. "Jesus arrived from Galilee at the Jordan coming to John, to be baptized by him. But John tried to prevent Him . . . But Jesus answering said to him, 'Permit it at this time; for in this way it is fitting for <u>us</u> to fulfill all righteousness.' Then he permitted Him."[p]

Jesus said "If anyone wishes to come after Me, let him . . . follow Me."[q] The believer in Christ must obediently follow his Lord through the waters of baptism to fulfill all righteousness. Further, the believer should be baptized to obey the command of Christ: "Go therefore and make disciples of all the nations, baptizing them in the

[1] Rom 6:4, Page 212.
[m] Acts 8:36, Page 172.
[n] Acts 8:37, Page 172.
[o] Acts 10:47, Page 177.
[p] Matt. 3:13, 14a, 15, Page 3.
[q] Matt. 16:24, Page 24.

name of the Father and the Son and the Holy Spirit, teaching them to observe all that I commanded you."ʳ Peter obeyed the instructions of Christ as he ministered the word in the House of Cornelius who said to him: "We are all here present before God to hear all that you have been commanded by the Lord."ˢ Then Peter preached the gospel and as a result Cornelius and all his group were saved. Then Peter asked: "Surely no one can refuse the water for these to be baptized who have received the Holy Spirit just as we did, can he? And he ordered them to be baptized in the name of Jesus Christ."ᵗ

Since immersion of believers is commanded it imposes upon him a responsibility to obey Christ. Therefore the question,

When Should Believers Be Baptized?

The New Testament teaches that the command to be baptized should be obeyed by the believer as soon as possible based on the accounts recorded in the following instances:

At Once

"Look! Water! What prevents me from being baptized?"ᵘ It was an urgent request. The new believer in Jesus was on a journey and desired to stop and to be baptized at once.

Same Hour

"And he took them that very hour of the night (midnight) and washed their wounds, and immediately he was baptized."ᵛ The jailer felt his need and asked, "What must I do to be saved? And they said, believe on the Lord Jesus and you shall be saved. And they spoke the Word of the Lord to him."ʷ He believed, was saved, and obeyed the command to be baptized the same hour he was saved.

ʳMatt. 28:19, 20a, Page 45.
ˢActs 10:33b, Page 176.
ᵗActs 10:47, 48, Page 177.
ᵘActs 8:36, Page 172.
ᵛActs 16:33, Page 186.
ʷActs 16:30, 31, 32, Page 186.

Same Day

"So then, those who had received his Word were baptized; And there were added <u>that day</u> about three thousand souls!"[x]

Three Days After Being Saved

The Apostle Paul was saved while enroute from Jerusalem to Damascus. "And he was three days without sight."[y] "And a certain Ananias," said: "Brother Saul, receive your sight," and now <u>why do you delay</u>? Arise and be baptized."[aa]

Jesus taught His followers to <u>disciple, dip,</u> and <u>then develop</u> those saved. "Go therefore and make disciples of all the nations, baptizing them in the name of the Father and the Son and the Holy Spirit, teaching them to observe all that I commanded you; and lo, I am with you always, even to the end of the age."[bb] The early church obeyed Jesus by baptizing believers as soon as possible.

Now we ask the question,

What Does Immersion Do?

Immersion shows the obedience of the believer.

<u>Obedience</u> to Christ's command to be immersed reveals the believer's love for the Savior. This is shown in the scriptures:

"If you love me, you will keep My commandments."[cc] "We know that we have come to know Him, if we keep His commandments. The one who says, I have come to know Him, and does not keep His commandments is a liar, and the truth is not in Him, but whoever keeps His word, in him the love of God has truly been perfected."[dd]

<u>An Object</u> lesson is taught by immersion so that viewers may learn the gospel story. Immersion conveys the picture of the gospel. It is God's first century method of Audio-visual education. The candidate

[x]Acts 2:41, Page 163.
[y]Acts 9:9, Page 173.
[aa]Acts 22:12, 13, 16, Page 196.
[bb]Matt. 28:19, 20, Page 45.
[cc]John 14:15, Page 146.
[dd]1 John 2:3, 4, 5, Page 322.

pantomimes the gospel story: "that Christ died for our sins according to the scriptures, and that He was <u>buried</u>, and that He was raised on the third day according to the scriptures."ᶜᶜ

This is to be continued by every believer until Christ comes to earth again. "You proclaim the Lord's death until He comes."ᶠᶠ

CONCLUSION

The conclusion of the teaching reveals God's method of Audio-visual education. He has ever pictured the gospel of grace. Beginning with the first man, Adam, the Bible teaches that God's plan of salvation was to be portrayed by the believer. Adam taught his sons, Cain and Abel, to bring an offering to the Lord. "And in course of time Cain brought to the Lord an offering of the fruit of the ground. And Abel brought of the first-born of his flock and the fat portions. And the Lord had respect and regard for his offering. But for Cain and his offering He had no respect or regard."ᵍᵍ

The animal slain on an altar to carry out the requirements of the law in the Old Testament was a type or symbol of the Lamb of God. "For the life (the animal soul) is the blood, and I have given it for you upon the altar to make atonement for your souls; for it is the blood that makes atonement, by reason of the life (which it represents)."ʰʰ

Each sacrifice pointed like an index finger to Calvary. It showed the believer's faith that God would provide a substitute to die in the believer's place to pay for his sin. It was faith in God's word and not the sacrifice of the animal that saved. "For it is impossible for the blood of bulls and goats to take away sins."ⁱⁱ "For the law, since it has only a shadow of the good things to come and not the very form of things, can never by the same sacrifices year by year which they offer continually make perfect those who draw near". . . . Then he said, "Behold I have come to do thy will! He takes away the first in order

ᶜᶜ1 Cor. 15:3, 4, Page 242.

ᶠᶠ1 Cor. 11:26, Page 237.

ᵍᵍGen. 4:3, 4, 5, The Amplified Old Testament, Zondervan Publishing House, Grand Rapids, Michigan, 1964.

ʰʰLeviticus 17:11.

ⁱⁱHeb. 10:4, Page 303.

to establish the second. By this will we have been sanctified through the offering of the body of Jesus Christ once for all."[ii]

As under the first covenant the believer showed his faith by a sacrifice, so under the new covenant the believer shows his faith by the ordinances of baptism and the Lord's Supper. The believer's faith in the death of Christ on the Cross for sins, His burial in the grave, and His resurrection is portrayed in the baptism of the believer in water. The believer is "buried with Him through baptism into death, in order that as Christ was raised from the dead through the glory of the Father so we too might walk in newness of life."[kk] The believer must be saved before baptism to show what he believes. And in like manner as the sacrifice in the Old Testament did not save, neither does the act of baptism save the believer. It is faith in God's word that saves and is bestowed by grace.

SUGGESTION

Now study "How you show you are saved." Page 45.

Scripture No. 1, Sec. 2, Matthew 28:18-20. Please read that chain of scriptures and references until you have completed the teaching.

[ii]Heb. 10:1-9, 10, Page 303.
[kk]Rom. 6:4, Page 212.

I have read the six references to the Plan presenting the Person of Salvation, beginning on pages 186, and ending on page 219. I repented of my sins and in prayer claimed the promise of Romans 10:13, page 219. I confessed Christ publicly according to Matthew 10:32, page 13 on the

_____ day of _____ 19_____ .

_____ Signature

Your name

BAPTISMAL CERTIFICATE

I, the undersigned ordained minister, baptized

_____

Your name

in _____ Church of

_____ City _____ State

on the _____ day of _____ 19_____

_____ Signature

Minister

COMMITMENT TO STUDY GOD'S WORD

I receive this gift in the spirit in which it is given. I recognize it as a Bible study aid with notes, helps, and four chains of references that lead from the basic truths to maturity in the Christian faith.

I promise to read the first chain of six Scriptures and references beginning on page 186 at least two times within the next two days. Then during the coming week I will read the next three chains of reference beginning on pages 45, 270, and 150. I plan to read my Bible daily as instructed on page xiii and will begin reading on page 122.

I will pray daily for the guidance of the Holy Spirit in the study of the Soul Winner's New Testament (John 16:13, page 149).

This commitment made this _____ day

of _____ , 19____ .

_____
Signature of person receiving gift

The Gift of this Soul Winner's New Testament
is presented as a part of the Outreach Ministry of